Economics for Business

We work with leading authors to develop the
strongest educational materials in economics,
bringing cutting-edge thinking and best learning
practice to a global market.

Under a range of well-known imprints, including
Financial Times Prentice Hall, we craft high quality
print and electronic publications which help readers
to understand and apply their content,
whether studying or at work.

To find out about the complete range of our
publishing please visit us on the World Wide Web at:
www.pearsoneduc.com

SECOND EDITION

Economics for Business

John Sloman
and Mark Sutcliffe

FINANCIAL TIMES

Prentice Hall

An imprint of **Pearson Education**

Harlow, England · London · New York · Reading, Massachusetts · San Francisco · Toronto · Don Mills, Ontario · Sydney
Tokyo · Singapore · Hong Kong · Seoul · Taipei · Cape Town · Madrid · Mexico City · Amsterdam · Munich · Paris · Milan

Pearson Education Limited
Edinburgh Gate
Harlow
Essex CM20 2JE
England

and Associated Companies throughout the world

Visit us on the World Wide Web at:
www.pearsoneduc.com

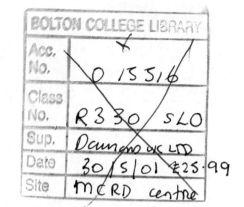

First published by Prentice Hall 1998
Second edition 2001

© John Sloman and Mark Sutcliffe 1998
© Pearson Education 2001

The rights of John Sloman and Mark Sutcliffe to be
identified as authors of this Work have been asserted
by them in accordance with the Copyright, Designs, and
Patents Act 1988.

ISBN 0–273–65187–0 PPR

British Library Cataloguing-in-Publication Data
A catalogue record for this book is available from the British Library

Library of Congress Cataloging-in-Publication Data
Sloman, John, 1947–
    Economics for business/John Sloman and Mark Sutcliffe.—2nd ed.
        p. cm.
    Includes bibliographical references and index.
    ISBN 0-273-65187-0 (pbk.)
    1. Economics. 2. Business. 3. Commerce. 4. Great Britain—Economic
policy—1945– 5. Great Britain—Commercial policy. I. Sutcliffe, Mark. II.
Title.

HB171.5 .S6353 1998
330–dc21   2001023002

Set in Sabon and Franklin Gothic
Typeset by 3
Printed and bound by Ashford Colour Press Ltd, Gosport

Contents

PART B

Background to demand

PART C

Background to supply

PART **D**

Supply: short-run profit maximisation

PART **E**

Supply: alternative strategies

PART **F**

The firm in the factor market

PART **G**

The relationship between government and business

PART **H**

Business in the international environment

PART **J**

Macroeconomic policy

Preface

To the student

If you are studying economics on a business studies degree or diploma, then this book is written for you. Although we cover all the major principles of economics, the focus throughout is on the world of business. For this reason we also cover several topics that do not appear in traditional economics textbooks.

As well as making considerable use of business examples throughout the text, we have included many case studies (in boxes). These illustrate how economics can be used to understand particular business problems or aspects of the business environment. Many of these case studies cover issues that you are likely to read about in the newspapers. Some cover general business issues; others look at specific companies.

We hope that, in using this book, you will share some of our fascination for economics. It is a subject that is highly relevant to the world in which we live. And it is a world where many of our needs are served by business – whether as employers or as producers of the goods and services we buy. After graduating, you will probably take up employment in business. A thorough grounding in economic principles should prove invaluable in the business decisions you may well have to make.

Our aim throughout the book is to make this intriguing subject clear for you to understand and as relevant as possible to you as a student of business.

The written style is direct and straightforward, with short paragraphs to aid rapid comprehension. Definitions of all key terms are given in the margin, with defined terms appearing in bold. Summaries are given at the end of each chapter, with points numbered according to the section in which they appeared. These summaries should help you in reviewing the material you have covered and in revising for exams. Each chapter finishes with a series of questions. These can be used to check your understanding of the chapter and help you to see how its material can be applied to various business problems.

We hope you enjoy the book and come to appreciate the crucial role that economics plays in all our lives, and in particular in the practice of business.

Good luck and *bon appetit*.

To the tutor

The aim of this book is to provide a course in economic principles as they apply to the business environment. It is designed to be used by first-year undergraduates on business studies degrees and diplomas where economics is taught from the business perspective. It is also suitable for students studying economics on MBA, DMS and various professional courses.

Being essentially a book on economics, we cover all the major topics found in standard economics texts – indeed, much of the material in the principles sections is drawn directly from *Economics* (fourth edition). But in addition there are several specialist business chapters and sections to build upon and enliven the subject for business studies students. These have been fully updated and revised for this new edition. The following are some examples of these additional topics:

- The business environment
- Business organisations
- Characteristics theory
- Marketing the product
- Alternative aims of firms
- Growth strategy
- Strategic alliances
- The small-firm sector
- Pricing in practice
- Government and the firm, including policies towards research and technology development (R&TD) and policies towards training
- Government and the market, including environmental policy and transport policy
- Financial markets
- The multinational corporation
- Trading blocs
- Monetary union.

The text is split into 31 chapters. Each chapter is kept relatively short to enable the material to be covered in a single lecture or class. Each chapter finishes with review questions, which can be used for seminars or discussion sessions.

The chapters are grouped into 10 parts:

- Part A *Business and economics* (Chapters 1–5) establishes the place of business within the economy, the relevance of economics to business decision making and the operation and functioning of the market economy.

- Part B *Background to demand* (Chapters 6–8) considers the consumer, how consumer behaviour can be predicted and how, via advertising and marketing, consumer demand can be influenced.

- Part C *Background to supply* (Chapters 9 and 10) focuses on business costs, revenue and profits.

- Part D *Supply: short-run profit maximisation* (Chapters 11 and 12) presents the traditional analysis of market structures and the implications that such structures have for business conduct and performance.

- Part E *Supply: alternative strategies* (Chapters 13–16) considers various alternative theories of the firm. It also examines how business size can influence business actions, and how pricing strategies differ from one firm to another and how these strategies are influenced by the market conditions in which firms operate.

- Part F *The firm in the factor market* (Chapters 17 and 18) focuses upon the market for labour and the market for capital. It examines what determines the factor proportions that firms use.

- Part G *The relationship between government and business* (Chapters 19–21) establishes the theoretical rationale behind government intervention in the economy, and then assesses the relationship between the government and the individual firm and the government and the market.

- Part H *Business in the international environment* (Chapters 22–4): after establishing the basis of international trade and the benefits that accrue from it, the emphasis of the remaining chapters is to consider how the world trading system has changed with the development and proliferation of the multinational corporation, and the expansion of regional trading agreements.

- Part I *The macroeconomic environment* (Chapters 25–8) considers the macroeconomic framework in which firms operate. We focus upon the principal economic variables, investigate the role of money in the economy, and briefly outline the theoretical models underpinning the relationships between these variables.

- Part J *Macroeconomic policy* (Chapters 29–31) examines the mechanics of government intervention at a macro level as well as its potential benefits and drawbacks. Demand-side and supply-side policy and economic policy co-ordination between countries are all considered.

Special features

The book contains the following special features:

- A direct and straightforward written style; short paragraphs to aid rapid comprehension. The aim all the time is to provide maximum clarity.

- (*New to this edition*) Attractive double-page opening sections for each of the 10 Parts of the book. These contain an introduction to the material covered and an article from the *Financial Times* on one of the topics.

- All technical terms are highlighted and clearly defined in the margin on the page they appear. This feature has proved very popular in the three editions of *Economics* and is especially useful for students when revising.

- A comprehensive index, including reference to all defined terms. This enables students to look up a definition as required and to see it used in context.

- Additional applied material to that found in the text can be found in the boxes within each chapter. All boxes include questions so as to relate the material back to the chapter in which the box is located. The extensive use of applied material makes learning much more interesting for students and helps to bring the subject alive. This is particularly important for business students who need to relate economic theory to their other subjects and to the world of business generally.

- Detailed summaries appear at the end of each chapter with the points numbered by the chapter section in which they are made. These allow the students not only to check their comprehension of chapter's contents, but also to get a clear overview of the material they have been studying.

■ Each chapter concludes with a series of review questions to test students' understanding of the chapter's salient points. These questions can be used for seminars or as set work to be completed in the students' own time.

■ A careful and consistent use of colour and shading. The tint used for the second colour allows several different shades to be achieved. The object is to make the text more attractive to students and easier to use by giving clear signals as to the book's structure.

■ (*New to this edition*) A detailed Web Appendix. You can easily access any of these sites from the book's own Web site (at http://www.booksites.net/sloman). When you enter the site, click on Student Resources and then on Hot Links in the left-hand panel. You will find all the sites from the Web Appendix listed. Click on the one you want and the 'hot link' will take you straight to it.

Supplements

Web site

Visit the book's Web site at

http://www.booksites.net/sloman

This has a range of materials available for students and tutors.

For students

■ Study material designed to help you improve your results.

■ *Economics in the News* features on topical stories, with analysis and links to key concepts and pages in the book.

■ Up-to-date *Case Studies* with questions for self study.

■ Hotlinks to over 200 Web sites given in the book's Web Appendix and referenced throughout the text.

■ Self-test questions.

■ Answers to questions in the book.

For tutors

■ A secure password-protected site with material designed to help you teach.

■ A section dedicated to issues in teaching and learning.

■ Customisable lecture plans in PowerPoint, including animated diagrams.

■ Key models as full-colour animated PowerPoint slide shows.

■ Downloadable PowerPoint slides and OHTs of all figures and most tables from the book.

■ Further case studies to supplement your teaching.

CD-ROM (new edition)

The tutor's CD has been thoroughly revised to take account of the changes in the second edition. It also contains various new features. It is available free of charge from Pearson Education to tutors using the book as a course text. It contains the following:

■ PowerPoint® slide shows in full colour for use with a data projector in lectures and classes. These can also be made available to students by loading them on to a local network. All PowerPoint files are small enough to copy to a 3½″ disk (for portability) and are available in PowerPoint 97 and 95 versions. The CD contains several types of these slide shows:
   - All figures from the book and most of the tables. Each figure is built up in a logical sequence, thereby allowing tutors to show them in lectures in an animated form.
   - A range of models. These show how the key models used in the book are developed. There are 38 of these models and each one builds up in around 20 to 50 screens.
   - Lecture plans. These are a series of bullet-point lecture plans. There is one for each chapter of the book. Each one can be easily edited, with points added, deleted or moved, so as to suit particular lectures. A consistent use of colour is made to show how the points tie together. The lecture plans are also available in Word®.
   - Lecture plans with integrated diagrams. These lecture plans include animated diagrams and charts at the appropriate points.

■ (*New feature*) PowerPoint slides for printing onto acetate for use with a conventional OHP. These are reverse image slides (i.e. dark lines on a clear background) designed to minimise printer ink. They can be printed in colour, or in black and white (and grey). These slides contain the figures, models, lecture plans and lecture plans with integrated diagrams referred to above.

■ Multiple-choice, short answer and true-false questions. This very large test bank is completely redesigned and contains many new questions. It is more flexible and easier to use.

■ Case studies. These can be reproduced and used for classroom exercises or for student assignments.

The CD also contains supplementary material from John's *Economics* (4th edition) and *Essentials of Economics* (2nd edition).

Case Studies and Answer Pack

For those tutors who prefer a hard-copy version of the case studies and answers to end-of-chapter questions, packs are available from Pearson Education.

WinEcon and BusEcon

Most UK higher education institutions now have *WinEcon* on their network. This is a comprehensive computer-based learning programme for introductory economics, developed by the Economics consortium of the Teaching and

Learning Technology Programme (TLTP). The Consortium has been developing a version of *WinEcon* for students studying economics on a business studies programme. This version is called *BusEcon* and is particularly suitable for use with this book. Further details on the *WinEcon* and *BusEcon* software are available from Blackwells publishers. There is also a Web site for information on the software: http://www.webecon.bris.ac.uk/winecon/

Acknowledgements

As with the first edition, the task of writing has been made much easier by the support we've had from many people. Thanks to the whole team at Pearson Education, and especially to Paula Harris and Natasha Dupont for all the hard work they've put in. Thanks too to the many users of the book who have given us feedback. We always value their comments.

John and Mark

Thanks, as always, to my family and especially to Alison, who continues to show remarkable patience. Her support has been brilliant. Thanks too to Tony Flegg, my 'office mate' at UWE, and a user of the book. His comments and eye for fine detail have been invaluable.

John

It feels like only yesterday that John and I wrote the first edition of this book. Thanks to all my students over the last three years who have commented on the book's contents – for good or bad! And thanks, as always, to my family, who have commented on my absence while writing. Do I hear the kettle again, Sheila?

Mark

A Companion Web Site accompanies

ECONOMICS FOR BUSINESS:
Second Edition

by **John Sloman** and **Mark Sutcliffe**

Visit the *Economics for Business,* Companion Web Site at *www.booksites.net/sloman* where you will find valuable teaching and learning material including:

For Lecturers:
- PowerPoint slides of figures, lecture plans and models
- Case Studies

For Students:
- Hot links to over 200 websites
- Case Studies
- Economics in the News
- Self-test questions

Publisher's acknowledgements

We are grateful to the following for permission to reproduce copyright material:

Tables 8.1, 8.2, 8.3 and 8.5 from *Advertising Statistics Yearbook 2000*, NTC Publications Ltd; Tables 8.4(a) and 8.4(b) reprinted with permission of ACNielsen MMS, Madison House, High Street, Sunninghill, Berkshire, SL5 9NP, Tel. 01344 627 553; 1999; Figure 14.1 from *Non-Price Decisions*, Palgrave Publishers Ltd (Koutsoyiannis, A. 1982); Figure 14.2 from *The Economist*, 8 July 2000, © The Economist Newspaper Ltd, London 8.7.00; Figure in Box 14.2 based on information provided by Thomson Financial Securities; Tables 15.3 and 15.4 from *Statistical News Release*, Department of Trade and Industry 7 August 2000, Crown Copyright is reproduced with the permission of the Controller of Her Majesty's Stationery Office; Table 15.5 from *Understanding the Small-Business Sector*, published by Routledge reprinted with permission from ITBP Ltd (Storey, D. J. 1994); Figure in Box 16.1 from Predatory pricing in *Economic Review*, February, Philip Allan Updates (Stewart, G. 1997); Tables (a) and (b) in Box 16.2 from *Bank of England Quarterly Bulletin*, May 1996, reprinted with permission of Publications Group, Bank of England; Table in Box 17.2 from *First Report of the Low Pay Commission*, Department of Trade and Industry 1998 (http://www.lowpay.gov.uk/IR/lowpay/summary.htm), Crown Copyright is reproduced with the permission of the Controller of Her Majesty's Stationery Office; Tables (a) and (b) in Box 20.2 from *R&D Scoreboard, 2000*, Department of Trade and Industry, Crown Copyright is reproduced with the permission of the Controller of Her Majesty's Stationery Office; Table 21.1 from *Evaluating Economic Instruments for Environmental Policy*, copyright Organisation for Economic Co-operation and Development 1977 (OECD 1997); Table 21.2 from *Annual Abstract of Statistics 2000*, Office for National Statistics, National Statistics © Crown Copyright 2001; Figure 22.2, Figure (b) in Box 22.2 and Figures 22.3 and 22.4 from *Trade Statistics*, World Trade Organization (WTO, 2000); Tables in Box 22.2 based on information in WTO web site http://www.wto.org/english/res_e/statis_e/webpub_e.xls, reprinted with permission of World Trade Organization; Table in Box 24.1 from *Bank of England Inflation Report*, February 1998, reprinted with permission of Publications Group, Bank of England; Tables 25.1 and 25.2 from *UK National Income and Expenditure*, Office for National Statistics, National Statistics © Crown Copyright 1999.

Building Group plc for an abridged extract from *Building* 27.9.1991; Christian Aid for an extract from 'Fair Shares Transnational companies, the WTO and the world's poorest communities'; Department of trade and Industry http://www.innovation.gov.uk/finance for an extract from 'Highlights of the Scoreboard' from *R & D Scoreboard* © Crown copyright; Economist Newspapers Ltd for extracts from articles appearing in Box 5.3 taken from

The Economist 3.2.96 © The Economist Newspaper Ltd 1996 and an article appearing in Box 4.2 from *The Economist* 24.7.99 © The Economist Newspaper Ltd 1999; Guardian Newspapers Limited for extracts from the articles 'Skills shortage may cost Europe £37bn' by Steve Shipside in *The Guardian* 23.3.00 and 'Mersey beats faster to the hi-tech sound' by Anne Hyland in *The Guardian* 6.6.00; The Independent Newspaper (UK) Limited for an extract from the article 'A price war hotter than a vindaloo' by Jim White in *The Independent* 8.10.93; the authors J. Lipsky, J and K. Parker 1997 for an extract from an article published in *The Financial Times* 13.10.97 appearing in Box 24.1; Net Profit Publications for an article 'E-commerce offers a wider net for corporate buying' published in *The Financial Times*, © Net Profit is a publisher of electronic business case studies, analysis and reports, see www.netprofiteurope.com, (Bowen, D. and Charlton, E. 2000).

We are grateful to the Financial Times Limited for permission to reprint the following material:

An extract from an article dated 26.05.00 in Box 8.1 © *Financial Times* 26.05.00; an extract from an article dated 22.02.00 in Box 17.3, © *Financial Times* 22.02.00; an extract from an article in Box 19.3 from FT.COM, © *Financial Times*; a table taken from an article dated 19.11.96 in Box 23.1 © *Financial Times* 19.11.96; an extract from an article dated 27.11.99 in Box 30.1 © *Financial Times*, 27 November, 1999.

'Economic turnaround set to release region's e-business potential', © *Financial Times*, 06.09.00; 'Coca-Cola loses its fizz', © *Financial Times*, 18.09.00; Extract from an article dated 13.06.00, 'The downsizing era "...tore up the implicit contract of employment which had, for decades, tied people to their companies..."' © *Financial Times*, 13.06.00; 'Ryanair attacks Lufthansa on pricing policy', © *Financial Times*, 14.06.00; 'The urge to merge takes on a different form', © *Financial Times*, 30.06.00; 'Work in progress', © *Financial Times*, 30.06.00; 'Building bridges across the skills gap', © *Financial Times*, 05.10.00; 'The single currency has had a significant effect on investment, although the UK – outside the euro-zone – stays ahead of the pack', © *Financial Times*, 4.10.99; 'Input prices put pressure on margins, © *Financial Times*, 07/08.10.00; 'Interest rates held after MPC split', © *Financial Times*, 21.09.00.

While every effort has been made to trace the owners of copyright material, in a few cases this has proved impossible and we take this opportunity to offer our apologies to any copyright holders whose rights we have unwittingly infringed.

Business and economics

THE FINANCIAL TIMES, 6 SEPTEMBER 2000

Economic turnaround set to release region's e-business potential

By ANDREW FISHER

The tide has turned dramatically in Asia's IT markets. A few years ago, many companies were fighting for survival in the face of the financial storms that swept across the region. The potential of the internet was the last thing on their minds.

But today, as the crises have ebbed and confidence is back – though its return has been patchy – the most far-sighted are investing keenly in online business.

Among the big Asian countries, Japan, South Korea and Taiwan have the best prospects of developing powerful internet-related ventures. China clearly has huge potential, but this is some way from being realised. At the other end of the scale, many companies in Hong Kong and Singapore are aggressively pursuing electronic commerce strategies.

As the e-commerce wave strengthens, traditional business practices will be overturned. Cosy relationships, such as Japan's keiretsu or corporate families, will be shaken up and many wholesalers and middlemen will be forced to shift online or go out of business.

Japan accounts for just over half the Asia–Pacific online retail market, followed by Korea. Online retail revenue per capita in Japan, however, lags behind the US, the UK and Germany, as well as Korea and Australia. Most IT industry attention, though, is focused on the B2B market because of its size and the big corporate contracts involved. The heavyweights of global IT, such as IBM, Sun Microsystems, Oracle and Cisco, are heavily involved in Asia and keen to expand their presence.

Mark Hoffmann, head of Commerce One, the US e-commerce software company, sees a bright future on the Asian B2B scene. 'It's exploding,' he says. 'Asia is behind (the US), but it's not behind by much. There's some pretty impressive stuff going on out there.'

Bill Gates, head of Microsoft, recently said he was 'incredibly optimistic' about Asia's future.

'Its countries are rapidly increasing their investments in technologies and infrastructure needed to connect businesses, governments and educational systems,' he commented. 'The opportunities for Asia to become a driving force behind the digital economy on the global stage are tremendous.'

Businesses play a key role in all our lives. Whatever their size, and whatever the goods or services they provide, they depend on us as consumers to buy their products.

But just as businesses rely on us for their income, so equally many of us rely on firms for our income. The wages we earn depend on our employer's success, and that success in turn depends on us as suppliers of labour.

And it is not just as customers and workers that we are affected by business. The success of business in general affects the health of the whole economy and thus the lives of us all.

The extract opposite from the *Financial Times* provides a good illustration of this. It was not so long ago (1997/8) that south-east Asia was in deep crisis and the global economy was on the verge of a major recession. Yet today south-east Asia has recovered much of what it lost and is set for a revolution in e-commerce. Not only will this benefit economies in the region, but it will have a profound impact on economies all around the world.

In Part A of this book we shall consider the relationship between business and economics. Chapters 1 to 3 look at the types of environment in which businesses operate, the different ways in which they are organised and the role of economists in analysing business behaviour. Then in Chapters 4 and 5 we will examine the operation of markets. As consumers, we buy from firms and they sell to us. This process of buying and selling involves *demand* and *supply*. As we shall see, the interaction of demand and supply then determines the market price of the product and the profit the firm makes.

The 'theory of business' leads to a life of obstruction, because theorists do not see the business, and the men of business will not reason out the theories.

Walter Bagehot (1826–77), *Economics Studies*, ed. W. Hutton, vol. I, pp. 9–10

key terms

The business environment
Production
Firms
Industries
Scarcity
Macroeconomics
Microeconomics
Circular flow of income
Principal and agent
Business organisation
Price taker
Perfectly competitive market
Price mechanism
Demand
Supply
Equilibrium price and quantity
Shifts in demand and supply
Price elasticity of demand and supply
Income and cross elasticities of demand
Speculation
Risk and uncertainty

1

The business environment and business economics

What is business economics?

What is the role of *business economics*? What will you be studying in this book?

Clearly we will be studying *firms*: the environment in which they operate, the decisions they make, and the effects of these decisions – on themselves, on their customers, on their employees, on their business rivals and on the public at large.

But what particular aspects of business does the *economist* study? Firms are essentially concerned with using inputs to make output. Inputs cost money and output earns money. The difference between the revenue earned and the costs incurred constitutes the firm's profit. Firms will normally want to make as much profit as possible, or at the very least to avoid a decline in profits. In order to meet these and other objectives, managers will need to make choices: choices of what types of output to produce, how much to produce and at what price; choices of what techniques of production to use, how many workers to employ and of what type, what suppliers to use for raw materials, equipment, etc. In each case, when weighing up alternatives, managers will want to make the best choices. Business economists study these choices. They study economic decision making by firms.

The study of decision making can be broken down into three stages.

The external influences on the firm (the 'business environment'). Here we are referring to the various factors that affect the firm that are largely outside its direct control. Examples are the competition it faces, the prices it pays for raw materials, the state of the economy (e.g. whether growing or in recession) and the level of interest rates. Businesses will need to obtain a clear understanding of their environment before they can set about making the right decisions.

Internal decisions of the firm. Given a knowledge of these external factors, how do firms then decide on prices, output, inputs, marketing, investment, etc? Here the business economist can play a major role in helping firms achieve their business objectives.

The external effects of business decision making. When the firm has made its decisions and acted on them, how do the results affect the firm's rivals, its customers and the wider public? In other words, what is the impact of a firm's decision making on people *outside* the firm? Are firms' actions in the public interest, or is there a case for government intervention?

What do business economists do?

Our study of business will involve three types of activity:

- *Description*. For example, we will be describing the objectives of businesses (e.g. making profit of increasing market share), the types of market in which firms operate (e.g. competitive or non-competitive) and the constraints on decision making (e.g. the costs of production, the level of consumer demand and the state of the economy).
- *Analysis*. For example, we will analyse how a firm's costs and profits are likely to vary with the amount of output it produces and what would be the consequences of a change in consumer demand or a change in the price charged by rivals. We will also analyse the upswings and downswings in the economy: something that will have a crucial bearing on the profitability of many companies.
- *Recommendations*. Given the objectives of a firm, the business economist can help to show how those objectives can best be met. For example, if a firm wants to maximise its profits, the business economist can advise on what prices to change, how much to invest, how much to advertise, etc. Of course, any such recommendations will only be as good as the data on which they are based. In an uncertain environment, recommendations will necessarily be more tentative.

In this chapter, as an introduction to the subject of business economics, we shall consider the place of the firm within its business environment, and assess how these external influences are likely to shape and determine its actions. In order to discuss the relationship between a business's actions and its environment, we first need to define what the business environment is.

1.1 The business environment

It is normal to identify four dimensions to the business environment: political/legal, economic, social/cultural and technological.

Political/legal factors. Firms will be directly affected by the actions of government and other political events. These might be major events affecting the whole of the business community, such as the collapse of communism, the Gulf War or a change of government. Alternatively, they may be actions affecting just one part of the economy. For example, an anti-smoking campaign by the government will affect the tobacco industry. Similarly, businesses will be affected by the legal framework in which they operate. Examples include industrial relations legislation, product safety standards, regulations governing pricing in the privatised industries and laws preventing collusion between firms to keep prices up.

Economic factors. Economic factors can range from big to small, from local to national to international, from current to future; from the rising costs of raw materials to the market entry of a new rival, from the forthcoming Budget to the instability of international exchange rates, from the current availability of investment funds to the likely future cash flow from a new product. Business must constantly take such factors into account when devising and acting upon its business strategy.

It is normal to divide the economic environment in which the firm operates into two levels:

- *The microeconomic environment.* This includes all the economic factors that are *specific* to a particular firm operating in its own particular market. Thus one firm may be operating in a highly competitive market, whereas another may not; one firm may be faced by rapidly changing consumer tastes (e.g. a designer clothing manufacturer), while another may be faced with a virtually constant consumer demand (e.g. a potato merchant); one firm may face rapidly rising costs, whereas another may find that costs are constant or falling.
- *The macroeconomic environment.* This is the *national* and *international* economic situation in which business as a whole operates. Business in general will fare much better if the economy is growing than if it is in recession. In examining the macroeconomic environment, we will also be looking at the policies that governments adopt in their attempt to steer the economy, since these policies, by affecting things such as taxation, interest rates and exchange rates, will have a major impact on firms.

Social/cultural factors. This aspect of the business environment concerns social attitudes and values. These include attitudes towards working conditions and the length of the working day, equal opportunities for different groups of people (whether by ethnicity, gender, physical attributes, etc.), the nature and purity of products, the use and abuse of animals, and images portrayed in advertising. The social/cultural environment also includes social trends, such as an increase in the average age of the population, or changes in attitudes towards seeking paid employment while bringing up small children. In recent times, various ethical issues, especially concerning the protection of the environment, have had a big impact on the actions of business and the image that many firms seek to present.

Technological factors. Over the last twenty years the pace of technological change has quickened. This has had a huge impact not only on how firms produce products, but also on how their business is organised. The use of robots and other forms of computer-controlled production has changed the nature of work for many workers. It has also created a wide range of new opportunities for businesses, many of which are yet to be realised. The information-technology revolution is also enabling much more rapid communication and making it possible for many workers to do their job from home or while travelling.

The division of the factors affecting a firm into political, economic, social and technological is known as a **PEST analysis**, and is widely used by business enterprises to audit their environment and to help them establish a strategic approach to their business activities. It is nevertheless important to recognise that there is a great overlap and interaction among these four sets of factors. Laws and government policies reflect social attitudes; technological factors determine economic ones, such as costs and productivity; technological progress often reflects the desire of researchers to meet social needs; and so on.

As well as such interaction, we must also be aware of the fact that the business environment is constantly changing. Some of these changes are gradual,

definition
PEST analysis Where the political, economic, social and technological factors shaping a business environment are assessed by a business so as to devise future business strategy.

BOX 1.1

The UK defence industry
Structure–conduct–performance

With the collapse of communism and the ending of the Cold War, defence industries around the world have been faced with fundamental changes in their business environment.

A PEST analysis (see page 5) can reveal some of the most important changes. When conducting such an analysis not only are relevant factors identified, but it is possible to distinguish between strengths and weaknesses. The table shows a PEST analysis carried out on the UK defence sector.

The most significant threat to this sector has come from political change (i.e. the decline in the perceived external threat) and its economic consequences (i.e. the reduction in defence expenditure). World military expenditure declined at a rate of 7.2 per cent per annum between 1988 and 1993. UK military expenditure as a percentage of GDP fell from a 5.2 per cent peak in 1985 to 3.8 per cent in 1994). Businesses within the defence sector have responded to this threat, not only by rationalising their business activities, but, most crucially, by seeking out partners in order to establish collaborative ventures. By pursuing such a strategy, they are able to share the huge research and development (R&D) costs that are associated with products within this sector, and subsequently they spread the risk of new product development.

The development of the Eurofighter is in many respects a classic example of this approach. The Eurofighter was developed by the UK, Germany, Italy and Spain in the mid-1990s, with development costs alone amounting to some £35 billion. Industry analysts suggest that, as technology becomes more expensive, many products, such as Eurofighter, will no longer be feasible for any individual company, or even country, to develop alone. As such the conduct of business will involve working with, rather than against, potential business rivals.

As well as reducing R&D costs, collaborative business ventures also represent a way in which businesses with distinct specialisms can focus their production in these specialist areas and operate within niche markets. For example, British Aerospace has specialised in the production of aircraft wings and GEC in military electronics.

Although collaborative ventures and rising specialisation seem the most likely direction in which the defence industry will develop, there are several alternative strategies that businesses within this sector could adopt. For example, a business might seek to strengthen its market position by merging with or taking over its rivals, either domestically based or overseas. Alternatively, businesses within the defence sector might look to diversify, and locate business activities in non-defence markets. Such a strategy crucially depends upon the ability to transfer technology between different markets, and ultimately between different products.

some are revolutionary. To be successful, a business will need to adapt to these changes and, wherever possible, take advantage of them. Ultimately, the better business managers understand the environment in which they operate, the more likely they are to be successful, either in exploiting ever changing opportunities or in avoiding potential disasters.

Although we shall be touching on political, social and technological factors, it is economic factors which will be our main focus of concern when examining the business environment.

1.2 The structure of industry

One of the most important and influential elements of the business environment is the *structure of industry*. How a firm performs depends on the state of its particular industry and the amount of competition it faces. A knowledge of the

Even given the structural change of many markets within the defence sector, such markets still remain dominated by relatively few producers, which, given the specialist nature of their business, acts as an effective barrier to new firms entering the market.

In search of maintaining performance (profitability, market share, etc.), companies in the defence sector have had to adjust rapidly in the face of a changing world political situation. Crucially for European producers, the impact of this has been to reduce competition and enhance collaboration – a far safer alternative.

Question

In what ways have the defence industries responded to the ending of the Cold War?

PEST analysis of the UK defence sector

	Strengths	*Weaknesses*
Political	Industry is a powerful lobby group – ability to influence government	End of the Cold War
		Cuts in defence spending
		Lack of long-term government action
Economic	Skilled labour force	Economic specialism creates dependency
	Specialist service	Vulnerable to world economic activity
		Impact upon regional economy of defence cutbacks such as regional unemployment
		Costs of restructuring
		Direction in restructuring: i.e. what markets to locate in
Social	Proactive management culture	
	Union commitment to business	
Technological	High technology base	Need for constant innovation
		R&D cost

structure of an industry is therefore crucial if we are to understand business behaviour and its likely outcomes.

In this section we will consider how the production of different types of goods and services are classified and how firms are located into different industrial groups.

Classifying production

When analysing production it is common to distinguish three broad categories:

- **Primary production.** This refers to the production and extraction of natural resources such as minerals and sources of energy. It also includes output from agriculture.
- **Secondary production.** This refers to the output of the manufacturing and construction sectors of the economy.

> **definition**
>
> **Primary production**
> The production and extraction of natural resources, plus agriculture.

> **definition**
>
> **Secondary production**
> The production from manufacturing and construction sectors of the economy.

Figure 1.1

Output of industrial sectors (as % of GDP)

Source: Based on *UK National Accounts (Blue Book)* (ONS, 2000).

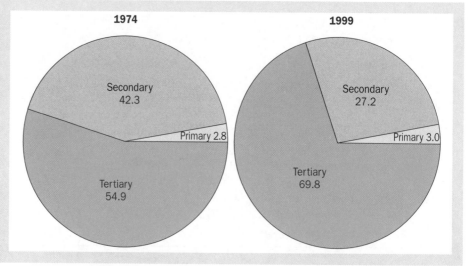

Figure 1.2

Employment by industrial sector (% of total employees)

Source: Based on *Labour Market Trends* (ONS, various editions).

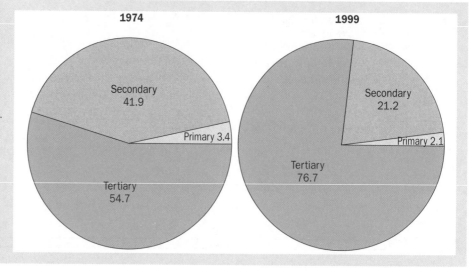

● **Tertiary production**. This refers to the production of services, and includes a wide range of sectors such as finance, the leisure industry, retailing and transport.

definition

Tertiary production
The production from the service sector of the economy.

definition

Gross Domestic Product (GDP)
The value of output produced within the country over a twelve-month period.

Figures 1.1 and 1.2 show the share of output (or **gross domestic product (GDP)**) and employment of these three sectors in 1974 and 1999. They illustrate how the tertiary sector has expanded rapidly. In 1999, it contributed some 70 per cent to total output and employed approximately 77 per cent of all workers. By contrast, the share of output and employment of the secondary sector has declined. In 1999, it accounted for only some 27 per cent of output and 21 per cent of employment.

This trend is symptomatic of a process known as **deindustrialisation** – a decline in the share of the secondary sector in GDP. Many commentators argue that this process of deindustrialisation is inevitable and that the existence of a large and growing tertiary sector in the UK economy reflects its maturity.

Others are more sceptical. They argue that the UK still relies heavily on manufacturing industry for employment, and more importantly for export earnings. Even though the tertiary sector is a large employer, as most services tend to be labour intensive, the output from such production tends to be consumed domestically and little is exported overseas. The reason for this is that the vast majority of service production tends to be provided in the country in which the service is demanded. Thus a strong manufacturing base is still required if the UK is to play its way in the world, and be able to purchase its much needed imports.

The classification of production into primary, secondary and tertiary allows us to consider broad changes in the economy. However, if we require a more comprehensive analysis of the structure of industry and its changes over time, then such a general classification is of little value. What we need to do is to classify firms into particular industries. In the following section we identify the classification process used in the UK and the EU.

Classifying firms into industries

An industry refers to a group of firms that produce a particular category of product. Thus we could refer to the electrical goods industry, the holiday industry, the aircraft industry or the insurance industry. Industries can then be grouped together into broad **industrial sectors**, such as manufacturing industry, or mining and quarrying, or construction, or transport.

Classifying firms into industrial groupings and subgroupings has a number of purposes. It helps us to analyse various trends in the economy and to identify areas of growth and areas of decline. It helps to identify parts of the economy with specific needs, such as training or transport infrastructure. Perhaps most importantly, it helps economists and business people to understand and predict the behaviour of firms that are in direct competition with each other. In such cases, however, it may be necessary to draw the boundaries of an industry quite narrowly.

To illustrate this, take the case of the vehicle industry. The vehicle industry produces cars, lorries, vans and coaches. The common characteristic of these vehicles is that they are self-propelled road transport vehicles. In other words, we could draw the boundaries of an industry in terms of the broad physical or technical characteristics of the products it produces. The problem with this type of categorisation, however, is that these products may not be substitutes in an *economic* sense. If I am thinking of buying a new vehicle to replace my car, I am hardly likely to consider buying a coach or a lorry! Lorries are not in competition with cars. If we are to group products together with are genuine competitors for each other, we will want to divide industries into more narrow categories. For example, we could classify cars into several groups according to size, price, function, engine capacity, etc.: e.g. luxury, saloon (of various size categories), estate (again of various size categories), seven seater and sports.

On the other hand, if we draw the boundaries of an industry too narrowly, we may end up ignoring the effects of competition from another closely related industry. For example, if we are to understand the pricing strategies of electricity supply companies in the household market, it might be better to focus on the whole domestic fuel industry.

Thus how narrowly or broadly we draw the boundaries of an industry depends on the purposes of our analysis.

> **definition**
> **Deindustrialisation**
> The decline in the contribution to production of the manufacturing sector of the economy.

> **definition**
> **Industry**
> A group of firms producing a particular product or service.

> **definition**
> **Industrial sector**
> A grouping of industries producing similar products or services.

Standard Industrial Classification

The formal system under which firms are grouped into industries is known as the **Standard Industrial Classification (SIC)**. The SIC was first introduced in 1948. Its aim was to promote the collection by various government departments and non-governmental agencies of a uniform and comparable body of data on industry. Since 1948 the SIC has been periodically revised. Revisions to the SIC have been made in order to reflect changes in the UK's industrial structure, such as those resulting from the growth in new products and the new industries associated with them.

The most recent revision in 1992 was initiated as a response to the EU's desire to establish a new Europe-wide classification system. Such a revision was seen as a crucial requirement for the effective monitoring of business in the EU's 'internal market' (the system whereby there are not supposed to be any artificial barriers to trade between EU members).

Table 1.1   **Standard Industrial Classification 1992**

Section	Subsection
A Agriculture, hunting and forestry	
B Fishing	
C Mining and quarrying	CA Mining and quarrying of energy producing materials
	CB Mining and quarrying except energy producing materials
D Manufacturing	DA Manufacture of food products, beverages and tobacco
	DB Manufacture of textiles and textile products
	DC Manufacture of leather and leather products
	DD Manufacture of wood and wood products
	DE Manufacture of pulp, paper and paper products; publishing and printing
	DF Manufacture of coke, refined petroleum products and nuclear fuel
	DG Manufacture of chemicals, chemical products and man-made fibres
	DH Manufacture of rubber and plastic products
	DI Manufacture of other non-metallic mineral products
	DJ Manufacture of basic metals and fabricated metal products
	DK Manufacture of machinery and equipment not elsewhere classified
	DL Manufacture of electrical and optical equipment
	DM Manufacture of transport equipment
	DN Manufacturing not elsewhere classified
E Electricity, gas and water supply	

Section	Subsection
F Construction	
G Wholesale and retail trade, repair of motor vehicles and personal and household goods	
H Hotels and restaurants	
I Transport, storage and communication	
J Financial intermediation	
K Real estate, renting and business activities	
L Public administration and defence; compulsory social security	
M Education	
N Health and social work	
O Other community, social and personal service activities	
P Private households with employed persons	
Q Extra-territorial organisations and bodies	

Source: Based on *Standard Industrial Classification 1992* (CSO).

SIC(92) is divided into seventeen sections (A–Q), each representing a production classification (see Table 1.1). Two of the sections (C and D) are in turn divided into subsections. Sections or subsections are then divided into divisions; divisions are divided into groups; groups are divided into classes; and some classes are further divided into subclasses. Table 1.2 gives an example of how a manufacturer of cardboard boxes would be classified according to this system.

In total, SIC(92) has 17 sections, 16 subsections, 60 divisions, 222 groups, 503 classes and 142 subclasses.

Changes in the structure of the UK economy

Given such a classification, how has UK industry changed over time? Figures 1.3 and 1.4 show the changes in output and employment of the various sectors identified by the SIC from 1980 to 1985, from 1985 to 1990, and from 1990 to 1995.

Table 1.2   The classification of the manufacture of cardboard boxes

Section D	Manufacturing (comprising divisions 15 to 37)
Subsection DE	Manufacture of pulp, paper and paper products; publishing and printing (comprising divisions 21 and 22)
Division 21	Manufacture of pulp, paper and paper products (comprising groups 21.1 and 21.2)
Group 21.2	Manufacture of articles of paper and paperboard (comprising classes 21.21 to 21.25)
Class 21.21	Manufacture of corrugated paper and paperboard and of containers of paper and paperboard (comprising subclasses 21.21/1 and 21.21/2)
Subclass 21.21/2	Manufacture of cartons, boxes, cases and other containers

Source: Based on *Standard Industrial Classification 1992* (CSO).

Figure 1.3
GDP by industry
(1980 = 100)

Source: Based on *UK National Accounts (Blue Book)* (ONS, 2000).

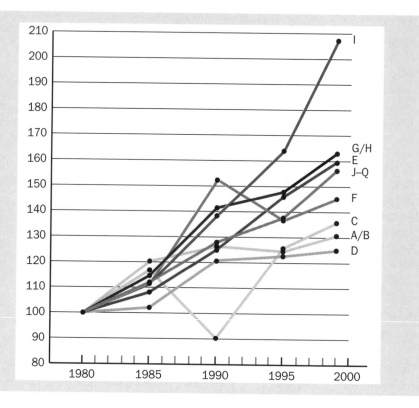

Figure 1.4
Employment by industry (1980 = 100)

Source: Based on *Annual Abstract of Statistics* (ONS, 2000).

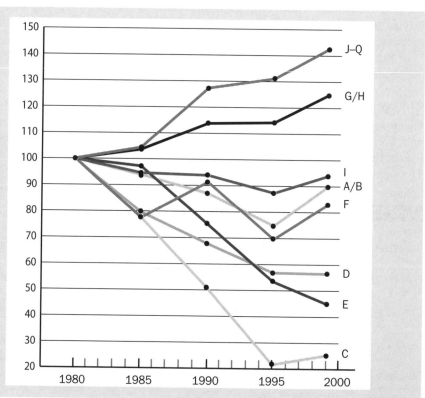

The figures reveal that only mining and quarrying (C) experienced a decline in output between 1985 and 1990 (reflecting the decline in the coal industry). However, the construction industry (F) declined after 1990, and manufacturing (D) remained largely stagnant. By contrast, the service sectors (G–O), and especially the finance and banking sector (J and K) and the transport, storage and communication sector (I), have grown very rapidly.

In respect to employment, a similar, although more dramatic, pattern emerges. Only the retail trade (G and H), finance and banking (J and K) and other services (L–O) have seen an increase in employment over the whole twenty-year period. In all the other sectors, employment has fallen, and in mining and quarrying (C), electricity, gas and water supply (E) and manufacturing (D), the fall has been dramatic.

If we examine the subsections and divisions within the SIC, we can get a more detailed picture of how the structure of industry has changed. For example, we find that the process of deindustrialisation has not been experienced by all manufacturing industries. Certain divisions, such as instrument and electrical engineering, are in fact among the fastest growing in the whole UK economy. It is the more traditional manufacturing industries, such as metal manufacturing, which have experienced a substantial decline.

In respect to employment, there are again substantial variations between divisions. Thus whereas the financial services sector has seen a rapid growth in employment, there has been a decline in employment in parts of the retail banking sector (fewer counter staff are required in high street banks, given the growth in cash machines, direct debits, debit cards, etc.). And whereas there has been a decline in employment in primary industries (such as agriculture and mining) and traditional manufacturing industries (such as shipbuilding and metal manufacturing), there has been a growth in employment in some of the more 'high-tech' industries.

Analysing industrial concentration

The SIC also enables us to address wider issues such as changes in **industrial concentration**.

When we examine the size structure of UK industry, we find that some sectors are dominated by large business units (those employing more than 500 people), whereas in others it is small and medium-sized enterprises (SMEs) that dominate.

Table 1.3 shows that in the manufacturing sector (D) 39.2 per cent of all workers were employed by large firms in 1998, and such firms accounted for 51.8 per cent of the sector's turnover. The *number* of large manufacturing firms, however, was a mere 1150, compared with 330 985 SMEs. In some sectors, the bulk of output is produced by small or medium-sized firms. This is especially true in the service sector, but also in agriculture, forestry and fishing, and in construction. In other sectors, production is highly concentrated in just a few firms. This is especially so in industries such as electricity, gas and water supply, and in the mining and quarrying sector. In most of these cases, production involves large-scale capital equipment and thus would not suit small firms.

We will be examining industrial structure and the scale of enterprises at several points in the book.

> **definition**
>
> **Industrial concentration**
> The degree to which an industry is dominated by large business enterprises.

Table 1.3	Number of businesses, employment and turnover by industrial sector: 1998			
Sector	Size of business	Number of businesses (and % of sector)	Employment (% of sector)	Turnover (% of sector)
All	SMEs[a]	3 654 440 (99.9)	61.5	59.9
	Large firms[b]	3 445 (0.1)	38.5	40.1
A/B	SMEs	192 835 (99.9)	99.9	99.5
	Large firms	5 (0.1)	0.1	0.1
C	SMEs	5 445 (99.5)	44.8	40.3
	Large firms	30 (0.5)	55.2	59.7
D	SMEs	330 985 (99.7)	60.8	48.2
	Large firms	1 150 (0.3)	39.2	51.8
E	SMEs	300 (88.2)	na	na
	Large firms	40 (11.8)	na	na
F	SMEs	728 570 (99.9)	89.1	80.8
	Large firms	130 (0.1)	10.9	19.2
G	SMEs	553 715 (99.9)	56.9	65.3
	Large firms	485 (0.1)	43.1	34.7
H	SMEs	153 190 (99.9)	60.9	56.5
	Large firms	130 (0.1)	39.1	43.5
I	SMEs	210 855 (99.9)	43.7	48.2
	Large firms	215 (0.1)	56.3	51.8
J	SMEs	65 710 (99.7)	28.4	51.4
	Large firms	225 (0.3)	72.6	48.6
K	SMEs	736 480 (99.9)	76.2	79.4
	Large firms	440 (0.1)	23.8	20.6
M	SMEs	100 905 (99.9)	na	na
	Large firms	25 (0.1)	na	na
N	SMEs	202 790 (99.8)	44.2	34.9
	Large firms	455 (0.2)	55.8	65.1
O	SMEs	373 135 (99.9)	80.5	64.7
	Large firms	110 (0.1)	19.5	35.3

Source: Based on *Small and Medium-sized Enterprises Report* (Department of Trade and Industry, 1999).
[a] Firms with fewer than 500 employees.
[b] Firms with 500 or more employees.
na Figures not available

1.3 The determinants of business performance

Structure–conduct–performance

It should be apparent from our analysis thus far that business performance is strongly influenced by the market structure within which the firm operates. This is known as the *structure–conduct–performance paradigm.*

A business operating in a highly competitive market structure will conduct its activities differently from a business in a market with relatively few competitors. For example, the more competitive the market, the more aggressive the business may have to be in order to sell its product and remain competitive. The less competitive the market structure, the greater the chance that collusion between producers might be the preferred strategy, as this reduces the excesses and uncertainties that outright competition might produce.

Such conduct will in turn influence how well businesses perform. Performance can be measured by several different indicators, such as current profitability or profitability over the longer term, market share or growth in market share, and changes in share prices or share prices relative to those of other firms in the industry or to other firms in general, to name some of the most commonly used.

Throughout the book, we shall be seeing how market structure affects business conduct, and how business conduct affects business performance.

It would be wrong, however, to argue that business performance is totally shaped by external factors such as market structure. In fact, the internal aims and organisation of business may be very influential in determining success.

Internal aims and organisation

Economists have traditionally based their analysis of business activity on the assumption that its prime goal is the maximisation of profits. In the past, this was largely true. In the eighteenth and nineteenth centuries, enterprises were managed by the business owner: the true 'entrepreneur'. However, as businesses grew throughout the nineteenth century, and as the range of products became larger and production processes became more complex, so the managerial role became ever more specialist. Owners (the shareholders) and managers became increasingly distinct groups.

This distinction between owners and managers is crucial when we attempt to establish precisely what the objectives of business might be. Whose objectives are we referring to: those of the owner, or those of the manager who controls the assets of the business enterprise? As we shall see in Chapters 3 and 13, the objectives of managers and owners may well be at odds. Managers may pursue a range of objectives, and it could well be that these objectives conflict with each other. Thus a manager might like to maximise profits and also to maximise sales. The means to increase sales may be to cut prices, but that may have the effect of reducing profits. Thus managers may have to content themselves with merely achieving a *satisfactory* level of each goal.

It is not only the aims of a business that affect its performance. Performance also depends on the following:

- Internal structure. The way in which the firm is organised (e.g. into departments or specialised units) will affect its costs, its aggressiveness in the market, its willingness to innovate, etc.
- Information. The better informed a business is about its markets, about its costs of production, about alternative techniques and about alternative products it could make, the better will it be able to fulfil its goals.
- The competence of management. The performance of a business will depend on the skills, experience, motivation, dedication and sensitivity of its managers.
- The quality of the workforce. The more skilled and the better motivated is a company's workforce, the better will be its results.
- Systems. The functioning of any organisation will depend on the systems in place: information systems, systems for motivation (rewards, penalties,

team spirit, etc.), technical systems (for sequencing production, for quality control, for setting specifications), distributional systems (transport, ordering and supply), financial systems (for accounting and auditing), and so on.

We shall be examining many of these features of internal organisation in subsequent chapters.

SUMMARY

1a Business economics is about the study of economic decisions made by business and the influences upon this. It is also concerned with the effects that this decision making has upon other businesses and the performance of the economy in general.

1b The business environment refers to the environment within which business decision making takes place. It is commonly divided into four dimensions: political, economic, social and technological.

1c The economic dimension of the business environment is divided into two: the microeconomic environment and the macroeconomic environment. The micro environment analyses factors specific to a particular firm in a particular market. The macro environment considers how national and international economic circumstances affect all business.

2a Production is divided into being primary, secondary or tertiary. The contribution to output of these different sectors of production has changed over time. Most recently in the UK the tertiary sector has grown and the secondary sector contracted.

2b Firms are classified into industries and industries into sectors. Such classification enables us to chart changes in industrial structure over time and to assess changing patterns of industrial concentration.

3 The performance of a business is determined by a wide range of both internal and external factors, such as business organisation, the aims of owners and managers, and market structure.

REVIEW QUESTIONS

1 Assume you are a UK car manufacturer and are seeking to devise a business strategy for the twenty-first century. Conduct a PEST analysis on the UK car industry and evaluate the various strategies that the business might pursue.

2 What is the Standard Industrial Classification (SIC)? In what ways might such a classification system be useful? Can you think of any limitations or problems such a system might have over time?

3 In Chapter 1 we have identified some of the major changes in the UK's industrial structure and concentration in recent times. What were these changes and what might they tell us about changes in the British economy?

4 Outline the main determinants of the business performance. Distinguish whether these are micro- or macroeconomic.

Economics and the world of business

2.1 What do economists study?

Tackling the problem of scarcity

We have looked at various aspects of the business environment and the influences on firms. We have also looked at some of the economic problems that businesses face. But what contribution can economists make to the analysis of these problems and to recommending solutions?

To answer this question we need to go one stage back and ask what it is that economists study in general. What is it that makes a problem an *economic* problem? The answer is that there is one central problem faced by all individuals and all societies. This is the problem of *scarcity*.

We define scarcity as 'the excess of human wants over what can actually be produced'.

Of course, we do not all face the problem of scarcity to the same degree. A poor person unable to afford enough to eat or a decent place to live will hardly see it as a 'problem' that a rich person cannot afford a second Rolls-Royce. But economists do not claim that we all face an *equal* problem of scarcity. The point is that people, both rich and poor, want more than they can have and this will cause them to behave in certain ways. Economics studies that behaviour.

Two of the key elements in satisfying wants are **consumption** and **production**. As far as consumption is concerned, economics studies how much the population spends; what the pattern of consumption is in the economy; and how much people buy of particular items. The business economist, in particular, studies consumer behaviour; how sensitive consumer demand is to changes in prices, advertising, fashion and other factors; and how the firm can seek to persuade the consumer to buy its products.

As far as production is concerned, economics studies how much the economy produces in total; what influences the rate of growth of production; and why the production of some goods increases and others falls. The business economist tends to focus on the role of the firm in this process: what determines the output of individual businesses and the range of products they produce; what techniques firms use and why; and what determines their investment decisions and how many workers they employ.

The production of goods and services involves the use of inputs, or factors of production as they are often called. These are of three broad types:

- Human resources: **labour**. The labour force is limited both in number and in skills.

---

definition

Scarcity
The excess of human wants over what can actually be produced to fulfil these wants.

definition

Consumption
The act of using goods and services to satisfy wants. This will normally involve purchasing the goods and services.

definition

Production
The transformation of inputs into outputs by firms in order to earn profit (or meet some other objective).

definition

Factors of production (or resources)
The inputs into the production of goods and services: labour, land and raw materials, and capital.

definition

Labour
All forms of human input, both physical and mental, into current production.

- Natural resources: **land and raw materials**. The world's land area is limited, as are its raw materials.
- Manufactured resources: **capital**. Capital consists of all those inputs that themselves have had to be produced in the first place. The world has a limited stock of capital: a limited supply of factories, machines, transportation and other equipment. The productivity of capital is limited by the state of technology.

We will be studying the use of these resources by firms for the production of goods and services: production to meet consumer demand – production which will thus help to reduce the problem of scarcity.

Demand and supply

We said that economics is concerned with consumption and production. Another way of looking at this is in terms of *demand* and *supply*. It is quite likely that you already knew that economics had something to do with demand and supply. In fact, demand and supply and the relationship between them lie at the very centre of economics. But what do we mean by the terms, and what is their relationship with the problem of scarcity?

Demand is related to wants. If goods and services were free, people would simply demand whatever they wanted. Such wants are virtually boundless: perhaps only limited by people's imagination. *Supply*, on the other hand, is limited. It is related to resources. The amount that firms can supply depends on the resources and technology available.

Given the problem of scarcity, given that human wants exceed what can actually be produced, *potential* demands will exceed *potential* supplies. Society therefore has to find some way of dealing with this problem. Somehow it has to try to match demand and supply. This applies at the level of the economy overall: *aggregate* demand will need to be balanced against *aggregate* supply. In other words, total spending in the economy will need to balance total production. It also applies at the level of individual goods and services. The demand and supply of cabbages will need to balance, as will the demand and supply of video recorders, cars, houses and haircuts.

But if potential demand exceeds potential supply, how are *actual* demand and supply to be made equal? Either demand has to be curtailed, or supply has to be increased, or a combination of the two. Economics studies this process. It studies how demand adjusts to available supplies, and how supply adjusts to consumer demands.

The business economist studies the role of firms in this process: how they respond to demand, or, indeed, try to create demand for their products; how they combine their inputs to achieve output in the most efficient way; how they decide the amount to produce and the price to charge their customers; and how they make their investment decisions. Not only this, the business economist also considers the wider environment in which firms operate and how they are affected by it: the effect of changes in the national and international economic climate, such as upswings and downswings in the economy, and changes in interest rates and exchange rates. In short, the business economist studies supply: how firms' output is affected by a range of influences, and how firms can best meet their objectives.

definition

Land (and raw materials)
Inputs into production that are provided by nature: e.g. unimproved land and mineral deposits in the ground.

definition

Capital
All inputs into production that have themselves been produced: e.g. factories, machines and tools.

Dividing up the subject

Economics is traditionally divided into two main branches – *macroeconomics* and *microeconomics*, where 'macro' means big, and 'micro' means small.

Macroeconomics is concerned with the economy as a whole. It is thus concerned with **aggregate demand** and **aggregate supply**. By 'aggregate demand' we mean the total amount of spending in the economy, whether by consumers, by overseas customers for our exports, by the government, or by firms when they buy capital equipment or stock up on raw materials. By 'aggregate supply' we mean the total national output of goods and services.

Microeconomics is concerned with the individual parts of the economy. It is concerned with the demand and supply of *particular* goods and services and resources: cars, butter, clothes and haircuts; electricians, secretaries, blast furnaces, computers and coal.

Business economics, because it studies firms, is largely concerned with microeconomic issues. Nevertheless, given that businesses are affected by what is going on in the economy as a whole, it is still important for the business economist to study the macroeconomic environment and its effects on individual firms.

2.2 Business economics: the macroeconomic environment

Because things are scarce, societies are concerned that their resources are being used as *fully as possible*, and that over time the national output should *grow*. Governments are keen to boast to their electorate how much the economy has grown since they have been in charge!

The achievement of growth and the full use of resources is not easy, however, as witness the periods of high unemployment and stagnation that have occurred from time to time throughout the world (for example, in the 1930s, the early 1980s and the early 1990s). Furthermore, attempts by governments to stimulate growth and employment have often resulted in inflation and balance of payments crises. Even when societies do achieve growth, it is often short lived. Economies have often experienced cycles, where periods of growth alternate with periods of stagnation, such periods varying from a few months to a few years.

Macroeconomics, then, studies the determination of national output and its growth over time. It also studies the problems of stagnation, unemployment, inflation, the balance of international payments and cyclical instability, and the policies adopted by governments to deal with these problems.

Macroeconomic problems are closely related to the balance between aggregate demand and aggregate supply.

If aggregate demand is *too high* relative to aggregate supply, inflation and balance of payments deficits are likely to result.

- **Inflation** refers to a general rise in the level of prices throughout the economy. If aggregate demand rises substantially, firms are likely to respond by raising their prices. After all, if demand is high, they can probably still sell as much as before (if not more) even at the higher prices, and thus make more profits. If firms in general put up their prices, inflation results.

---

definition

Macroeconomics
The branch of economics that studies economic aggregates (grand totals): e.g. the overall level of prices, output and employment in the economy.

definition

Aggregate demand
The total level of spending in the economy.

definition

Aggregate supply
The total amount of output in the economy.

definition

Microeconomics
The branch of economics that studies individual units: e.g. households, firms and industries. It studies the interrelationships between these units in determining the pattern of production and distribution of goods and services.

definition

Rate of inflation
The percentage increase in the level of prices over a twelve-month period.

● **(Current account) balance of payments deficits**[1] are the excess of imports over exports. If aggregate demand rises, people are likely to buy more imports. In other words, part of the extra expenditure will go on Japanese videos, German cars, French wine, etc. Also if inflation is high, home-produced goods will become uncompetitive with foreign goods. We are likely, therefore, to buy more foreign imports, and foreigners are likely to buy fewer of our exports.

If aggregate demand is *too low* relative to aggregate supply, unemployment and recession may well result.

● A recession is where output in the economy declines: in other words, growth becomes negative. A recession is associated with a low level of consumer spending. If people spend less, shops are likely to find themselves with unsold stocks. As a result they will buy less from the manufacturers, which in turn will cut down on production.
● Unemployment is likely to result from cutbacks in production. If firms are producing less, they will need a smaller labour force.

Macroeconomic *policy*, therefore, tends to focus on the balance of aggregate demand and aggregate supply. It can be **demand-side policy**, which seeks to influence the level of spending in the economy. This in turn will affect the level of production, prices and employment. Or it can be **supply-side policy**. This is designed to influence the level of production directly: for example, by trying to create more incentives for workers or business people.

Macroeconomic policy and its effects on business

Both demand-side and supply-side policy will affect the business environment. Take demand-side policy. If there is a recession, the government might try to boost the level of spending (aggregate demand) by cutting taxes, increasing government spending or reducing interest rates. If consumers respond by purchasing more, then this will clearly have an effect on businesses. But firms will want to be stocked up ready for an upsurge in consumer demand. Therefore, they will want to estimate the effect on their own particular market of a boost to aggregate demand. Studying the macroeconomic environment and the effects of government policy, therefore, is vital for firms when forecasting future demand for their product.

It is the same with supply-side policy. The government may introduce tax incentives for firms to invest, or for people to work harder; it may introduce new training schemes; it may build new motorways. These policies will affect firms' costs and hence the profitability of production. So, again, firms will want to predict how government policies are likely to affect them, so that they can plan accordingly.

The circular flow of income

One of the most useful diagrams for illustrating the macroeconomic environment and the relationships between producers and consumers is the *circular flow of income* diagram. This is illustrated in Figure 2.1.

---

[1] The current account excludes investments and financial movements into and out of the country. Such movements are called the 'financial account'.

definition

Current account balance of payments
Exports of goods and services minus imports of goods and services. If exports exceed imports, there is a 'current account surplus' (a positive figure). If imports exceed exports, there is a 'current account deficit' (a negative figure).

definition

Recession
A period where national output falls for a few months or more.

definition

Unemployment
The number of people who are actively looking for work but are currently without a job. (Note that there is much debate as to who should officially be counted as unemployed.)

definition

Demand-side policy
Government policy designed to alter the level of aggregate demand, and thereby the level of output, employment and prices.

definition

Supply-side policy
Government policy that attempts to alter the level of aggregate supply directly.

BOX 2.1

Looking at macroeconomic data
Assessing different countries' macroeconomic performance

Rapid economic growth, low unemployment, low inflation and the avoidance of current account deficits are the major macroeconomic policy objectives of most governments round the world. To help them achieve these objectives they employ economic advisers. But when we look at the performance of various economies, the success of government macroeconomic policies seems decidedly 'mixed'.

The table shows data for the USA, Japan, Germany and the UK from 1978 to 2001.

If the government does not have much success in managing the economy it could be for the following reasons:

● Economists have incorrectly analysed the problems and hence have given the wrong advice.

● Economists disagree and hence have given conflicting advice.
● Economists have based their advice on inaccurate forecasts.
● Governments have not heeded the advice of economists.
● There is little else that governments could have done: the problems were insoluble.

Questions

1 Has the UK generally fared better or worse than the other three countries?
2 Was there a common pattern in the macroeconomic performance of each of the four countries over these 24 years?

Macroeconomic performance of four industrialised economies (average annual figures)

	Unemployment (% of workforce)				Inflation (%)				Economic growth (%)				Balance on current account (% of national income)			
	USA	Japan	Germany	UK	USA	Japan	Germany	UK	USA	Japan	Germany	UK	USA	Japan	Germany	UK
1978–80	6.3	2.1	3.2	5.8	9.7	5.1	4.1	13.2	2.5	4.9	2.9	1.4	−0.2	−0.1	−0.3	0.6
1981–3	8.8	2.4	7.7	11.2	6.6	3.2	5.0	8.4	1.0	3.4	0.3	1.3	−0.5	0.9	0.4	1.8
1984–6	7.1	2.6	6.9	11.4	3.3	1.6	1.4	4.8	4.8	3.7	2.4	2.6	−3.2	3.6	2.9	0.3
1987–9	5.6	2.5	6.0	8.3	3.7	1.2	1.4	5.7	3.7	5.1	2.9	3.9	−2.8	2.8	4.4	−3.0
1990–2	6.6	2.1	4.5	8.7	4.2	2.7	3.4	6.4	1.5	3.3	4.3	−0.3	−0.7	2.2	0.5	−2.2
1993–5	6.2	2.8	8.2	9.6	2.8	0.6	3.0	2.5	3.1	0.8	1.0	3.2	−1.5	2.7	−0.9	−0.8
1996–8	4.9	3.6	9.4	7.2	2.3	0.8	1.4	3.0	4.0	1.4	1.5	2.8	−2.0	2.3	−0.2	0.2
1999–2001	4.4	5.0	8.5	5.8	2.4	0.0	1.2	2.3	4.0	1.4	2.5	2.4	−4.2	2.7	−0.3	−1.7

Source: Datastream

The consumers of goods and services are labelled 'households'. Some members of households, of course, are also workers, and in some cases are the owners of other factors of production too, such as land. The producers of goods and services are labelled 'firms'.

Firms and households are in a twin 'demand and supply' relationship.

First, on the right-hand side of the diagram, households demand goods and services, and firms supply goods and services. In the process, exchange takes place. In a money economy (as opposed to a **barter economy**), firms exchange goods and services for money. In other words, money flows from households to firms in the form of consumer expenditure, while goods and services flow the other way – from firms to households.

definition

Barter economy
An economy where people exchange goods and services directly with one another without any payment of money. Workers would be paid with bundles of goods.

Figure 2.1
Circular flow of goods and incomes

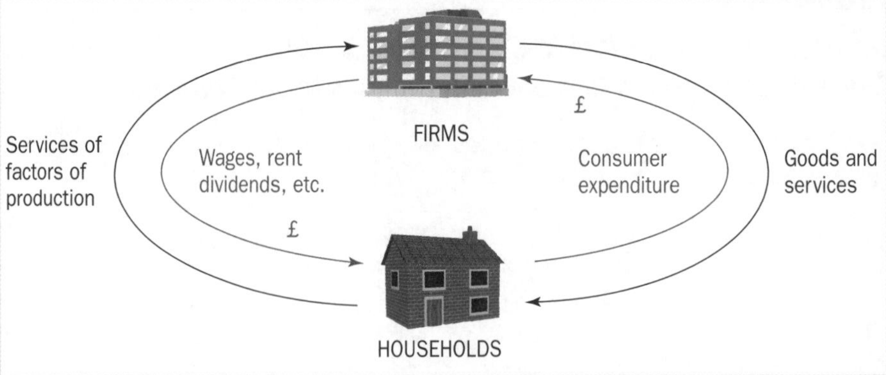

Services of factors of production

Wages, rent dividends, etc.

£

FIRMS

Consumer expenditure

£

Goods and services

HOUSEHOLDS

This coming together of buyers and sellers is known as a **market** – whether it be a street market, a shop, an auction, a mail-order system or whatever. Thus we talk about the market for apples, the market for oil, for cars, for houses, for televisions and so on.

Second, firms and households come together in the market for factors of production. This is illustrated on the left-hand side of the diagram. This time the demand and supply roles are reversed. Firms demand the use of factors of production owned by households – labour, land and capital. Households supply them. Thus the services of labour and other factors flow from households to firms, and in exchange firms pay households money – namely, wages, rent, dividends and interest. Just as we referred to particular goods markets, so we can also refer to particular factor markets – the market for bricklayers, for secretaries, for hairdressers, for land, etc.

There is thus a circular flow of incomes. Households earn incomes from firms and firms earn incomes from households. The money circulates. There is also a circular flow of goods and services, but in the opposite direction. Households supply factor services to firms, which then use them to supply goods and services to households.

Macroeconomics is concerned with the total size of the flow. If consumers choose to spend more, firms will earn more from the increased level of sales. They will probably respond by producing more or raising their prices, or some combination of the two. As a result, they will end up paying more out to workers in the form of wages, and to shareholders in the form of profits. Households will thus have gained additional income. This will then lead to an additional increase in consumer spending, and, therefore, a further boost to production. To summarise: increased spending generates additional income, which, in turn, generates additional spending, and so on as additional incomes flow round and round the circular flow of income.

The effect does not go on indefinitely, however. When households earn additional incomes, not all of it is spent: not all of it recirculates. Some of the additional income will be saved; some will be paid in taxes; and some will be spent on imports (and will not thus stimulate domestic production). The bigger these 'withdrawals', as they are called, the less will production go on being stimulated.

It is important for firms to estimate the eventual effect of an initial rise in consumer demand (or a rise in government expenditure, for that matter). Will there

key terms

Market
The interaction between buyers and sellers.

be a boom in the economy, or will the rise in demand merely fizzle out? A study of macroeconomics helps business people to understand the effects of changes in aggregate demand, and the effects that such changes will have on their own particular business.

We examine the macroeconomic environment and the effects on business of macroeconomic policy in Chapters 25–31.

2.3 Business economics: microeconomic choices

Microeconomics and choice

Because resources are scarce, choices have to be made. There are three main categories of choice that must be made in any society:

- *What* goods and services are going to be produced and in what quantities, given that there are not enough resources to produce all the things that people desire? How many cars, how much wheat, how much insurance, how many pop concerts, how many coats, etc. will be produced?
- *How* are things going to be produced, given that there is normally more than one way of producing things? What resources are going to be used and in what quantities? What techniques of production are going to be adopted? Will cars be produced by robots or by assembly-line workers? Will electricity be produced from coal, oil, gas, nuclear fission, renewable resources or a mixture of these?
- *For whom* are things going to be produced? In other words, how is the nation's income going to be distributed? After all, the higher your income, the more you can consume of the nation's output. What will be the wages of farm workers, printers, cleaners and accountants? How much will pensioners receive? How much profit will owners of private companies receive or will state-owned industries make?

All societies have to make these choices, whether they be made by individuals, by groups or by the government. These choices can be seen as *micro*economic choices, since they are concerned not with the *total* amount of national output, but with the *individual* goods and services that make it up: what they are, how they are made, and who gets the incomes to buy them.

Choice and opportunity cost

Choice involves sacrifice. The more food you choose to buy, the less money you will have to spend on other goods. The more food a nation produces, the fewer resources will there be for producing other goods. In other words, the production or consumption of one thing involves the sacrifice of alternatives. This sacrifice of alternatives in the production (or consumption) of a good is known as its **opportunity cost**.

If the workers on a farm can produce either 1000 tonnes of wheat or 2000 tonnes of barley, then the opportunity cost of producing 1 tonne of wheat is the 2 tonnes of barley forgone. The opportunity cost of buying a textbook is the new pair of jeans you also wanted that you have had to go without. The opportunity cost of working overtime is the leisure you have sacrificed.

> **definition**
>
> **Opportunity cost**
> The cost of any activity measured in terms of the best alternative forgone.

BOX 2.2

The opportunity costs of studying economics
What are you sacrificing?

You may not have realised it, but you probably consider opportunity costs many times a day. The reason is that we are constantly making choices: what to buy, what to eat, what to wear, whether to go out, how much to study and so on. Each time we make a choice to do something, we are in effect rejecting doing some alternative. This alternative forgone is the opportunity cost of our action.

Sometimes the opportunity costs of our actions are the direct monetary costs we incur. Sometimes it is more complicated.

Take the opportunity costs of your choices as a student of economics.

Buying a textbook costing £26.95
This does involve a direct money payment. What you have to consider is the alternatives you could have bought with the £26.95. You then have to weigh up the benefit from the best alternative against the benefit of the textbook.

Question
What might prevent you from making the best decision?

Coming to classes
You may or may not be paying course fees. Even if you are, there is no extra (marginal) monetary cost in coming to classes once the fees have been paid. You will not get a refund by skipping classes!

So are the opportunity costs zero? No: by coming to classes you are *not* working in the library; you are *not* having an extra hour in bed; you are *not* sitting drinking coffee with friends, and so on. If you are making a rational decision to come to classes, then you will consider such possible alternatives.

Question
If there are several other things you could have done, is the opportunity cost the sum of all of them?

Revising for an economics exam
Again, the opportunity cost is the best alternative to which you could have put your time. This might be revising for some *other* exam. You will probably want to divide your time sensibly between your subjects. A *sensible* decision is not to revise economics on any given occasion if you will gain a greater benefit from revising for another subject. In such a case the (marginal) opportunity cost of revising economics exceeds the (marginal) benefit.

Choosing to study at university or college
What are the opportunity costs of being a student in higher education?

At first it might seem that the costs would include the following:

- Tuition fees.
- Books, stationery, etc.
- Accommodation expenses.
- Transport.
- Food, entertainment and other living expenses.

But adding these up does not give the opportunity cost. The opportunity cost is the sacrifice entailed by going to university or college rather than doing something else. Let us assume that the alternative is to take a job that has been offered. The correct list of opportunity costs of higher education would include:

- Books, stationery, etc.
- *Additional* accommodation and transport expenses over what would have been incurred by taking the job.
- Wages that would have been earned in the job *less* any student grant received.

Note that tuition fees are not included because it is assumed that these are paid by the student's local education authority.

Questions
1 Why is the cost of food not included?
2 Make a list of the benefits of higher education.
3 Is the opportunity cost to the individual of attending higher education different from the opportunity costs to society as a whole?

Rational choices

Economists often refer to **rational choices**. By this is simply meant the weighing-up of the *costs* and *benefits* of any activity, whether it be firms choosing what and how much to produce, workers choosing whether to take a particular job or to work extra hours, or consumers choosing what to buy.

Imagine you are doing your shopping in a supermarket and you want to buy some meat. Do you spend a lot of money and buy best steak, or do you buy cheap mince instead? To make a rational (i.e. sensible) decision, you will need to weigh up the costs and benefits of each alternative. Best steak may give you a lot of enjoyment, but it has a high opportunity cost: because it is expensive, you will need to sacrifice quite a lot of consumption of other goods if you decide to buy it. If you buy the mince, however, although you will not enjoy it so much, you will have more money left over to buy other things: it has a lower opportunity cost.

Thus rational decision making, as far as consumers are concerned, involves choosing those items that give you the best value for money: i.e. the *greatest benefit relative to cost*.

The same principles apply to firms when deciding what to produce. For example, should a car firm open up another production line? A rational decision will again involve weighing up the benefits and costs. The benefits are the revenues that the firm will earn from selling the extra cars. The costs will include the extra labour costs, raw material costs, costs of component parts, etc. It will be profitable to open up the new production line only if the revenues earned exceed the costs entailed: in other words, if it earns a profit.

In the more complex situation of deciding which model of car to produce, or how many of each model, the firm must weigh up the relative benefits and costs of each: i.e. it will want to produce the most profitable product mix.

Marginal costs and benefits

In economics we argue that rational choices involve weighing up **marginal costs** and **marginal benefits**. These are the costs and benefits of doing a little bit more or a little bit less of a given activity. They can be contrasted with the *total* costs and benefits of the activity.

Take a familiar example. What time will you set the alarm clock to go off tomorrow morning? Let us say that you have to leave home at 8.30. Perhaps you will set the alarm for 7.00. That will give you plenty of time to get up and get ready, but it will mean a relatively short night's sleep. Perhaps then you will decide to set it for 7.30 or even 8.00. That will give you a longer night's sleep, but much more of a rush in the morning to get ready.

So how do you make a rational decision about when the alarm should go off? What you have to do is to weigh up the costs and benefits of *additional* sleep. Each extra minute in bed gives you more sleep (the marginal benefit), but gives you more of a rush when you get up (the marginal cost). The decision is therefore based on the costs and benefits of *extra* sleep, not on the *total* costs and benefits of a whole night's sleep.

This same principle applies to rational decisions made by consumers, workers and firms. For example, the car firm we were considering just now will weigh up the marginal costs and benefits of producing cars: in other words, it will

---

definition

Rational choices
Choices that involve weighing up the benefit of any activity against its opportunity cost.

---

definition

Marginal costs
The additional cost of doing a little bit more (or *1 unit* more if a unit can be measured) of an activity.

---

definition

Marginal benefits
The additional benefits of doing a little bit more (or *1 unit* more if a unit can be measured) of an activity.

compare the costs and revenue of producing *additional* cars. If additional cars add more to the firm's revenue than to its costs, it will be profitable to produce them.

Microeconomic choices and the firm

All economic decisions made by firms involve choices. The business economist studies these choices and their results.

We will look at the choices of how much to produce, what price to charge the customer, how many inputs to use, what type of inputs to use and in what combination, whether to expand the scale of the firm's operations, whether to invest in new plant, whether to engage in research and development, whether to merge with or take over another company, whether to diversify into other markets, whether to export. The right choices (in terms of best meeting the firm's objectives) will vary according to the type of market in which the firm operates, its predictions about future demand, its degree of power in the market, the actions and reactions of competitors, the degree and type of government intervention, the current tax regime, the availability of finance, and so on. In short, we will be studying the whole range of economic choices made by firms and in a number of different scenarios.

In all these cases, the owners of firms will want the best possible choices to be made: i.e. those choices that best meet the objectives of the firm. Making the best choices, as we have seen, will involve weighing up the marginal benefits against the marginal opportunity costs of each decision.

SUMMARY

1a The central economic problem is that of scarcity. Given that there is a limited supply of factors of production (labour, land and capital), it is impossible to provide everybody with everything they want. Potential demands exceed potential supplies.

1b The subject of economics is usually divided into two main branches: macroeconomics and microeconomics.

2a Macroeconomics deals with aggregates such as the overall levels of unemployment, output, growth and prices in the economy.

2b The macroeconomic environment will be an important determinant of a business's profitability.

3a Microeconomics deals with the activities of individual units within the economy: firms, industries, consumers, workers, etc. Because resources are scarce, people have to make choices. Society has to choose by some means or other *what* goods and services to produce, *how* to produce them and *for whom* to produce them. Microeconomics studies these choices.

3b Rational choices involve weighing up the marginal benefits of each activity against its marginal opportunity costs. If the marginal benefit exceeds the marginal cost, it is rational to choose to do more of that activity.

3c Businesses are constantly faced with choices: how much to produce, what inputs to use, what price to charge, how much to invest, etc. We will study these choices.

REVIEW QUESTIONS

1 Virtually every good is scarce in the sense we have defined it. There are, however, a few exceptions. Under *certain circumstances*, water and air are not scarce. When and where might this be true for (a) water and (b) air?

Why is it important to define water and air very carefully before deciding whether they are scarce or abundant? Under circumstances where they are *not* scarce, would it be possible to charge for them?

2   Which of the following are macroeconomic issues, which are microeconomic ones and which could be either depending on the context?
    (a) Inflation.
    (b) Low wages in certain service industries.
    (c) The rate of exchange between the pound and the Deutschmark.
    (d) Why the price of cabbages fluctuates more than that of cars.
    (e) The rate of economic growth this year compared with last year.
    (f) The decline of traditional manufacturing industries.

3   Make a list of three things you did yesterday. What was the opportunity cost of each?

4   A washing machine manufacturer is considering whether to produce an extra batch of 1000 washing machines. How would it set about working out the marginal opportunity cost of so doing?

5   How would a firm use the principle of weighing up marginal costs and marginal benefits when deciding whether (a) to take on an additional worker; (b) to offer overtime to existing workers?

6   We identified three categories of withdrawal from the circular flow of income. What were they? There are also three categories of 'injection' of expenditure into the circular flow of income. What do you think they are?

APPENDIX

Some techniques of economic analysis

When students first come to economics, many are worried about the amount of mathematics they will encounter. Will it all be equations and graphs, and will there be lots of hard calculations to do and difficult theories to grasp?

As you will see if you glance through the pages of this book, there are many diagrams and tables and a few equations. But this does not mean that there are many mathematical techniques that you will have to master. In fact there are relatively few techniques, but they are ones which we use many times in many different contexts. You will find that, if you are new to the subject, you will very quickly become familiar with these techniques. If you are not new to the subject, perhaps you could reassure your colleagues who are!

Diagrams as pictures

In many cases, we use diagrams simply to provide a picture of a relationship. Just as a photograph in a newspaper can often provide a much more vivid picture of an event than any description in words, so too a diagram in economics

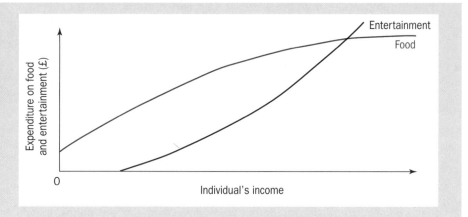

can often picture a relationship with a vividness and clarity that could never be achieved by description alone.

For example, we may observe that as people's incomes rise, they spend a lot more on entertainment and only a little more on food. We can picture this relationship very nicely by the use of a simple graph.

In Figure 2.2, an individual's income is measured along the horizontal axis and the expenditure on food and entertainment is measured up the vertical axis. There are just two lines on this diagram: the one showing how the person's expenditure on entertainment rises as income rises, the other how the expenditure on food rises as income rises. Now we could use a diagram like this to plot actual data. But we may simply be using it as a sketch – as a picture. In this case we do not necessarily need to put figures on the two axes. We are simply showing the relative *shapes* of the two curves. These shapes tell us that the person's expenditure on entertainment rises more quickly than that on food, and that above a certain level of income the expenditure on entertainment becomes greater than that on food.

If you were to describe in words all the information that this sketch graph depicts, you would need several lines of prose.

Figure 2.1 (the circular flow diagram) was an example of a sketch designed to give a simple, clear picture of a relationship: a picture stripped of all unnecessary detail.

Representing real-life statistics

In many cases we will want to depict real-world data. We may want to show, for example, how the level of business investment has fluctuated over a given period of time, or we may want to depict the market shares of the different firms within a given industry. In the first case we will need to look at time-series data. In the second we will look at cross-section data.

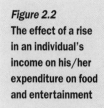

definition

Time-series data
Information depicting how a variable (e.g. the price of eggs) changes over time.

Time-series data

Table 2.1 shows annual percentage changes in investment in the European Union between 1980 and 2000.

A table like this is a common way of representing **time-series data**. It has the

Table 2.1	Investment in the EU: percentage changes from previous year																			
1980	1981	1982	1983	1984	1985	1986	1987	1988	1989	1990	1991	1992	1993	1994	1995	1996	1997	1998	1999	2000
1.8	−5.0	−1.5	0.4	1.5	2.6	3.9	5.4	8.5	7.0	4.1	−0.3	−0.3	−5.8	2.6	3.5	2.3	3.3	5.7	5.1	5.6

Source: Adapted from *OECD Economic Outlook*, December (OECD, 2000).

advantage of giving the precise figures, and is thus a useful reference if we want to test any theory and see if it predicts accurately.

Notice that in this particular table the figures are given annually. Depending on the period of time over which we want to see the movement of a variable, it may be more appropriate to use a different interval of time. For example, if we wanted to see how investment had changed over the last 50 years, we might use intervals of five years or more. If, however, we wanted to see how investment had changed over the course of a year, we would probably use monthly figures.

Time-series data can also be shown graphically. In fact the data from a table can be plotted directly on to a graph. Figure 2.3 plots the data from Table 2.1. Each dot on the graph corresponds to one figure from the table. The dots are then joined up to form a single line.

Thus if you wanted to find the annual percentage change in investment in the EU at any time between 1980 and 2000, you would simply find the appropriate date on the horizontal axis, read vertically upward to the line you have drawn, then read across to find the annual rate of change in investment.

Although a graph like this cannot give you quite such an accurate measurement of each point as a table does, it gives a much more obvious picture of how the figures have moved over time and whether the changes are getting bigger (the curve getting steeper) or smaller (the curve getting shallower). We can also

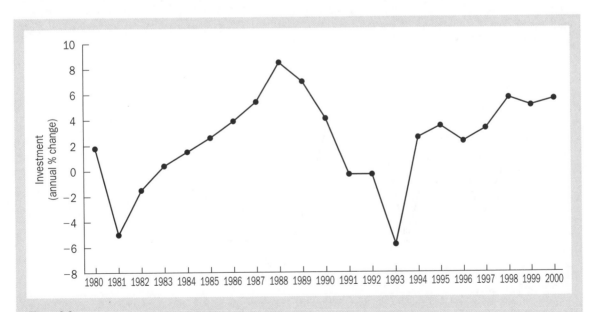

Figure 2.3

Investment in the EU: percentage changes from previous year

Table 2.2 National income in the EU: percentage changes from previous year (economic growth rates)

1980	1981	1982	1983	1984	1985	1986	1987	1988	1989	1990	1991	1992	1993	1994	1995	1996	1997	1998	1999	2000
1.4	0.1	0.9	1.8	2.4	2.6	2.8	2.9	4.1	3.6	3.0	1.8	1.1	−0.4	2.7	2.4	1.6	2.5	2.7	2.3	3.4

Source: Adapted from *OECD Economic Outlook*, December (OECD, 2000).

read off what the likely figure would be for some point *between* two observations.

It is also possible to combine *two* sets of time-series data on one graph to show their relative movements over time. Table 2.2 shows annual percentage changes in EU national income (i.e. economic growth rates) for the same time period.

Figure 2.4 plots these data along with those from Table 2.1. This enables us to get a clear picture of how annual changes in investment and in national income moved in relation to each other over the period in question.

Cross-section data

Cross-section data show different observations made at the *same point in time*. For example, they could show the quantities of food and clothing purchased at

> **key terms**
>
> **Cross-section data**
> Information showing how a variable (e.g. the consumption of eggs) differs between different groups or different individuals at a given time.

BOX 2.3

Representation of data

An example of a technique which can be used to analyse an economic problem is a time-series graph. The diagram is an example of a time-series graph and shows the relationship between the growth in output (GDP) and in investment in the UK between 1982 and 2000.

Questions

1 Explain the trends which can be seen from the graph.
2 Construct a general theory, based on the graph, about the relationship between investment and GDP.
3 How would you describe this type of 'model building'?

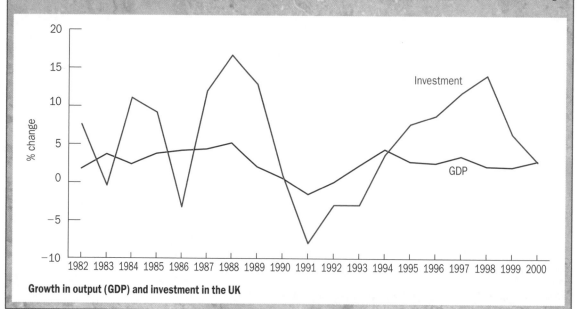

Growth in output (GDP) and investment in the UK

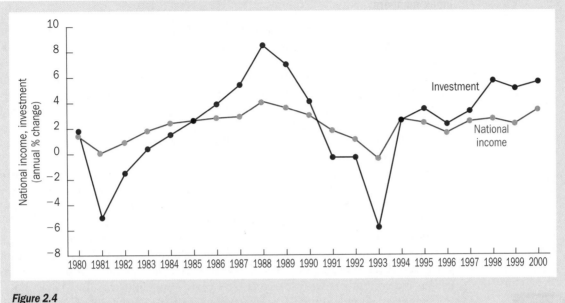

Figure 2.4
Economic growth and changes in investment in the EU

various levels of household income, or the costs to a firm or industry of producing various quantities of a product.

Table 2.3 gives an example of cross-section data. It shows the percentage shares of the UK's largest brewers in 1985 and 1999. Cross-section data like these are often represented in the form of a chart. Figure 2.5 shows the data as a *bar chart*, and Figure 2.6 as a *pie chart*.

It is possible to represent cross-section data at two or more different points in time, thereby presenting the figures as a time series. In Table 2.3, figures are given for just two years. With a more complete time series we could graph the movement of the market shares of each of the brewers over time.

Table 2.3	Market shares of the largest brewers		
1985 (%)		*2000* (%)	
Bass	22	Interbrew (Bass, Whitbread)	32
Allied Lyons (Carlsberg)	13	Scottish and Newcastle	30
Grand Met (Watneys)	12	Carlsberg-Tetley	13
Whitbread	11	Diageo (Guinness)	5
Scottish and Newcastle	10	Others	20
Courage	9		
Others	23		
	100		100

Source: *Various newspaper articles.*

Index numbers

Time-series data are often expressed in terms of **index numbers**. Consider the data in Table 2.4. It shows index numbers of manufacturing output in the UK from 1980 to 1999.

One year is selected as the **base year**, and this is given the value of 100. In our example this is 1995. The output for other years is then shown by their percentage variation from 100. For 1981 the index number is 75.9. This means that manufacturing output was 24.1 per cent lower in 1981 than in 1995. The index number for 1998 is 102.0. This means that manufacturing output was 2 per cent higher than in 1995.

The use of index numbers allows us to see clearly any upward and downward movements, and to make an easy comparison of one year with another. For example, Table 2.4 shows quite clearly that output fell from 1980 to 1982 and did not regain its 1980 level until after 1984.

Index numbers are very useful for comparing two or more time series of data. For example, suppose we wanted to compare the growth of manufacturing output with that of the service industries. To do this we simply express both sets of figures as index numbers with the same base year. This is illustrated in Table 2.5.

The figures show a quite different pattern for the two sectors. The growth of the service industries was much more steady and more rapid.

Using index numbers to measure percentage changes

To find the annual percentage growth rate in any one year, we simply look at the percentage change in the index from the previous year. To work this out, we use the following formula:

$$\left(\frac{I_t - I_{t-1}}{I_{t-1}}\right) \times 100$$

where I_t is the index in the year in question and I_{t-1} is the index in the previous year.

definition

Index number
The value of a variable expressed as 100 plus or minus its percentage deviation from a base year.

definition

Base year (for index numbers)
The year whose index number is set at 100.

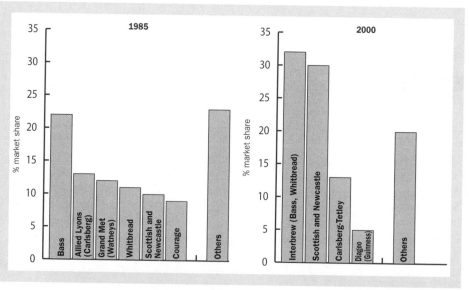

Figure 2.5
Market shares of the largest brewers

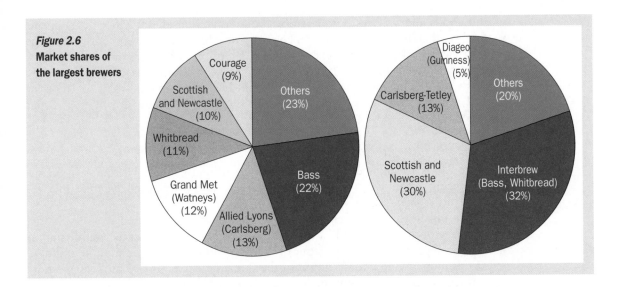

Figure 2.6
Market shares of the largest brewers

Thus to find the growth rate in manufacturing output from 1987 to 1988, we first see how much the index has risen $I_t - I_{t-1}$. The answer is $94.1 - 87.7 = 6.4$. But this does *not* mean that the growth rate is 6.4 per cent. According to our formula, the growth rate is equal to:

$$\frac{94.1 - 87.7}{87.7} \times 100$$

$$= 6.4/87.7 \times 100$$

$$= 7.3\%$$

The price index

Perhaps the best known of all price indices is the **retail price index** (**RPI**) (in the USA known as the *consumer price index (CPI)*). It is an index of the prices

> **definition**
> **Retail price index (RPI)**
> An index of the prices of goods bought by a typical household.

Table 2.4   **UK manufacturing output: 1995 = 100**

1980	1981	1982	1983	1984	1985	1986	1987	1988	1989	1990	1991	1992	1993	1994	1995	1996	1997	1998	1999
80.9	75.9	75.8	77.5	80.3	82.6	83.7	87.7	94.1	97.9	97.7	92.8	92.8	94.1	98.5	100.0	100.4	101.7	102.0	101.9

Source: Based on *Economic Trends* (ONS) various years.

Table 2.5   **UK manufacturing and service industry output: 1995 = 100**

	1980	1981	1982	1983	1984	1985	1986	1987	1988	1989	1990	1991	1992	1993	1994	1995	1996	1997	1998	1999
Output of manufacturing	80.9	75.9	75.8	77.5	80.3	82.6	83.7	87.7	94.1	97.9	97.7	92.8	92.8	94.1	98.5	100.0	100.4	101.7	102.0	101.9
Output of services	67.8	68.0	69.0	71.3	74.0	76.3	79.4	82.7	86.5	88.3	89.5	89.3	89.7	92.5	96.8	100.0	103.3	107.8	111.7	114.5

Source: Based on *Economic Trends* (ONS) various years.

of goods and services purchased by the average household. Movements in this index, therefore, show how the cost of living has changed. Annual percentage increases in the RPI are the commonest definition of the rate of inflation. Thus if the RPI went up from 100 to 110 over a twelve-month period, we would say that the rate of inflation was 10 per cent. If it went up from 150 to 162 over 12 months, the rate of inflation would be $(162 - 150)/150 \times 100 = 8$ per cent.

The use of weighted averages

The RPI is a **weighted average** of the prices of many items. The index of manufacturing output that we looked at above was also a weighted average: an average of the output of many individual products.

To illustrate how a weighted average works, consider the case of a weighted average of the output of just three industries, A, B and C. Let us assume that in the base year (year 1) the output of A was £7 million, of B £2 million and of C £1 million, giving a total output of the three industries of £10 million. We now attach weights to the output of each industry to reflect its proportion of total output. Industry A is given a weight of 0.7 because it produces seven-tenths of total output. Industry B is given a weight of 0.2 and industry C of 0.1. We then simply multiply each industry's index by its weight and add up all these figures to give the overall industry index.

The index for each industry in year 1 (the base year) is 100. This means that the weighted average index is also 100. Table 2.6 shows what happens to output in year 2. Industry A's output falls by 10 per cent, giving it an index of 90 in year 2. Industry B's output rises by 10 per cent and industry C's output rises by 30 per cent, giving indices of 110 and 130, respectively. But as you can see from the table, despite the fact that two of the three industries have had a rise in output, the total industry index has *fallen* from 100 to 98. The reason is that industry A is so much larger than the other two that its decline in output outweighs their increase.

The retail prices index is a little more complicated. The reason is that it is calculated in two stages. First, products are grouped into categories such as food, clothing and services. A weighted average index is worked out for each group. Thus the index for food would be the weighted average of the indices for bread, potatoes, cooking oil, etc. Second, a weight is attached to each of the groups in order to work out an overall index.

Table 2.6 **Constructing a weighted average index**

Industry	Weight	Year 1 Index	Year 1 Index times weight	Year 2 Index	Year 2 Index times weight
A	0.7	100	70	90	63
B	0.2	100	20	110	22
C	0.1	100	10	130	13
Total	1.0		100		98

Functional relationships

Business economists frequently examine how one economic variable affects another: how the purchases of cars are affected by their price; how consumer expenditure is affected by taxes, or by incomes; how the cost of producing washing machines is affected by the price of steel; how business investment is affected by changes in interest rates. These relationships are called functional relationships. We will need to express these relationships in a precise way. This can be done in the form of a table, as a graph or as an equation.

Simple linear functions

These are relationships which when plotted on a graph produce a straight line. Let us take an imaginary example of the relationship between total saving in the economy (S) and the level of national income (Y). This functional relationship can be written as:

$$S = f(Y)$$

This is simply shorthand for saying that saving is a function of (i.e. depends on) the level of national income.

If we want to know just *how much* will be saved at any given level of income, we will need to spell out this functional relationship. Let us do this in each of the three ways.

As a table. Table 2.7 gives a selection of values of Y and the corresponding level of S. It is easy to read off from the table the level of saving at one of the levels of national income listed. It is clearly more difficult to work out the level of saving if national income were £23.4 billion or £47.4 billion.

As a graph. Figure 2.7 plots the data from Table 2.7. Each of the dots corresponds to one of the points in the table. By joining the dots up into a single line we can easily read off the value for saving at some level of income other than those listed in the table. A graph also has the advantage of allowing us to see the relationship at a glance.

It is usual to plot the *independent variable* (i.e. the one that does not depend on the other) on the horizontal or *x*-axis, and the *dependent variable* on the vertical or *y*-axis. In our example, saving *depends* on national income. Thus saving is the dependent variable and national income is the independent variable.

> **definition**
>
> **Functional relationships**
> The mathematical relationships showing how one variable is affected by one or more others.

Table 2.7	A saving function
National income (£bn per year)	Total saving (£bn per year)
0	0
10	2
20	4
30	6
40	8
50	10

Figure 2.7
A graph of the
saving function:
S = 0.2Y

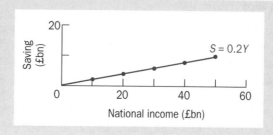

As an equation. The data in the table can be expressed in the equation:

$$S = 0.2Y$$

This has the major advantage of being precise. We could work out *exactly* how much would be saved at any given level of national income.

This particular function starts at the origin of the graph (i.e. the bottom left-hand corner). This means that when the value of the independent variable is zero, so too is the value of the dependent variable. Frequently, however, this is not the case in functional relationships. For example, when people have a zero income, they will still have to live, and thus will draw from their past savings: they will have *negative* saving.

When a graph does not pass through the origin, its equation will have the form:

$$y = a + bx$$

where this time y stands for the dependent variable (not 'income') and x for the independent variable, and a and b will have numbers assigned in an actual equation. For example, the equation might be:

$$y = 4 + 2x$$

This would give Table 2.8 and Figure 2.8.

Notice two things about the relationship between the equation and the graph:

- The point where the line crosses the vertical axis (at a value of 4) is given by the constant (a) term. If the a term were negative, the line would cross the vertical axis *below* the horizontal axis.
- The slope of the line is given by the b term. The slope is 2/1: for every 1 unit increase in x there is a 2 unit increase in y.

Table 2.8 $y = 4 + 2x$

x	y
0	4
1	6
2	8
3	10
4	12
5	14
.	.
.	.

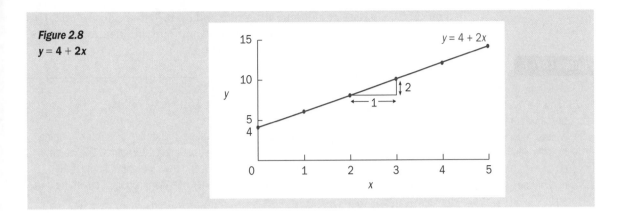

Figure 2.8
y = 4 + 2x

Non-linear functions

These are functions where the equation involves a squared term (or other power terms). Such functions will give a curved line when plotted on a graph. As an example, consider the following equation:

$$y = 4 + 10x - x^2$$

Table 2.9 and Figure 2.9 are based on it.

Table 2.9	$y = 4 + 10x - x^2$
x	y
0	4
1	13
2	20
3	25
4	28
5	29
6	28
.	.
.	.
.	.

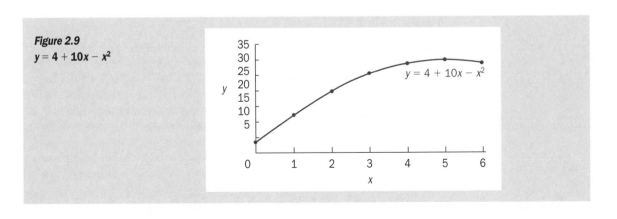

Figure 2.9
y = 4 + 10x − x²

As you can see, y rises at a decelerating rate and eventually begins to fall. This is because the negative x^2 term is becoming more and more influential as x rises, and eventually begins to outweigh the $10x$ term.

SUMMARY

1 Diagrams in economics can be used as pictures: to sketch a relationship so that its essentials can be perceived at a glance.

2 Tables, graphs and charts are also used to portray real-life data. These can be time-series data or cross-section data or both.

3 Presenting time-series data as index numbers gives a clear impression of trends and is a good way of comparing how two or more series (perhaps originally measured in different units) have changed over the same time period. A base year is chosen and the index for that year is set at 100. The percentage change in the value of a variable is given by the percentage change in the index. The formula is:

$$\left(\frac{I_t - I_{t-1}}{I_{t-1}}\right) \times 100$$

4 Several items can be included in one index by using a weighted value for each of the items. The weights must add up to 1 and each weight will reflect the relative importance of that particular item in the index.

5 Functional relationships can be expressed as an equation, a table or a graph. In the linear (straight-line) equation $y = a + bx$, the a term gives the vertical intercept (the point where the graph crosses the vertical axis) and the b term gives the slope. When there is a power term (e.g. $y = a + bx + cx^2$), the graph will be a curve.

REVIEW QUESTIONS TO APPENDIX

1 What are the relative advantages and disadvantages of presenting information in (a) a table; (b) a graph; (c) an equation?

2 If the RPI went up from 125 to 130 over twelve months, what would be the rate of inflation over that period?

3 On a diagram like Figure 2.8, draw the graphs for the following equations.

$y = -3 + 4x$

$y = 15 - 3x$

4 What shaped graph would you get from the following equations?

$y = -6 + 3x + 2x^2$

$y = 10 - 4x + x^2$

If you cannot work out the answer, construct a table like Table 2.9 and then plot the figures on a graph.

Business organisations

If you decide to grow strawberries in your garden or allotment, or if you decide to put up a set of shelves in your home, then you have made a production decision. Most production decisions, however, are not made by the individuals who will consume the product. Most production decisions are made by firms: whether by small one-person businesses or by giant multinational corporations, such as General Motors or Sony.

In this chapter we are going to investigate the firm: what is its role in the economy; what are the goals of firms; how do firms differ in respect to their legal status; and in what ways are they organised internally?

3.1 The nature of firms

Economists have traditionally paid little attention to the ways in which firms operate and to the different roles they might take. Firms were often seen merely as organisations for producing output and employing inputs in response to market forces. Virtually no attention was paid to just how firms were organised and how different forms of organisation would influence their behaviour. The firm was seen as a 'black box': inputs were fed in one end, they were used in the most efficient way, and output then emerged from the other end. But do firms have a more significant function to play in respect to resource allocation and production, and does their internal organisation affect their decisions? The answer to these questions is clearly yes.

Complex production

Very few goods or services are produced by one person alone. Most products require a complex production process that will involve many individuals. But how are these individuals to be organised in order to produce such goods and services? Two very different ways are:

- within markets via price signals;
- within firms via a hierarchy of managerial authority.

In the first of these two ways, each stage of production would involve establishing a distinct contract with each separate producer. Assume that you wanted to purchase a woollen jumper. You would need to enter a series of separate contracts: to have the jumper designed, to buy the wool, to get the wool spun, to get it dyed, to have the jumper knitted. There are many other stages in the production and distribution process that might also be considered. With each contract a price will have to be determined, and that price will reflect current market conditions. In most cases, such a form of economic organisation would prove to be highly inefficient and totally impractical. Consider the number of contracts that might be necessary if you wished to purchase a motor car!

With the second way of organising production, a single firm (or just a few firms) replaces the market. The co-ordination of the conversion of inputs into output takes place *within* the firm: not through the market mechanism, but by management issuing orders as to what to produce and the manner in which this is to take place. Hence the distinguishing feature of the firm is that the price mechanism plays little if any role in allocating resources within it.

The benefits of organising production within firms

The function of the firm is to bring together a series of production and distribution operations, doing away with the need for individuals to enter into narrowly specified contracts. If you want a woollen jumper, you go to a woollen jumper retailer.

The key advantage of organising production and distribution through firms, as opposed to the market, is that it involves lower **transaction costs**. Transaction costs are the costs of making economic arrangements about production, distribution and sales. The transaction costs associated with individual contracts made through the market are likely to be substantial for the following reasons:

- The *uncertainty* in framing contracts. It is unlikely that decision makers will have perfect knowledge of the production process. Given, then, that such contracts are established on imperfect information, they are consequently subject to error.
- The *complexity* of contracts. Many products require many stages of production. The more complex the product, the greater the number of contracts that would have to be made. The specifications within contracts may also become more complex, requiring high levels of understanding and knowledge of the production process. The more complex contracts become, the poorer is likely to be the quality of decision making, and the higher the costs of production.
- *Monitoring* contracts. Entering into a contract with another person may require that you monitor whether the terms of the contract are fulfilled. This may incur a significant time cost for the individual, especially if a large number of contracts require monitoring.
- *Enforcing* contracts. If one party breaks its contract, the legal expense of enforcing the contract or recouping any losses may be significant. Many individuals might find such costs prohibitive, and as a consequence be unable to pursue broken contracts through the legal system.

What is apparent is that, for most goods, the firm represents a superior way to organise production. The actions of management replace the price signals of the market and overcome many of the associated transaction costs.

definition
Transaction costs
Those costs incurred when making economic contracts in the market place.

Goals of the firm

Economists have traditionally assumed that firms will want to maximise profits. The 'traditional theory of the firm', as it is called, shows how much output firms should produce and at what price, in order to make as much profit as possible. But do firms necessarily want to maximise profits?

It is reasonable to assume that the *owners* of firms will want to maximise profits: this much most of the critics of the traditional theory accept. The question is, however, whether the owners make the decisions about how much to produce and at what price.

The divorce of ownership from control

As businesses steadily grew over the eighteenth and nineteenth centuries, many owner-managers were forced, however reluctantly, to devolve some responsibility for the running of the business to other individuals. These new managers brought with them technical skills and business expertise, a crucial prerequisite for a modern successful business enterprise. The managerial revolution that was to follow, in which business owners (shareholders) and managers became distinct groups, called into question what the precise goals of the business enterprise might now be. This debate was to be further fuelled by the development of the **joint-stock company**, in which the ownership of the enterprise was progressively dispersed over a large number of shareholders. The growth in the joint-stock company was a direct consequence of business owners looking to raise large amounts of investment capital in order to maintain or expand business activity.

This twin process of managerial expansion and widening share ownership led Berle and Means[1] to argue that the *ownership* of stocks and shares in an enterprise no longer meant *control* over its assets. They subsequently drew a distinction between 'nominal ownership', namely getting a return from investing in a business, and 'effective ownership', which is the ability to control and direct the assets of the business. The more dispersed nominal ownership becomes, the less and less likely it is that there will be effective ownership by shareholders. This issue will be considered in more detail in Chapter 13.

As you will discover in section 3.2, the modern company is *legally* separate from its owners. Hence the assets are legally owned by the business itself. Consequently, the group *in charge* of the business is that which controls the use of these assets: i.e. the group which determines the business's objectives and implements the necessary procedures to secure them. In most companies this group is the managers.

Berle and Means argued that, as a consequence of this transition from owner to manager control, conflicts are likely to develop between the goals of managers and those of the owners.

But what are the objectives of managers? Will they want to maximise profits, or will they have some other aim?

Managers may be assumed to want to maximise their *own* interests. This may well involve pursuits that conflict with profit maximisation. They may, for example, pursue higher salaries, greater power or prestige, greater sales, better working conditions or greater popularity with their subordinates. Different managers in the same firm may well pursue different aims.

Managers will still have to ensure that *sufficient* profits are made to keep shareholders happy, but that may be very different from *maximising* profits.

Alternative theories of the firm to those of profit maximisation, therefore, tend to assume that large firms are profit 'satisficers'. That is, managers strive

definition
Joint-stock company
A company where ownership is distributed between a large number of shareholders

[1] Adolf A. Berle and Gardiner C. Means, *The Modern Corporation and Private Property* (Macmillan, 1933).

hard for a minimum target level of profit, but are less interested in profits above this level.

Such theories fall into two categories: first, those theories that assume that firms attempt to maximise some other aim, provided that sufficient profits are achieved; and second, those theories that assume that firms pursue a number of potentially conflicting aims, of which sufficient profit is merely one. These alternative theories are examined more fully in Chapter 13.

The principal/agent relationship

Can the owners of a firm ever be sure that their managers will pursue the business strategy most appropriate to achieving the owners' goals (which traditional economic theory tells us is the maximisation of profit)? This is an example of what is known as the **principal–agent problem**. One of the features of a complex modern economy is that people (principals) have to employ others (agents) to carry out their wishes. If you want to go on holiday, it is easier to go to a travel agent to sort out the arrangements than to do it all yourself. Likewise, if you want to buy a house, it is more convenient to go to an estate agent.

The crucial advantage that agents have over their principals is specialist knowledge and information. This is frequently the basis upon which agents are employed. For example, owners employ managers for their specialist knowledge of a market or their understanding of business practice. But this situation of **asymmetric information** – that one party (the agent) knows more than the other (the principal) – means that it will be very difficult for the principal to judge in whose interest the agent is operating. Are the manager's own goals rather than the goals of the owner being pursued? It is the same in other walks of life. The estate agent trying to sell you a house may not tell you about the noisy neighbours or that the vendor is prepared to accept a much lower price. A second-hand car dealer may 'neglect' to tell you about the rust on the underside of the car, or that it had a history of unreliability.

Principals may attempt to reconcile the fact that they have imperfect information, and are thus in an inherently weak position, in the following ways:

> **definition**
>
> **Principal–agent problem**
> One where people (principals), as a result of lack of knowledge, cannot ensure that their best interests are served by their agents.

- *Monitoring* the performance of the agent. Shareholders could monitor the performance of their senior managers through attending annual general meetings. The managers could be questioned by shareholders and ultimately replaced if their performance is seen as unsatisfactory.
- Establishing a series of *incentives* to ensure that agents act in the principals' best interest. For example, managerial pay could be closely linked to business performance.

> **definition**
>
> **Asymmetric information**
> A situation in which one party in an economic relationship knows more than another.

Within any firm there will exist a complex chain of principal–agent relationships – between workers and managers, between junior managers and senior managers, between senior managers and directors, and between directors and shareholders. All groups will hold some specialist knowledge which might be used to further their own distinct goals. Predictably, the development of effective monitoring and evaluation programmes and the creation of performance-related pay schemes have been two central themes in the development of business practices in recent years – a sign that the principal is looking to fight back.

Staying in business

Aiming for profits, sales, salaries, power, etc. will be useless if the firm does not survive! Trying to *maximise* any of the various objectives may be risky. For example, if a firm tries to maximise its market share by aggressive advertising or price cutting, it might invoke a strong response from its rivals. The resulting war may drive it out of business. Some of the managers may easily move to other jobs and may actually gain from the experience, but the majority are likely to lose. Concern with survival, therefore, may make firms cautious.

Not all firms, however, make survival the top priority. Some are adventurous and are prepared to take risks. Adventurous firms are most likely to be those dominated by a powerful and ambitious individual – an individual prepared to take gambles.

The more dispersed the decision-making power is in the firm, and the more worried managers are about their own survival, the more cautious are their policies likely to be: preferring 'tried and trusted' methods of production, preferring to stick with products that have proved to be popular, and preferring to expand slowly and steadily.

If a firm is too cautious, however, it may not after all survive. It may find that it loses markets to more aggressive competitors. Ultimately, therefore, if a firm is concerned to survive, it must be careful to balance caution against keeping up with competitors, ensuring that the customer is sufficiently satisfied and that costs are kept sufficiently low by efficient management and the introduction of new technology.

The efficient operation of the firm may be strongly influenced by its internal organisational structure. We will consider this in more detail in section 3.3, but first we must consider how the *legal* structure of the firm might influence its conduct within the market place.

3.2 The firm as a legal entity

The legal structure of the firm is likely to have a significant impact on its conduct, and subsequent performance, within the market place. There are several types of firm, each with a distinct legal status.

The sole proprietor

This is where the business is owned by just one person. Usually such businesses are small, with only a few employees. Retailing, building and farming are typical areas to find sole proprietorships. Such businesses are easy to set up and may require only a relatively small initial capital investment. They may well flourish if the owner is highly committed to the business, and they can be very flexible to changing market conditions. They suffer two main disadvantages, however:

- Limited scope for expansion. Finance is limited to what the owner can raise personally. Also there is a limit to the size of an organisation that one person can effectively control.
- Unlimited liability. The owner is personally liable for any losses that the business might make. This could result in the owner's house, car and other assets being seized to pay off any outstanding debts.

BOX 3.1

Managers and owners
High salaries and corporate goals

In 2000, the annual median salary plus bonuses for the chief executives of the top 100 UK companies was over £740 000. Average earnings in the UK in 2000 were only £22 000. What is more, executive pay is increasing by some 10 per cent per year compared to under 5 per cent for average earnings.

The earnings of senior executives in the USA are substantially higher still. A normal remuneration package for those at the top of large companies in the USA is more than £20 million per year.

The awards given to executive 'fat cats' have met with considerable protest in recent years. So how can such high pay awards to top executives be justified? The two main arguments put forward to justify such generosity are as follows:

- 'The best cost money.' Failure to offer high rewards may encourage the top executives within an industry to move elsewhere.
- 'High rewards motivate.' High rewards are likely to motivate not only top executives, but also those below them. Managers, especially those in the middle of the business hierarchy, will compete for promotion and seek to do well with such high rewards on offer.

In addition to using high salaries to motivate managers, shareholders, who ultimately determine the pay of top executives, have been keen to modify the manner in which top executives receive their rewards, in order to provide additional incentives. Increasingly there has been greater reliance on payouts of shares and share 'options', rather than on salaries and short-term bonuses. The justification for such a move is that giving rewards in the form of shares links the interests of managers, owners and investors. In such an environment, a rational 'reward-maximising' manager will always be seeking to enhance share value, and this will be linked to the company's success. As such, the need for monitoring managerial activity diminishes.

The drawback of simply giving shares (as opposed to share options) to top managers concerns how they might respond to *risk*. They might be 'risk averse' and seek to protect the value of their shares, preferring to avoid risky ventures that might jeopardise profits and cause share prices to fall. But in doing this, they will fail to embark on projects which could potentially be very profitable (albeit risky) and thereby fail to *add* value to investors' shares. Because of this, the giving of share *options* to top managers has become more prevalent.

Share options give top managers the right to buy shares at a set price. If the share value goes above this level, the manager makes the difference. If the share price falls below this level, the manager can exercise the option *not* to buy. In such circumstances, top managers are shielded from the risks of failure, but encouraged to do as well as possible.

All the above arguments imply that there should be a clear link between the remuneration top managers receive, whether as salary, bonuses or share options, and the performance of the business. A survey conducted by *Management Today* and William Mercer in July 1999[1] considered those companies that made up the FTSE 350 (the top 350 companies in the Financial Times Stock Exchange Index), and ranked these companies by total shareholder return (TSR). TSR is the theoretical capital growth rate that a shareholder would have received over a three-year period, assuming that all dividends were reinvested. They found that the correlation between reward and performance was far from clear.

> Five of the most highly rewarded FTSE company executives in Britain last year were Charles Brady of Amvescap at £4 million, Robert Wilson of Rio Tinto at almost £2 million, Peter Job of Reuters at £1.6 million, Sir Colin Southgate of EMI at £1 million and Sir Richard Evans of British Aerospace at £1.9 million. Of these, only Amvescap made it into the top 50 in the TSR lists, at 41. British Aerospace came close. In contrast, Reuters, EMI, and Rio Tinto were down among the dogs.[2]

CEO	Salary (£)	Bonus (£)	LTIP (£)	Total Remuneration (£)
FTSE Leaders				
Kevin Lomax, MISYS	285 717	329 287	193 228	808 232
Mike Kinski, Stagecoach	372 000	250 000	80 069	630 069
David Prosser, Legal & General	440 000	400 000	361 215	1 201 215
Chris Gent, Vodafone	587 000	0	3 246 985	3 833 985
Peter Ellwood, Lloyds TSB	475 000	199 000	940 797	1 614 797
Sir Dick Evans, British Aerospace	501 000	175 000	1 194 250	1 870 250
Francis Mackay, Compass Group	425 000	138 000	1 418 654	1 981 654
Peter Burt, Bank of Scotland	277 000	90 000	785 382	1 152 382
Sir Ronnie Frost, Hays	250 000	94 000	123 981	467 981
Charles Brady, Amvescap	335 000	2 412 000	1 383 000	4 080 000
FTSE Laggards				
Christopher Collins, Hanson	310 000	155 000	544 223	1 009 223
Robert Wilson, Rio Tinto	669 000	144 000	1 179 548	1 992 548
Sir Colin Southgate, EMI Group	543 300	105 000	361 600	1 010 400
Tony Hales, Allied Domecq	460 000	165 000	732 065	1 357 065
Danny Rosenkrantz, The BOC Group	473 000	290 000	0	763 000
Charles Miller Smith, ICI	550 000	0	78 489	700 439
Bob Ayling, British Airways	450 000	0	0	450 000
Peter Job, Reuters	522 000	255 000	815 938	1 592 938

The report also examined the effectiveness of long-term incentive plans (LTIPs), the executive remuneration system recommended by Sir Richard Greenbury, following his investigation into executive pay. LTIPs are essentially stock option/share bonus schemes, where the bonus is payable upon the business achieving above average performance. The report found little or no relationship between LTIPs and business performance. As the table indicates, chief executive officers (CEOs) of many of the poor performing companies (the 'laggards') received LTIPs greater than or at least comparable to the FTSE leaders!

The conclusion is that LTIPs alone do not ensure corporate success. Also, as the *Management Today* article remarks,

It does not follow, simply because shares have fallen, that executives have performed badly. In some cases, it could have been a lot worse without their efforts.

Questions

1 Explain how the above might illustrate the principal–agent relationship.

2 In the UK, many of the highest-paid executives head former public utilities. Why might the giving of very high rewards to such individuals be a source of public concern?

[1] *Management Today* (July 1999)
[2] *ibid.*

The partnership

This is where two or more people own the business. In most partnerships there is a legal limit of 20 partners. Partnerships are common in the same fields as sole proprietorships. They are also common in the professions: solicitors, accountants, surveyors, etc. With more owners, there is more scope for expansion. More finance can be raised and the partners can each specialise in one aspect of the business.

Partners, however, still have unlimited liability. This problem could be very serious. The mistakes of one partner could jeopardise the personal assets of all the other partners.

Where large amounts of capital are required and/or when the risks of business failure are relatively high, partnerships are not an appropriate form of organisation. In such cases it is best to form a company (or 'joint-stock company' to give it its full title).

Companies

A company is legally separate from its owners. This means that it can enter into contracts and own property. Any debts are *its* debts, not the owners'.

Each owner has a share in the company. The size of their share holdings will vary from one shareholder to another and will depend on the amount they invest. Each shareholder will receive his or her share of the company's distributed profit. The payments to shareholders are called 'dividends'.

The owners have only *limited liability*. This means that, if the company goes bankrupt, the owners will lose the amount of money they have invested in the company, but no more. Their personal assets cannot be seized. This has the advantage of encouraging people to become shareholders, and indeed large companies may have thousands of shareholders – some with very small holdings and others, including institutional shareholders such as pension funds, with very large holdings. Without the protection of limited liability, many of these investors would never put their money into any company that involved even the slightest risk.

Shareholders often take no part in the running of the firm. They may elect a board of directors which decides broad issues of company policy. The board of directors in turn appoints managers who make the day-to-day decisions. There are two types of companies: public and private.

Public limited companies. Don't be confused by the title. A public limited company is still a private enterprise: it is not a nationalised industry. It is 'public' because it can offer new shares publicly: by issuing a prospectus, it can invite the public to subscribe to a new share issue. In addition, many public limited companies are quoted on the Stock Exchange. This means that existing shareholders can sell some or all of their shares on the Stock Exchange. The prices of these shares will be determined by demand and supply. A public limited company must hold an annual shareholders' meeting.

Private limited companies. Private limited companies cannot offer their shares publicly. Shares have to be sold privately. This makes it more difficult for private limited companies to raise finance, and consequently they tend to be smaller than public companies. They are, however, easier to set up than public companies.

Consortia of firms

It is common, especially in large civil engineering projects that involve very high risks, for many firms to work together as a consortium. The Channel Tunnel and Thames Barrier are products of this form of business organisation. Within the consortium one firm may act as the managing contractor, while the other members may provide specialist services. Alternatively, management may be more equally shared.

Co-operatives

These are of two types.

Consumer co-operatives. These, like the old high street Co-ops, are officially owned by the consumers. Consumers in fact play no part in the running of these co-ops. They are run by professional managers.

Producer co-operatives. These are firms that are owned by their workers, who share in the firm's profit according to some agreed formula. They are sometimes formed by people in the same trade coming together: for example, producers of handicraft goods. At other times they are formed by workers buying out their factory from the owners; this is most likely if it is due to close, with a resultant loss of jobs. Producer co-operatives, although still relatively few in number, have grown in recent years.

Public corporations

These are state-owned enterprises such as the BBC, the Bank of England and nationalised industries.

They have a legal identity separate from the government. The corporation is run by a board, but the members of the board are appointed by the relevant government minister. The boards have to act within various terms of reference laid down by Act of Parliament. Profits of public corporations that are not re-invested accrue to the Treasury. Since 1980 many public corporations have been 'privatised': that is, they have been sold directly to other firms in the private sector (such as Austin Rover to British Aerospace) or to the general public through a public issue of shares (such as British Gas).

The issue of privatisation is considered in Chapter 21.

3.3 The internal organisation of the firm

The internal operating structures of firms are frequently governed by their size. Small firms tend to be centrally managed, with decision making operating through a clear managerial hierarchy. In large firms, however, the organisational structure tends to be more complex, although technological change is forcing many organisations to reassess the most suitable organisational structure for their business.

U-form

In small to medium-sized firms, the managers of the various departments – marketing, finance, production, etc. – are normally directly responsible to a chief

Figure 3.1
U-form business organisation

Chief executive
Production
Finance
Sales
Purchasing

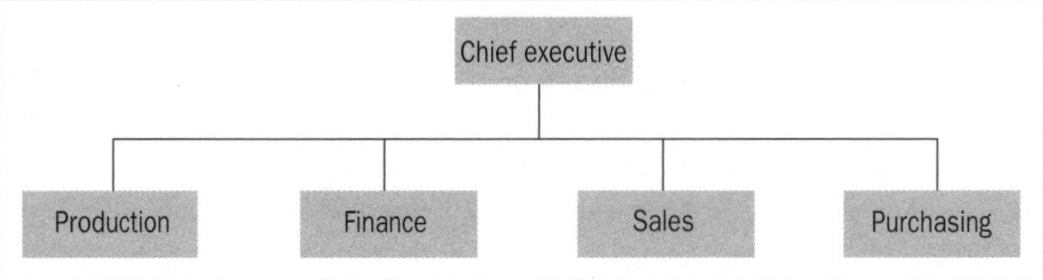

executive, whose function is to co-ordinate their activities: relaying the firm's overall strategy to them and being responsible for interdepartmental communication. We call this type of structure **U (unitary) form** (see Figure 3.1).

definition
U-form business organisation
One in which the central organisation of the firm (the chief executive or a managerial team) is responsible both for the firm's day-to-day administration and for formulating its business strategy.

When firms expand beyond a certain size, however, a U-form structure is likely to become inefficient. This inefficiency arises from difficulties in communication, co-ordination and control. It becomes too difficult to manage the whole organisation from the centre. The problem is that the chief executive suffers from **bounded rationality** – a limit on the rate at which information can be absorbed and processed. As the firm grows, more decisions are required. This leads to less time per decision and ultimately poorer decisions. The chief executive effectively loses control of the firm.

In attempting to regain control, it is likely that a further managerial layer will be inserted. The chain of command thus becomes lengthened as the chief executive must now co-ordinate and communicate via this intermediate managerial level. This leads to the following problems:

definition
Bounded rationality
Individuals are limited in their ability to absorb and process information. People think in ways conditioned by their experiences (family, education, peer groups, etc.).

- Communication costs increase.
- Messages and decisions may be misinterpreted and distorted.
- The firm experiences a decline in organisational efficiency as various departmental managers, freed from central control, seek to maximise their personal departmental goals.

M-form

To overcome these organisational problems, the firm can adopt an **M (multi-divisional) form** of managerial structure (see Figure 3.2).

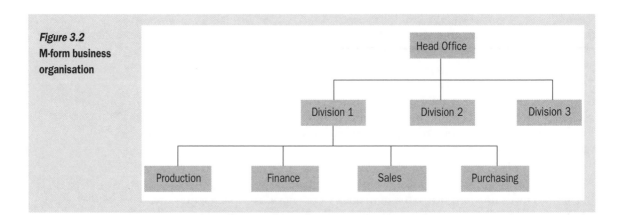

Figure 3.2
M-form business organisation

Head Office
Division 1
Division 2
Division 3
Production
Finance
Sales
Purchasing

This suits medium to large firms. The firm is divided into a number of 'divisions'. Each division could be responsible for a particular product or group of products, or a particular market (e.g. a specific country). The day-to-day running and even certain long-term decisions of each division would be the responsibility of the divisional manager(s). This leads to the following benefits:

● Reduced length of information flows.
● The chief executive being able to concentrate on overall strategic planning.
● An enhanced level of control, with each division being run as a mini 'firm', competing with other divisions for the limited amount of company resources available.

The flat organisation

The shift towards the M-form organisational structure was primarily motivated by a desire to improve the process of decision making within the business. This involved adding layers of management. Recent technological innovations, especially in respect to computer systems such as E-mail and management information systems, have encouraged many organisations to think again about how to establish an efficient and effective organisational structure. The **flat organisation** is one that fully embraces the latest developments in information technology, and by so doing is able to reduce the need for a large group of middle managers. Senior managers, through these new information systems, can communicate easily and directly with those lower in the organisational structure. Middle managers are effectively bypassed.

The speed of information flows reduces the impact of bounded rationality on the decision-making process. Senior managers are able to re-establish and, in certain cases, widen their span of control over the business organisation.

In many respects the flat organisation represents a return to the U-form structure. It is yet to be seen whether we also have a return to the problems associated with this type of organisation.

Multinationals and business organisation

Further types of business organisation which we might identify are closely linked to the expansion and development of the multinational enterprise. Such organisational structures have developed as a response to these businesses attempting to control their business activities on a global scale. Three forms of multinational business organisation are identified below.

H-form. The H-form or **holding company** is in many respects a variation on the M-form structure. A holding company (or parent company) is one which owns a controlling interest in other subsidiary companies. These subsidiaries, in turn, may also have controlling interests in other companies.

H-form organisational structures can be highly complex. While the parent company has ultimate control over its various subsidiaries, it is likely that both tactical and strategic decision making is left to the individual companies within the organisation. Many multinationals are organised along the lines of an inter-

definition

M-form business organisation
One in which the business is organised into separate departments, such that responsibility for the day-to-day management enterprise is separated from the formulation of the business's strategic plan.

definition

Flat organisation
One in which technology enables senior managers to communicate directly with those lower in the organisational structure. Middle managers are bypassed.

definition

Holding company
A business organisation in which the present company holds interests in a number of other companies or subsidiaries.

BOX 3.2

Downsizing and business reorganisation
The case of IBM

During the 1980s and 1990s many businesses, especially in the USA, undertook large-scale reorganisation. One result was mass redundancies, as major corporations attempted to 'downsize'.

The initial wave of downsizing consisted mainly of companies which were suffering from falling profits. Their objective was to reduce costs and thereby bolster their profits. Later, downsizing began to be practised by companies doing well in their various markets. These included companies such as General Electric (104 000 redundancies between 1980 and 1990), Procter and Gamble (13 000) and AT&T (40 000). Such companies practised downsizing not out of desperation, but as a means of improving their performance. By reducing the size of their headquarters and removing layers of managerial bureaucracy, and even in many cases breaking up the business into smaller units, it was hoped that the business would become more flexible and ultimately more efficient.

In addition, businesses have been increasingly focusing upon 'core competencies'. What this means is that peripheral or non-core activities have been axed. In effect, businesses have sought to become more specialist and produce those goods or services where they can do better than their rivals.

The case of IBM presents one of the most dramatic examples. In 1987, IBM employed 406 000 people. By 1995, its workforce had shrunk to 202 000. This wave of downsizing started in the late 1980s as IBM's profits began to fall, largely as a consequence of failing to pre-dict the rise of the workstation and the decline of the mainframe computer, on which IBM's profits had largely depended. In 1991, desperate measures were undertaken to revive IBM's declining position. The chairman of IBM, John Akers, announced that the company was to be split into thirteen autonomous units, nine of which were manufacturing and development businesses. These were to act as suppliers to the remaining four units, which were concerned with marketing and servicing. Between these units there was to operate an internal market with a series of negotiated transfer prices. It was hoped that such a radical reorganisation would enable IBM to compete more effectively in a world market where the speed of technological change was intensifying, and where the number of small business with new and innovative products was growing rapidly.

In the USA, the initial wave of downsizing and business reorganisation was met with horror, as so many people were put out of work. It has been estimated that between 1980 and 1995 the largest 100 American firms shed 25 per cent of their workforce, the equivalent of 4 million workers. More recently, however, views concerning the impact of downsizing have been revised. What has happened in many cases is that businesses, now that they have got back to their core competencies, are looking to expand as their market positions have strengthened. In addition, many activities conducted by businesses, such as catering, building maintenance and the operation and running of computer systems,

---

definition

Integrated international enterprise
One in which an international company pursues a single business strategy. It co-ordinates the business activities of its subsidiaries across different countries.

national holding company, where overseas subsidiaries pursue their own independent strategy. Electra Flemming Holdings Ltd represents a good example of an H-form business organisation. Figure 3.3 shows the firm's organisational structure and the range of assets it owns.

Integrated international enterprise. The **integrated international enterprise** is an organisational structure where a company's international subsidiaries, rather than pursuing independent business strategies, co-ordinate and integrate their activities in pursuit of shared corporate aims and objectives. The co-ordination of such activities can be either at a regional level – for example, within the European market – or on a truly global scale. In such an organisation, the distinction between parent company and subsidiary is of less relevance than the

are things they cannot do without. As such, companies have been forced into 'outsourcing': that is, funding another company to provide the service for them. These other companies have then absorbed most of the redundant labour.

It appears that if downsizing is truly successful, then it is a self-eliminating process. As the new lean and efficient company betters its rivals, so the demand for its product rises, and with it the demand for labour.

If unsuccessful, the slimming of business may turn into anorexia, which is not healthy. Some companies that have cut their costs drastically have found that the quality of their operations has suffered, leading to a fall in revenue: a fall that may be greater than the fall in costs. The result is a reduction in profit.

Recent developments

Strong economic growth in both the USA and UK has revealed a further legacy for business of the downsizing trend of the 1990s: recruiting and holding on to staff. The downsizing era

> ... tore up the implicit contract of employment which had, for decades, tied people to their companies. Under that contract, workers gave commitment and loyalty, in return for job security until retirement.[1]

Companies now find that, with workers in short supply, especially in key areas such as computer or Internet technicians, they are in a constant battle to recruit and retain their services. Commitment and loyalty are at premium. In the USA.

> Besides signing-on bonuses and share options, employers are offering free meals, manicures on company premises and laptop computers. Employees who announce they are leaving are often offered large pay increases to change their minds. ... British companies are also competing to offer better pay and perks. Norfrost, the Scottish freezer manufacturer, even allows staff to bring their dogs to work.[2]

Employees once again seem to be of value, but without the tradition of commitment and loyalty lost during the era of downsizing, employers are having to stretch to ever greater lengths to hold on to this valuable resource.

Questions

1 Why might downsizing fail to improve the economic position of a business?
2 What side-effects, other than on levels of employment, might widespread downsizing have on the national economy?

[1] *Financial Times* (13/6/00)
[2] *ibid*

---

identification of a clear corporate philosophy which dominates business goals and policy.

Transnational association. A further form of multinational business organisation is the **transnational association**. Here the business headquarters holds little equity investment in its subsidiaries. These are largely owned and managed by local people. These subsidiaries receive from the headquarters managerial and technical assistance, in exchange for contractual agreements that output produced by the subsidiary is sold to the headquarters. Such output is most likely to take the form of product components rather than finished products. The headquarters then acts as an assembler, marketer or distributor of such output, or some combination of all three. The main advantage of organising

definition
Transnational association
A form of business organisation in which the subsidiaries of a company in different countries are contractually bound to the parent company to provide output to or receive inputs from other subsidiaries.

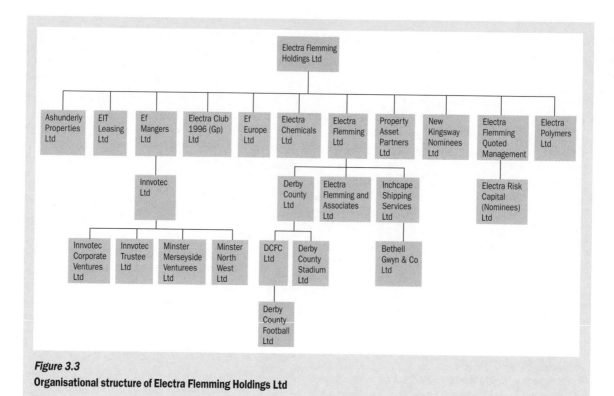

Figure 3.3
Organisational structure of Electra Flemming Holdings Ltd

international business in this way is that it reduces costs. This form of organisation is known as **global sourcing** and involves the international business using distinct production sites to produce large numbers of single components. With the transnational association, the headquarters still retains the decisive role in integrating business activity.

The organisational structures and issues surrounding multinational corporations will be investigated more fully in Chapter 23.

SUMMARY

1a The firm's role in the economy is to eliminate the need for making individual contracts through the market, and to provide a more efficient way to organise production.

1b Using the market to establish a contract is not costless. Transaction costs will mean that the market is normally less efficient than the firm as an allocator of resources.

1c The divorce of ownership from control implies that the objectives of owners and managers may diverge, and similarly the objectives of one manager from another. Hence the goals of firms may be diverse. What is more, as ownership becomes more

dispersed, so the degree of control by owners diminishes yet further.

1d Managers might pursue maximisation goals other than profit, or look to achieve a wide range of targets in which profit acts as a constraint on other business aims.

1e The problem of managers not pursuing the same goals as the owners is an example of the *principal–agent problem*. Agents (in this case the managers) may not always carry out the wishes of their principals (in this case the owners). Because of asymmetric information, managers are able to pursue their own aims, just so long as they produce

SUMMARY

results that will satisfy the owners. The solution for owners is for there to be better means of monitoring the performance of managers, and incentives for the managers to behave in the owners' interests.

2a The legal status of the firm will influence both its actions and performance within the market place.

2b There are several types of legal organisation of firms: the sole proprietorship, the partnership, the private limited company, the public limited company, consortia of firms, co-operatives and public corporations. In the first two cases, the owners have unlimited liability: the owners are personally liable for any losses the business might make. With companies, however, shareholders' liability is limited to the amount they have invested. This reduced risk encourages people to invest in companies.

3a The relative success of a business organisation will be strongly influenced by its organisational structure. As a firm grows, its organisational structure will need to evolve in order to account for the business's growing complexity. This is particularly so if the business looks to expand overseas.

3b As firms grow, so they tend to move from a U-form to an M-form structure. In recent years, however, with the advance of information technology, many firms have adopted a flat organisation – a return to U-form.

3c Multinational companies often adopt relatively complex forms of organisation. These vary from a holding company (H-form) structure, to the integrated international enterprise, to transnational associations.

REVIEW QUESTIONS

1 What is meant by the term 'transaction costs'? Explain why the firm represents a more efficient way of organising economic life than relying on individual contracts.

2 Explain why the business objectives of owners and managers are likely to diverge. How might owners attempt to ensure that managers act in their interests and not in the managers' own interests?

3 Compare and contrast the relative strengths and weaknesses of the partnership and the public limited company.

4 Conduct an investigation into a recent large building project, such as the Channel Tunnel. Identify what firms were involved and the roles and responsibilities they had. Outline the advantages and disadvantages that such business consortia might have.

5 If a business is thinking of reorganisation, why and in what ways might new technology be an important factor in such considerations?

6 What problems are multinational corporations, as opposed to domestic firms, likely to have in respect to organising their business activity? What alternative organisational models might multinationals adopt? To what extent do they overcome the problems you have identified?

4 The working of competitive markets

4.1 Business in a competitive market

If a firm wants to increase its profits, should it raise its prices, or should it lower them? Should it increase its output, or should it reduce it? Should it modify its product, or should it keep the product unchanged? The answer to these and many other questions is that it depends on the market in which the firm operates. If the market is buoyant, it may well be a good idea for the firm to increase its output in anticipation of greater sales. It may also be a good idea to raise the price of its product in the belief that consumers will be willing to pay more. If, however, the market is declining, the firm may well decide to reduce output, or cut prices, or diversify across into an alternative product.

The firm is thus greatly affected by its market environment, an environment that is often outside the firm's control and subject to frequent changes. For many firms, prices are determined not by them, but by the market. Even where they do have some influence over prices, the influence is only slight. They may be able to put prices up a small amount, but if they raise them too much, they will find that they lose sales to their rivals.

The market dominates a firm's activities. The more competitive the market, the greater this domination becomes. In the extreme case, the firm may have no power at all to change its price: it is what we call a **price taker**. It has to accept the market price as given. If the firm attempts to raise the price above the market price, it will simply be unable to sell its product: it will lose all its sales to its competitors. Take the case of farmers selling wheat. They have to accept the price as dictated by the market. If individually they try to sell above the market price, no one will buy.

In competitive markets, consumers too are price takers. When we go into shops we have no control over prices. We have to accept the price as given. For example, when you get to the supermarket checkout, you cannot start haggling with the checkout operator over the price of a can of beans or a tub of margarine.

So how does a competitive market work? For simplicity we will examine the case of a **perfectly competitive market**. This is where both producers and consumers are too numerous to have any control over prices whatsoever: a situation where everyone is a price taker.

(Clearly, in other markets, firms will have some discretion over the prices they charge. For example, a manufacturing company such as Ford will have some discretion over the prices it charges for its Fiestas or Mondeos. In such cases the firm has some 'market power'. We will examine different degrees of market power in Chapters 11 and 12.)

definition

Price taker
A person or firm with no power to be able to influence the market price.

definition

Perfectly competitive market (preliminary definition)
A market in which all producers and consumers of the product are price takers. (There are other features of a perfectly competitive market; these are examined in Chapter 11.)

The price mechanism

In a **free market** individuals are free to make their own economic decisions. Consumers are free to decide what to buy with their incomes: free to make demand decisions. Firms are free to choose what to sell and what production methods to use: free to make supply decisions. The resulting demand and supply decisions of consumers and firms are transmitted to each other through their effect on *prices*: through the **price mechanism**.

The price mechanism works as follows. Prices respond to *shortages* and *surpluses*. Shortages cause prices to rise. Surpluses cause prices to fall.

If consumers decide they want more of a good (or if producers decide to cut back supply), demand will exceed supply. The resulting *shortage* will cause *the price of the good to rise*. This will act as an incentive to producers to supply more, since production will now be more profitable. On the other hand, it will discourage consumers from buying so much. *Price will continue rising until the shortage has thereby been eliminated*.

If, on the other hand, consumers decide they want less of a good (or if producers decide to produce more), supply will exceed demand. The resulting *surplus* will cause *the price of the good to fall*. This will act as a disincentive to producers, who will supply less, since production will now be less profitable. It will encourage consumers to buy more. *Price will continue falling until the surplus has thereby been eliminated*.

The same analysis can be applied to labour (and other factor) markets, except that here the demand and supply roles are reversed. Firms are the demanders of labour. Households are the suppliers. If the demand for a particular type of labour exceeded its supply, the resulting shortage would drive up the wage rate (i.e. the price of labour), thus reducing firms' demand for that type of labour and encouraging more workers to take up that type of job. Wages would continue rising until demand equalled supply: until the shortage was eliminated.

Likewise if there were a surplus of a particular type of labour, the wage would fall until demand equalled supply.

The effect of changes in demand and supply

How will the price mechanism respond to changes in consumer demand or producer supply? After all, the pattern of consumer demand changes over time. For example, people may decide they want more CDs and fewer cassettes. Likewise the pattern of supply also changes. For example, changes in technology may allow the mass production of microchips at lower cost, while the production of hand-built furniture becomes relatively expensive.

In all cases of changes in demand and supply, the resulting changes in *price* act as both *signals* and *incentives*.

A change in demand

A rise in demand is signalled by a rise in price. This then acts as an incentive for supply to rise. What in effect is happening is that the high price of these goods relative to their costs of production is signalling that consumers are willing to see resources diverted from other uses. Firms respond by doing just that. They divert resources from goods with lower prices relative to costs (and hence lower profits) to those goods that are more profitable.

definition

Free market
One in which there is an absence of government intervention. Individual producers and consumers are free to make their own economic decisions.

definition

The price mechanism
The system in a market economy whereby changes in price in response to changes in demand and supply have the effect of making demand equal to supply.

A fall in demand is signalled by a fall in price. This then acts as an incentive for supply to fall. These goods are now less profitable to produce.

A change in supply

A rise in supply is signalled by a fall in price. This then acts as an incentive for demand to rise. A fall in supply is signalled by a rise in price. This then acts as an incentive for demand to fall.

The interdependence of markets

The interdependence of goods and factor markets

A rise in demand for a good will raise its price and profitability. Firms will respond by supplying more. But to do this they will require more inputs. Thus the demand for the inputs will rise, which, in turn, will raise the price of the inputs. The suppliers of inputs will respond to this incentive by supplying more. This can be summarised as follows:

Goods market

- Demand for the good rises.
- This creates a shortage.
- This causes the price of the good to rise.
- This eliminates the shortage by choking off some of the demand and encouraging firms to produce more.

Factor market

- The increased supply of the good causes an increase in the demand for factors of production (i.e. inputs) used in making it.
- This causes a shortage of those inputs.
- This causes their prices to rise.
- This eliminates their shortage by choking off some of the demand and encouraging the suppliers of inputs to supply more.

It can thus be seen that changes in goods markets will cause changes in factor markets. Figure 4.1 summarises this sequence of events. (It is common in economics to summarise an argument like this by using symbols.)

Figure 4.1
The price mechanism: the effect of a rise in demand

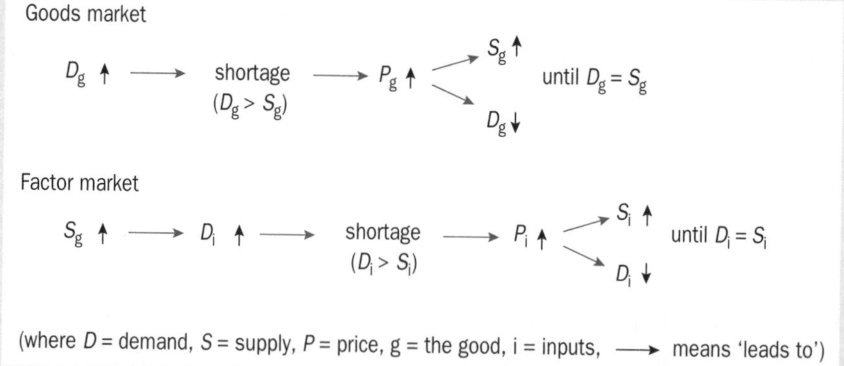

Goods market

$$D_g \uparrow \longrightarrow \text{shortage} \longrightarrow P_g \uparrow \nearrow \begin{matrix} S_g \uparrow \\ \\ D_g \downarrow \end{matrix} \quad \text{until } D_g = S_g$$
$$(D_g > S_g)$$

Factor market

$$S_g \uparrow \longrightarrow D_i \uparrow \longrightarrow \text{shortage} \longrightarrow P_i \uparrow \nearrow \begin{matrix} S_i \uparrow \\ \\ D_i \downarrow \end{matrix} \quad \text{until } D_i = S_i$$
$$(D_i > S_i)$$

(where D = demand, S = supply, P = price, g = the good, i = inputs, $\longrightarrow$ means 'leads to')

Interdependence exists in the other direction too: factor markets affect goods markets. For example, the discovery of raw materials will lower their price. This will lower the costs of production of firms using these raw materials and increase the supply of the finished goods. The resulting surplus will lower the price of the good, which, in turn, will encourage consumers to buy more.

The interdependence of different goods markets

A rise in the price of one good will encourage consumers to buy alternatives. This will drive up the price of alternatives. This in turn will encourage producers to supply more of the alternatives.

Let us now turn to examine each side of the market – demand and supply – in more detail.

4.2 Demand

The relationship between demand and price

The headlines announce, 'Major crop failures in Brazil and East Africa: coffee prices soar.' Shortly afterwards you find that coffee prices have doubled in the shops. What do you do? Presumably you will cut back on the amount of coffee you drink. Perhaps you will reduce it from, say, six cups per day to two. Perhaps you will give up drinking coffee altogether.

This is simply an illustration of the general relationship between price and consumption: *when the price of a good rises, the quantity demanded will fall.* This relationship is known as the **law of demand**. There are two reasons for this law:

- People will feel poorer. They will not be able to afford to buy so much of the good with their money. The purchasing power of their income (their *real income*) has fallen. This is called the **income effect** of a price rise.
- The good will now be dearer relative to other goods. People will thus switch to alternative or 'substitute' goods. This is called the **substitution effect** of a price rise.

Similarly, when the price of a good falls, the quantity demanded will rise. People can afford to buy more (the income effect), and they will switch away from consuming alternative goods (the substitution effect).

Therefore, returning to our example of the increase in the price of coffee, we will not be able to afford to buy as much as before, and we will probably drink more tea, cocoa, fruit juices or even water instead.

The amount by which the quantity demanded falls will depend on the size of the income and substitution effects.

The size of the income effect depends primarily on the proportion of income spent on the good. Thus the more coffee we buy in the first place, the more likely it is that we will be forced to cut down on the amount we buy if the price goes up. In other words, the bigger the proportion of income spent on the good, the bigger will be the effect of a price rise on people's real income, and the more they will reduce the quantity they demand.

The size of the substitution effect depends primarily on the number and

definition

The law of demand
The quantity of a good demanded per period of time will fall as the price rises and rise as the price falls, other things being equal (*ceteris paribus*).

definition

Income effect
The effect of a change in price on quantity demanded arising from the consumer becoming better or worse off as a result of the price change.

definition

Substitution effect
The effect of a change in price on quantity demanded arising from the consumer switching to or from alternative (substitute) products.

closeness of substitute goods. Thus if you are quite happy to drink tea instead of coffee, a rise in the price of coffee will cause you to cut your consumption of coffee considerably, and correspondingly to increase your consumption of tea.

A word of warning: be careful about the meaning of the words **quantity demanded**. They refer to the amount consumers are willing and able to purchase at a given price over a given time period (for example, a week, or a month, or a year). They do *not* refer to what people would simply *like* to consume. You might like to own a Rolls-Royce, but your demand for Rolls-Royces will almost certainly be zero.

The demand curve

Consider the hypothetical data in Table 4.1. The table shows how many kilos of potatoes per month would be purchased at various prices.

Columns (2) and (3) show the **demand schedules** for two individuals, Tracey and Darren. Column (4), by contrast, shows the total **market demand schedule**. This is the total demand by all consumers. To obtain the market demand schedule for potatoes, we simply add up the quantities demanded at each price by *all* consumers: i.e. Tracey, Darren and everyone else who demands potatoes. Notice that we are talking about demand *over a period of time* (not at a *point* in time). Thus we would talk about daily demand or weekly demand or annual demand or whatever.

The demand schedule can be represented graphically as a **demand curve**. Figure 4.2 shows the market demand curve for potatoes corresponding to the schedule in Table 4.1. The price of potatoes is plotted on the vertical axis. The quantity demanded is plotted on the horizontal axis.

Point *E* shows that at a price of 20p per kilo, 100 000 tonnes of potatoes are demanded each month. When the price falls to 16p we move down the curve to point *D*. This shows that the quantity demanded has now risen to 200 000 tonnes per month. Similarly, if price falls to 12p, we move down the curve again to point *C*: 350 000 tonnes are now demanded. The five points on the graph (*A–E*) correspond to the figures in columns (1) and (4) of Table 4.1. The graph also enables us to read off the likely quantities demanded at prices other than those in the table.

A demand curve could also be drawn for an individual consumer. Like market demand curves, individuals' demand curves generally slope downward from left to right: they have negative slope.

Two points should be noted at this stage:

> **definition**
>
> **Quantity demanded**
> The amount of a good that a consumer is willing and able to buy at a given price over a given period of time.

> **definition**
>
> **Demand schedule for an individual**
> A table showing the different quantities of a good that a person is willing and able to buy at various prices over a given period of time.

> **definition**
>
> **Market demand schedule**
> A table showing the different total quantities of a good that consumers are willing and able to buy at various prices over a given period of time.

> **definition**
>
> **Demand curve**
> A graph showing the relationship between the price of a good and the quantity of the good demanded over a given time period. Price is measured on the vertical axis; quantity demanded is measured on the horizontal axis. A demand curve can be for an individual consumer or a group of consumers, or more usually for the whole market.

Table 4.1 **The demand for potatoes (monthly)**

	Price (pence per kg) (1)	Tracey's demand (kg) (2)	Darren's demand (kg) (3)	Total market demand (tonnes: 000s) (4)
A	4	28	16	700
B	8	15	11	500
C	12	5	9	350
D	16	1	7	200
E	20	0	6	100

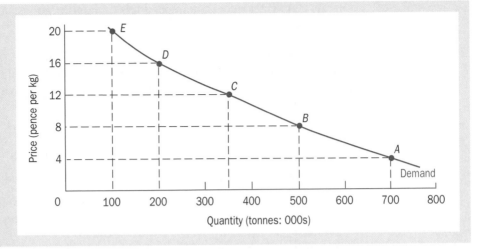

Figure 4.2
Market demand curve for potatoes (monthly)

- In textbooks, demand curves (and other curves too) are only occasionally used to plot specific data. More frequently they are used to illustrate general theoretical arguments. In such cases the axes will simply be price and quantity, with the units unspecified.
- The term 'curve' is used even when the graph is a straight line! In fact, when using demand curves to illustrate arguments we frequently draw them as straight lines.

Other determinants of demand

Price is not the only factor that determines how much of a good people will buy. Demand is also affected by the following.

Tastes. The more desirable people find the good, the more they will demand. Tastes are affected by advertising, by fashion, by observing other consumers, by considerations of health and by the experiences from consuming the good on previous occasions.

The number and price of substitute goods (i.e. competitive goods). The higher the price of **substitute goods**, the higher will be the demand for this good as people switch from the substitutes. For example, the demand for coffee will depend on the price of tea. If tea goes up in price, the demand for coffee will rise.

The number and price of complementary goods. **Complementary goods** are those that are consumed together: cars and petrol, shoes and polish, bread and butter. The higher the price of complementary goods, the fewer of them will be bought and hence the less the demand for this good. For example, the demand for compact discs will depend on the price of CD players. If the price of CD players goes up, so that fewer are bought, the demand for CDs will fall.

Income. As people's incomes rise, their demand for most goods will rise. Such goods are called **normal goods**. There are exceptions to this general rule, how-

definition
Substitute goods A pair of goods which are considered by consumers to be alternatives to each other. As the price of one goes up, the demand for the other rises.

definition
Complementary goods A pair of goods consumed together. As the price of one goes up, the demand for both goods will fall.

definition
Normal goods Goods whose demand rises as people's incomes rise.

ever. As people get richer, they spend less on **inferior goods**, such as cheap margarine, and switch to better quality goods.

Distribution of income. If, for example, national income were redistributed from the poor to the rich, the demand for luxury goods would rise. At the same time, as the poor got poorer, they might have to turn to buying inferior goods, whose demand would also rise.

Expectations of future price changes. If people think that prices are going to rise in the future, they are likely to buy more now before the price does go up.

To illustrate these six determinants let us look at the demand for butter.

- Tastes: if it is heavily advertised, demand is likely to rise. If, on the other hand, there is a cholesterol scare, people may demand less for health reasons.
- Substitutes: if the price of margarine goes up, the demand for butter is likely to rise as people switch from one to the other.
- Complements: if the price of bread goes up, people will buy less bread and hence less butter to spread on it.
- Income: if people's incomes rise, they may well turn to consuming butter rather than margarine.
- Income distribution: if income is redistributed away from the poor, they may have to give up consuming butter and buy cheaper margarine instead, or simply buy less butter and be more economical with the amount they use.
- Expectations: if it is announced in the news that butter prices are expected to rise in the near future, people are likely to buy more now and stock up their freezers while current prices last.

Movements along and shifts in the demand curve

A demand curve is constructed on the assumption that 'other things remain equal' (*ceteris paribus*). In other words, it is assumed that none of the determinants of demand, other than price, changes. The effect of a change in price is then simply illustrated by a movement along the demand curve: for example, from point *B* to point *D* in Figure 4.2 when price rises from 8p to 16p per kilo.

What happens, then, when one of these other determinants changes? The answer is that we have to construct a whole new demand curve: the curve shifts. If a change in one of the other determinants causes demand to rise – say, income rises – the whole curve will shift to the right. This shows that at each price more will be demanded than before. Thus in Figure 4.3 at a price of *P*, a quantity of Q_0 was originally demanded. But now, after the increase in demand, Q_1 is demanded. (Note that D_1 is not necessarily parallel to D_0.)

If a change in a determinant other than price causes demand to fall, the whole curve will shift to the left.

To distinguish between shifts in and movements along demand curves, it is usual to distinguish between a change in *demand* and a change in the *quantity demanded*. A shift in demand is referred to as a **change in demand**, whereas a movement along the demand curve as a result of a change in price is referred to as a **change in the quantity demanded**.

definition
Inferior goods Goods whose demand falls as people's incomes rise.

definition
Change in demand The term used for a shift in the demand curve. It occurs when a determinant of demand *other* than price changes.

definition
Change in the quantity demanded The term used for a movement along the demand curve to a new point. It occurs when there is a change in price.

Figure 4.3
An increase in
demand

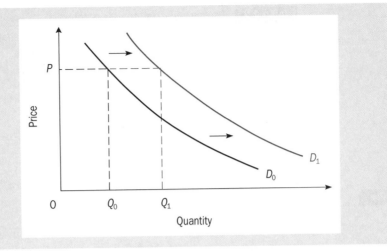

4.3 Supply

Supply and price

Imagine you are a farmer deciding what to do with your land. Part of your land is in a fertile valley. Part is on a hillside where the soil is poor. Perhaps, then, you will consider growing vegetables in the valley and keeping sheep on the hillside.

Your decision will depend to a large extent on the price that various vegetables will fetch in the market, and likewise the price you can expect to get from sheep and wool. As far as the valley is concerned, you will plant the vegetables that give the best return. If, for example, the price of potatoes is high, you will probably use a lot of the valley for growing potatoes. If the price gets higher, you may well use the whole of the valley, perhaps being prepared to run the risk of potato disease. If the price is very high indeed, you may even consider growing potatoes on the hillside, even though the yield per acre is much lower there. In other words, the higher the price of a particular crop, the more you are likely to grow in preference to other crops.

This illustrates the general relationship between supply and price: *when the price of a good rises, the quantity supplied will also rise.* There are three reasons for this:

● As firms supply more, they are likely to find that, beyond a certain level of output, costs rise more and more rapidly.

In the case of the farm we have just considered, once potatoes have to be grown on the hillside, the costs of producing them will increase. Also if the land has to be used more intensively, say by the use of more and more fertilisers, again the cost of producing extra potatoes is likely to rise quite rapidly. It is the same for manufacturers. Beyond a certain level of output, costs are likely to rise rapidly as workers have to be paid overtime and as machines approach their full capacity. If higher output involves higher costs of production, producers will need to get a higher price if they are to be persuaded to produce extra output.

Table 4.2	The supply of potatoes (monthly)		
	Price of potatoes (pence per kg)	Farmer X's supply (tonnes)	Total market supply (tonnes: 000s)
a	4	50	100
b	8	70	200
c	12	100	350
d	16	120	530
e	20	130	700

- The higher the price of the good, the more profitable it becomes to produce. Firms will thus be encouraged to produce more of it by switching from producing less profitable goods.
- Given time, if the price of a good remains high, new producers will be encouraged to set up in production. Total market supply thus rises.

The first two determinants affect supply in the short run. The third affects supply in the long run. We distinguish between short-run and long-run supply later in section 5.4.

The supply curve

The amount that producers would like to supply at various prices can be shown in a **supply schedule**. Table 4.2 shows a monthly supply schedule for potatoes, both for an individual farmer (farmer X) and for all farmers together (the whole market).

The supply schedule can be represented graphically as a **supply curve**. A supply curve may be an individual firm's supply curve or a market supply curve (i.e. that of the whole industry).

Figure 4.4 shows the *market* supply curve of potatoes. As with demand curves, price is plotted on the vertical axis and quantity on the horizontal axis. Each of the points *a–e* correspond to a figure in Table 4.2. Thus for example, a price rise from 12p per kilogram to 16p per kilogram will cause a movement

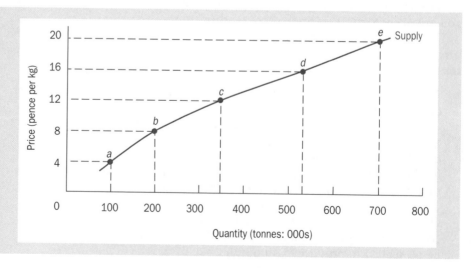

Figure 4.4
Market supply curve of potatoes (monthly)

along the supply curve from point c to point d: total market supply will rise from 350 000 tonnes per month to 530 000 tonnes per month.

Not all supply curves will be upward sloping (positively sloped). Sometimes they will be vertical, or horizontal, or even downward sloping. This will depend largely on the time period over which firms' response to price changes is considered. This question is examined in the next chapter (pages 84–5).

Other determinants of supply

Like demand, supply is not determined simply by price. The other determinants of supply are as follows.

The costs of production. The higher the costs of production, the less profit will be made at any price. As costs rise, firms will cut back on production, probably switching to alternative products whose costs have not risen so much.

The main reasons for a change in costs are as follows:

- Change in input prices: costs of production will rise if wages, raw material prices, rents, interest rates or any other input prices rise.
- Change in technology: technological advances can fundamentally alter the costs of production. Consider, for example, how the microchip revolution has changed production methods and information handling in virtually every industry in the world.
- Organisational changes: various cost savings can be made in many firms by reorganising production.
- Government policy: costs will be lowered by government subsidies and raised by various taxes.

The profitability of alternative products (substitutes in supply). If some alternative product (**a substitute in supply**) becomes more profitable to supply than before, producers are likely to switch from the first good to this alternative. Supply of the first good falls. Other goods are likely to become more profitable if:

- their price rises;
- their cost of production falls.

For example, if the price of carrots goes up, or the cost of producing carrots comes down, farmers may decide to produce more carrots. The supply of potatoes is therefore likely to fall.

The profitability of goods in joint supply. Sometimes when one good is produced, another good is also produced at the same time. These are said to be **goods in joint supply**. An example is the refining of crude oil to produce petrol. Other grade fuels will be produced as well, such as diesel and paraffin. If more petrol is produced, due to a rise in demand, then the supply of these other fuels will rise too.

Nature, 'random shocks' and other unpredictable events. In this category we would include the weather and diseases affecting farm output, wars affecting the supply of imported raw materials, the breakdown of machinery, industrial disputes, earthquakes, floods and fire, etc.

The aims of producers. A profit-maximising firm will supply a different quantity from a firm that has a different aim, such as maximising sales.

> **definition**
>
> **Substitutes in supply**
> These are two goods where an increased production of one means diverting resources away from producing the other.

> **definition**
>
> **Goods in joint supply**
> These are two goods where the production of more of one leads to the production of more of the other.

Expectations of future price changes. If price is expected to rise, producers may temporarily reduce the amount they sell. Instead they are likely to build up their stocks and only release them on to the market when the price does rise. At the same time they may plan to produce more, by installing new machines, or taking on more labour, so that they can be ready to supply more when the price has risen.

To illustrate some of these determinants, let us consider the example of butter. What would cause the supply of butter to rise?

- A reduction in the costs of producing butter. This could be caused, say, by a reduction in the price of nitrogen fertiliser. This would encourage farmers to use more fertiliser, which would increase grass yields, which in turn would increase milk yields per acre. Alternatively, new technology may allow more efficient churning of butter. Or again, the government may decide to give subsidies to farmers to produce more butter.
- A reduction in the profitability of producing cream or cheese. If these products become less profitable, due say to a reduction in their price, due in turn to a reduction in consumer demand, more butter is likely to be produced instead.
- An increase in the profitability of skimmed milk. If consumers buy more skimmed milk, then an increased supply of skimmed milk is likely to lead to an increase in the supply of butter and other cream products, since they are jointly produced with skimmed milk.
- If weather conditions are favourable, grass yields and hence milk yields are likely to be high. This will increase the supply of butter and other milk products.
- If butter producers expect butter prices to rise in the future, they may well decide to release less on to the market now and put more into frozen storage until the price does rise.

Movements along and shifts in the supply curve

The principle here is the same as with demand curves. The effect of a change in price is illustrated by a movement along the supply curve: for example, from point *d* to point *e* in Figure 4.4 when price rises from 16p to 20p. Quantity supplied rises from 530 000 to 700 000 tonnes.

Figure 4.5
Shifts in the supply curve

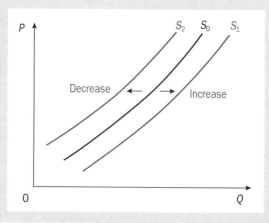

If any other determinant of supply changes, the whole supply curve will shift. A rightward shift illustrates an increase in supply. A leftward shift illustrates a decrease in supply. Thus in Figure 4.5, if the original curve is S_0, the curve S_1 represents an increase in supply, whereas the curve S_2 represents a decrease in supply.

A movement along a supply curve is often referred to as a **change in the quantity supplied**, whereas a shift in the supply curve is simply referred to as a **change in supply**.

4.4 Price and output determination

Equilibrium price and output

We can now combine our analysis of demand and supply. This will show how the actual price of a product and the actual quantity bought and sold are determined in a free and competitive market.

Let us return to the example of the market demand and market supply of potatoes, and use the data from Tables 4.1 and 4.2. These figures are given again in Table 4.3.

What will be the price and output that actually prevail? If the price started at 4p per kilogram, demand would exceed supply by 600 000 tonnes ($A - a$). Consumers would be unable to obtain all they wanted and would thus be willing to pay a higher price. Producers, unable or unwilling to supply enough to meet the demand, will be only too happy to accept a higher price. The effect of the shortage, then, will be to drive up the price. The same would happen at a price of 8p per kilogram. There would still be a shortage; price would still rise. But as the price rises, the quantity demanded falls and the quantity supplied rises. The shortage is progressively eliminated.

What would happen if the price started at a much higher level: say at 20p per kilogram? In this case supply would exceed demand by 600 000 tonnes ($e - E$). The effect of this surplus would be to drive the price down as farmers competed against each other to sell their excess supplies. The same would happen at a price of 16p per kilogram. There would still be a surplus; price would still fall.

In fact, only one price is sustainable. This is the price where demand equals supply: namely 12p per kilogram, where both demand and supply are 350 000 tonnes. When supply matches demand the market is said to **clear**. There is no shortage and no surplus.

definition
Change in the quantity supplied The term used for a movement along the supply curve to a new point. It occurs when there is a change in price.

definition
Change in supply The term used for a shift in the supply curve. It occurs when a determinant other than price changes.

definition
Market clearing A market clears when supply matches demand, leaving no shortage or surplus.

Table 4.3	The market demand and supply of potatoes (monthly)	
Price of potatoes (pence per kg)	Total market demand (tonnes: 000s)	Total market supply (tonnes: 000s)
4	700 (A)	100 (a)
8	500 (B)	200 (b)
12	350 (C)	350 (c)
16	200 (D)	530 (d)
20	100 (E)	700 (e)

BOX 4.1

UK house prices
The ups and downs of the housing market

If you are thinking of buying a house sometime in the future, then you may well follow the fortunes of the housing market with some trepidation. In the late 1980s there was a housing price explosion in the UK: in fact, between 1984 and 1989 house prices *doubled*. In 1984 the average price of a house was £30 952; by 1989 it was £61 163. If similar increases were to occur again, many people might find that owning a home of their own remains just a dream.

House prices since the early 1980s
The diagram shows what happened to house prices in the period 1983 to 1998. There was rapid house price inflation up to 1989. It reached a peak in 1988, when average house prices rose by 23.3 per cent in that one year alone.

In their rush to buy a house before prices rose any further, many people in this period borrowed as much as they were able. Building societies and banks at that time had plenty of money to lend and were only too willing to do so. Many people, therefore, took out very large mortgages. In 1983 the average new mortgage was 2.08 times average annual earnings. By 1989 this figure had risen to 3.44.

After 1989 there followed a period of *falling* prices.

From 1990 to 1995, house prices fell by 12.2 per cent. As a result of this, many people found themselves in a position of *negative equity*. This is the situation where the size of their mortgage is greater than the value of their house. In other words, if they sold their house, they would end up still owing money! For this reason many people found that they could not move house.

Then in 1996, house prices began to recover. Was this good news or bad news? For those trapped in negative equity, it was good news. It was good news also for old people who wished to move into a retirement home and who had a house to sell. It was bad news, however, for the first-time buyer! As we shall see in many parts of this book, what is good news for one person is often bad news for another.

The determinants of house prices
House prices are determined by demand and supply. If demand rises (i.e. shifts to the right) or if supply falls (i.e. shifts to the left), the equilibrium price of houses will rise. Similarly, if demand falls or supply rises, the equilibrium price will fall.

So why did house prices rise so rapidly in the 1980s, only to fall in the early 1990s? The answer lies primarily

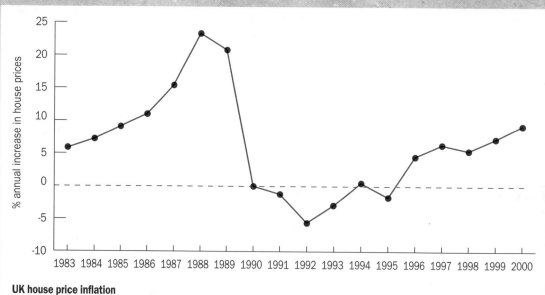

UK house price inflation

in changes in the *demand* for housing. Let us examine the various factors that affected the demand for houses.

Incomes (actual and anticipated). The second half of the 1980s was a period of rapidly rising incomes. The economy was experiencing an economic 'boom'. Many people wanted to spend their extra incomes on housing: either buying a house for the first time, or moving to a better one. What is more, many people thought that their incomes would continue to grow, and were thus prepared to stretch themselves financially in the short term by buying an expensive house, confident that their mortgage payments would become more and more affordable over time.

The early 1990s, by contrast, was a period of recession, with rising unemployment and much more slowly growing incomes. People had much less confidence about their ability to afford large mortgages.

The desire for home ownership. The prime minister in the 1980s, Mrs Thatcher, put great emphasis on the virtues of home ownership: her vision was one of a home-owning democracy. Certainly, the mood of the age was very much that it was desirable to own one's home. This fuelled the growth in demand.

The cost of mortgages. During the second half of the 1980s, mortgage interest rates were generally falling. This meant that people could afford larger mortgages, and thus afford to buy more expensive houses. In 1989, however, this trend was reversed. Mortgage interest rates were now rising. Many people found it difficult to maintain existing payments, let alone to take on a larger mortgage.

The availability of mortgages. In the late 1980s, mortgages were readily available. Banks and building societies were prepared to accept smaller deposits on houses, and to grant mortgages of 3½ times a person's annual income, compared with 2½ times in the early 1980s. In the early 1990s, however, banks and building societies were more cautious about granting mortgages. They were aware that, with falling house prices, rising unemployment and the growing problem of negative equity, there was a growing danger that borrowers would default on payments.

Speculation. In the 1980s, people generally believed that house prices would continue rising. This encouraged people to buy as soon as possible, and to take out the biggest mortgage possible, before prices went up any further. There was also an effect on supply. Those with houses to sell held back until the last possible moment in the hope of getting a higher price. The net effect was for a rightward shift in the demand curve for houses and a leftward shift in the supply curve. The effect of this speculation, therefore, was to help bring about the very effect that people were predicting (see section 5.4).

In the early 1990s, the process was reversed. People thinking of buying houses held back, hoping to buy at a lower price. People with houses to sell tried to sell as quickly as possible before prices fell any further. Again the effect of this speculation was to aggravate the fall in prices.

What of the future?

In 1996, house prices began to rise again, but with interest rates rising too and with people more cautious after the experience on the early 1990s, the increase in house prices was much more modest than that in the 1980s. Whether the early 2000s will be another period of rapidly rising prices depends very much on the factors listed above. If the economy booms, if interest rates are low, if mortgages are readily available, and if people believe that prices will rise, there may well be another boom in house prices. It is unlikely, however, that the boom will be as great as in the late 1980s. Political parties are only too well aware of the dangers of allowing too much money to be available for mortgages too cheaply.

Questions

1 Draw supply and demand diagrams to illustrate what was happening to house prices (a) in the second half of the 1980s; (b) in the early 1990s.
2 Are there any factors on the *supply* side that contribute to changes in house prices? If so, what are they?
3 Find out what has happened to house prices over the last three years. Attempt an explanation of what has happened.

This price, where demand equals supply, is called the **equilibrium price**. By **equilibrium** we mean a point of balance or a point of rest: in other words, a point towards which there is a tendency to move. In Table 4.3, if the price starts at other than 12p per kilogram, there will be a tendency for it to move towards 12p. The equilibrium price is the only price at which producers' and consumers' wishes are mutually reconciled: where the producers' plans to supply exactly match the consumers' plans to buy.

Demand and supply curves

The determination of equilibrium price and output can be shown using demand and supply curves. Equilibrium is where the two curves intersect.

Figure 4.6 shows the demand and supply curves of potatoes corresponding to the data in Table 4.3. Equilibrium price is P_e (12p) and equilibrium quantity is Q_e (350 000 tonnes).

At any price above 12p, there would be a surplus. Thus at 16p there is a surplus of 330 000 tonnes $(d - D)$. More is supplied than consumers are willing and able to purchase at that price. Thus a price of 16p fails to clear the market. Price will fall to the equilibrium price of 12p. As it does so, there will be a movement along the demand curve from point D to point C, and a movement along the supply curve from point d to point c.

At any price below 12p, there would be a shortage. Thus at 8p there is a shortage of 300 000 tonnes $(B - b)$. Price will rise to 12p. This will cause a movement along the supply curve from point b to point c and along the demand curve from point B to point C.

Point Cc is the equilibrium: where demand equals supply.

Movement to a new equilibrium

The equilibrium price will remain unchanged only so long as the demand and supply curves remain unchanged. If either of the curves shifts, a new equilibrium will be formed.

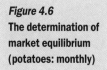

definition

Equilibrium price
The price where the quantity demanded equals the quantity supplied: the price where there is no shortage or surplus.

definition

Equilibrium
A position of balance. A position from which there is no inherent tendency to move away.

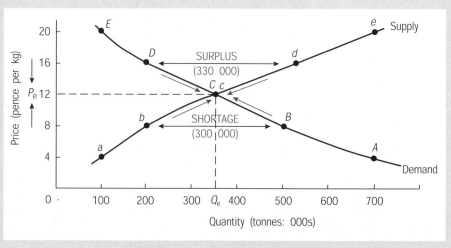

Figure 4.6
The determination of market equilibrium (potatoes: monthly)

Figure 4.7
The effect of a shift
in the demand curve

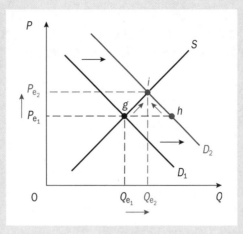

A change in demand

If one of the determinants of demand changes (other than price), the whole demand curve will shift. This will lead to a movement *along* the *supply* curve to the new intersection point.

For example, in Figure 4.7, if a rise in consumer incomes led to the demand curve shifting to D_2, there would be a shortage of $h - g$ at the original price P_{e1}. This would cause price to rise to the new equilibrium P_{e2}. As it did so there would be a movement along the supply curve from point g to point i, and along the new demand curve (D_2) from point h to point i. Equilibrium quantity would rise from Q_{e1} to Q_{e2}.

The effect of the shift in demand, therefore, has been a movement *along* the supply curve from the old equilibrium to the new: from point g to point i.

A change in supply

Likewise, if one of the determinants of supply changes (other than price), the

Figure 4.8
The effect of a shift
in the supply curve

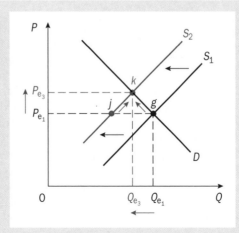

BOX 4.2

The heyday of the auction
A revolution in the working of the price mechanism?

An example of supply and demand in action is the 'Internet auction'. This is similar to a regular auction, where people bid for items put up for sale, and the highest bidder wins. The price is that bid by the highest bidder. With an Internet auction, the bidding is on-line.

The following extracts are from an article appearing in *The Economist* of 24 July 1999. It considers the rise of Internet auctions and compares them with other forms of price setting.

As an example of all that is frothy, faddish and foolhardy about investment in Internet shares, you might be tempted to choose eBay... This is a company that made its name by helping people to buy and sell, for example, beanie babies, second-hand surf-boards and other stuff that would otherwise end up as junk. But while eBay's share price may be crazy, it would be wrong to dismiss the company as just another symptom of a mania. There is method in this madness. *On-line auctions* may be one of the most valuable innovations wrought by the Internet.

Economists have long recognised the virtues of auctions. In 1880, Léon Walras, a French economist, described the entire price mechanism as an auctioneer. The 'Walrasian auctioneer' would call out a price, see how many buyers and sellers there were and, if these did not balance, adjust the price until demand equalled supply.

But in practice, for most of human history, auctions have not played a starring role in the price-setting process. Mostly they have been limited to agricultural and other commodity markets, fine art and antiques, and – of increasing importance in recent decades – some types of financial securities

Two other forms of price-setting have been dominant: one-to-one negotiation (haggling); and the non-negotiable menu of prices offered by seller to buyer. These two approaches are not bad: the price mechanism based on them obviously does a much better job of allocating scarce resources than do centrally planned systems that eschew prices altogether.

But each method has important flaws. When there is a menu, the most that people will reveal about their demand for a given product is whether or not they are willing to buy at the listed price. So unless the seller has, from other sources, an intimate knowledge of supply and demand conditions, the price he sets may have highly inefficient consequences. Moreover, menu prices can be 'sticky' – slow to adjust to changes in the balance of supply and demand.

One-to-one haggling has the advantages of inter-

whole supply curve will shift. This will lead to a movement *along* the *demand* curve to the new intersection point.

For example, in Figure 4.8, if costs of production rose, the supply curve would shift to the left: to S_2. There would be a shortage of $g - j$ at the old price of P_{e1}. Price would rise from P_{e1} to P_{e3}. Quantity would fall from Q_{e1} to Q_{e3}. In other words, there would be a movement along the demand curve from point g to point k, and along the new supply curve (S_2) from point j to point k.

To summarise: a shift in one curve leads to a movement along the other curve to the new intersection point.

Sometimes a number of determinants might change. This may lead to a shift in *both* curves. When this happens, equilibrium simply moves from the point where the old curves intersected to the point where the new ones intersect.

action and dialogue, which improve the chances of reaching a mutually beneficial outcome. But it also carries a big risk: that the seller or buyer may not be negotiating with the best person (i.e. the one willing to pay the most, or sell for least).

Auctions can overcome these shortcomings by soliciting a wide range of bids from many people. And the Internet, thanks to its cheap interconnection of millions of people, makes well-functioning auctions far easier. They are now possible for many goods and services that used to rely on haggling or menus. And even in markets where auctions have long been used to set prices, the Internet can make them much more sophisticated than ever before.

So far, the leading on-line auctions are fairly simple, but highly popular, affairs. Already eBay boasts 2.4m sale-items in 1,627 categories. One reason for its success, and for that of the auctions more recently offered by uBid, Amazon, Yahoo! and others, is that they are entertaining. America is now full of auction addicts crowing about their latest success or bemoaning a near miss. Yet the phenomenon has also introduced useful economic efficiencies, creating big new markets by bringing together a large number of participants – the 'eBay community' alone boasts 3.8m members.

Steve Kaplan, an economist at the University of Chicago, points out that on-line auctions have a big economic advantage over traditional on-line menu-priced sites, such as that pioneered by Amazon. Such sites cut out the cost of going to the shops, and make it cheaper to compare prices with other retailers. But Amazon's customers are no better off if it attracts more users. Whereas the more buyers and sellers turn up on eBay, the better their chances of getting a good deal, as the auction becomes deeper and more liquid.

. . . Needless to say, fixed prices are not going to disappear. Taking part in on-line auctions is time-consuming (and nerve-wracking). Economic theory suggests they are most useful in particular circumstances: when there is uncertainty about what is the right price. This could be for one of two reasons. Either the value of a product is a matter of private taste and opinion – such as a Van Gogh painting or a rare Spice Girls doll. Or the value is likely to be similar for everyone, but it is not obvious to the seller what it is – such as a rail-operating franchise or a radio-bandwidth licence.

Questions

1 What are the advantages of on-line auctions to (a) purchasers; (b) sellers?
2 In what ways do firms using traditional 'menu-based' pricing respond to an increase in demand for their product?

SUMMARY

1a A firm is greatly affected by its market environment. The more competitive the market, the less discretion the firm has in determining its price. In the extreme case of a perfect market, the price is entirely outside the firm's control. The price is determined by demand and supply in the market, and the firm has to accept this price: the firm is a price taker.

1b In a perfect market, price changes act as the mechanism whereby demand and supply are balanced. If there is a shortage, price will rise until the shortage is eliminated. If there is a surplus,

price will fall until that is eliminated.

2a When the price of a good rises, the quantity demanded per period of time will fall. This is known as the 'law of demand'. It applies both to individuals' demand and to the whole market demand.

2b The law of demand is explained by the income and substitution effects of a price change.

2c The relationship between price and quantity demanded per period of time can be shown in a table (or 'schedule') or as a graph. On the graph, price is plotted on the vertical axis and quantity demanded per period of time on the horizontal axis. The resulting demand curve is downward sloping (negatively sloped).

2d Other determinants of demand include tastes, the number and price of substitute goods, the number and price of complementary goods, income, the distribution of income and expectations of future price changes.

2e If price changes, the effect is shown by a movement along the demand curve. We call this effect 'a change in the quantity demanded'.

2f If any other determinant of demand changes, the whole curve will shift. We call this effect 'a change in demand'. A rightward shift represents an increase in demand; a leftward shift represents a decrease in demand.

3a When the price of a good rises, the quantity supplied per period of time will usually also rise. This applies both to individual producers' supply and to the whole market supply.

3b There are two reasons in the short run why a higher price encourages producers to supply more: (a) they are now willing to incur higher costs per unit associated with producing more; (b) they will switch to producing this product and away from now less profitable ones. In the long run there is a third reason: new producers will be attracted into the market.

3c The relationship between price and quantity supplied per period of time can be shown in a table (or schedule) or as a graph. As with a demand

curve, price is plotted on the vertical axis and quantity per period of time on the horizontal axis. The resulting supply curve is upward sloping (positively sloped).

3d Other determinants of supply include the costs of production, the profitability of alternative products, the profitability of goods in joint supply, random shocks and expectations of future price changes.

3e If price changes, the effect is shown by a movement along the supply curve. We call this effect 'a change in the quantity supplied'.

3f If any determinant *other* than price changes, the effect is shown by a shift in the whole supply curve. We call this effect 'a change in supply'. A rightward shift represents an increase in supply; a leftward shift represents a decrease in supply.

4a If the demand for a good exceeds the supply, there will be a shortage. This will lead to a rise in the price of the good.

4b If the supply of a good exceeds the demand, there will be a surplus. This will lead to a fall in the price.

4c Price will settle at the equilibrium. The equilibrium price is the one that clears the market: the price where demand equals supply. This is shown in a demand and supply diagram by the point where the two curves intersect.

4d If the demand or supply curves shift, this will lead either to a shortage or to a surplus. Price will therefore either rise or fall until a new equilibrium is reached at the position where the supply and demand curves *now* intersect.

REVIEW QUESTIONS

1 Using a diagram like Figure 4.1, summarise the effect of (a) a reduction in the demand for a good; (b) a reduction in the costs of production of a good.

2 Referring to Table 4.1, assume that there are 200 consumers in the market. Of these, 100 have schedules like Tracey's and 100 have schedules like Darren's. What would be the total market demand schedule for potatoes now?

3 Again referring to Table 4.1, draw Tracey's and Darren's demand curves for potatoes on one diagram. (Note that you will use the same vertical scale as in Figure 4.2, but you will need a quite different horizontal scale.) At what price is their demand the same? What explanations could there be for the quite different shapes of their two demand curves? (This question is explored in the next chapter.)

4 The price of pork rises and yet it is observed that the sales of pork increase. Does this mean that the demand curve for pork is upward sloping? Explain.

5 Refer to the list of determinants of supply (see pages 63–4). For what reasons might (a) the supply of potatoes fall; (b) the supply of leather rise?

6 This question is concerned with the supply of oil for central heating. In each case consider whether there is a movement along the supply curve (and in which direction) or a shift in it (and whether left or right): (a) new oil fields start up in production; (b) the demand for central heating rises; (c) the price of gas falls; (d) oil companies anticipate an upsurge in the demand for central-heating oil; (e) the demand for petrol rises; (f) new technology decreases the costs of oil refining; (g) all oil products become more expensive.

7 The price of cod is much higher today than it was 20 years ago. Using demand and supply diagrams, explain why this should be so.

8 The number of owners of compact disc players has grown rapidly and hence the demand for compact discs has also grown rapidly. Yet the prices of CDs has fallen. Why? Use a supply and demand diagram to illustrate your answer.

9 What will happen to the equilibrium price and quantity of butter in each of the following cases? You should state whether demand or supply or both have shifted and in which direction: (a) a rise in the price of margarine; (b) a rise in the demand for yoghurt; (c) a rise in the price of bread; (d) a rise in the demand for bread; (e) an expected increase in the price of butter in the near future; (f) a tax on butter production; (g) the invention of a new, but expensive, process of removing all cholesterol from butter, plus the passing of a law which states that butter producers must use this process. In each case assume *ceteris paribus*.

10 If both demand and supply change, and if we know in which direction they have shifted but not by how much, why is it that we will be able to predict the direction in which *either* price or quantity will change, but not both? (Clue: consider the four possible combinations and sketch them if necessary: *D* left, *S* left; *D* right, *S* right; *D* left, *S* right; *D* right, *S* left.)

Business in a market environment

In Chapter 4 we examined how prices are determined in perfectly competitive markets: by the interaction of market demand and market supply. In such markets, although the *market* demand curve is downward sloping, the demand curve faced by the individual firm will be horizontal. This is illustrated in Figure 5.1.

The market price is P_m. The individual firm can sell as much as it likes at this market price: it is too small to have any influence on the market – it is a price taker. It will not force the price down by producing more because, in terms of the total market, this extra would be an infinitesimally small amount. If a farmer doubled the output of wheat sent to the market, it would be too small an increase to affect the world price of wheat!

In practice, however, many firms are not price takers; they have some discretion in choosing their price. Such firms will face a downward-sloping demand curve. If they raise their price, they will sell less; if they lower their price, they will sell more. But firms will want to know more than this. They will want to know just *how much* the quantity demanded will fall. In other words, they will want to know how *responsive* demand is to a rise in price. This responsiveness is measured using a concept called 'elasticity'.

5.1 Price elasticity of demand

The responsiveness of quantity demanded to a change in price

The demand for an individual firm

For any firm considering changing its price, it is vital to know the likely effect

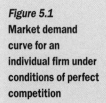

Figure 5.1
Market demand curve for an individual firm under conditions of perfect competition

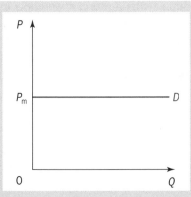

Figure 5.2
The demand for an individual firm's product

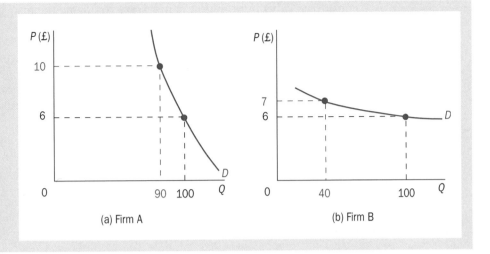

(a) Firm A

(b) Firm B

on the quantity demanded. Take the case of two firms facing very different demand curves. These are shown in Figure 5.2.

Firm A can raise its price quite substantially – from £6 to £10 – and yet its level of sales only falls by a relatively small amount – from 100 units to 90 units. This firm will probably be quite keen to raise its price. After all, it could make significantly more profits on each unit sold (assuming no rise in costs per unit), and yet only sell slightly fewer units.

Firm B, however, will think twice about raising its price. Even a relatively modest increase in price – from £6 to £7 – will lead to a substantial fall in sales from 100 units to 40 units. What is the point of making a bit more profit on those units it manages to sell, if in the process it ends up selling a lot fewer units? In such circumstances the firm may contemplate lowering its price.

The responsiveness of market demand

Economists too will want to know how responsive demand is to a change in price: except in this case it is the responsiveness of *market* demand that is being

Figure 5.3
Market supply and demand

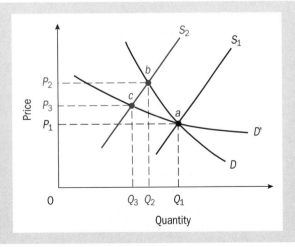

considered. This information is necessary to enable them to predict the effects of a shift in supply on the market price of a product.

Figure 5.3 shows the effect of a shift in supply with two quite different demand curves (D and D'). Assume that initially the supply curve is S_1, and that it intersects with both demand curves at point a, at a price of P_1 and a quantity of Q_1. Now supply shifts to S_2. What will happen to price and quantity? Economists will want to know! The answer is that it depends on the shape of the demand curve. In the case of demand curve D, there is a relatively large rise in price (to P_2) and a relatively small fall in quantity (to Q_2): equilibrium is at point b. In the case of demand curve D', however, there is only a relatively small rise in price (to P_3), but a relatively large fall in quantity (to Q_3): equilibrium is at point c.

Given the importance of knowing the responsiveness of demand to a change in price, we will need some way of measuring this responsiveness. *Elasticity* is the measure we use.

Defining price elasticity of demand

What we will want to compare is the size of the change in quantity demanded of a given product with the size of the change in price. **Price elasticity of demand** does just this. It is defined as follows:

$$P\epsilon_D = \frac{\text{Proportionate (or percentage) change in quantity demanded}}{\text{Proportionate (or percentage) change in price}}$$

If, for example, a 20 per cent rise in the price of a product causes a 10 per cent fall in the quantity demanded, the price elasticity of demand will be:

$$-10\%/20\% = -0.5$$

Three things should be noted at this stage about the figure that is calculated for elasticity.

The use of proportionate or percentage measures

Elasticity is measured in proportionate or percentage terms for the following reasons:

- It allows comparison of changes in two qualitatively different things, which are thus measured in two different types of unit: i.e. it allows comparison of quantity changes (quantity demanded) with monetary changes (price).
- It avoids the problem of what size units to use. For example, an increase from £2 to £4 is 2 price units. An increase from 200 pence to 400 pence is 200 price units. By measuring this change in proportionate or percentage terms, the same result is obtained whichever price unit is used, thus avoiding the problems of a merely apparent difference in price change.
- It is the only sensible way of deciding *how big* a change in price or quantity is. Take a simple example. An item goes up in price by £1. Is this a big increase or a small increase? We can answer this only if we know what the original price was. If a can of beans goes up in price by £1, that is a huge price increase. If, however, the price of a house goes up by £1, that is a tiny price increase. In other words, it is the percentage or proportionate increase in price that we look at in deciding how big a price rise it is.

---

definition

Price elasticity of demand
A measure of the responsiveness of quantity demanded to a change in price.

The sign (positive or negative)

If price increases (a positive figure), the quantity demanded will fall (a negative figure). If price falls (a negative figure), the quantity demanded will rise (a positive figure). Thus price elasticity of demand will be negative: a positive figure is being divided by a negative figure (or vice versa).

The value (greater or less than 1)

If we now ignore the sign and just concentrate on the value of the figure, this tells us whether demand is **elastic** or **inelastic**.

Elastic ($\epsilon > 1$). This is where a change in price causes a proportionately larger change in the quantity demanded. In this case the price elasticity of demand will be greater than 1, since we are dividing a larger figure by a smaller figure.

Inelastic ($\epsilon < 1$). This is where a change in price causes a proportionately smaller change in the quantity demanded. In this case the price elasticity of demand will be less than 1, since we are dividing a smaller figure by a larger figure.

Unit elastic ($\epsilon = 1$). **Unit elasticity** is where the quantity demanded changes proportionately the same as price. This will give an elasticity equal to 1, since we are dividing a figure by itself.

The determinants of price elasticity of demand

The demand for some goods will be highly price elastic: only a small percentage change in price will be necessary to cause a large percentage change in the quantity demanded. The demand for other goods by contrast will be highly price *in*elastic: even large percentage changes in price will have relatively little effect on the quantity demanded. But why will the price elasticity of demand vary from one good to another? What determines price elasticity of demand?

The number and closeness of substitute goods

This is the most important determinant. The more substitutes there are for a good, and the closer they are, the greater will be the price elasticity of demand. The reason is that people will be able to switch to the substitutes when the price of the good rises. The more numerous the substitutes and the closer they are, the more people will switch: in other words, the bigger will be the substitution effect of a price rise.

    For example, the price elasticity of demand for a particular brand of a product will probably be fairly high, especially if there are many other, similar brands. If its price goes up, people can simply switch to another brand: there is a large substitution effect. By contrast the demand for a product in general will normally be pretty inelastic. If the price of food in general goes up, demand for food will fall only slightly. People will buy a little less, since they cannot now afford so much: this is the *income* effect of the price rise. But there is no alternative to food that can satisfy our hunger: there is therefore virtually no *substitution* effect.

---

definition

Elastic
If demand is (price) elastic, then any change in price will cause the quantity demanded to change proportionately more. (Ignoring the negative sign) it will have a value greater than 1.

definition

Inelastic
If demand is (price) inelastic, then any change will cause the quantity demanded to change by a proportionately smaller amount. (Ignoring the negative sign) it will have a value less than 1.

definition

Unit elasticity
When the price elasticity of demand is unity, this is where quantity demanded changes by the same proportion as the price. Price elasticity is equal to −1.

The proportion of income spent on the good

The higher the proportion of our income that is spent on a good, the more we will be forced to cut consumption when its price rises: the bigger will be the income effect and the more elastic will be the demand.

Thus salt has a very low price elasticity of demand. This is because we spend such a tiny fraction of our income on salt that we would find little difficulty in paying a relatively large percentage increase in its price: the income effect of a price rise would be very small. By contrast, there will be a much bigger income effect when a major item of expenditure rises in price. For example, if mortgage interest rates rise (the 'price' of loans for house purchase), people may have to cut down substantially on their demand for housing – being forced to buy somewhere much smaller and cheaper, or to live in rented accommodation.

The time period

When price rises, people may take a time to adjust their consumption patterns and find alternatives. The longer the time period after a price change, then, the more elastic is the demand likely to be.

5.2 The importance of price elasticity of demand to business decision making

definition

Total (sales) revenue (TR)
The amount a firm earns from its sales of a product at a particular price. $TR = P \times Q$. Note that we are referring to *gross* revenue: that is, revenue before the deduction of taxes or any other costs.

A firm's sales revenue

One of the most important applications of price elasticity of demand concerns its relationship with a firm's sales revenue. The **total sales revenue** (**TR**) of a firm is simply price times quantity:

$$TR = P \times Q$$

For example, 3000 units (*Q*) sold at £2 per unit (*P*) will earn the firm £6000 (*TR*). This is shown graphically in Figure 5.4 as the area of the shaded rectangle. But why? The area of a rectangle is simply its height multiplied by its length.

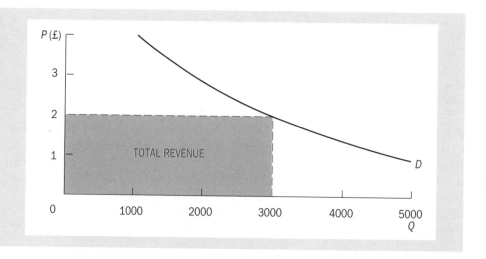

Figure 5.4
Total revenue

But *TR* is simply price (the height of the shaded rectangle) multiplied by quantity (the length of the rectangle).

Let us assume that a firm wants to increase its total revenue. What should it do? Should it raise its price or lower it? The answer depends on the price elasticity of demand.

Elastic demand and sales revenue

As price rises, so quantity demanded falls, and vice versa. When demand is elastic, quantity changes proportionately more than price. Thus the change in quantity has a bigger effect on total revenue than does the change in price. This can be summarised as follows:

P rises; *Q* falls proportionately more; therefore *TR* falls.

P falls: *Q* rises proportionately more; therefore *TR* rises.

In other words, total revenue changes in the same direction as *quantity*.

This is illustrated in Figure 5.5. Demand is elastic between points *a* and *b*. A rise in price from £4 to £5 causes a proportionately larger fall in quantity demanded: from 20 to 10. Total revenue *falls* from £80 (the striped area) to £50 (the shaded area).

When demand is elastic, then, a rise in price will causes a fall in total revenue. If a firm wants to increase its revenue, it should *lower* its price.

Inelastic demand and sales revenue

When demand is inelastic, it is the other way around. Price changes proportionately more than quantity. Thus the change in price has a bigger effect on total revenue than does the change in quantity. To summarise the effects:

P rises; *Q* falls proportionately less; *TR* rises.

P falls; *Q* rises proportionately less; *TR* falls.

In other words, total revenue changes in the same direction as *price*.

This is illustrated in Figure 5.6. Demand is inelastic between points *a* and *c*. A rise in price from £4 to £8 causes a proportionately smaller fall in quantity

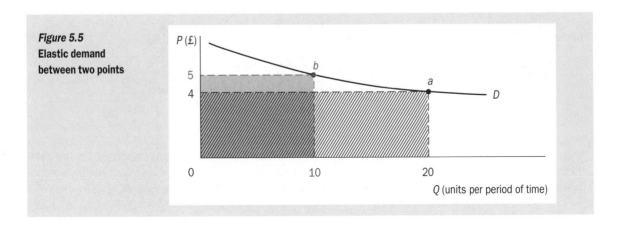

Figure 5.5
Elastic demand
between two points

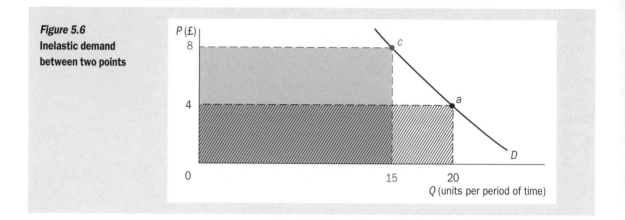

Figure 5.6
Inelastic demand
between two points

demanded: from 20 to 15. Total revenue *rises* from £80 (the striped area) to £120 (the shaded area).

If a firm wants to increase its revenue in this case, therefore, it should *raise* its price.

Special cases

Figure 5.7 shows three special cases: (a) a totally inelastic demand ($P\epsilon_D = 0$), (b) an infinitely elastic demand ($P\epsilon_D = \infty$) and (c) a unit elastic demand ($P\epsilon_D = -1$).

Totally inelastic demand

This is shown by a vertical straight line. No matter what happens to price, quantity demanded remains the same. It is obvious that the more the price is raised, the bigger will be the revenue. Thus in Figure 5.7(a), P_2 will earn a bigger revenue than P_1.

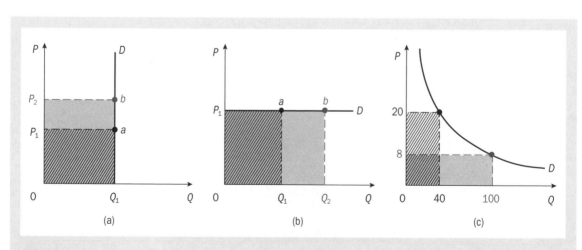

Figure 5.7
(a) Totally inelastic demand ($P\epsilon_D = 0$); (b) Infinitely elastic demand ($P\epsilon_D = \infty$); (c) Unit elastic demand ($P\epsilon_D = -1$)

Infinitely elastic demand

This is shown by a horizontal straight line. At any price above P_1 demand is zero. But at P_1 (or any price below) demand is 'infinitely' large.

This seemingly unlikely demand curve is in fact relatively common. Many firms that are very small (like the small-scale grain farmer) are price takers. They have to accept the price as given by supply and demand in the *whole market*. If individual farmers were to try to sell above this price, they would sell nothing at all. At this price, however, they can sell to the market all they produce. (Demand is not *literally* infinite, but as far as the farmer is concerned it is.) In this case, the more the individual farmer produces, the more revenue will be earned. In Figure 5.7(b), more revenue is earned at Q_2 than at Q_1.

Unit elastic demand

This is where price and quantity change in exactly the same proportion. Any rise in price will be exactly offset by a fall in quantity, leaving total revenue unchanged. In Figure 5.7(c), the striped area is exactly equal to the shaded area: in both cases total revenue is £800.

You might have thought that a demand curve with unit elasticity would be a straight line at 45° to the axes. Instead it is a curve called a *rectangular hyperbola*. The reason for its shape is that the proportionate *rise* in quantity must equal the proportionate *fall* in price (and vice versa). As we move down the demand curve, in order for the *proportionate* (or percentage) change in both price and quantity to remain constant, there must be a bigger and bigger *absolute* rise in quantity and a smaller and smaller absolute fall in price. For example, a rise in quantity from 200 to 400 is the same proportionate change as a rise from 100 to 200, but its absolute size is double. A fall in price from £5 to £2.50 is the same percentage as a fall from £10 to £5, but its absolute size is only half.

5.3 Other elasticities

Firms are interested to know the responsiveness of demand not just to a change in price: they will also want to know the responsiveness of demand to changes in other determinants, such as consumers' incomes and the prices of substitute or complementary goods to theirs. They will want to know the **income elasticity of demand** – the responsiveness of demand to a change in consumers' incomes (Y); and the **cross-price elasticity of demand** – the responsiveness of demand for their good to a change in the price of another (whether a substitute or a complement).

Income elasticity of demand ($Y\epsilon_D$)

We define the income elasticity of demand for a good as follows:

$$Y\epsilon_D = \frac{\text{Proportionate (or percentage) change in quantity demanded}}{\text{Proportionate (or percentage) change in income}}$$

For example, if a 2 per cent rise in consumer incomes causes an 8 per cent rise in a product's demand, then its income elasticity of demand will be:

> **definition**
>
> **Income elasticity of demand**
> The responsiveness of demand to a change in consumer incomes: the proportionate change in demand divided by the proportionate change in income.

> **definition**
>
> **Cross-price elasticity of demand**
> The responsiveness of demand for one good to a change in the price of another: the proportionate change in demand for one good divided by the proportionate change in price of the other.

8%/2% = 4

Note that in the case of a normal good, the figure for income elasticity will be positive: a *rise* in income leads to a *rise* in demand (a positive figure divided by a positive figure gives a positive answer).

Determinants of income elasticity of demand

Degree of 'necessity' of the good. In a developed country, the demand for luxury goods expands rapidly as people's incomes rise, whereas the demand for more basic goods, such as bread, rises only a little. Thus items such as cars and foreign holidays have a high income elasticity of demand, whereas items such as potatoes and bus journeys have a low income elasticity of demand.

The demand for some goods actually decreases as income rises. These are inferior goods such as cheap margarine. As people earn more, so they switch to butter or better quality margarine. Inferior goods have a negative income elasticity of demand: a *rise* in income leads to a *fall* in demand (a negative figure divided by a positive figure gives a negative answer).

The rate at which the desire for a good is satisfied as consumption increases. The more quickly people become satisfied, the less their demand will expand as income increases.

The level of income of consumers. Poor people will respond differently from rich people to a rise in their incomes. For example, for a given rise in income, poor people may buy a lot more butter, whereas rich people may buy only a little more.

Income elasticity of demand and the firm

Income elasticity of demand is an important concept to firms considering the future size of the market for their product. If the product has a high income elasticity of demand, sales are likely to expand rapidly as national income rises, but may also fall significantly if the economy moves into recession.

Firms may also find that some parts of their market have a higher income elasticity of demand than others, and may thus choose to target their marketing campaigns on this group. For example, middle-income groups may have a higher income elasticity of demand for hi-fi products than lower-income groups (who are unlikely to be able to afford such products even if their incomes rise somewhat) or higher-income groups (who can probably afford them anyway, and thus would not buy much more if their incomes rose).

Cross-price elasticity of demand ($C_{\epsilon_{D_{ab}}}$)

This is often known by its less cumbersome title of cross elasticity of demand. It is a measure of the responsiveness of demand for one product to a change in the price of another (either a substitute or a complement). It enables us to predict how much the demand curve for the first product will shift when the price of the second product changes. We define cross-price elasticity as follows:

$$C_{\epsilon_D} = \frac{\text{Proportionate (or percentage) change in demand for good a}}{\text{Proportionate (or percentage) change in price of good b}}$$

If good b is a *substitute* for good a, a's demand will *rise* as b's price rises. For example, the demand for bicycles will rise as the price of public transport rises. In this case, cross elasticity will be a positive figure. If b is *complementary* to a, however, a's demand will *fall* as b's price rises and thus as the quantity of b demanded falls. For example, the demand for petrol falls as the price of cars rises. In this case, cross elasticity will be a negative figure.

Cross-price elasticity of demand and the firm

The major determinant of cross elasticity of demand is the closeness of the substitute or complement. The closer it is, the bigger will be the effect on the first good of a change in the price of the substitute or complement, and hence the greater will be the cross elasticity – either positive or negative.

Firms will wish to know the cross elasticity of demand for their product when considering the effect on the demand for their product of a change in the price of a rival's product (a substitute). If firm b cuts its price, will this make significant inroads into the sales of firm a? If so, firm a may feel forced to cut its prices too; if not, then firm a may keep its price unchanged. The cross-price elasticities of demand between a firm's product and those of each of its rivals are thus vital pieces of information for a firm when making its production, pricing and marketing plans.

Similarly, a firm will wish to know the cross-price elasticity of demand for its product with any complementary good. Car producers will wish to know the effect of petrol price increases on the sales of their cars.

Price elasticity of supply ($P\epsilon_S$)

Just as we can measure the responsiveness of demand to a change in one of the determinants of demand, so too we can measure the responsiveness of supply to a change in one of the determinants of supply. The **price elasticity of supply** refers to the responsiveness of supply to a change in price. We define it as follows:

$$P\epsilon_S = \frac{\text{Proportionate (or percentage) change in quantity supplied}}{\text{Proportionate (or percentage) change in price}}$$

Thus if a 15 per cent rise in the price of a product causes a 30 per cent rise in the quantity supplied, the price elasticity of supply will be:

30%/15% = 2

In Figure 5.8 curve S_2 is more elastic between any two prices than curve S_1. Thus, when price rises from P_1 to P_2 there is a larger increase in quantity supplied with S_2 (namely, Q_1 to Q_3) than there is with S_1 (namely, Q_1 to Q_2).

Determinants of price elasticity of supply

The amount that costs rise as output rises. The less the additional costs of producing additional output, the more firms will be encouraged to produce for a given price rise: the more elastic will supply be.

Supply is thus likely to be elastic if firms have plenty of spare capacity, if they can readily get extra supplies of raw materials, if they can easily switch away from producing alternative products and if they can avoid having to introduce

definition

Price elasticity of supply
The responsiveness of quantity supplied to a change in price: the proportionate change in quantity supplied divided by the proportionate change in price.

Figure 5.8
Price elasticity of supply

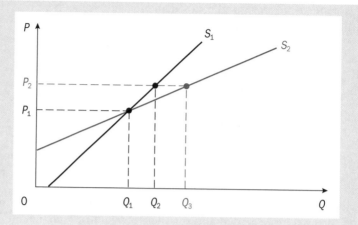

overtime working (at higher rates of pay). If all these conditions hold, costs will be little affected by a rise in output and supply will be relatively elastic. The less these conditions apply, the less elastic will supply be.

Time period (see Figure 5.9)
● Immediate time period. Firms are unlikely to be able to increase supply by much immediately. Supply is virtually fixed, or can vary only according to available stocks. Supply is highly inelastic. In the diagram S_I is drawn with $P\epsilon_S = 0$. If demand increases to D_2, supply will not be able to respond. Price will rise to P_2. Quantity will remain at Q_1. Equilibrium will move to point *b*.
● Short run. If a slightly longer time period is allowed to elapse, some inputs can be increased (e.g. raw materials), while others will remain fixed (e.g. heavy machinery). Supply can increase somewhat. This is illustrated by S_S. Equilibrium will move to point *c* with price falling again, to P_3, and quantity rising to Q_3.
● Long run. In the long run, there will be sufficient time for all inputs to be increased and for new firms to enter the industry. Supply, therefore, is likely

Figure 5.9
Supply in different time periods

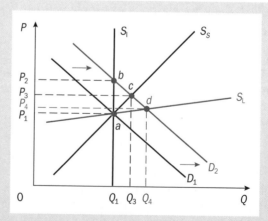

BOX 5.1

The market for leather
A case study in demand and supply

Some markets are subject to considerable price fluctuations. The magnitude of these fluctuations depends on the amount by which demand and/or supply curves shift, and the price elasticity of demand and supply. The following extract, taken from an article in *The Independent* of 9 May 1994, considers price fluctuations in the market for sheepskin and cattle hides.

> Prices of sheepskin and cattle hides have soared in recent months as suppliers have struggled to meet demand. According to the British Leather Confederation, UK abattoir prices of sheepskin are now £7 to £7.50 compared with just under £1 in autumn 1990, Oxhides (steers and heifers) fetch £40 against a low of £17 to £18 in the first quarter of 1991, although traders and tanners believe the market has now peaked, at least for the moment.
>
> ... Normal laws of supply and demand do not apply as skins and hides are a by-product of the meat, wool and dairy industries. In the past 12 to 18 months, demand for leather goods has risen, yet the UK cattle kill was 9 per cent down in 1993 from the previous year and the lamb kill was 7 per cent down. Falling demand for red meat and a significant rise in the live export of UK lambs, particularly to France, are the main reasons.
>
> UK tanners have been left short of quality raw material and prices have risen steeply. However, consumers' resistance to higher prices of finished goods prevented increases being passed on and the tanners' margins have been squeezed.
>
> There is little prospect of the by-product status

of skins and hides changing. In the UK, the value of a cattle hide is only 7 to 10 per cent of the total carcass and the value of a sheepskin 10 to 15 per cent of the carcass. Farmers are more concerned about selling the meat.

> Lack of a homogeneous raw material hampers the creation of an international market. Sheepskins are graded according to climate. Higher quality skins from temperate zones are further divided, with UK skins usually fetching a premium price over New Zealand domestics. South African Capes are considered high quality, but the supply is limited.

Questions
1 Why had the supply of skins and hides fallen despite a rise in demand? Illustrate this using a demand and supply diagram.
2 According to the article, which of the following are likely to be relatively elastic and which relatively inelastic: (a) the price elasticity of supply of raw skins and hides; (b) the price elasticity of demand for raw skins and hides; (c) the price elasticity of demand for finished products made with skins and hides? Explain the reasoning behind your answers.
3 Given the answer to Q2, demonstrate with demand and supply curves why there had been a substantial rise in price of raw skins and hides which had nevertheless not been passed on in higher prices for finished goods made with skins and hides.
4 Why does the lack of a homogeneous raw material exacerbate the problem of price stability?

to be highly elastic. This is illustrated by curve S_1. Long-run equilibrium will be at point *d* with price falling back even further, to P_4, and quantity rising all the way to Q_4. In some circumstances the supply curve may even slope downward. (See the section on economies of scale in Chapter 9.)

The measurement of price elasticity of supply

A vertical supply curve has zero elasticity. It is totally unresponsive to a change in price. A horizontal supply curve has infinite elasticity. There is no limit to the amount supplied at the price where the curve crosses the vertical axis.

When two supply curves cross, the steeper one will have the lower price

Figure 5.10
Unit elastic supply curves

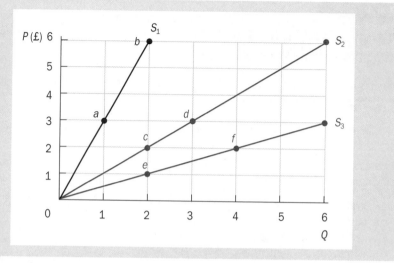

elasticity of supply. Any straight-line supply curve starting at the origin, however, will have an elasticity equal to 1 throughout its length, *irrespective of its slope*. This perhaps rather surprising result is illustrated in Figure 5.10. This shows three supply curves, each with a different slope, but each starting from the origin. On each curve two points are marked. In each case there is the *same* proportionate rise in Q as in P. For example, in curve S_1 a doubling in price from £3 to £6 leads to a doubling of output from 1 unit to 2 units.

This demonstrates nicely that it is not the *slope* of a curve that determines its elasticity, but its proportionate change.

Other supply curves' elasticity will vary along their length. In such cases we have to refer to the elasticity between two points on the curve.

5.4 The time dimension of market adjustment

The full adjustment of price, demand and supply to a situation of disequilibrium will not be instantaneous. It is necessary, therefore, to analyse the time path which supply takes in responding to changes in demand, and which demand takes in responding to changes in supply.

Short-run and long-run adjustment

As we have already seen, elasticity varies with the time period under consideration. The reason is that producers and consumers take time to respond to a change in price. The longer the time period, the bigger the response, and thus the greater the elasticity of supply and demand.

This is illustrated in Figures 5.11 and 5.12. In both cases, as equilibrium moves from points a to b to c, there is a large short-run price change (P_1 to P_2) and a small short-run quantity change (Q_1 to Q_2), but a small long-run price change (P_1 to P_3) and a large long-run quantity change (Q_1 to Q_3).

Figure 5.11
Response of supply to an increase in demand

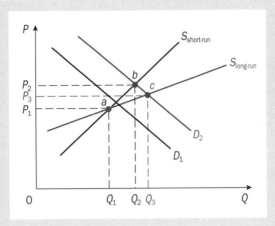

Figure 5.12
Response of demand to an increase in supply

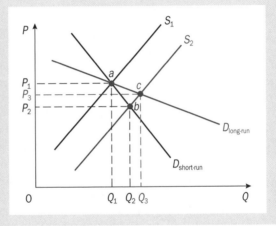

Time lags in production: the cobweb

When goods take a time to produce, there will be a time lag between a change in production decisions and a change in the actual supply coming on to the market. Thus the actual supply at one time will depend on that planned at a previous time. For example, the quantity that farmers harvest now will depend on what they planted earlier.

Since supply decisions depend on price, supply at any time will depend on price at a previous time.

These time lags can lead to price fluctuations. This is illustrated in Figure 5.13: the **cobweb diagram**. To keep the analysis as simple as possible, we make two important assumptions:

- Firms' production plans, once made, are fully carried out; they end up supplying precisely the amount they had planned to.
- There is an initial disequilibrium in the market: either demand or supply has shifted. The result is that price is now above the intersection of the new demand and supply curves.

> **definition**
>
> **Cobweb diagram**
> A diagram showing the path of price and quantity adjustment over time, given a lag between the decision to supply and the goods coming to market. The path has a shape like a cobweb.

Figure 5.13
(a) Convergent cobweb (damped oscillations)
(b) Divergent cobweb (explosive oscillations)

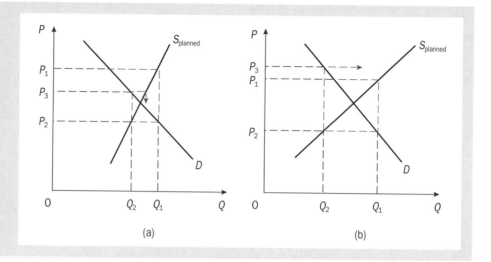

(a)

(b)

The diagrams show just the new demand and supply curves. Note that the supply curve is the *planned* supply curve. The *actual* supply coming on to the market will be the amount planned in the previous time period.

Assume that the initial (disequilibrium) price is P_1. At P_1 producers plan to supply Q_1. Thus in the next time period Q_1 is actually supplied. But in order for Q_1 to be sold, price falls to P_2. Producers, seeing that price has fallen to P_2, now only plan to supply Q_2 for the next time period. So in the next time period Q_2 duly comes on to the market. Price now has to rise to P_3 to clear the market.

This process continues with both price and quantity oscillating.

Whether these oscillations get smaller or larger depends on the shape of the demand and supply curves. If the supply curve is steeper than the demand curve (Figure 5.13(a)), the oscillations will be damped: they will get smaller over time. This is called a **convergent cobweb**. If the demand curve is steeper than the supply curve, however, the oscillations will be explosive: they will get larger over time. This is called a **divergent cobweb**.

In practice, cobwebs will not be as clear cut as in the diagram for a number of reasons:

definition

Convergent cobweb
A cobweb where the path converges on the equilibrium point. The price oscillations get smaller over time.

definition

Divergent cobweb
A cobweb where the path gets further and further away from the 'equilibrium' point. The price oscillations get larger over time.

- Producers may anticipate price fluctuations and not simply rely on current prices.
- Demand and supply curves may shift in the meantime.
- There may be a lag in demand adjustment as well as in supply adjustment.
- Plans may not be fulfilled. For example, farmers may experience a better or worse harvest than anticipated.
- Producers may use stocks. They may draw on stocks when prices are high and build stocks when prices are low. Thus supply released on to the market will not fluctuate so much. This in turn will reduce price fluctuations.

Nevertheless cobweb effects have been observed in various markets. Historically, 'hog' cycles and potato cycles have been identified which show clear fluctuations in pig meat and potato prices.

Speculation

In a world of shifting demand and supply curves, prices do not stay the same. Sometimes they go up; sometimes they come down. We have just seen this in the case of the cobweb theory, where prices of foodstuffs can oscillate up and down.

If prices are likely to change in the foreseeable future, this will affect the behaviour of buyers and sellers *now*. If, for example, it is now December and you are thinking of buying a new winter coat, you might decide to wait until the January sales, and in the meantime make do with your old coat. If, on the other hand, when January comes you see a new summer dress in the sales, you might well buy it now and not wait until the summer for fear that the price will have gone up by then. Thus a belief that prices will go up will cause people to buy now; a belief that prices will come down will cause them to wait.

The reverse applies to sellers. If you are thinking of selling your house and prices are falling, you will want to sell it as quickly as possible. If, on the other hand, prices are rising sharply, you will wait as long as possible so as to get the highest price. Thus a belief that prices will come down will cause people to sell now; a belief that prices will go up will cause them to wait.

This behaviour of looking into the future and making buying and selling decisions based on your predictions is called **speculation**. Speculation is often based on current trends in price behaviour. If prices are currently rising, people may try to decide whether they are about to peak and go back down again, or whether they are likely to go on rising. Having made their prediction, they will then act on it. This speculation will thus affect demand and supply, which in turn will affect price. Speculation is commonplace in many markets: the stock exchange, the foreign exchange market and the housing market are three examples. Large firms often employ specialist buyers who choose the right time to buy inputs, depending on what they anticipate will happen to their price.

Speculation tends to be **self-fulfilling**. In other words, the actions of speculators tend to bring about the very effect on prices that speculators had anticipated. For example, if speculators believe that the price of ICI shares is about to rise, they will buy more ICI shares. But by doing this they will ensure that the price *will* rise. The prophecy has become self-fulfilling.

Speculation can either help to reduce price fluctuations or aggravate them: it can be stabilising or destabilising.

Stabilising speculation

Speculation will tend to have a **stabilising** effect on price fluctuations when suppliers and/or demanders believe that a change in price is only *temporary*.

An initial fall in price. In Figure 5.14, demand has shifted from D_1 to D_2; equilibrium has moved from point a to point b, and price has fallen to P_2. How do people react to this fall in price?

Given that they believe this fall in price to be only temporary, suppliers *hold back*, expecting prices to rise again: supply shifts from S_1 to S_2. After all, why supply now when, by waiting, they could get a higher price?

Buyers *increase* their purchases, to take advantage of the temporary fall in price. Demand shifts from D_2 to D_3.

The equilibrium moves to point c, with price rising back towards P_1.

definition

Speculation
This is where people make buying or selling decisions based on their anticipations of future prices.

definition

Self-fulfilling speculation
The actions of speculators tend to cause the very effect that they had anticipated.

definition

Stabilising speculation
This is where the actions of speculators tend to reduce price fluctuations.

BOX 5.2

Adjusting to oil price shocks
Short-run and long-run demand and supply responses

Between December 1973 and June 1974, the Organisation of Petroleum Exporting Countries (OPEC) put up the price of oil from $3 to $12 per barrel. It was further raised to over $30 in 1979. In the late 1980s the price fluctuated, but the trend was downward. Except for a sharp rise at the time of the Gulf War in 1990, the trend continued in the early 1990s. By 1996 the price was fluctuating around $16 per barrel: in real terms (i.e. after correcting for inflation), roughly the level prior to 1973.

The situation for OPEC deteriorated further in the late 1990s, following the recession in the Far East. Oil demand fell by some 2 million barrels per day. By early 1999, the price had fallen to around $10 per barrel – a mere $2.70 in 1973 prices! In response, OPEC members agreed to cut production by 4.3 million barrels per day. The objective was to push the price back up to around $18–$20 per barrel. But, with the Asian economy recovering and the world generally experiencing more rapid economic growth, the price rose rapidly, reaching over $35 in late 2000. The effect was to trigger protests around the world, with pressure on governments to cut fuel taxes.

The price movements can be explained using simple demand and supply analysis.

The initial rise in price

OPEC raised the price from P_1 to P_2. To prevent surplus at that price, OPEC members restricted their output by agreed amounts. This had the effect of shifting the supply curve to S_2, with Q_2 being produced. This reduction in output needed to be only relatively small because the short-run demand for oil was highly price

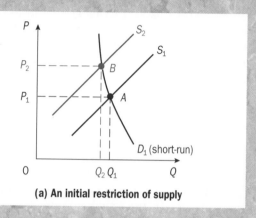

(a) An initial restriction of supply

inelastic: for most uses there are no substitutes in the short run.

Long-run effects on demand

The long-run demand for oil was more elastic. With high oil prices persisting, people tried to find ways of cutting back on consumption. People bought smaller cars. They converted to gas or solid-fuel central heating. Firms switched

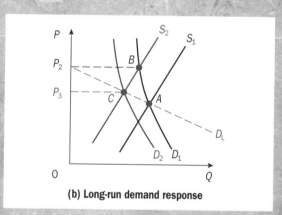

(b) Long-run demand response

An initial rise in price. In Figure 5.15, demand has shifted from D_1 to D_2. Price has risen from P_1 to P_2.

Suppliers bring their goods to market now, before price falls again. Supply shifts from S_1 to S_2. Demanders, however, hold back until price falls. Demand shifts from D_2 to D_3. The equilibrium moves to point c, with price falling back towards P_1.

to other fuels. Less use was made of oil-fired power stations for electricity generation. Energy-saving schemes became widespread both in firms and in the home.

This had the effect of shifting the short-run demand curve from D_1 to D_2. Price fell back from P_2 to P_3. This gave a long-run demand curve of D_L: the curve that joins points A and C.

The fall in demand was made bigger by a world recession in the early 1980s.

Long-run effects on supply

With oil production so much more profitable, there was an incentive for non-OPEC oil producers to produce oil. Prospecting went on all over the world and large oil fields were discovered and opened up in the North Sea, Alaska, Mexico, China and elsewhere.

In addition, OPEC members were tempted to break their 'quotas' (their allotted output) and sell more oil.

The net effect was an increase in world oil supplies. This is shown by a shift in the supply curve to S_3. Equilibrium price thus fell back to P_1 (point D).

Note that the supply curves in these diagrams are all *short-run* supply curves, since each one shows supply for a particular number of oil fields.

Drawing a long-run supply curve is more difficult: it depends when in the story we start and what assumptions we make.

We could draw a long-run supply curve linking points E and F. The reasoning is as follows. After the limiting of supply to S_2, OPEC members would have supplied at point E, had the price remained at P_1. After some years with the price set at P_2 or thereabouts, more suppliers enter the market. The supply curve shifts to S_3. Had the demand curve not shifted, equilibrium would then have

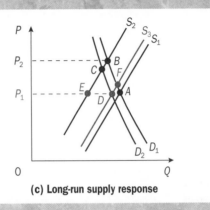

(c) Long-run supply response

moved to point F: the intersection of S_3 and the original demand. A long-run supply curve thus links points E and F.

Back to square one

By the late 1990s, with the oil price as low as $10 per barrel, OPEC once more cut back supply. The story had come full circle. This cut-back is illustrated in diagram (a).

The trouble this time was that the world was recovering from recession. Demand was shifting to the right. The effect was that the price rose above the $18–$20 per barrel OPEC target. In September 2000, OPEC agreed to increase its production in order to bring the price down to around $25 from the $35 mark it had reached. In other words, they agreed to shift the supply curve back to the right somewhat.

Question

Give some examples of things that could make the demand for oil more elastic. What specific policies could the government take to make demand more elastic?

A good example of stabilising speculation is that which occurs in agricultural commodity markets. Take the case of wheat. When it is harvested in the autumn there will be a plentiful supply. If all this wheat were to be put on the market, the price would fall to a very low level. Later in the year, when most of the wheat would have been sold, the price would then rise to a very high level. This is all easily predictable.

Figure 5.14
**Stabilising
speculation: initial
price fall**

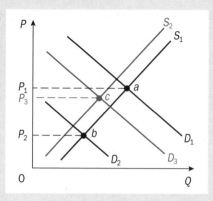

Figure 5.15
**Stabilising
speculation: initial
price rise**

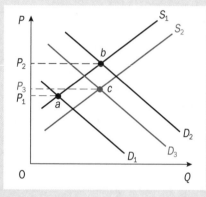

So what do farmers do? The answer is that they speculate. When the wheat is harvested they know its price will tend to fall, and so instead of bringing it all to market they put a lot of it into store. The more price falls, the more they will put into store *anticipating that the price will later rise*. But this holding back of supplies prevents prices from falling. In other words, it stabilises prices.

Later in the year, when the price begins to rise, they will gradually release grain on to the market from the stores. The more the price rises, the more will they release on to the market *anticipating that the price will fall again by the time of the next harvest*. But this releasing of supplies will again stabilise prices by preventing them rising so much.

Rather than the farmers doing the speculation, it could be done by grain merchants. When there is a glut of wheat in the autumn, and prices are relatively low, they buy wheat on the grain market and put it into store. When there is a shortage in the spring and summer, they sell wheat from their stores. In this way they stabilise prices just as the farmers did when they were the ones that operated the stores.

Destabilising speculation

Speculation will tend to have a **destabilising** effect on price fluctuations when suppliers and/or buyers believe that a change in price heralds similar changes to come.

Figure 5.16
Destabilising speculation: initial price fall

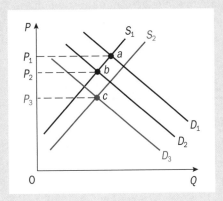

An initial fall in price. In Figure 5.16 demand has shifted from D_1 to D_2 and price has fallen from P_1 to P_2. This time, believing that the fall in price heralds further falls in price to come, suppliers sell now before the price does fall. Supply shifts from S_1 to S_2. And demanders wait: they wait until price does fall further. Demand shifts from D_2 to D_3.

Their actions ensure that the price does fall further: to P_3.

An initial rise in price. In Figure 5.17, a price rise from P_1 to P_2 is caused by a rise in demand from D_1 to D_2. Suppliers wait until the price rises further. Supply shifts from S_1 to S_2. Demanders buy now before any further rise in price. Demand shifts from D_2 to D_3.

As a result the price continues to rise: to P_3.

Conclusion

In some circumstances, then, the action of speculators can help keep price fluctuations to a minimum (stabilising speculation). This is most likely when markets are relatively stable in the first place, with only moderate underlying shifts in demand and supply.

In other circumstances, however, speculation can make price fluctuations much worse. This is most likely in times of uncertainty, when there are significant

Figure 5.17
Destabilising speculation: initial price rise

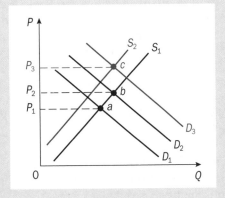

changes in the determinants of demand and supply. Given this uncertainty, people may see price changes as signifying some trend. They then 'jump on the bandwagon' and do what the rest are doing, and further fuel the rise or fall in price.

5.5 Dealing with uncertainty

Risk and uncertainty

When price changes are likely to occur, buyers and sellers will try to anticipate them. Unfortunately, on many occasions no one can be certain just what these price changes will be. Take the case of stocks and shares. If you anticipate that the price of, say, BP shares is likely to go up substantially in the near future, you may well decide to buy some now and then sell them later after the price has risen. But you cannot be certain that they will go up in price: they may fall instead. If you buy the shares, therefore, you will be taking a gamble.

Now gambles can be of two types. The first is where you know the odds. Let us take the simplest case of a gamble on the toss of a coin. Heads you win; tails you lose. You know that the odds of winning are precisely 50 per cent. If you bet on the toss of a coin, you are said to be operating under conditions of **risk**. *Risk is when the probability of an outcome is known.*

The second form of gamble is the more usual. This is where the odds are not known or are known only roughly. Gambling on the Stock Exchange is like this. You may have a good idea that a share will go up in price, but is it a 90 per cent chance, an 80 per cent chance or what? You are not certain. Gambling under these sorts of conditions is known as operating under **uncertainty**. *This is when the probability of an outcome is not known.*

You may well disapprove of gambling and want to dismiss people who engage in it as foolish or morally wrong. But 'gambling' is not just confined to horses, cards, roulette and the like. Risk and uncertainty pervade the whole of economic life and decisions are constantly having to be made whose outcome cannot be known for certain. Even the most morally upright person will still have to decide which career to go into, whether and when to buy a house, or even something as trivial as whether or not to take an umbrella when going out. Each of these decisions and thousands of others are made under conditions of uncertainty (or occasionally risk).

We shall be examining how risk and uncertainty affect economic decisions at several points throughout the book. For example, in the next chapter we will see how it affects people's attitudes and actions as consumers, and how taking out insurance can help to reduce their uncertainty. At this point, however, let us focus on firms' attitudes when supplying goods.

A simple way that suppliers can reduce risks is by holding stocks. Take the case of the wheat farmers we saw in the previous section. At the time when they are planting the wheat in the spring, they are uncertain as to what the price of wheat will be when they bring it to market. If they keep no stores of wheat, they will just have to accept whatever the market price happens to be at harvest time. If, however, they have storage facilities, they can put the wheat into store if the price is low and then wait until it goes up. Alternatively, if the price of wheat is high at harvest time, they can sell it straight away. In other words, they can wait until the price is right.

BOX 5.3

The role of the speculator

... the greed of bond traders drives up interest rates, and so harms output and jobs. Stockmarkets punish companies that invest in their workers instead of boosting profits. The managers of pensions and mutual funds flood emerging markets with capital, then pull the plug on a whim. Even governments quail before the might of speculators. When they set their exchange rate at a vulnerable level, speculators sell the currency forcing them to devalue.[1]

This commonly held, yet largely unfair, view of the speculator emphasises all that might be bad in the speculators' business. In fact, speculators play a crucially important role in economic affairs, and it is this side of the speculators' actions that are largely ignored and taken for granted.

For example, take share prices. A firm's share price reflects the market estimation of the business's future prospects. A falling share price implies that the market's view of the firm is deteriorating, making it more expensive for the company to raise new finance in the stock market. The more expensive finance is for the business, the fewer investments it will make, which if the market is correct is desirable, as firms with better prospects will receive not only more but cheaper finance.

The criticism of this position is that speculators frequently get things wrong. They focus too much on the short term and on the current profitability of the business, ignoring long-run prospects and opportunities

But is there any basis to this criticism? *The Economist* of 3 February 1996 thinks not.

Shares derive their worth from a firm's underlying assets. If the market in which these shares are traded 'undervalued' them, anyone who bought such a share would be getting a bargain: they would receive a windfall in the future when the firm's long-term investment paid off. It would then be easy for a few clever investors to exploit the market's short-sightedness. For example, if it were true, as it is sometimes said, that the market attaches too little value to corporate R & D, a few investors could make a bundle by buying shares in firms with large R & D budgets. In the process, of course, these firms' prices would rise until they were no longer undervalued.

If this sounds abstract, consider the concrete evidence that investors care about the long term. The shares of many bio-technology or software firms, some of which have never made a profit, continue to fetch dizzying prices in the stockmarket. Indeed, a common criticism of stockmarket speculators is that they push the prices of high-tech firms too high. In other words, they seem to care too much, not too little, about the long term.

By far the greatest criticism of speculators is the volatility they create by shifting prices up and down, apparently at a whim. But even this might be explained away as a virtue, as the speculators are simply responding to changing economic conditions, either at the level of the firm or within the economy generally. The speculators are adjusting their decisions in line with changing circumstances. In other words, they are being efficient, although this does not necessarily imply that their decisions are correct!

[1] *The Economist*, 3 February 1996.

Question

How might it be beneficial for the economy if speculators were less efficient?

Although the keeping of stocks will substantially reduce uncertainty, it can never eliminate it. The farmer when planting the wheat cannot know just how good a harvest it will be. If it is a very good harvest, the market price is likely to remain low for a long time after the harvest, since farmers generally have full barns and are all anxious to sell at the moment when prices begin to rise. Also there is the problem that storage costs money. Thus the farmer must weigh up the possible benefits in terms of higher prices of waiting longer before selling against the additional storage costs involved.

Dealing in futures markets

Another way of reducing or even eliminating uncertainty is by dealing in **futures** or **forward markets**. Let us examine the activities first of sellers and then of buyers.

Sellers

Suppose you are a farmer and want to store grain to sell some time in the future, expecting to get a better price then than now. The trouble is that there is a chance that the price will go down. Given this uncertainty, you may be unwilling to take a gamble.

An answer to your problem is provided by the *commodity futures market*. This is a market where prices are agreed between sellers and buyers *today* for delivery at some specified date in the *future*.

For example, if it is 20 October today, you could be quoted a price *today* for delivery in six months' time (i.e. on 20 April). This is known as the six-month **future price**. Assume that the six-month future price is £60 per tonne. If you agree to this price and make a six-month forward contract, you are agreeing to sell a specified amount of wheat at £60 on 20 April. No matter what happens to the **spot price** (i.e. the current market price) in the meantime, your selling price has been agreed. The spot price could have fallen to £30 (or risen to £100) by April, but your selling price when 20 April arrives is fixed at £60. There is thus *no risk to you whatsoever of the price going down*. You will, of course, lose out if the spot price is *more* than £60 in April.

Buyers

Now suppose that you are a flour miller. In order to plan your expenditures, you would like to know the price you will have to pay for wheat, not just today, but also at various future dates. In other words, if you want to take delivery of wheat at some time in the future, you would like a price quoted *now*. You would like the risks removed of prices going *up*.

Let us assume that today (20 October) you want to *buy* the same amount of wheat on 20 April that a farmer wishes to sell on that same date. If you agree to the £60 future price, a future contract can be made with the farmer. You are then guaranteed that purchase price, no matter what happens to the spot price in the meantime. There is thus *no risk to you whatsoever of the price going up*. You will, of course, lose out if the spot price is *less* than £60 in April.

The determination of the future price

Prices in the futures market are determined in the same way as in other markets: by demand and supply. For example, the six-month wheat price or the three-month coffee price will be that which equates the demand for those futures with the supply. If the five-month sugar price is currently £200 per tonne and people expect by then, because of an anticipated good beet harvest, that the spot price for sugar will be £150 per tonne, there will be few who will want to buy the futures at £200 (and many who will want to sell). This excess of supply of futures over demand will push the price down.

Speculators

Many people operate in the futures market who never actually handle the commodities themselves. They are neither producers nor users of the commodities.

> **definition**
>
> **Futures or forward market**
> A market in which contracts are made to buy or sell at some future date at a price agreed today.

> **definition**
>
> **Future price**
> A price agreed today at which an item (e.g. commodities) will be exchanged at some set date in the future.

> **definition**
>
> **Spot price**
> The current market price.

They merely speculate. Such speculators may be individuals, but they are more likely to be financial institutions.

Let us take a simple example. Suppose that the six-month (April) coffee price is £1000 per tonne and that you, as a speculator, believe that the spot price of coffee is likely to rise above that level between now (October) and six months' time. You thus decide to buy 20 tonnes of April coffee futures now.

But you have no intention of taking delivery. After four months, let us say, true to your prediction, the spot price (February) has risen and as a result the April price (and other future prices) have risen too. You thus decide to *sell* 20 tonnes of April (two-month) coffee futures, whose price, let us say, is £1200. You are now 'covered'.

When April comes, what happens? You have agreed to buy 20 tonnes of coffee at £1000 per tonne and to sell 20 tonnes of coffee at £1200 per tonne. All you do is hand the futures contract to buy to the person to whom you agreed to sell. They sort out delivery between them and you make £200 per tonne profit.

If, however, your prediction had been wrong and the price had *fallen*, you would have made a loss. You would have been forced to sell coffee contracts at a lower price than you had bought them.

Speculators in the futures market thus incur risks, unlike the sellers and buyers of the commodities, for whom the futures market eliminates risk. Financial institutions offering futures contracts will charge for the service: for taking on the risks.

SUMMARY

1a Price elasticity of demand measures the responsiveness of demand to a change in price. It is defined as the proportionate (or percentage) change in quantity demanded divided by the proportionate (or percentage) change in price.

1b If quantity demanded changes proportionately more than price, the figure for elasticity will be greater than 1 (ignoring the sign): it is elastic. If the quantity demanded changes proportionately less than price, the figure for elasticity will be less than 1: it is inelastic. If they change by the same proportion, the elasticity has a value of 1: it is unit elastic.

1c Given that demand curves are downward sloping, price elasticity of demand will have a negative value.

1d Demand will be more elastic the greater the number and closeness of substitute goods, the higher the proportion of income spent on the good and the longer the time period that elapses after the change in price.

1e Demand curves normally have different elasticities along their length. We can thus normally refer only to the specific value for elasticity between two points on the curve or at a single point.

2a It is important for firms to know the price elasticity of demand for their product whenever they are considering a price change. The reason is that the effect of the price change on the firm's sales revenue will depend on the product's price elasticity.

2b When the demand for a firm's product is price elastic, a rise in price will lead to a reduction in consumer expenditure on the good and hence to a reduction in the total revenue of the firm.

2c When demand is price inelastic, however, a rise in price will lead to an increase in total revenue for the firm.

3a Income elasticity of demand measures the responsiveness of demand to a change in income. For normal goods it has a positive value. Demand will be more income elastic the more luxurious the good and the less rapidly demand is satisfied as consumption increases.

3b Cross-price elasticity of demand measures the responsiveness of demand for one good to a change in the price of another. For substitute goods the value will be positive; for complements it will be

SUMMARY

negative. The cross-price elasticity will be greater the closer the two goods are as substitutes or complements.

3c Price elasticity of supply measures the responsiveness of supply to a change in price. It has a positive value. Supply will be more elastic the less costs per unit rise as output rises and the longer the time period.

4a A complete understanding of markets must take into account the time dimension.

4b Given that producers and consumers take a time to respond fully to price changes, we can identify different equilibria after the elapse of different lengths of time. Generally, short-run supply and demand tend to be less price elastic than long-run supply and demand. As a result any shifts in demand or supply curves tend to have a relatively bigger effect on price in the short run and a relatively bigger effect on quantity in the long run.

4c If there is a time lag between the decision to supply and the supply coming on to the market, price oscillations are likely to occur. High prices cause producers to plan to supply more. This extra supply when it comes on to the market depresses market price. Producers respond by planning to produce less. When this reduced supply comes to market, market price will rise again. The path that these oscillations trace out on a demand and supply diagram is shaped like a cobweb. These cobwebs can be convergent or divergent depending on the shape of the demand and supply curves.

4d People often anticipate price changes and this will affect the amount they demand or supply. This speculation will tend to stabilise price fluctuations if people believe that the price changes are only temporary. However, speculation will tend to destabilise these fluctuations (i.e. make them more severe) if people believe that prices are likely to continue to move in the same direction as at present (at least for some time).

5a A lot of economic decision making is made under conditions of risk or uncertainty.

5b Risk is when the probability of an outcome occurring is known. Uncertainty is when the probability is not known.

5c One way of reducing risks is to hold stocks. If the price of a firm's product falls unexpectedly, it can build up stocks rather than releasing its product on to the market. If the price later rises, it can then release stocks on to the market. Similarly with inputs: if their price falls unexpectedly, firms can build up their stocks, only to draw on them later if input prices rise.

5d A way of eliminating risk and uncertainty is to deal in the futures markets. When firms are planning to buy or sell at some point in the future, there is the danger that price could rise or fall unexpectedly in the meantime. By agreeing to buy or sell at some particular point in the future at a price agreed today (a 'future' price), this danger can be eliminated. The bank or other institution offering the price (the 'speculator') is taking on the risk, and will charge for this service.

REVIEW QUESTIONS

1 Why does price elasticity of demand have a negative value, whereas price elasticity of supply has a positive value?

2 Rank the following in ascending order of elasticity: jeans, black Levi jeans, black jeans, black Levi 501 jeans, trousers, outer garments, clothes.

3 How might a firm set about making the demand for its brand less elastic?

4 Will a general item of expenditure like food or clothing have a price elastic or inelastic demand?

5 Assuming that a firm faces an inelastic demand and wants to increase its total revenue, *how much* should it raise its price? Is there any limit?

6 Can you think of any examples of goods which have a totally inelastic demand (a) at *all* prices; (b) over a particular price range?

7 Which of these two pairs are likely to have the highest cross-price elasticity of demand: two brands of coffee, or coffee and tea?

8 What shaped demand and supply curves would give a stable cobweb: i.e. one where price fluctuations persist with the same magnitude?

9 Would speculation help to stabilise the price fluctuations associated with the cobweb effect? How would speculation work here?

10 Redraw Figures 5.14–5.17, only this time assume that it was an initial shift in supply that caused price to change in the first place.

11 Give some examples of decisions you have taken recently that were made under conditions of uncertainty. With hindsight do you think you made the right decisions? Explain.

12 What methods can a firm use to reduce risk and uncertainty?

13 If speculators believed that the price of cocoa in six months was going to be *below* the six-month future price quoted today, how would they act?

B Background to demand

FT

THE FINANCIAL TIMES, JULY 18 2000

Coca-Cola loses its fizz

It is end of an era for Coca-Cola. Some 114 years after Dr John Styth Pemberton first concocted the drink in the basement of his Atlanta home, its decades of supremacy as the world's most valuable brand seem about to draw to a close.

In a moment that may come to symbolise the new economy's triumph over the old, a study to be published today will show that Coca-Cola is on the point of being ousted from the top of the global league table by Microsoft, a name invented only 25 years ago.

The Coca-Cola brand is still reckoned to be worth a phenomenal $72.5 billion (£48.3 billion) in terms of its earnings potential. But its value has tumbled 13 per cent in the last year, while the value of Microsoft's brand is estimated to have increased 24 per cent to $70.2 billion.

Coca-Cola is not the only old economy brand to have lost value as new economy brands have gained. Some of the worst performers in the league table are Kodak, Heinz, Xerox, Wrigley's, Hertz, Burger King, Johnnie Walker, Guinness and Pampers, all of which show declines.

In contrast, most new economy brands show double-digit percentage gains in value, and technology companies now account for four of the top five brands. The only loser is Ericsson, whose value is estimated to have plunged 47 per cent – reflecting the success of Nokia, its biggest rival.

Nearly all the brands that have lost value in the rankings belong to companies in the food, drink or consumer packaged goods businesses. These sectors also account for many of the lowest gainers: McDonald's, Marlboro, Gillette and Kellogg's, for example, all saw relatively small increases in brand value. So did Nestlé, Unilever and Diageo, with their big portfolios of mature brands.

Until now companies such as Coca-Cola, H J Heinz and Kellogg had been around so long that their brands looked indestructible, and seemed destined to command the top slots in the global league table for as long as anyone could foresee.

It is still hard to imagine a day when these famous names will cease to dominate the supermarket shelves. But when a brand as powerful as Coca-Cola can lose 13 per cent of its value in just a year, it is possibly time to ask whether the lifespan of these brands is infinite, or something less.

If a business is to be successful, it must be able to predict the strength of demand for its products and be able to respond to any changes in consumer tastes. It will also want to know how its customers are likely to react to changes in its price or its competitors' prices, or to changes in income. In other words, it will want to know the price, cross-price and income elasticities of demand for its product. The better the firm's knowledge of its market, the better will it be able to plan its output to meet demand, and the more able will it be to choose its optimum price, product design, marketing campaigns, etc.

In Chapter 6 we will go behind the demand curve to gain a better understanding of consumer behaviour. We will consider how economists analyse consumer satisfaction and how it varies with the amount consumed. We will then relate this to the shape of the demand curve.

Then, in Chapter 7, we will investigate how data on consumer behaviour can be collected and the problems that businesses face in analysing such information and using it to forecast changes in demand.

Chapter 8 explores how firms can expand and develop their markets by the use of various types of non-price competition. It looks at ways in which firms can differentiate their products from those of their rivals. It also considers how a business sets about deriving a marketing strategy, and assesses the role and implications of product advertising. If Coca-Cola is to 'retain its fizz' (see article opposite) it is important that it gets its marketing strategy right.

> **All forecasting is in an important sense backward-looking – vividly compared to steering a ship by its wake.**
>
> Ralph Harris, 'Models or markets', in J.B. Ramsey, *Economic Forecasting – Models or Markets?* (1977), p. 86
>
> **Doing business without advertising is like winking at a girl in the dark. You know what you are doing, but nobody else does.**
>
> Steuart Henderson Britt

key terms

Marginal utility
Rational consumer
Adverse selection
Moral hazard
Product characteristics
Indifference curves
Efficiency frontier
Demand function
Forecasting
Non-price competition
Product differentiation
Product marketing
Advertising

Demand and the consumer

6.1 Marginal utility theory

Given our limited incomes, we have to make choices about what to buy. You may have to choose between that new economics textbook you feel you ought to buy and going to a rock concert, between a new pair of jeans and a meal out, between saving up for a car and having more money to spend on everyday items, and so on. Business managers are interested in finding out what influences your decisions to consume, and how they might price or package their product to increase their sales.

In this section it is assumed that as consumers we behave 'rationally': that we consider the relative costs and benefits of our purchases in order to gain the maximum satisfaction possible from our limited incomes. Sometimes we may act 'irrationally'. We may purchase goods impetuously with little thought to their price or quality. In general, however, it is a reasonably accurate assumption that people behave rationally.

This does not mean that you get a calculator out every time you go shopping! When you go round the supermarket, you are hardly likely to look at every item on the shelf and weigh up the satisfaction you think you would get from it against the price on the label. Nevertheless, you have probably learned over time the sort of things you like and the prices they cost. You can probably make out a 'rational' shopping list quite quickly.

With major items of expenditure such as a house, a car, a carpet or a foreign holiday, we are likely to take much more care. Take the case of a foreign holiday: you will probably spend quite a long time browsing through brochures comparing the relative merits of various holidays against their relative costs, looking for a holiday that gives good value for money. This is rational behaviour.

Total and marginal utility

People buy goods and services because they get satisfaction from them. Economists call this satisfaction 'utility'.

An important distinction must be made between *total utility* and *marginal utility*.

Total utility (*TU*) is the total satisfaction that a person gains from all those units of a commodity consumed within a given time period. Thus if Tracey drank 10 cups of tea a day, her daily total utility from tea would be the satisfaction derived from those 10 cups.

Marginal utility (*MU*) is the additional satisfaction gained from consuming one *extra* unit within a give period of time. Thus we might refer to the marginal utility that Tracey gains from her third cup of tea of the day or her eleventh cup.

definition
Total utility The total satisfaction a consumer gets from the consumption of all the units of a good consumed within a given time period.

definition
Marginal utility The extra satisfaction gained from consuming one extra unit of a good within a given time period.

103

Diminishing marginal utility

Up to a point, the more of a commodity you consume, the greater will be your total utility. However, as you become more satisfied, each extra unit you consume will probably give you less additional utility than previous units. In other words, your marginal utility falls, the more you consume. This is known as the **principle of diminishing marginal utility**. For example, the second cup of tea in the morning gives you less additional satisfaction than the first cup. The third cup gives less satisfaction still.

At some level of consumption, your total utility will be at a maximum. No extra satisfaction can be gained by the consumption of further units within that period of time. Thus marginal utility will be zero. Your desire for tea may be fully satisfied at twelve cups per day. A thirteenth cup will yield no extra utility. It may even give you displeasure (i.e. negative marginal utility).

The optimum level of consumption: the simplest case – one commodity

Just how much of a good should people consume if they are to make the best use of their limited income? To answer this question we must tackle the problem_of how to measure utility. The problem is that utility is subjective. There is no way of knowing what another person's experiences are really like. Just how satisfying does Brian find his first cup of tea in the morning? How does his utility compare with Tracey's? We do not have utility meters that can answer these questions!

One solution to the problem is to measure utility with money. In this case, total utility becomes the value that people place on their consumption, and marginal utility becomes the amount of money that a person would be prepared to pay to obtain one more unit: in other words, what that extra unit is worth to that person. If Darren is prepared to pay 30p to obtain an extra packet of crisps, then that packet yields him 30p worth of utility: $MU = 30p$.

So how many packets should he consume if he is to act rationally? To answer this we need to introduce the concept of **consumer surplus**.

Marginal consumer surplus

Marginal consumer surplus (MCS) is the difference between what you are willing to pay for one more unit of a good and what you are actually charged. If Darren was willing to pay 30p for another packet of crisps which in fact cost him only 25p, he would be getting a marginal consumer surplus of 5p.

$$MCS = MU - P$$

Total consumer surplus

Total consumer surplus (TCS) is the sum of all the marginal consumer surpluses you have obtained from all the units of a good you have consumed. It is the difference between the total utility from all the units and your expenditure on them. If Darren consumes 4 packets of crisps, and if he would have been prepared to spend £1.40 on them and only had to spend £1.00, then his total consumer surplus is 40p.

$$TCS = TU - TE$$

where TE is the total expenditure on a good: i.e. $P \times Q$.

(Note that total expenditure (*TE*) is a similar concept to total revenue (*TR*). They are both defined as $P \times Q$. But in the case of total expenditure, *Q* is the quantity *purchased* by the consumer(s) in question, whereas in the case of total revenue, *Q* is the quantity *sold* by the firm(s) in question.)

Rational consumer behaviour

Let us define **rational consumer behaviour** as the attempt to maximise (total) consumer surplus. How do people set about doing this?

People will go on purchasing additional units as long as they gain additional consumer surplus: in other words, as long as the price they are prepared to pay exceeds the price they are charged ($MU > P$). But as more units are purchased, so they will experience diminishing marginal utility. They will be prepared to pay less and less for each additional unit. Their marginal utility will go on falling until $MU = P$: that is, until no further consumer surplus can be gained. At that point, they will stop purchasing additional units. Their optimum level of consumption has been reached: consumer surplus has been maximised. Were they to continue to purchase beyond this point, *MU* would be less than *P*, and thus they would be paying more for the last units than they were worth to them.

The process of maximising consumer surplus can be shown graphically. Let us take the case of Tina's annual purchases of petrol. Tina has her own car, but as an alternative she can use public transport or walk. To keep the analysis simple, let us assume that Tina's parents bought her the car and pay the licence duty, and that Tina does not have the option of selling the car. She does, however, have to buy the petrol. The current price is 80p per litre. Figure 6.1 shows her consumer surplus.

If she were to use just a few litres per year, she would use them for very important journeys for which no convenient alternative exists. For such trips she may be prepared to pay up to 110p per litre. For the first few litres, then, she is getting a marginal utility of around 110p per litre, and hence a marginal consumer surplus of around 30p (i.e. 110p – 80p).

By the time her annual purchase is around 250 litres, she would only be prepared to pay around 100p for additional litres. The additional journeys, although still important, would be less vital. Perhaps these are journeys where she could have taken public transport, albeit at some inconvenience. Her marginal consumer surplus at 250 litres is 20p (i.e. 100p – 80p).

definition

Rational consumer behaviour
The attempt to maximise total consumer surplus.

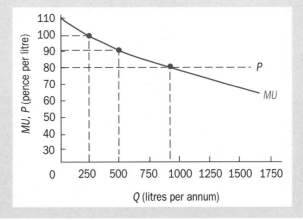

Figure 6.1
Tina's consumer surplus from petrol

Figure 6.2
Consumer surplus

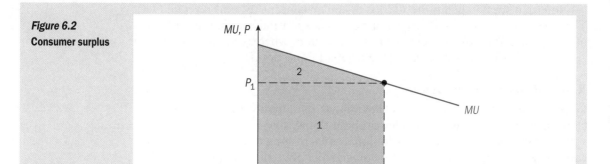

Gradually additional litres give less and less additional utility as fewer and fewer important journeys are undertaken. The 500th litre yields 91p worth of extra utility. Marginal consumer surplus is now 11p (i.e. 91p − 80p).

By the time she gets to the 900th litre, Tina's marginal utility has fallen to 80p. There is no additional consumer surplus to be gained. Her total consumer surplus is at a maximum. She thus buys 900 litres, where $P = MU$.

Her total consumer surplus is the sum of all the marginal consumer surpluses: the sum of all the 900 vertical lines between the price and the MU curve. This is represented by the total *area* between the dashed P line and the MU curve.

This analysis can be expressed in general terms. In Figure 6.2, if the price of a commodity is P_1, the consumer will consume Q_1. The person's total expenditure (TE) is P_1Q_1, shown by area 1. Total utility (TU) is the area under the marginal utility curve: i.e. areas 1 + 2. Total consumer surplus ($TU − TE$) is shown by area 2.

Marginal utility and the demand curve for a good

An individual's demand curve

Individual people's demand curves for any good will be the same as their marginal utility curve for that good, measured in money.

This is demonstrated in Figure 6.3, which shows the marginal utility curve for

Figure 6.3
**An individual
person's demand
curve**

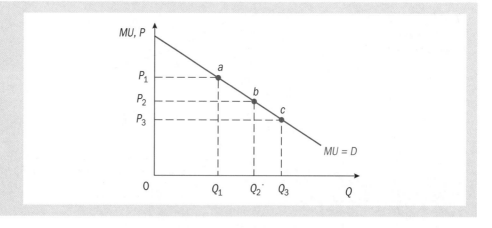

a particular person and a particular good. If the price of the good were P_1, the person would consume Q_1: where $MU = P$. Thus point a would be one point on that person's demand curve. If the price fell to P_2, consumption would rise to Q_2, since this is where $MU = P_2$. Thus point b is a second point on the demand curve. Likewise if price fell to P_3, Q_3 would be consumed. Point c is a third point on the demand curve.

Thus as long as individuals seek to maximise consumer surplus and hence consume where $P = MU$, their demand curve will be along the same line as their marginal utility curve.

The market demand curve

The market demand curve will simply be the (horizontal) sum of all individuals' demand curves and hence MU curves.

The shape of the demand curve. The price elasticity of demand will reflect the rate at which MU diminishes. If there are close substitutes for a good, it is likely to have an elastic demand, and its MU will diminish slowly as consumption increases. The reason is that increased consumption of this product will be accompanied by *decreased* consumption of the alternative product(s). Since total consumption of this product *plus* the alternatives has increased only slightly (if at all), the marginal utility will fall only slowly.

For example, the demand for a given brand of petrol is likely to have a fairly high price elasticity, since other brands are substitutes. If there is a cut in the price of Texaco petrol (assuming the prices of other brands stay constant), consumption of Texaco will increase a lot. The MU of Texaco petrol will fall slowly, since people consume less of other brands. Petrol consumption *in total* may be only slightly greater and hence the MU of petrol only slightly lower.

Shifts in the demand curve. How do *shifts* in demand relate to marginal utility? For example, how would the marginal utility of (and hence demand for) margarine be affected by a rise in the price of butter? The higher price of butter would cause less butter to be consumed. This would increase the marginal utility of margarine, since if people are using less butter, their desire for margarine is higher. The MU curve (and hence the demand curve) for margarine thus shifts to the right.

Weaknesses of the one-commodity version of marginal utility theory

A change in the consumption of one good will affect the marginal utility of substitute and complementary goods. It will also affect the amount of income left over to be spent on other goods. Thus a more satisfactory explanation of demand would involve an analysis of choices between goods, rather than looking at one good in isolation. We examine such choices in section 6.3.

What is more, deriving a demand curve from a marginal utility curve measured in money, assumes that money itself has a constant marginal utility. The trouble is, it does not. If people have a rise in income, they will consume more. Other things being equal, the marginal utility of the goods they consume will diminish. Thus an extra £1 of consumption will bring less satisfaction than previously. In other words, it is likely that *the marginal utility of money diminishes as income rises*.

BOX 6.1

The marginal utility revolution: Jevons, Menger, Walras
Solving the diamonds–water paradox

What determines the market value of a good? We already know the answer: demand and supply. So if we find out what determines the position of the demand and supply curves, we will at the same time be finding out what determines a good's market value.

This might seem obvious. Yet for years economists puzzled over just what determines a good's value.

Some economists like Karl Marx and David Ricardo concentrated on the supply side. For them, value depended on the amount of resources used in producing a good. This could be further reduced to the amount of *labour* time embodied in the good. Thus, according to the *labour theory of value*, the more labour that was directly involved in producing the good, or indirectly in producing the capital equipment used to make the good, the more valuable would the good be.

Other economists looked at the demand side. But here they came across a paradox.

Adam Smith in the 1760s gave the example of water and diamonds. 'How is it', he asked, 'that water which is so essential to human life, and thus has such a high "value-in-use", has such a low market value (or "value-in-exchange")? And how is it that diamonds which are relatively so trivial have such a high market value?' The answer to this paradox had to wait over a hundred years until the marginal utility revolution of the 1870s. William Stanley Jevons (1835–82) in England, Carl Menger (1840–1921) in Austria, and Leon Walras (1834–1910) in Switzerland all independently claimed that the source of the market value of a good was its *marginal* utility, not its *total* utility.

This was the solution to the diamonds–water paradox. Water, being so essential, has a high total utility: a high 'value in use'. But for most of us, given that we consume so much already, it has a very low marginal utility. Do you leave the cold tap running when you clean your teeth? If you do, it shows just how trivial water is to you *at the margin*. Diamonds, on the other hand,

although they have a much lower total utility, have a much higher marginal utility. There are so few diamonds in the world, and thus people have so few of them, that they are very valuable at the margin. If, however, a new technique were to be discovered of producing diamonds cheaply from coal, their market value would fall rapidly. As people had more of them, so their marginal utility would rapidly diminish.

Marginal utility still only gives the demand side of the story. The reason why the marginal utility of water is so low is that *supply* is so plentiful. Water is very expensive in Saudi Arabia! In other words, the full explanation of value must take into account both demand *and* supply.

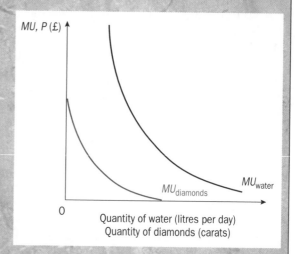

Question

The diagram illustrates a person's *MU* curves of water and diamonds. Assume that diamonds are more expensive than water. Show how the *MU* of diamonds will be greater than the *MU* of water. Show also how the *TU* of diamonds will be less than the *TU* of water. (Remember: *TU* is the area under the *MU* curve.)

Unless a good occupies only a tiny fraction of people's expenditure, a fall in its price will mean that their real income has increased: i.e. they can afford to purchase more goods in general. As they do so, the marginal utility of their money will fall. We cannot, therefore, legitimately use money to measure utility in an absolute sense. We can, however, still talk about the relative utility we get from various goods for a given increase in expenditure.

What is more, the assumptions of diminishing marginal utility and of the consumer making rational choices by considering whether it is 'worth' paying the price being charged are quite realistic assumptions about consumer behaviour. It is important for businesses to realise that the demand for their product tends to reflect consumers' perceptions of the *marginal* utility they expect to gain, rather than the *total* utility.

6.2 Demand under conditions of risk and uncertainty

The problem of imperfect information

So far we have assumed that when people buy goods and services, they know exactly what price they will pay and how much utility they will gain. In many cases this is a reasonable assumption. When you buy a bar of chocolate, you clearly do know how much you are paying for it and have a very good idea how much you will like it. But what about a video recorder, or a car, or a washing machine, or any other **consumer durable**? In each of these cases you are buying something that will last you a long time, and the further into the future you look, the less certain you will be of its costs and benefits to you.

Take the case of a washing machine costing you £400. If you pay cash, your immediate outlay involves no uncertainty: it is £400. But washing machines can break down. In two years' time you could find yourself with a repair bill of £100. This cannot be predicted and yet it is a price you will have to pay, just like the original £400. In other words, when you buy the washing machine, you are uncertain as to the full 'price' it will entail over its lifetime.

If the costs of the washing machine are uncertain, so too are the benefits. You might have been attracted to buy it in the first place by the manufacturer's glossy brochure, or by the look of it, or by adverts on TV, in magazines, etc. When you have used it for a while, however, you will probably discover things you had not anticipated. The spin dryer does not get your clothes as dry as you had hoped; it is noisy; it leaks; the door sticks; and so on.

Buying consumer durables thus involves uncertainty. So too does the purchase of assets, whether a physical asset such as a house or financial assets such as shares. In the case of assets, the uncertainty is over their future *price*. If you buy shares in a recently privatised industry, what will happen to their price? Will they shoot up in price, thus enabling you to sell them at a large profit, or will they fall? You cannot know for certain.

Attitudes towards risk and uncertainty

So how will uncertainty affect people's behaviour? The answer is that it depends on their attitudes towards taking a gamble. To examine these attitudes let us assume that a person does at least know the *odds* of the gamble. In other words, the person is operating under conditions of *risk* rather than *uncertainty*.

To illustrate different attitudes towards risk, consider the case of gambling that a particular number will come up on the throw of a dice. There is a one in six chance of this happening. Would you gamble? It depends on what odds you were offered and on your attitude to risk.

Odds can be of three types. They can be *favourable* odds. This is where on average you will gain. If, for example, you were offered odds of 10 to 1 on the throw of a dice, then for a £1 bet you would get nothing if you lost, but you would get £10 if your number came up. Since your number should come up on average one time in every six, on average you will gain. The longer you go on playing, the more money you are likely to win. If the odds were 6 to 1, they would be *fair* odds. On average you would break even. If, however, they were less than 6 to 1, they would be described as *unfavourable*. On average you would lose.

There are three possible categories of attitude towards risk.

Risk neutral. This is where a person will take a gamble if the odds are favourable; not take a gamble if the odds are unfavourable; and be indifferent about taking a gamble if the odds are fair.

Risk loving. This is where a person is prepared to take a gamble even if the odds are unfavourable. The more risk loving a person is, the worse the odds he or she will be prepared to accept.

Risk averse. This is where a person may not be prepared to take a gamble even if the odds are favourable. The more risk averse the person is, the better would have to be the odds before he or she could be enticed to take a gamble. Few people are *totally risk averse* and thus totally unwilling to take a gamble. If I offered people a bet on the toss of a coin such that tails they pay me 10p and heads I pay them £100, few would refuse (unless on moral grounds).

Diminishing marginal utility of income and attitudes towards risk taking

Avid gamblers may be risk lovers. People who spend hours in the betting shop or at the race track may enjoy the risks, knowing that there is always the chance that they might win. On average, however, such people will lose. After all, the bookies have to take their cut and thus the odds are generally unfavourable.

Most people, however, for most of the time are risk averters. We prefer to avoid insecurity. But why? Is there a simple reason for this? Economists use marginal utility analysis to explain why.

They argue that the gain in utility to people from an extra £100 is less than the loss of utility from forgoing £100. Imagine your own position. You have probably adjusted your standard of living to your income (or are trying to!). If you unexpectedly gained £100, that would be very nice: you could buy some new clothes or have a weekend away. But if you lost £100, it could be very hard indeed. You might have very serious difficulties in making ends meet. Thus if you were offered the gamble of a 50:50 chance of winning or losing £100, you would probably decline the gamble.

This risk-averting behaviour accords with the principle of *diminishing marginal utility*. Up to now in this chapter we have been focusing on the utility from the consumption of individual goods: Tracey and her cups of tea; Darren and his packets of crisps. In the case of each individual good, the more we consume, the less satisfaction we gain from each additional unit: the marginal utility falls. But the same principle applies if we look at our *total* consumption. The higher our level of total consumption, the less additional satisfaction will be gained from each additional £1 spent. What we are saying here is that there is a **diminishing**

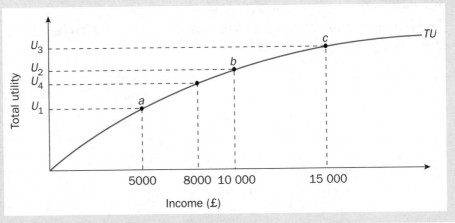

Figure 6.4
The total utility of income given diminishing marginal utility of income

marginal utility of income. The more you earn, the lower will be the utility from each *extra* £1. If people on low incomes earn an extra £100, they will feel a lot better off: the marginal utility they will get from that income will be very high. If rich people earn an extra £100, however, their gain in utility will be less.

Why, then, does a diminishing marginal utility of income make us risk averters? The answer is illustrated in Figure 6.4, which shows the *total* utility you get from your income.

The slope of this curve gives the *marginal* utility of your income. As the marginal utility of income diminishes, so the curve gets flatter. A rise in income from £5000 to £10 000 will cause a movement along the curve from point *a* to point *b*. Total utility rises from U_1 to U_2. A similar rise in income from £10 000 to £15 000, however, will lead to a move from point *b* to point *c*, and hence a *smaller* rise in total utility from U_2 to U_3.

Now assume that your income is £10 000 and you are offered a chance of gambling £5000 of it. You are offered the fair odds of a 50:50 chance of gaining an extra £5000 (i.e. doubling it) or losing it. Effectively, then, you have an equal chance of your income rising to £15 000 or falling to £5000.

At an income of £10 000, your total utility is U_2. If your gamble pays off and as a result your income rises to £15 000, your total utility will rise to U_3. If it does not pay off, you will be left with only £5000 and a utility of U_1. Given that you have a 50:50 chance of winning, your *average* expected utility will be midway between U_1 and U_3 (i.e. $\frac{(U_1 + U_3)}{2}$) = U_4. But this is the utility that would be gained from an income of £8000. Given that you would prefer U_2 to U_4 you will choose not to take the gamble.

Thus risk aversion is part of rational utility-maximising behaviour.

On most occasions we will not know the odds of taking a gamble. In other words, we will be operating under conditions of *uncertainty*. This could make us very cautious indeed. The more pessimistic we are, the more cautious we will be.

Insurance: a way of removing risks

Insurance is the opposite of gambling. It takes the risk away. If, for example, you risk losing your job if you are injured, you can remove the risk of loss of income by taking out an appropriate insurance policy.

definition

Diminishing marginal utility of income
Where each additional pound earned yields less additional utility.

BOX 6.2

Problems for unwary insurance companies
'Adverse selection' and 'moral hazard'

Adverse selection

This is where the people taking out insurance are those who have the highest risk.

For example, suppose that a company offers medical insurance. It surveys the population and works out that the average person requires £200 of treatment per year. The company thus sets the premium at £250 (the extra £50 to cover its costs and provide a profit). But it is likely that the people most likely to take out the insurance are those most likely to fall sick: those who have been ill before, those whose families have a history of illness, those in jobs that are hazardous to health, etc. These people on average may require £500 of treatment per year. The insurance company would soon make a loss.

But cannot the company then simply raise premiums to £550 or £600? It can, but the problem is that it will thereby be depriving the person of *average* health of reasonably priced insurance.

The answer is for the company to discriminate more carefully between people. You may have to fill out a questionnaire so that the company can assess your own particular risk and set an appropriate premium. There may need to be legal penalties for people caught lying!

Moral hazard

This is where having insurance makes you less careful and thus increases your risk to the company. For example, if your bicycle is insured against theft, you may be less concerned to go through the hassle of chaining it up each time you leave it.

Again, if insurance companies work out risks by looking at the *total* number of bicycle thefts, these figures will understate the risks to the company because they will include thefts from *uninsured* people who are likely to be more careful.

The problem of moral hazard occurs in many other walks of life. A good example is that of debt. If someone else is willing to pay your debts (e.g. your parents) it is likely to make you less careful in your spending! This argument has been used by some rich countries for not cancelling the debts of poor countries.

Given that people are risk averters, they will be prepared to pay the premiums even though they give them 'unfair odds'. The total premiums paid to insurance companies will be *more* than the amount the insurance companies pay out: that is, after all, how the companies make a profit.

But does this mean that the insurance companies are less risk averse than their customers? Why is it that the insurance companies are prepared to shoulder the risks that their customers were not? The answer is that the insurance company is able to **spread its risks**.

The spreading of risks

If there is a one in a hundred chance of your house burning down each year, although it is only a small chance it would be so disastrous that you are simply not prepared to take the risk. You thus take out house insurance and are prepared to pay a premium of *more than* 1 per cent (one in a hundred).

The insurance company, however, is not just insuring you. It is insuring many others at the same time. If your house burns down, there will be approximately 99 others that do not. The premiums the insurance company has collected will be more than enough to cover its payments. The more houses it insures, the smaller will be the variation in the proportion that actually burn down each year.

This is an application of the **law of large numbers**. What is unpredictable for an individual becomes highly predictable in the mass. The more people the insurance company insures, the more predictable is the total outcome.

What is more, the insurance company will be in a position to estimate just what the risks are. It can thus work out what premiums it must charge in order to make a profit. With individuals, however, the precise risk is rarely known. Do you know your chances of living to 70? Almost certainly you do not. But a life assurance company will know precisely the chances of a person of your age, sex and occupation living to 70! It will have the statistical data to show this. In other words, an insurance company will be able to convert your *uncertainty* into their *risk*.

The spreading of risks does not just require that there should be a large number of policies. It also requires that the risks should be **independent**. If any insurance company insured 1000 houses *all in the same neighbourhood*, and then there were a major fire in the area, the claims would be enormous. The risks of fire were not independent. The company would, in fact, have been taking a gamble on a single event. If, however, it provides fire insurance for houses scattered all over the country, the risks *are* independent.

Another way in which insurance companies can spread their risks is by **diversification**. The more types of insurance a company offers (car, house, life, health, etc.), the greater is likely to be the independence of the risks.

6.3 The characteristics approach to analysing consumer demand

As we concluded in the last section, to get a better understanding of consumer demand, we need to analyse how consumers choose *between* products. In other words, we must look at products, not in isolation, but in relation to other products. Any firm wanting to understand the basis on which consumers demand its products will want to know why they might choose *its* product rather than those of its rivals. A car manufacturer will want to know why consumers might choose one of its models rather than those of its competitors.

Such choices depend not only on price but on the characteristics of the products. If you were buying a car, in addition to its price you would consider features such as style, performance, comfort, reliability, durability, fuel economy, safety and various added features (such as air conditioning, stereo system, air bags, electric windows, etc.). Car manufacturers will thus design their cars to make them as attractive as possible to consumers, relative to the cost of manufacture. In fact, most firms will constantly try to find ways of improving their products to make them more appealing to consumers.

What we are saying here is that consumers derive utility from the various characteristics that a product possesses. To understand choices, then, we need to look at the attributes of different products and how these influence consumer choices between them. **Characteristics theory** (sometimes called 'attributes theory') was developed by the economist Kelvin Lancaster[1] in the mid-1960s to analyse such choices and to relate them to the demand for a product.

---

[1] K. Lancaster, 'A New Approach to Consumer Theory', *Journal of Political Economy*, 74 (April 1966), pp. 132–57

definition

Law of large numbers
The larger the number of events of a particular type, the more predictable will be their average outcome.

definition

Independent risks
Where two risky events are unconnected. The occurrence of one will not affect the likelihood of the occurrence of the other.

definition

Diversification
Where a firm expands into new types of business.

definition

Characteristics (or attributes) theory
The theory that demonstrates how consumer choice between different varieties of a product depends on the characteristics of these varieties, along with prices of the different varieties, the consumer's budget and the consumer's tastes.

Characteristics theory is based on four key assumptions:

- All products possess various characteristics.
- Different brands possess them in different proportions.
- The characteristics are measurable: they are 'objective'.
- The characteristics (along with price and consumers' incomes) determine consumer choice.

Identifying and plotting products' characteristics

Let us take a simple case of a product where consumers base their choice between brands on price and just two characteristics. For example, assume that consumers choose between different brands of breakfast cereal on the basis of taste and health-giving properties. To keep the analysis simple, let us assume that taste is related to the amount of sugar in the cereal and that health-giving properties are related to the amount of fibre.

Plotting the characteristics of different brands

The combinations of these two characteristics, sugar and fibre, can be measured on a diagram. In Figure 6.5, the quantity of sugar is measured on the horizontal axis and the quantity of fibre on the vertical axis. One brand, Healthbran, contains a lot of fibre, but only a little sugar. Another, Tastyflakes, contains a lot of sugar, but only a little fibre.

The ratio of the two attributes, fibre and sugar, in each of the two brands is given by the slope of the two rays out from the origin. Thus by consuming a certain amount of Healthbran, given by point h_1 on the Healthbran ray, the consumer is getting f_1 of fibre and s_1 of sugar. The consumption of more Healthbran is shown by a movement up the ray, say to h_2. At this point the consumer gets f_2 of fibre and s_2 of sugar. Notice that the ratio of fibre to sugar is the same in both cases. The ratio is given by f_1/s_1 ($= f_2/s_2$), which is simply the slope of the Healthbran ray.

The consumer of Tastyflakes can get relatively more sugar, but less fibre.

Figure 6.5
The characteristics of two brands of breakfast cereal

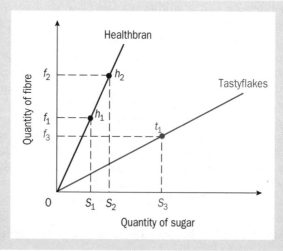

Thus consumption at point t_1 gives s_3 of sugar, but only f_3 of fibre. The ratio of fibre to sugar for Tastyflakes is given by the slope of its ray, which is f_3/s_3.

Any number of rays can be put on the diagram, each one representing a particular brand. In each case, the ratio of fibre to sugar is given by the slope of the ray.

Changes in a product's characteristics. If a firm decides to change the mix of characteristics of a product, the slope of the ray will change. Thus if Healthbran were made sweeter, its ray would become shallower.

The budget constraint

The amount that a consumer buys of a brand will depend in part on the consumer's budget and on the price of the product. Assume that, given the current price of Healthbran, Jane's budget for breakfast cereals allows her to buy at h_1 per month: in other words, the amount of Healthbran that gives f_1 of fibre and s_1 of sugar. (This assumes that she only buys Healthbran and not some other brand too.)

A change in the budget. If she allocates more of her income to buying breakfast cereal, and sticks with Healthbran, she would move up the ray: say, to h_2. In other words, by buying more Healthbran, she would be buying more fibre and more sugar. Similarly, a reduction in expenditure on a product would be represented by a movement down its ray.

A change in price. If a product rises in price and the budget allocated to it remains the same, less will be purchased. There will be a movement down its ray.

The efficiency frontier

In practice, many consumers will buy a mixture of brands. Some days you may prefer one type of breakfast cereal, some days you may prefer another type. People get fed up with consuming too much of one brand or variety: they experience diminishing marginal utility from that particular mix of characteristics. You may allocate a certain amount of money for a summer holiday each year, but you may well want to go to a different place each year, since each place has a different mix of characteristics.

Assume that, given her current budget for breakfast cereals, the prices of Healthbran and Tastyflakes allow Jane to buy at either point *a* or point *b* in Figure 6.6. By switching completely from Healthbran to Tastyflakes, her consumption of fibre would go down from f_1 to f_2, and her consumption of sugar would go up from s_1 to s_2. She could, however, spend part of her budget on Healthbran and part on Tastyflakes. In fact, she could consume anywhere along the straight line joining points *a* and *b*. This line is known as the **efficiency frontier**. For example, by buying some of each brand, she could consume at point *c*, giving her f_3 of fibre and s_3 of sugar.

If she did consume at point *c*, how much of the two characteristics would she get from each of the two brands? This is shown in Figure 6.7 by drawing two lines from point *c*, each one parallel to one of the two rays. Consumption of the

definition
Efficiency frontier A line showing the maximum attainable combinations of two characteristics for a given budget. These characteristics can be obtained by consuming one or a mixture of two brands or varieties of a product.

Figure 6.6
The efficiency frontier

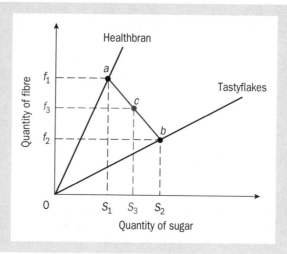

two brands takes place at points d and e respectively, giving her f_h units of fibre and s_h units of sugar from Healthbran, and f_t units of fibre and s_t units of sugar from Tastyflakes. The total amount of fibre and sugar from the two brands will be f_3 $(= f_h + f_t)$ and s_3 $(= s_h + s_t)$.[2]

It is easily possible to show an efficiency frontier between several brands, each with their own particular blend of characteristics. This is illustrated in Figure 6.8, which shows the case of four breakfast cereals, each with different combinations of fibre and sugar.

Any of the four points through which the efficiency frontier passes can change if the price of that brand changes. So if Oatybix went up in price, point b would move down the Oatybix ray, thereby altering the shape of the efficiency frontier.

Figure 6.7
Consuming a mixture of two products

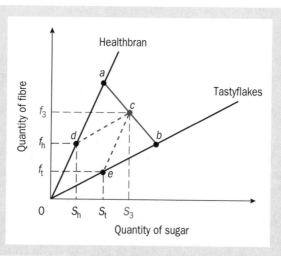

[2] This follows because of the shape of the parallelogram $Odce$. Being a parallelogram makes the distance $f_3 - f_h$ equal to $f_t - O$. Thus adding f_h and f_t gives f_3, which must correspond to point c. Similarly the distance $s_3 - s_t$ must equal $s_h - O$. Thus adding s_h and s_t gives s_3, which also must correspond to point c.

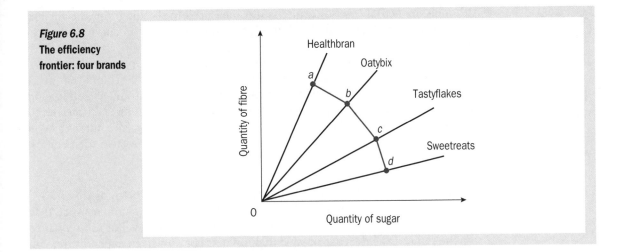

Figure 6.8
The efficiency frontier: four brands

If any of the brands changed their mix of characteristics, then the respective ray would pivot. If the consumer's budget changed, then the whole efficiency frontier would move parallel up or down all the rays.

The optimum level of consumption

Indifference curves

We have seen that by switching between brands, consumers can obtain different mixtures of characteristics. But what, for any given consumer, is the optimum mixture? This can be shown by examining a consumer's preferences, and the way we do this is to construct **indifference curves**. This is illustrated in Figure 6.9, which shows five indifference curves, labelled I_1 to I_5.

An indifference curve shows all the different combinations of the two characteristics that yield an equal amount of satisfaction or utility. Thus any combination of characteristics along curve I_1 represents the same given level of utility. The consumer is, therefore, 'indifferent' between all points along curve I_1.

> **definition**
>
> **Indifference curve**
> A line showing all those combinations of two characteristics of a good between which a consumer is indifferent: i.e. those combinations that give a particular level of utility.

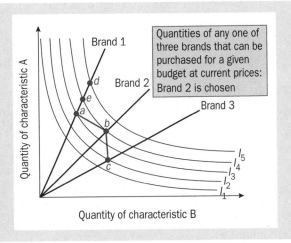

Figure 6.9
Choosing between brands

Although the actual level of utility is not measured in the diagram, the further out the curve, the higher the level of utility. Thus all points on curve I_5 are preferred to all points along curve I_4, and all points along curve I_4 are preferred to all points along curve I_3, and so on. In fact, indifference curves are rather like contours on a map. Each contour represents all points on the ground that are a particular height above sea level. You can have as many contours as you like on the map, depending at what interval you draw them: 100 metre, 25 metre, 10 metre, or whatever. Similarly you could have as many indifference curves as you like on an *indifference map*. In Figure 6.9, we have drawn just five such curves, as that is all that is necessary to illustrate consumer choice.

The shape of indifference curves. Indifference curves are drawn as downward sloping. The reason is that if consumers get less of one characteristic, they would need more of the other to compensate, if their total level of utility was to stay the same. Take the case of washing powder. For any given expenditure, you would only be prepared to give up a certain amount of one characteristic, say whiteness, if you got more of another characteristic, such as softness.

Notice that the indifference curves are not drawn as straight lines. They are bowed in towards the origin. The reason is that people generally are willing to give up less and less of one characteristic for each additional unit of another. For example, if you were buying a new PC, you might be prepared to give up some RAM to get extra hard disk space, but for each extra GB of disk space you would probably be prepared to give up less and less RAM. We call this a **diminishing marginal rate of substitution** between the two characteristics. The reason is that you get diminishing marginal utility from any characteristic the more of it you consume, and are thus prepared to give up less and less of another characteristic (whose marginal utility rises as you have less of it).

Indifference curves for different consumers. Different consumers will have different indifference maps. The indifference map in Figure 6.9 is drawn for a particular consumer, say James. If another consumer, Henry, gets relatively more satisfaction from characteristic B than does James, Henry's indifference curves would be steeper. In other words, he would be prepared to give up more units of A to get a certain amount of B than would James.

The optimum combination of characteristics

We are now in a position to see how a 'rational' consumer would choose between brands. Figure 6.9 shows the rays for three brands of a product, with, at given prices, the efficiency frontier passing through points a, b and c. The consumer would choose to consume Brand 2, since point b is on a higher indifference curve than point a (Brand 1), which in turn is on a higher indifference curve than point c (Brand 3).

Sometimes the consumer will choose to purchase a mixture of brands. This is shown in Figure 6.10, which takes the simple case of just two brands in the market. By consuming at point a (i.e. a combination of point b on the Brand 1 ray and point c on the Brand 2 ray), the consumer is on a higher indifference curve than by consuming only Brand 1 (point d) or Brand 2 (point e).

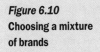

Figure 6.10
Choosing a mixture of brands

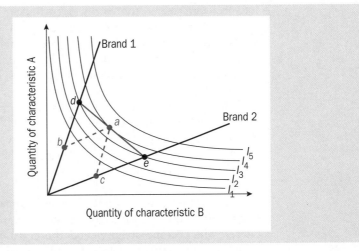

Response to changes

We can now show how consumers would respond to changes in price, income, product characteristics and tastes.

Changes in price. Referring back to Figure 6.9, if the price of a brand changes, there is a shift in the efficiency frontier, so that it crosses the ray for that brand at a different point. For example, if the price of Brand 1 fell, there would be a movement of the efficiency frontier up the Brand 1 ray from point *a*. If the price fell far enough that the efficiency frontier now passed through point *d*, the consumer would switch from consuming just Brand 2 to just Brand 1. If the price fell less than this, so that the efficiency frontier passed through point *e*, then the consumer would buy a mixture of both brands. The optimum consumption point would lie on an indifference curve a little above I_4.

We can relate this analysis to the concept of cross-price elasticity of demand (see page 82). If two products are very close substitutes, they will have a high cross-price elasticity of demand. But what makes them close substitutes? The answer is that they are likely to have similar characteristics; their rays will have a similar slope. Even a slight rise in the price of one of them (i.e. a small movement along its ray) can lead the consumer to switch to the other. This will occur when the rays are close together: when they have a similar slope.

Changes in income. If there is a change in consumer incomes, so that people allocate a bigger budget to the product in question, then there will be a parallel movement outwards of the efficiency frontier. Whether this will involve consumers switching between brands depends on the shape of the indifference map.

Changes in the characteristics of a product (real or perceived). If consumers believe that a brand now yields relatively more of characteristic B than A, the ray will become less steep. How far out will the efficiency point be on this new ray? This depends on the total perceived amount of the two characteristics that is obtained from the given budget spent on this brand.

To illustrate this, consider Figure 6.11. The firm producing Brand 1 changes its specifications, so that for a given budget a lot more characteristic B can be obtained and a little more characteristic A. The result is that the brand's ray shifts inwards and the efficiency frontier which originally connected points *a* and *b*, now connects points *c* and *b*. In this case the consumer represented by the indifference curves shown switches consumption from Brand 2 at point *b* to Brand 1 at point *c*.

If there is a proportionate increase in both characteristics (i.e. the brand has generally improved), the slope of the ray will not change. Instead, there will be a movement of the efficiency frontier outward along the ray. Graphically the effect is the same as a fall in the price of the product: more of both characteristics can be obtained for a given budget.

Changes in tastes. If consumers' tastes change, their whole indifference map will change. If characteristic B now gives more utility relative to A than before, the curves will become steeper, and the consumer is likely to choose a product which yields relatively more of characteristic B (i.e. one with a relatively shallow ray).

Clearly firms will attempt to predict such changes in tastes and will try, through product design, advertising and marketing, to shift the ray for their brand in the desired direction (downwards in the above case). They will also try to persuade consumers that the product is generally better (i.e. has more of all characteristics) and thereby move outward the point where the efficiency frontier crosses the brand's ray.

Usefulness of the characteristics approach

Characteristics analysis can help us understand the nature of consumer choice. When we go shopping and compare one product with another, it is the differences in the features of the various brands, along with price, that determine which products we end up buying. If firms, therefore, want to compete effectively with their rivals, it is not enough to compete solely in terms of price, it is important to focus on the specifications of their product and how these compare with those of their rivals' products.

Figure 6.11
A change in the characteristics of Brand 1

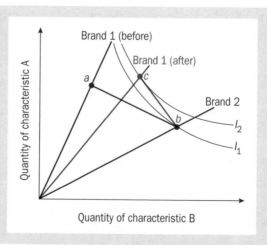

Characteristics analysis can help firms study the implications of changing their product's specifications (and of their rivals changing theirs). It also allows firms to analyse the effects of changes in their price, or their rivals' prices; the effects of changes in the budgets of various types of consumer; the effects of changes in consumer tastes; and the effects of repositioning themselves in the market.

Take the producer of Brand 1 in Figure 6.12. Clearly the firm would like to persuade consumers like the one illustrated to switch away from Brand 2 to Brand 1. It could do this by lowering its price. But a small reduction in price will have no effect on this consumer. Only when the price has fallen far enough for the efficiency frontier to rise nearly to point *d* will the consumer start switching; and only when the price has fallen further still, so that the efficiency frontier passes through a point a little above point *d*, will the consumer switch completely.

An alternative would be for the firm to reposition its product. It could introduce more of characteristic B into its product, thereby swinging the Brand 1 ray clockwise towards the Brand 2 ray. Clearly, it would have to be careful about its price too. The closer its brand became in quality to Brand 2, the more elastic would demand become, since Brand 1 would now be a closer substitute for Brand 2. In the extreme case of its ray becoming the same as that for Brand 2, its price would have to be low enough for the consumer to buy at or above point *b*. Depending on consumer tastes (and hence the shape of the indifference curves), it may choose to reposition its brand between the Brand 2 and Brand 3 rays. Again, a careful mix of product characteristics and price may enable it to capture a larger share of the market.

Another alternative would be for the firm to attempt to influence consumer tastes. In Figure 6.12, if it could persuade consumers to attach more value to characteristic A, the indifference curves would become shallower (i.e. less characteristic A would now be needed to give consumers a given level of utility). If the curves swung downwards enough, point *a* could be now on a higher indifference curve than point *b*. The consumer concerned would switch from Brand 2 to Brand 1. Clearly, the more consumers are influenced in this way, the more will sales of Brand 1 rise.

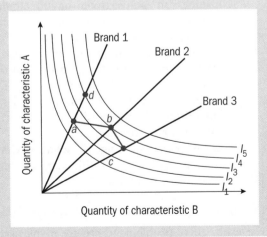

Figure 6.12
Options open to the firm producing Brand 1

If a firm is thinking of launching a new product, again it will need to see how the characteristics of its product compare with those of the existing firms in the market. It will need to see where its ray would be compared with those of other firms, and whether the price it is thinking of charging would enable it to take sales off its rivals.

Limitations of characteristics analysis

Characteristics analysis, as we have seen, can help firms to understand their position in the market and the effects of changing their strategy. Nevertheless it cannot provide firms with a complete analysis of demand. There are four key limitations of the approach:

- It is sometimes difficult to identify and measure characteristics in a clear and unambiguous way. Take our case of breakfast cereals. Fibre content might be simply measured, but taste is not. We took sugar content as an indicator of taste, but taste is much more subtle and complex than mere sweetness. But, at least with taste we could use sweetness as a guide. Some other characteristics are more difficult still to measure, with no simple approximation that we can use. Take the look or design of a product, whether it be furniture, clothing, a painting or a car. What makes it visually appealing depends on the personal tastes of the consumer, and such tastes are virtually impossible to quantify.
- Most products have several characteristics. The analysis we have been examining, however, is limited to just two characteristics: one on each axis. It is possible, however, by using mathematical analysis to extend the number of characteristics. Nevertheless, the more characteristics that are included in the analysis, the more complex it becomes.
- Indifference curves, whilst being a good means of understanding consumer choice in theory, have practical limitations. To draw an indifference map for just one consumer would be very difficult, given that consumers often would find it hard having to imagine a series of combinations of characteristics between which they were indifferent. To draw indifference curves for millions of consumers would be virtually impossible. At best, therefore, they can provide a rough guide to consumer choice.

  Nevertheless, many markets divide into different **market segments** with consumers in each segment having similar tastes (and hence similar sets of indifference curves). For example, different models of car fall into different groups (such as medium-sized saloons, high-performance small cars, people carriers and small 'tall' cars), as do different types of restaurant and different types of holiday. Thus a tour operator will first identify the particular segment of the market it is aiming for (e.g. a young person's package holiday with the characteristics of guaranteed sunshine and plenty of nightlife) and then position itself in that particular market relative to its rival tour operators.
- Consumer tastes change. In what way consumer tastes will change, and how these changes will influence the shape of the indifference curves, is very difficult to predict.

Conclusions

Despite these problems, there are many useful insights that firms can gain from

definition

Market segment
A part of a market for a product where the demand is for a particular variety of that product.

the analysis. For example, in Figure 6.12, with the efficiency frontier passing through points *a*, *b* and *c*, even without drawing any indifference curves, it is clear that consumers would prefer Brand 2 to either Brand 1 or 3, unless (a) characteristic A were especially desirable relative to characteristic B (i.e. the indifference curves, if drawn, would be very shallow), in which case the consumer might buy Brand 1; or (b) characteristic B were especially desirable relative to characteristic A (i.e. the indifference curves, if drawn, would be very steep), in which case Brand 3 might be purchased. Firms, through their market research, could gain considerable information about consumer attitudes towards the two characteristics and thus the general shape, if not precise position, of indifference curves.

What is clear is that firms need good information about the demand for their products and to develop a careful marketing strategy. In Chapter 7 we look at how firms attempt to get information about demand, and in Chapter 8 we examine how firms set about developing, marketing and advertising their products.

SUMMARY

1a Economists call consumer satisfaction 'utility'. Marginal utility diminishes as consumption increases. This means that total utility will rise less and less rapidly as people consume more. At a certain point, total utility will reach a maximum, at which point marginal utility will be zero. Beyond this point, total utility will fall; marginal utility will be negative.

1b Consumers will attempt to maximise their total utility. They will do this by consuming more of a good as long as its marginal utility to them (measured in terms of the price they are prepared to pay for it) exceeds its price. They will stop buying additional amounts once *MU* has fallen to equal the price. At this point, the consumer's surplus will be maximised.

1c An individual's demand curve lies along the same line as the individual's marginal utility curve. The market demand curve is the sum of all individuals' marginal utility curves.

2a When people buy consumer durables they may be uncertain of their benefits and any additional repair and maintenance costs. When they buy financial assets they may be uncertain of what will happen to their price in the future. Buying under these conditions of imperfect knowledge is therefore a form of gambling. When we take such gambles, if we know the odds we are said to be operating under conditions of *risk*. If we do not know the odds we are said to be operating under conditions of *uncertainty*.

2b People can be divided into risk lovers, risk averters

and those who are risk neutral. Because of the diminishing marginal utility of income it is rational for people to be risk averters (unless gambling is itself pleasurable).

2c Insurance is a way of eliminating risks for policy holders. Being risk averters, people are prepared to pay premiums in order to obtain insurance. Insurance companies, on the other hand, are prepared to take on these risks because they can spread them over a large number of policies. According to the law of large numbers, what is unpredictable for a single policy holder becomes highly predictable for a large number of them provided that their risks are independent of each other.

3a Consumers buy products for their characteristics. Characteristics can be plotted on a diagram and a ray drawn out from the origin for each product. The slope of the ray gives the amount of the characteristic measured on the vertical axis relative to the amount measured on the horizontal axis.

3b The amount purchased will depend on the consumer's budget. An efficiency frontier can be drawn showing the maximum quantity of various alternative brands (or combinations of them) that can be purchased for that budget.

3c An indifference map can be drawn on the same diagram. The map shows a series of indifference curves, each one measuring all the alternative combinations of two characteristics that give the consumer a given level of utility. The consumer is

SUMMARY

thus indifferent between all combinations along an indifference curve. Indifference curves further out to the right represent higher levels of utility and thus preferred combinations. Indifference curves are bowed in to the origin. This reflects a diminishing marginal rate of substitution between characteristics.

3d The optimum combination of characteristics is where the efficiency frontier is tangential to (i.e. just touches) the highest indifference curve. The 'rational' consumer will thus purchase at this point.

3e A change in a product's price, or a change in the consumer's budget, is represented by a movement along the product's ray. A change in the mix of characteristics of a product is represented by a

swing in the ray (i.e. a change in its slope). A change in consumer tastes is represented by a shift in the indifference curves. They will become steeper if tastes shift towards the characteristic measured on the horizontal axis.

3f Although (a) some characteristics are difficult or impossible to measure, (b) only two characteristics can be measured on a simple two-dimensional diagram and (c) the position of indifference curves is difficult to identify in practice, characteristics theory gives useful insights into the process of consumer choice. It can help firms analyse the implications of changing their or their rivals' product's specifications, changes in consumer tastes and changes in their or their rivals' prices.

REVIEW QUESTIONS

1 Do you ever purchase things irrationally? If so, what are they and why is your behaviour irrational?

2 If you buy something in the shop on the corner when you know that the same item could have been bought more cheaply two miles up the road in the supermarket, is you behaviour irrational? Explain.

3 How would marginal utility and market demand be affected by a rise in the price of a complementary good?

4 Why do we get less consumer surplus from goods where our demand is relatively price elastic?

5 Explain why the price of a good is no reflection of the *total* value that consumers put on it.

6 Give some examples of risk taking or gambling where the odds are (a) unfavourable; (b) fair; (c) favourable.

7 If people are generally risk averse, why do so many people around the world take part in national lotteries?

8 Why are insurance companies unwilling to provide insurance against losses arising from war or 'civil insurrection'? Name some other events where it would be impossible to obtain insurance.

9 Make a list of characteristics of shoes. Which of these could be easily measured and which are more 'subjective'?

10 If two houses had identical characteristics, except that one was near a noisy airport and the other was in a quiet location, and if the market price

of the first house was £80 000 and the second was £100 000, how would that help us to put a value on the characteristic of peace and quiet?

11 Assume that Rachel is attending university and likes to eat a meal at lunchtime. Assume that she has three options of where to eat: the university refectory, a nearby pub or a nearby restaurant. Apart from price, she takes into account the quality of the food and the pleasantness of the surroundings when choosing where to eat.

Sketch her indifference map for the two characteristics, food quality and pleasantness of surroundings. Now, making your own assumptions about which locations provide which characteristics, the prices they charge and Rachel's weekly budget for lunches, sketch the rays for the three locations and draw a weekly efficiency frontier. Mark Rachel's optimum consumption point.

Now illustrate the following (you might need to draw separate diagrams):

(a) A rise in the price of meals at the local pub, but no change in the price of meals at the other two locations.

(b) A shift in Rachel's tastes in favour of food quality relative to pleasantness of surroundings.

(c) The refectory is refurbished and is now a much more attractive place to eat.

12 Why would consumption at a point inside the efficiency frontier not be 'rational'?

Demand and the firm

Given our analysis in Chapter 6, how might a business set about discovering the wants of consumers and hence the intensity of demand? The more effectively a business can identify such wants, the more likely it is to increase its sales and be successful. The clearer idea it can gain of the rate at which the typical consumer's utility will decline as consumption increases, the better estimate it can make of the product's price elasticity. Also the more it can assess the relative utility to the consumer of its product compared with those of its rivals, the more effectively will it be able to compete by differentiating its product from theirs. In this chapter we shall consider the alternative strategies open to business for collecting data on consumer behaviour, and how it can help business managers to estimate and forecast patterns of demand.

7.1 Estimating demand functions

If a business is to make sound strategic decisions, it must have a good understanding of its market. It must be able to predict things such as the impact of an advertising campaign, or the consequences of changing a brand's price or specifications. It must also be able to predict the likely growth (or decline) in consumer demand, both in the near future and over the longer term. The problem is that information on consumer behaviour can be costly and time consuming to acquire, and there is no guarantee as to its accuracy. As a result, business managers are frequently making strategic decisions with imperfect knowledge, never fully knowing whether the decision they have made is the 'best' one: i.e. the one which yields the most profit or sales, or best meets some other more specific strategic objective (such as driving a competitor from a segment of a market).

But despite the fact that the information which a firm acquires is bound to be imperfect, it is still usually better than relying on hunches or 'instinct'. The firm having obtained information on consumer behaviour, there are two main uses to which it can be put:

- Estimating demand functions. Here the information is used to show the relationship between the quantity demanded and the various determinants of demand, such as price, consumers' incomes, advertising, the price of substitute and complementary goods, etc. Once this relationship (known as a *demand function*) has been established, it can be used to predict what would happen to demand if one of its determinants changed.
- Forecasting future demand. Here the information is used to project future sales potential. This can then be used as the basis for output and investment plans.

In this section we concentrate on the first of these two uses. We examine methods for gathering data on consumer behaviour and then see how these data can be used to estimate a demand function.

Methods of collecting data on consumer behaviour

There are three general approaches to gathering information about consumers. These are: **observations of market behaviour, market surveys** and **market experiments**.

Market observations

The firm can gather data on how demand for its product has changed over time. Virtually all firms will have detailed information of their sales broken down by week, and/or month, and/or year. They will probably also have information on how sales have varied from one part of the market to another.

In addition, the firm will need to obtain data on how the various determinants of demand (such as price, advertising and the price of competitors' products) have themselves changed over time. Firms are likely to have much of this information already: for example, the amount spent on advertising and the prices of competitors' products. Other information might be relatively easy to obtain by paying an agency to do the research.

Having obtained this information, the firm can then use it to estimate how changes in the various determinants have affected demand in the past, and hence what effect they will be likely to have in the future (we examine this estimation process later in this section).

Even the most sophisticated analysis based on market observations, however, will suffer from one major drawback. Relationships that held in the past will not necessarily hold in the future. Consumers are human, and humans change their minds. Their perceptions of products change (something that the advertising industry relies on!) and their tastes change. Such changes can often not be predicted from an examination of past sales trends, no matter how many factors, such as income and the price of competitors' products, are taken into account.

It is for these reasons that many firms turn to market surveys or market experiments to gain more information about the future.

Market surveys

It is not uncommon to be stopped in a city centre, or to have a knock at the door, and be asked whether you would kindly answer the questions of some market researcher. If the research interviewer misses you, then a postal questionnaire may well seek out the same type of information. A vast quantity of information can be collected in this way. It is a relatively quick and cheap method of data collection. Questions concerning all aspects of consumer behaviour might be asked, such as those relating to present and future patterns of expenditure, or how a buyer might respond to changing product specifications or price, both of the firm in question and of its rivals.

A key feature of the market survey is that it can be targeted at distinct consumer groups, thereby reflecting the specific information requirements of a business. For example, businesses selling luxury goods will be interested only in

> **definition**
>
> **Observations of market behaviour**
> Information gathered about consumers from the day-to-day activities of the business within the market.

> **definition**
>
> **Market surveys**
> Information gathered about consumers, usually via a questionnaire, that attempts to enhance the business's understanding of consumer behaviour.

> **definition**
>
> **Market experiments**
> Information gathered about consumers under artificial or simulated conditions. A method used widely in assessing the effects of advertising on consumers.

consumers falling within higher income brackets. Other samples might be drawn from a particular age group or gender, or from those with a particular lifestyle, such as eating habits.

The major drawback with this technique concerns the accuracy of the information acquired. Accurate information requires various conditions to be met.

A random sample. If the sample is not randomly selected, it may fail to represent a cross-section of the population being surveyed. As a result, it may be subject to various forms of research bias. For example, the sample might not contain the correct gender and racial balance. The information might then over-emphasise the views of a particular group (e.g. white men).

Clarity of the questions. It is important for the questions to be phrased in an unambiguous way, so as not to mislead the respondent.

Avoidance of leading questions. It is very easy for the respondent to be led into giving the answer the firm wants to hear. For example, when asking whether the person would buy a new product that the firm is thinking of launching, the questionnaire might make the product sound really desirable. The respondents might, as a result, say that they would buy the product, but later, when they see the product in the shops, they might realise that they do not want it.

Willingness of respondents. People might refuse to answer particular questions, possibly due to their personal nature. This may then lead to partial or distorted information.

Truthful response. It is very tempting for respondents who are 'keen to please' to give the answer that they think the questioner wants, or for other somewhat reluctant respondents to give 'mischievous' answers. In other words, people may lie!

Stability of demand. By the time the product is launched, or the changes to an existing product are made, time will have elapsed. The information may then be out of date. Consumer demand may have changed, as tastes and fashions have shifted, or as a result of the actions of competitors. The essence of the problem of market surveys is that they ask consumers what they are likely to do. People can and do change their mind.

As well as surveying consumers, businesses might survey other businesses, or panels of experts within a particular market. Both could yield potentially valuable information to the business.

Market experiments

Rather than asking consumers questions and getting them to *imagine* how they *would* behave, the market experiment involves observing consumer *behaviour* under simulated conditions. It can be used to observe consumer reactions to a new product or to changes in an existing product.

A simple experiment might involve consumers being asked to conduct a blind taste test for a new brand of toothpaste. The experimenter will ensure that the same amount of paste is applied to the brush, and that the subjects swill their mouths prior to tasting a further brand. Once the experiment is over, the 'consumers' are quizzed about their perceptions of the product.

The demand for butter[1]
A real-world demand function

The following is an estimate of the UK's market demand curve for butter. It has been estimated (using a computer regression package) from actual data for the years 1992–9.

$$Q_d = 21.39 - 10.88P_b + 12.36P_m + 0.29Y$$

where: Q_d is the quantity of butter sold in grams per person per week.

P_b is the 'real' price of butter: i.e. the price of butter in pence per kg, divided by the retail price index (RPI) (1990 = 100).

P_m is the 'real' price of margarine (calculated in the same way as butter).

Y is the real personal disposable income of households: i.e. household income after tax, expressed as an index (1990= 100).

From this economists could forecast what would happen to the demand for butter if any of three variables – the price of butter, the price of margarine or income – changed.

Question

From this equation, calculate what would happen to the demand for butter if:
(a) The price of butter went up by 1p per kg and the RPI was 100.
(b) The price of margarine went up by 1p per kg and the RPI was 200.
(c) The index of personal disposable incomes went up by 1 point.

There is a serious problem with estimated demand functions like these: they assume that *other* determinants of demand have not changed. In the case of this demand-for-butter function, one of the other determinants *did* change. This was tastes – during the 1980s and 1990s there was a massive shift in demand from

butter and margarine to low fat spreads, partly for health reasons, and partly because of an improvement in the taste for these products and a greater range available. The following table shows this shift.

Consumption of butter, margarine and spreads (grams per person per week)

	Butter	Margarine	Low-fat spreads
1986	64	116	30
1992	41	79	51
1997	38	26	77

Source: Based on *National Food Survey* (MAFF) various years.

Assuming that this shift in taste took place steadily over time, a new demand equation was estimated for the same years:

$$Q_d = 16.4 - 8.63P_b + 6.67P_m + 0.5Y - 1.16TIME$$

where the *TIME* term is as follows: 1992 = 1, 1993 = 2, 1994 = 3, etc.

Because of the large changes, over just a few years, in the nature and variety of low fat spreads, it is not possible to include the price (or prices) of these products in an equation in any meaningful way. But clearly, their presence on the market has shifted the demand curve for butter, and continues to do so, and hence makes the estimated equations less reliable for forecasting the demand for butter.

Questions

1 How does the introduction of the *TIME* term affect the relationship between the demand for butter and (a) the price of margarine and (b) personal disposable income?

2 Is butter a normal good or an inferior good?

[1]Calculations by W. Thurlow.

The nature of the experiment can be far more intricate than this. For example, a *laboratory shop* might be set up to simulate a real shopping experience. In this 'shop', products can be displayed, packaged and priced in a variety of ways. Consumers could be given a certain amount of money and asked to spend it as they choose in the shop. The experiment could be repeated a number of times to establish the effects of changing prices, or layout, or the mix of products on the shelves. At the end of the experiment, the reasons behind the subjects' preferences can be explored.

This type of experiment can be used to test the effectiveness of advertising. People could be shown an advertisement for a product, and then, after a certain amount of time, be given money to spend in the laboratory shop, where the new product is on sale. The laboratory shop can be manipulated in a variety of ways so as to yield sufficient information as to what the optimum marketing strategy for a product or product range might be.

The major drawback with this approach to measuring consumer behaviour is that consumers might modify their behaviour because they realise that their actions are being monitored. For example, consumers in the laboratory shop might spend more time looking at price than they would otherwise, simply because they might believe that this is what a *good*, rational consumer would do. Under normal conditions it might simply be habit, or something 'irrational' such as the colour of the packaging, that determines which product they select.

Another type of market experiment involves confining a marketing campaign to a particular town or region. The campaign could involve advertising, or giving out free samples, or discounting the price, or introducing an improved version of the product, but each confined to that particular locality. Sales in that area are then compared with sales in other areas in order to assess the effectiveness of the various campaigns.

Using the data to estimate demand functions

Once the business has undertaken its market analysis, what will it do with the information? How can it use its new knowledge to aid its decision making?

One way the information might be used is for the business to attempt to estimate the relationship between the quantity demanded and the various factors that influence demand. This would then enable the firm to predict how the demand for the product would be likely to change if one or more of the determinants of demand changed.

We can represent the relationship between the demand for a product and the determinants of demand in the form of an equation. This is called a **demand function**. It can be expressed in general terms or with specific values attached to the determinants.

General form of a demand function

In its general form the demand function is effectively a list of the various determinants of demand.

$$Q_d = f(P_g, T, P_{s_1}, P_{s_2}...P_{s_n}, P_{c_1}, P_{c_2}...P_{c_m}, Y, B, P_{g_{t+1}}^e)$$

This is merely saying in symbols that the quantity demanded (Q_d) is a 'function of' (f) – i.e. depends on – the price of the good itself (P_g), tastes (T), the price of substitute goods ($P_{s_1}, P_{s_2}, ...P_{s_n}$), the price of complementary goods ($P_{c_1}, P_{c_2}, ...P_{c_m}$), total consumer incomes (Y), the distribution of income (B), and the expected price of the good (P_g^e) at some future time ($t+1$). The equation is thus just a form of shorthand.

Note that this function could be extended by dividing determinants into subcategories. For example, income could be broken down by household type, age, gender or any other characteristic. Similarly, instead of having one term labelled 'tastes', we could identify various characteristics of the product or its marketing that determine tastes.

In this general form, there are no numerical values attached to each of the determinants. As such, the function has no predictive value for the firm.

Estimating demand equations

To make predictions, the firm must use its survey or experimental data to assign *values* to each of the determinants. These values show just how much demand will change if any one of the determinants changes (while the rest are held constant). For example, suppose that an electricity distributor reckons that there are three main determinants of demand (Q_d) for the electricity it supplies: its price (P), total consumer incomes (Y) and the price of gas (P_g). It will wish to assign values to the terms a, b, c and d (known as *coefficients*) in the following equation:

$$Q_d = a + bP + cY + dP_g$$

But how are the values of the coefficients to be estimated? This is done using a statistical technique called **regression analysis**. To conduct regression analysis, a number of observations must be used. For example, the electricity company could use its market observations (or the results from various surveys or experiments).

To show how these observations are used, let us consider the very simplest case: that of the effects of changes in just one determinant – for example, price. In this case the demand equation would simply be of the form $Q_d = a + bP$ (where the value of b would be negative).

The observations might be like those illustrated in Figure 7.1. The points show the amounts of electricity per time period actually consumed at different prices. We could, by eye, construct a demand curve through these points. Regression analysis is a technique that allows us to obtain the line of best fit. (We do not explain regression analysis in this book, but most business statistics texts cover the topic.)

Of course, in reality, there are many determinants of the demand for electricity. That is one reason why the observed points in Figure 7.1 do not all fall exactly along the line. Demand varies at each different price according to what

Figure 7.1
Consumption of electricity at different prices

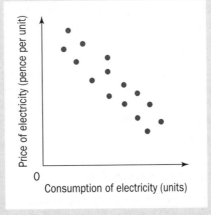

is happening to the other determinants. The other major reason is if the observed points are based on different samples, where each sample is not identical in composition and tastes.

Regression analysis can also be used to determine more complex relationships: to derive the equation that best fits the data on changes in a number of variables. Unlike a curve on a diagram, which simply shows the relationship between two variables, an equation can show the relationship between several variables. Regression analysis can be used to find the 'best fit' equation from data on changes in a number of variables.

For example, using regression analysis with data on changes in the quantity of electricity consumed resulting from changes in price, consumer incomes and the price of gas, the following equation might be estimated:

$$Q_d = 2000 - 500P + 0.4Y + 200P_g$$

where Q_d is measured in millions of gigawatts per annum, P in pence per kilowatt hour, Y in £ millions and P_g in pence per kilowatt hour.

Thus if the price of electricity were 5p per kilowatt hour, consumer incomes were £20 billion and the price of gas were 2p per kilowatt hour, then the demand for electricity would be 7900 million gigawatts per annum. This is calculated as follows:

$$Q_d = 2000 - (500 \times 5) + (0.4 \times 20\,000) + (200 \times 2)$$
$$= 2000 - 2500 + 8000 + 400$$
$$= 7900$$

The branch of economics that applies statistical techniques to economic data is known as **econometrics**. The problem with using such techniques, however, is that they cannot produce equations and graphs that allow totally reliable predictions to be made. The data on which the equations are based are often incomplete or unreliable, and the underlying relationships on which they are based (often ones of human behaviour) may well change over time.

7.2 Forecasting demand

Demand functions are useful in that they show what will happen to demand *if* one of the determinants changes. But businesses will want to know more than the answer to an 'If ... then' question. They will want to know what will actually happen to the determinants and, more specifically, what will happen to demand itself. In other words, they will want *forecasts* of future demand. After all, if demand is going to increase, they may well want to invest *now* so that they have the extra capacity to meet the extra demand. But it will be a costly mistake to invest in extra capacity if demand is not going to increase.

We now, therefore, turn to examine some of the forecasting techniques used by business.

Simple time-series analysis

Simple time-series analysis involves directly projecting from past sales data into the future. Thus if it is observed that sales of a firm's product have been grow-

definition
Econometrics
The branch of economics which applies statistical techniques to economic data.

ing steadily by 3 per cent per annum for the last few years, the firm can use this to predict that sales will continue to grow at approximately the same rate in the future. Similarly, if it is observed that there are clear seasonal fluctuations in demand, as in the case of the demand for holidays or ice cream or winter coats, then again it can be assumed that fluctuations of a similar magnitude will continue into the future. In other words, using simple time-series analysis assumes that demand in the future will continue to behave in the same way as in the past.

Using simple time-series analysis in this way can be described as 'black box' forecasting. No *explanation* is offered as to *why* demand is behaving in this way: any underlying model of demand is 'hidden in a black box'. In a highly stable market environment, where the various factors affecting demand change very little or, if they do, change very steadily or regularly, such time-series analysis can supply reasonably accurate forecasts. The problem is that, without closer examination of the market, the firm cannot know whether changes in demand of the same magnitude as in the past will continue into the future. Just because demand has followed a clear pattern in the past, it does not inexorably follow that it will continue to exhibit the same pattern in the future. After all, the determinants of demand may well have changed. Successful forecasting, therefore, will usually involve a more sophisticated analysis of trends.

The decomposition of time paths

One way in which the analysis of past data can be made more sophisticated is to identify different elements in the time path of sales. Figure 7.2 illustrates one such time path: the (imaginary) sales of woollen jumpers by firm X. It is shown by the continuous red line, labelled 'Actual sales'.

Four different sets of factors normally determine the shape of a time path like this.

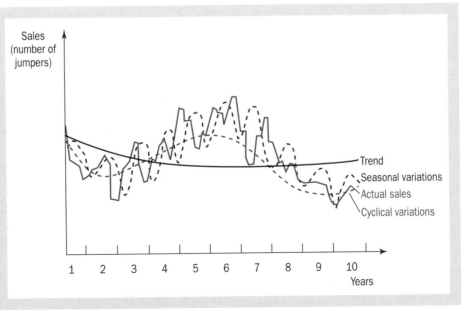

Figure 7.2
(Imaginary) sales of woollen jumpers

Trends. These are increases or decreases in demand over a number of years. In our example, there is a long-term decrease in demand for this firm's woollen jumpers up to year 7 and then a recovery in demand thereafter.

Trends may reflect factors such as changes in population structure, or technological innovation or longer-term changes in fashion. Thus if wool were to become more expensive over time compared with other fibres, or if there were a gradual shift in tastes away from woollen jumpers and towards acrylic or cotton jumpers, or towards sweatshirts, this could explain the long-term decline in demand up to year 7. A gradual shift in tastes back towards natural fibres, and to wool in particular, or a gradual reduction in the price of wool, could then explain the subsequent recovery in demand.

Alternatively, trends may reflect changes over time in the structure of an industry. For example, an industry might become more and more competitive with new firms joining. This would tend to reduce sales for existing firms (unless the market were expanding very rapidly).

Cyclical fluctuations. In practice, the level of actual sales will not follow the trend line precisely. One reason for this is the cyclical upswings and downswings in business activity in the economy as a whole. In some years incomes are rising rapidly and thus demand is buoyant. In other years, the economy will be in recession, with incomes falling. In these years, demand may well also fall. In our example, in boom years people may spend much more on clothes (including woollen jumpers), whereas in a recession, people may make do with their old clothes. The cyclical variations line is thus above the trend line in boom years and below the trend line during a recession.

Seasonal fluctuations. The demand for many products also depends on the time of year. In the case of woollen jumpers, the peak demand is likely to be as winter approaches or just before Christmas. Thus the seasonal variations line is above the cyclical variations line in winter and below it in summer.

Short-term shifts in demand or supply. Finally, the actual sales line will also reflect various short-term shifts in demand or supply, causing it to diverge from the smooth seasonal variations line.

There are many reasons why the demand curve might shift. A competitor might increase its price, or there may be a sudden change in fashion, caused, say, by a pop group deciding to wear woollen jumpers for their new video: what was once seen as unfashionable by many people now suddenly becomes fashionable! Alternatively, there may be an unusually cold or hot, or wet or dry spell of weather.

Likewise there are various reasons for sudden shifts in supply conditions. For example, there may be a sheep disease which ruins the wool of infected sheep. As a result, the price of wool goes up, and sales of woollen jumpers falls.

These sudden shifts in demand or supply conditions are often referred to as 'random shocks' because they are usually unpredictable and temporarily move sales away from the trend. (Note that *long-term* shifts in demand and supply will be shown by a change in the trend line itself.)

Even with sophisticated time-series analysis, which breaks time paths into their constituent elements, there is still one major weakness: time-series analysis is merely a projection of the *past*. Most businesses will want to anticipate *changes* to sales trends – to forecast any deviations from the current time path. One method for doing this is *barometric forecasting*.

Barometric forecasting

Assume that you are a manager of a furniture business and are wondering whether to invest in new capital equipment. You would only want to do this if the demand for your product was likely to rise. You will probably, therefore, look for some indication of this. A good barometer of future demand for furniture would be the number of new houses being built. People will tend to buy new furniture some months after the building of their new house has commenced.

It is common for businesses to use **leading indicators** such as housing starts when attempting to predict the future. In fact some leading indicators, such as increased activity in the construction industry, rises in Stock Exchange prices, a depreciation of the rate of exchange and a rise in industrial confidence, are good indicators of a general upturn in the economy.

Barometric forecasting is a technique whereby forecasts of demand in industry A are based on an analysis of time-series data for industry (or sector, or indicator) B, where changes in B normally precede changes in A. If B rises by x per cent, it can be assumed (other things being equal) that A will change by y per cent.

Barometric forecasting is widely used to predict *cyclical* changes: the effects of the upswings and downswings in the economy. It is thus useful not only for individual firms, but also for governments, which need to plan their policies to counteract the effects of the business cycle: the unemployment associated with recessions, or the inflation associated with booms in the economy.

Barometric forecasting suffers from two major weaknesses. The first is that it only allows forecasting a few months ahead – as far ahead as is the time lag between the change in the leading indicator and the variable being forecasted. The second is that it can only give a general indication of changes in demand. It is simply another form of time-series analysis. Just because a relationship existed in the past between a leading indicator and the variable being forecasted, it cannot be assumed that exactly the same relationship will exist in the future.

Normally, then, firms use barometric forecasting merely to give them a rough guide as to likely changes in demand for their product: i.e. whether it is likely to expand or contract, and by 'a lot' or by 'a little'. Nevertheless information on leading indicators is readily available in government or trade statistics.

To get a more precise forecast, firms must turn to their demand function, and estimate the effects of predicted changes in the determinants of the demand for their product.

Using demand functions in forecasts

We have seen in section 7.1 how demand functions can be used to show the effects of changes in the determinants of demand. For example, in the following model:

$$Q_d = a + bP + cP_s + dY + eA$$

where the demand for the product (Q_d) is determined by its price (P), the price

---

> **definition**
>
> **Leading indicators**
> Indicators that help predict future trends in the economy.

> **definition**
>
> **Barometric forecasting**
> A technique used to predict future economic trends based upon analysing patterns of time-series data.

of a substitute product (P_s), consumer incomes (Y) and advertising (A), the parameters (b, c, d and e) show the effects on Q_d of changes in the determinants.

In order to forecast the demand for its product (the **dependent variable**), the firm will need to obtain values for P, P_s, Y and A (the **independent variables**). The firm itself chooses what price to charge and how much to advertise, and thus will decide the values of P and A. Forecasts of consumer incomes are readily available from the government's Office for National Statistics (ONS) or from private forecasting agencies. As far as P_s is concerned, here the firm will have to make an informed guess. Most firms will have a pretty good idea of the likely policies of their competitors.

Obviously, the accuracy of the forecasts will depend on the accuracy of the model as a description of the past relationship between demand and its determinants. Fortunately, this can be tested using various econometric techniques, and the reliability of the model can be determined. What is more, once the forecast is made, it can be compared with the actual outcome and the new data can be used to refine the model and improve its predictive power for next time.

The major strength of these econometric models is that they attempt to show how the many determinants affect demand. They also allow firms to feed in different assumptions to see how they will affect the outcome. Thus one forecast might be based on the assumption that the major competitor raises its price by x per cent, another that it raises its price by y per cent, and another that it leaves its price unchanged. The firm can then see how sensitive its sales will be to these possible changes. This is called **sensitivity analysis** and its use allows the firm to assess just how critical its assumptions are: would a rise in its rival's price by x per cent rather than y per cent make all the difference between a profit and a loss, or would it make little difference?

Econometric models can be highly complex, involving several equations and many variables. For example, there might be a separate variable for each of the prices and specifications of all the various products in competition with this one.

Problems with econometric forecasting

But despite the apparent sophistication of some of the econometric models used by firms or by forecasting agencies, the forecasts are often wrong.

One reason for this is that the variables specified in the model do not explain all the variation in the demand for the product. In order to take some account of these missing independent variables, it is normal to include an *error term* (r). But this error term will probably cover a number of unspecified determinants which are unlikely to move together over time. It does not therefore represent a stable or predictable 'determinant'. The larger the error term, the less confident we can be about using the equation to predict future demand.

Another reason for the inaccuracy of forecasts is that certain key determinants are difficult, if not impossible, to measure with any accuracy. This is a particular problem with subjective variables like taste and fashion. How can taste be modelled?

Perhaps the biggest weakness of using demand functions for forecasting is that the forecasts are themselves based on forecasts of what will happen to the various determinants. Take the cases of just two determinants: the specifications of competitors' products and consumer tastes. Just what changes will competitors make to their products? Just how will tastes change in the future? Consider the problems a clothing manufacturer might have in forecasting demand for a

definition

Dependent variable
That variable whose outcome is determined by other variables within an equation.

definition

Independent variables
Those variables that determine the dependent variable, but are themselves determined independently of the equation they are in.

definition

Sensitivity analysis
Assesses how sensitive an outcome is to different variables within an equation.

range of clothing! Income, advertising and the prices of the clothing will all be significant factors determining demand, but so too will be the range offered by other manufacturers and also people's perception of what is and what is not fashionable. But predicting changes in competitors' products and changes in fashion is notoriously difficult.

This is not to say that firms should give up in their attempt to forecast demand. Rather it suggests that they might need to conduct more sophisticated market research, and even then to accept that forecasts can only give an approximate indication of likely changes to demand.

SUMMARY

1a Businesses seek information on consumer behaviour so as to predict market trends and improve strategic decision making.

1b One source of data is the firm's own information on how its sales have varied in the past with changes in the various determinants of demand, such as consumer incomes and the prices of competitors' products.

1c Another source of data is market surveys. These can generate a large quantity of cheap information. Care should be taken, however, to ensure that the sample of consumers investigated reflects the target consumer group.

1d Market experiments involve investigating consumer behaviour within a controlled environment. This method is particularly useful when considering new products where information is scarce.

1e Armed with data drawn from one or more of these sources, the business manager can attempt to estimate consumer demand using various statistical techniques, such as regression analysis.

1f The estimation of the effects on demand of a change in a particular variable, such as price, depends upon the assumption that all other factors that influence demand remain constant. However, factors that influence the demand for a product are

constantly changing, hence there will always be the possibility of error when estimating the impact of change.

2a It is not enough to know what will happen to demand if a determinant changes. Businesses will want to forecast what will actually happen to demand. To do this they can use a variety of methods: time-series analysis, barometric forecasting and econometric modelling.

2b Time-series analysis bases future trends on past events. Time-series data can be decomposed into different elements: trends, seasonal fluctuations, cyclical fluctuations and random shocks.

2c Barometric forecasting involves making predictions based upon changes in key leading indicators.

2d If a firm has estimated its demand function (using econometric techniques), it can then feed into this model forecasts of changes in the various determinants of demand and use the model to predict the effect on demand. The two main problems with this approach are: the reliability of the demand function (although this can be tested using econometric techniques), and the reliability of forecasts of changes in the various determinants of demand.

REVIEW QUESTIONS

1 What are the relative strengths and weaknesses of using (a) market observations, (b) market surveys and (c) market experiments as means of gathering evidence on consumer demand?

2 You are working for a record company which is thinking of signing up some new bands. What market observations, market surveys and market experiments could you conduct to help you decide which bands to sign?

3 You are about to launch a new range of cosmetics, but you are still to decide upon the content and structure of your advertising campaign. Consider how market surveys and market experiments might be used to help you assess consumer perceptions of the product. What limitations might each of the research methods have in helping you gather data?

4 The following is an estimate of the UK's market demand curve for instant coffee. It has been derived (using a computer regression package) from actual data for the years 1973–85.

$$Q_c = 0.042 - 0.068P_c + 0.136P_T + 0.0067Y$$

where: Q_c is the quantity of instant coffee purchased in ounces per person per week;

P_c and P_T are respectively the 'real' prices of instant coffee and tea, calculated by dividing their market prices in pence per lb by the retail price index for all food (*RPI*) (1980 = 100);

Y is an index of real personal disposable income (1980 = 100): i.e. household income after tax.

The following table gives the prices of coffee and tea and real disposable income for three years (1973, 1985 and 1990).

Year	Market price of coffee (Mp_c) (pence per lb)	RPI of all food (1980 = 100)	Real price of coffee ($P_c = MP_c/$ RPI $\times$ 100)	Market price of tea (MP_T) (pence per lb)	Real price of tea ($P_T = MP_T/$ RPI $\times$ 100)	Index of real disposable income (Y) (1980 = 100)
1973	111.33	35.20		35.53		89.30
1985	511.65	131.40		184.39		106.10
1990	585.19	165.89		212.77		128.62

(a) Fill in the columns for the real price of coffee (P_c) and the real price of tea (P_T).

(b) Use the above equation to estimate the demand for instant coffee in 1973.

(c) Calculate the percentage growth in the market over the 13-year sample period (1973–85).

(d) The equation was used to forecast the demand for instant coffee in 1990. Purchases were estimated at 0.7543 ounces per person per week.

  (i) Verify this from the equation.

  (ii) The actual level of purchases is recorded as 0.48 ounces per week. Suggest reasons why the equation seriously over-estimates the level of demand for 1990.

5 Outline the alternative methods a business might use to forecast demand. How reliable do you think such methods are?

6 Imagine that you are an airline attempting to forecast demand for seats over the next two or three years. What, do you think, could be used as leading indicators?

Products, markets and advertising

For most firms, selling their product is not simply a question of estimating demand and then choosing an appropriate price and level of production. In other words, they do not simply take their market as given. Instead they will seek to *influence* demand. They will do this by developing their product and differentiating it from those of their rivals, and then marketing it by advertising and other forms of product promotion.

What firms are engaging in here is **non-price competition**. In such situations the job of the manager can be quite complex. It is likely to involve making a series of strategic decisions, not just concerning price, but also concerning each product's design and quality, its marketing and advertising, and the provision of various forms of after-sales service.

Central to non-price competition is **product differentiation**. Most firms' products differ in various ways from those of their rivals. Take the case of washing machines. Although all washing machines wash clothes, and as such are close substitutes for each other, there are many differences between brands. They differ not only in price, but also in their capacity, their styling, their range of programmes, their economy in the use of electricity, hot water and detergent, their reliability, their noise, their after-sales service, etc. Firms will attempt to design their product so that they can stress its advantages (real or imaginary) over the competitor brands. Just think of the specific features of particular models of car, hi-fi equipment or brands of cosmetic, and then consider the ways in which these features are stressed by advertisements. In fact, think of virtually any advertisement and consider how it stresses the features of that particular brand.

8.1 Product differentiation

Features of a product

A product has many dimensions, and a strategy to differentiate a product may focus on one or more of these dimensions.

Technical standards. These relate to the product's level of technical sophistication: how advanced it is in relation to the current state of technology. This would be a very important product dimension if, for example, you were purchasing a PC. Similarly, if you were purchasing a car, you might be concerned whether it had such features as anti-locking brakes or air bags, or had a catalytic converter. The incorporation of technical advances is likely to affect aspects such as performance, safety, ease of use and comfort.

Quality standards. These relate to aspects such as the quality of the materials used in the product's construction and the care taken in assembly. These will affect the product's durability and reliability. The purchase of consumer durables, such as televisions, hi-fi and toys, will be strongly influenced by quality standards.

Design characteristics. These relate to the product's direct appeal to the consumer in terms of appearance or operating features. Examples of design characteristics are colour, style and even packaging. The demand for fashion products such as clothing will be strongly influenced by design characteristics.

Service characteristics. This aspect is not directly concerned with the product itself, but with the support and back-up given to the customer after the product has been sold. Servicing, product maintenance and guarantees would be included under this heading. When purchasing a new car, the quality of after-sales service might strongly influence the choice you make.

Any given product will possess a 'bundle' of the above attributes. Within any product category, each brand is likely to have a different mix of technical and quality standards and design and service characteristics. Consumers will select the bundle of attributes they most prefer. One consumer may be willing to accept lower technical standards for a better service agreement; another may want the highest technical standards and care little about the product's appearance. Different dimensions of the product will guide consumer choice. The fact that these different dimensions exist means that producers can focus the marketing of their product on factors other than price.

If a business is to benefit from the differentiation of its product from those of its rivals, consumers must be made aware of the differences. Thus an important part of non-price competition is advertising. As will be discussed more fully in section 8.3, good advertising will shape a product's image and stress to the consumer its desirable qualities, whether these are its technical, quality, design or service characteristics.

Vertical and horizontal product differentiation

When firms are seeking to differentiate their product from those of their rivals, one important distinction they must consider is that between *vertical* and *horizontal* differentiation.

Vertical product differentiation. This is where products differ in quality, with some being perceived as superior and others as inferior. In general, the better the quality, the more expensive will the product be. Take the case of a stereo cassette recorder. The cheaper (inferior) models will just have basic functions. As you move up the price range, so the models will have more and better functions, such as Dolby B, C and S, soft touch controls, better frequency response and automatic bias selection.

Vertical product differentiation will usually be in terms of the quantity and quality of functions and/or the durability of the product (often a reflection of the quality of the materials used and the care spent in making the product).

> **definition**
>
> **Vertical product differentiation**
> Where a firm's product differs from its rivals' products in respect to quality.

Thus a garment will normally be regarded as superior if it is better made and uses high-quality cloth. In general, the vertical quality differences between products will tend to reflect differences in production costs.

Horizontal product differentiation. This refers to differences between products that are not generally regarded as superior or inferior, but merely reflections of the different tastes of different consumers. One person may prefer black shoes and another brown. One may prefer milk chocolate, another plain. Within any product range there may be varieties which differ in respect to style, design, flavour, colour, etc. Such attributes are neither 'good' nor 'bad', simply different. Take a product like cosmetics. Within any one range, there is likely to be a considerable variety of colours, textures or perfumes, catering for the particular preferences of particular consumers.

Horizontal differences within a range do not significantly alter the costs of

> **definition**
>
> **Horizontal product differentiation**
> Where a firm's product differs from its rivals' products, although the products are seen to be of a similar quality.

BOX 8.1

Brands and own-brands
What's in a name?

The rise of supermarket own-brands during the 1990s has been phenomenal. Their market penetration in the UK has been so great that, by 1995, 54.5 per cent of all sales in the major supermarket chains were of own-branded products. In 1992, just three years earlier, the figure had been a mere 27 per cent. What makes this rise even more striking is that it followed a period when branded products dominated the market and seemed to be growing in strength. During the 1980s, the profits of companies such as Kellogg's and Heinz were increasing by as much as 15 per cent a year.

As Alan Mitchell argues in *Marketing Week* (6 December 1996), the brand system seemed to be unassailable.

> Brand manufacturers commanded economies of scale in both sourcing and production which enabled them to offer superior value to consumers. Mass advertising helped to drive the demand that, in turn, promoted mass production by keeping brands top of consumer awareness. National distribution created mass presence and availability, driving sales and reinforcing brands' share of mind.
>
> And the healthy margins generated by the synergy between mass production, advertising and distribution, allowed manufacturers to invest in research and development and offer genuinely improved products. This in turn, created new reassurance of value for money and extra sales, thereby adding impetus to the virtuous circle.

However, towards the end of the 1980s, things started to go horribly wrong for branded products:

● The economic boom came to an end, and the UK went into recession, with the result that consumers became more price conscious.
● Supermarkets began to develop a more extensive range of own-label products.

As Alan Mitchell points out:

> New technologies [were] allowing own-label manufacturers to produce smaller batch runs at lower costs: so the benefits of economies of scale [declined].
>
> Own-label products also lay claim to cost advantages, both on marketing and distribution – a few dedicated trucks from factory to retailer regional distribution centre are nothing compared with the cost of a fleet serving every retailer, wholesaler, and convenience shop.
>
> This means all the paraphernalia of advertising, distribution, and new product development that made the brand manufacturing model so powerful decades ago is unravelling, and becoming an enormous cost burden instead – a burden that adds up to 50 per cent on to the final consumer price and allows retailers to undercut brands while creaming off higher margins. The virtuous cycle goes into reverse, and becomes a vicious circle.

Such were the cost advantages of the own-label

production, and it is common for the different varieties to have the same price. A pot of red paint is likely to be the same price as a pot of blue (of the same brand). The point is that the products, although horizontally different, are of comparable quality.

In practice, most product ranges will have a mixture of horizontal and vertical differentiation. For example, some of the differences between different makes and models of motor car will be vertical (e.g. luxury or basic internal fittings, acceleration and fuel consumption); some will be horizontal (e.g. hatchback or saloon, colour and style).

Market segmentation

Different features of a product will appeal to different consumers. This applies both to vertically differentiated features and to horizontally differentiated ones.

alternative that, for many products, the price discrepancy between brands and own-brands had become staggering, forcing brand manufacturers to make substantial price cuts. For example, the dairy producer Kraft was forced to slash prices on many of its cheese products, which in many cases were some 45 per cent more expensive than own-label alternatives.

The position of branded products has been further undermined. Technology has not only pushed down costs, but also raised the *quality* of products, making it easier for own-label producers to copy established brands, and in many cases to innovate themselves.

In addition, so as not to be left out, many famous branded goods manufacturers also make own-label products. Such actions might in fact be ultimately self-defeating, since they have resulted in a change in consumer perceptions regarding own-brands. Consumer surveys increasingly show that consumers perceive few discernible differences between branded products and own-brands. As a result, a product's price becomes far more significant in determining purchase.

What are brand manufacturers to do? Can they afford to increase advertising to strengthen brand identity, and, even if they did, would consumers care? What is apparent is that the ability of brand manufacturers to bolster sagging profits by pushing up prices is no longer a viable option. Like the own-brand manufacturer, established brand manufacturers must seek to cut costs if they are to maintain profit margins on existing products.

There is another strategy, however, that they can pursue. This is to extend a brand to new products and use the brand image to promote them. Not only will this help raise revenue but it will also reduce the producer's reliance on a single product.

Virgin, for example, has long since ceased to mean a record store. Sir Richard Branson has stretched the brand to embrace an airline, trains, finance, soft drinks, mobile phones, holidays, bridal wear and cinemas – and this week, he launched Virgin Cars, an online car buying service. ... Coca-Cola has been around much longer than Virgin, its name has meant a soft drink for 114 years. But in the past few months it has also come to mean funky clothing after the US and UK launch of Coca-Cola Ware, a range of discreetly branded T-shirts, denims and drawstring pants aimed at the teens and 20s market.[1]

[1] *Financial Times* (26/5/2000)

Questions

1 How has the improvement in the quality of own-brands affected the price elasticity of demand for branded products? What implications does this have for the pricing strategy of brand manufacturers?

2 Do the brand manufacturers have any actual or potential cost advantages over own-brand manufacturers?

Where features are quite distinct, and where particular features or groups of features can be seen to appeal to a particular category of consumers, it might be useful for producers to divide the market into segments. Taking the example of cars again, the market could be divided into luxury cars, large, medium and small family cars, sports cars, multi-terrain vehicles, six-seater people carriers, etc. Each type of car occupies a distinct market segment, and within each segment the individual models are likely to be both horizontally and vertically differentiated from competitor models.

When consumer tastes change over time, or where existing models do not cater for every taste, a firm may be able to identify a new segment of the market – a **market niche**. Take a product like margarine. In recent years, various market niches have been developed: sunflower margarines, olive oil margarines, soya margarines, low-fat margarines, ultra-low-fat margarines, margarines with a percentage of butter, low-fat dairy spreads, etc. These have mixtures of various *characteristics*: taste, source of fat/oil (e.g. sunflower), type of fat (polyunsaturated/monounsaturated/saturated), percentage of fat, ease of spreading from the fridge, etc. It is the combination of these characteristics that distinguishes one brand from another.

Having identified the appropriate market niche for its product, the marketing division within the firm will then set about targeting the relevant consumer group(s) and developing an appropriate strategy for promoting the product. In the next section we will explore more closely those factors which are likely to influence a business's marketing strategy.

8.2 Marketing the product

What is marketing?

There is no single accepted definition of marketing. It is generally agreed, however, that marketing covers the following activities: establishing the strength of consumer demand in existing parts of the market, and potential demand in new niches; developing an attractive and distinct image for the product; informing potential consumers of various features of the product; fostering a desire by consumers for the product; and, in the light of all these, persuading consumers to buy the product.

Clearly, marketing must be seen within the overall goals of the firm. There would be little point in spending vast sums of money in promoting a product if it led to only a modest increase in sales and sales revenue.

Product/market strategy

definition
Market niche
A part of a market (or new market) that has not been filled by an existing brand or business.

Once the nature and strength of consumer demand (both current and potential) have been identified, the business will set about meeting and influencing this demand. In most cases it will be hoping to achieve a growth in sales. To do this, one of the first things the firm must decide is its *product/market strategy*. This will involve addressing two major questions:

- Should it focus on promoting its existing product, or should it develop new products?

● Should it focus on gaining a bigger share of its existing market, or should it seek to break into new markets?

In 1957 Igor Ansoff illustrated these choices in what he called a **growth vector matrix**. This is illustrated in Figure 8.1.

The four boxes show the possible combinations of answers to the above questions: Box A – *market penetration* (existing product, existing market); Box B – *product development* (new product, existing market); Box C – *market development* (existing product, new market); Box D – *diversification* (new product, new market).

Market penetration. In the market penetration strategy, the business will seek not only to retain current customers, but to expand its customer base with existing products in existing markets. Of the four strategies, this is generally the least risky: the business will be able to play to its product strengths and draw on its knowledge of the market. The business's marketing strategy will tend to focus upon aggressive product promotion and distribution. Such a strategy, however, is likely to lead to fierce competition from existing business rivals, especially if the overall market is not expanding and if the firm can therefore gain an increase in sales only by taking market share from its rivals.

Product development. Product development strategies will involve introducing new models and designs in existing markets. This may involve either vertical differentiation (for example, the introduction of an upgraded model) or horizontal differentiation (the introduction of a new style).

Market development. With a market development strategy the business will seek increased sales of current products by expanding into new markets. These may be in a different geographical location (for example, overseas), or new market segments. Alternatively, the strategy may involve finding new uses and applications for the product.

Diversification. A diversification strategy will involve the business expanding into new markets with new products. Of all the strategies, this is the most risky given the unknown factors that the business is likely to face.

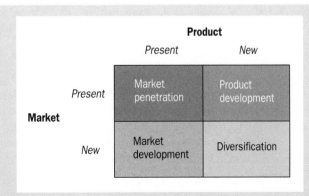

Figure 8.1
Growth vector components

Source: I. Ansoff, *Corporate Strategy* (McGraw-Hill, 1965); 'Strategies for diversification', *Harvard Business Review* (September–October 1957).

Once the product/market strategy has been decided upon, the business will then attempt to devise a suitable *marketing strategy*. This will involve looking at the marketing mix.

The marketing mix

In order to differentiate the firm's product from those of its rivals, there are four variables that can be adjusted. These are as follows:

- Product.
- Price.
- Place (distribution).
- Promotion.

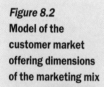

Marketing mix
The mix of product, price, place (distribution) and promotion that will determine a business's marketing strategy.

The particular combination of these variables, known as 'the four Ps', represents the business's **marketing mix,** and it is around a manipulation of them that the business will devise its marketing strategy.

Figure 8.2 illustrates the various considerations that might be taken into account when looking at product, price, place and promotion.

Product considerations. These involve issues such as quality and reliability, as well as branding, packaging and after-sales service.

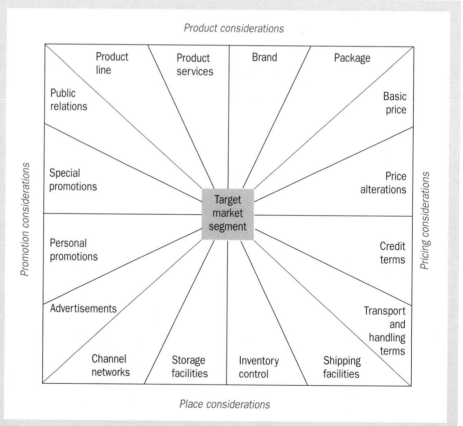

Figure 8.2
Model of the customer market offering dimensions of the marketing mix

Source: Based on H.A. Lipson and J.R. Darling, *Introduction to Marketing: an administrative approach* (John Wiley & Sons, Inc., 1971).

Pricing considerations. These involve not only the product's basic price in relation to those of competitors' products, but also opportunities for practising price discrimination (the practice of charging different prices in different parts of the market: Chapter 16), offering discounts to particular customers, and adjusting the terms of payment for the product.

Place considerations. These focus on the product's distribution network, and involve issues such as where the business's retail outlets should be located, what warehouse facilities the business might require, and how the product should be transported to the market.

Promotion considerations. These focus primarily upon the amount and type of advertising the business should use. In addition, promotion issues might also include selling techniques, special offers, trial discounts and various other public relations 'gimmicks'.

Every product is likely to have a distinct marketing *mix* of these four variables. Thus we cannot talk about an ideal value for one (e.g. the best price), without considering the other three. What is more, the most appropriate mix will vary from product to product and from market to market. If you wanted to sell a Rolls-Royce, you would be unlikely to sell any more by offering free promotional gifts or expanding the number of retail outlets. You might sell more Rolls-Royces, however, if you were to improve their specifications or offer more favourable methods of payment.

What the firm must seek to do is to estimate how sensitive demand is to the various aspects of marketing. The greater the sensitivity (elasticity) in each case, the more the firms should focus on that particular aspect. It must be careful, however, that changing one aspect of marketing does not conflict with another. For example, there would be little point in improving the product's quality, if at the same time promotional gimmicks were used which were associated in the minds of consumers with inferior, 'mass consumption' products.

Another consideration that must be taken into account is the stage in the product's life cycle. The most appropriate marketing mix for a new and hence unfamiliar product, and one which may be facing little in the way of competition, may well be totally inappropriate for a product that is long established and may be struggling against competitors to maintain its market share.

8.3 Advertising

One of the most important aspects of marketing is advertising. The major aim of advertising is to sell more products, and business spends a vast quantity of money on advertising to achieve this goal. By advertising, the business will not only be informing the consumer of the product's existence and availability, but also deliberately attempting to persuade and entice the consumer to purchase the good. In doing so, it will tend to stress the specific and unique qualities of this firm's product over those of its rivals. This will be discussed in more detail below.

Advertising facts and figures

Advertising and the state of the economy

Advertising expenditure, like other business expenditure, is subject to the cyclical movement of the national economy. Indeed, advertising is particularly sensitive to the ups and downs in the economy. In times of rising demand and growing profitability of business, expenditure on advertising tends to rise substantially. Conversely, when economic growth slows, and product demand falls, advertising budgets will be cut. Thus between 1984 and 1989, when real GDP increased by 22 per cent, advertising expenditure increased by 48 per cent in real terms, and in 1994, another year of strong economic growth, advertising expenditure increased by 8.5 per cent in real terms, to stand at a total of £10.2 billion. These figures compare with a 15 per cent fall in advertising expenditure in real terms between 1989 (the peak of the 1980s boom) and 1991 (a year of recession) (see Table 8.1). Since 1991, advertising expenditure in constant prices (i.e. after removing the effects of inflation) has increased every year (see Table 8.1).

Advertising media

When considering advertising expenditure by the main categories of media, we can see a long historical trend over which total press advertising has fallen from a high of 84.7 per cent in 1938 (although it reached a peak of nearly 90 per cent in 1953) to 58.3 per cent in 1999. By contrast, advertising on television (which only started in the UK in the mid-1950s) now accounts for over 32 per cent of total advertising expenditure. Other types of advertising – posters, radio and cinema – account for less than 10 per cent between them. Table 8.2 gives more details.

Product sectors

The distribution of advertising expenditure by product sectors shows that over

Table 8.1 Total advertising expenditure (including direct mail)

	At current prices (£bn)	At constant (1995) prices (£bn)	As a percentage of	
			Gross value added	Household expenditure
1985	5.05	7.96	1.57	2.45
1986	5.80	8.84	1.70	2.54
1987	6.57	9.61	1.75	2.61
1988	7.61	10.62	1.82	2.69
1989	8.64	11.18	1.88	2.78
1990	8.93	10.55	1.79	2.65
1991	8.53	9.53	1.64	2.38
1992	8.86	9.54	1.63	2.35
1993	9.14	9.68	1.60	2.29
1994	10.14	10.48	1.68	2.42
1995	11.03	11.03	1.74	2.51
1996	12.08	11.79	1.80	2.58
1997	13.33	12.62	1.87	2.68
1998	14.40	13.17	1.92	2.73
1999	15.31	13.80	1.95	2.73

Source: *Advertising Statistics Yearbook 2000* (NTC Publications Ltd).

Table 8.2 Total advertising expenditure excluding direct mail (% of total)

	1938	1958	1978	1988	1990	1992	1994	1995	1996	1997	1998	1999
National newspapers	25.4	18.9	15.8	15.5	14.9	14.6	14.7	14.5	14.1	14.1	14.3	14.4
Regional newspapers	27.1	24.1	25.8	21.8	21.6	20.7	20.6	19.8	19.3	19.1	18.8	18.6
Consumer magazines	15.3	13.3	8.5	6.8	6.8	5.9	5.5	5.4	5.5	5.6	5.6	5.4
Business and professional	11.9	10.0	10.1	9.9	9.9	9.4	8.6	9.1	9.5	9.5	9.5	9.5
Directories	0.0	1.2	2.7	5.2	6.2	6.6	6.5	6.5	6.5	6.3	6.1	6.2
Press production costs	5.1	5.2	5.1	5.0	5.2	5.4	5.2	5.2	5.2	4.9	4.9	4.8
Total press	84.7	72.7	68.0	64.2	64.7	62.6	61.1	60.4	60.1	59.6	59.2	58.3
Television	0.0	19.3	25.8	30.0	29.3	31.2	31.8	31.7	31.7	31.7	31.7	32.2
Outdoor and transport	8.5	6.0	3.6	3.4	3.5	3.6	3.9	4.2	4.4	4.7	4.8	4.8
Radio	3.4	0.4	1.9	2.0	2.1	2.0	2.7	3.0	3.2	3.4	3.6	3.8
Cinema	3.4	1.6	0.7	0.4	0.5	0.6	0.6	0.7	0.7	0.8	0.8	0.9
Total	100.0	100.0	100.0	100.0	100.0	100.0	100.0	100.0	100.0	100.0	100.0	100.0

Source: *Advertising Statistics Yearbook 2000* (NTC Publications Ltd).

27 per cent of advertising expenditure is for consumables: i.e. food, drink, cosmetics, etc. A further 21 per cent is for consumer durables such as household appliances and equipment. Both these sectors tend to be dominated by just a few firms producing each type of product. This type of market is known as 'oligopoly', which is Greek for 'few sellers'. Oligopolists often compete heavily in terms of product differentiation and advertising. (Oligopoly is examined in Chapter 12.)

Details of the allocation of advertising expenditure between the different product sectors are given in Table 8.3.

Table 8.3 Advertising expenditure by product sector

	1986	1987	1988	1989	1990	1991	1992
Retail	13.8	13.2	12.6	12.3	12.4	13.4	14.7
Industrial	8.7	8.2	7.7	8.7	7.4	6.5	6.7
Financial	10.2	11.0	11.4	10.9	10.5	9.1	7.8
Government	3.3	3.3	3.1	3.3	3.2	3.2	2.9
Services	8.5	8.7	9.5	10.0	10.8	11.2	11.3
Durables	20.5	20.2	20.2	20.2	19.6	19.6	19.4
Consumables	35.0	35.4	35.5	34.6	36.1	36.9	37.2
Total	100.0	100.0	100.0	100.0	100.0	100.0	100.0

	1993	1994	1995	1996	1997	1998	1999
Retail	16.6	16.5	17.9	18.2	18.0	18.9	19.0
Industrial	7.1	7.8	7.7	9.2	9.9	8.9	9.1
Financial	8.5	10.2	9.7	9.4	8.8	8.3	8.7
Government	2.4	2.2	2.5	2.3	2.4	2.3	2.9
Services	11.1	10.4	10.7	10.7	10.3	11.1	11.8
Durables	19.0	19.4	20.2	20.8	21.2	21.4	21.0
Consumables	35.4	33.5	31.2	29.3	29.3	29.1	27.4
Total	100.0	100.0	100.0	100.0	100.0	100.0	100.0

Source: *Advertising Statistics Yearbook 2000* (NTC Publications Ltd).

If we take the 25 companies with the highest advertising expenditure, most are within the consumables and consumer durables sectors. The same applies to the 25 most advertised brands (see Table 8.4).

The advertising/sales ratio

If we wished to consider the intensity of advertising within a given product sector, we could construct an **advertising/sales ratio**. This relates the total expenditure on advertising for a particular product to the total value of product sales. A selection of products and their advertising/sales ratios can be seen in Table 8.5.

Hair colourants have the highest advertising/sales ratio at 34.5 per cent. This tells us that 34.5 per cent of all earnings by firms producing hair colourants go on advertising their product. At the other extreme, hairdressers spend only 0.04 per cent of their sales revenue on advertising their product.

The wide variation in advertising intensity can be put down to two factors: market structure and product characteristics. As mentioned above, oligopolistic markets are likely to see high advertising outlays. But what types of product will be the most heavily advertised? There are three main categories here.

definition

Advertising/sales ratio
A ratio that reflects the intensity of advertising within a

Table 8.4 **The top advertisers and advertising brands: 2000**

(a) The top 25 advertisers

Rank 2000	Rank 1999	Advertiser	Total spending on advertising (£000)
1	1	Procter & Gamble	135,999
2	4	BT – British Telecom	113,596
3	2	COI – Central Office of Information	102,758
4	3	Renault UK	72,039
5	5	Vauxhall	63,106
6	6	L'Oréal Golden	60,643
7	8	Ford	58,410
8	10	Van der Bergh	54,968
9	21	DFS Northern Upholstery	51,579
10	13	Lever Brothers	50,603
11	–	British Sky Broadcasting	49,730
12	9	Kellogg's (GB)	48,098
13	12	Volkswagen	48,021
14	16	Peugeot	47,796
15	–	Vodafone	47,781
16	7	Mars	47,470
17	–	MBNA International Bank	46,310
18	11	Elida Fabergé	45,110
19	18	McDonald's	42,370
20	15	J Sainsbury	42,076
21	–	Toyota (GB)	40,607
22	–	BCA Book Club	39,968
23	25	Pedigree Masterfoods	39,346
24	19	BT Cellnet	38,394
25	22	British Gas	37,492

(b) The top 25 brands

Rank 2000	Brand	Total spending on advertising (£000)
1	McDonald's – Restaurants	42,351
2	Barclaycard – Credit Card	29,515
3	Sainsbury's – Product Range	28,909
4	B&Q – Product Range	28,670
5	Morgan Stanley Dean Witter – Credit	28,302
6	AOL – Internet access	27,860
7	PC World – Computer Superstore	27,612
8	Ondigital – Television System	27,437
9	Homebase – Product Range	25,696
10	BCA – Product Range	25,670
11	DFS – Product Range	24,773
12	One2One – Mobile Phone Network	24,007
13	Time Computers – Computer Dealer	23,040
14	Sky – Satellite Television	22,462
15	Tiny Computers – Computer Dealer	21,393
16	Currys – Product Range	19,709
17	Claims Direct – Legal Advisors	19,672
18	BT – Internet Services	19,661
19	Capital One – Credit Card	19,171
20	Egg – Visa Card	18,036
21	Littlewoods – Catalogue	17,952
22	Renault – Clio Range	17,937
23	Daily Telegraph Newspaper	17,761
24	Renault – Scenic Range	16,843
25	Asda – Product Range	16,663

Source: Data supplied by A C Nielsen MMS.

The first category is goods that represent a large outlay for consumers (e.g. furniture, electrical goods and other consumer durables). Consumers will not want to make a wrong decision: it would be an expensive mistake. They will thus tend to be cautious in their purchasing decision and will be likely to search for information before selecting a particular product. Advertisers will seek to provide information (but, of course, only information relating to their particular product).

The second category is new products which producers are attempting to establish on the market. The third category is goods, such as baby care products, which experience constant changes in their customer base.

Products with the lowest advertising/sales ratio will, by contrast, tend to be those goods whose specifications change very little, or where competition is minimal. For example, fish has a ratio of 0.37 per cent and bus travel 0.15 per cent.

Before we move on to consider the aims of advertising, we need to introduce one note of caution when considering the advertising/sales ratio. Many products with low ratios, such as motor cars with a ratio of 2.29 per cent and soft drinks

Table 8.5	Advertising/sales ratios: 1998 (ranked by advertising/sales ratio)
Product category	Advertising/sales ratio (%)
Hair colourants	34.53
Indigestion remedies	20.92
Shampoos	18.35
Soap, toilet	16.59
Cold treatments	8.40
Eye make-up	6.76
Coffee, total	4.94
Watches	4.34
Greenhouses and garden sheds	4.01
Magazines, total	3.74
Books	3.03
Motor cars, new	2.29
Soft drinks, carbonated	1.95
Cheese	1.67
Paints	1.33
Bottled water	1.22
Kitchen furniture	1.13
Fast food/take-away	1.02
Air travel	0.89
Curtains and blinds	0.41
Stockbrokers' fees	0.13
Personal stereos (incl. CD)	0.13
Men's underwear	0.08
Fresh vegetables	0.07
Hairdressing	0.04

Source: *Advertising Statistics Yearbook 2000* (NTC Publications Ltd).

with 1.95 per cent, are clearly products that are heavily advertised. What the advertising/sales ratio does not reveal is the *absolute* amount spent on advertising. Only 2.29 per cent of revenue from the sales of cars is spent on advertising. But this commands significantly more advertising space and time than the 34.53 per cent of revenue that is spent on hair colourants. Thus in 1998, £615 million was spent on advertising cars, compared with only £36 million on advertising hair colourants. A better way of measuring the intensity of advertising might be to consider the air time or column centimetres in the press that a product or sector buys.

The intended effects of advertising

We have argued that the main aim of advertising is to sell more of the product. But when we are told that brand X will make us more beautiful, enrich our lives, wash our clothes whiter, give us get-up-and-go, give us a new taste sensation or make us the envy of our friends, just what are the advertisers up to? Are they merely trying to persuade consumers to buy more?

In fact, there is a bit more to it than this. Advertisers are trying to do two things:

- Shift the product's demand curve to the right.
- Make it less price elastic.

This is illustrated in Figure 8.3. D_1 shows the original demand curve with price at P_1 and sales at Q_1. D_2 shows the curve after an advertising campaign. The rightward shift allows an increased quantity (Q_2) to be sold at the original price. If, at the same time, the demand is made less elastic, the firm can also raise its price and still experience an increase in sales. Thus in the diagram, price can be raised to P_2 and sales will be Q_3 – still substantially above Q_1. The total gain in revenue is shown by the shaded area.

How can advertising bring about this new demand curve?

Shifting the demand curve to the right. This will occur if the advertising brings the product to more people's attention and if it increases people's desire for the product.

Making the demand curve less elastic. This will occur if the advertising creates greater brand loyalty. People must be led to believe (rightly or wrongly) that competitors' brands are inferior. This will allow the firm to raise its price above that of its rivals with no significant fall in sales. There will only be a small substitution effect of this price rise because consumers have been led to believe that there are no close substitutes.

The more successful an advertising campaign is, the more it will shift the demand curve to the right and the more it will reduce the price elasticity of demand.

Assessing the effects of advertising

The supporters of advertising claim that not only is it an important freedom for firms, but also it provides specific benefits for the consumer. By contrast, critics of advertising suggest that it can impose serious costs on the consumer and on society in general. In this section we will assess the basis of this difference.

The arguments put forward in favour of advertising include the following:

Figure 8.3
The effect of advertising on the demand curve

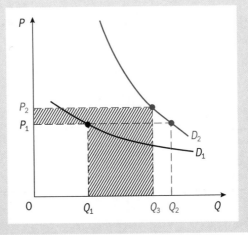

BOX 8.2

Advertising and the long run
Promoting quality[1]

If brand communications are an investment, we should expect them to produce long-term benefits. Indeed, we need to do so, for it is rare for advertising to pay for itself through increased profits in the short term. Recognising this fact should focus our attention on the role of advertising (in particular) as a tool for building a brand over time. If our advertising and other brand communications are successful, we will not merely attain short-term sales targets, relatively cost-effectively, but we will also be creating a brand that has momentum and staying power.[2]

It is relatively straightforward to measure the short-term impact of an advertising campaign; a simple before and after assessment of sales will normally give a good indication of the advertising's effectiveness. But what about the medium and longer-term effects of an advertising campaign? How will sales and profits be affected over, say, a five-year period?

The typical impact of advertising on a product's sales is shown in Figure (a). Assume that there is an advertising campaign for the product between time t_1 and t_2. There is a direct effect on sales while the advertising lasts and shortly afterwards. Sales rise from S_1 to S_2. After a while (beyond time t_3), the direct effect of the advertising begins to wear off, and wears off completely by time t_4. This is illustrated by the dashed line. But the higher level of sales declines much more slowly, given that many of the new customers continue to buy the product out of habit. Sales will eventually level off (at point t_5). It is likely, however, that sales will not return to the original level of S_1; there will be some new customers who will stick with the product over the long term. This long-term effect is shown by the increase in sales from S_1 to S_3.

But just what is this long-term effect? One way to explore the impact of advertising over the long run is to evaluate how advertising and profitability in general are linked.

In Figure (b) the argument is made that advertising shapes the key element of profitability, namely relative customer value. Customer value is determined by the product's perceived quality (and hence utility) relative to price. The more that advertising can enhance the perceived quality of a product, the more it will increase the product's profitability.

How this benefits the business over the longer term is best seen through examples.

Andrex has been using the 'puppy' to advertise its toilet tissues since 1972. It has, through this series of commercials, maintained a strong brand image and a per-

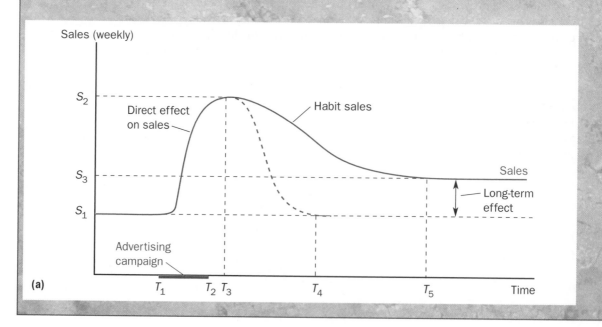

(a)

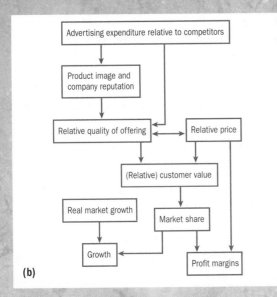

(b)

A study conducted in 1998 charted the profitability of 183 UK companies that all experienced recession in relation to their respective industries in the early 1990s. Of the 183 companies, 110 chose to cut their advertising expenditure, 53 chose to maintain it, and the remaining 20 increased it. The survey found that those which increased spending on advertising saw their profits suffer less than those which cut or maintained their advertising. They were nearly twice as profitable as the cutters and three times more profitable than those who maintained their advertising budgets.

The study also examined longer-term effects. It found that those which increased or maintained their advertising expenditure were the fastest to increase profits once the recession was over. Those that cut spending on advertising found that over the first two years of recovery their profits only increased by half the rate of those companies which had increased their advertising expenditure.

The Nescafé Gold Blend advertising campaign, 'the romance', offers a good example of how a premium-priced product managed to grow and capture market share during the recession of the early 1990s, when it might have been expected that consumers would be looking to save money and buy a cheaper alternative. During the recessionary years, Nescafé maintained its £5 million per year budget for the Gold Blend brand. It is estimated that the £5 million per year spent on advertising yielded extra long-term sales of some £50 million per year.

The message of this example and the others identified above is that advertising should seek to promote a product's quality. This is the key to long-term sales and profits. What is also apparent is that successful brands have advertising campaigns which have been consistent over time. A brand image of quality is not created overnight, but once it is established it can endure and yield profits over the longer term.

ception of high quality. As a result, its share of the market is consistently at about 30 per cent. It has also been able to charge a price premium of around 30 per cent for its product. It is estimated that the past 10 years' worth of advertising has cost approximately £54 million but has led to extra sales worth at least £300 million.

PG Tips is another brand that leads its respective market. The UK tea market has been dominated by PG Tips since 1958, when it became market leader, a position it still holds today. The 'chimp' adverts have established a clear brand image, enabling PG Tips to hold its ground in a highly competitive market and charge a price premium. (Blind tests have revealed that consumers cannot distinguish between any of the leading tea brands!) Market analysis shows that PG Tips has a price elasticity of demand of −0.4 compared with its nearest rival, Tetley, which has an elasticity of −1.4. It is estimated that over the past 20 years advertising the PG Tips brand has cost £100 million but generated in the region of £2 billion in extra sales.

An alternative way to illustrate the impact of advertising on longer-term profitability is to assess how companies approach advertising in a recession. What happens when advertising expenditure is cut, and how quickly does profitability return once the recession is over and advertising expenditure once again begins to rise?

Questions

1 How are long-run profits and advertising linked?

2 Why does quality 'win out' in the end?

[1] Adapted from *Admap* (July/August 1999)

[2] *ibid*, p. 17

- Advertising provides information to consumers on what products are available.
- Advertising may be necessary in order to introduce new products. Without it, firms would find it difficult to break into markets in which there were established brands. In other words, it is a means of breaking down barriers to the entry of new firms and products.
- It can aid product development by helping the firm emphasise the special features of its product.
- It may encourage price competition, if prices feature significantly in the advertisement.
- By increasing sales, it may allow the firm to gain economies of scale (see section 9.4), which in turn will help to keep prices down.

On the other side, the following arguments are put forward against advertising:

- Advertising is designed to persuade people to buy the product. Consumers do not have perfect information and may thus be misled into purchasing goods whose qualities may be inferior to those goods which are not advertised.
- Scarcity is defined as the excess of human wants over the means of fulfilling them. Advertising is used to *create* wants. It could thus be argued to increase scarcity.
- It increases materialism.
- Advertising costs money: it uses resources. These resources could be put to alternative uses in producing more goods.
- If there are no reductions in costs to be gained from producing on a larger scale, the costs of advertising will tend to raise the price paid by the consumer. Even if the firm has potential economies of scale, it may be prevented from expanding its sales by retaliatory advertising from its rivals.
- Advertising can create a barrier to the entry of new firms by promoting brand loyalty to *existing* firms' products. New firms may not be able to afford the large amount of advertising necessary to create a new brand image, whereas existing firms can spread the cost of their advertising over their already large number of sales. In other words, there are economies of scale in advertising which act as a barrier to entry.

  This barrier is strengthened if existing firms sell many brands each (for example, in the washing powder industry many brands are produced by just two firms). This makes it even harder for new firms successfully to introduce a new brand, since the consumer already has so many to choose from.

  The fewer the competitors, the less elastic will be the demand for each individual firm, and the higher, therefore, will be the profit-maximising price.
- People are constantly subjected to advertisements, whether on television, in magazines, on bill-boards, etc., and often find them annoying, tasteless or unsightly. Thus advertising imposes costs on society in general. These costs are external to the firm: that is, they do not cost the firm money, and hence are normally ignored by the firm.

The effects of advertising on competition, costs and prices are largely an empirical issue, and clearly these effects will differ from one product to another.

However, many of the arguments presented here involve judgements as to whether the effects are socially desirable or undesirable. Such judgements involve questions of taste and morality: things that are questions of opinion and cannot be resolved empirically.

SUMMARY

1a When firms seek to differentiate their product from those of their competitors, they can adjust one or more of four dimensions of the product: its technical standards, its quality, its design characteristics, and the level of customer service.

1b Products can be vertically and horizontally differentiated from one another. Vertical differentiation is where products are superior or inferior to others. Horizontal differentiation is where products differ, but are of a similar quality.

2a Marketing involves developing a product image and then persuading consumers to purchase it.

2b A business must choose an appropriate product/market strategy. Four such strategies can be identified: market penetration (focusing on existing product and market); product development (new product in existing market); market development (existing product in new markets); diversification (new products in new markets).

2c The marketing strategy of a product involves the manipulation of four key variables: product, price, place and promotion. Every product has a distinct marketing mix. The marketing mix is likely to change over the product's life cycle.

3a Advertising expenditure is cyclical, expanding and contracting with the upswings and downswings of the economy.

3b Most advertising expenditure goes on consumables and durable goods.

3c The advertising intensity within a given product sector can be estimated by considering the advertising/sales ratio. The advertising/sales ratio is likely to be higher the more oligopolistic the market, the more expensive the product, the newer the product, and the more the customer base for a product is subject to change.

3d The aims of advertising are to increase demand and make the product less price elastic.

3e Supporters of advertising claim that it: provides consumers with information; brings new products to consumers' attention; aids product development; encourages price competition; and generates economies of scale through increasing sales.

3f Critics of advertising claim that it: distorts consumption decisions; creates wants; pushes up prices; creates barriers to entry; and produces unwanted side effects, such as being unsightly.

REVIEW QUESTIONS

1 How might we account for the growth in non-price competition within the modern developed economy?

2 Distinguish between vertical and horizontal product differentiation. Give examples of goods that fall into each category.

3 Consider how the selection of the product/market strategy (market penetration, market development, product development and diversification) will influence the business's marketing mix. Identify which elements in the marketing mix would be most significant in developing a successful marketing strategy.

4 Why might the advertising/sales ratio be a poor guide to the degree of exposure of the consumer to advertisements for a particular category of product?

5 Imagine that 'Sunshine' sunflower margarine, a well-known brand, is advertised with the slogan, 'It helps you live longer' (the implication being that butter and margarines high in saturates shorten your life). What do you think would happen to the demand curve for a supermarket's *own* brand of sunflower margarine? Consider both the direction of shift and the effect on elasticity. Will the elasticity differ markedly at different prices? How will this affect the pricing policy and sales of the supermarket's own brand? Could the supermarket respond other than by adjusting the price of its margarine?

6 On balance, does advertising benefit (a) the consumer; (b) society in general?

C Background to supply

THE FT REPORTS...

THE FINANCIAL TIMES, 13 JUNE 2000

E-commerce offers a wider net for corporate buying

BUY ONLINE EXCHANGES WILL TRANSFORM PROCUREMENT

David Bowen and Emma Charlton

If you are looking for an e-commerce investment that is a little safer than a dotcom, may we suggest buying an office furniture manufacturer in eastern Europe or south-east Asia?

Why? The answer lies in the rash of recent announcements about "procurement hubs", "online exchanges" and "trading communities". Whatever they are called, they are all designed to transform the most unglamorous area: corporate purchasing, especially for non-production goods. And one of the most significant effects will be to bring new low-cost suppliers into hitherto exclusive supply chains. This will have negative consequences for manufacturers in more expensive countries.

Our study of electronic procurement in Europe reveals an extraordinary level of interest among purchasing executives in France, Germany and the UK. Although only 14 per cent of respondents to our survey have installed any sort of internet-based purchasing system, 59 per cent are considering one. Moreover, 75 per cent think the internet will be "very" or "extremely" important for procurement in three years' time.

In broad terms, the new procurement systems allow employees to order goods directly from their PCs, either through an intranet or a Website.

Orders are automatically channelled to suppliers, often via a hub that acts as a host for their online catalogues. The catalogues hold the company's negotiated prices, as well as authorisation rules that ensure the right people buy only what they are allowed to.

It is not difficult to see why there is so much enthusiasm for such systems. As Scott Walker, in charge of procurement of US forestry giant Weyerhaeuser, told us: "The returns on investment are so large they are unbelievable." Cost-savings come in administration and in the actual cost of the item: centrally negotiated discounts can be enforced across the whole organisation.

In Part C we turn to supply. In other words, we will focus on the amount that firms produce. In Parts D and E we shall see how the supply decision is affected by the environment in which a firm operates, and in particular by the amount of competition it faces. In this part of the book, however, we take a more general look at supply and its relationship to profit.

Profit is made by firms earning more from the sale of goods than the goods cost to produce. A firm's total profit ($T\Pi$) is thus the difference between its total sales revenue (TR) and its total costs of production (TC):

$$T\Pi = TR - TC$$

(Note that we use the Greek Π (pi) for 'profit'.)

Businesses can increase their profitability either by increasing their revenue (by selling more of their product or adjusting their price) or by reducing their costs of production. It would appear that many of the advances in e-commerce, as described in the *Financial Times* report, offer businesses the opportunity both to sell more and also to lower their costs of production – a clear incentive for any business to embrace the opportunities that e-commerce has to offer.

In order, then, to discover how a firm can maximise its profit, or even get a sufficient level of profit, we must first consider what determines costs and revenue. Chapter 9 examines costs. Chapter 10 considers revenue, and then puts costs and revenue together to examine profit.

> The profit motive is the driving force of a private enterprise economy. It is the desire for profits that motivates the continuation of production and the accumulation of capital.
>
> D. Fusfeld,
> *Economics* (1988),
> p. 27

key terms

Opportunity cost
Explicit and implicit costs
Law of diminishing (marginal) returns
Returns to scale (increasing, constant and decreasing)
Economies of scale (internal)
External economies of scale
Diseconomies of scale
Specialisation and division of labour
Fixed and variable factors
Fixed and variable costs
Total average and marginal costs and revenue
Price takers and price choosers
Profit maximisation
Normal profit
Supernormal profit

Costs of production

9.1 The meaning of costs

Opportunity cost

When measuring costs, economists always use the concept of opportunity cost. As we saw in Chapter 2, opportunity cost is the cost of any activity measured in terms of the *sacrifice* made in doing it: in other words, the cost measured in terms of the opportunities forgone. The more food you choose to buy, the less money you will have to spend on other goods. Thus the opportunity cost of an extra £5 spent in the supermarket is the £5 worth of other goods you will now have to go without. Similarly, the more food a nation produces, the less resources will there be for producing other goods. In other words, the production or consumption of one thing involves the sacrifice of alternatives. If a car manufacturer can produce 10 small saloon cars with the same amount of inputs as it takes to produce 6 large saloon cars, then the opportunity cost of producing 1 small car is 0.6 of a large car. If a taxi and car hire firm uses its cars as taxis, then the opportunity cost includes not only the cost of employing taxi drivers and buying fuel, but also the sacrifice of rental income from hiring its vehicles out.

Measuring a firm's opportunity costs

Just how do we measure a firm's opportunity cost? First we must discover what factors of production it has used. Then we must measure the sacrifice involved in using them. To do this it is necessary to put factors into two categories.

Factors not owned by the firm: explicit costs

The opportunity cost of those factors not already owned by the firm is simply the price that the firm has to pay for them. Thus if the firm uses £100 worth of electricity, the opportunity cost is £100. The firm has sacrificed £100 which could have been spent on something else.

These costs are called **explicit costs** because they involve direct payment of money by firms.

Factors already owned by the firm: implicit costs

When the firm already owns factors (e.g. machinery) it does not as a rule have to pay out money to use them. Their opportunity costs are thus **implicit costs**. They are equal to what the factors *could* earn for the firm in some alternative use, either within the firm or hired out to some other firm.

> **definition**
> **Opportunity cost**
> Cost measured in terms of the next best alternative forgone.

> **definition**
> **Explicit costs**
> The payments to outside suppliers of inputs.

> **definition**
> **Implicit costs**
> Costs which do not involve a direct payment of money to a third party, but which nevertheless involve a sacrifice of some alternative.

BOX 9.1

The fallacy of using historic costs
Or there's no point crying over spilt milk

'What's done is done.'

'Write it off to experience.'

'You might as well make the best of a bad job.'

These familiar sayings are all everyday examples of a simple fact of life: once something has happened, you cannot change the past. You have to take things as they are *now*.

If you fall over and break your leg, there is little point in saying, 'If only I hadn't done that I could have gone on that skiing holiday; I could have taken part in that race; I could have done so many other things (sigh).' Wishing things were different won't change history. You have to manage as well as you can *with* your broken leg.

It is the same for a firm. Once it has purchased some inputs, it is no good then wishing it hadn't. It has to accept that it has now got them, and make the best decisions about what to do with them.

Take a simple example. The local greengrocer in early December decides to buy 100 Christmas trees for £10 each. At the time of purchase this represents an opportunity cost of £10 each, since the £10 could have been spent on something else. The greengrocer estimates that there is enough local demand to sell all 100 trees at £15 each, thereby making a reasonable profit (even after allowing for handling costs).

But the estimate turns out to be wrong. On 23 December there are still 50 trees unsold. What should be done? At this stage the £10 that was paid for the trees is irrelevant. It is a historic cost. It cannot be recouped: the trees cannot be sold back to the wholesaler!

In fact the opportunity cost is now zero. It might even be negative if the greengrocer has to pay to dispose of any unsold trees. It might, therefore, be worth selling the trees at £10, £5 or even £1. Last thing on Christmas Eve it might even be worth giving away any unsold trees.

Question

Why is the correct price to charge (for the unsold trees) the one at which the price elasticity of demand equals –1? (Assume no disposal costs.)

Here are some examples of implicit costs:

- A firm owns some buildings. The opportunity cost of using them is the rent it could have received by letting them out to another firm.
- A firm draws £100 000 from the bank out of its savings in order to invest in new plant and equipment. The opportunity cost of this investment is not just the £100 000 (an explicit cost), but also the interest it thereby forgoes (an implicit cost).
- The owner of the firm could have earned £15 000 per annum by working for someone else. This £15 000 is the opportunity cost of the owner's time.

> **definition**
>
> **Historic costs**
> The original amount the firm paid for factors it now owns.

If there is no alternative use for a factor of production, as in the case of a machine designed to produce a specific product, and if it has no scrap value, the opportunity cost of using it is *zero*. In such a case, if the output from the machine is worth more than the cost of all the *other* inputs involved, the firm might as well use the machine rather than let it stand idle.

What the firm paid for the machine – its **historic cost** – is irrelevant. Not using the machine will not bring that money back. It has been spent. These are sometimes referred to as 'sunk costs'.

> **definition**
>
> **Replacement costs**
> What the firm would have to pay to replace factors it currently owns.

Likewise, the **replacement cost** is irrelevant. That should be taken into account only when the firm is considering replacing the machine.

9.2 Production in the short run

The cost of producing any level of output will depend on the amount of inputs used and the price that the firm must pay for them. Let us first focus on the quantity of inputs used.

The production function: using inputs to produce output

It is usual in economics to group inputs or 'factors of production' into three categories:

Labour. This category includes all working people of whatever type: electricians, secretaries, doctors, managers, unskilled workers, etc.

Land. This category includes not only land, but all natural resources.

Capital. This includes all manufactured inputs: plant, tools, machinery, etc. (Note that we are referring here to physical capital, not *financial* capital. In other words, we are not referring to the *money* used to finance investment.)

Some economists include a fourth category: **entrepreneurship**. In a capitalist economy, the owners of firms organise the other three factors, and take the risks of being in business. Entrepreneurship is this organisational activity.

The relationship between output and inputs can be shown in a **production function**. A production function shows the relationship between the amount of factors used and the amount of output generated per period of time (e.g. per day, per month or per year). It can be expressed in algebraic form as follows:

$$TPP = f(F_1, F_2, F_3 \ldots F_n)$$

This merely states that total output – or **total physical product** (*TPP*) – depends on (i.e. is a function of) the quantity of factors (F_1, F_2, etc.) that are used. Numerical examples of production functions are given in the following sections.

Firms are likely to employ many different types of workers, raw materials, tools and machines. In simple economic models, however, it is usually assumed that firms employ only one type of labour, one type of land and one type of capital. In more complex models, this assumption can be relaxed.

The simplest model of all assumes just two factors of production: for example, labour and capital, or labour and land. In the case of labour and capital, the production function would be in the form:

$$TPP = f(K, L)$$

where K and L are the quantities of capital and labour employed.

Although in the case of most firms these two-factor production functions are a considerable abstraction from reality, useful generalisations can nevertheless be made about the relationship between production and costs.

Before we go on, let us review what we have established so far:

- Firms will want to know what output they should produce to maximise profit, or at least to gain a particular level of profit.
- The level of profit depends on costs and revenue.
- Costs depend on the amount of inputs used.
- The amount of inputs used depends on the amount of output produced.

---

definition

Entrepreneurship
The initiating and organising of the production of new goods, or the introduction of new techniques, and the risk taking associated with it.

---

definition

Production function
The mathematical relationship between the output of a good and the inputs used to produce it. It shows how output will be affected by changes in the quantity of one or more of the inputs.

---

definition

Total physical product
The total output of a product per period of time that is obtained from a given amount of inputs.

- The relationship between output and inputs is shown in the production function.

Let us now examine the production function in more detail. To start with we must distinguish between short-run and long-run production functions.

Short-run and long-run changes in production

If a firm wants to increase production, it will take time to acquire a greater quantity of certain inputs. For example, a manufacturer can use more electricity by turning on switches, but it might take a long time to obtain and install more machines, and longer still to build a second or third factory.

If, then, the firm wants to increase output in a hurry, it will only be able to increase the quantity of certain inputs. It can use more raw materials, more fuel, more tools and possibly more labour (by hiring extra workers or offering overtime to its existing workforce). But it will have to make do with its existing buildings and most of its machinery.

The distinction we are making here is between **fixed factors** and **variable factors**. A *fixed* factor is an input that cannot be increased within a given time period (e.g. buildings). A *variable* factor is one that can.

The distinction between fixed and variable factors allows us to distinguish between the **short run** and the **long run**.

The short run is a time period during which at least one factor of production is fixed. In the short run, then, output can be increased only by using more variable factors. For example, if a shipping line wanted to carry more passengers in response to a rise in demand, it could accommodate more passengers on existing sailings if there was space. It could increase the number of sailings with its existing fleet, by hiring more crew and using more fuel. But in the short run it could not buy more ships: there would not be time for them to be built.

The long run is a time period long enough for all inputs to be varied. Given long enough, a firm can build a second factory and install new machines.

The actual length of the short run will differ from firm to firm. It is not a fixed period of time. Thus if it takes a farmer a year to obtain new land, buildings and equipment, the short run is any time period up to a year and the long run is any time period longer than a year. But if it takes a shipping company three years to obtain an extra ship, the short run is any period up to three years and the long run is any period longer than three years.

For the remainder of this chapter we will concentrate on *short-run* production and costs. We will look at the long run in the next chapter.

Production in the short run: the law of diminishing returns

Production in the short run is subject to *diminishing returns*. You may well have heard of 'the law of diminishing returns': it is one of the most famous of all 'laws' of economics. To illustrate how this law underlies short-run production, let us take the simplest possible case where there are just two factors: one fixed and one variable.

Take the case of a farm. Assume the fixed factor is land and the variable factor is labour. Since the land is fixed in supply, output per period of time can be increased only by increasing the number of workers employed. But imagine what would happen as more and more workers crowded on to a fixed

---

definition

Fixed factor
An input that cannot be increased in supply within a given time period.

definition

Variable factor
An input that *can* be increased in supply within a given time period.

definition

Short run
The period of time over which at least one factor is fixed.

definition

Long run
The period of time long enough for *all* factors to be varied.

BOX 9.2

Followers of fashion

For many products, style is a key component to their success. Two such products are clothing and cars. Both markets exhibit 'fashion price cycles'. In recent times, however, whereas seasonal price variations for clothes have become more pronounced, those for cars have diminished. The extract below, taken from *The Economist* of 23 December 1995, explores the factors affecting the price of fashion products, and in particular looks at the role of costs.

According to standard economic theory, Giorgio Armani, a world-famous Italian fashion designer, runs a simple business. His company combines inputs of labour (seamstresses), capital (dyeing and weaving machines) and raw materials (cloth) to make clothes with the best possible trade-off between cost and quality. He then calculates what the demand is for his designs, and estimates how many units he can make without marginal costs exceeding marginal revenues. He sells these at the market-clearing price, and earns just enough profit to compensate him for his investment of time and money.

The flaw of this stylised view is that it ignores the most important thing that designers such as Mr Armani sell: fashion itself.

The article observes that the prices of fashion-sensitive goods, such as clothing and cars, follow well-established 'fashion cycles'. At the beginning of the season, prices are set at a high level. Then, as the season progresses, prices gradually fall, only to rise again as new styles are introduced for the next season.

The main reason for this is uncertainty. When producers introduce a new line they do not know how successful it will be. To avoid selling it for less than is necessary, they initially set a high price, then lower it for lines that do not sell well. A good way to measure the importance of fashion, therefore, is to look at the variation in seasonal prices.

Over the past few decades, seasonal price variations for women's clothing have become more pronounced. However, prices in the American car market, which also tend to follow a 'fashion' cycle, have displayed the opposite trend.

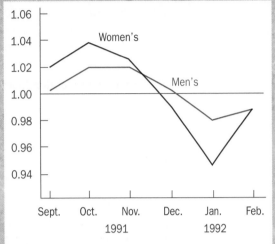

Clothing prices, relative to the average

Clothing prices, relative to the average

The explanation for these differences, claims the article, is to be found in changes in technology in the two industries.

Advances in the textile industry, such as the development of sophisticated electronic weaving, have made it cheaper for designers to revamp their lines each season. But in the car industry, it has become more costly to make radical style changes each year. Although new technology has made it easier to change the size and shape of a car's body, the costs of doing so as a share of the total production costs have actually risen.

Questions

1 If consumers are aware that unsuccessful lines of clothing will fall in price as the season progresses, why do they buy when prices are set high at the start of the season? What does this tell us about the shape of the demand curve for a given fashion product (a) at the start, and (b) at the end of the season?

2 What has happened to fixed costs as a proportion of total costs in the production of cars? How has this affected car design strategy?

3 How might we account for the changing magnitudes of the fashion price cycles of clothing and cars? What role do fixed costs play in the explanation?

area of land. The land cannot go on yielding more and more output indefinitely. After a point the additions to output from each extra worker will begin to diminish.

We can now state the **law of diminishing (marginal) returns**. It says that: *when increasing amounts of a variable factor are used with a given amount of a fixed factor, there will come a point when each extra unit of the variable factor will produce less extra output than the previous unit.*

The short-run production function: total product

Let us now see how the law of diminishing returns affects total output (*TPP*).

In the simple case of the farm with only two factors – namely, a fixed supply of land ($\bar{L}n$) and a variable supply of farm workers (Lb) – the production function would be:

$$TPP = f(\bar{L}n, Lb)$$

The production function can also be expressed in the form of a table or a graph. Table 9.1 and Figure 9.1 show a hypothetical production function for a farm producing wheat. They show how wheat output per year varies as extra workers are employed on a fixed amount of land.

With nobody working on the land, output will be zero (point *a*). As the first farm workers are taken on, wheat output initially rises more and more rapidly. The assumption behind this is that with only one or two workers efficiency is low, since the workers are spread too thinly. With more workers, however, they can work together – each, perhaps, doing some specialist job – and thus they can use the land more efficiently. In Figure 9.1, output rises more and more rapidly up to the employment of the third worker (point *b*).

After point *b*, however, diminishing marginal returns set in: output rises less and less rapidly, and the *TPP* curve correspondingly becomes less steeply sloped.

When point *d* is reached, wheat output is at a maximum: the land is yielding as much as it can. Any more workers employed after that are likely to get in each other's way. Thus beyond point *d*, output is likely to fall again: eight workers produce less than seven workers.

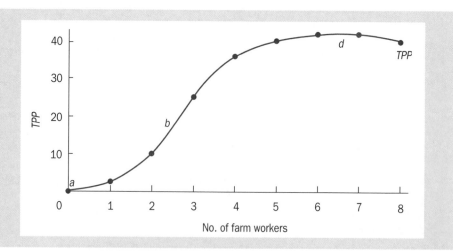

Figure 9.1
Wheat production per year from a particular farm

The short-run production function: average and marginal product

In addition to total physical product, two other important concepts are illustrated by a production function: namely, **average physical product** (**APP**) and **marginal physical product** (**MPP**).

Average physical product

This is output (*TPP*) per unit of the variable factor (*Qv*). In the case of the farm, it is the output of wheat per worker.

$$APP = TPP/Qv$$

Thus in Table 9.1, the average physical product of labour when four workers are employed is 36/4 = 9 tonnes.

Marginal physical product

This is the *extra* output (Δ*TPP*) produced by employing *one more* unit of the variable factor.

Thus in Table 9.1 the marginal physical product of the fourth worker is 12 tonnes. The reason is that, by employing the fourth worker, wheat output has risen from 24 tonnes to 36 tonnes: a rise of 12 tonnes.

In symbols, marginal physical product is given by:

$$MPP = \Delta TPP/\Delta Qv$$

Thus in our example:

$$MPP = 12/1 = 12$$

The reason why we divide the increase in output (Δ*TPP*) by the increase in the quantity of the variable factor (Δ*Qv*) is that some variable factors can be increased only in multiple units. For example, if we wanted to know the *MPP* of fertiliser and we found out how much extra wheat was produced by using an extra 20 kg bag, we would have to divide this output by 20 (Δ*Qv*) to find the *MPP* of *one* more kilogram.

Let us return to the data given in Table 9.1. From these figures we can derive figures for *APP* and *MPP*. This is done in Table 9.2.

Note that the figures for *MPP* are entered in the spaces between the other

---

definition
Average physical product (APP) Total output (*TPP*) per unit of the variable factor in question: *APP = TPP/Qv*.

definition
Marginal physical product (MPP) The extra output gained by the employment of one more unit of the variable factor: *MPP = ΔTPP/ΔQv*.

Table 9.1 **Wheat production per year from a particular farm**

Quantity of variable factor: number of workers employed (Lb)	Total physical product: output of wheat in tonnes per year (TPP)
0	0
1	3
2	10
3	24
4	36
5	40
6	42
7	42
8	40

	Number of workers (Lb)	TPP	APP (= TPP/Lb)	MPP (= ΔTPP/ΔLb)
Table 9.2	**Wheat production per year from a particular farm (tonnes)**			
a	0	0	–	
	1	3	3	3
	2	10	5	7
b	3	24	8	14
c	4	36	9	12
	5	40	8	4
	6	42	7	2
d	7	42	6	0
	8	40	5	-2

figures. The reason is that *MPP* can be seen as the *difference* in output *between* one level of input and another. Thus in the table the difference in output between five and six workers is 2 tonnes.

These figures can be represented graphically. Figure 9.2 shows *TPP* on one graph and *APP* and *MPP* on another.

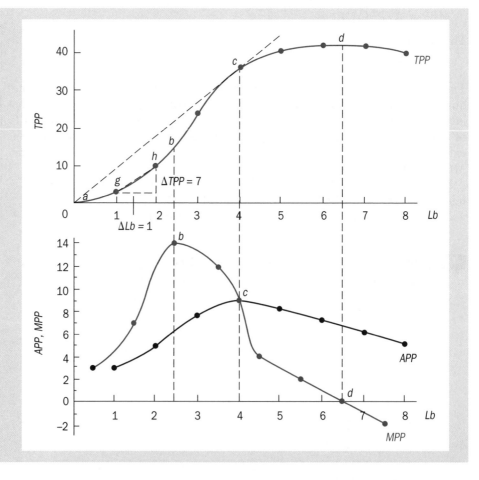

Figure 9.2
Wheat production per year (tonnes)

- The *MPP* between two points is equal to the slope of the *TPP* curve between those two points. For example, when the number of workers increases from 1 to 2 ($\Delta Lb = 1$), *TPP* rises from 3 to 10 tonnes ($\Delta TPP = 7$). *MPP* is thus 7: the slope of the line between points *g* and *h*.
- *MPP* rises at first: the slope of the *TPP* curve gets steeper.
- *MPP* reaches a maximum at point *b*. At that point the slope of the *TPP* curve is at its steepest.
- After point *b*, diminishing returns set in. *MPP* falls. *TPP* becomes less steep.
- *APP* rises at first. It continues rising as long as the addition to output from the last worker (*MPP*) is greater than the average output (*APP*): the *MPP* pulls the *APP* up. This continues beyond point *b*. Even though *MPP* is now falling, the *APP* goes on rising as long as the *MPP* is still above the *APP*. Thus *APP* goes on rising to point *c*.
- Beyond point *c*, *MPP* is below *APP*. New workers add less to output than the average. This pulls the average down: *APP* falls.
- As long as *MPP* is greater than zero, *TPP* will go on rising: new workers add to total output.
- At point *d*, *TPP* is at a maximum (its slope is zero). An additional worker will add nothing to output: *MPP* is zero.
- Beyond point *d*, *TPP* falls. *MPP* is negative.

9.3 Costs in the short run

Having looked at the background to costs in the short run, we now turn to examine short-run costs themselves. We will be examining how costs change as a firm changes the amount it produces. Obviously, if it is to decide how much to produce, it will need to know just what the level of costs will be at each level of output.

Costs and inputs

A firm's costs of production will depend on the factors of production it uses. The more factors it uses, the greater will its costs be. More precisely, this relationship depends on two elements.

The productivity of the factors. The greater their physical productivity, the smaller will be the quantity of them that is needed to produce a given level of output, and hence the lower will be the cost of that output. In other words, there is a direct link between *TPP*, *APP* and *MPP* and the costs of production.

The price of the factors. The higher their price, the higher will be the costs of production.

In the short run, some factors are fixed in supply. Their total costs, therefore, are fixed, in the sense that they do not vary with output. Rent on land is a **fixed cost**. It is the same whether the firm produces a lot or a little.

The cost of variable factors, however, does vary with output. The cost of raw materials is a **variable cost**. The more that is produced, the more raw materials are used and therefore the higher is their total cost.

> **definition**
>
> **Fixed costs**
> Total costs that do not vary with the amount of output produced.

> **definition**
>
> **Variable costs**
> Total costs that do vary with the amount of output produced.

Table 9.3	Total costs for firm X		
Output (Q)	TFC (£)	TVC (£)	TC (£)
0	12	0	12
1	12	10	22
2	12	16	28
3	12	21	33
4	12	28	40
5	12	40	52
6	12	60	72
7	12	91	103
.	.	.	.
.	.	.	.
.	.	.	.

Total cost

The **total cost** (*TC*) of production is the sum of the *total variable costs* (TVC) and the *total fixed costs* (TFC) of production.

$$TC = TVC + TFC$$

Consider Table 9.3 and Figure 9.3. They show the total costs for an imaginary firm for producing different levels of output (Q). Let us examine each of the three cost curves in turn.

Total fixed cost (TFC)

In our example, total fixed cost is assumed to be £12. Since this does not vary with output, it is shown by a horizontal straight line.

Total variable cost (TVC)

With a zero output, no variable factors will be used. Thus TVC = 0. The TVC curve, therefore, starts from the origin.

definition

Total cost(*TC*)
The sum of total fixed costs (*TFC*) and total variable costs(*TVC*): *TC* = *TFC* + *TVC*.

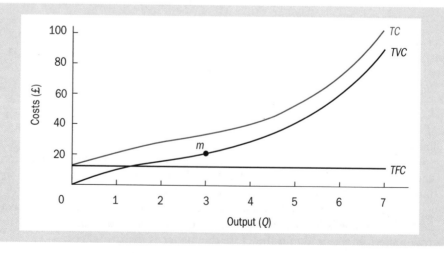

Figure 9.3
Total costs for firm X

The shape of the *TVC* curve follows from the law of diminishing returns. Initially, *before* diminishing returns set in, *TVC* rises less and less rapidly as more variable factors are added. For example, in the case of a factory with a fixed supply of machinery, initially as more workers are taken on the workers can do increasingly specialist tasks and make a fuller use of the capital equipment. This corresponds to the portion of the *TPP* curve that rises more rapidly (up to point *b* in Figure 9.1).

As output is increased beyond point *m* in Figure 9.3, diminishing returns set it. Given that extra workers (the extra variable factors) are producing less and less extra output, the extra units of output they do produce will be costing more and more in terms of wage costs. Thus *TVC* rises more and more rapidly. The *TVC* curve gets steeper. This corresponds to the portion of the *TPP* curve that rises less rapidly (between points *b* and *d* in Figure 9.1).

Total cost (TC)

Since $TC = TVC + TFC$, the *TC* curve is simply the *TVC* curve shifted vertically upwards by £12.

Average and marginal cost

Average cost *(AC)* is cost per unit of production.

$$AC = TC/Q$$

Thus if it costs a firm £2000 to produce 100 units of a product, the average cost would be £20 for each unit (£2000/100).

Like total cost, average cost can be divided into the two components, fixed and variable. In other words, average cost equals **average fixed cost** ($AFC = TFC/Q$) plus **average variable cost** ($AVC = TVC/Q$).

$$AC = AFC + AVC$$

Marginal cost *(MC)* is the *extra* cost of producing *one more unit*: that is, the rise in total cost per one unit rise in output.

$$MC = \frac{\Delta TC}{\Delta Q}$$

To explain this formula, consider the following two examples.

Example 1

A firm is currently producing 100 units of output at a cost of £2000. It now increases its output to 101 units and its total cost rises to £2030. It has thus incurred an extra cost of £30 to produce this 101st unit. Thus the marginal cost of the 101st unit is £30.

Putting these figures into the formula gives:

$$MC = \frac{\Delta TC}{\Delta Q} = \frac{(£2030 - £2000)}{101 - 100} = \frac{£30}{1}$$

But why do we have to divide the rise in cost by 1? In cases like this, where output can be increased one unit at a time, it is obviously not necessary to divide the rise in cost by the rise in output. Marginal cost is simply the rise in costs of

> **definition**
>
> **Average (total) cost (AC)**
> Total cost (fixed plus variable) per unit of output: $AC = TC/Q = AFC + AVC$.

> **definition**
>
> **Average fixed cost (AFC)**
> Total fixed cost per unit of output: $AFC = TFC/Q$.

> **definition**
>
> **Average variable cost (AVC)**
> Total variable cost per unit of output: $AVC = TVC/Q$.

> **definition**
>
> **Marginal cost (MC)**
> The cost of producing one more unit of output: $MC = \Delta TC/\Delta Q$.

Table 9.4	Costs						
Output (Q) (units)	TFC (£)	AFC (TFC/Q) (£)	TVC (£)	AVC (TVC/Q) (£)	TC (TFC + TVC) (£)	AC (TC/Q) (£)	MC (ΔTC/ΔQ) (£)
0	12	–	0	–	12	–	
1	12	12	10	10	22	22	10
2	12	6	16	8	28	14	6
3	12	4	21	7	33	11	5
4	12	3	28	7	40	10	7
5	12	2.4	40	8	52	10.4	12
6	12	2	60	10	72	12	20
7	12	1.7	91	13	103	14.7	31

producing that extra unit. There are cases, however, where output can only be increased in batches . . .

Example 2

Assume that a firm is currently producing 1 000 000 boxes of matches a month. It now increases output by 1000 boxes, (another batch): $\Delta Q = 1000$. As a result its total costs rise by £30: $\Delta TC = £30$. What is the cost of producing *one* more box of matches? It is:

$$MC = \frac{\Delta TC}{\Delta Q} = \frac{£30}{1000} = 3p$$

(Note that all marginal costs are variable, since, by definition, there can be no extra fixed costs as output rises.)

Given the *TFC*, *TVC* and *TC* for each output, it is possible to derive the *AFC*, *AVC*, *AC* and *MC* for each output using the above definitions. For example, using the data of Table 9.3, Table 9.4 can be constructed.

What will be the shapes of the *MC*, *AFC*, *AVC* and *AC* curves? These follow from the nature of the *MPP* and *APP* curves that we looked at in section 9.2. You will (hopefully) recall that the typical shapes of the *APP* and *MPP* curves are like those illustrated in Figure 9.4.

Figure 9.4
Average and marginal physical product

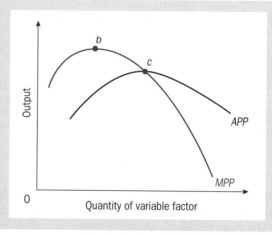

Figure 9.5
Average and marginal costs

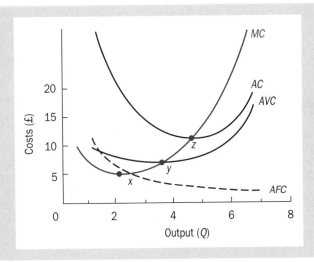

Marginal cost (MC)

The shape of the *MC* curve follows directly from the law of diminishing returns. Initially, in Figure 9.5, as more of the variable factor is used, extra units of output cost less than previous units. *MC* falls. This corresponds to the rising portion of the *MPP* curve in Figure 9.4 and the portion of the *TVC* curve in Figure 9.3 to the left of point *m*.

Beyond a certain level of output, diminishing returns set in. This is shown as point *x* in Figure 9.5 and corresponds to point *b* in Figure 9.4 (and point *m* in Figure 9.3). Thereafter *MC* rises as *MPP* falls. Additional units of output cost more and more to produce, since they require ever increasing amounts of the variable factor.

Average fixed cost (AFC)

This falls continuously as output rises, since *total* fixed costs are being spread over a greater and greater output.

Average variable cost (AVC)

The shape of the *AVC* curve depends on the shape of the *APP* curve. As the average product of workers rises (up to point *c* in Figure 9.4), the average labour cost per unit of output (the *AVC*) falls: up to point *y* in Figure 9.5. Thereafter, as *APP* falls, *AVC* must rise.

Average (total) cost (AC)

This is simply the vertical sum of the *AFC* and *AVC* curves. Note that, as *AFC* gets less, the gap between *AVC* and *AC* narrows.

The relationship between average cost and marginal cost

This is simply another illustration of the relationship that applies between *all* averages and marginals.

As long as new units of output cost less than the average, their production must pull the average cost down. That is, if *MC* is less than *AC*, *AC* must be falling. Likewise, if new units cost more than the average, their production must drive the average up. That is, if *MC* is greater than *AC*, *AC* must be rising. Therefore, the *MC* crosses the *AC* at its minimum point (point *z* in Figure 9.5).

Since all marginal costs are variable, the same relationship holds between *MC* and *AVC*.

BOX 9.3

Short-run cost curves in practice
When fixed factors are divisible

Are short-run cost curves always the shape depicted in this chapter? The answer is no. Sometimes, rather than being U-shaped, the *AVC* and *MC* curves are flat bottomed, like the curves in the diagram. Indeed, they may be constant (and equal to each other) over a *substantial* range of output.

The reason for this is that sometimes fixed factors may not have to be in full use all the time. Take the case of a firm with 100 identical machines, each one requiring one person to operate it. Although the firm cannot use *more* than the 100 machines, it could use fewer: in other words, some of the machines could be left idle. Assume, for example, that instead of using 100 machines, the firm uses only 90. It would need only 90 operatives and 90 per cent of the raw materials. Similarly, if it used only 20 machines, its total variable costs (labour and raw materials) would be only 20 per cent. What we are saying here is that *average* variable cost remains constant – and over a very large range of output: using anything from 1 machine to 100 machines.

The reason for the constant *AVC* (and *MC*) is that by varying the amount of fixed capital used, the *propor-*

tions used of capital, labour and raw materials can be kept the same and hence the average and marginal productivity of labour and raw materials will remain constant.

Only when all machines are in use (at Q_1) will *AVC* start to rise if output is further expanded. Machines may then have to work beyond their optimal speed, using more raw materials per unit of output (diminishing returns to raw materials), or workers may have to work longer shifts with higher (overtime) pay.

Questions

1 Assume that a firm has 5 identical machines, each operating independently. Assume that with all 5 machines operating normally, 100 units of output are produced each day. Below what level of output will *AVC* and *MC* rise?

2 Manufacturing firms like the one we have been describing will have other fixed costs (such as rent and managerial overheads). Does the existence of these affect the argument that the *AVC* curve will be flat bottomed?

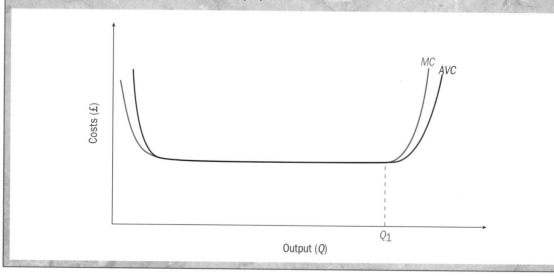

9.4 Production in the long run

In the long run *all* factors of production are variable. There is time for the firm to build a new factory (maybe in a different part of the country), to install new machines, to use different techniques of production, and in general to combine its inputs in whatever proportion and in whatever quantities it chooses.

In the long run, then, a firm will have to make a number of decisions: about the scale of its operations, the location of its operations and the techniques of production it will use. These decisions will affect the costs of production. It is important, therefore, to get them right.

The scale of production

If a firm were to double all of its inputs – something it could do in the long run – would it double its output? Or would output more than double or less than double? We can distinguish three possible situations.

Constant returns to scale. This is where a given percentage increase in inputs will lead to the same percentage increase in output.

Increasing returns to scale. This is where a given percentage increase in inputs will lead to a larger percentage increase in output.

Decreasing returns to scale. This is where a given percentage increase in inputs will lead to a smaller percentage increase in output.

Notice the terminology here. The words 'to scale' mean that *all* inputs increase by the same proportion. Decreasing returns to *scale* are therefore quite different from *diminishing* marginal returns (where only the *variable* factor increases). The differences between marginal returns to a variable factor and returns to scale are illustrated in Table 9.5.

In the short run, input 1 is assumed to be fixed in supply (at 3 units). Output can be increased only by using more of the variable factor (input 2). In the long run, however, both input 1 and input 2 are variable.

> **definition**
> **Economies of scale**
> When increasing the scale of production leads to a lower cost per unit of output.

Economies of scale

The concept of increasing returns to scale is closely linked to that of **economies of scale**. A firm experiences economies of scale if costs per unit of output fall as the scale of production increases. Clearly, if a firm is getting increasing returns

Table 9.5	Short-run and long-run increases in output					
	Short run			Long run		
Input 1	Input 2	Output		Input 1	Input 2	Output
3	1	25		1	1	15
3	2	45		2	2	35
3	3	60		3	3	60
3	4	70		4	4	90
3	5	75		5	5	125

to scale from its factors of production, then as it produces more, it will be using smaller and smaller amounts of factors per unit of output. Other things being equal, this means that it will be producing at a lower unit cost.

There are a number of reasons why firms are likely to experience economies of scale. Some are due to increasing returns to scale; some are not.

Specialisation and division of labour. In large-scale plants, workers can do more simple repetitive jobs. With this **specialisation and division of labour**, less training is needed; workers can become highly efficient in their particular job, especially with long production runs; there is less time lost in workers switching from one operation to another; supervision is easier. Workers and managers can be employed who have specific skills in specific areas.

Indivisibilities. Some inputs are of a minimum size. They are indivisible. The most obvious example is machinery. Take the case of a combine harvester. A small-scale farmer could not make full use of one. They only become economical to use, therefore, on farms above a certain size. The problem of **indivisibilities** is made worse when different machines, each of which is part of the production process, are of a different size. For example, if there are two types of machine, one producing 6 units a day, the other packaging 4 units a day, a minimum of 12 units per day will have to be produced, involving two production machines and three packaging machines, if all machines are to be fully utilised.

The 'container principle'. Any capital equipment that contains things (blast furnaces, oil tankers, pipes, vats, etc.) will tend to cost less per unit of output, the larger its size. The reason has to do with the relationship between a container's volume and its surface area. A container's cost will depend largely on the materials used to build it and hence roughly on its *surface area*. Its output will depend largely on its *volume*. Large containers have a bigger volume relative to surface area than do small containers. For example, a container with a bottom, top and four sides, with each side measuring 1 metre, has a volume of 1 cubic metre and a surface area of 6 square metres (6 surfaces of 1 square metre each). If each side were now to be doubled in length to 2 metres, the volume would be 8 cubic metres and the surface area 24 square metres (6 surfaces of 4 square metres each). Thus an eightfold increase in capacity has been gained at only a fourfold increase in the container's surface area, and hence an approximate fourfold increase in cost.

Greater efficiency of large machines. Large machines may be more efficient, in the sense that more output can be gained for a given amount of inputs. For example, only one worker may be required to operate a machine whether it be large or small. Also, a large machine may make more efficient use of raw materials.

By-products. With production on a large scale, there may be sufficient waste products to enable them to make some by-product.

Multistage production. A large factory may be able to take a product through several stages in its manufacture. This saves time and cost moving the semi-

---

definition

Specialisation and division of labour
Where production is broken down into a number of simpler, more specialised tasks, thus allowing workers to acquire a high degree of efficiency.

definition

Indivisibilities
The impossibility of dividing a factor into smaller units.

finished product from one firm or factory to another. For example, a large card-board-manufacturing firm may be able to convert trees or waste paper into cardboard and then into cardboard boxes in a continuous sequence.

All the above are examples of **plant economies of scale**. They are due to an individual factory or workplace or machine being large. There are other economies of scale that are associated with the firm being large – perhaps with many factories.

Organisational. With a large firm, individual plants can specialise in particular functions. There can also be centralised administration of the firms. Often, after a merger between two firms, savings can be made by **rationalising** their activities in this way.

Spreading overheads. Some expenditures are economic only when the *firm* is large, such as research and development: only a large firm can afford to set up a research laboratory. This is another example of indivisibilities, only this time at the level of the firm rather than the plant. The greater the firm's output, the more these **overhead costs** are spread.

Financial economies. Large firms may be able to obtain finance at lower interest rates than small firms. They may be able to obtain certain inputs cheaper by buying in bulk.

Economies of scope. Often a firm is large because it produces a range of products. This can result in each individual product being produced more cheaply than if it was produced in a single-product firm. The reason for these **economies of scope** is that various overhead costs and financial and organisational economies can be shared between the products. For example, a firm that produces a whole range of CD players, cassette recorders, amplifiers and tuners can benefit from shared marketing and distribution costs and the bulk purchase of electronic components.

Diseconomies of scale

When firms get beyond a certain size, costs per unit of output may start to increase. There are several reasons for such **diseconomies of scale**:

- Management problems of co-ordination may increase as the firm becomes larger and more complex, and as lines of communication get longer. There may be a lack of personal involvement by management.
- Workers may feel 'alienated' if their jobs are boring and repetitive, and if they feel an insignificantly small part of a large organisation. Poor motivation may lead to shoddy work.
- Industrial relations may deteriorate as a result of these factors and also as a result of the more complex interrelationships between different categories of worker.
- Production-line processes and the complex interdependencies of mass production can lead to great disruption if there are hold-ups in any one part of the firm.

Whether firms experience economies or diseconomies of scale will depend on the conditions applying in each individual firm.

---

definition

Plant economies of scale
Economies of scale that arise because of the large size of the factory.

definition

Rationalisation
The reorganising of production (often after a merger) so as to cut out waste and duplication and generally to reduce costs.

definition

Overheads
Costs arising from the general running of an organisation, and only indirectly related to the level of output.

definition

Diseconomies of scale
Where costs per unit of output increase as the scale of production increases.

definition

Economies of scope
When increasing the range of products produced by a firm reduces the cost of producing each one.

BOX 9.4

Liverpool: the home of the Beatles and computer games!
Industrial clusters and the location of business

Michael Porter, a world-famous writer on business strategy, argues that for a business to be truly competitive both domestically and internationally, it must be part of an 'industrial cluster'. An industrial cluster is a geographic area in which like businesses locate, along with those which supply to and distribute for the industry. This geographic proximity creates a 'tinderbox of innovation': it establishes a skills base, and helps businesses work together to create an alliance network, through which ideas, information and joint ventures flow.

Such clusters were crucial during the industrial revolution. They enabled countries such as Britain to establish world dominance in many areas of manufacturing. Iron and steel production and fabrication in Sheffield, and textiles in Nottingham, were both sites of intense industrial clustering.

The value of such clustering remains today. They may no longer be industrial, but the key competitive advantages they generate remain. For example, the dominance of high technology markets by US business is due in no small part to Silicon Valley, the location of a vibrant cluster of hi-tech business. Such hi-tech clusters exist in the UK: the area surrounding Cambridge is probably the most dominant. However, clusters can be found elsewhere.

The following extract, taken from *The Guardian* of 6 June 2000, reports on the cluster of computer games manufacturers appearing around Liverpool and the impact this is having on the region.

It is a strange statistic. It sounds spurious. But nevertheless it is trotted out locally with dead-pan confidence: 70 per cent of Japanese computer games are designed within a 30 mile radius of Liverpool. Forget the wit and the tourists on their Magical Mystery tours. Liverpudlians now live and work in an e-port, churning out computer games, software and web designers at a rate that suggests the creative juices of the north-west are flowing as fast as they have for decades.

And just a glance at the new structures of steel and glass springing up around the old docks says this city has got a serious case of the new economy.

'Obviously the new technology-related businesses are fast growing and a very important aspect of our regional economy' said John Burrows, the North-West Development Agency's business development director. The agency is now fielding 300 inquiries annually from large hi-tech firms, which are considering investing in the area and want to rationalise their European operations. Sony saw the potential early and bought Psygnosis back in 1993 to support its Playstation business. Now a queue has formed to follow Sony's Liverpool lead. The French games giant Infogames has also been

Location

In the long run, a firm can move to a different location. The location will affect the cost of production, since locations differ in terms of the availability and cost of raw materials, suitable land and power supply, the qualifications, skills and experience of the labour force, wage rates, transport and communications networks, the cost of local services, and banking and financial facilities. In short, locations differ in terms of the availability, suitability and cost of the factors of production.

Transport costs will be an important influence on a firm's location. Ideally, a firm will wish to be as near as possible to both its raw materials and the market for its finished product. When market and raw materials are in different locations, the firm will minimise its transport costs by locating somewhere between the two. In general, if the raw materials are more expensive to transport than the finished product, the firm should locate as near as possible to the

drawn in to the hub of creativity and bought another gaming group, Ocean. Another of Europe's largest game developers, Rage Software, is also based on Merseyside – but has remained independent, with a full listing on the London stock market.

The growth of hi-tech business has helped to offset the demise of manufacturing and port industries which drove unemployment in the region to almost 20 per cent in the depths of the recession in the early 1990s. The latest figure is 9.5 per cent. It has also lifted house prices, boosted new restaurants and bars – and left salesmen at glitzy car showrooms rubbing their hands with glee. Almost £1 billion in investment finance from the European Development Fund has contributed to Liverpool's economic revival and its increasing attractiveness to business.

While the north-west doesn't have London or Heathrow on its doorstop to lure the likes of Microsoft, the half-hour drive to Manchester's international airport is almost adequate, says Burrows. The argument of a better quality of life goes a long way with many of the companies which have decided to locate in Liverpool and the surrounding area. Housing is cheaper than in the south-east, commuting is easy and there is a thriving cultural scene. And of course Liverpool is one of the few British cities apart from London with what amounts to a world brand.

Amaze, an Internet company that emerged from Liverpool University and which now employs 125 people, does not consider its location a disadvantage. Stuart Melhuish, chief executive of the web design and software company, admits Liverpool can be a difficult location for long-distance travel. But he adds: 'We are in the e-business, location isn't necessarily an issue. The reality is with our client handling skills we can work with customers remotely.' It boasts clients such as pharmaceuticals group Warner Lambert, Saatchi and Saatchi and Volkswagen. Melhuish said a lot of Amaze's employees were graduates – and the company relied on the surrounding universities, which he listed as a major plus for the region. 'Creativity is definitely one of the region's strengths,' he said. 'Finding a way to ensure that talent pool stays in the north-west is the difficult thing.'

Questions

1 The principal economic advantage of an industrial cluster is that it gains external economies of scale. Identify the main ways in which such economies of scale might be realised.
2 What adverse impacts might industrial clustering have on Liverpool?

raw materials. This will normally apply to firms whose raw materials are heavier or more bulky than the finished product. Thus heavy industry, which uses large quantities of coal and various ores, tends to be concentrated near the coal fields or near the ports. If, on the other hand, the finished product is more expensive to transport (e.g. bread or beer), the firm will probably be located as near as possible to its market.

When raw materials or markets are in many different locations, transport costs will be minimised at the 'centre of gravity'. This location will be nearer to those raw materials and markets whose transport costs are greater per mile.

The size of the whole industry

As an *industry* grows in size, this can lead to **external economies of scale** for its member firms. This is where a firm, whatever its own individual size, benefits

> **definition**
> **External economies of scale**
> Where a firm's costs per unit of output decrease as the size of the whole *industry* grows.

from the *whole industry* being large. For example, the firm may benefit from having access to specialist raw material or component suppliers, labour with specific skills, firms that specialise in marketing the finished product, and banks and other financial institutions with experience of the industry's requirements. What we are referring to here is the **industry's infrastructure**: the facilities, support services, skills and experience that can be shared by its members.

The member firms of a particular industry might experience **external diseconomies of scale**. For example, as an industry grows larger, this may create a growing shortage of specific raw materials or skilled labour. This will push up their prices, and hence the firms' costs.

The optimum combination of factors

In the long run, all factors can be varied. The firm can thus choose what techniques of production to use: what design of factory to build, what types of machine to buy, how to organise the factory, and whether to use highly automated processes or more labour-intensive techniques. It must be very careful in making these decisions. Once it has built its factory and installed the machinery, these then become fixed factors of production, maybe for many years: the subsequent 'short-run' time period may in practice last a very long time!

For any given scale, how should the firm decide what technique to use? How should it decide the optimum 'mix' of factors of production?

The profit-maximising firm will obviously want to use the least costly combination of factors to produce any given output. It will therefore substitute factors, one for another, if by so doing it can reduce the cost of a given output. What, then, is the optimum combination of factors?

The simple two-factor case

Take first the simplest case where a firm uses just two factors: labour (L) and capital (K). The least-cost combination of the two will be where:

$$\frac{MPP_L}{P_L} = \frac{MPP_K}{P_K}$$

In other words, it is where the extra product (MPP) from the last pound spent on each factor is equal. But why should this be so? The easiest way to answer this is to consider what would happen if they were not equal.

If they were not equal, it would be possible to reduce cost per unit of output, by using a different combination of labour and capital. For example, if:

$$\frac{MPP_L}{P_L} > \frac{MPP_K}{P_K}$$

more labour should be used relative to capital, since the firm is getting a greater physical return for its money from extra workers than from extra capital. As more labour is used per unit of capital, however, diminishing returns to labour set in. Thus MPP_L will fall. Likewise, as less capital is used per unit of labour, the MPP_K will rise. This will continue until:

$$\frac{MPP_L}{P_L} = \frac{MPP_K}{P_K}$$

At this point, the firm will stop substituting labour for capital.

---

definition

Industry's infrastructure
The network of supply agents, communications, skills, training facilities, distribution channels, specialised financial services, etc. that support a particular industry.

definition

External diseconomies of scale
Where a firm's costs per unit of output increase as the size of the whole industry increases.

Since no further gain can be made by substituting one factor for another, this combination of factors or 'choice of techniques' can be said to be the most efficient. It is the least-cost way of combining factors for any given output. Efficiency in this sense of using the optimum factor proportions is known as **technical** or **productive efficiency**.

The multifactor case

Where a firm uses many different factors, the least-cost combination of factors will be where:

$$\frac{MPP_a}{P_a} = \frac{MPP_b}{P_b} = \frac{MPP_c}{P_c} \cdots = \frac{MPP_n}{P_n}$$

where a … n are different factors of production.

The reasons are the same as in the two-factor case. If any inequality exists between the MPP/P ratios, a firm will be able to reduce its costs by using more of those factors with a high MPP/P ratio and less of those with a low MPP/P ratio until the ratios all become equal.

A major problem for a firm in choosing the least-cost technique is in predicting future factor price changes.

If the price of a factor were to change, the MPP/P ratios would cease to be equal. The firm, to minimise costs, would then like to alter its factor combinations until the MPP/P ratios once more become equal. The trouble is that, once it has committed itself to a particular technique, it may be several years before it can switch to an alternative one. Thus if a firm invests in labour-intensive methods of production and is then faced with an unexpected wage rise, it may regret not having chosen a more capital-intensive technique.

Postscript: decision making in different time periods

We have distinguished between the short run and the long run. Let us introduce two more time periods to complete the picture. The complete list then reads as follows.

Very short run (immediate run). All factors are fixed. Output is fixed. The supply curve is vertical. On a day-to-day basis, a firm may not be able to vary output at all. For example, a flower seller, once the day's flowers have been purchased from the wholesaler, cannot alter the amount of flowers available for sale on that day. In the very short run, all that may remain for a producer to do is to sell an already-produced good.

Short run. At least one factor is fixed in supply. More can be produced, but the firm will come up against the law of diminishing returns as it tries to do so.

Long run. All factors are variable. The firm may experience constant, increasing or decreasing returns to scale. But although all factors can be increased or decreased, they are of a fixed *quality*.

Very long run. All factors are variable, *and* their quality and hence productivity can change. Labour productivity can increase as a result of education, training,

> **definition**
>
> **Technical or productive efficiency**
> The least-cost combination of factors for a given output.

experience and social factors. The productivity of capital can increase as a result of new inventions (new discoveries) and innovation (putting inventions into practice).

Improvements in factor quality will increase the output they produce: *TPP*, *APP* and *MPP* will rise. These curves will shift vertically upward.

Just how long the 'very long run' is will vary from firm to firm. It will depend on how long it takes to develop new techniques, new skills or new work practices.

It is important to realise that decisions *for* all four time periods can be made *at* the same time. Firms do not make short-run decisions *in* the short run and long-run decisions *in* the long run. They can make both short-run and long-run decisions today. For example, assume that a firm experiences an increase in consumer demand and anticipates that it will continue into the foreseeable future. It thus wants to increase output. Consequently, it makes the following four decisions *today*:

- *(Very short run)* It accepts that for a few days it will not be able to increase output. It informs its customers that they will have to wait. It may temporarily raise prices to choke off some of the demand.
- *(Short run)* It negotiates with labour to introduce overtime working as soon as possible, to tide it over the next few weeks. It orders extra raw materials from its suppliers. It launches a recruitment drive for new labour so as to avoid paying overtime longer than is necessary.
- *(Long run)* It starts proceedings to build a new factory. The first step may be to discuss requirements with a firm of consultants.
- *(Very long run)* It institutes a programme of research and development and/or training in an attempt to increase productivity.

Although we distinguish these four time periods, it is the middle two we are primarily concerned with. The reason for this is that there is very little that the firm can do in the *very* short run. And in the *very* long run, although the firm will obviously want to increase the productivity of its inputs, it will not be in a position to make precise calculations of how to do it. It will not know precisely what inventions will be made, or just what will be the results of its own research and development.

9.5 Costs in the long run

When it comes to making long-run production decisions, the firm has much more flexibility. It does not have to operate with plant and equipment of a fixed size. It can expand the whole scale of its operations. All its inputs are variable, and thus the law of diminishing returns does not apply. The firm may experience economies of scale or diseconomies of scale, or its average costs may stay constant as it expands the scale of its operations.

Since there are no fixed factors in the long run, there are no long-run fixed costs. For example, the firm may rent more land in order to expand its operations. Its rent bill therefore goes up as it expands its output.

All costs, then, in the long run are variable costs.

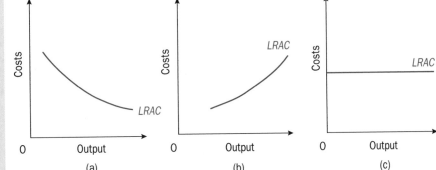

Figure 9.6
Alternative long-run average cost curves
(a) Economies of scale
(b) Diseconomies of sale
(c) Constant costs

Long-run average costs

Long-run average cost *(LRAC)* curves can take various shapes.

If the firm experiences economies of scale, its *LRAC* curve will fall as the scale of production increases (diagram (a) in Figure 9.6). This, after all, is how we define economies of scale: namely, a reduction in average costs as the scale of production increases. If diseconomies of scale predominate, the *LRAC* curve will rise (diagram (b)). Alternatively, if the firm experiences neither economies nor diseconomies of scale, the *LRAC* curve will be horizontal (diagram (c)).

It is often assumed that, as a firm expands, it will initially experience economies of scale and thus face a downward-sloping *LRAC* curve. After a point, however, all such economies will have been achieved and thus the curve will flatten out. Then (possibly after a period of constant *LRAC*), the firm will get so large that it will start experiencing diseconomies of scale and thus a rising *LRAC*. At this stage, production and financial economies begin to be offset by the managerial problems of running a giant organisation.

The effect of this is to give a L-shaped or saucer shaped curve, as in Figure 9.7.

> **definition**
>
> **Long-run average cost (*LRAC*) curve**
> A curve that shows how average cost varies with output on the assumption that *all* factors are variable. (It is assumed that the least-cost method of production will be chosen for each output.)

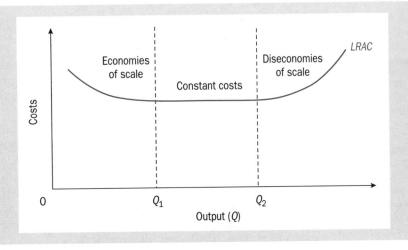

Figure 9.7
A typical long-run average cost curve

Assumptions behind the long-run average cost curve

We make three key assumptions when constructing long-run average cost curves.

Factor prices are given. At each output, a firm will be faced with a given set of factor prices. If factor prices *change*, therefore, both short- and long-run cost curves will shift. Thus an increase in wages would shift the curves upwards.

It may be the case, however, that factor prices will be different at *different* levels of output. For example, one of the economies of scale that many firms enjoy is the ability to obtain bulk discount on raw materials and other supplies. In such cases the curve does *not* shift. The different factor prices are merely experienced at different points along the curve, and are reflected in the shape of the curve. Factor prices are still given for any particular level of output.

The state of technology and factor quality are given. These are assumed to change only in the *very* long run. If a firm gains economies of scale, it is because it is being able to exploit *existing* technologies and make better use of the existing availability of factors of production.

Firms choose the least-cost combination of factors for each output. The assumption here is that firms operate efficiently: that they choose the cheapest possible way of producing any level of output. In other words, at every point along the LRAC curve the firm will adhere to the cost-minimising formula:

$$\frac{MPP_a}{P_a} = \frac{MPP_b}{P_b} = \frac{MPP_c}{P_c} \cdots = \frac{MPP_n}{P_n}$$

where a ... n are the various factors that the firm uses.

If the firm did not choose the optimum factor combination, it would be producing at a point above the LRAC curve.

Long-run marginal costs

The relationship between long-run average and **long-run marginal cost** curves is just like that between any other averages and marginals. Diagrams (a) to (c) in Figure 9.8 show this relationship in the three cases we looked at in Figure 9.6.

If there are economies of scale (diagram (a)), additional units of output will add less to costs than the average. The *LRMC* curve must be below the *LRAC* curve and thus pulling the average down as output increases. If there are diseconomies of scale (diagram (b)), additional units of output will cost more than the average. The *LRMC* curve must be above the *LRAC* curve, pulling it up. If there are no economies or diseconomies of scale, so that the *LRAC* curve is horizontal, any additional units of output will cost the same as the average and thus leave the average unaffected (diagram (c)).

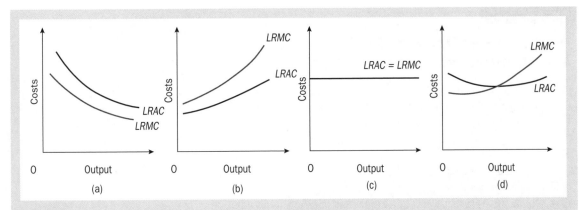

Figure 9.8
The relationship between long-run average and marginal costs
(a) Economies of scale (b) Diseconomies of scale (c) Constant costs (d) Initial economies of scale, then diseconomies of scale

The relationship between long-run and short-run average cost curves

Take the case of a firm which has just one factory and faces a short-run average cost curve illustrated by $SRAC_1$ in Figure 9.9.

In the long run, it can build more factories. If it thereby experiences economies of scale (due, say, to savings on administration), each successive factory will allow it to produce with a new lower $SRAC$ curve. Thus with two factories it will face curve $SRAC_2$; with three factories curve $SRAC_3$, and so on. Each $SRAC$ curve corresponds to a particular amount of the factor that is fixed in the short run: in this case, the factory.

From this succession of short-run average cost curves we can construct a long-run average cost curve. This is shown in Figures 9.10 and 9.11.

If a firm could only build factories of a particular size, the $LRAC$ curve would be 'wavy' as in Figure 9.10. Up to output Q_1, it would be cheaper to use just one factory, but for an output between Q_1 and Q_2 it would be cheaper to use

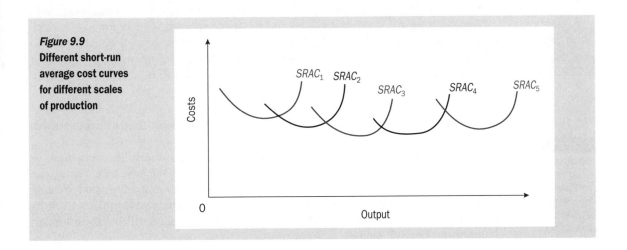

Figure 9.9
Different short-run average cost curves for different scales of production

BOX 9.5

Minimum efficient scale
The extent of economies of scale in practice

One of the most important studies of economies of scale was made in the late 1980s by C.F. Pratten.[1] Pratten found strong evidence that many firms, especially in manufacturing, experienced substantial economies of scale.

In a few cases long-run average costs fell continuously as output increased. For most firms, however, they fell up to a certain level of output and then remained constant.

There are two methods commonly used to measure the extent of economies of scale. The first involves identifying a *minimum efficient scale* (*MES*). The *MES* is the size beyond which no significant additional economies of scale can be achieved: in other words, the point where the *LRAC* curve flattens off. In Pratten's studies he defined this level as the minimum scale above which any possible doubling in scale would reduce average costs by less than 5 per cent (i.e. virtually the bottom of the *LRAC* curve). In the diagram *MES* is shown at point *a*.

The *MES* can be expressed in terms either of an individual factory or of the whole firm. Where it refers to the minimum efficient scale of an individual factory, the *MES* is known as the *minimum efficient plant size* (*MEPS*).

The *MES* can then be expressed as a percentage of the total size of the market or of total domestic production. The table shows *MES* for various plants and firms. The first column shows *MES* as a percentage of total UK production. The second column shows *MES* as a percentage of total EU production.

Expressing *MES* as a percentage of total output gives an indication of how competitive the industry could be. In some industries (such as shoes and tufted carpets), economies of scale were exhausted (i.e. *MES*

was reached) with plants or firms that were still small relative to total UK production and even smaller relative to total EU production. In such industries there would be room for many firms and thus scope for considerable competition.

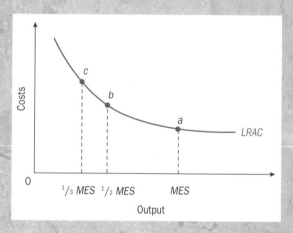

In other industries, however, even if a single plant or firm were large enough to produce the whole output of the industry in the UK, it would still not be large enough to experience the full potential economies of scale: the *MES* is greater than 100 per cent. Examples include factories producing cellulose fibres, and car manufacturers. In such industries there is no possibility of competition. In fact, as long as the *MES* exceeds 50 per cent there will not be room for more than one firm large enough to gain full economies of scale. In this case the industry is said to be a *natural monopoly*. As we shall see in the next few chapters, when competition is lacking consumers may suffer by firms charging prices considerably above costs.

---

two factories. Likewise between Q_2 and Q_3 it would be cheaper to use three factories.

It is usual, however, to show the *LRAC* curve as a smooth line tangential to the *SRAC* curves (as in Figure 9.11). This is known as the **envelope curve**. The assumption here is that the short-run fixed factor(s) can be varied by *any* amount in the long run. For example, factories of any size could be built or existing ones could be expanded. The result is that there will be an unlimited number of *SRAC* curves.

definition

Envelope curve
A long-run average cost curve drawn as the tangency points of a series of short-run average cost curves.

Product	MES as % of production		% additional cost at 1\2 MES
	UK	EU	
Individual plants			
Cellulose fibres	125	16	3
Rolled aluminium semi-manufactures	114	15	15
Refrigerators	85	11	4
Steel	72	10	6
Electric motors	60	6	15
TV sets	40	9	9
Cigarettes	24	6	1.4
Ball-bearings	20	2	6
Beer	12	3	7
Nylon	4	1	12
Bricks	1	0.2	25
Tufted carpets	0.3	0.04	10
Shoes	0.3	0.03	1
Firms			
Cars	200	20	9
Lorries	104	21	7.5
Mainframe computers	> 100	n.a.	5
Aircraft	100	n.a.	5
Tractors	98	19	6

Sources: C.F. Pratten (1988); M. Emerson, *The Economics of 1992* (Oxford University Press, 1988).

of *MES*. The normal fractions used are ½ or ⅓ *MES*. This is illustrated in the diagram. Point *b* corresponds to ½ *MES*; point *c* to ⅓ *MES*. The greater the percentage by which *LRAC* at point *b* or *c* is higher than at point *a*, the greater will be the economies of scale to be gained by producing at *MES* rather than at ½ *MES* or ⅓ *MES*. For example, in the table there are greater economies of scale to be gained from moving from ½ *MES* to *MES* in the production of electric motors than in cigarettes.

The main purpose of Pratten's study was to determine whether the creation of a large internal EU market with no trade barriers by the end of 1992 would significantly reduce costs and increase competition. The table suggests that in all cases, other things being equal, the EU market is large enough for firms to gain the full economies of scale *and* for there to be enough firms for the market to be competitive.

Questions

1 Why might a firm operating with one plant achieve *MEPS* and yet not be large enough to achieve *MES*? (Clue: are all economies of scale achieved at plant level?)

2 Why might a firm producing bricks have an *MES* which is only 0.2 per cent of total EU production and yet face little effective competition from other EU countries?

[1] C.F. Pratten, 'A survey of the economies of scale', in *Research on the 'Costs of Non-Europe'*, vol. 2 (Office for Official Publications of the European Communities, 1988).

The second way of measuring the extent of economies of scale is to see how much costs would increase if production were reduced to a certain fraction

Long-run cost curves in practice

Firms do experience economies of scale. Some experience continuously falling *LRAC* curves, as in Figure 9.6(a). Others experience economies of scale up to a certain output and thereafter constant returns to scale.

Evidence is inconclusive on the question of diseconomies of scale. There is little evidence to suggest the existence of *technical* diseconomies, but the possibility of diseconomies due to managerial and industrial relations problems cannot be ruled out.

Figure 9.10
Constructing long-run average cost curves from short-run average cost curves: factories of fixed size

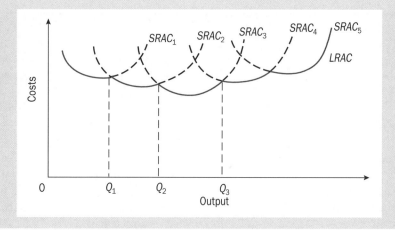

Figure 9.11
Constructing long-run average cost curves from short-run average cost curves: choice of factory size

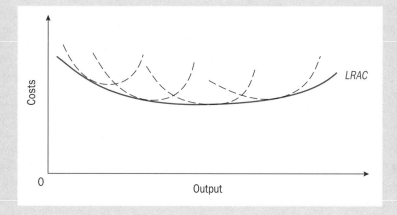

SUMMARY

1a When measuring costs of production, we should be careful to use the concept of opportunity cost.

1b In the case of factors not owned by the firm, the opportunity cost is simply the explicit cost of purchasing or hiring them. It is the price paid for them.

1c In the case of factors already owned by the firm, it is the implicit cost of what the factor could have earned for the firm in its next best alternative use.

2a A production function shows the relationship between the amount of inputs used and the amount of output produced from them (per period of time).

2b In the short run it is assumed that one or more factors (inputs) are fixed in supply. The actual length of the short run will vary from industry to industry.

2c Production in the short run is subject to diminishing returns. As greater quantities of the variable factor(s) are used, so each additional unit of the variable factor will add less to output than previous units: total physical product will rise less and less rapidly.

2d As long as marginal physical product is above average physical product, average physical product will rise. Once MPP has fallen below APP, however, APP will fall.

3a With some factors fixed in supply in the short run, their total costs will be fixed with respect to output. In the case of variable factors, their total cost will increase as more output is produced and hence as more of them are used.

3b Total cost can be divided into total fixed and total variable cost. Total variable cost will tend to

SUMMARY

increase less rapidly at first as more is produced, but then, when diminishing returns set in, it will increase more and more rapidly.

3c Marginal cost is the cost of producing one more unit of output. It will probably fall at first (corresponding to the part of the *TVC* curve where the slope is getting shallower), but will start to rise as soon as diminishing returns set in.

3d Average cost, like total cost, can be divided into fixed and variable costs. Average fixed cost will decline as more output is produced. The reason is that the total fixed cost is being spread over a greater and greater number of units of output. Average variable cost will tend to decline at first, but once the marginal cost has risen above it, it must then rise.

4a In the long run, a firm is able to vary the quantity it uses of all factors of production. There are no fixed factors.

4b If it increases all factors by the same proportion, it may experience constant, increasing or decreasing returns to scale.

4c Economies of scale occur when costs per unit of output fall as the scale of production increases. This can be due to a number of factors, some of which are directly caused by increasing (physical) returns to scale. These include the benefits of specialisation and division of labour, the use of larger and more efficient machines, and the ability to have a more integrated system of production. Other economies of scale arise from the financial and administrative benefits of large-scale organisations.

4d Long-run costs are also influenced by a firm's location. The firm will have to balance the need to be as near as possible both to the supply of its raw materials and to its market. The optimum balance will depend on the relative costs of transporting the inputs and the finished product.

4e To minimise costs per unit of output, a firm should choose that combination of factors which gives an equal marginal product for each factor relative to its price: i.e. $MPP_a/P_a = MPP_b/P_b = MPP_c/P_c$, etc. (where a, b and c are different factors). If the MPP/P ratio for any factor is greater than that for another, more of the first should be used relative to the second.

4f Four distinct time periods can be distinguished. In addition to the short- and long-run periods, we can also distinguish the very-short- and very-long-run periods. The very short run is when all factors are fixed. The very long run is where not only the quantity of factors but also their quality is variable (as a result of changing technology, etc.).

5a In the long run, all factors are variable. There are thus no long-run fixed costs.

5b When constructing long-run cost curves, it is assumed that factor prices are given, that the state of technology is given and that firms will choose the least-cost combination of factors for each given output.

5c The *LRAC* curve can be downward sloping, upward sloping or horizontal, depending in turn on whether there are economies of scale, diseconomies of scale or neither. Typically, *LRAC* curves are drawn as <-shaped (sometimes with a flat bottom), or as saucer-shaped curved. As output expands, initially there are economies of scale. When these are exhausted, the curve will become flat. When the firm becomes very large, it may begin to experience diseconomies of scale. If this happens, the *LRAC* curve will begin to slope upward again.

5d The long-run marginal cost curve will be below the *LRAC* curve when *LRAC* is falling, above it when *LRAC* is rising and equal to it when *LRAC* is neither rising nor falling.

5e An envelope curve can be drawn which shows the relationship between short-run and long-run average cost curves. The *LRAC* curve envelops the short-run *AC* curves: it is tangential to them.

REVIEW QUESTIONS

1 Are all explicit costs variable costs? Are all variable costs explicit costs?

2 Up to roughly how long is the short run in the following cases?
   (a) A mobile disco firm;

(b) Electricity power generation;

(c) A small grocery retailing business;

(d) 'Superstore Hypermarkets plc'.

In each case, specify your assumptions.

3 Given that there is a fixed supply of land in the world, what implications can you draw from Figure 9.2 about the effects of an increase in world population for food output per head?

4 The following are some costs incurred by a shoe manufacturer. Decide whether each one is a fixed cost or a variable cost or has some element of both.

(a) The cost of leather;

(b) The fee paid to an advertising agency;

(c) Wear and tear on machinery;

(d) Business rates on the factory;

(e) Electricity for heating and lighting;

(f) Electricity for running the machines;

(g) Basic minimum wages agreed with the union;

(h) Overtime pay;

(i) Depreciation of machines as a result purely of their age (irrespective of their condition).

5 Assume that you are required to draw a *TVC* curve corresponding to Figure 9.1. What will happen to this *TVC* curve beyond point *d*?

6 Why is the minimum point of the *AVC* curve at a lower level of output than the minimum point of the *AC* curve?

7 Which economies of scale are due to increasing returns to scale and which are due to other factors?

8 What economies of scale is a large department store likely to experience?

9 Why are many firms likely to experience economies of scale up to a certain size and then diseconomies of scale after some point beyond that?

10 Why are bread and beer more expensive to transport per mile than the raw materials used in their manufacture?

11 Name some industries where external economies of scale are gained. What are the specific external economies in each case?

12 How is the opening up of trade and investment between eastern and western Europe likely to affect the location of industries within Europe that have (a) substantial economies of scale; (b) little or no economies of scale?

13 If factor X costs twice as much as factor Y ($P_X/P_Y = 2$), what can be said about the relationship between the *MPP*s of the two factors if the optimum combination of factors is used?

14 Could the long run and the very long run ever be the same length of time?

15 Examine Figure 9.6. What would (a) the firm's long-run total cost curve, and (b) its long-run marginal cost curve look like in each of these three cases?

16 Under what circumstances is a firm likely to experience a flat-bottomed *LRAC* curve?

10 Revenue and profit

10.1 Revenue

In this chapter we will identify the output and price at which a firm will maximise its profits, and how much profit will be made at that level. Remember that we defined a firm's total profit ($T\Pi$) as its total revenue minus its total costs of production.

$$T\Pi = TR - TC$$

In the previous two chapters we have looked at costs in some detail. We must now turn to the revenue side of the equation. As with costs, we distinguish between three revenue concepts: total revenue (TR), average revenue (AR) and marginal revenue (MR).

Total, average and marginal revenue

Total revenue (TR)

Total revenue is the firm's total earnings per period of time from the sale of a particular amount of output (Q).

For example, if a firm sells 1000 units (Q) per month at a price of £5 each (P), then its monthly total revenue will be £5000: in other words, £5 × 1000 ($P \times Q$). Thus:

$$TR = P \times Q$$

Average revenue (AR)

Average revenue is the amount the firm earns per unit sold. Thus:

$$AR = TR/Q$$

So if the firm earns £5000 (TR) from selling 1000 units (Q), it will earn £5 per unit. But this is simply the price! Thus:

$$AR = P$$

(The only exception to this is when the firm is selling its products at different prices to different consumers. In this case AR is simply the (weighted) average price.)

Marginal revenue (MR)

Marginal revenue is the extra total revenue gained by selling one more unit (per time period). So if a firm sells an extra 20 units this month compared with what

---

definition

Total revenue
A firm's total earnings from a specified level of sales within a specified period: $TR = P \times Q$.

definition

Average revenue
Total revenue per unit of output. When all output is sold at the same price, average revenue will be the same as price: $AR = TR/Q = P$.

definition

Marginal revenue
The extra revenue gained by selling one or more unit per time period: $MR = \Delta TR/\Delta Q$.

it expected to sell, and in the process earns an extra £100, then it is getting an extra £5 for each extra unit sold: $MR = £5$. Thus:

$$MR = \Delta TR/\Delta Q$$

We now need to see how each of these three revenue concepts (TR, AR and MR) varies with output. We can show this relationship graphically in the same way as we did with costs.

The relationship will depend on the market conditions under which a firm operates. A firm which is too small to be able to affect market price will have different-looking revenue curves from a firm which is able to choose the price it charges. Let us examine each of these two situations in turn.

Revenue curves when price is not affected by the firm's output

Average revenue

If a firm is very small relative to the whole market, it is likely to be a **price taker**. That is, it has to accept the price given by the intersection of demand and supply in the whole market. But, being so small, it can sell as much as it is capable of producing at that price. This is illustrated in Figure 10.1.

Diagram (a) shows market demand and supply. Equilibrium price is £5. Diagram (b) looks at the demand for an individual firm which is tiny relative to the whole market. (Look at the difference in the scale of the horizontal axes in the two diagrams.)

Being so small, any change in the firm's output will be too insignificant to affect the market price. The firm thus faces a horizontal demand 'curve' at this price. It can sell 200 units, 600 units, 1200 units or whatever without affecting this £5 price.

Average revenue is thus constant at £5. The firm's average revenue curve must therefore lie along exactly the same line as its demand curve.

Marginal revenue

In the case of a horizontal demand curve, the marginal revenue curve will be the same as the average revenue curve, since selling one more unit at a constant

> **definition**
>
> **Price taker**
> A firm that is too small to be able to influence the market price.

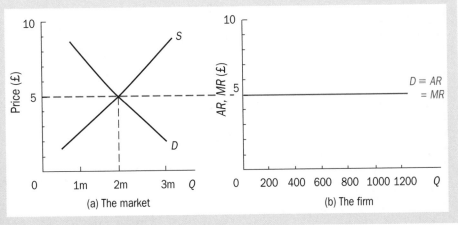

Figure 10.1
Deriving a firm's **AR** and **MR**: price-taking firm

(a) The market

(b) The firm

Table 10.1	Deriving total revenue	
Quantity (units)	Price ≡ AR = MR(£)	TR (£)
0	5	0
200	5	1000
400	5	2000
600	5	3000
800	5	4000
1000	5	5000
1200	5	6000
.	.	.
.	.	.
.	.	.

price (*AR*) merely adds that amount to total revenue. If an extra unit is sold at a constant price of £5, an extra £5 is earned.

Total revenue

Table 10.1 shows the effect on total revenue of different levels of sales with a constant price of £5 per unit.

As price is constant, total revenue will rise at a constant rate as more is sold. The *TR* 'curve' will therefore be a straight line through the origin, as in Figure 10.2.

Revenue curves when price varies with output

The three curves (*TR*, *AR* and *MR*) will look quite different when price does vary with the firm's output.

If a firm has a relatively large share of the market, it will face a downward-sloping demand curve. This means that if it is to sell more, it must lower the

Figure 10.2
Total revenue curve for a price-taking firm

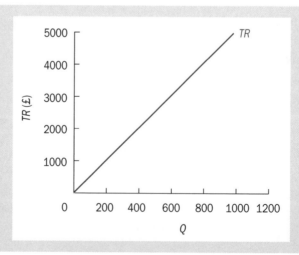

price. But it could also choose to raise its price. If it does so, however, it will have to accept a fall in sales.

Average revenue

Remember that average revenue equals price. If, therefore, the price has to be reduced to sell more output, average revenue will fall as output increases.

Table 10.2 gives an example of a firm facing a downward-sloping demand curve. The demand curve (which shows how much is sold at each price) is given by the first two columns.

Note that, as in the case of a price-taking firm, the demand curve and the *AR* curve lie along exactly the same line. The reason for this is simple: $AR = P$, and thus the curve relating price to quantity (the demand curve) must be the same as that relating average revenue to quantity (the *AR* curve).

Marginal revenue

When a firm faces a downward-sloping demand curve, marginal revenue will be less than average revenue, and may even be negative. But why?

If a firm is to sell more per time period, it must lower its price (assuming it does not advertise). This will mean lowering the price not just for the extra units it hopes to sell, but also for those units it would have sold had it not lowered the price.

Thus the marginal revenue is the price at which it sells the last unit, *minus* the loss in revenue it has incurred by reducing the price on those units it could otherwise have sold at the higher price. This can be illustrated with Table 10.2.

Assume that price is currently £7. Two units are thus sold. The firm now wishes to sell an extra unit. It lowers the price to £6. It thus gains £6 from the sale of the third unit, but loses £2 by having to reduce the price by £1 on the two units it could otherwise have sold at £7. Its net gain is therefore £6 − £2 = £4. This is the marginal revenue: it is the extra revenue gained by the firm from selling one more unit. (Note that in Table 10.2 the figures for *MR* are entered in the spaces between the figures for the other three columns.)

There is a simple relationship between marginal revenue and *price elasticity of demand*. Remember from Chapter 5 (see p. 79) that if demand is price elastic, a *decrease* in price will lead to a proportionately larger increase in the quantity demanded and hence an *increase* in revenue. Marginal revenue will thus be posi-

Table 10.2	Revenues for a firm facing a downward-sloping demand curve		
Q (units)	P = AR (£)	TR (£)	MR (£)
1	8	8	
			8
2	7	14	
			6
3	6	18	
			2
4	5	20	
			0
5	4	20	
			−2
6	3	18	
			−4
7	2	14	
.	.	.	.
.	.	.	.

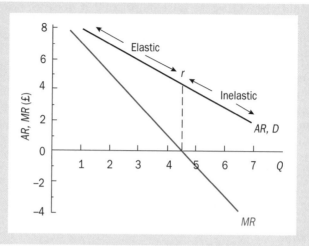

Figure 10.3
AR and **MR** curves for a firm facing a downward-sloping demand curve

tive. If, however, demand is inelastic, a decrease in price will lead to a proportionately smaller increase in sales. In this case the price reduction will more than offset the increase in sales and as a result revenue will fall. Marginal revenue will be negative.

If, then, marginal revenue is a positive figure (i.e. if sales per time period are 4 units or less in Figure 10.3), the demand curve will be elastic at that point, since a rise in quantity sold (as a result of a reduction in price) would lead to a rise in total revenue. If, on the other hand, marginal revenue is negative (i.e. at a level of sales of 5 or more units in Figure 10.3), the demand curve will be inelastic at that point, since a rise in quantity sold would lead to a *fall* in total revenue.

Thus the demand (*AR*) curve of Figure 10.3 is elastic to the left of point *r* and inelastic to the right.

Total revenue

Total revenue equals price times quantity. This is illustrated in Table 10.2. The *TR* column from Table 10.2 is plotted in Figure 10.4.

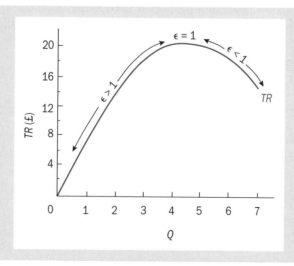

Figure 10.4
Total revenue for a firm facing a downward-sloping demand curve

Unlike in the case of a price-taking firm, the *TR* curve is not a straight line. It is a curve that rises at first and then falls. But why? As long as marginal revenue is positive (and hence demand is price elastic), a rise in output will raise total revenue. However, once marginal revenue becomes negative (and hence demand is inelastic), total revenue will fall. The peak of the *TR* curve will be where *MR* = 0. At this point, the price elasticity of demand will be equal to -1.

Shifts in revenue curves

We saw in Chapter 4 that a change in *price* will cause a movement along a demand curve. It is similar with revenue curves, except that here the causal connection is in the other direction. Here we ask what happens to revenue when there is a change in the firm's *output*. Again the effect is shown by a movement along the curves. The assumption here is that the price charged will be that which will ensure that the output is sold. Thus the causal sequence is: price determines the output that can be sold (a movement along the demand curve); this then determines the level of revenue earned (a movement along the three revenue curves).

A change in any *other* determinant of demand, such as tastes, income or the price of other goods, will shift the demand curve. By affecting the price at which each level of output can be sold, it will cause a shift in all three revenue curves. An increase in revenue is shown by a vertical shift upwards; a decrease by a shift downwards.

10.2 Profit maximisation

We are now in a position to put costs and revenue together to find the output at which profit is maximised, and also to find out how much that profit will be.

There are two ways of doing this. The first and simpler method is to use total cost and total revenue curves. The second method is to use marginal and average cost and marginal and average revenue curves. Although this method is a little more complicated (but only a little!), it is more useful when we come to compare profit maximising under different market conditions.

We will look at each method in turn. In both cases we will concentrate on the short run: namely, that period in which one or more factors are fixed in supply. In both cases we take the case of a firm facing a downward-sloping demand curve.

Short-run profit maximisation: using total curves

Table 10.3 shows the total revenue figures from Table 10.2. It also shows figures for total cost. These figures have been chosen so as to produce a *TC* curve of a typical shape.

Total profit (*TΠ*) is found by subtracting *TC* from *TR*. Check this out by examining the table. Where *TΠ* is negative, the firm is making a loss. Total profit is maximised at an output of 3 units: namely, where there is the greatest gap between total revenue and total costs. At this output, total profit is £4 (£18 − £14).

Table 10.3

Q (units)	TR (£)	TC (£)	TΠ (£)
0	0	6	−6
1	8	10	−2
2	14	12	2
3	18	14	4
4	20	18	2
5	20	25	−5
6	18	36	−18
7	14	56	−42
.	.	.	.
.	.	.	.
.	.	.	.

The *TR*, *TC* and *TΠ* curves are plotted in Figure 10.5. The size of the maximum profit is shown by the arrows.

Short-run profit maximisation: using average and marginal curves

Table 10.4 is based on the figures in Table 10.3.

Finding the maximum profit that a firm can make is a two-stage process. The first stage is to find the profit-maximising output. To do this we use the *MC* and *MR* curves. The second stage is to find out just how much profit is at this output. To do this we use the *AR* and *AC* curves.

Stage 1: Using marginal curves to arrive at the profit-maximising output

There is a very simple **profit-maximising rule**: if profits are to be maximised, *MR* must equal *MC*. From Table 10.4 it can be seen that *MR* = *MC* at an output of 3. This is shown as point *e* in Figure 10.6.

definition

Profit-maximising rule
Profit is maximised where marginal revenue equals marginal cost.

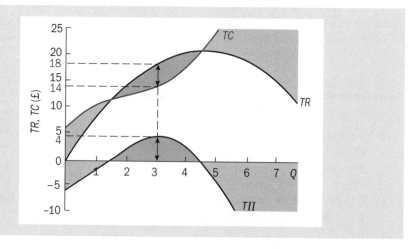

Figure 10.5
Finding maximum profit using totals curves

Table 10.4

Q (units)	P = AR (£)	TR (£)	MR (£)	TC (£)	AC (£)	MC (£)	TΠ (£)	AΠ (£)
0	9	0		6	–		−6	–
			8			4		
1	8	8		10	10		−2	−2
			6			2		
2	7	14		12	6		2	1
			4			2		
3	6	18		14	4⅔		4	1⅓
			2			4		
4	5	20		18	4½		2	½
			0			7		
5	4	20		25	5		−5	−1
			−2			11		
6	3	18		36	6		−18	−3
			−4			20		
7	2	14		56	8		−42	−6
.	.	.	.	.	.	.	.	.
.	.	.	.	.	.	.	.	.
.	.	.	.	.	.	.	.	.

But why are profits maximised when $MR = MC$? The simplest way of answering this is to see what the position would be if MR did not equal MC.

Referring to Figure 10.6, at a level of output below 3, MR exceeds MC. This means that by producing more units there will be a bigger addition to revenue (MR) than to cost (MC). Total profit will *increase. As long as MR exceeds MC, profit can be increased by increasing production.*

At a level of output above 3, MC exceeds MR. All levels of output above 3 thus add more to cost than to revenue and hence *reduce* profit. *As long as MC exceeds MR, profit can be increased by cutting back on production.*

Profits are thus maximised where $MC = MR$: at an output of 3. This can be confirmed by reference to the *TΠ* column in Table 10.4.

Students worry sometimes about the argument that profits are maximised when $MR = MC$. Surely, they say, if the last unit is making no profit, how can profit be at a *maximum*? The answer is very simple. If you cannot *add* anything more to a total, the total must be at the maximum. Take the simple analogy of going up a hill. When you cannot go any higher, you must be at the top.

Figure 10.6
Finding the profit-maximising output using the marginal curves

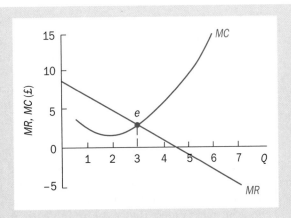

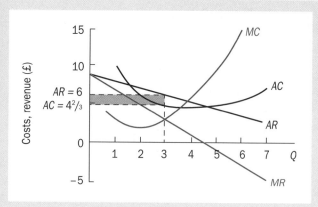

Figure 10.7
Measuring the maximum profit using average curves

Stage 2: Using average curves to measure the size of the profit

Once the profit-maximising output has been discovered, we now use the average curves to measure the *amount* of profit at the maximum. Both marginal and average curves corresponding to the data in Table 10.4 are plotted in Figure 10.7.

First, average profit ($A\Pi$) is found. This is simply $AR - AC$. At the profit-maximising output of 3, this gives a figure for $A\Pi$ of £6 − £4⅔ = £1⅓. Then total profit is obtained by multiplying average profit by output:

$$T\Pi = A\Pi \times Q$$

This is shown as the shaded area. It equals £1⅓ × 3 = £4. This can again be confirmed by reference to the $T\Pi$ column in Table 10.4.

Some qualifications

Long-run profit maximisation

Assuming that the AR and MR curves are the same in the long run as in the short run, long-run profits will be maximised at the output where MR equals the *long-run MC*. The reasoning is the same as with the short-run case.

The meaning of 'profit'

One element of cost is the opportunity cost to the owners of the firm incurred by being in business. This is the minimum return that the owners must make on their capital in order to prevent them from eventually deciding to close down and perhaps move into some alternative business. It is a *cost* since, just as with wages, rent, etc., it has to be covered if the firm is to continue producing. This opportunity cost to the owners is sometimes known as **normal profit**, and is included in the cost curves.

What determines this normal rate of profit? It has two components. First, someone setting up in business invests capital in it. There is thus an opportunity cost. This is the interest that could have been earned by lending it in some risk-less form (e.g. by putting it in a savings account in a bank). Nobody would set up a business unless they expected to earn at least this rate of profit. Running a business is far from riskless, however, and hence a second element is a return to compensate for risk. Thus:

Normal profit (%) = rate of interest on a riskless loan + a risk premium

The risk premium varies according to the line of business. In those with fairly predictable patterns, such as food retailing, it is relatively low. Where outcomes are very uncertain, such as mineral exploration or the manufacture of fashion garments, it is relatively high.

Thus if owners of a business earn normal profit, they will (just) be content to remain in that industry. If they earn more than normal profit, they will also (obviously) prefer to stay in this business. If they earn less than normal profit, then after a time they will consider leaving and using their capital for some other purpose.

Given that normal profits are included in costs, any profit that is shown diagrammatically (e.g. the shaded area in Figure 10.7) must therefore be over and above normal profit. It is known by several alternative names: **supernormal profit, pure profit, economic profit, abnormal profit, producer's surplus** or sometimes simply **profit**. They all mean the same thing: the excess of profit over normal profit.

> **definition**
>
> **Supernormal profit**
> (also known as **pure profit, economic profit, abnormal profit, producer's surplus or simply profit**)
> The excess of total profit above normal profit.

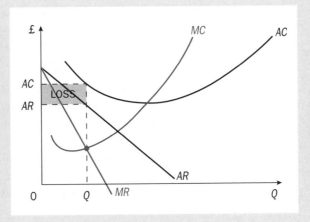

Figure 10.8
Loss-minimising output

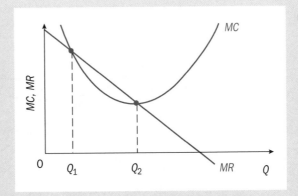

Figure 10.9
Choosing the profit-maximising output when *MC* = *MR* at more than one output

Loss minimising

It may be that there is no output at which the firm can make a profit. Such a situation is illustrated in Figure 10.8: the *AC* curve is above the *AR* curve at all levels of output.

In this case, the output where $MR = MC$ will be the loss-minimising output. The amount of loss at the point where $MR = MC$ is shown by the shaded area in Figure 10.8.

When MC = MR at two different outputs

Figure 10.9 illustrates a case where $MR = MC$ at two different points. Which is the one that maximises profit? The answer is Q_2. At Q_1, a move in either direction would *increase* profit (or reduce loss). For example, as output is increased above Q_1, *MR* becomes greater than *MC* and thus output should increase further: *away* from Q_1 and toward Q_2.

The rule for profit maximisation, then, can be redefined as: the firm should produce where $MR = MC$ *provided that* above that output *MC* exceeds *MR* and below that output *MR* exceeds *MC*.

Whether or not to produce at all

The short run. Fixed costs have to be paid even if the firm is producing nothing at all. Rent has to be paid, business rates have to be paid, etc. Providing, therefore, that the firm is more than covering its *variable* costs, it can go some way to paying off these fixed costs and therefore will continue to produce.

It will shut down if it cannot cover its variable costs: that is, if the *AVC* curve is above, or the *AR* curve is below, that illustrated in Figure 10.10. This situation is known as the **short-run shut-down point**.

The long run. All costs are variable in the long run. If, therefore, the firm cannot cover its long-run average costs (which include normal profit), it will close down. The **long-run shut-down point** will be where the *AR* curve is tangential to the *LRAC* curve.

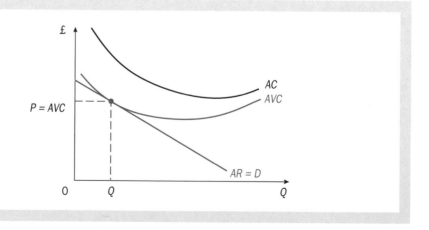

Figure 10.10
The short-run shut-down point

REVIEW QUESTIONS

1   Draw a downward-sloping demand curve. Now put in scales of your own choosing for both axes. Read off various points on the demand curve and use them to construct a table showing price and quantity. Use this table to work out the figures for a marginal revenue column. Now use these figures to draw an *MR* curve.

2   Copy Figures 10.3 and 10.4 (which are based on Table 10.2). Now assume that incomes have risen and that, as a result, two more units per time period can be sold at each price. Draw a new table and plot the resulting new *AR*, *MR* and *TR* curves on your diagrams. Are the new curves parallel to the old ones? Explain.

3   What can we say about the slope of the *TR* and *TC* curves at the maximum-profit point? What does this tell us about marginal revenue and marginal cost?

4 Using the following information, construct a table like Table 10.3.

Q	0	1	2	3	4	5	6	7
P	12	11	10	9	8	7	6	5
TC	2	6	9	12	16	21	28	38

Use your table to draw diagrams like Figures 10.5 and 10.7. Use these two diagrams to show the profit-maximising output and the level of maximum profit. Confirm your findings by reference to the table you have constructed.

5 The following table shows the average cost and average revenue (price) for a firm at each level of output.

Output	1	2	3	4	5	6	7	8	9	10
AC (£)	7.00	5.00	4.00	3.30	3.00	3.10	3.50	4.20	5.00	6.00
AR (£)	10.00	9.50	9.00	8.50	8.00	7.50	7.00	6.50	6.00	5.50

(a) Construct a table to show *TC, MC, TR* and *MR* at each level of output (put the figures for *MC* and *MR* mid-way between the output figures).
(b) Using *MC* and *MR* figures, find the profit-maximising output.
(c) Using *TC* and *TR* figures, check your answer to (b).
(d) Plot the *AC, MC, AR* and *MR* figures on a graph.
(e) Mark the profit-maximising output and the *AR* and *AC* at this output.
(f) Shade in an area to represent the level of profits at this output.

6 Normal profits are regarded as a cost (and are included in the cost curves). Explain why.

7 What determines the size of normal profit? Will it vary with the general state of the economy?

8 A firm will continue producing in the short run even if it is making a loss, providing it can cover its variable costs. Explain why. Just how long will it be willing to continue making such a loss?

9 Would there ever be a point in a firm attempting to continue in production if it could not cover its *long-run* average (total) costs?

10 The price of pocket calculators and digital watches fell significantly in the years after they were first introduced and at the same time demand for them increased substantially. Use cost and revenue diagrams to illustrate these events. Explain the reasoning behind the diagram(s) you have drawn.

11 In February 2000, Unilever, the giant consumer products company, announced that it was to cut 25 000 jobs, close 100 plants and rely more on the internet to purchase its supplies. It would use part of the money saved to increase promotion of its leading brands, such as Dove skincare products, Lipton tea, Omo detergents and Calvin Klein cosmetics. The hope was to boost sales and increase profits. If it meets these targets, what is likely to have happened to its total costs, total revenue, average costs and average revenue? Give reasons for your answer.

D

Supply: short-run profit maximisation

THE FINANCIAL TIMES, 14 JUNE 2000

Ryanair attacks Lufthansa on pricing policy

Kevin Done

Ryanair, the leading European low cost airline, has accused Lufthansa, the German carrier, of using "predatory pricing" and unfair competition in an attempt to drive it off its routes between the UK and Germany.

The Dublin-based airline said yesterday that it had filed a formal complaint with the European Commission.

The move by Ryanair against Lufthansa follows similar action taken earlier this year by Go, the no-frills airline subsidiary of British Airways, which accused the German group of abusing its dominant position to force it to withdraw its service from London Stansted to Munich.

Michael O'Leary, Ryanair's chief executive, said: "It is clear that Lufthansa is engaged in a policy of below-cost pricing on those routes where it faces competition from Ryanair and other low-cost airlines."

He said that unless the European Commission intervened to restrain this "abusive behaviour" by Lufthansa, the prospects of spreading low-fare services in Germany would be diminished.

Lufthansa had already forced Go off the Stansted–Munich service "by these unfair means".

Ryanair said the German carrier, which already served both Heathrow and Gatwick airports from Frankfurt, has announced that it would also fly to Stansted, as soon as Ryanair announced its own service last year.

Ryanair said Lufthansa was willing to suffer considerable short-term losses so it could "eliminate competition from low-cost carriers in the German market by abusing its dominant position."

Lufthansa last night rejected the accusation. "We are perfectly entitled to defend vigorously our home market," it said. "We are not going to stand by and be rolled over by no-frills competitors that cannot stand the heat. The UK market is very important for us."

As we saw in Chapter 10, a firm's profits are maximised where its marginal cost equals its marginal revenue. But we will want to know more than this.

- What determines the *amount* of profit that a firm will make? Will profits be large, or just enough for the firm to survive, or so low that it will be forced out of business?
- Will the firm produce a high level of output or a low level?
- Will it be producing efficiently?
- Will the price charged to the consumer be high or low?
- And, more generally, will the consumer benefit from the decisions that a firm makes?

The answers to all these questions depend on the amount of *competition* that a firm faces. A firm in a highly competitive environment will behave quite differently than a firm facing little or no competition. If Lufthansa, for example, faces competition in carrying passengers between the UK and Germany, then it will behave quite differently from if it were the sole carrier. Ryanair claims that Lufthansa will exploit its monopoly position and charge higher fares, once competition has been driven from the market.

In Part D we will look at *different types of market structure*: from highly competitive markets at one end of the spectrum ('perfect competition'), to ones with no competition at all at the other ('monopoly'). We will also look at the intermediate cases of 'imperfect competition': monopolistic competition (where there are quite a lot of firms competing against each other) and oligopoly (where there are just a few).

> The natural price, or the price of free competition ... is the lowest which can be taken, not upon every occasion indeed, but for any considerable time together ... [It] is the lowest which the sellers can commonly afford to take, and at the same time continue their business.
>
> Adam Smith (1723–90),
> *Wealth of Nations*, ed. Cannan,
> Vol. I, Book I, Chapter VII,
> p. 63

Profit maximisation under perfect competition and monopoly

11.1 Alternative market structures

It is traditional to divide industries into categories according to the degree of competition that exists between the firms within the industry. There are four such categories.

At one extreme is **perfect competition**, where there are very many firms competing. Each firm is so small relative to the whole industry that it has no power to influence price. It is a price taker. At the other extreme is **monopoly**, where there is just one firm in the industry, and hence no competition from *within* the industry. In the middle comes **monopolistic competition**, where there are quite a lot of firms competing and where there is freedom for new firms to enter the industry, and **oligopoly**, where there are only a few firms and where entry of new firms is restricted.

To distinguish more precisely between these four categories, the following must be considered:

- How freely can firms enter the industry: is entry free or restricted? If it is restricted, just how great are the barriers to the entry of new firms?
- The nature of the product. Do all firms produce an identical product, or do firms produce their own particular brand or model or variety?
- The degree of control the firm has over price. Is the firm a price taker or can it choose its price, and if it can, how will changing its price affect its profits? What we are talking about here is the nature of the demand curve it faces. How elastic is it? If it puts up its price, will it lose (a) all its sales (a horizontal demand curve), or (b) a large proportion of its sales (a relatively elastic demand curve), or (c) just a small proportion of its sales (a relatively inelastic demand curve)?

Table 11.1 shows the differences between the four categories.

The market structure under which a firm operates will determine its behaviour. Firms under perfect competition behave quite differently from firms that are monopolists, which behave differently again from firms under oligopoly or monopolistic competition.

This behaviour (or 'conduct') will in turn affect the firm's performance: its prices, profits, efficiency, etc. In many cases it will also affect other firms' performance: *their* prices, profits, efficiency, etc. The collective conduct of all the firms in the industry will affect the whole industry's performance.

Economists thus see a causal chain running from market structure to the performance of that industry.

Structure → Conduct → Performance

---

definition

Perfect competition
A market structure in which there are many firms; where there is freedom of entry to the industry; where all firms produce an identical product; and where all firms are price takers.

definition

Monopoly
A market structure where there is only one firm in the industry.

definition

Monopolistic competition
A market structure where, like perfect competition, there are many firms and freedom of entry into the industry, but where each firm produces a differentiated product and thus has some control over its price.

definition

Oligopoly
A market structure where there are few enough firms to enable barriers to be erected against the entry of new firms.

Table 11.1	Features of the four market structures				
Type of market	*Number of firms*	*Freedom of entry*	*Nature of product*	*Examples*	*Implication for demand curve for firm*
Perfect competition	Very many	Unrestricted	Homogeneous (undifferentiated)	Cabbages, carrots (these approximate to perfect competition)	Horizontal. The firm is a price taker
Monopolistic competition	Many/several	Unrestricted	Differentiated	Builders, restaurants	Downward sloping, but relatively elastic. The firm has some control over price
Oligopoly	Few	Restricted	1. Undifferentiated or 2. Differentiated	1. Cement 2. Cars, electrical appliances	Downward sloping, relatively inelastic but depends on reactions of rivals to a price change
Monopoly	One	Restricted or completely blocked	Unique	Local water company, train operators (over particular routes)	Downward sloping, more inelastic than oligopoly. Firm has considerable control over price

First, we look at the two extreme market structures: perfect competition and monopoly. Then we turn to look at the two intermediate cases of monopolistic competition and oligopoly (Chapter 12).

These two intermediate cases are sometimes referred to collectively as **imperfect competition**. The vast majority of firms in the real world operate under imperfect competition. It is still worth studying the two extreme cases, however, because they provide a framework within which to understand the real world. Some industries tend more to the competitive extreme, and thus their performance corresponds to some extent to perfect competition. Other industries tend more to the other extreme: for example, when there is one dominant firm and a few much smaller firms. In such cases, their performance corresponds more to monopoly.

11.2 Perfect competition

The theory of perfect competition illustrates an extreme form of capitalism. In it firms are entirely subject to market forces. They have no power whatsoever to affect the price of the product. The price they face is that determined by the interaction of demand and supply in the whole *market*.

Assumptions

The model of perfect competition is built on four assumptions:

- Firms are *price takers*. There are so many firms in the industry that each one produces an insignificantly small proportion of total industry supply,

BOX 11.1

Concentration ratios
Measuring the degree of competition

We can get some indication of how competitive a market is by observing the number of firms: the more the firms, the more competitive the market would seem to be. However, this does not tell us anything about how *concentrated* the market might be. There may be *many* firms (suggesting a situation of perfect competition or monopolistic competition), but the largest two firms might produce 95 per cent of total output. This would make these two firms more like oligopolists.

Thus even though a large number of producers may make the market *seem* highly competitive, this could be deceiving. Another approach, therefore, to measuring the degree of competition is to focus on the level of concentration of firms.

The simplest measure of industrial concentration involves adding together the market share of the largest so many firms: e.g. the largest three or the largest five. This would give what is known as the '3-firm' or '5-firm concentration ratio'.

The table shows the 5-firm concentration ratios of selected industries in the UK. As you can see, there is an enormous variation in the degree of concentration from one industry to another.

One of the main reasons for this is differences in the percentage of total industry output at which economies of scale are exhausted. If this occurs at a low level of output, there will be room for several firms in the industry which are all benefiting from the maximum economies of scale. Take the case of tufted carpets. As the table in Box 9.5 showed (see page 189), economies of scale are exhausted at less than 1 per cent of total industry output. It is not surprising that the largest five firms in the carpet industry account for only 21.8 per cent of output. In the case of steel, however, with a minimum efficient plant size at 72 per cent of industry output, the largest five firms account for 95.3

per cent of output (most of which is produced by one firm, British Steel).

Differences in the extent of economies of scale are not the only cause of differences in concentration. The degree of concentration will also depend on the barriers to entry of other firms into the industry (see page 220) and on various factors such as transport costs and historical accident. It will also depend on how varied the products are within any one industrial category. For example, in categories as large as 'clothing' and 'toys and sports goods' there is room for many firms, each producing a specialised range of products. Within each sub-category, e.g. tennis racquets, there may be relatively few firms producing.

So is the degree of concentration a good guide to the degree of competitiveness of the industry? The answer is that it is *some* guide, but on its own it can be misleading. In particular it ignores the degree of competition from abroad, and from other areas within the country. Thus the five largest UK motor vehicle manufacturers may produce 82.9 per cent of UK vehicle output, but these manufacturers face considerable competition from imported cars and lorries. On the other hand, the five largest water suppliers may account for only 49.7 per cent of UK output, but within their own regions of the country they have a monopoly.

Questions

1. What are the advantages and disadvantages of using a 5-firm concentration ratio rather than a 10-firm, 3-firm or even a 1-firm ratio?
2. Why are some industries like bread baking and brewing relatively concentrated, in that a few firms produce a large proportion of total output, and yet there are also many small producers?

Industry	5-firm concentration ratio	Industry	5-firm concentration ratio
Tobacco products	99.5	Water supply	49.7
Iron and steel	95.3	Footwear	48.2
Asbestos goods	89.8	Bread, biscuits, etc.	47.0
Motor vehicles and engines	82.9	Carpets	21.8
Cement, lime and plaster	77.7	Clothing	20.7
Grain milling	62.3	Bolts, nuts and springs	11.4
		Processing of plastics	8.8

Source: Based on *Business Monitor PA 1002* (HMSO, 1995).

and therefore has *no power whatsoever* to affect the price of the product. It faces a horizontal demand 'curve' at the market price: the price determined by the interaction of demand and supply in the whole market.

- There is complete *freedom of entry* of new firms into the industry. Existing firms are unable to stop new firms setting up in business. Setting up a business takes time, however. Freedom of entry therefore applies in the long run. An extension of this assumption is that there is complete factor mobility in the long run. If profits are higher than elsewhere, capital will be freely attracted into that industry. Likewise, if wages are higher than for equivalent work elsewhere, workers will freely move into that industry and will meet no barriers.
- All firms produce an *identical product*. (The product is 'homogeneous'.) There is therefore no branding or advertising.
- Producers and consumers have *perfect knowledge* of the market. That is, producers are fully aware of prices, costs and market opportunities. Consumers are fully aware of price, quality and availability of the product.

These assumptions are very strict. Few, if any, industries in the real world meet these conditions. Certain agricultural markets perhaps are closest to perfect competition. The market for fresh vegetables is an example.

The short run and the long run

Before we can examine what price, output and profits will be, we must first distinguish between the short run and the long run as they apply to perfect competition.

In the **short run**, the number of firms is fixed. Depending on its costs and revenue, a firm might be making large profits, small profits, no profits or a loss; and in the short run it may continue to do so.

In the **long run**, however, the level of profits will affect entry into and exit from the industry. If profits are high, new firms will be attracted into the industry, whereas if losses are being made, firms will leave.

This leads us to the distinction we made in Chapter 10: that between *normal* and *supernormal* profits. Let us examine them in the context of perfect competition.

Normal profit. This is the level of profit that is just enough to persuade firms to stay in the industry in the long run, but not high enough to attract new firms. If less than normal profits are made, firms will leave the industry in the long run.

Supernormal profit. This is any profit above normal profit. If supernormal profits are made, new firms will be attracted into the industry in the long run.

The short-run equilibrium of the firm

The determination of price, output and profit in the short run under perfect competition can best be shown in a diagram.

Figure 11.1 shows a short-run equilibrium for both industry and a firm under perfect competition. Both parts of the diagram have the same scale for the vertical axis. The horizontal axes have totally different scales, however. For example, if the horizontal axis for the firm were measured in, say, thousands of

definition

The short run under perfect competition
The period during which there is too little time for new firms to enter the industry.

definition

The long run under perfect competition
The period of time which is long enough for new firms to enter the industry.

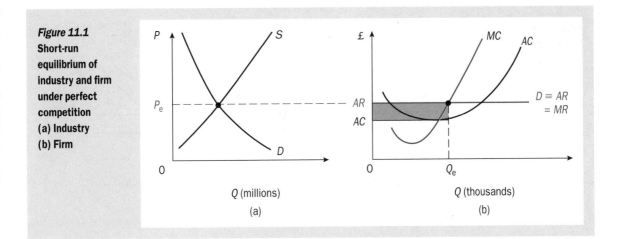

Figure 11.1
Short-run equilibrium of industry and firm under perfect competition
(a) Industry
(b) Firm

units, the horizontal axis for the whole industry might be measured in millions or tens of millions of units, depending on the number of firms in the industry.

Let us examine the determination of price, output and profit in turn.

Price

The price is determined in the industry by the intersection of demand and supply. The firm faces a horizontal demand (or average revenue) 'curve' at this price. It can sell all it can produce at the market price (P_e), but nothing at a price above P_e.

Output

The firm will maximise profit where marginal cost equals marginal revenue ($MR = MC$), at an output of Q_e. Note that, since the price is not affected by the firm's output, marginal revenue will equal price. The reason is that the firm is not having to reduce its price in order to sell more. An extra unit produced will therefore earn its full price for the firm. Thus the firm's MR 'curve' and D 'curve' are the same horizontal straight line.

Profit

If the average cost (AC) curve (which includes normal profit) dips below the average revenue (AR) 'curve', the firm will earn supernormal profit. Super-normal profit per unit at Q_e is the vertical difference between AR and AC at Q_e. Total supernormal profit is the shaded rectangle in Figure 11.1.

What happens if the firm cannot make a profit at *any* level of output? This situation would occur if the AC curve were above the AR curve at all points. This is illustrated in Figure 11.2 where the market price is P_1. In this case, the point where $MC = MR$ represents the *loss-minimising* point (where loss is defined as anything less than normal profit). This amount of the loss is represented by the shaded rectangle.

As we saw in Chapter 10, whether the firm is prepared to continue making a loss in the short run or whether it will close down immediately depends on whether it can cover its *variable* costs. Provided price is above average variable

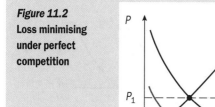

Figure 11.2
Loss minimising under perfect competition

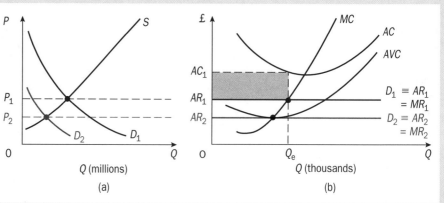

cost (AVC), the firm will continue producing in the short run: it can pay its variable costs and go some way to paying its fixed costs. It will shut down in the short run only if the market price falls below P_2 in Figure 11.2.

The long-run equilibrium of the firm

In the long run, if typical firms are making supernormal profits, new firms will be attracted into the industry. Likewise, if existing firms can make supernormal profits by increasing the scale of their operations, they will do so, since all factors of production are variable in the long run.

The effect of the entry of new firms and/or the expansion of existing firms is to increase industry supply. This is illustrated in Figure 11.3.

The industry supply curve shifts to the right. This in turn leads to a fall in price. Supply will go on increasing, and price falling, until firms are making only normal profits. This will be when price has fallen to the point where the demand 'curve' for the firm just touches the bottom of its long-run average cost curve.

Figure 11.3
Long-run equilibrium under perfect competition
(a) Industry (b) Firm

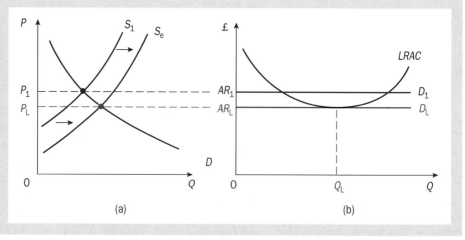

Q_L is thus the long-run equilibrium output of the firm, with P_L the long-run equilibrium price.

Since the $LRAC$ curve is tangential to all possible short-run AC curves (see section 9.5), the full long-run equilibrium will be as shown in Figure 11.4 where:

$$LRAC = AC = MC = MR = AR$$

The incompatibility of perfect competition and substantial economies of scale

Why is perfect competition so rare in the real world – if it even exists at all? One important reason for this has to do with economies of scale.

In many industries, firms may have to be quite large if they are to experience the full potential economies of scale. But perfect competition requires there to be *many* firms. Firms must therefore be small under perfect competition: too small in most cases for economies of scale.

Once a firm expands sufficiently to achieve economies of scale, it will usually gain market power. It will be able to undercut the prices of smaller firms, which will thus be driven out of business. Perfect competition is destroyed.

Perfect competition could only exist in any industry, therefore, if there were no (or virtually no) economies of scale.

Does the firm benefit from operating under perfect competition?

Under perfect competition the firm faces a constant battle for survival. If it becomes less efficient than other firms, it will make less than normal profits and be driven out of business. If it becomes more efficient, it will earn supernormal profits. But these supernormal profits will not last for long. Soon other firms, in order to survive themselves, will be forced to copy the more efficient methods of the new firm.

It is the same with the development of new products. If a firm is able to produce a new product that is popular with consumers, it will be able to gain a temporary advantage over its rivals. But again, any supernormal profits will last only as long as it takes other firms to respond. Soon the increase in supply

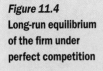

Figure 11.4
Long-run equilibrium
of the firm under
perfect competition

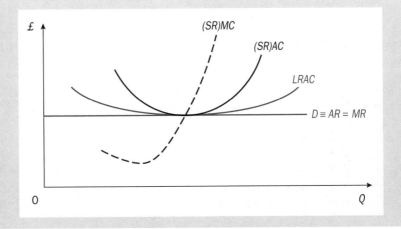

BOX 11.2

E-commerce
A modern form of perfect competition?

'Anyone who fails to become an e-business will become an ex-business.' (Phil Lawler, managing director of Hewlett-Packard)

'In 5 years' time, all companies will be Internet companies, or they won't be companies at all.' (Andy Grove, Chairman of Intel)[1]

The massive growth in companies selling over the Internet has raised many questions. Will all companies become Internet companies? Is this the beginning of the end of shops as we know them? Will we all be caught up in a web, where big companies swallow up little ones, and where we, as consumers, end up with no power at all?

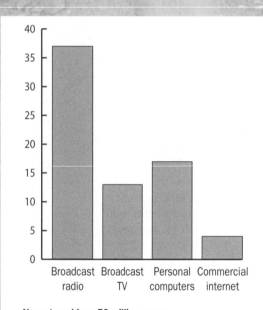

Years to achieve 50 million users

Source: US Commerce Department.

In practice, e-commerce could have large benefits for consumers. These include not only the obvious benefits of being able to do your shopping from your own home, but also of having a wider choice of products and at more reasonable prices. But why should prices be more reasonable? The answer is that e-commerce has the potential to make markets more competitive: in fact, in many cases, pretty close to *perfectly* competitive.

Moving markets back towards perfect competition?

To see the extent to which e-commerce is making markets more competitive, let's look at the assumptions of perfect competition.

Large number of firms. The growth of e-commerce has led to many new firms starting up in business. It's not just large firms like Amazon.com that are providing increased competition for established firms, but the thousands of small on-line companies that are being established every day. Many of these firms are selling directly to us as consumers. This is known as 'B2C' e-commerce (business-to-consumers). But many more are selling to other firms ('B2B'). More and more companies, from the biggest to the smallest, are transferring their purchasing to the Web and are keen to get value for money.

The reach of the Web is global. This means that firms, whether conventional or Web-based, are having to keep an eye on the prices and products of competitors in the rest of the world, not just in the local neighbourhood. Firms' demand curves are thus becoming very price elastic. This is especially so for goods that are cheap to transport, or for services such as insurance and banking.

Perfect knowledge. If you go shopping to buy a new household item and want to get the best deal, then it can take you some time going from shop to shop comparing prices. If, however, you go on-line to buy the same item, you can very rapidly compare prices. Search engines can quickly locate a list of alternative suppliers. Alternatively you can use an on-line shopping mall, such as ShopSmart.com. Better still, you can use a 'shopping bot', such as evenbetter.com, mySimon.com or RuSure.com. These Websites automatically inform you of the best available prices. And improved information is not confined to prices. 'Shopping agents', such as Frictionless.com give additional information on quality and service.

The competition through increased information over the Internet extends beyond e-commerce: it spills over to shops. As people increasingly compare prices in shops with prices on-line, so shops are having to be more and more competitive with their on-line counterparts.

Freedom of entry. Internet companies often have lower start-up costs than their conventional rivals. Their premises are generally much smaller, with no 'shop-front' costs and lower levels of stock holding. Marketing costs can also be relatively low, especially given the ease with which companies can be located with search engines and shopping bots. Internet companies are often smaller and more specialist, relying on Internet 'outsourcing' (buying parts, equipment and other supplies through the Internet), rather than making everything themselves. They are also more likely to use delivery firms rather than having their own transport fleet.

All this makes it relatively cheap for new firms to set up and begin trading over the Internet. Also, if the set-up costs are relatively low, there is less to lose if the company fails. This makes it more tempting for small firms to 'have a go'. It is also relatively easy for large firms to 'diversify' across into new businesses, especially if they are already trading on the Internet.

Identical products. With the use of shopping agents, customers can compare the prices of different firms for supplying identical products. This makes price competition very intense.

Not only do these factors make markets more price competitive, they also bring other benefits. Costs are driven down, as firms economise on stock holding, rely more on outsourcing and develop more efficient relationships with suppliers. The competition also encourages innovation, which improves quality and the range of products.

Is there a limit to e-commerce?

In 20 years, will we be doing all our shopping on the net? Will the only shopping malls be virtual ones? Although e-commerce is revolutionising some markets, it is unlikely that things will go anything like that far.

For a start, going out shopping is itself an enjoyable experience. Many people like wandering round the shops, meeting friends, seeing what takes their fancy, trying on clothes, browsing through CDs and so on. 'Retail therapy' for many is an important means of 'de-stressing'. Also, with 'real shopping' you can see the goods and assess how much you like them. Then, of course, if you buy something, you can take it home with you straight away, rather than waiting for it to be delivered.

With on-line shopping, you have to rely on the Web. Access may be slow and frustrating. 'Surfing' may instead become 'wading'. Then if you do buy something, you may not know how long you will have to wait to be delivered, or whether it will even arrive!

The Internet may reduce the costs of producing some items, but not all. With heavy or bulky items, or items where special deliveries have to be made, the extra distribution costs may outweigh cost savings elsewhere.

Finally there is the role of big companies. They do not like to see their powerful position in the market threatened and are likely to try to dominate Internet sales, thereby reducing the market's competitiveness. Amazon.com may have gained a foothold in the market, but large established booksellers are retaliating. Waterstones and Blackwells are now heavily promoting their Internet sales. Amazon.com may survive, but it will be difficult for new general booksellers to break into the market. As in any market, large powerful firms will try to erect barriers to the entry of new firms. The movement towards perfect competition is likely to be strongly resisted!

Questions

1 Why may the Internet work better for replacement buys than for new purchases?

2 Give three examples of products that are particularly suitable for selling over the Internet and three that are not. Explain your answer.

[1] Quotes from 'The net imperative', *The Economist*, (26 June 1999)

of the new product will drive the price down and eliminate these supernormal profits. Similarly, the firm must be quick to copy new products developed by its rivals. If it does not, it will soon make a loss and be driven out of the market.

Thus being in perfect competition is a constant battle for survival. It might benefit the consumer, but most firms in such an environment would love to be able to gain some market power: power to be able to restrict competition and to retain supernormal profits into the long run.

The extreme case of market power is that of monopoly: a firm that faces no competition – at least not from *within* its industry. Monopoly is the subject of the next section.

11.3 Monopoly

What is a monopoly?

This may seem a strange question because the answer seems obvious. A monopoly exists when there is only one firm in the industry.

But whether an industry can be classed as a monopoly is not always clear. It depends how narrowly the industry is defined. For example, a textile company may have a monopoly on certain types of fabric, but it does not have a monopoly on fabrics in general. The consumer can buy fabrics other than those supplied by the company. A rail company may have a monopoly over rail services between two cities, but it does not have a monopoly over public transport between these two cities. People can travel by coach or air. They could also use private transport.

To some extent, the boundaries of an industry are arbitrary. What is more important for a firm is the amount of monopoly *power* it has, and that depends on the closeness of substitutes produced by rival industries. In many countries, there is a monopoly supplier of electricity. They also have virtually no rivals in supplying power for lighting and running many domestic appliances. In the case of heating, however, they may have serious rivals in the form of coal, oil and gas.

Barriers to entry

For a firm to maintain its monopoly position, there must be barriers to the entry of new firms. Barriers also exist under oligopoly, but in the case of monopoly they must be high enough to block the entry of new firms. Barriers can take various forms.

definition
Natural monopoly A situation where long-run average costs would be lower if an industry were under monopoly than if it were shared between two or more competitors.

Economies of scale. If the monopolist's costs go on falling significantly up to the output that satisfies the whole market, the industry may not be able to support more than one producer. This case is known as **natural monopoly**. It is particularly likely if the market is small. For example, two bus companies might find it unprofitable to serve the same routes, each running with perhaps only half-full buses, whereas one company with a monopoly of the routes could make a profit. Electricity transmission via a national grid is another example of a natural monopoly.

Even if a market could support more than one firm, a new entrant is unlikely to be able to start up on a very large scale. Thus the monopolist which is already experiencing economies of scale can charge a price below the cost of the new entrant and drive it out of business. If, however, the new entrant is a firm already established in another industry, it may be able to survive this competition.

Product differentiation and brand loyalty. If a firm produces a clearly differentiated product, where the consumer associates the product with the brand, it will be very difficult for a new firm to break into that market. Rank Xerox invented, and patented, the plain paper photocopier. After this legal monopoly (see below) ran out, people still associated photocopiers with Rank Xerox. It is still not unusual to hear someone say that they are going to 'Xerox the article' or, for that matter, 'Hoover their carpet' or use a 'biro' (meaning a ballpoint pen). This barrier can occur even though the market is potentially big enough for two firms, each gaining all the available economies of scale. In other words, the problem for the new firm is not in being able to produce at low enough costs, but in being able to produce a product sufficiently attractive to consumers who are loyal to the familiar brand.

Lower costs for an established firm. An established monopoly is likely to have developed specialised production and marketing skills. It is more likely to be aware of the most efficient techniques and the most reliable and/or cheapest suppliers. It is likely to have access to cheaper finance. It is thus operating on a lower cost curve. New firms would therefore find it hard to compete and would be likely to lose any price war.

Ownership of, or control over, key factors of production. If a firm governs the supply of vital inputs (say, by owning the sole supplier of some component part), it can deny access to these inputs to potential rivals. On a world scale, the de Beers company has a monopoly in fine diamonds because all diamond producers market their diamonds through de Beers.

Ownership of, or control over, wholesale or retail outlets. Similarly, if a firm controls the outlets through which the product must be sold, it can prevent potential rivals from gaining access to consumers.

Legal protection. The firm's monopoly position may be protected by patents on essential processes, by copyright, by various forms of licensing (allowing, say, only one firm to operate in a particular area) and by tariffs (i.e. customs duties) and other trade restrictions to keep out foreign competitors. Examples of monopolies based on patents include nylon (Du Pont) and instant cameras (Polaroid).

Mergers and takeovers. The monopolist can put in a takeover bid for any new entrant. The sheer threat of takeovers may discourage new entrants.

Aggressive tactics. An established monopolist can probably sustain losses for longer than a new entrant. Thus it could start a price war, mount massive advertising campaigns, offer attractive after-sales service, introduce new brands to compete with new entrants, and so on.

Intimidation. The monopolist may resort to various forms of harassment, legal or illegal, to drive a new entrant out of business.

Equilibrium price and output

Since there is, by definition, only one firm in the industry, the firm's demand curve is also the industry demand curve.

Compared with other market structures, demand under monopoly will be relatively inelastic at each price. The monopolist can raise its price and consumers have no alternative firm to turn to within the industry. They either pay the higher price, or go without the good altogether.

Unlike the firm under perfect competition, the monopoly firm is thus a 'price maker'. It can choose what price to charge. Nevertheless, it is still constrained by its demand curve. A rise in price will reduce the quantity demanded. This is illustrated in Figure 11.5.

As with firms in other market structures, a monopolist will maximise profit where $MR = MC$. In Figure 11.5 profit is maximised at Q_m. The supernormal profit obtained is shown by the shaded area.

These profits will tend to be larger, the less elastic is the demand curve (and hence the steeper is the MR curve), and thus the bigger is the gap between MR and price (AR). The actual elasticity will depend on whether reasonably close substitutes are available in *other* industries. The demand for a rail service will be much less elastic (and the potential for profit greater) if there is no bus service to the same destination.

Since there are barriers to the entry of new firms, a monopolist's supernormal profits will not be competed away in the long run. The only difference, therefore, between short-run and long-run equilibrium is that in the long run the firm will produce where $MR = long\text{-}run\ MC$.

Comparing monopoly with perfect competition

Because it faces a different type of market environment, the monopolist will produce a quite different output and at a quite different price from a perfectly competitive industry.

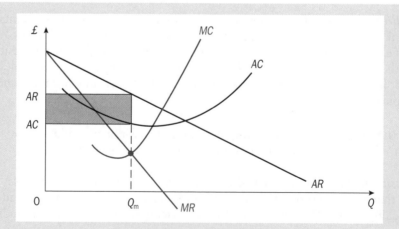

Figure 11.5
Profit maximising under monopoly

Let us compare the two.

The monopolist will produce a lower output at a higher price in the short run. Figure 11.6 compares the profit-maximising position for an industry under monopoly with that under perfect competition. Note that we are comparing the monopoly with the whole *industry* under perfect competition. That way we can assume, for the sake of comparison, that they both face the same demand curve. We also assume for the moment that they both face the same cost curves.

The monopolist will produce Q_1 at a price of P_1. This is where $MC = MR$.

If the same industry were under perfect competition, however, it would produce at Q_2 and P_2 – a higher output and a lower price. But why? The reason for this is that for each of the firms in the industry – and it is at this level that the decisions are made – marginal revenue is the same as price. Remember that the *firm* under perfect competition faces a perfectly elastic demand (AR) curve, which also equals MR (see Figure 11.1). Thus producing where $MC = MR$ also means producing where $MC = P$. When *all* firms under perfect competition do this, price and quantity in the *industry* will be given by P_2 and Q_2 in Figure 11.6.

The monopolist may also produce a lower output at a higher price in the long run. Under perfect competition, freedom of entry eliminates supernormal profit and forces firms to produce at the bottom of their $LRAC$ curve. The effect, therefore, is to keep long-run prices down. Under monopoly, however, barriers to entry allow profits to remain supernormal in the long run. The monopolist is not forced to operate at the bottom of the AC curve. Thus, other things being equal, long-run prices will tend to be higher, and hence output lower, under monopoly.

Costs under monopoly. The sheer survival of a firm in the long run under perfect competition requires that it uses the most efficient known technique, and develops new techniques wherever possible. The monopolist, however, sheltered by barriers to entry, can still make large profits even if it is not using the most efficient technique. It has less incentive, therefore, to be efficient.

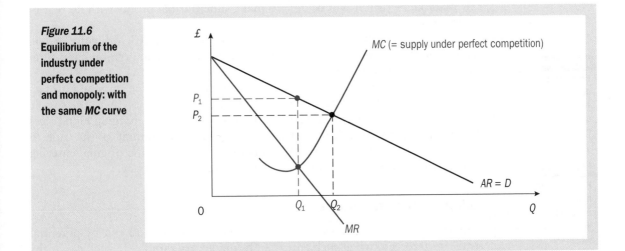

Figure 11.6
Equilibrium of the industry under perfect competition and monopoly: with the same *MC* curve

On the other hand, the monopoly may be able to achieve substantial economies of scale due to larger plant, centralised administration and the avoidance of unnecessary duplication (e.g. a monopoly water company would eliminate the need for several sets of rival water mains under each street). If this results in an *MC* curve substantially below that of the same industry under perfect competition, the monopoly may even produce a *higher* output at a *lower* price.

Another reason why a monopolist may operate with lower costs is that it can use part of its supernormal profits for research and development and investment. It may not have the same *incentive* to become efficient as the perfectly competitive firm which is fighting for survival, but it may have a much greater *ability* to become efficient than has the small firm with limited funds.

Although a monopoly faces no competition in the goods market, it may face an alternative form of competition in financial markets. A monopoly, with potentially low costs, which is currently run inefficiently, is likely to be subject to a takeover bid from another company. This **competition for corporate control** may thus force the monopoly to be efficient in order to prevent being taken over.

Innovation and new products. The promise of supernormal profits, protected perhaps by patents, may encourage the development of new (monopoly) industries producing new products.

11.4 Potential competition or potential monopoly?

The theory of contestable markets

Potential competition

In recent years, economists have developed the theory of contestable markets. This theory argues that what is crucial in determining price and output is not whether an industry is *actually* a monopoly or competitive, but whether there is the real *threat* of competition.

If a monopoly is protected by high barriers to entry – say that it owns all the raw materials – then it will be able to make supernormal profits with no fear of competition.

If, however, another firm *could* take over from it with little difficulty, it will behave much more like a competitive firm. The threat of competition has a similar effect to actual competition.

As an example, consider a catering company that is given permission by a factory to run its canteen. The catering company has a monopoly over the supply of food to the workers in that factory. If, however, it starts charging high prices or providing a poor service, the factory could offer the running of the canteen to an alternative catering company. This threat may force the original catering company to charge 'reasonable' prices and offer a good service.

Perfectly contestable markets

A market is perfectly contestable when the costs of entry and exit by potential rivals are zero, and when such entry can be made very rapidly. In such cases, the

---

definition

Competition for corporate control
The competition for the control of companies through takeovers.

definition

Perfectly contestable market
A market where there is free and costless entry and exit.

moment the possibility of earning supernormal profits occurs, new firms will enter, thus driving profits down to a normal level. The sheer threat of this happening, so the theory goes, will ensure that the firm already in the market will (a) keep its prices down, so that it just makes normal profits, and (b) produce as efficiently as possible, taking advantage of any economies of scale and any new technology. If the existing firm did not do this, entry would take place and potential competition would become actual competition.

Contestable markets and natural monopolies

So why in such cases are the markets not *actually* perfectly competitive? Why do they remain monopolies?

The most likely reason has to do with economies of scale and the size of the market. To operate on a minimum efficient scale, the firm may have to be so large relative to the market that there is only room for one such firm in the industry. If a new firm does come into the market, then one or other of the two firms will not survive the competition. The market is simply not big enough for both of them.

If, however, there are no entry or exit costs, new firms will be perfectly willing to enter even though there is only room for one firm, provided they believe that they are more efficient than the existing firm. The existing firm, knowing this, will be forced to produce as efficiently as possible and with only normal profit.

The importance of costless exit

Setting up in a new business usually involves large expenditures on plant and machinery. Once this money has been spent, it becomes fixed costs. If these fixed costs are no higher than those of the existing firm, then the new firm could win the battle. But, of course, there is always the risk that it might lose.

But does losing the battle really matter? Can the firm not simply move to another market?

It does matter if there are substantial costs of exit. This will be the case if the capital equipment cannot be transferred to other uses. In this case these fixed costs are known as **sunk costs**. The losing firm is left with capital equipment it cannot use. The firm may therefore be put off entering in the first place. The market is not perfectly contestable, and the established firm can make supernormal profit.

If, however, the capital equipment can be transferred, the exit costs will be zero (or at least very low), and new firms will be more willing to take the risks of entry. For example, a rival coach company may open up a service on a route previously operated by only one company, and where there is still only room for one operator. If the new firm loses the resulting battle, it can still use the coaches it has purchased. It simply uses them for a different route. The cost of the coaches is not a sunk cost.

Costless exit, therefore, encourages firms to enter an industry, knowing that, if unsuccessful, they can always transfer their capital elsewhere.

The lower the exit costs, the more contestable the market. This implies that firms already established in other similar markets may provide more effective competition against monopolists, since they can simply transfer capital from

> **definition**
>
> **Sunk costs**
> Costs that cannot be recouped (e.g. by transferring assets to other uses).

BOX 11.3

Windows cleaning
Microsoft, the Internet and the US Justice Department

On 18 May 1998, the US government initiated its biggest competition case for 20 years: it sued Microsoft, the world's largest software company. It accused Microsoft of abusing its market power and seeking to crush its rivals. A verdict was reached on 7 June 2000, when Federal Judge Thomas Penfield Jackson ruled that Microsoft be split in two to prevent it operating as a monopoly. One company would produce and market the *Windows* operating system; the other would produce and market the applications software, such as *Microsoft Office* and the Web browser, *Internet Explorer*. The judge ruled that Microsoft had broken competition law ('anti-trust' law) by abusing its dominant position in the computer operating system market.

The case against Microsoft had been building for many years, but it was with the release of *Windows 98* that the US government decided to act. Windows, owned by Microsoft, is the operating system installed on more than 95 per cent of the world's personal computers. With *Windows 98*, Microsoft integrated its own Internet browser, *Internet Explorer*, into the Windows system. But it is in this area of Internet browsers that Microsoft faces stiff competition from Netscape Communications, which controls over 60 per cent of the market. US anti-trust officials argued that the integration of Microsoft's Internet browser with its operating system would stifle competition in Internet software. In other words, by controlling the operating software, Microsoft could force its Internet browser on to consumers and computer manufacturers.

The US Justice Department alleged that Microsoft had committed the following anti-competitive actions:

- Back in May 1995, Microsoft attempted to collude with Netscape Communications to divide the Internet browser market. Netscape Communications refused.
- Microsoft had forced personal computer manufacturers to install *Internet Explorer* in order to obtain a *Windows 95* operating licence.
- Microsoft insisted that PC manufacturers conformed to a Microsoft front screen for Windows. This included specified icons, one of which was Microsoft's *Internet Explorer*.
- It had set up reciprocal advertising arrangements with America's largest Internet service providers, such as America Online. Here Microsoft would promote

America Online via Windows. In return, America Online would not promote Netscape's browsers.

In the face of these alleged abuses of its monopoly position, the US Justice Department argued that Microsoft should be required to do the following:

- Remove the integrated browser from its *Windows 98* package, or include access to rival products.
- End its practice of forcing PC manufacturers to install its Internet browser in order to gain a Windows licence.
- Allow PC manufacturers to determine the opening screen when using the Windows system.
- End agreements with Internet service providers that solely promoted Microsoft products.

Microsoft, in its defence, argued that the integration of its own browser into the Windows system was a natural part of the process of product innovation and development. Microsoft officials claimed that accusations of unfair trading practices were not founded: it was simply attempting to improve the quality of its product. If Microsoft was to do nothing with its Windows product, it would, over time, lose its dominant market position, and be replaced by a more innovative and superior product manufactured by a rival software producer. Bill Gates, the founder of Microsoft, reiterated this point. He argued:

> This suit is all about Microsoft's right to innovate on behalf of consumers, the right to integrate new technologies into the operating system as they develop.[1]

In this respect, Microsoft could be seen to be operating in the consumer's interest. The argument is that, in an environment where technology is changing rapidly, Microsoft's control over standards gives the user a measure of stability, knowing that any new products and applications will be compatible with existing ones. In other words, new software can be incorporated into existing systems.

Joel Klein, head of the US Anti-trust Division, was quick to recognise this argument, but pointed out that the problem with Microsoft was not its use of technology, but its behaviour. If Microsoft was to operate a monopoly in the area of operating systems, then it had an obligation to behave in a manner that was not anti-competitive and detrimental to the interests of consumers, whether in terms of price or choice. As he stated:

> Inventors and investors cannot and will not develop and market innovative software programs if they know that Microsoft can use its Windows monopoly to block the distribution of their programs and to force consumers to buy Microsoft's competing products.[2]

Network effects

The key issue in respect to Microsoft then, was not so much the browser war, but far more fundamentally to do with the operating system, and how Microsoft used its ownership of this system to extend its leverage into other related high-technology markets.

> An operating system attracts software developed around that operating system, thereby discouraging new competition since any alternative faces not only the challenge of creating a better operating system but competing against a whole array of already existing software applications. Businesses train employees in one technology and are reluctant to abandon that investment in training, while the existence of a pool of people trained in that technology encourages other businesses to adopt that technology. And as desktop software has to be able to work with client–server networks and an array of other technologies, it becomes nearly impossible to abandon an established set of technology standards that tie those different parts together. These so-called 'network effects' give an incredible anti-competitive edge to companies like Microsoft that control so many different parts of the network.[3]

Network effects arise when consumers of a product benefit from it being used by *other* consumers. The more people that use it, the greater the benefit to each individual user. The problem for the consumer in such a scenario is that these network effects can lead to the establishment of a monopoly producer and hence to higher prices. There is also the problem of whether the best product is being produced by the monopolist. In such an instance, the consumer may be 'locked in' to using an inferior product or technology with limited opportunity (if any) to change.

Microsoft had been able to use consumer lock-in to drive competitors from the market. Where choice did

exist, for example in Internet browsers, Microsoft was using its operating system dominance to rectify its inferior market position.

Judge Jackson not only ordered the split up of Microsoft. He ordered the company to modify its behaviour. This included doing the following:

- Giving computer manufacturers more freedom in configuring their systems and in selling or promoting non-Microsoft software.
- Charging the same price for *Windows* to each of the top 20 computer manufacturers.
- Giving equal access to technical information to other software vendors as to its own agents.

Microsoft vowed to fight the ruling on appeal. Whether, then, the court's ruling and Microsoft's reaction to it will end up generating more genuine competition in computer operating systems and software remains to be seen.

Questions

1 In what respects might Microsoft's behaviour be deemed to have been: (a) against the public interest; (b) in the public interest?

2 In December 1998, America Online (AOL) announced it was to acquire Netscape Communications, and to form an alliance with Sun Microsystems. The state of South Carolina subsequently dropped its anti-trust suit against Microsoft, stating that 'the forces of competition are working'. Bill Gates remarked on hearing news of the merger, 'It's hard to believe that the Government can still press their case with a straight face. Three of the biggest competitors are banking together and yet the Government is still trying to slow us down.' Should the AOL–Netscape merger alter attitudes towards the recent business practices of Microsoft?

3 The problem with being locked-in to a product or technology is only a problem if such a product can be clearly shown to be inferior to an alternative. What difficulties might there be in establishing such a case?

---

[1] *Financial Times*, 21/5/98
[2] *ibid.*
[3] N. Newman, From MS Word to MS World: How Microsoft is Building a Global Monopoly (1997), www.netaction.org/msoft/world

one market to another. For example, studies of airlines in the USA show that entry to a particular route may be much easier for an established airline, which can simply transfer planes from one route to another.

Costless exit can also allow effective potential competition for oligopolies. As we shall see in Chapter 12, if an oligopolistic market is contestable, this will reduce the level of supernormal profits that can be made, just as it does with a monopoly.

Hit-and-run competition

When entry and exit costs are low, and entry can be made speedily, firms may engage in **hit-and-run** tactics. They may enter a market for a short period when high profits can be made, and then quickly withdraw again.

For example, a small goods delivery company may set up a rival parcels service to the national postal service at Christmas time over certain major routes if the national service has high (monopoly) postal charges. The fear of such competition may prevent the national service from charging high prices in the first place. Similarly, a local builder serving a small village may suddenly find itself facing competition after a storm from 'cowboy' operators offering to mend roofs cheaply for cash. The fear of this may again dissuade the local builder from raising its prices, even if several roofs have been damaged.

Assessment of the theory

Simple monopoly theory merely focuses on the existing structure of the industry and makes no allowance for potential competition. The theory of contestable markets, however, goes much further and examines the *size* of entry barriers and exit costs. The bigger these are, the less contestable the market and therefore the greater the monopoly power of the existing firm. Various attempts have been made to measure monopoly power in this way.

One criticism of the theory, however, is that it does not take sufficient account of the possible reactions of the established firm. There may be no cost barriers to entry or exit (i.e. a perfectly contestable market), but the established firm may let it be known that any firm that dares to enter will face all-out war! This may act as a deterrent to entry. In the meantime, the established firm may charge high prices and make supernormal profits.

If a monopoly operates in a perfectly contestable market, it might bring the 'best of both worlds' for the consumer. Not only will it be able to achieve low costs through economies of scale, but also the potential competition will keep profits and hence prices down.

SUMMARY

1a There are four alternative market structures under which firms operate. In ascending order of firms' market power, they are: perfect competition, monopolistic competition, oligopoly and monopoly.

1b The market structure under which a firm operates will affect its conduct and its performance.

2a The assumptions of perfect competition are: a very large number of firms, complete freedom of entry, a homogeneous product and perfect knowledge of the good and its market by both producers and consumers.

2b In the short run, there is not time for new firms to

enter the market, and thus supernormal profits can persist. In the long run, however, any supernormal profits will be competed away by the entry of new firms.

2c The short-run equilibrium for the firm will be where the price, as determined by demand and supply in the market, is equal to marginal cost. At this output the firm will be maximising profit.

2d The long-run equilibrium will be where the market price is just equal to firms' long-run average cost.

2e There are no substantial economies of scale to be gained in a perfectly competitive industry. If there were, the industry would cease to be perfectly competitive as the large, low-cost firms drove the small high-cost ones out of business.

3a A monopoly is where there is only one firm in an industry. In practice, it is difficult to determine where a monopoly exists because it depends on how narrowly an industry is defined.

3b Barriers to the entry of new firms will normally be necessary to protect a monopoly from competition. Such barriers include economies of scale (making the firm a natural monopoly or at least giving it a cost advantage over new (small) competitors), control over supplies of inputs or over outlets, patents or copyright, and tactics to eliminate competition (such as takeovers or aggressive advertising).

3c Profits for the monopolist (as for other firms) will be maximised where $MC = MR$.

3d If demand and cost curves are the same in a monopoly and a perfectly competitive industry, the monopoly will produce a lower output and at a higher price than the perfectly competitive industry.

3e On the other hand, any economies of scale will in part be passed on to consumers in lower prices, and the monopolist's high profits may be used for research and development and investment, which in turn may lead to better products at possibly lower prices.

4a Potential competition may be as important as actual competition in determining a firm's price and output strategy.

4b The threat of this competition is greater, the lower are the entry and exit costs to and from the industry. If the entry and exit costs are zero, the market is said to be *perfectly* contestable. Under such circumstances, an existing monopolist will be forced to keep its profits down to the normal level if it is to resist entry of new firms. Exit costs will be lower, the lower are the sunk costs of the firm.

4c Hit-and-run competition can be an important feature of highly contestable markets.

4d The theory of contestable markets provides a more realistic analysis of firms' behaviour than theories based simply on the *existing* number of firms in the industry.

REVIEW QUESTIONS

1 Why do economists treat normal profit as a cost of production? What determines (a) the level and (b) the rate of normal profit for a particular firm?

2 Why is perfect competition so rare?

3 Why does the market for fresh vegetables approximate to perfect competition, whereas that for frozen or tinned ones does not?

4 Illustrate on a diagram similar to Figure 11.3 what would happen in the long-run if price were initially below P_L.

5 As an illustration of the difficulty in identifying monopolies, try to decide which of the following are monopolies: British Telecom; your local evening newspaper; British Gas; the village post office; the Royal Mail; Interflora;

the London Underground; ice creams in the cinema; Guinness; food on trains; TippEx; the board game 'Monopoly'.

6 Try this brain teaser. A monopoly would be expected to face an inelastic demand. After all, there are no direct substitutes. And yet, if it produces where $MR = MC$, MR must be positive, demand must therefore be *elastic*. Therefore the monopolist must face an elastic demand! Can you solve this conundrum?

7 For what reasons would you expect a monopoly to charge (a) a higher price, and (b) a lower price than if the industry were operating under perfect competition?

8 In which of the following industries are exit costs likely to be low: (a) steel production; (b) market gardening; (c) nuclear power generation; (d) specialist financial advisory services; (e) production of fashion dolls; (f) production of a new drug; (g) contract catering; (h) mobile discos; (i) car ferry operators? Are these exit costs dependent on how narrowly the industry is defined?

9 Think of three examples of monopolies (local or national) and consider how contestable their markets are.

Profit maximisation under imperfect competition

Very few markets in practice can be classified as perfectly competitive or as a pure monopoly. The vast majority of firms do compete with other firms, often quite aggressively, and yet they are not price takers: they do have some degree of market power. Most markets, therefore, lie between the two extremes of monopoly and perfect competition, in the realm of 'imperfect competition'.

There are two types of imperfect competition: namely, monopolistic competition and oligopoly. Under monopolistic competition there will normally be quite a large number of relatively small firms, whereas under oligopoly there will normally only be a few – say, between two and twenty.

12.1 Monopolistic competition

We will start by looking at monopolistic competition. This was a theory developed in the 1930s by the American economist Edward Chamberlin. Monopolistic competition is nearer to the competitive end of the spectrum. It can best be understood as a situation where there are a lot of firms competing, but where each firm does nevertheless have some degree of market power (hence the term 'monopolistic' competition): each firm has some discretion as to what price to charge for its products.

Assumptions of monopolistic competition

- There is *quite a large number of firms*. As a result, each firm has an insignificantly small share of the market and, therefore, its actions are unlikely to affect its rivals to any great extent. What this means is that each firm in making its decisions does not have to worry about how its rivals will react. It assumes that what its rivals choose to do will *not* be influenced by what it does.

    This is known as the assumption of **independence**. (As we shall see later, this is not the case under oligopoly. There we assume that firms believe that their decisions *do* affect their rivals, and that their rivals' decisions will affect them. Under oligopoly we assume that firms are *inter*dependent.)
- There is *freedom of entry* of new firms into the industry. If any firm wants to set up in business in this market, it is free to do so.

In these two respects, therefore, monopolistic competition is like perfect competition.

- Unlike perfect competition, however, each firm produces a product or provides a service that is in some way different from its rivals. As a result, it can raise its price without losing all its customers. Thus its demand curve is downward sloping, albeit relatively elastic given the large number of competitors to whom customers can turn. This is known as the assumption of **product differentiation**.

Petrol stations, chemist shops, hairdressers and builders are all examples of monopolistic competition.

A typical feature of monopolistic competition is that, although there are many firms in the industry, there is only one firm in a particular location. This applies particularly in retailing. There may be many newsagents in a town, but only one in a particular street. In a sense, therefore, it has a local monopoly. People may be prepared to pay higher prices there to avoid having to go elsewhere.

It is similar with the general food store. Once a week people may go to the supermarket where prices are cheaper, but if they run out of one or two items during the week, they will go to the shop on the corner, even though it is dearer.

Equilibrium of the firm

Short run

As with other market structures, profits are maximised at the output where $MC = MR$. The diagram will be the same as for the monopolist, except that the AR and MR curves will be more elastic. This is illustrated in Figure 12.1(a). As with perfect competition, it is possible for the monopolistically competitive firm to make supernormal profit in the short run. This is shown as the shaded area.

Just how much profit the firm will make in the short run depends on the strength of demand: the position and elasticity of the demand curve. The further to the right the demand curve is relative to the average cost curve, and the less elastic the demand curve is, the greater will be the firm's short-run profit. Thus a firm facing little competition and whose product is considerably differentiated from its rivals may be able to earn considerable short-run profits.

Take the case of a petrol station near a new housing estate. If it is the only one in the neighbourhood, it will have considerable market power. It may face a relatively high and inelastic demand. Motorists may have to travel a long way

definition

Product differentiation
When one firm's product is sufficiently different from its rivals' to allow it to raise the price of the product without customers all switching to the rivals' products. A situation where a firm faces a downward-sloping demand curve.

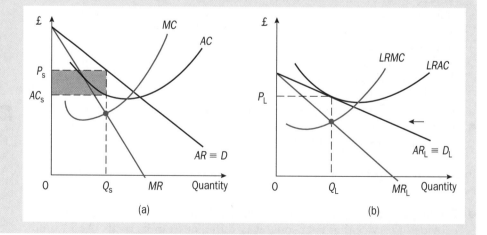

Figure 12.1
Equilibrium of the firm under monopolistic competition
(a) Short run
(b) Long run

to get to the next filling station. *Some* motorists may be prepared to do just that if the price of its petrol is high. Others, however, may find it inconvenient to go to another station, or may have to use extra petrol to do so (thus cancelling out any cost advantage). In the short run, therefore, it may be able to charge a high price and make large supernormal profits.

Long run

If typical firms are earning supernormal profit, new firms will enter the industry in the long run. In the case of the petrol station we were looking at just now, new ones are likely to open in the neighbourhood: not necessarily in the same place, but maybe at the other end of the estate.

As new firms enter, they will take some of the customers away from established firms. The demand for the established firms' products will therefore fall. Their demand (AR) curve will shift to the left, and will continue doing so as long as supernormal profits remain and thus new firms continue entering.

Long-run equilibrium will be reached when only normal profits remain: when there is no further incentive for new firms to enter. This is illustrated in Figure 12.1(b). The firm's demand curve settles at D_L, where it is tangential to (i.e. just touches) the firm's *LRAC* curve. Output will be Q_L: where $AR_L = LRAC$. (At any other output, *LRAC* is greater than *AR* and thus less than normal profit would be made.)

Limitations of the model

There are various problems in applying the model of monopolistic competition to the real world:

- Information may be imperfect. Firms will not enter an industry if they are unaware of the supernormal profits currently being made, or if they underestimate the demand for the particular product they are considering selling.
- Given that the firms in the industry produce different products, it is difficult if not impossible to derive a demand curve for the industry as a whole. Thus the analysis has to be confined to the level of the firm.
- Firms are likely to differ from each other, not only in the product they produce or the service they offer, but also in their size and in their cost structure. What is more, entry may not be *completely* unrestricted. Two petrol stations could not set up in exactly the same place – on a busy crossroads, say. Thus although the typical or 'representative' firm may only earn normal profit in the long run, other firms may be able to earn long-run supernormal profit. They may have some cost advantage or produce a product that is impossible to duplicate perfectly.
- Existing firms may make supernormal profits, but if a new firm entered, this might reduce everyone's profits below the normal level. Thus a new firm will not enter and supernormal profits will persist into the long run. An example would be a small town with two chemist's shops. They may both make more than enough profit to persuade them to stay in business. But if a third set up (say midway between the other two), there would not be enough total sales to allow them all to earn even normal profit. This is a problem of *indivisibilities*. Given the overheads of a chemist's shop, it is

not possible to set up one small enough to take away just enough customers to leave the other two with normal profits.

● One of the biggest problems with the simple model outlined in the previous section is that it concentrates on price and output decisions. In practice, the profit-maximising firm under monopolistic competition will also need to decide the exact variety of product to produce, and how much to spend on advertising it. This will lead the firm to take part in non-price competition (which we examined in Chapter 8).

Comparing monopolistic competition with perfect competition and monopoly

Comparison with perfect competition

It is often argued that monopolistic competition leads to a less efficient allocation of resources than perfect competition.

Figure 12.2 compares the long-run equilibrium positions for two firms. One firm is under perfect competition and thus faces a horizontal demand curve. It will produce an output of Q_1 at a price of P_1. The other is under monopolistic competition and thus faces a downward-sloping demand curve. It will produce the lower output of Q_2 at the higher price of P_2. A crucial assumption here is that a firm would have the *same* long-run average cost (*LRAC*) curve in both cases. Given this assumption, we can make the following two predictions about monopolistic competition:

● Less will be sold and at a higher price.
● Firms will not be producing at the least-cost point.

By producing more, firms would move to a lower point on their *LRAC* curve. Thus firms under monopolistic competition are said to have **excess capacity**. In Figure 12.2 this excess capacity is shown as $Q_1 - Q_2$. In other words, monopolistic competition is typified by quite a large number of firms (e.g. petrol stations), all operating at less than optimum output, and thus being forced to charge a price above that which they could charge if they had a bigger turnover. How often have you been to a petrol station and had to queue for the pumps?

So how does this affect the consumer? Although the firm under monopolistic competition may charge a higher price than under perfect competition, the difference may be very small. Although the firm's demand curve is downward sloping, it is still likely to be highly elastic due to the large number of substitutes.

> **definition**
>
> **Excess capacity (under monopolistic competition)**
> In the long run, firms under monopolistic competition will produce at an output below their minimum-cost point.

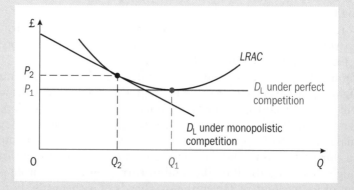

Figure 12.2
Long-run equilibrium of the firm under perfect and monopolistic competition

BOX 12.1

Curry wars
Competition hotter than a vindaloo

The growth in the popularity of Indian food in the 1980s and 1990s has led to the proliferation of restaurants and take-away outlets. The close geographic proximity of many such businesses on a well-known street in Bristol led to what became known as the 'Curry War'.

The restaurants had appeared to exist alongside one another quite happily, providing a range of Indian food. In line with the assumptions of monopolistic competition, the restaurants competed in terms of non-price factors such as comfort, advertising and opening hours. Business boomed.

Then with the recession of the early 1990s a price war suddenly erupted. Take-away prices were slashed at first by 20 and 30 per cent, and eventually by 50 per cent at the war's peak. Similar price cuts for dining-in meals were soon to follow. As the war grew more intense, many restaurants saw their profits fall. This was particularly true for those restaurants which tried to resist cutting their prices.

Due to the geographical proximity and cultural links of these businesses, the cut-throat nature of such competition was eventually averted. The local traders' association formed what amounted to a curry cartel. Minimum prices were fixed for curries and prices rose once again.

But as prices in Bristol were rising, prices in other towns were plummeting. On 8 October 1993 *The Independent* reported on a new curry war in Hampstead.

> Mr Khan looked around the Fleet Tandoori, packed, on a Tuesday night, with lager-swilling curry-shovellers, and expressed himself delighted with his night's work.
>
> 'We are doing this for the hard-pressed consumer,' he said. 'We are the consumer's friend. At our prices the consumer can eat at the Fleet for dinner every night for less than the cost of breakfast.'
>
> It may seem unlikely, but if you want a cheap curry to warm you up this autumn, forget Brick Lane, Bradford or the Balti houses of Birmingham. Head instead for Hampstead, the plushest of London districts, where you can indulge in Bombay duck, onion bhaji and vindaloo and still have enough change from a fiver for a packet of extra strong mints ...
>
> ... The opening skirmishes came in September, when the Light of Kashmir restaurant, operating in Hampstead since 1962, started a 'Sunday Madness' promotion, halving, at a stroke, its prices.
>
> ... Within a fortnight, the restaurant had extended its half-price offer to Saturdays and thence to every night of the week ... Two doors down on Fleet Road's parade of shops, on the other side of a Mexican restaurant that offers an 'eat-all-you-like buffet' for just £4.99, is the Fleet Tandoori. A week after the Light started its Seven-Day Madness, a sign appeared outside the Fleet advertising meals at half price.
>
> ... What has upset Mr Khan ... is that all the curry men of Fleet Road are friends and neighbours from way back ... Over the years they have shared staff, poached each other's chefs, cartelled their prices. But the recession put an end to this camaraderie.

Questions

1 What impact do you think curry wars have on other types of take-away and restaurant meals in the same geographic area? What is the relevance of the concepts of price and cross-price elasticities of demand to these effects?

2 Why are curry wars likely to last only a limited period of time?

3 Collusion between restaurants suggests that they are operating under oligopoly, not monopolistic competition. Do you agree?

Furthermore, the consumer may benefit from monopolistic competition by having a greater variety of products to choose from. Each firm may satisfy some particular requirement of particular consumers.

Comparison with monopoly

The arguments are very similar here to those when comparing perfect competition and monopoly.

On the one hand, freedom of entry for new firms and hence the lack of long-run supernormal profits under monopolistic competition are likely to help keep prices down for the consumer and encourage cost saving. On the other hand, monopolies are likely to achieve greater economies of scale and have more funds for investment and research and development.

12.2 Oligopoly

Oligopoly occurs when just a few firms between them share a large proportion of the industry.

There are, however, significant differences in the structure of industries under oligopoly, and similarly significant differences in the behaviour of firms. The firms may produce a virtually identical product (e.g. metals, chemicals, sugar, petrol). Most oligopolists, however, produce differentiated products (e.g. cars, soap powder, soft drinks, electrical appliances). Much of the competition between such oligopolists is in terms of the marketing of their particular brand. Marketing practices may differ considerably from one industry to another.

The two key features of oligopoly

Despite the differences between oligopolies, there are two crucial features that distinguish oligopoly from other market structures.

Barriers to entry

Unlike firms under monopolistic competition, there are various barriers to the entry of new firms. These are similar to those under monopoly (see page 220). The size of the barriers, however, will vary from industry to industry. In some cases entry is relatively easy, whereas in others it is virtually impossible.

Interdependence of the firms

definition

Interdependence (under oligopoly)
One of the two key features of oligopoly. Each firm will be affected by its rivals' decisions. Likewise its decisions will affect its rivals. Firms recognise this interdependence. This recognition will affect their decisions.

Because there are only a few firms under oligopoly, each firm will have to take account of the others. This means that they are mutually dependent: they are **interdependent**. Each firm is affected by its rivals' actions. If a firm changes the price or specification of its product, for example, or the amount of its advertising, the sales of its rivals will be affected. The rivals may then respond by changing their price, specification or advertising. No firm can therefore afford to ignore the actions and reactions of other firms in the industry.

It is impossible, therefore, to predict the effect on a firm's sales of, say, a change in its price without first making some assumption about the reactions of other firms. Different assumptions will yield different predictions. For this reason there is no single generally accepted theory of oligopoly. Firms may react differently and unpredictably.

Competition and collusion

Oligopolists are pulled in two different directions:

- The interdependence of firms may make them wish to *collude* with each other. If they can club together and act as if they were a monopoly, they could jointly maximise industry profits.
- On the other hand, they will be tempted to *compete* with their rivals to gain a bigger share of industry profits for themselves.

These two policies are incompatible. The more fiercely firms compete to gain a bigger share of industry profits, the smaller these industry profits will become! For example, price competition drives down the average industry price, while competition through advertising raises industry costs. Either way, industry profits fall.

Sometimes firms will collude. Sometimes they will not. The following sections examine first **collusive oligopoly** (both open and tacit), and then **non-collusive oligopoly**.

Equilibrium of industry under collusive oligopoly

When firms under oligopoly engage in collusion, they may agree on prices, market share, advertising expenditure, etc. Such collusion reduces the uncertainty they face. It reduces the fear of engaging in competitive price cutting or retaliatory advertising, both of which could reduce total industry profits.

A formal collusive agreement is called a **cartel**. The cartel will maximise profits if it acts like a monopoly: if the members behave as if they were a single firm. This is illustrated in Figure 12.3.

The total market demand curve is shown with the corresponding market MR curve. The cartel's MC curve is the *horizontal* sum of the MC curves of its members (since we are adding the *output* of each of the cartel members at each level of marginal cost). Profits are maximised at Q_1 where $MC = MR$. The cartel must therefore set a price of P_1 (at which Q_1 will be demanded).

Having agreed on the cartel price, the members may then compete against each other using *non-price competition*, to gain as big a share of resulting sales (Q_1) as they can.

> **definition**
>
> **Collusive oligopoly**
> When oligopolists agree (formally or informally) to limit competition between themselves. They may set output quotas, fix prices, limit product promotion or development, or agree not to 'poach' each other's markets.

> **definition**
>
> **Non-collusive oligopoly**
> When oligopolists have no agreement between themselves – formal, informal or tacit.

> **definition**
>
> **Cartel**
> A formal collusive agreement.

Figure 12.3
Profit-maximising cartel

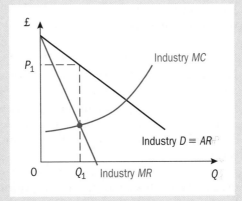

Alternatively, the cartel members may somehow agree to divide the market between them. Each member would be given a **quota**. The sum of all the quotas must add up to Q_1. If the quotas exceeded Q_1, either there would be output unsold if price remained fixed at P_1, or the price would fall.

But if quotas are to be set by the cartel, how will it decide the level of each individual member's quota? One way is to set quotas at the level that will minimise overall industry costs. To do this, each firm should be instructed to produce a level of output such that all firms' marginal costs are the *same*. If they were *not* the same, if firm A's *MC* were greater than firm B's, total costs would be reduced by switching some of industry production from A to B. In fact, by constructing an industry *MC* curve which is the horizontal sum of the members' *MC* curves, we are assuming that, at any given *industry* marginal cost, each member's *MC* will be that same level.

The trouble with this cost-minimising solution to carving up the market between the members is that members may have very different costs. In this case, the members with lower costs will be given a high quota, whereas the members with the high costs may be given a very low quota or no quota at all. Clearly it would not be in the interests of the high-cost producers to agree to such quotas!

A more likely method would be for the cartel to divide the market between the members according to their current market share. That is the solution most likely to be accepted as 'fair'.

In many countries cartels are illegal, being seen by the government as a means of driving up prices and profits and thereby as being against the public interest. Government policy towards cartels is examined in Chapter 20.

Where open collusion is illegal, firms may simply break the law, or get round it. Alternatively, firms may stay within the law, but still *tacitly* collude by watching each other's prices and keeping theirs similar. Firms may tacitly 'agree' to avoid price wars or aggressive advertising campaigns.

Tacit collusion

One form of **tacit collusion** is where firms keep to the price that is set by an established leader. The leader may be the largest firm: the firm which dominates the industry. This is known as **dominant firm price leadership**. Alternatively, the price leader may simply be the one that has proved to be the most reliable one to follow: the one that is the best barometer of market conditions. This is known as **barometric firm price leadership**. Let us examine each of these two types of price leadership in turn.

Dominant firm price leadership

How does the leader set the price? This depends on the assumptions it makes about its rivals' reactions to its price changes. If it assumes that rivals will simply follow it by making exactly the same percentage price changes up or down, then a simple model can be constructed. This is illustrated in Figure 12.4. The leader assumes that it will maintain a constant market share (say 50 per cent).

The leader will maximise profits where its marginal revenue is equal to its marginal cost. It knows its current position on its demand curve (say, point *a*). It then estimates how responsive its demand will be to industry-wide price

---

definition

Quota (set by a cartel)
The output that a given member of a cartel is allowed to produce (production quota) or sell (sales quota).

definition

Tacit collusion
When oligopolists take care not to engage in price cutting, excessive advertising or other forms of competition. There may be unwritten 'rules' of collusive behaviour such as price leadership.

definition

Dominant firm price leadership
When firms (the followers) choose the same price as that set by a dominant firm in the industry (the leader).

definition

Barometric firm price leadership
Where the price leader is the one whose prices are believed to reflect market conditions in the most satisfactory way.

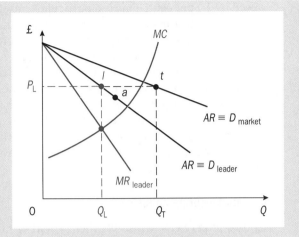

Figure 12.4
A price leader aiming to maximise profits for a given market share

changes and thus constructs its demand and *MR* curves on that basis. It then chooses to produce Q_L at a price of P_L: at point *l* on its demand curve (where $MC = MR$). Other firms then follow that price. Total market demand will be Q_T, with followers supplying that portion of the market not supplied by the leader: namely, $Q_T - Q_L$.

There is one problem with this model. That is the assumption that the followers will want to maintain a constant market share. It is possible that, if the leader raises its price, the followers may want to supply more, given that the new price (= *MR* for a price-taking follower) may well be above their marginal cost. On the other hand, the followers may decide merely to maintain their market share for fear of invoking retaliation from the leader, in the form of price cuts or an aggressive advertising campaign.

Barometric firm price leadership

A similar exercise can be conducted by a barometric firm. Although the firm is not dominating the industry, its price will be followed by the others. It merely tries to estimate its demand and *MR* curves – assuming, again, a constant market share – and then produces where $MR = MC$ and sets price accordingly.

In practice, which firm is taken as the barometer may frequently change. Whether we are talking about oil companies, car producers or banks, any firm may take the initiative in raising prices. If the other firms are merely waiting for someone to take the lead – say, because costs have risen – they will all quickly follow suit. For example, if one of the bigger building societies or banks raises its mortgage rates by 1 per cent, this is likely to stimulate the others to follow suit.

Other forms of tacit collusion

An alternative to having an established leader is for there to be an established set of simple 'rules of thumb' that everyone follows.

One such example is **average cost pricing**. Here producers, instead of equating *MC* and *MR*, simply add a certain percentage for profit on top of average costs. Thus, if average costs rise by 10 per cent, prices will automatically be

definition

Average cost pricing
Where a firm sets its price by adding a certain percentage for (average) profit on top of average cost.

raised by 10 per cent. This is a particularly useful rule of thumb in times of inflation, when all firms will be experiencing similar cost increases.

Another rule of thumb is to have certain **price benchmarks**. Thus clothes may sell for £9.95, £14.95 or £19.95 (but not £12.31 or £16.42). If costs rise, then firms simply raise their price to the next benchmark, knowing that other firms will do the same. Average cost pricing, benchmark pricing and other pricing strategies are considered in more detail in Chapter 16.

Rules of thumb can also be applied to advertising (e.g. you do not criticise other firms' products, only praise your own); or to the design of the product (e.g. lighting manufacturers tacitly agreeing not to bring out an everlasting light bulb).

Factors favouring collusion

Collusion between firms, whether formal or tacit, is more likely when firms can clearly identify with each other or some leader and when they trust each other not to break agreements. It will be easier for firms to collude if the following conditions apply:

- There are only very few firms, all well known to each other.
- They are open with each other about costs and production methods.
- They have similar production methods and average costs, and are thus likely to want to change prices at the same time and by the same percentage.
- They produce similar products and can thus more easily reach agreements on price.
- There is a dominant firm.
- There are significant barriers to entry and thus there is little fear of disruption by new firms.
- The market is stable. If industry demand or production costs fluctuate wildly, it will be difficult to make agreements, partly due to difficulties in predicting and partly because agreements may frequently have to be amended. There is a particular problem in a declining market where firms may be tempted to undercut each other's price in order to maintain their sales.
- There are no government measures to curb collusion.

Non-collusive oligopoly: the breakdown of collusion

In some oligopolies, there may be only a few (if any) factors favouring collusion. In such cases, the likelihood of price competition is greater.

Even if there is collusion, there will always be the temptation for individual oligopolists to 'cheat', by cutting prices or by selling more than their allotted quota. The danger, of course, is that this would invite retaliation from the other members of the cartel, with a resulting price war. Price would then fall and the cartel could well break up in disarray.

When considering whether to break a collusive agreement, even if only a tacit one, a firm will ask: (1) 'How much can we get away with without inviting retaliation?' and (2) 'If a price war does result, will we be the winners? Will we succeed in driving some or all of our rivals out of business and yet survive ourselves, and thereby gain greater market power?'

definition
Price benchmark This is a price which is typically used. Firms, when raising prices, will usually raise it from one benchmark to another.

The position of rival firms, therefore, is rather like that of generals of opposing armies or the players in a game. It is a question of choosing the appropriate *strategy*: the strategy that will best succeed in outwitting your opponents. The strategy that a firm adopts will, of course, be concerned not just with price, but also with advertising and product development.

The firm's choice of strategy will depend on (a) how it thinks its rivals will react to any price changes or other changes it makes; (b) its willingness to take a gamble. Economists have developed **game theory**, which examines the best strategy that a firm can adopt for each assumption about its rivals' behaviour.

Non-collusive oligopoly: game theory

Simple dominant strategy games

The simplest case is where there are just two firms with identical costs, products and demand. They are both considering which of two alternative prices to charge. Table 12.1 shows typical profits they could each make.

Let us assume that at present both firms (X and Y) are charging a price of £2 and that they are each making a profit of £10 million, giving a total industry profit of £20 million. This is shown in the top left-hand box (A).

Now assume they are both (independently) considering reducing their price to £1.80. In making this decision, they will need to take into account what their rival might do, and how this will affect them. Let us consider X's position. In our simple example there are just two things that its rival, firm Y, might do. Either Y could cut its price to £1.80, or it could leave its price at £2. What should X do?

One alternative is to go for the cautious approach and think of the worst thing that its rival could do. If X kept its price at £2, the worst thing for X would be if its rival Y cut its price. This is shown by box C: X's profit falls to £5 million. If, however, X cut its price to £1.80, the worst outcome would again be for Y to cut its price, but this time X's profit only falls to £8 million. In this case, then, if X is cautious, it will *cut its price to £1.80*. Note that Y will argue along similar lines, and if it is cautious, it too will cut its price to £1.80. This policy of adopting the safer strategy is known as **maximin**. Following a maximin strategy, the firm will opt for the alternative that will *max*imise its *mini*mum possible profit.

An alternative strategy is to go for the optimistic approach and assume that your rivals react in the way most favourable to you. Here the firm will go for

definition
Game theory (or the theory of games) The study of alternative strategies that oligopolists may choose to adopt, depending on their assumptions about their rivals' behaviour.

definition
Maximin The strategy of choosing the policy whose worst possible outcome is the least bad.

Table 12.1 Profits for firms A and B at different prices

		X's price £2	X's price £1.80
Y's price	£2	**A** £10m each	**B** £5m for Y £12m for X
	£1.80	**C** £12m for Y £5m for X	**D** £8m each

the strategy that yields the highest possible profit. In X's case this will be again to cut price, only this time on the optimistic assumption that firm Y will leave its price unchanged. If firm X is correct in its assumption, it will move to box B and achieve the maximum possible profit of £12 million. This strategy of going for the maximum possible profit is known as **maximax**. Note that again the same argument applies to Y. Its maximax strategy will be to cut price and hopefully end up in box C.

Given that in this 'game' *both* approaches, maximin and maximax, lead to the *same* strategy (namely, cutting price), this is known as a **dominant strategy game**.

But given that both X and Y will be tempted to reduce prices, they will end up earning a lower profit (£8 million profit each in box D) than if they had charged the higher price (£10 million profit each in box A). Thus collusion, rather than a price war, would have benefited both, and yet both would be tempted to cheat and cut prices. This is known as the **prisoners' dilemma**.

More complex games with no dominant strategy

More complex 'games' can be devised with more than two firms, many alternative prices, differentiated products and various forms of non-price competition (e.g. advertising). In such cases, the cautious (maximin) strategy may suggest a different policy (e.g. do nothing) from the high-risk (maximax) strategy (e.g. cut prices substantially).

In many situations, firms will have a number of different options open to them and a number of possible reactions by rivals. In such cases, the choice facing firms may be many. They may opt for a compromise strategy between maximax and maximin. This could be a strategy that is more risky than the maximin one, but with the chance of a higher profit; but not as risky as the maximax one, but where the maximum profit possible is not so high.

The usefulness of game theory

The advantage of the game-theory approach is that the firm does not need to know which response its rivals will make. It does, however, need to be able to measure the effect of each possible response. This will be virtually impossible to do when there are many firms competing and many different responses that could be made. The approach is only useful, therefore, in relatively simple cases, and even here the estimates of profit from each outcome may amount to no more than a rough guess.

It is thus difficult for an economist to predict with any accuracy what price, output and level of advertising the firm will choose. This problem is compounded by the difficulty of predicting the type of strategy – safe, high risk, compromise – that the firm will adopt.

In some cases, firms may compete hard for a time (in price or non-price terms) and then realise that maybe no one is winning. Firms may then jointly raise prices and reduce advertising. Later, after a period of tacit collusion, competition may break out again. This may be sparked off by the entry of a new firm, by the development of a new product design, by a change in market demand, or simply by one or more firms no longer being able to resist the temptation to 'cheat'. In short, the behaviour of particular oligopolists may change quite radically over time.

---

definition

Maximax
The strategy of choosing the policy which has the best possible outcome.

---

definition

Dominant strategy game
Where the *same* policy is suggested by different strategies.

---

definition

Prisoners' dilemma
Where two or more firms (or people), by attempting independently to choose the best strategy for whatever the other(s) are likely to do, end up in a worse position than if they had co-operated in the first place.

Non-collusive oligopoly: the kinked demand curve

In 1939 a theory of non-collusive oligopoly was developed simultaneously on both sides of the Atlantic: in America by Paul Sweezy and in Britain by R.L. Hall and C.J. Hitch. This **kinked demand curve** theory has since become perhaps the most famous of all theories of oligopoly. The model seeks to explain how it is that, even when there is no collusion at all between oligopolists, prices can nevertheless remain stable.

The theory is based on two asymmetrical assumptions:

- If an oligopolist cuts its price, its rivals will feel forced to follow suit and cut theirs, to prevent losing customers to the first firm.
- If an oligopolist raises its price, however, its rivals will *not* follow suit since, by keeping their prices the same, they will thereby gain customers from the first firm.

On these assumptions, each oligopolist will face a demand curve that is *kinked* at the current price and output (see Figure 12.5). A rise in price will lead to a large fall in sales as customers switch to the now lower-priced rivals. The firm will thus be reluctant to raise its price. Demand is relatively elastic above the kink. On the other hand, a fall in price will bring only a modest increase in sales, since rivals lower their prices too and therefore customers do not switch. The firm will thus also be reluctant to reduce its price. Demand is relatively inelastic below the kink. Thus oligopolists will be reluctant to change prices at all.

This price stability can be shown formally by drawing in the firm's marginal revenue curve, as in Figure 12.6.

To see how this is done, imagine dividing the diagram into two parts either side of Q_1. At quantities less than Q_1 (the left-hand part of the diagram), the MR curve will correspond to the shallow part of the AR curve. At quantities greater than Q_1 (the right-hand part), the MR curve will correspond to the steep part of the AR curve. To see how this part of the MR curve is constructed, imagine extending the steep part of the AR curve back to the vertical axis. This and the corresponding MR curve are shown by the dotted lines in Figure 12.6.

As you can see, there will be a gap between points *a* and *b*. In other words, there is a vertical section of the MR curve between these two points.

definition
Kinked demand theory The theory that oligopolists face a demand curve that is kinked at the current price: demand being significantly more elastic above the current price than below. The effect of this is to create a situation of price stability.

Figure 12.5
Kinked demand curve for a firm under oligopoly

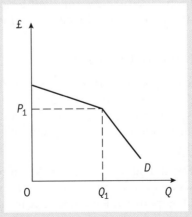

Figure 12.6
Stable price under conditions of a kinked demand curve

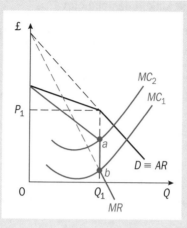

Profits are maximised where $MC = MR$. Thus, if the MC curve lies anywhere between MC_1 and MC_2 (i.e. between points a and b), the profit-maximising price and output will be P_1 and Q_1. Thus prices will remain stable *even with a considerable change in costs*.

Despite its simple demonstration of the real-world phenomenon of price stability, the model does have two major limitations.

- Price stability may be due to *other* factors. Firms may not want to change prices too frequently, as it will involve modifying price lists, working out new revenue predictions and revaluing stocks of finished goods, and it may also upset customers. Price stability, therefore, is not proof of the accuracy of the model.
- Although the model can help to explain price stability, it does not explain how prices are set in the first place. To do this, some other model would be required (see Chapter 16 for an analysis of pricing in practice). This is a serious limitation in terms of inflation, when oligopolists, like other firms, will raise prices in response to higher costs and higher demand. What the model does predict, however, is that the price will be raised only after marginal cost has risen above MC_2 in Figure 12.6, and that once it has been raised, a new kink will form at that price. Price will then remain fixed at that level until higher costs once more force a further price rise.

Oligopoly and the consumer

When oligopolists act collusively and jointly maximise industry profits, they are in effect acting together as a monopoly. In such cases, prices may be very high. This is clearly not in the best interests of consumers.

Furthermore, in two respects, oligopoly may be more disadvantageous than monopoly:

- Depending on the size of the individual oligopolists, there may be less scope for economies of scale to mitigate the effects of market power.
- Oligopolists are likely to engage in much more extensive advertising than a monopolist.

These problems will be less severe, however, if oligopolists do not collude, if there is some degree of price competition and if barriers to entry are weak.

Moreover, the power of oligopolists in certain markets may to some extent be offset if they sell their product to other powerful firms. Thus oligopolistic producers of baked beans or soap powder sell a large proportion of their output to giant supermarket chains, which can use their market power to keep down the price at which they purchase these products. This phenomenon is known as **countervailing power**.

In some respects, oligopoly may be more beneficial to the consumer than other market structures:

● Oligopolists, like monopolists, can use part of their supernormal profit for research and development. Unlike monopolists, however, oligopolists will have a considerable *incentive* to do so. If the product design is improved, this may allow the firm to capture a larger share of the market, and it may be some time before rivals can respond with a similarly improved product. If, in addition, costs are reduced by technological improvement, the resulting higher profits will enable the firm better to withstand a price war should one break out.

● Non-price competition through product differentiation may result in greater choice for the consumer. Take the case of stereo equipment. Non-price competition has led to a huge range of different products of many different specifications, each meeting the specific requirements of different consumers.

It is difficult to draw any general conclusions, since oligopolies differ so much in their performance.

Oligopoly and contestable markets

The theory of contestable markets has been applied to oligopoly as well as to monopoly, and similar conclusions are drawn.

The lower the entry and exit costs for new firms, the more difficult it will be for oligopolists to collude and make supernormal profits. If oligopolists do form a cartel (whether legal or illegal), this will be difficult to maintain if it very soon faces competition from new entrants. What a cartel has to do in such a situation is to erect entry barriers, thereby making the 'contest' more difficult. For example, the cartel could form a common research laboratory, denied to outsiders. It might attempt to control the distribution of the finished product by buying up wholesale or retail outlets. Or it might simply let it be known to potential entrants that they will face all-out price, advertising and product competition from all the members if they should dare to set up in competition.

The industry is thus likely to behave competitively if entry and exit costs are low, with all the benefits and costs to the consumer of such competition – even if the new firms do not actually enter. However, if entry and/or exit costs are high, the degree of competition will simply depend on the relations between existing members of the industry.

> **definition**
>
> **Countervailing power**
> When the power of a monopolistic/oligopolistic seller is offset by powerful buyers who can prevent the price from being pushed up.

BOX 12.2

Rip-off Britain
Evidence of oligopolistic collusion?

In recent years there have been repeated allegations that British consumers are paying much higher prices than their European counterparts on a wide range of goods. The car industry, the large supermarket chains and the banks have all been charged with 'ripping-off' the consumer. Such has been the level of concern, that all three industries have been referred to the Competition Commission (see section 20.1).

Car industry

The clearest evidence of anti-competitive pricing behaviour in the UK car industry came with the admission by Volvo in July 1999 that it had entered secret agreements to keep British car prices high. This appeared to be just the tip of an iceberg, with car manufacturers fixing prices through the system of selective and exclusive distribution (SED). In other words, manufacturers would only supply through 'official' dealers who would sell at the list price (or at small agreed 'discounts').

When we consider the difference in price between identical models in Britain and mainland Europe the discrepancies are huge. The Competition Commission report, published in April 2000, found that car buyers in Britain were paying on average some 10 to 12 per cent more than those in France, Germany and Italy for the same models. For 58 of the 71 models analysed by the Commission, the UK price was at least 20 per cent higher than in the cheapest country. The Commission concluded that British car buyers were paying around 10 per cent too much for new cars, or some £1100 for an average car.

The price discrepancies between Britain and Europe were maintained by car manufacturers blocking cheaper European cars coming into the UK. Manufacturers have been accused of adopting a number of anti-competitive practices. These include threatening mainland European car dealers with losing their dealership if they sell to British buyers, and delaying the delivery date of right-hand drive models to mainland European dealers in the hope that British buyers will change their minds and go back to a British dealership.

Supermarkets

The Competition Commission enquiry into supermarkets, which began in April 1999, followed a nine-month investigation by the Office of Fair Trading into the major supermarket chains' business activities. The OFT identified three major areas of concern: the use of barriers to entry, the lack of effective price competition, and the relationship between the large supermarket chains and their suppliers.

The main issue concerns the major supermarket chains' huge buying and selling power. They have been able to drive costs down by forcing suppliers to offer discounts. Many suppliers, such as growers, have found their profit margins cut to the bone. However, these cost savings have not been passed on from supplier to shopper. The supermarket chains have adopted a system of 'shadow pricing', a form of tacit collusion whereby they all observe each other's prices and ensure that they remain at similar levels: often similarly high levels rather than similarly low levels! This has limited the extent of true price competition, and the resulting high prices have seen profits grow as costs have been driven ever downwards.

Since the OFT referral, the £6.7 billion take-over of Asda by Wal-Mart, the world's largest retailer, with a reputation of being a ruthless price cutter, promised to

---

SUMMARY

1a Monopolistic competition occurs where there is free entry to the industry and quite a large number of firms operating independently of each other, but where each firm has some market power as a result of producing differentiated products or services.

1b In the short run, firms can make supernormal profits. In the long run, however, freedom of entry will drive profits down to the normal level. The long-run equilibrium of the firm is where the (downward-sloping) demand curve is tangential to the long-run average cost curve.

1c The long-run equilibrium is one of excess capacity. Given that the demand curve is downward sloping, its tangency point with the *LRAC* curve will not be at

change the whole issue of pricing in the supermarket sector. Of the supermarket chains, Asda has always been one of the cheapest. With the Wal-Mart take-over, the drive to cut prices gained fresh momentum. Asda planned to slash prices on hundreds of products, with most seeing some price reduction.

Tesco in response, striving to maintain its position as the UK's number one supermarket retailer, launched its own price-cutting campaign. It was determined not to get left behind in the price-cutting war.

Despite these apparent price wars, the Competition Commission was still concerned that competition was being restricted. It sought to answer a number of questions. Is price competition limited to a relatively small number of frequently purchased items, and at stores which face the most local competition? Are cost reductions 'being rapidly and fully passed through to consumers'? Is 'the pattern of prices and margins across different types of product, including branded and own label products, related to costs to the extent that would be expected in a fully competitive market? This would include products persistently sold at a loss, which may benefit consumers in the short term but which may distort competition and consumer choice, and may adversely affect the supply or availability of such products in the longer term.'[1]

One solution suggested by the Competition Commission would be to force supermarkets to publish their prices on the Internet, thereby allowing consumers or consumers' organisations to make easy comparisons of the prices charged by different supermarkets.

Banks

According to a Treasury report, chaired by Don Cruickshank,[2] UK banks are making excessive profits of some £3 billion to £5 billion per year, with bank customers paying up to £400 a year too much in charges and interest rates. The report found that current accounts were the least competitive product. They pay little or no interest to customers in credit and charge exorbitant amounts if you go overdrawn. But it was not just current accounts: mortgages, savings accounts, credit cards and personal loans were all identified as often being poor products.

Banks have tight control over cheque clearing, money transmission systems and cash machines. This makes it difficult for new competitors to enter the market. For example, a new bank without an extensive network of cash machines would find it difficult to attract customers, given the hefty charges for using other banks' machines. In addition, bank customers are often unwilling to consider changing accounts, fearing that this will involve a lot of time and expense.

Small businesses were found to be facing even more excessive charges. The government thus asked the Competition Commission to inquire into this particular aspect of the provision of banking services.

Questions

1 Identify the main barriers to entry in the supermarket and banking sectors.

2 In what forms of tacit collusion are firms in the three industries likely to engage?

[1] 'Supply of Groceries from Multiple Stores Monopoly Inquiry: Annex 2 To Issues Letter' (Competition Commission, 2000)
[2] 'Competition in UK Banking: a Report to the Chancellor of the Exchequer' (TSO, 2000)

SUMMARY

the bottom of the *LRAC* curve. Increased production would thus be possible at *lower* average cost.

1d In practice, supernormal profits may persist into the long run: firms have imperfect information; entry may not be completely unrestricted; there may be a problem of indivisibilities; firms may use non-price competition to maintain an advantage over their rivals.

1e Monopolistically competitive firms, because of excess capacity, may have higher costs, and thus higher prices, than perfectly competitive firms, but consumers may gain from a greater diversity of products.

1f Monopolistically competitive firms may have less economies of scale than monopolies and conduct

SUMMARY

less research and development, but the competition may keep prices lower than under monopoly. Whether there will be more or less choice for the consumer is debatable.

2a An oligopoly is where there are just a few firms in the industry with barriers to the entry of new firms. Firms recognise their mutual dependence.

2b Oligopolists will want to maximise their joint profits. This will tend to make them collude to keep prices high. On the other hand, they will want the biggest share of industry profits for themselves. This will tend to make them compete.

2c Whether they compete or collude depends on the conditions in the industry. They are more likely to collude if there are few of them; if they are open with each other; if they have similar products and cost structures; if there is a dominant firm; if there are significant entry barriers; if the market is stable; and if there is no government legislation to prevent collusion.

2d Collusion can be open or tacit.

2e A formal collusive agreement is called a 'cartel'. A cartel aims to act as a monopoly. It can set price and leave the members to compete for market share, or it can assign quotas. There is always a temptation for cartel members to 'cheat' by undercutting the cartel price if they think they can get away with it and not trigger a price war.

2f Tacit collusion can take the form of price leadership. This is where firms follow the price set by either a dominant firm in the industry or one seen as a reliable 'barometer' of market conditions. Alternatively, tacit collusion can simply involve following various rules of thumb such as average cost pricing and benchmark pricing.

2g Non-collusive oligopolists will have to work out a price strategy. This will depend on their attitudes towards risk and on the assumptions they make about the behaviour of their rivals. Game theory examines various strategies that firms can adopt when the outcome of each is not certain. They can adopt a low-risk 'maximin' strategy of choosing the policy that has the least-bad worst outcome, or a high-risk 'maximax' strategy of choosing the policy with the best possible outcome, or some compromise.

2h Because firms are likely to face a kinked demand curve, they are likely to keep their prices stable unless there is a large shift in costs or demand.

2i Whether consumers benefit from oligopoly depends on the particular oligopoly and how competitive it is; whether there is any countervailing power; whether the firms engage in extensive advertising and of what type; whether product differentiation results in a wide range of choice for the consumer; how much of the profits are ploughed back into research and development; and how contestable the market is. Since these conditions vary substantially from oligopoly to oligopoly, it is impossible to state just how well or how badly oligopoly in general serves the consumer's interest.

REVIEW QUESTIONS

1 Think of ten different products or services and estimate roughly how many firms there are in the market. You will need to decide whether 'the market' is a local one, a national one or an international one. In what ways do the firms compete in each of the cases you have identified?

2 Imagine there are two types of potential customer for jam sold by a small food shop. One is the person who has just run out and wants some now. The other is the person who looks in the cupboard, sees that the pot of jam is less than half full and thinks, 'I will soon need some more.' How will the price elasticity of demand differ between these two customers?

3 Why may a food shop charge higher prices than supermarkets for 'essential items' and yet very similar prices for delicatessen items?

4 How will the position and shape of a firm's short-run demand curve depend on the prices that rivals charge?

5 Assuming that a firm under monopolistic competition can make supernormal profits in the short run, will there be any difference in the long-run and short-run elasticity of demand? Explain.

6 Firms under monopolistic competition generally have spare capacity. Does this imply that if, say, half of the petrol stations were closed down, the consumer would benefit? Explain.

7 Will competition between oligopolists always reduce total industry profits?

8 In which of the following industries is collusion likely to occur: bricks, beer, margarine, cement, crisps, washing powder, blank audio or video cassettes, carpets?

9 Draw a diagram like Figure 12.4. Illustrate what would happen if there were a rise in market demand.

10 Devise a box diagram like that in Table 12.1, only this time assume that there are three firms, each considering the two strategies of keeping price the same or reducing it by a set amount. Is the game still a 'dominant strategy game'?

11 What are the limitations of game theory in predicting oligopoly behaviour?

12 Which of the following are examples of effective countervailing power?
   (a) A power station buying coal from a large local coal mine.
   (b) A large factory hiring a photocopier from Rank Xerox.
   (c) Marks and Spencer buying clothes from a garment manufacturer.
   (d) A small village store (but the only one for miles around) buying food from a wholesaler.

Is it the size of the purchasing firm that is important in determining its power to keep down the prices charged by its suppliers?

E
Supply: alternative strategies

THE FT REPORTS...

THE FINANCIAL TIMES, 30 JUNE 2000

The urge to merge takes on a different form

Traditionally, mergers and acquisitions were top-down affairs. Chief executives came together with the help of their investment bankers, agreed on a combination, then proceeded with the arduous task of stitching together their operations.

But in the internet era, the process is starting to work in a different way. Corporate executives and investment bankers are focusing their efforts at the bottom – figuring out ways to integrate operations, without formally combining companies.

An example of this trend has been a flurry of deals creating business-to-business, or B2B, exchanges. In such arrangements, companies join forces to build internet market places, while stopping short of other corporate links.

In June, Morgan Stanley provided advice and financing for a computer, electronic and telecommunications market place. Called e2open.com, it brings together such leading tech players as Hitachi, IBM, LG Electronics, Matsushita Electric, Nortel Networks, Seagate Technology, Solectron and Toshiba.

The presence of so many high-tech companies in an internet exchange was a particularly telling endorsement of the model, since they were all sophisticated enough to strike out of their own should they have wanted to do so.

The B2B exchanges respond to the needs of companies that do a lot of outsourcing. In the past, Mr Mamdani a managing director in Morgan Stanley's merger and acquisition practice says, companies would buy suppliers to make sure essential goods and services would be available. Now, they can obtain the same kind of certainty of supply by linking up through the internet.

"The ability to share information allows you to capture efficiencies through greater integration with suppliers and distributors without having those activities housed in the same corporate shell" he says. "You don't need to own everything."

The old economy analogy would be a case where competing industrial companies joined together to push for roads or port facilities so they could ship their products to customers.

M any small companies, especially those facing fierce competition, may be forced to pursue profit as their overriding goal, merely to survive. The maximum profit they can make may be only just enough for them to stay in business in the long term (i.e. normal profit).

With large companies, however, where mere survival is not the overriding concern, the pursuit of short-run profit is likely to be only one of many business objectives. The modern business enterprise is often a complex organisation, with many different departments and divisions. What is more, the ownership and control of the firm are often in totally different hands: i.e. shareholders and managers. With many competing interests there are often several objectives being pursued simultaneously.

In Part E we will consider what these alternative objectives might be and the strategies that businesses might adopt in their pursuit.

In Chapter 13 we will outline various alternative theories of the firm – alternative, that is, to the traditional theory of short-run profit maximisation. Then, in Chapter 14, we will focus on one particular theory: that of growth maximisation.

> The typical entrepreneur is no longer the bold and tireless businessman of Marshall, or the sly rapacious Moneybags of Marx, but a mass of inert shareholders, indistinguishable from rentiers, who employ salaried managers to run their concerns.
>
> Joan Robinson (1903–83),
> *An Essay on Marxian Economics*,
> 1947, Chapter III, p. 18

Chapter 15 looks at the small-firm sector, and compares the objectives and behaviour of small firms with those of their bigger rivals.

Finally, in Chapter 16, we will look at alternative pricing strategies and how they vary with market structure and the different aims that firms might pursue.

key terms

Profit satisficing
Managerial utility
Behavioural theories
  of the firm
Organisational slack
Takeover constraint
Horizontal and
  vertical integration
Diversification
Merger
Enterprise
Cost-based pricing
Price discrimination
Transfer pricing

Alternative theories of the firm

13.1 Problems with traditional theory

The traditional profit-maximising theories of the firm have been criticised for being unrealistic. The criticisms are mainly of two sorts: (a) that firms wish to maximise profits, but for some reason or other are unable to do so; or (b) that firms have aims other than profit maximisation. Let us examine each in turn.

Difficulties in maximising profit

One criticism of traditional theory sometimes put forward is that firms do not use *MR* and *MC* concepts. This may be true, but firms could still arrive at maximum profit by trial and error adjustments of price, or by finding the output where *TR* and *TC* are furthest apart. Provided they end up maximising profits, they will be equating *MC* and *MR*, even if they do not know it! In this case, traditional models will still be useful in predicting price and output.

The main difficulty in trying to maximise profits is a lack of information.

Firms may well use accountants' cost concepts not based on opportunity cost (see section 9.1). If it is thereby impossible to measure true profit, a firm will not be able to maximise profit except by chance.

More importantly, firms are unlikely to know precisely (or even approximately) their demand curves and hence their *MR* curves. Even though (presumably) they will know how much they are selling at the moment, this only gives them one point on their demand curve and no point at all on their *MR* curve. In order to make even an informed guess about marginal revenue, they must have some idea of how responsive demand will be to a change in price. But how are they to estimate this price elasticity? Market research may help. But even this is frequently very unreliable. Such information takes time to acquire and act on, by which time market conditions may have changed, thus making the information out of date. The firm will thus have to decide whether the possibly small benefit from market research is worth its cost.

The biggest problem in estimating the firm's demand curve is in estimating the actions and reactions of *other* firms and their effects. Collusion between oligopolists or price leadership would help, but there will still be a considerable area of uncertainty, especially if the firm faces competition from abroad. Even other *industries'* products may be substitutes or complements to some degree, and thus changes in their price or quality will affect the firm's demand curve.

Game theory may help a firm decide its price and output strategy: it may choose to sacrifice the chance of getting the absolute maximum profit (the high-risk, maximax option), and instead go for the safe strategy of getting probably at least reasonable profits (maximin). But even this assumes that it knows the consequences for its profits of each of the possible reactions of its rivals. In reality, it will not even have this information to any degree of certainty, because it simply will not be able to predict just how consumers will respond to each of its rivals' alternative reactions.

Finally, there is the problem in deciding the *time period* over which the firm should be seeking to maximise profits. Firms operate in a changing environment. Demand curves shift; supply curves shift. Some of these shifts occur as a result of factors outside the firm's control, such as changes in competitors' prices and products, or changes in technology. Some, however, change as a direct result of a firm's policies, such as an advertising campaign, the development of a new improved product, or the installation of new equipment. The firm is not, therefore, faced with static cost and revenue curves from which it can read off its profit-maximising price and output. Instead it is faced with a changing (and often highly unpredictable) set of curves. If it chooses a price and an output that maximise profits this year, it may as a result jeopardise profits in the future.

Let us take a simple example. The firm may be trying to decide whether to invest in new expensive equipment. If it does, its costs will rise in the short run and thus short-run profits will fall. On the other hand, if the quality of the product thereby increases, demand is likely to increase over the longer run. Also variable costs are likely to decrease if the new equipment is more efficient in its use of fuel or raw materials, or requires less labour per unit of output to operate it. In other words, long-run profit is likely to increase, but probably by a highly uncertain amount.

Given these extreme problems in deciding profit-maximising price and output, firms may adopt simple rules of thumb for pricing. These are examined in Chapter 16.

Alternative aims

An even more fundamental attack on the traditional theory of the firm is that firms do not even *aim* to maximise profits (even if they could).

The traditional theory of the firm assumes that it is the *owners* of the firm that make price and output decisions. It is reasonable to assume that owners *will* want to maximise profits: this much most of the critics of the traditional theory accept. The question is, however, whether the owners do in fact make the decisions.

In Chapter 3 we saw that in public limited companies there is generally a separation of ownership and control. The shareholders are the owners and presumably will want the firm to maximise profits so as to increase their dividends and the value of their shares. Shareholders elect directors. Directors in turn employ professional managers, who are often given considerable discretion in making decisions. But what are the objectives of managers? Will *they* want to maximise profits, or will they have some other aim?

Managers may be assumed to want to *maximise their own utility*. This may well involve pursuits that conflict with profit maximisation. They may, for example, pursue higher salaries, greater power or prestige, better working conditions, greater sales, etc. Different managers in the same firm may well pursue different aims.

Managers will still have to ensure that *sufficient* profits are made to keep shareholders happy, but that may be very different from *maximising* profits.

Alternative theories of the firm to those of profit maximisation, therefore, tend to assume that large firms are **profit satisficers**. That is, managers strive hard for a minimum target level of profit, but are less interested in profits above this level.

Such theories fall into two categories: first those theories that assume that firms attempt to maximise some other aim, provided that sufficient profits are achieved (these are examined in section 13.2); and second, those theories that assume that firms pursue a number of potentially conflicting aims, of which sufficient profit is merely one (these theories are examined in section 13.3).

13.2 Alternative maximising theories

Long-run profit maximisation

The traditional theory of the firm is based on the assumption of *short-run* profit maximisation. Many actions of firms may be seen to conflict with this aim and yet could be consistent with the aim of **long-run profit maximisation**. For example, policies to increase the size of the firm or the firm's share of the market may involve heavy advertising or low prices to the detriment of short-run profits. But if this results in the firm becoming larger, with a larger share of the market, the resulting economic power may enable the firm to make larger profits in the long run.

At first sight, a theory of long-run profit maximisation would seem to be a realistic alternative to the traditional short-run profit-maximisation theory. In practice, however, the theory is not a very useful predictor of firms' behaviour and is very difficult to test.

One question is whether long-run profit maximisation is merely the result of managers pursuing other aims, or whether it is the prime aim itself.

What is more, 'long-run maximisation' could be an excuse for virtually any policy. When challenged as to why the firm had, say, undertaken expensive research, or high-cost investment, or engaged in a damaging price war, the managers could reply, 'Ah, yes, but in the long run it will pay off.' This is very difficult to refute (until it is too late!).

If long-run profit maximisation *is* the prime aim, the means of achieving it are extremely complex. The firm will need a plan of action for prices, output, investment, etc., stretching from now into the future. But today's prices and marketing decisions affect tomorrow's demand. Therefore, future demand curves cannot be taken as given. Similarly, today's investment decisions will affect tomorrow's costs. Therefore, future cost curves cannot be taken as given. These shifts in demand and cost curves will be very difficult to estimate with any precision. Quite apart from this, the actions of competitors, suppliers, unions and so on are difficult to predict. Thus the picture of firms making precise calculations of long-run profit-maximising prices and outputs is a false one.

A precise theory of long-run profit maximisation is therefore not useful in explaining how firms actually behave. Either the theory would be too simplistic to be realistic, because there could be no simple formula for predicting price and output and the level of investment, or it would have to be so complex that it would be quite unworkable.

It may be useful, however, simply to observe that firms, when making current

> **definition**
>
> **Profit satisficing**
> Where decision makers in a firm aim for a target level of profit rather than the absolute maximum level.

> **definition**
>
> **Long-run profit maximisation**
> An alternative theory which assumes that managers aim to shift cost and revenue curves so as to maximise profits over some longer time period.

BOX 13.1

In search of long-run profits
The video games war

Traditional economic theory argues that firms will seek to maximise their short-run profits, and therefore adopt a range of strategies to achieve this goal. There are, however, plenty of examples from the world of business to suggest that firms often take a longer-term perspective. One recent example, which has been part of a long-running video games war between Sony, Sega and Nintendo, was the pricing decision taken by Sony and Sega in the face of renewed competition from Nintendo.

The following extract is taken from the *Financial Times* of 1–2 March 1997, and relays some of the actions and intentions of the market's major players at the time. It is clear that long-run profits seem a major motivating factor.

Sony, the Japanese consumer electronics group, fired the latest salvo in the video games war yesterday by reducing the price of its PlayStation games console by £70 to £129.99 on the eve of the launch of the Nintendo 64 system.

The Nintendo 64, which goes on sale in the UK today with a recommended retail price of £249.99, is based on 64-bit technology which makes it faster and more powerful than PlayStation and Saturn, both of which are 32-bit consoles.

Since their launch in autumn 1995, the Sony and Sega systems have dominated the video games market ... However, the Nintendo 64 has achieved significant sales in Japan, since its introduction there last July, and in North America, where it sold 1.7 million systems between its September debut and Christmas.

In the 18 months that PlayStation and Saturn have been on the market, Sony and Sega have adopted a strategy of pricing the consoles as cheaply as possible to establish a large base of players to whom they can sell the highly profitable software.

Sony has reduced the price of the PlayStation, the best-selling games system in the UK, having sold a total of 750 000 consoles, from £299.99 in September 1995 to £199.99 last May. Sega followed suit by cutting Saturn's price.

Sony's latest cut is intended to stop the Nintendo 64 from taking future sales from PlayStation. Sega will discuss the pricing issue at this weekend's meeting, but it plans to start a promotion on Monday, giving away two free games with each new Saturn console.

As part of the offensive against Nintendo 64, Sony has decided to widen the price range of its PlayStation software by launching a 'Platinum

price, output and investment decisions, try to judge the approximate effect on new entrants, consumer demand, future costs, etc., and try to avoid decisions that would appear to conflict with long-run profits. Often this will simply involve avoiding making decisions (e.g. cutting price) that may stimulate an unfavourable reaction from rivals (e.g. rivals cutting their price).

Managerial utility maximisation

The theory of profit maximisation came under increasing attack during the 1950s and 1960s, when a whole range of new and alternative theories were developed. The common element of these theories was the replacing of profit maximising by a profit constraint.

Provided that satisfactory levels of profit were achieved, managers were seen to be free to pursue a whole range of discretionary policies: that is, they were free to maximise their own utility.

Much of the pioneering work in the field of **managerial utility maximisation**

Range' of past bestsellers, priced at £19.99 each, compared with up to £49.99 for new games.

Since 1997, the industry and the strategies of the businesses operating in it have changed very little, although it would seem that Sony has stolen a march on its rivals. Sony's ruthless price-cutting strategy has seen the PlayStation's price tumble below £100 with any number of free games included, and software prices have also been cut with a range of budget titles now on offer called PlayStation Classics, which sell for under £10. Over its six years, 70 million PlayStations have been sold, and in 1999 the product accounted for 40 per cent of Sony's turnover. With this foundation, Sony is looking to ensure that its PlayStation 2, launched in 2000, continues its dominance. With a DVD facility, and crucially in marketing terms, backward compatibility (i.e. PlayStation games can be played on PlayStation 2), Sony will hope to expand its market share.

Does this mean an end to cost cutting and a longer-run view of profits, now that Sony has seen off its main rivals? The answer is probably no. Games consoles, the hardware, are not upgradeable. As a result, products like the PlayStation are cyclical, in so far as they mature and then require replacement as technological innovation moves on. At that stage there is an opportunity for new rivals to enter the market and threaten the dominance of the market leader. The games market is worth an estimated $11 billion and as such the rewards for a successful product are immense. Such rewards have not gone unnoticed by the likes of Microsoft, which hopes, in the latter part of 2001, to launch its X-box to challenge the PlayStation. Nintendo, in development with Matsushita, is developing the Dolphin to challenge them both.

It would be a poor business strategy not to look to the future in this ever changing market, and so long as competition remains, and products need replacing over a period of time, then long-run profits are likely to be the goal rather than the maximisation of profits over the short-run.

Questions

1 Why might a business wish to maximise long-run profits?
2 How does the maximisation of long-run profits conflict with the maximisation of short-run profits?
3 What factors might favour collusion in the video games market? What factors might make collusion unlikely?

was done by O.E. Williamson. He identified a number of factors that would determine a manager's utility. These included the following:

- Salary.
- Security.
- Dominance – including status, power and prestige.
- Professional excellence.

Of these variables, only salary was directly measurable. The rest would have to be measured indirectly through other variables that reflected them. For this purpose Williamson developed the concept of 'expense preference'. This was a means of illustrating the satisfaction that managers gained from spending money – in particular, on *staff*, on *perks* (such as company cars and a plush office) and on *discretionary investment*. He suggested that such spending reflected the manager's power, status, prestige, security and professional excellence.

Increased *spending on staff* was suggested by Williamson to be equivalent to promotion. Power, status and prestige would all be enhanced as the staff under the manager's control grew in number. The number of staff was a symbol of the manager's professional importance.

Emoluments (perks) in the form of expense accounts, company cars, etc., reflect the manager's position within the firm. The higher the level of perks, the more secure and dominant the manager is likely to be.

Discretionary investment by managers is possible when earnings above the minimum profit constraint are achieved. This allows managers to expand staff and perks and undertake any other projects that the manager wishes to pursue. How the money is invested is at the manager's discretion.

Having identified these factors that influence a manager's utility, Williamson developed several models in which managers maximise their utility function. He used these models to predict managerial behaviour under various conditions and argued that they performed better than traditional profit-maximising theory. To support these claims he conducted a number of case studies. These showed, for example, that staff and perks were cut during recessions and expanded during booms, and that new managers were frequently able to cut staff without influencing the productivity of firms.

Although Williamson's work has produced and stimulated a whole range of investigations into the behaviour of managers, the evidence gathered remains inconclusive. Many economists suggest that the nature of the market in which the firm operates will determine which of the theories is the most relevant: profit maximisation, managerial utility or some other.

Sales revenue maximisation (short run)

Perhaps the most famous of all alternative theories of the firm is that developed by William Baumol in the late 1950s. This is the theory of **sales revenue maximisation**. Unlike the theories of long-run profit maximisation and managerial utility maximisation, it is easy to identify the price and output that meet this aim – at least in the short run.

So why should managers want to maximise their firm's sales revenue? The answer is that the success of managers, and especially sales managers, may be judged according to the level of the firm's sales. Sales figures are an obvious barometer of the firm's health. Managers' salaries, power and prestige may depend directly on sales revenue. The firm's sales representatives may be paid commission on their sales. Thus sales revenue maximisation may be a more dominant aim in the firm than profit maximisation, particularly if it has a dominant sales department.

Sales revenue will be maximised at the top of the TR curve at output Q_1 in Figure 13.1. Profits, by contrast, would be maximised at Q_2. Thus, for given total revenue and total cost curves, sales revenue maximisation will tend to lead to a higher output and a lower price than profit maximisation. In other words, the firm will operate on a lower point on its demand curve.

The firm will still have to make sufficient profits, however, to keep the shareholders happy. Thus firms can be seen to be operating with a profit constraint. They are *profit satisficers*.

The effect of this profit constraint is illustrated in Figure 13.2. The diagram shows a total profit ($T\Pi$) curve. (This is found by simply taking the difference between TR and TC at each output.) Assume that the minimum acceptable

---

definition
Sales revenue maximisation An alternative theory of the firm which assumes that managers aim to maximise the firm's short-run total revenue.

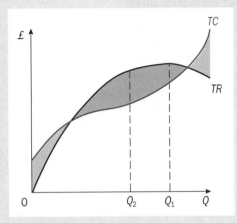

Figure 13.1
Sales revenue maximising output

profit is Π (whatever the output). Any output greater than Q_3 will give a profit less than Π. Thus the sales revenue maximiser who is also a profit satisficer will produce Q_3 not Q_1. Note, however, that this output is still greater than the profit-maximising output Q_2.

If the firm could maximise sales revenue and still make more than the minimum acceptable profit, it would probably spend this surplus profit on advertising to increase revenue further. This would have the effect of shifting the *TR* curve upward and also the *TC* curve (since advertising costs money).

Sales revenue maximisation will tend to involve more advertising than profit maximisation. Ideally the profit-maximising firm will advertise up to the point where the marginal revenue of advertising equals the marginal cost of advertising (assuming diminishing returns to advertising). The firm aiming to maximise sales revenue will go beyond this, since further advertising, although costing more than it earns the firm, will still add to total revenue. The firm will continue advertising until surplus profits above the minimum have been used up.

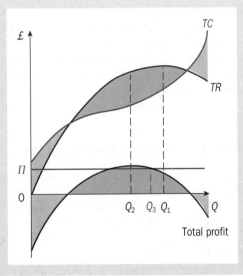

Figure 13.2
Sales revenue maximising with a profit constraint

Growth maximisation

Rather than aiming to maximise *short-run* revenue, managers may take a longer-term perspective and aim for **growth maximisation** in the size of the firm. They may gain utility directly from being part of a rapidly growing 'dynamic' organisation; promotion prospects are greater in an expanding organisation, since new posts tend to be created; large firms may pay higher salaries; managers may obtain greater power in a large firm.

Growth is probably best measured in terms of a growth in sales revenue, since sales revenue (or 'turnover') is the simplest way of measuring the size of a business. An alternative would be to measure the capital value of a firm, but this will depend on the ups and downs of the stock market and is thus a rather unreliable method.

If a firm is to maximise growth, it needs to be clear about the time period over which it is setting itself this objective. For example, maximum growth over the next two or three years might be obtained by running factories to absolute maximum capacity, cramming in as many machines and workers as possible, and backing this up with massive advertising campaigns and price cuts. Such policies, however, may not be sustainable in the longer run. The firm may simply not be able to finance them. A longer-term perspective (say, 5–10 years) may therefore require the firm to 'pace' itself, and perhaps to direct resources away from current production and sales into the development of new products that have a potentially high and growing long-term demand.

Equilibrium for a growth-maximising firm

What will a growth-maximising firm's price and output be? Unfortunately, there is no simple formula for predicting this.

In the short run, the firm may choose the profit-maximising price and output – so as to provide the greatest funds for investment. On the other hand, it may be prepared to sacrifice some short-term profits in order to mount an advertising campaign. It all depends on the strategy it considers most suitable to achieve growth.

In the long run, prediction is more difficult still. The policies that a firm adopts will depend crucially on the assessments of market opportunities made by managers. But this involves judgement, not fine calculation. Different managers will judge a situation differently.

One prediction can be made. Growth-maximising firms are likely to diversify into different products, especially as they approach the limits to expansion in existing markets.

Alternative growth strategies are considered in Chapter 14.

Alternative maximising theories and the consumer

It is difficult to draw firm conclusions about how the behaviour of firms in these alternative maximising theories will affect the consumer's interest.

In the case of sales revenue maximisation, a higher output will be produced than under profit maximisation, but the consumer will not necessarily benefit from lower prices, since more will be spent on advertising – costs that will be passed on to the consumer.

In the case of growth and long-run profit maximisation, there are many possible policies that a firm could pursue. To the extent that a concern for the long run encourages firms to look to improved products, new products and new techniques, the consumer may benefit from such a concern. To the extent, however, that growth encourages a greater level of industrial concentration through merger, so the consumer may lose from the resulting greater level of monopoly power.

As with the traditional theory of the firm, the degree of competition that a firm faces is a crucial factor in determining just how responsive it will be to the wishes of the consumer.

13.3 Multiple aims

Satisficing and the setting of targets

Firms may have more than one aim. For example, they may try to achieve increased sales revenue *and* increased profit. The problem with this is that, if two aims conflict, it will not be possible to maximise both of them. For example, sales revenue will probably be maximised at a different price and output from that at which profits are maximised. Where firms have two or more aims, a compromise may be for targets to be set for individual aims which are low enough to achieve simultaneously, and yet which are sufficient to satisfy the interested parties.

Such target setting is also likely when the maximum value of a particular aim is unknown. If, for example, the maximum achievable profit is unknown, the firm may well set a target for profit which it feels is both satisfactory and achievable.

Behavioural theories of the firm: the setting of targets

A major advance in alternative theories of the firm has been the development of **behavioural theories**.[2] Rather than setting up a model to show how various objectives could in theory be achieved, behavioural theories of the firm are based on observations of how firms *actually* behave.

Large firms are often complex institutions with several departments (sales, production, design, purchasing, personnel, finance, etc.). Each department is likely to have its own specific set of aims and objectives, which may possibly come into conflict with those of other departments. These aims in turn will be constrained by the interests of shareholders, workers, customers and creditors, who will need to be kept sufficiently happy.

Behavioural theories do not lay down rules of how to *achieve* these aims, but rather examine what these aims are, the motivations underlying them, the conflicts that can arise between aims, and how these conflicts are resolved.

It is assumed that targets will be set for production, sales, profit, stock holding, etc. If, in practice, target levels are not achieved, a 'search' procedure will be started to find what went wrong and how to rectify it. If the problem cannot be rectified, managers will probably adjust the target downwards. If, on the

definition
Behavioural theories of the firm Theories that attempt to predict the actions of firms by studying the behaviour of various groups of people within the firm and their interactions under conditions of potentially conflicting interests.

[2] See in particular: R.M. Cyert and J.G. March, *A Behavioural Theory of the Firm* (Prentice Hall, 1963).

BOX 13.2

Stakeholder power?
Who governs the firm?

The concept of the 'stakeholder economy' became fashionable in the late 1990s. Rather than the economy being governed by big business, and rather than businesses being governed in the interests of shareholders (many of whom are big institutions, such as insurance companies and pension funds), the economy should serve the interests of everyone. But what does this mean for the governance of firms?

The stakeholders of a firm include customers, employees (from senior managers to the lowest-paid workers), shareholders, suppliers, lenders and the local and national communities.

The supporters of a stakeholding economy argue that *all* these interest groups ought to have a say in the decisions of the firm. Trades unions or workers' councils ought to be included in decisions affecting the workforce, or indeed all company decisions. They could be represented on decision-making bodies and perhaps have seats on the board of directors. Alternatively, the workforce might be given the power to elect managers.

Banks or other institutions lending to firms ought to be included in investment decisions. In Germany, where banks finance a large proportion of investment, banks are represented on the boards of most large companies.

Local communities ought to have a say in any projects (such as new buildings or the discharge of effluent) that affect the local environment. Customers ought to have more say in the quality of products being produced, for example by being given legal protection against the production of shoddy or unsafe goods. Where interest groups cannot be directly represented in decision making, then companies ought to be regulated by the government in order to protect the interests of the various groups. For example, if farmers

and other suppliers to supermarkets are paid very low prices, then the purchasing behaviour of the supermarkets could be regulated by some government agency.

But is this vision of a stakeholder economy likely to become reality? Trends in the international economy suggest that the opposite might be occurring. The growth of multinational corporations, with their ability to move finance and production to wherever it is most profitable, has weakened the power of employees, local interest groups and even national governments.

Employees in one part of the multinational may have little in the way of common interests with employees in another. In fact, they may vie with each other, for example over which plant should be expanded or closed down. What is more, many firms are employing a larger and larger proportion of casual, part-time, temporary or agency workers. With these new 'flexible labour markets' such employees have far less say in the company than permanent members of staff: they are 'outsiders' to decision making within the firm (see section 17.7).

Also, the widespread introduction of share incentive schemes for managers (whereby managers are rewarded with shares), has increasingly made profits their driving goal. Finally, the policies of opening up markets and deregulation, policies that were adopted by many governments round the world up to the mid-1990s, has again weakened the power of many stakeholders.

Question

Are customers' interests best served by profit-maximising firms, answerable primarily to shareholders, or by firms where various stakeholder groups are represented in decision taking?

other hand, targets are easily achieved, managers may adjust them upwards. Thus the targets to which managers aspire depend to a large extent on the success in achieving *previous* targets. Targets are also influenced by expectations of demand and costs, by the achievements of competitors and by expectations of competitors' future behaviour. For example, if it is expected that the economy is likely to move into recession, sales and profit targets may be adjusted downwards.

If targets conflict, the conflict will be settled by a bargaining process between managers. The outcome of the bargaining, however, will depend on the power and ability of the individual managers concerned. Thus a similar set of conflicting targets may be resolved differently in different firms.

Behavioural theories of the firm: organisational slack

Since changing targets often involves search procedures and bargaining processes and is therefore time consuming, and since many managers prefer to avoid conflict, targets tend to be changed fairly infrequently. Business conditions, however, often change rapidly. To avoid the need to change targets, therefore, managers will tend to be fairly conservative in their aspirations. This leads to the phenomenon known as **organisational slack**.

When the firm does better than planned, it will allow slack to develop. This slack can then be taken up if the firm does worse than planned. For example, if the firm produces more than it planned, it will build up stocks of finished goods and draw on them if production subsequently falls. It would not, in the meantime, increase its sales target or reduce its production target. If it did, and production then fell below target, the production department might not be able to supply the sales department with its full requirement.

Thus keeping targets fairly low and allowing slack to develop allows all targets to be met with minimum conflict.

Multiple goals: some predictions of behaviour

Conservatism

Some firms may be wary of unnecessary change. Change is risky. They may prefer to stick with tried and tested practices. 'If it works, stick with it.' This could apply to pricing policies, marketing techniques, product design and range, internal organisation of the firm, etc.

If something does not work, however, managers will probably change it, but again they may be conservative and only try a cautious change: perhaps imitating successful competitors.

This safe, satisficing approach makes prediction of any given firm's behaviour relatively easy. You simply examine its past behaviour. However, making generalisations about all such cautious firms is more difficult. Different firms are likely to have established different rules of behaviour depending on their own particular experiences of their market.

Comparison with other firms

Managers may judge their success by comparing their firm's performance with that of rival firms. For example, growing market share may be seen as a more important indicator of 'success' than simple growth in sales. Similarly, they may compare their profits, their product design, their technology or their industrial relations with those of rivals. To many managers it is *relative* performance that matters, rather than absolute performance.

What predictions can be made if this is how managers behave? The answer is that it depends on the nature of competition in the industry. The more

> **definition**
>
> **Organisational slack**
> When managers allow spare capacity to exist, thereby enabling them to respond more easily to changed circumstances.

profitable, innovative and efficient are the competitors, the more profitable, innovative and efficient will managers try to make their particular firm.

The further ahead of their rivals that firms try to stay, the more likely it is that there will be a 'snowballing' effect: each firm trying to outdo the other.

Satisficing and the consumer's interest

Firms with multiple goals will be satisficers. The greater the number of goals of the different managers, the greater is the chance of conflict and the more likely it is that organisational slack will develop. Satisficing firms are therefore likely to be less responsive to changes in consumer demand and changes in costs than profit-maximising firms. They may thus be less efficient.

On the other hand, such firms may be less eager to exploit their economic power by charging high prices, or to use aggressive advertising, or to pay low wages.

The extent to which satisficing firms do act in the public interest will, as in the case of other types of firm, depend to a large extent on the amount and type of competition they face, and their attitudes towards this competition. Firms that compare their performance with that of their rivals are more likely to be responsive to consumer wishes than firms that prefer to stick to well-established practices. On the other hand, they may be more concerned to 'manipulate' consumer tastes than the more traditional firm.

SUMMARY

1a There are two major types of criticism of the traditional profit-maximising theory: (a) firms may not have the information to maximise profits; (b) they may not even want to maximise profits.

1b Lack of information on demand and costs and on the actions and reactions of rivals, and a lack of use of opportunity cost concepts may mean that firms adopt simple 'rules of thumb' for pricing.

1c In large companies there is likely to be a divorce between ownership and control. The shareholders (the owners) may want maximum profits, but it is the managers who make the decisions, and managers are likely to aim to maximise their own utility rather than that of the shareholders. This leads to profit 'satisficing'. This is where managers aim to achieve sufficient profits to keep shareholders happy, but this is a secondary aim to one or more alternative aims.

1d Some alternative theories assume that there is a single alternative aim that firms seek to maximise. Others assume that managers have a series of (possibly conflicting) aims.

2a Rather than seeking to maximise short-run profits, a firm may take a longer-term perspective. It is very difficult, however, to predict the behaviour of a long-run profit-maximising firm, since (a) different managers are likely to make different judgements about how to achieve maximum profits, and (b) demand and cost curves may shift unpredictably both in response to the firm's own policies and as a result of external factors.

2b Managers may seek to maximise their own utility, which, in turn, will depend on factors such as salary, job security, power within the organisation and the achievement of professional excellence. Given, however, that managerial utility depends on a range of variables, it is difficult to use the theory to make general predictions of firms' behaviour.

2c Managers may gain utility from maximising sales revenue. However, they will still have to ensure that a satisfactory level of profit is achieved. The output of a firm which seeks to maximise sales revenue will be higher than that for a profit-maximising firm. Its level of advertising will also tend to be higher. Whether price will be higher or lower depends on the relative effects on demand and cost of the additional advertising.

2d Many managers aim for maximum growth of their organisation, believing that this will help their salaries, power, prestige, etc.

2e As with long-run profit-maximising theories, it is

SUMMARY

difficult to predict the price and output strategies of a growth-maximising firm. Much depends on the judgements of particular managers about growth opportunities.

3a In large firms, decisions are taken by, or influenced by, a number of different people, including various managers, shareholders, workers, customers, suppliers and creditors. If these different people have different aims, then a conflict between them is likely to arise. A firm cannot maximise more than one of these conflicting aims. The alternative is to seek to achieve a satisfactory target level of a number of aims.

3b Behavioural theories of the firm examine how managers and other interest groups actually behave, rather than merely identifying various equilibrium positions for output, price, investment, etc.

3c If targets were easily achieved last year, they are likely to be made more ambitious next year. If they were not achieved, a search procedure will be conducted to identify how to rectify the problem. This may mean adjusting targets downwards, in which case there will be some form of bargaining process between managers.

3d Life is made easier for managers if conflict can be avoided. This will be possible if slack is allowed to develop in various parts of the firm. If targets are not being met, the slack can then be taken up without requiring adjustments in other targets.

3e Satisficing firms may be less innovative, less aggressive and less willing to initiate change. If they do change, it is more likely to be in response to changes made by their competitors. Managers may judge their performance by comparing it with that of rivals.

3f Satisficing firms may be less aggressive in exploiting a position of market power. On the other hand, they may suffer from greater inefficiency.

REVIEW QUESTIONS

1 In the traditional theory of the firm, decision makers are often assumed to have perfect knowledge and to be able to act, therefore, with complete certainty. It is now widely accepted that in practice firms will be certain about very few things. Of the following: (a) production costs; (b) demand; (c) elasticity; (d) supply; (e) consumer tastes; (f) technology; (g) government policy, which might they be certain of? Which might they be uncertain of?

2 Make a list of six aims that a manager of a high street department store might have. Identify some conflicts that might arise between these aims.

3 When are increased profits in a manager's personal interest?

4 Draw a diagram with *MC* and *MR* curves. Mark the output (a) at which profits are maximised; (b) at which sales revenue is maximised.

5 Since advertising increases a firm's costs, will prices necessarily be lower with sales revenue maximisation than with profit maximisation?

6 We have seen that a firm aiming to maximise sales revenue will tend to produce more than a profit-maximising firm. This conclusion certainly applies under monopoly and oligopoly. Will it also apply under (a) perfect competition and (b) monopolistic competition, where in both cases there is freedom of entry?

7 A frequent complaint of junior and some senior managers is that they are frequently faced with new targets from above, and that this makes their life difficult. If their complaint is true, does this conflict with the hypothesis that managers will try to build in slack?

8 What evidence about firms' behaviour could be used to refute the argument that firms will tend to build in organisational slack and as a result be inherently conservative?

Growth strategy  14

Whether businesses wish to grow or not, many are forced to. The dynamic competitive process of the market drives producers on to expand in order to remain in the market place. If a business fails to grow, this may benefit its more aggressive rivals. They may secure a greater share of the market, leaving the first firm with reduced profits. Thus business growth is often vital if a firm is to survive.

The goal of business growth is closely linked to the key objectives of managers. As mentioned in Chapter 13, managerial status, prestige, promotion and salary might be more directly related to such a goal rather than that of profit maximisation. Business growth might also be essential if the business is successfully to manage change and deal with many of the inherent uncertainties of the business environment.

In this chapter we shall consider the various growth strategies open to firms and assess their respective advantages and disadvantages. First, however, we shall need to look at the relationship between a firm's growth and its profitability, and also at those factors which are likely to constrain the growth of the business.

14.1 Growth and profitability

In using traditional theories of the firm, economists often assume that there is a limit to the expansion of the firm: that there is a level of output beyond which profits will start to fall. The justification for this view can be found on both the supply side and the demand side.

On the supply side, it is assumed that if a firm grows beyond a certain size, it will experience rising long-run average costs. In other words, the long-run average cost curve is assumed to be U-shaped, possibly with a horizontal section at the bottom (see page 185). This argument is often based on the assumption that it is *managerial* diseconomies of scale which start driving costs up once a firm has expanded beyond a certain point: there are no more plant economies to be achieved (the firm has passed its **minimum efficient scale (MES)**); instead, the firm is faced with a more complex form of organisation, with longer lines of management, more difficult labour relations and a greater possibility of lack of effort going unnoticed.

On the demand side it is assumed that the firm faces a downward-sloping demand curve (and hence marginal revenue curve) for its product. Although this demand curve can be shifted by advertising and other forms of product promotion, finite demand naturally places a constraint on the expansion of the firm.

These two assumptions can be challenged, however. On the supply side, with a multidivisional form of organisation and systems in place for monitoring performance, it is quite possible to avoid diseconomies of scale.

As far as demand is concerned, although the demand (or at least its rate of

definition

Minimum efficient scale (MES)
The size of the individual factory or of the whole firm, beyond which no significant additional economies of scale can be gained. For an individual factory the MES is known as the *minimum efficient plant size* (MEPS).

growth) for any one product may be limited, the firm could diversify into new markets.

It is thus incorrect to say that there is a limit to the size of a business. An individual business may be able to go on expanding its capacity or diversifying its interests indefinitely. There does, however, exist an upper limit on the firm's *rate* of growth – the *speed* at which it can expand its capacity or diversify. The reason behind this constraint is that growth is determined by the profitability of the business. The growth rate/profitability relationship can operate in two ways:

- Growth depends upon profitability. The more profitable the firm, the more likely it is to be able to raise finance for investment.
- Growth affects profitability. In the short run, growth above a certain rate may *reduce* profitability. Some of the finance for the investment necessary to achieve growth may have to come from the firm's sales revenue. A firm wishing to expand its operations in an existing market will require greater advertising and marketing; and a firm seeking to diversify may have to spend considerable sums on market research and employing managers with specialist knowledge and skills. In both cases, investment is likely to be needed in new plant and machinery. In other words, the firm may have to sacrifice some of its short-run profits for the long-run gains that greater growth might yield.

But what about long-run profits? Will growth increase or decrease these? The answer depends on the nature of the growth. If growth leads to expansion into new markets in which demand is growing, or to increased market power, or to increased economies of scale, then growth may well increase long-run profits – not only total profits, but the rate of profit on capital, or the ratio of profits to revenue. If, however, growth leads to diseconomies of scale, or to investment in risky projects, then growth may well be at the expense of long-run profitability.

To summarise: greater profitability may lead to higher growth, but higher growth, at least in the short run, may be at the expense of profits.

14.2 Constraints on growth

However much a firm may want to grow, it might simply not be possible. There are several factors that can restrict the ability of a business to expand.

Financial conditions. Financial conditions determine the ability of a firm to fund its growth. Growth can be financed in three distinct ways: by borrowing, by retaining profits or by the issue of new shares. The proportions of UK company investment financed from these three sources is shown in Table 14.1.

As you can see, the largest source of finance for investment in the UK is internal funds (i.e. ploughed-back profit). Nevertheless, until the recession of the early 1990s, there was a growing proportion of company investment financed by bank borrowing. In fact, as can be seen from the table, in 1989 borrowing from banks, etc. exceeded the level of **internal funds** used for business investment. With this one exception, however, internal funds remain the major way of financing investment in the UK. The principal limitation in achieving growth via this means is that such funds are linked to business profitability, and this in turn is subject to the cyclical nature of economic activity – to the booms

Table 14.1	Sources of capital funds of UK industrial and commercial companies				
Year	Total from all sources (£ million)	Internal funds[a] (%)	Borrowing from banks, etc. (%)	Shares and debentures (%)	Overseas sources (%)
1970	6336	60.7	22.4	3.2	13.7
1980	28 913	66.1	22.3	4.9	6.7
1986	48 715	58.5	21.6	12.5	7.4
1987	79 475	49.6	21.1	25.3	4.0
1988	99 874	40.8	39.6	11.5	8.1
1989	108 025	32.7	41.7	14.9	10.7
1990	88 058	37.5	33.2	16.2	13.1
1992	53 452	68.3	−5.3	26.8	10.2
1994	86 469	72.9	−2.3	26.9	2.5
1996	144 501	53.0	20.0	19.0	8.0
1997	135 050	41.7	8.7	30.2	19.4

[a] Includes grants and tax relief.

Source: Based on *Financial Statistics* (ONS, various issues).

and slumps that the economy experiences. Profitability tends to fall in a recession along with the level of sales. In such times it is often difficult for a firm to afford new investment.

The *borrowing* of finance to fund expansion may be constrained by a wide range of factors, from the availability of finance in the banking sector, to the creditworthiness of the business.

The *issuing of new shares* to fund growth depends not only on confidence within the stock market in general, but on the stock market's assessment of the potential performance of the individual firm in particular. It should be noted that finance from this source is not open to all firms. For most small and medium-sized enterprises (i.e. those not listed on the Stock Exchange), raising finance through issuing new shares must be done privately, and normally this source of finance is very limited.

Shareholder confidence. Whichever way growth is financed – internal funds, borrowing or new share issues – the likely outcome in the short run is a reduction in the firm's share dividend. If the firm *retains* too much *profit*, there will be less to pay out in dividends. Similarly, if the firm *borrows* too much, the interest payments that it incurs are likely to make it difficult to maintain the level of dividends to shareholders. Finally, if it attempts to raise capital by a *new issue of shares*, the distributed profits will have to be divided between a larger number of shares. Whichever way it finances investment, therefore, the more it invests, the more the dividends on shares in the short run will probably fall. This could lead shareholders to sell their shares, unless they are confident that *long*-run profits and hence dividends will rise again, thus causing the share price to remain high in the long run. If shareholders do *not* have this confidence, they may well sell their shares. This will cause share prices to fall. If they fall too far, the firm runs the risk of being taken over and certain managers risk losing their jobs.

This **takeover constraint**, therefore, requires that the growth-maximising firm distribute sufficient profits to avoid being taken over. Hence the rate of business

definition
Takeover constraint The effect that the fear of being taken over has on a firm's willingness to undertake projects that reduce distributed profits.

growth is influenced by shareholder demands and expectations and the fear of takeover.

The converse to this situation is also true. If a business fails to grow fast enough, it may be that a potential buyer sees the firm as a valuable acquisition, whose resources might be put to more profitable use over the longer term. Hence businesses must avoid being overcautious and paying high share dividends, but, as a result, failing to invest and failing to exploit their true potential.

The likelihood of takeover depends in large part on the stock market's assessment of the firm's potential: how is the firm's investment strategy perceived to affect its future performance and profitability? The views of the stock market are reflected in the **valuation ratio** of the firm. This is the ratio of the stock market value of the firm's shares (the number of issued shares times the current share price) to the book value of the firm's assets. A low ratio means that the real assets of the business are effectively undervalued: that they can be purchased at a low market price. The business is thus likely to be more attractive to potential bidders. Conversely, firms with a high valuation ratio are seen as overvalued and are unlikely to be the target of takeover bids.

In the long run, a rapidly growing firm may find its profits increasing, especially if it can achieve economies of scale and a bigger share of the market. These profits can then be used to finance further growth. The firm will still not have unlimited finance, however, and therefore will still be faced by the takeover constraint if it attempts to grow too rapidly.

Demand conditions. Our analysis of business growth has shown that finance for growth is largely dependent upon the business's profitability. The more profit it makes, the more it can draw on internal funds; the more likely financial institutions will be to lend; and the more readily will new share issues be purchased by the market. The profitability of a business is in turn dependent upon market demand and demand growth. If the firm is operating in an expanding market, profits are likely to grow and finance will be relatively easy to obtain.

If, on the other hand, the firm's existing market becomes saturated, it will find that profits and sales are unlikely to rise unless it diversifies into related or non-related markets. One means of overcoming this demand constraint is to expand overseas, either by attempting to increase export sales or by locating new production facilities in foreign markets.

Managerial conditions. The growth of a firm is usually a planned process, and as such must be managed. Such management is carried out by the firm's management team. But the management team will be limited in respect to the number of individuals, their knowledge and abilities. For example, it might lack entrepreneurial vision, or various organisational skills.

Equally, as with other resources within the business, the management team might grow, or alternatively its composition might change in order to reflect the new needs of the growing business. However, new managers take time to be incorporated into, and become part of, an effective management team. They must undergo a period of training and become integrated into their new firm, as well as join a team of managers accustomed to working together. The rate of growth of business is thus constrained by this process of managerial expansion.

The skills and abilities of the management team will influence not only the rate of growth, but also its direction. Whether the firm diversifies into new

---

definition

Valuation ratio
The ratio of stock market value to book value. The stock market value is an assessment of the firm's past and anticipated future performance. The book value is a calculation of the current value of the firm's assets.

markets, or concentrates on redefining old or new products within existing markets, will greatly depend upon available managerial abilities.

In the sections below we will explore the alternative growth strategies open to businesses and the various advantages and limitations that such strategies present.

14.3 Alternative growth strategies

In pursuit of growth, a firm will seek to increase its markets: whether at home or internationally. In either case the firm will need to increase its capacity. This may be achieved by one or both of the following:

- **Internal expansion.** This is where a business looks to expand its productive capacity by adding to existing plant or by building new plant.
- **External expansion.** This is where a business grows by merging with other firms or by taking them over.

Whether the business embarks upon internal or external expansion, a number of alternative growth paths are open to the business. Figure 14.1 shows these various routes.

> **definition**
>
> **Internal expansion**
> Where a business adds to its productive capacity by adding to existing or by building new plant.

> **definition**
>
> **External expansion**
> Where business growth is achieved by merging with or taking over businesses within a market or industry.

Internal expansion

In order to achieve additional sales, the business must seek new demand in order to justify investment in additional capacity. There are three main ways of doing this:

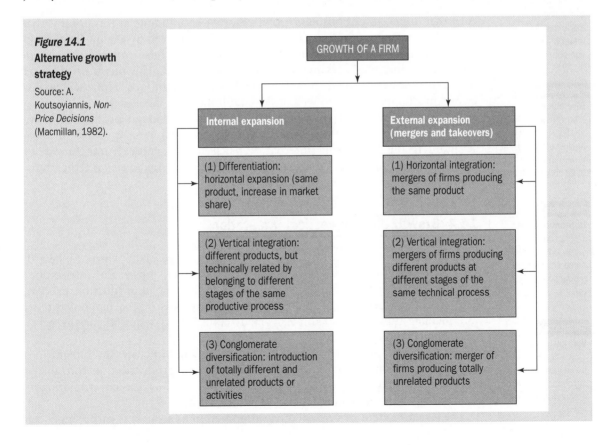

Figure 14.1
Alternative growth strategy

Source: A. Koutsoyiannis, *Non-Price Decisions* (Macmillan, 1982).

GROWTH OF A FIRM

Internal expansion

External expansion (mergers and takeovers)

(1) Differentiation: horizontal expansion (same product, increase in market share)

(2) Vertical integration: different products, but technically related by belonging to different stages of the same productive process

(3) Conglomerate diversification: introduction of totally different and unrelated products or activities

(1) Horizontal integration: mergers of firms producing the same product

(2) Vertical integration: mergers of firms producing different products at different stages of the same technical process

(3) Conglomerate diversification: merger of firms producing totally unrelated products

- The firm can expand or **differentiate its product** within existing markets, by, for example, updating or restyling its product, or improving its technical characteristics.
- Alternatively, the business might seek to expand via **vertical integration**. This involves the firm expanding within the same product market, but at a different stage of production. For example, a car manufacturer might wish to produce its own components ('backward vertical integration') or distribute and sell its own car models ('forward vertical integration').
- As a third option, the business might seek to expand outside of its current product range, and move into new markets. This is known as a process of **diversification**.

External expansion (growth through mergers and takeovers)

Similar growth paths can be pursued via external expansion. However, in this case the business does not create the productive facilities itself, but purchases existing production. As Figure 14.1 identifies, we can distinguish three types of merger: horizontal, vertical and conglomerate.

- A **horizontal merger** is where two firms at the same stage of production within an industry merge.
- A **vertical merger**, is where businesses at different stages of production within the same industry merge. As such we might identify backward and forward vertical mergers for any given firm involved in the merger.
- A **conglomerate merger** is where firms in totally unrelated industries merge.

A further dimension of business growth that we should note at this point is that all of the above-mentioned growth paths can be achieved by the business looking beyond its national markets. In other words, the business might decide to become multinational and invest in expansion overseas. This raises a further set of issues, problems and advantages that a business might face. These will be discussed in Chapter 23 when we consider multinational business.

We have already considered business expansion through product differentiation in Chapter 8. In this chapter, therefore, we will focus on the other possibilities facing the firm: internal expansion via vertical integration or diversification, and external expansion via merger or takeover (whether horizontal, vertical or conglomerate).

14.4 Growth through vertical integration

Vertical integration, as we have seen, can be of two types: backward or forward. Backward integration (or, as it is sometimes known, 'upstream' integration) involves the business expanding into earlier stages of the production process, such as the extraction or refinement of raw materials or the manufacture of intermediate inputs: for example, various components required for the product's final assembly.

Forward integration (or, as it is sometimes known, 'downstream' integration) involves the business expanding into later stages of production, or into distribution or retailing. Such expansion might involve the business co-ordinating its own haulage and managing its own retail network.

The level or extent of vertical integration within a business is surprisingly dif-

---

> **definition**
>
> **Product differentiation**
> In the context of growth strategies, this is where a business upgrades existing products or services so as to make them different from those of rival firms.

> **definition**
>
> **Vertical integration**
> A business growth strategy that involves expanding within an existing market, but at a different stage of production. Vertical integration can be 'forward', such as moving into distribution or retail, or 'backward', such as expanding into extracting raw materials or producing components.

> **definition**
>
> **Diversification**
> A business growth strategy in which a business expands into new markets outside of its current interests.

> **definition**
>
> **Horizontal merger**
> Where two firms in the same industry at the same stage of the production process merge.

> **definition**
>
> **Vertical merger**
> Where two firms in the same industry at different stages in the production process merge.

ficult to measure. The reason lies in the difficulty of defining exactly what constitutes a 'stage' of production: just how far could the productive process be divided up, such that the individual stages could realistically be undertaken by separate firms? Where does one stage finish and another start? This is a very difficult judgement to make.

One way of assessing the level of vertical integration within a business is to distinguish between its *primary production* operation and its *auxiliary* operations. Auxiliary operations are those stages of production which either supply inputs or contribute to the downstream output of the primary production operation. Once a business's primary production operation is identified, the extent of vertical integration should become more apparent. If we wish to measure the degree of vertical integration, one widely used method is to estimate the ratio of the level of employment in auxiliary production to the total level of employment within the business. The higher this figure, the greater the degree of vertical integration.

A classic example of a vertically integrated firm is a steel manufacturer. Excluding distribution we might argue that there are seven distinct stages of production. These involve: the mining of the ore; the preparation of the ore for use; the smelting of the ore to produce pig iron; the refining of the pig iron to produce steel; the production of semi-finished steel products (the rolling stage); the production of finished steel components, such as pipes; and finally the last stage, fabrication, which involves the manufacture of steel products. If we were to include aspects of distribution and retailing, the stages in steel production would be considerable. We can also see that the steel producer's primary production operation – refining (and possibly smelting) – is in fact a very small part of the overall manufacture of steel products.

Why vertical integration?

We can identify a number of reasons why a business might wish to expand via vertical integration.

Greater efficiency

When vertical integration results in a fall in a business's long-run average costs, it is effectively experiencing various economies of scale. We can identify four categories under which vertical integration might lead to cost savings.

> *Production economies.* These occur when a business, through integration, lowers its costs by performing *complementary* stages of production within a single business unit. The classic example of this is the steel manufacturer combining the furnacing and milling stages of production, saving the costs that would have been required to reheat the iron had such operations been undertaken by independent businesses. Clearly, for most firms, the performing of more than one stage on a single site is likely to reduce transport costs, as semi-finished products no longer have to be moved from one plant to another.

> *Co-ordination economies.* Such economies arise from the internal structure of the business and its ability to transfer intermediate products between its various divisions. The business is able to avoid purchasing and selling expenses, including those related to the marketing and advertising of the product(s).

> **definition**
> **Conglomerate merger**
> Where two firms in different industries merge.

Managerial economies. Even though each production stage or division might have its own management or administrative team, economies can be gained from having a single source of supervision.

Financial economies. A vertically integrated business may gain various financial economies. Given the link between vertical integration and business size, such companies may be more able to negotiate favourable deals from key suppliers. In respect to finance, the additional security (and hence confidence) that a vertically integrated business can offer (see below) means that it might be able to secure lower borrowing rates of interest from the financial markets.

For a more detailed analysis of economies of scale, you should refer back to Chapter 9.

Reduced uncertainty

A business that is not vertically integrated may find itself subject to various uncertainties in the market place. Examples include: uncertainty over future price movements, supply reliability or access to markets.

Backward vertical integration will enable the business to control its supply chain. Without such integration the firm may feel very vulnerable, especially if there are only a few suppliers within the market. In such cases the suppliers would be able to exert considerable control over price. Alternatively, suppliers may be unreliable. For example, Lucas, the car components manufacturer, had very poor industrial relations during the 1970s and was frequently closed as a result of strike action. This had a significant impact on the performance of car manufacturers supplied by Lucas.

Forward vertical integration creates greater certainty in so far as it gives the business guaranteed access to distribution and retailing on its own terms. As with supply, forward markets might be dominated by large monopsonist(s) which are able not only to dictate price, but also to threaten market foreclosure (being shut out from a market). Forward vertical integration can remove the possibility of such events occurring.

Monopoly power

Forward or backward vertical integration may allow the business to acquire a greater monopoly/monopsony position in the market. Depending upon the type of vertical integration, the business might be able to set prices both for final products and for factor inputs.

Barriers to entry

Vertical integration may give the firm greater power in the market by enabling it to erect entry barriers to potential competitors. For example, a firm that undertakes backward vertical integration and acquires a key input resource can effectively close the market to potential new entrants, either by simply refusing to supply a competitor, or by charging a very high price for the factor such that new firms face an absolute cost disadvantage.

A further barrier to entry might arise from an increase in the minimum ef-ficient size of the business. As the firm becomes more integrated, it is likely to experience greater economies of scale (i.e. long-run average costs that go on falling below their previous minimum level). New entrants are then forced to come into the market at the level of integration that existing firms are operating under. Failure to do so will mean that new entrants will be operating at an instant cost disadvantage, and hence will be less competitive.

Problems with vertical integration

The major problem with vertical integration as a form of expansion is that the security it gives the business may reduce its ability to respond to changing market demands. A business that integrates, either backward or forward, ties itself to particular supply sources or particular retail outlets. If, by contrast, it were free to choose between suppliers, inputs might be obtained at a lower price than the firm could achieve by supplying itself. Equally, the ability to shift between retail outlets would allow the firm to locate in the best market positions. This may not be possible if it is tied to its own retail network.

As with all business strategy, one course of action may well preclude the pursuit of an alternative. The decision of the business to expand its operations via vertical integration means that resources will be diverted to this goal. The potential advantages from other growth strategies, such as the spreading of risk through diversification, are lost. This is not a problem of vertical integration as such, but it represents the opportunity costs of selecting this strategy to the *exclusion* of others.

Tapered vertical integration

How can a firm gain the benefits of vertical integration but avoid the costs? One alternative means of expansion is **tapered vertical integration**. This is where a business begins producing some of an input itself, while still buying some from another firm (often through subcontracting). This growth strategy is different from a situation where you are relying totally on subcontractors to provide supply (which we will explore in section 14.7). For example, Coca-Cola and Pepsi are large vertically integrated enterprises. They have, as part of their operations, wholly-owned bottling subsidiaries. However, in certain markets they subcontract to independent bottlers both to produce and to market their product.

The advantages of both making and buying an input are:

- The firm, by making an input or providing a service in-house, will have information concerning the costs and profitability of such an operation. Such information helps in the negotiation of contracts with independent producers. In addition, the firm will be able to use the threat of producing more itself to ensure that independent suppliers do not exploit their supply position, which they might be able to do if they held a monopolistic position within the supply chain. The firm is not totally at the mercy of an independent third party over which it has no control.
- The firm does not require the same level of capital outlay that would be required if it were to rely solely on an input or service produced by itself. As such it is able to externalise some of the costs and risks of its business operations.

The major drawback with this growth strategy is that shared production might fail to generate economies of scale, and is hence less efficient than might otherwise be the case. In other words, if Coca-Cola bottled all its own cola, then it

> **definition**
>
> **Tapered vertical integration**
> Where a firm is partially integrated with an earlier stage of production: where it produces *some* of an input itself and buys some from another firm.

might achieve significantly greater economies of scale then by sharing bottling with other firms. None might be large enough to achieve the efficiency gains that a single production site might generate.

Other significant costs with subcontracting are largely borne by the firm doing the subcontracted work, not by the contractor. Many small and medium-sized enterprises (SMEs), which might see doing subcontracted work for a large firm as a means of expanding their business and hence of growing themselves, find that the relationship between them and the large firm is often a highly unequal one. SMEs find that they not only bear some of the large firm's risk, but are easily expendable. Such vulnerability intensifies, the greater the proportion of the SME's production that is done for a particular customer. When a high level of reliance occurs, the SME finds that its business is, in essence, vertically integrated with its customer, but without the benefits that such a position should confer.

14.5 Growth through diversification

Diversification is the process whereby a firm shifts from being a single-product to a multiproduct producer. Such products need not cover similar activities. We can in fact identify four directions in which diversification might be undertaken:

- Using the existing technological base and market area.
- Using the existing technological base and new market area.
- Using a new technological base and existing market area.
- Using a new technological base and new market area.

Categorising the strategies in this way would suggest that the direction of diversification is largely dependent upon both the nature of technology and the market opportunities open to the firm. But the ability to capitalise on these features depends on the experience, skills and market knowledge of the managers of the business. In general, diversification is likely to occur in areas where the business can use and adapt existing technology and knowledge to its advantage.

The diversification of Amstrad, the personal computer manufacturer, into the mobile telephone market is a good example of where a business's current technology and market knowledge are being applied to a distinct new product.

Why diversification?

There are three principal factors which might encourage a business to diversify.

Stability. So long as a business produces a single product in a single market, it is vulnerable to changes in that market's conditions. If a farmer produces nothing but potatoes, and the potato harvest fails, the farmer is ruined. If however, the farmer produces a whole range of vegetable products, or even diversifies into livestock, then he or she is less subject to the forces of nature and the unpredictability of the market. Diversification therefore enables the business to *spread risk*.

Maintaining profitability. Businesses might also be encouraged to diversify if they wish to protect existing profit levels. It may be that the market in which a business is currently located is saturated and that current profitability is perceived to be at a maximum. Alternatively, the business might be in a market

BOX 14.1

'Panutilities'
A company of the future?

Who supplies your gas? Is it a gas utility? Who supplies your electricity? Is it an electricity utility? For many of us the answer to both questions is likely to be no. Ever since the major utility companies were privatised and deregulated, we have witnessed a steady attempt by many to diversify their business interests.

Initially such diversification was relatively narrowly focused. For example, energy suppliers began supplying other types of energy (e.g. Southern Electric supplying gas). However, the trend now is for broader diversification.

Centrica, formerly part of British Gas, is a case in point. In April 2000, it announced it would be moving into telecommunications. This would involve an alliance with Vodafone UK, which would provide the network for Centrica's mobile phone service, and with Torch Telecom and Cable and Wireless, which would provide

the network for Centrica's fixed-line service. Centrica planned to invest £150 million in the first two years of business. Through these alliances Centrica's telecom network will be run by others, leaving it to focus on customer services and billing, an area in which, through its gas and electricity provision, it has plenty of experience. In fact, Centrica will be looking to exploit this position, given its relationship with 14.8 million domestic gas users and a further 8 million electricity customers.

If the major utilities continue to diversify in this way, perhaps one day we will be able to receive just one bill from one service provider for all our major utility needs.

Question

Outline the main advantages to a business, such as Centrica, of a growth strategy based on diversification.

where demand is stagnant or declining. In such cases the business is likely to see a greater return on its investment by diversifying into new product ranges located in dynamic expanding markets.

Growth. If the current market is saturated, stagnant or in decline, diversification might be the only avenue open to the business if it wishes to maintain a high growth performance. In other words, it is not only the level of profits that may be limited in the current market, but also the growth of sales.

14.6 Growth through merger

A merger is a situation in which, as a result of mutual agreement, two firms decide to bring together their business operations. A **merger** is distinct from a takeover in so far as a **takeover** involves one firm bidding for another's shares (often against the will of the directors of the target firm). One firm thereby acquires another.

The distinction between merger and takeover is an important one. For example, an important difference is that, in order to acquire a firm, a business will require finance, whereas a merger might simply involve two firms swapping their existing shares for shares in the newly created merged company. A further difference might concern managerial relations between the two businesses. A merger implies that managers, through negotiation, have reached an agreement acceptable to both sides, whereas a takeover involves one group of managers, working in opposition to another group, looking to fend off the aggressor. The acquired firm usually finds its management team dismissed following such action!

In order to avoid confusion at this stage, we will use the term 'merger' to refer

definition

Merger
The outcome of a mutual agreement made by two firms to combine their business activities.

definition

Takeover
Where one business acquires another. A takeover may not necessarily involve mutual agreement between the two parties. In such cases, the takeover might be viewed as 'hostile'.

to *both* mergers ('mutual agreements') and takeovers ('acquisitions'), although where necessary we will draw a distinction between the two.

Why merge?

But why do firms want to merge with or take over others? Is it purely that they want to grow: are mergers simply evidence of the hypothesis that firms are growth maximisers? Or are there other motives that influence the predatory drive?

Merger for growth. If the aims of the decision makers within the firm are to maximise growth, mergers are an obvious means. They provide a much quicker means to growth than does internal expansion. Not only does the firm acquire new capacity, but also it acquires additional consumer demand. Building up this level of consumer demand by internal expansion might have taken a considerable length of time.

The telecommunications, media and technology (TMT) sector has seen many mergers in recent times where companies in different market segments have come together. The acquisition by America Online (AOL), the Internet group, of Time Warner brought together a firm strong in media distribution with a media content provider. The two businesses were clearly complementary and allowed AOL to grow and expand its range of media-based interests.

Merger for economies of scale. Once a firm has successfully merged with another, the constituent parts might be more effectively co-ordinated so as to reduce production costs. This may involve a process of 'rationalisation': reorganising the firm so as to remove any duplication of activities and to cut out waste. For example, a newly merged company will require only one head office, not two. On the marketing side, the two parts of the newly merged company may now share distribution and retail channels, benefiting from each other's knowledge and operation in distinct market segments or geographical locations.

The merger of Airbus Industries' partners, Aerospatiale-Matra of France, DaimlerChrysler Aerospace of Germany and Construcciones Aeronauticas of Spain, is estimated to save, through rationalisation, hundreds of millions of pounds annually. The newly created firm European Aeronautics Space and Defence Company (EADS) owns 80 per cent of Airbus, while BAE Systems of the UK owns the remaining 20 per cent. The rationalisation process was seen by many as necessary if Airbus was effectively to challenge its main rival Boeing of the USA.

Evidence for such motivation is sparse, however. The problem is in separating the desire to reduce costs from the desire to achieve other objectives. Reduced costs are a way of increasing profits and thereby of increasing the rate of growth. It is unlikely that managers will want to reduce costs for their own sake.

In fact, the evidence on costs suggests that most mergers result in few if any cost savings: either potential economies of scale are not exploited due to a lack of rationalisation, or diseconomies result from the disruptions of reorganisation or a lack of control over the acquired part of the organisation by the parent company. In many cases, managers seem to know little about the businesses that their companies have bought. New managers installed by the parent company are often seen as unsympathetic, and morale may go down.

Merger for monopoly power. Here the motive is to reduce competition and thereby gain greater market power and larger profits. With less competition, the firm will face a less elastic demand and be able to charge a higher percentage above marginal cost. What is more, the new more powerful company will be in a stronger position to regulate entry into the market by erecting effective entry barriers, thereby enhancing its monopoly position yet further.

Merger for increased market valuation. A merger can benefit shareholders of *both* firms if it leads to an increase in the stock market valuation of the merged firm. If both sets of shareholders believe that they will make a capital gain on their shares, then they are more likely to give the go-ahead for the merger.

In practice, however, there is little evidence to show that mergers lead to a capital gain. One possible reason for this is the lack of reduction in costs referred to above.

Merger to reduce uncertainty. Firms face uncertainty at two levels. The first is in their own markets. The behaviour of rivals may be highly unpredictable. Mergers, by reducing the number of rivals, can correspondingly reduce uncertainty. At the same time, they can reduce the *costs* of competition (e.g. reducing the need to advertise).

The second level of uncertainty is the macroeconomic one. Fluctuations in national and international economic activity can play havoc with a firm's sales and hence profits. Mergers can help to provide the firm with more protection against wider changes within the market place, such as those stemming from the economic actions of government.

Merger due to opportunity. A widely held theory concerning merger activity is that it occurs simply as a consequence of opportunities that may arise: opportunities that are often unforeseen. Therefore business mergers are largely unplanned and, as such, virtually impossible to predict. Dynamic business organisations will be constantly on the lookout for new business opportunities as they arise.

Other motives. A range of other merger motives have been advanced, although the empirical significance of these motives is largely untested. Such motives might include the following:

- Businesses merge with or take over others so as to avoid being the target of takeovers themselves.
- Merging with another firm so as to defend it from an unwanted predator (the 'White Knight' strategy).
- Asset stripping. This is where a firm takes over another and then breaks it up, selling off the profitable bits and probably closing down the remainder.
- Empire building. This is where owners or managers favour takeovers because of the power or prestige of owning or controlling several (preferably well-known) companies.
- Geographical expansion. The motive here is to broaden the geographical base of the company by merging with a firm in a different part of the country or the world.

Mergers will generally have the effect of increasing the market power of those firms involved. This could lead to less choice and higher prices for the consumer. For this reason, mergers have become the target for government competition policy. Such policy is the subject of Chapter 20.

BOX 14.2

Merger activity
A European perspective

Mergers[1] within Europe have been predominantly horizontal rather than vertical or conglomerate. This has led to a steady increase in concentration within a wide range of manufacturing and service-sector industries in a number of European countries, especially in the UK, France, Germany, Holland and Sweden. Research suggests that such merger activity has led to few gains in efficiency and only minimal improvements in competitiveness.

Main motives for mergers and joint ventures in the EC: 1988/9–1991/2

Strengthening of market position	648
Expansion	419
Restructuring (including rationalisation and synergy)	158
Complementarity	72
Diversification	55
Co-operation	13
Research and development	3
Other	73
Total cases specifying reasons	1441

Source: *Reports on Competition Policy* (Commission of the European Communities, various years).

Pre single market (1993)

The table shows the main motives given for industrial mergers and acquisitions in the European Community between 1988/9 and 1991/2. Clearly the desire to gain greater market power and market share was the driving force behind mergers in the EC.

For most of the 1980s, the majority of mergers occurring in Europe were within national boundaries. But as inter-EC trade grew and as Europe was increasingly seen by business as a 'single market', so an increasing proportion of mergers were 'cross-border'. The proportion of total EC mergers that were between companies in different member states grew from 8.3 per cent in 1987/8 to 20.5 per cent in 1992/3.

An important factor explaining the increase in inter-EC mergers was the process of dismantling barriers to trade to create a true 'common market' by 1993. Firms took the opportunity to establish a European network and restructure their operations as well as to expand productive capacity.

A notable feature of European merger activity is the size of the firms involved. In 1986–7, 57 per cent of merger activity involved firms with sales over €1 billion and 23 per cent over €5 billion. By 1990/91 this had risen to 87 per cent and 45 per cent respectively. The larger the firms involved, the more likely they are to be involved in cross-border mergers rather than purely domestic ones. The implication of these trends is that markets are becoming increasingly concentrated.

Since 1993

When the single market came into being in January 1993, many commentators predicted that there would be a new wave of merger activity as companies, faced with new competition, would be forced to rationalise, or would take the opportunity to expand their operations in other EU countries.

As it turned out, the recession gripping Europe caused merger activity initially to decline (see the diagram). The main determinant of merger activity in the short run remains the overall state of the economy. When an economy moves into recession, so merger activity also declines.

After 1994 the growth in mergers in the EU resumed. There were several explanations for this:

● A recovery in growth throughout the EU.
● A growing process of 'globalisation'. With the dismantling of trade barriers around the world and increasing financial deregulation, so international competition has increased. Companies have felt the need to become bigger in order to compete more effectively.
● Falling interest rates, making investment in the stock-market more attractive than saving in a bank.
● A deepening of the single market, making Europe-wide operation by companies easier.
● An increasing conviction that there would be a successful move to a single currency, making it easier for companies to operate on an EU-wide basis.

As 1999 approached, and with it the arrival of the euro, so merger activity reached fever pitch. In 1998 there were over 2000 deals targeting EU companies.

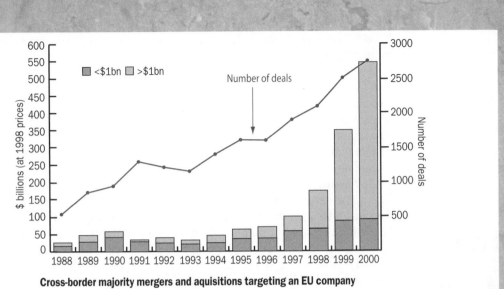

Cross-border majority mergers and aquisitions targeting an EU company

Source: Based on information provided by Thomson Financial Securities Data.

The total value of these deals was $170 billion (see the diagram). Sixty-three per cent of this value came from 28 deals worth more than $1 billion each. The largest were two mergers between European pharmaceutical companies – a $35 billion marriage of Zeneca of the UK and Astra of Sweden, and a $23 billion union of Germany's Hoechst and France's Rhône-Poulenc.

Other sectors in which merger activity has been rife are financial services and the privatised utilities sector. In the UK, in particular, most of the privatised water and electricity companies have been taken over, with buyers attracted by the sector's monopoly profits. French and US buyers have been prominent.

Many of the deals in the EU are 'hostile'. In other words, the company being taken over does not want to be. The deals are often concluded after prolonged boardroom battles, with bosses of the acquiring company seeking opportunities to build empires, and bosses of the target company attempting all sorts of manoeuvres to avoid being taken over. This may involve them seeking deals with alternative, more 'friendly' companies. Generally companies are increasingly using the services of investment banks to help them in the process of making or warding off deals.

Despite the growing number of horizontal mergers, there has also been a tendency for companies to become more focused, by selling off parts of their business which are not seen as 'core activities'. For example, not long after its takeover of Wellcome, Glaxo decided to concentrate on the production of *prescription* drugs, and as a consequence to sell its share of Warner Wellcome, which produced non-prescription drugs. Another example was Volvo. After unsuccessfully attempting to merge with Renault in 1993, it subsequently divested itself of several companies that it owned in a variety of industries, ranging from banking and finance to food, matches and pharmaceuticals.

This trend of horizontal mergers and conglomerate and vertical de-mergers has allowed companies to increase their market power in those specific sectors where they have expertise. Consumers may gain from lower costs, but the motives of the companies are largely to gain increased market power – something of dubious benefit to consumers.

Question

Are the motives for merger likely to be different in a recession from in a period of rapid economic growth?

[1] When we refer to 'mergers' this also includes acquisitions (i.e. takeovers).

14.7 Growth through strategic alliance

The term **strategic alliance** is used to cover a wide range of alternative collaborative arrangements. These might involve businesses working together on a project, or sharing information, or even sharing productive resources.

Such working relationships might be long term. An example is Airbus Industries, a consortium of European aircraft manufacturers, which was created in the late 1960s. Alternatively, the collaboration between businesses might be just for a single project. An example here is the company set up to build the Channel Tunnel, Trans Manche Link.

Such agreements also vary in respect to their formality. At one extreme, the alliance might entail creating a new jointly-owned enterprise. At the other extreme, the working agreement might be totally informal, with businesses remaining largely independent of one another. In addition, alliances vary in respect to their focus. Some agreements might focus upon very specific stages in the supply chain. An example would be two car manufacturers collaborating on engine design. Other agreements might be more free ranging and flexible. An example here would be two car manufacturers looking to develop a new type of car.

One of the best known sets of alliances in recent years has been in the airline industry. According to *The Economist*,[1] 'there were no fewer than 579 bilateral partnerships [in 2000], involving the 220 main airlines. That is an increase of nearly 50% over the last four years. From these airlines have emerged five large groupings [see Figure 14.2], plus a host of joint-marketing deals.'

Types of alliance

There are many types of alliance between businesses.

Joint ventures. A **joint venture** is where two or more firms decide to create, and jointly own, a new independent organisation. The creation of Cellnet by BT and Securicor is an example of such a strategy.

> **definition**
>
> **Strategic alliance**
> Where two firms work together, formally or informally, to achieve a mutually desirable goal.

> **definition**
>
> **Joint venture**
> Where two or more firms set up and jointly own a new independent firm.

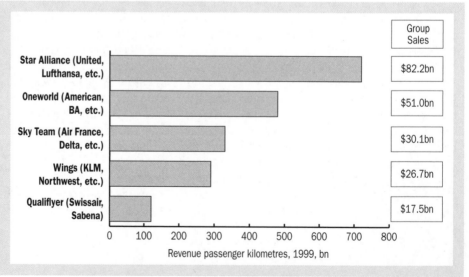

Figure 14.2
'Big Birds': Airline alliances

Source: *The Economist*, 8.7.00, p. 97 © The Economist Newspaper Limited, London, 8 July 2000.

	Group Sales
Star Alliance (United, Lufthansa, etc.)	$82.2bn
Oneworld (American, BA, etc.)	$51.0bn
Sky Team (Air France, Delta, etc.)	$30.1bn
Wings (KLM, Northwest, etc.)	$26.7bn
Qualiflyer (Swissair, Sabena)	$17.5bn

Revenue passenger kilometres, 1999, bn

Consortia. In recent years, many consortia have been created. Camelot, the company that runs the UK National Lottery, and Trans Manche Link, the company that built the Channel Tunnel, are two examples. A **consortium** is usually created for very specific projects, such as a large civil engineering work. As such they have a very focused objective and once the project is completed the consortium is usually dissolved. A consortium, however, like joint ventures, involves the creation of a new business to co-ordinate the activities of the partners and to oversee work on the project.

Franchising. A less formal strategic alliance is where a business agrees to **franchise** its operations to third parties. McDonald's and Coca-Cola are good examples of businesses that use a franchise network. In such a relationship the franchisee is responsible for manufacturing and/or selling, and the franchiser retains responsibility for branding and marketing.

Licensing. **Licensing** is where the owner of a patented product allows another company to produce it for a fee. Such a strategy is often seen in high-technology markets. For example, companies like Edios and Square, who create and manufacture games for the Playstation, have been given licences by Sony.

Subcontracting. Like licensing and franchising, **subcontracting** is a less formal source of strategic alliance, where companies maintain their independence. When a business subcontracts, it employs an independent business to manufacture or supply some service rather conduct the activity itself. Car manufacturers are major subcontractors. Given the multitude and complexity of components that are required to manufacture a car, the use of subcontractors to supply specialist items, such as brakes and lights, seems a logical way to organise the business. In Japan, for example, it has been found that the ten largest car manufacturers obtain as much as 75 per cent of their components from independent suppliers.

Networks. **Networks** are less formal than any of the above alliances. A network is where two or more businesses work collaboratively but without any formal relationship binding one to the other. Such a form of collaboration is highly prevalent in Japan. Rather than a formal contract regulating the behaviour of the partners to the agreement, their relationship is based upon an understanding of trust and loyalty.

Why form strategic alliances?

There are many reasons why firms may decide to set up a strategic alliance. Often these reasons are specific to a particular time or set of circumstances.

New markets. As a business expands, possibly internationally, it may well be advantageous to join with an existing player in the market. Such a business would have local knowledge and an established network of suppliers and distributors. Similar arguments apply if a business is seeking to diversify. Rather than developing the prerequisite skills, knowledge and networks necessary to succeed, the process might be curtailed by establishing an alliance with a firm already operating in the market.

[1] 'Dangerous Liaisons', *The Economist* (July 8 2000)

---

definition

Consortium
Where two or more firms work together on a specific project and create a separate company to run the project.

definition

Franchise
A formal agreement whereby a company uses another company to produce or sell some or all of its product.

definition

Licensing
Where the owner of a patented product allows another firm to produce it for a fee.

definition

Subcontracting
Where a firm employs another firm to produce part of its output or some of its input(s).

definition

Network
An informal arrangement between businesses to work together towards some common goal.

BOX 14.3

The global information economy and strategic alliances

The way forward for companies such as America Online?

The Marcar Management Institute of America announced in a report at the end of 1999 that, according to its estimates, the information economy would be worth $10.2 trillion by 2010, a staggering $7 trillion increase on the estimated value for 2000. It also suggested that this huge rise in value would be largely the consequence of the sector's dynamic nature and the integration of business via 'webs of alliances'. How significant are these alliances between business and how integrated are they?

The global information economy can be split into three sectors:

- *The create sector*: those businesses that produce information, i.e. publishers, newspapers, etc.

- *The move sector*: those businesses that specialise in the transfer of information, i.e. television, satellite communication, etc.
- *The use sector*: those businesses that provide those things necessary for others to access the information created and moved, i.e. computer manufacturers, software producers, etc.

The integration of business links across these three sectors is where the greatest gains are likely to be generated and the greatest value created.

America OnLine (AOL), for example, has positioned itself within the information economy not simply as a creator (where it has alliances with both the New York Times and Drkoop.com), but also in a web of alliances with businesses in both the move and use sectors as well.

INFOMATION VALUE CHAIN Create – Move – Use Information		
Create	**Move**	**Use**
content submarkets*	*transmission submarkets***	*application submarkets****
Information services	Internet	Internet applications
On-line providers	Satellite com	Multimedia services
CD-ROM	Wireless services	Browser software
Scanners	Enterprise networks	Laptops and portables
Magazines	Private networks	Messaging services
Music	Fiber optic equipment	Applications software
Books	Local area networks	Conferencing services
Financial records	Data communications	Video games
Maket research	Cable TV services	Peripherals
Newspapers	TV broadcasting	Personal computers
Printing	Long distance telephone	Consumer electronics
	Local telephone	Mainframes

(The left axis reads "Higher Growth rates Lower")

*Create, compile and package information **Facilitate transmission of and access to information ***Manipulate, apply and interact with information

Source: *The Global Information Economy 2020*, Marcar Management Institute of America, Inc (http://www.marcar.com/docs/pdf/EMCinfo2010.pdf)

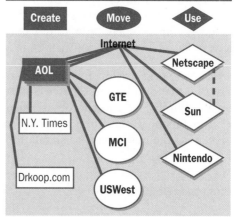

AMERICA ONLINE
Internet alliances boost growth

*Create, compile and package information **Facilitate transmission of and access to information ***Manipulate, apply and interact with information

Source: *The Global Information Economy 2020*, Marcar Management Institute of America, Inc (http://www.marcar.com/docs/pdf/EMCinfo2010.pdf)

Question

Outline the advantages and disadvantages to AOL from adopting such a growth strategy.

Risk sharing. Many business ventures might just be too risky for a solitary firm. Creating some form of strategic alliance spreads risk and creates opportunity. The Channel Tunnel and the consortium of firms that built it is one such example. The construction of the Channel Tunnel was a massive undertaking and far too risky for any single firm to embark upon. With the creation of a consortium, risk was spread, and the various consortium members were able to specialise in their areas of expertise.

Capital pooling. Projects that might have prohibitively high start-up costs, or running costs, may become feasible if firms co-operate and pool their capital. In addition, an alliance of firms, with their combined assets and credibility, may find it easier to generate finance, whether from investors in the stock market or from the banking sector.

The past 20 years have seen a flourishing of strategic alliances. They have become a key growth strategy for business both domestically and internationally. They are seen as a way of expanding business operations quickly without the difficulties associated with the more aggressive approach of acquisition or the more lengthy process of merger.

One sector in which the formation of strategic alliances is rife is that of the digital or information economy. Box 14.3 shows some of the recent developments in this area and assesses the implications for business and the economy.

SUMMARY

1a Business growth and business profitability are likely to be inversely related in the short run. A growing firm will bear certain additional costs, such as higher advertising and marketing bills.

1b In the long run, the relationship could be positive. A growing firm may take advantage of new market opportunities and may achieve greater economies of scale and increased market power. On the other hand, a rapidly growing firm may embark on various risky projects or projects with a low rate of return.

2a Constraints on business growth include (i) financial conditions, (ii) shareholder confidence, (iii) the level and growth of market demand and (iv) managerial conditions.

2b (i) Financial conditions determine the business's ability to raise finance. (ii) Shareholder confidence is likely to be jeopardised if a firm ploughs back too much profit into investment and distributes too little to shareholders. (iii) A firm is unlikely to be able to grow unless it faces a growing demand: either in its existing market, or by diversifying into new markets. (iv) The knowledge, skills and dynamism of the management team will be an important determinant of the firm's growth.

3a A business can expand either internally, or externally by merging with other firms.

3b Using either of these routes, there are three potential growth strategies open to business: product differentiation, vertical integration and diversification.

4a Vertical integration involves remaining in the same market, but expanding into a different stage of production.

4b Vertical integration can reduce a firm's costs through various economies of scale. It can also help to reduce uncertainty, as the vertically integrated business can hopefully secure supply routes and/or retail outlets. This strategy can also enhance the business's market power by enabling it to erect various barriers to entry.

4c A vertically integrated business will trade off the security of such a strategy with the reduced ability to respond to change and to exploit the advantages that the market might present.

4d Through a process of tapered vertical integration, many firms make part of a given input themselves and subcontract the production of the remainder to one or more other firms. By making a certain

SUMMARY

amount of an input itself, the firm is less reliant on suppliers, but does not require as much capital equipment as if it produced all the input itself.

5a The nature and direction of diversification depends upon the skills and abilities of managers, and the type of technology employed.

5b Diversification offers the business a growth strategy that not only frees it from the limitations of a particular market, but also enables it to spread its risks, and seek profit in potentially fast-growing markets.

6a There are three types of merger: horizontal, vertical and conglomerate. The type of merger adopted will be determined by the aims of business: that is,

whether to increase market power, improve business security or spread risks.

6b There is a wide range of motives for merger. Some have more statistical backing than others.

7a One means of achieving growth is through the formation of strategic alliances with other firms. They are a means whereby business operations can be expanded relatively quickly and at relatively low cost.

7b Types of strategic alliance include: joint ventures, consortia, franchising, licensing, subcontracting and networks.

7c Advantages of strategic alliances include easier access to new markets, risk sharing and capital pooling.

REVIEW QUESTIONS

1 Explain the relationship between a business's rate of growth and its profitability.

2 'Business managers must constantly tread a fine line between investing in business growth and paying shareholders an "adequate" dividend on their holdings.' Explain why this is such a crucial consideration.

3 Distinguish between internal and external growth strategy. Identify a range of factors which might determine whether an internal or external strategy is pursued.

4 What is meant by the term 'vertical integration'? Why might business wish to pursue such a growth strategy?

5 A firm can grow by merging with or taking over another firm. Such mergers or takeovers can be of three types: horizontal, vertical or conglomerate. Which of the following is an example of which type of merger (takeover)?
(a) A soft drinks manufacturer merges with a pharmaceutical company.
(b) A car manufacturer merges with a car distribution company.
(c) A large supermarket chain takes over a number of independent grocers.

6 To what extent will consumers gain or lose from the three different types of merger identified above?

7 Assume that an independent film company, which has up to now specialised in producing documentaries for a particular television broadcasting company, wishes to expand. Identify some possible horizontal, vertical and other closely related fields. What types of strategic alliances might it seek to form and with what types of company? What possible drawbacks might there be for it in such alliances?

The small-firm sector 15

How often do you hear of small business making it big? Not very often, and yet many of the world's major corporations began life as small businesses. From acorns have grown oak trees!

But small and large businesses are usually organised and run quite differently and face very different problems; and when a small business grows into a large one, it is transformed into a totally different organisation. An analogy is often drawn with the transformation of a caterpillar into a butterfly. They are still the same creature, yet they are so different that it is difficult to believe they are of the same genus. And so it is with large and small firms: they are still firms and yet their experience of business, the economy and management produces distinct and unique problems.

In this chapter we shall consider the place of the small firms within the economy: their strengths and weaknesses, their ability to grow and those factors that limit expansion. We shall also consider the role of government in respect to small-business policy, both in the UK and in the European Union.

15.1 Defining the small-firm sector

Unfortunately, there is no single agreed definition of a 'small' firm. In fact, a firm considered to be small in one sector of business, such as manufacturing, may be considerably different in size from one in, say, the road haulage business.

In 1971 the Bolton Committee,[1] set up to investigate the small-firm sector, attempted to resolve this problem by establishing both an *economic* and a *statistical* definition of a small firm. According to the Committee, a firm was deemed to be small if it satisfied each of the following three economic conditions:

- It should have a *small market share* and thus be unable to influence its business environment.
- It should be *managed by its owners*, and not involve a formalised management structure.
- It should not be part of a larger business organisation, and can thus *make its own business decisions*.

But just how small must a firm be in order to satisfy these conditions? The answer will vary from industry to industry. Recognising this, the Bolton Committee devised a series of statistical definitions of smallness according to the sector of the economy in which a firm is located. These definitions are given in Table 15.1.

---

[1] The Committee of Inquiry on Small Firms.

Table 15.1	Bolton Committee definitions of small companies	
Sector	*Upper limit*
Manufacturing	> 200 employees
Retail trades	> £450 000
Wholesale trades	> £1 700 000
Construction	
Mining, quarrying	> 25 employees
Motor trades	
Miscellaneous services	£450 000
Catering	All
Road transport	5 vehicles

Employment was used to identify smallness in manufacturing, construction, mining and motor trades, whereas turnover was the identifying criterion for small service-sector firms: retailing, wholesaling and others. Ownership criteria were used to identify a small catering firm, and the assets of the company identified a small road-transport business.

Although the Bolton Committee rightly recognised that what constitutes a small firm will vary from industry to industry, its attempt to define the small firm has been criticised in respect to both the economic conditions and the statistical definitions it adopted. Three major criticisms are as follows:

- Evidence suggests that the economic condition of *owner management* (i.e. a personalised management structure) is not compatible with the statistical definition of a small manufacturing firm as being one with up to 200 employees. Managerial structures have been found to become more formalised when the number of employees exceeds 100.
- Small firms tend to be specialist producers, operating in niche markets. As such, they may have a relatively *large* share of the segment of the market in which they are operating. The resulting market power gives them some control over price and profits. A small package-holiday company may have a tiny share of the total market, and yet, if it specialises in a particular type of holiday, such as for people with a particular hobby, it may have substantial market power in that segment of the market.
- The fact that there is no single criterion measuring smallness means that it is very difficult to compare like with like. Equally, the same criterion, such as employment, differs between sectors.

In recent years, the EU's definition of small and medium enterprises (SMEs) has become widely adopted by researchers, and is the basis on which all EU statistical data on SMEs are compiled. Three categories of SME are distinguished. These are shown in Table 15.2.

This subdivision of small firms into three categories allows us to distinguish features of enterprises that vary with the degree of smallness (e.g. practices of hiring and firing, pricing and investment strategies, competition and collusion, innovation). It also enables us to show changes over time in the size and composition of the small-firm sector. However, we might still question the adequacy of such a definition, given the diversity that can be found in business activity, organisational structure and patterns of ownership within the small-firm sector.

Table 15.2	EU SME definitions			
Criterion		Micro	Small	Medium
Maximum number of employees		9	49	249
Maximum annual turnover		–	€7 million	€40 million
Maximum annual balance sheet total		–	€5 million	€27 million
Maximum % owned by one, or jointly by several, enterprise(s) not satisfying the same criteria		–	25%	25%

Footnote: To qualify as an SME, both the employee and the independence criteria must be satisfied and either the turnover or the balance sheet total criteria

The small-firm sector in the UK

Failure to establish a clear definition of what is and what is not a small firm means that statistical estimates concerning the size of the small-firm sector are bound to be uncertain. In addition to this problem, official statistical sources regarding the UK's business structure and performance are widely dispersed over many publications. Two of the most important of these publications are as follows:

- *Annual Census of Production.* This draws on an annual sample of 20 000 businesses, and provides data on employment, output and wages.
- *VAT register.* The register is continually updated and covers all businesses above the VAT threshold and all those who register voluntarily. It provides data on business turnover and organisation.

These two sources are far from complete, however. All establishments between 1 and 20 employees, and 50 per cent of those between 20 and 40 employees are excluded from the Annual Census of Production. Businesses below the VAT threshold, and those not voluntarily registered, are obviously excluded from the VAT register.

One important source of data is the Department of Trade and Industry. Table 15.3 is taken from the DTI's *Small and Medium Enterprise Statistics* for 1999.

Table 15.3	Number of businesses, employment and turnover by size of enterprise, start 1999					
Size (number of employees)	Businesses (number)	Employment (000s)	Turnover[1] (£m ex VAT)	Businesses (%)	Employment (%)	Turnover (%)
None	2 324 340	2 708	90 463	63.2	12.5	4.7
1–4	963 615	2 395	221 986	26.2	11.0	11.4
5–9	201 835	1 459	123 029	5.5	6.7	6.3
10–19	109 280	1 533	149 451	3.0	7.1	7.7
20–49	46 955	1 462	147 505	1.3	6.7	7.6
50–99	14 450	1 011	102 860	0.4	4.7	5.3
100–199	8 165	1 131	116 638	0.2	5.2	6.0
200–249	1 570	349	38 633	–	1.6	2.0
250–499	3 220	1 121	149 275	0.1	5.2	7.7
500+	3 515	8 576	804 039	0.1	39.4	41.4
All	3 676 940	21 746	1 943 880	100.0	100.0	100.0
All with employee(s)	1 352 600	19 038	1 853 417	36.8	87.5	95.3

[1] Excluding finance sector
Source: *Statistical News Release* (DTI, 7/8/00)

It categorises business by number of employees and gives the total number of businesses, employment and turnover in each category.

The most significant feature of the data is that micro businesses (between 0 and 9 employees) accounted for 94.9 per cent of all businesses and provided 30.2 per cent of all employment. The table also shows that there were 3 660 475 micro and small businesses out of a total of 3 676 940 businesses: i.e. 99.6 per cent. Micro and small businesses also accounted for 48.6 per cent of employment and 43 per cent of turnover. From such information we can see that the small-firm sector clearly represents a very important part of the UK's industrial structure.

There are significant variations between sectors in the percentage of SMEs, whether by number of firms, employment or turnover. This is illustrated in Table 15.4.

Service providers (categories G to O in Table 15.4) contribute the overwhelming number of micro and small firms within the economy, accounting for 65.3 per cent of all micro and 69.8 per cent of all small firms.

Changes over time

How has the small-firm sector changed over time? The problems associated with definition and data collection make time-series analysis of the small-firm sector very difficult and prone to various inconsistencies. However, it is possible to identify certain indicators which show changes in the relative importance of the small-firm sector. In Figure 15.1 two such indicators are shown: the percentage of small firms within manufacturing by employment, and the level of self-employment among the labour force.

Table 15.4	SME share of businesses, employment and turnover by industry: start 1999				
	Businesses		Employment		Turnover[1]
	Total number	SME percentage share	Total employment (000s)	SME percentage share	SME percentage share
All industries[1]	3 676 940	99.8	21 746	55.4	51.0
A,B Agriculture, forestry & fishing	185 305	100.0	452	97.6	97.6
C Mining and quarrying	3 860	98.4	83	30.8	29.4
D Manufacturing	332 070	99.2	4 334	49.6	35.6
E Electricity, gas, water supply	325	86.9	139	2.6	6.9
F Construction	683 530	100.0	1 524	83.7	69.8
G Wholesale, retail & repairs	533 140	99.8	4 416	52.1	54.8
H Hotels & restaurants	154 400	99.8	1 598	55.6	52.9
I Transport, storage & communication	225 725	99.8	1 538	39.8	39.9
J Financial intermediation	59 455	99.4	1 043	21.1	35.5
K Real estate, business activities	800 515	99.9	3 146	69.6	73.1
M Education	107 850	99.9	255	83.8	86.5
N Health and social work	203 465	99.7	2 107	41.7	33.7
O Other social/personal services	387 295	99.9	1 111	76.7	64.1

[1] Finance sector excluded from turnover

Source: 'Small and Medium Enterprise (SME) Statistics for the UK, 1999' (*Statistical News Release*, DTI, 7/8/00)

Figure 15.1
The importance of small firms in the United Kingdom

Sources: D.J. Storey, *Understanding the Small Business Sector* (Routledge, 1994); *Labour market Trends* (ONS)

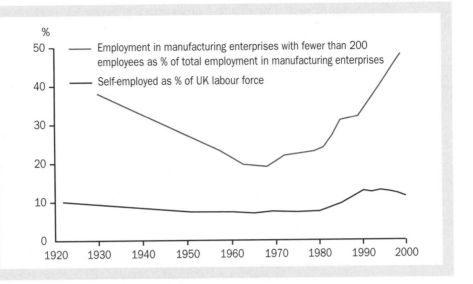

A similar trend is revealed in both data series: the percentage of small firms fell from the early part of the twentieth century, but from the mid-1960s began to rise again. What is the explanation for this rise in small businesses in recent years? A wide range of factors have been advanced to explain this phenomenon, and include the following.

The growth in the service sector of the economy. The opportunities for small businesses have increased due to various aspects of service provision. Many services are, by their nature, small in scale and/or specialist. For example, many small businesses have developed in the area of computer support and back-up.

The growth in niche markets. Rising consumer affluence creates a growing demand for specialist products and services. Key examples might be in textiles and in other fashion/craft-based markets. Such goods and services are likely to be supplied by small firms, in which economies of scale and hence price considerations are of less relevance.

New working practices which require greater labour force flexibility. Forms of employment such as **subcontracting** have become more pronounced, as businesses attempt to achieve certain cost and flexibility advantages over their rivals. This often forces individuals either to set up their own companies to provide such services, or to become self-employed.

A higher level of unemployment since the beginning of the 1980s. The higher the level of unemployment, the more people turned to self-employment as a more attractive alternative to being out of work.

The role of government. Government attitudes and policy initiatives shifted in favour of small business creation during the 1980s. The development of an **enterprise culture**, in which individuals were to be given the opportunity, and various financial incentives, to start their own businesses, was one of the

> **definition**
>
> **Subcontracting**
> The business practice where various forms of labour (frequently specialist) are hired for a given period of time. Such workers are not directly employed by the hiring business, but either employed by a third party or self-employed.

> **definition**
>
> **Enterprise culture**
> One in which individuals are encouraged to become wealth creators through their own initiative and effort.

principal aims of the Conservative government over the 1980s and 1990s. In section 15.3 we shall consider government policy initiatives in more detail.

The growth in small businesses in the UK has been pronounced since the early 1970s. But has a similar trend been apparent in other developed economies?

International comparisons

We have already seen the difficulties associated with the poor quality of data and the problems in defining the small-firm sector. These problems are particularly severe when it comes to making international comparisons. Best estimates suggest that the pattern in the UK is *not* generally repeated elsewhere. In most countries, both within Europe (e.g. Germany and France) and outside Europe (e.g. the USA and Japan), there has been no clear trend towards a growing small-firm sector, and in some cases the proportion of small businesses has declined. Italy is the only country, apart from the UK, where there has been a definite growth in the small-firm sector.

Investigations into self-employment rates among OECD countries between 1965 and 1987 reveal that, although self-employment is rising for most countries (for Japan and Holland it is, in fact, falling), the increase did not start until the mid-1970s, almost ten years later than in the UK.[2] This may well reflect the more significant and rapid structural changes taking place within the UK economy over this period.

In the rest of this chapter we shall put the definitional and statistical problems regarding the small-firm sector to one side, and focus on the role that SMEs play within the economy and at what determines their success or failure.

15.2 The survival, growth and failure of small businesses

Evidence suggests that a small business stands a significantly higher chance of failure than a large business, and yet many small businesses survive and some grow. What characteristics distinguish a successful small business from one that is likely to fail? The following section looks at this issue.

Competitive advantage and the small-firm sector

The fact that many small businesses do survive, and some manage to grow, suggests that they must have some edge over their larger rivals. The following have been found to be the key competitive advantages that small firms might hold.

Flexibility. Small firms are more able to respond to changes in market conditions and to meet customer requirements effectively. For example, they may be able to develop or adapt products for specific needs. Small firms may also be able to make decisions quickly, avoiding the bureaucratic and formal decision-making processes that typify many larger companies.

Quality of service. Small firms are more able to deal with customers in a personal manner and offer a more effective after-sales service.

[2] D.J. Storey, *Understanding the Small Business Sector* (Routledge, 1994).

BOX 15.1

The Dyson Dual Cyclone vacuum cleaner
A small business redefining the Hoover

In 1995, Dyson Appliances recorded turnover of £55 million. By 1996, with sales of 30 000 vacuum cleaners and a turnover of £8 million a month, Dyson Appliances was outperforming the market's major players, Hoover and Electrolux.

The tale of the Dyson Dual Cyclone vacuum cleaner records the successful and dramatic rise of James Dyson. As a budding entrepreneur, in the early 1980s he invented a revolutionary bagless vacuum cleaner, which worked, in effect, by creating a mini cyclone, whereby a high-speed air vortex pushed dust particles to the side of a collector. Without a bag, the suction power of the cleaner would not diminish over time, unlike conventional vacuums. When he initially developed this product (there were 5000 prototypes before a marketable product was finalised), neither Electrolux nor Hoover was interested – largely because of the profits they made from selling bags!

After an early and unsuccessful attempt to launch the project, Dyson managed to secure a deal with a Japanese company to produce and sell his product in Japan, where his vacuum retailed for a staggering £1200. At this price, it was unlikely to yield the mass sales Dyson hoped for, even given the superiority of the product. Thus Dyson set out to manufacture the product himself.

Finding it difficult to raise capital and find backers, Dyson reinvested his profits from the Japanese sales, and managed to raise the £4.5 million required to design and patent his product, to establish a network of subcontractor suppliers, and to create an assembly plant in the UK. With his vacuum cleaner priced at £200, Dyson hoped to enter the market at an affordable price.

Today, Dyson's vacuum cleaner has 50 per cent of the UK market and accounts for one-fifth of all vacuum cleaner sales across Western Europe.

Not content to sit on his success, James Dyson, at the end of 1999, launched his robot cleaner, a £5 million project which he hopes will have the same impact on the cleaner market as his bagless vacuum. He is hoping that by 2005 worldwide sales from the robot vacuum will be in the region of £2 billion, a substantial increase over the £400 million that the company currently earns.

The Dyson Dual Cyclone vacuum cleaner is a classic example of how a small business with a revolutionary product can have a massive impact on a market, and within a short period of time become established as a market leader.

Questions
1 What conditions existed to enable James Dyson's small business to do so well in such a short period of time?

2 In retrospect, were Electrolux and Hoover correct not to produce the new type of vacuum cleaner? Should they do so now?

Production efficiency and low overhead costs. Small firms can avoid some of the diseconomies of scale that beset large companies. A small firm can benefit from: management that avoids waste; good labour relations; the employment of a skilled and motivated workforce; lower accommodation costs.

Product development. As we have seen, many small businesses operate in niche markets, offering specialist goods or services. The distinctiveness of such products gives the small firm a crucial advantage over its larger rivals. A successful small business strategy, therefore, would be to produce products that are clearly differentiated from those of large firms in the market, thereby avoiding head-on competition – competition which the small firm would probably not be able to survive.

Innovation. Small businesses, especially those located in high-technology markets, are frequently product or process innovators. Such businesses, usually through entrepreneurial vision, manage successfully to match such innovations to changing market needs. Many small businesses are, in this respect, path breakers or market leaders.

Small businesses do, however, suffer from a number of significant limitations.

Problems facing small businesses

The following points have been found to hinder the success of small firms.

Selling and marketing. Small firms face many problems in selling and marketing their products, especially overseas. Small firms are perceived by their customers to be less stable and reliable than their larger rivals. This lack of credibility is likely to hinder their ability to trade. This is a particular problem for 'new' small firms which have not had long enough to establish a sound reputation.

Funding R & D. Given the specialist nature of many small firms, their long-run survival may depend upon developing new products and processes in order to keep pace with changing market needs. Such developments may require significant R & D investment. However, the ability of small firms to attract finance is limited, as many of them have virtually no collateral and they are frequently perceived by banks as a highly risky investment.

Management skills. A crucial element in ensuring that small businesses not only survive but grow is the quality of management. If key management skills, such as being able to market a product effectively, are limited, then this will limit the success of the business.

Economies of scale. Small firms will have fewer opportunities and scope to gain economies of scale, and hence their costs are likely to be somewhat higher than their larger rivals. This will obviously limit their ability to compete on price.

The question often arises whether it is possible to distinguish between those small businesses which are likely to grow and prosper and those that are likely to fail. In the section below we will consider not only how businesses grow, but whether there is a key to success.

How do small businesses grow?

It is commonly assumed that all businesses wish to grow. But is it true? Do small businesses want to become big businesses? It may well be that the owners of a small firm have no aspirations to expand the operations of their enterprise. They might earn sufficient profits and experience a level of job satisfaction that would in no way be enhanced with a bigger business operation. In fact the negative aspects of big business – formalised management structure, less customer contact and a fear of failure – might reduce the owner's level of satisfaction.

If growth is a small business objective, what are the chances of success? Evidence from both the UK and the USA suggests that there is a positive relationship between business survival and growth: estimates suggest that for every 100 firms established, after a ten-year period only 40 will survive.

The process of growth

Small businesses are frequently perceived to grow in stages. The number of stages may vary depending on the nature of the business and on how each stage is defined, but typically we can identify five (see Table 15.5).

In the initial stage, *inception*, the entrepreneur plays the key role in managing the enterprise with little if any formalised management structure. In the next two stages we see the firm establish itself (the *survival* stage) and then *begin to grow*. The entrepreneur devolves management responsibility to non-owner managers. Such non-owner managers are able to add certain skills to the business which might enhance its chances of growth and success. The fourth and fifth phases, *expansion* and *maturity*, see the firm become more bureaucratic and rationalised; power within the organisation becomes more dispersed.

This picture of the growth of small businesses is *descriptive* rather than explanatory. To *explain* why a small firm grows we need to examine a number of factors. It is useful to group them under three headings – the entrepreneur, the firm and strategy.

The entrepreneur

Factors in this section relate predominantly to the attributes and experience of the individual entrepreneur. They include the following.

Entrepreneurial motivation and a desire to succeed. Motivation, drive and determination are clearly important attributes for a successful entrepreneur. On their own, however, they are unlikely to be sufficient. If motivation is not complemented with things such as good business knowledge and decision making, then a business is likely to fail irrespective of its owner's motives.

Educational attainment. Although educational attainment does not necessarily generate business success (indeed, it is often claimed that running a business is not an 'intellectual' activity), the level of education of an entrepreneur is positively related to the rate of growth of the firm.

Table 15.5 Management role and style in the five stages of small business growth

Stage	Top management role	Management style	Organisation structure
1. Inception	Direct supervision	Entrepreneurial, individualistic	Unstructured
2. Survival	Supervised supervision	Entrepreneurial, administrative	Simple
3. Growth	Delegation/ co-ordination	Entrepreneurial, co-ordinate	Functional, centralised
4. Expansion	Decentralisation	Professional, administrative	Functional, decentralised
5. Maturity	Decentralisation	Watchdog	Decentralised functional/product

Source: D.J. Storey, *Understanding the Small-Business Sector* (Routledge, 1994).

BOX 15.2

Hypergrowth companies
The secrets of exceptional business performance?

Of all the beasts in the corporate jungle, the most fascinating is the one that emerges from nowhere, grows at a phenomenal rate and, before too long, is challenging some of the bigger animals. Hypergrowth companies are known in America as fast-growth tigers, in Britain as baby sharks.[1]

On rare occasions companies appear in the market place that grow at a phenomenal rate. What special ingredients do such businesses have which enable them to perform so well?

Coopers and Lybrand, in a recent study of hypergrowth businesses, defined them as 'firms which have achieved an increase in both turnover and employment of 100 per cent over the last three years'.

They applied this criterion to 501 medium-sized enterprises. They found that 26 companies fell into the hypergrowth category. The 26 companies were found to have the following features:

- They tended to be young. Half were under 10 years old.
- 70 per cent of them were privately owned, with turnover ranging from £13 million to £50 million a year.

- The majority of them served a single market or supplied a single product or service.
- The niche markets in which they tended to be located were under-exploited by bigger businesses or in many cases completely ignored.
- Most of them were located in service industries, such as transport, professional services and finance.

As well as sharing the above features, hypergrowth companies were also found to follow very similar business strategies. These included the following:

- Improving the speed at which new products and services got to the market.
- Maintaining tight control over stocks.
- Fostering a close relationship with main suppliers and customers.
- Ensuring that the best use of new technology was made in all aspects of business.
- Recruiting managers from outside the main market of the business, so as to ensure expertise in other core business activities: for example, marketing and retailing.
- Adopting employee incentive schemes, which included share ownership programmes.

[1] *Management Today*, February 1996.

Prior management experience and business knowledge. Previous experience by the owner in the same or a related industry is likely to offer a small firm a far greater chance of survival and growth. 'Learning by doing' will enable the new business owner to avoid past mistakes or to take advantage of missed previous opportunities.

The firm

The following are the key characteristics of a small business that determine its rate of growth.

The age of the business. New businesses grow faster than mature businesses.

The sector of the economy in which the business is operating. A firm is more likely to experience growth if it is operating in a growing market. Examples include the financial services sector during the 1980s, and specialist high-technology sectors today.

● Keeping company borrowing low, with growth funded, as far as possible, from the reinvestment of profits.

The main challenge for hypergrowth companies is whether they maintain their dramatic growth over the longer term. There are essentially two competing views regarding the long-term sustainability of hypergrowth.

The first is that 'baby sharks' create a virtuous circle, where fast growth fuels itself. Profits and performance, if managed correctly, create the necessary conditions to maintain hypergrowth. Essentially, high growth leads to high profits, which lead to high investment, which, in turn, can lead to high growth.

The alternative view is that hypergrowth businesses are hypergrowth by successfully exploiting a particular market or opportunity: a 'niche market'. Once the niche attracts the attention of rival firms, the ability to maintain hypergrowth diminishes. Hypergrowth is ultimately only short term.

What does seem apparent from recent investigations is that the main threat to hypergrowth businesses comes from their relationship with larger companies in the market place. Findings show that hypergrowth companies tend, on balance, to have more large company customers and suppliers than other medium-sized enterprises. As the *Management Today* article states:

> The danger for hypergrowth middle-sized businesses is that they will be squeezed when they begin to become a serious threat. Either that or they get taken over by one of their bigger customers, suppliers or competitors and lose the edge that made them special in the first place.

Questions

1 In what respects do hypergrowth companies share the same characteristics as enterprises in the small business sector?

2 Why is there potentially greater opportunity for small businesses, rather than medium or large enterprises, to become hypergrowth companies?

3 It is apparent from the evidence that medium-sized businesses might find it difficult to maintain hypergrowth. Explain why. What additional problems, if any, might a small business face if it attempts to maintain hypergrowth in the long term?

Legal forms. Limited companies have been found to grow faster than sole proprietorships or partnerships. Evidence suggests that limited companies tend to have greater market credibility with both banks and customers.

Location. Small firms tend to be highly dependent for their performance on a localised market. Being in the right place is thus a key determinant of a small business's growth.

Strategy

Various strategies adopted by the small firm will affect its rate of growth. Strategies that are likely to lead to fast growth include the following.

Workforce and management training. Training is a form of investment. It adds to the firm's stock of human capital, and thereby increases the quantity, and possibly also the quality, of output per head. This, in turn, is likely to increase the long-term growth of the firm.

The use of external finance. Taking on additional partners, or, more significantly, taking on shareholders, will increase the finance available to firms and therefore allow a more rapid expansion.

Product innovation. Firms that introduce new products have been found on the whole to grow faster than those that do not.

Export markets. Even though small firms tend to export relatively little, export markets can frequently offer additional opportunities for growth. This is especially important when the firm faces stiff competition in the domestic market.

The use of professional managers. The devolving of power to non-owning managers is identified as a major characteristic of fast-growth small firms. Such managers, as previously mentioned, widen the skills and knowledge base of the organisation, and shift the reliance of the business away from the entrepreneur, whose skills might be limited to specific areas.

What the above factors suggest is that, if a small business is to be successful and subsequently grow, then it must consider its business strategy – the organisation of the business, and the utilisation of individuals' abilities and experience. It is a combination of these factors which is likely to generate success, and only those businesses that co-ordinate such characteristics are likely to grow. Conversely, those businesses that fail to embrace these key characteristics are likely to fall by the wayside.

A potentially crucial factor in aiding success is the contribution and role of public policy. In the next section we shall consider the attitude of the UK government to small business and the policy initiatives it has introduced. We will also assess how such initiatives differ from, complement or duplicate those provided by the EU.

15.3 Government assistance and the small firm

When the UK Labour government was elected in 1997, it stated that its principal economic objective was to develop a strategy that would enable the country to achieve its full economic potential. A key element of the strategy was the encouragement and promotion of entrepreneurial talent; and one way of achieving this was by supporting small and medium-sized enterprises.

SME policy in the UK

There are two principal objectives of UK policy towards SMEs:

- to encourage individuals to start-up their own business;
- to encourage SME growth and performance.

Let us consider these objectives in turn.

Small business start-up

In the UK, the level of small business start-ups is about three businesses per 100 adults. In the USA, it is over seven businesses per 100 adults. In attempting to close the gap, the UK government has adopted a wide range of measures to encourage people to set up in business.

Some of the most recent incentives have focused on pre-start-up support and have sought to foster a greater entrepreneurial spirit among the young. The new National Curriculum includes the study of enterprise and employment, and the government intends to spend £10 million from April 2000 to enhance its current programme of education–business links. The National Enterprise Campaign is designed to inspire young people to go into business by following the examples of well-known entrepreneurs. It has enlisted the support of people such as Sir Richard Branson, Sir Alan Sugar and James Dyson. The government hopes that they will act as ambassadors for business and be role-models and mentors for aspiring young entrepreneurs.

One of the most significant measures has been the creation of the Small Business Service (SBS). The SBS is designed to give small firms, or those thinking of setting up a small firm, easy access to advice and support. (Prior to the SBS, the large diversity of initiatives and regulations applying to small business meant that there was no clear point of reference for anyone seeking advice or guidance.) In addition to this, the SBS is designed to ensure that the interests and problems of small business are taken into account when the government formulates its economic policy

Financial assistance to those wishing to start up a small business can come from a number of sources. Small businesses pay only a 10 per cent rate of corporation tax, rising to 20 per cent (compared with a normal rate of 30 per cent), and receive a 40 per cent capital allowance for investment in plant and machinery. In addition to receiving favourable treatment under the tax system, small firms have access to a wide range of funds and grants.

The £30 million Phoenix Fund was created to help those wishing to set up a business in an area of high unemployment. As well as offering finance, the fund is also looking to recruit 1000 volunteer business mentors to offer help and advice in starting up and running a small business. It is also backing a programme of Entrepreneurial Scholarships, where entrepreneurs from deprived areas will be given the opportunity to develop management and business skills to help them set up and survive in business on their own.

Additional money can also be received if a business sets up in an area that receives some form of regional assistance. Regional Selective Assistance (RSA) grants are available for the creation of new businesses, as are Enterprise Grants. With Enterprise Grants, a small business can receive up to 15 per cent of its fixed capital costs.

The New Deal programme also offers help for the long-term unemployed who wish to become self-employed and start their own business. For those over 50, £3000 is available during the first year.

Small business growth

Policies to encourage small business growth have focused largely on providing assistance in raising finance. The most significant example is the Small Firm Loan Guarantee Scheme (SFLGS). Guarantees are available for periods of between 2 and 10 years on bank loans from £5000 to £100 000. The government guarantees 70 per cent of a bank loan against default (or 85 per cent in the case of businesses that have been trading for more than two years). These guarantees are given to small businesses that have insufficient collateral or where an investment is considered by the bank to be too high-risk.

In addition to this support, the government has set up a further £1 billion fund to widen and deepen the provision of venture capital for smaller enterprises. This fund is run by the SBS and the Regional Development Agencies.

In an attempt to draw in private venture capital funds, a programme of 'Corporate Venturing' is to be introduced. Corporate Venturing involves investment by larger companies in new or expanding small business. In order to encourage such relations, the investor will be able to claim corporation tax relief at 20 per cent on all investments in the smaller firm.

The creation of the National Business Angels Network is a similar initiative. Here private individuals, or 'angels', wishing to invest in growing business are brought together with companies that require investment.

Further measures to encourage the growth of the small business sector include tax credits for research and development by SMEs, and the granting of generous capital allowances on investments in measures to promote e-commerce.

Small-firm policy in the EU

The need for an EU policy for SMEs was first recognised in the Colonna report on industrial policy back in 1970. However, it was not until 1985 that the European Council gave top priority to SME policy.

Limited assistance was available for SMEs within the EU between 1970 and 1985. A division within DG-3[3] (the part of the European Commission dealing with industrial policy) was set up to work with the Business Co-operation Centre, which helped SMEs to establish co-operative ventures with other firms, and also provided limited subsidies for certain trade activities.

Further assistance might have been gained from other divisions. DG-1 (External Relations) gave SMEs priority budget allocations that promoted international business. DG-16 (Regional Development) provided a wide range of grants for business creation projects in depressed regions. DG-5 (Employment, Social Affairs and Education) encouraged local employment initiatives, with small business being seen as a prime source of job creation.

Such initiatives as these, however, were not co-ordinated, but instead were pursued as largely separate strategies. However, in 1983, the 'European Year of the SME and Craft Industry', the European Parliament focused its attention on the needs of SMEs and the crucial requirement of a co-ordinated and independent policy. As a result, an SME task force was established in June 1986. This task force had two functions:

- To co-ordinate the various policies towards SMEs within the different EU divisions.
- To develop a general programme to aid SMEs which did not substitute or

[3] DG stands for 'Directorate General'. There are 36 DGs in the European Commission, each headed by a director-general, who reports to one of 20 Commissioners. DGs are no longer known by number but by name: e.g. Economic and Financial Affairs, Social affairs, Consumer Protection, Enterprise.

interfere with national actions within the EU, but rather operated in a complementary way.

The EU's *SME Action Programme* was set out in 1986. Its thirteen points fell into two categories. The first seven points considered regulatory and administrative issues; the final six points considered ways to help the creation and development of SMEs. The thirteen points of the Action Programme are outlined in Table 15.6.

The most significant moves towards a fully integrated SME policy occurred in 1993 when, as part of the EU's enterprise policy, SME initiatives were given an independent budget of ECU112.2bn for the period 1993 to 1996. In conjunction with this, it was stated that the impact of community policies on SMEs was to be more tightly monitored, co-ordinated and scrutinised.

In January 2000 this goal came a step closer with the formation of an Enterprise DG, following a merger of the DGs for SMEs and for industry and innovation. The aim of the Enterprise DG is to promote entrepreneurship and innovation within the EU.

The major sources of financial support for SMEs are the Structural Fund and the European Investment Bank (EIB). The Structural Fund provides finance to help correct regional imbalance within the EU. For the programming period 1994–9, 15 to 20 per cent of the Structural Fund (€23–30 billion) was devoted to SME support. Since 1990, the EIB has invested in nearly 42 000 SMEs, with loans totalling more than €11 billion. This represents about 45 per cent of all the finance allocated by the EIB to industry and services.

A wide range of policy initiatives have also been adopted in order to encourage SMEs to participate in the EU's technology programme. In the 5th Framework programme, SMEs have been allocated at least 10 per cent of the fund's budget of €13 700 million. The Co-operative Research Action for Technology (CRAFT) programme is split into a number of projects. SME participation is greatest in three – Industrial and Material Technologies (IMT), Information Technologies (ESPRIT) and Transport. These areas account for 67 per cent of all SME participation and 66 per cent of all SME funding.

In addition to providing funding, the EU's policy is to act as a networking facility, setting up partnerships and disseminating information. The Innovation Relay Centre Network was set up to advise small business on technology and innovation, and to assist in developing links to partners or to potential buyers of technologies developed by SMEs.

Table 15.6	**EU SME Action Programme**	
Regulatory and administrative matters	*Initiatives to encourage the establishment and development of SMEs*
1. Promoting the spirit of enterprise	7. Improving the social environment of SMEs
2. Improving the administrative environment	8. Training
3. Monitoring the completion of the internal market	9. Information
	10. Exports
4. Adapting company law	11. Encouraging new firms and innovation
5. Adapting competition law	12. Co-operation between firms and regions
6. Improving the tax environment	13. Provision of capital

The EU's commitment to SMEs has clearly grown in recent years. The EU provides not only extensive finance, but also advice, training and channels for communication to other enterprises.

The EU has recognised the valuable role that SMEs play within the economy, not only as employers and contributors to output, but in respect to their ability to innovate and initiate technological change – vital components in a successful and thriving regional economy.

SUMMARY

1a The small-firm sector is difficult to define. Different criteria might be used. However, the level of employment tends to be the most widely used.

1b The difficulties in defining what a small firm is mean that measuring the size of the small-firm sector is also difficult and subject to a degree of error. However, it appears that in the UK the small-firm sector has been growing since the mid-1960s. This is the result of a variety of influences including: industrial structure, working practices, the level of unemployment, the role of government and consumer affluence.

1c The growth in the small-firm sector in the UK is not mirrored elsewhere in the major industrial nations other than in Italy.

2a Small firms survive because they provide or hold distinct advantages over their larger rivals. Such advantages include: greater flexibility, greater quality of service, production efficiency, low overhead costs and product innovation.

2b Small businesses are prone to high rates of failure, however. This is due to problems of credibility, finance and limited management skills.

2c Of those small businesses that manage to survive, a small fraction will grow. The growth of business tends to proceed through a series of stages, in which the organisation and management of the firm evolves, becoming less and less dependent upon the owner-manager.

2d Those small businesses that do grow are likely to have distinct characteristics relating to individual abilities, business organisation and business strategy. Combinations of variables from these three categories will tend to favour growth of the SME.

3a Government policy aimed at the small firm within the UK is particularly concerned with business start-ups, although we can also identify initiatives that look to stimulate growth and improve performance.

3b Small business policy within the EU seeks to complement national programmes. It provides a wide range of grants, projects and information for SMEs. A large emphasis is placed upon the development and transmission of technological innovations within the SME sector.

REVIEW QUESTIONS

1 Why is it so difficult to define the small-firm sector? What problems does this create?

2 'Small businesses are crucial to the vitality of the economy.' Explain.

3 Compare and contrast the competitive advantages held by both small and big business.

4 It is often argued that the success of a small business depends upon a number of conditions. Such conditions can be placed under the general headings of: the entrepreneur, the firm and the strategy. How are conditions under each of these headings likely to contribute to small business success?

5 Compare and contrast UK and EU approaches to SME policy.

Pricing strategy 16

How are prices determined in practice? Is there such a thing as an 'equilibrium price' for a product that will be charged to all customers and by all firms in the industry? In most cases the answer is no.

Take the case of the price of a rail ticket. On asking, 'What's the train fare to London?', you are likely to receive any of the following replies: Do you want an 'Apex' ticket (one booked in advance)? Do you want first or standard class? Do you want single or return? How old are you? Do you have a railcard (family, young person's, student, senior citizen's)? Do you want a day return, a 'saver', a 'super saver' or a period return? Will you be travelling back on a Friday? Will you be travelling out before 10 a.m? Will you be leaving London between 4 p.m. and 6 p.m.? Do you want to reserve a seat? Do you want to take advantage of our special low-priced winter Saturday fare?

How you respond to the above questions will determine the price you pay, a price that can vary several hundred per cent from the lowest to the highest. And it is not just train fares that vary in this way: air fares and holidays are other examples. Selling the same product to different groups of consumers at different prices is known as **price discrimination**. (We shall examine price discrimination in detail later in this chapter.) But prices for a product do not just vary according to the customer. They vary according to a number of other factors as well.

- The life cycle of the product. When a firm launches a product, it may charge a very different price from when the product has become established in the market, or, later, when it is beginning to be replaced by more up-to-date products.
- The aims of the firm. Is the firm aiming to maximise profits, or is it seeking to maximise sales or growth, or does it have a series of aims? Which aim or aims that it pursues will determine the price it charges?
- The competition that the firm faces. Firms operating under monopoly or collusive oligopoly are likely to charge very different prices from firms operating in highly competitive markets.
- Information on costs and demand. Firms in the real world may have very scant information about the demand for their product and for the products of their competitors. The firm may well attempt to forecast demand, but the further into the future it projects, the less reliable will the projections become. It is the same with information on costs: firms may have only a rough idea of how costs are likely to change over time. The picture of a firm choosing its price by a careful calculation of marginal cost and marginal revenue may be far from reality.

In this chapter we will explore the pricing strategies of business. We will identify different pricing models, show how a firm's pricing policy is likely to change

> **definition**
>
> **Price discrimination**
> Where a firm sells the same product at different prices.

over a product's life cycle, and how and under what circumstances businesses might practise price discrimination. We will also consider a number of other pricing issues, such as those linked to a multiproduct business and the use of a practice known as 'transfer pricing'.

16.1 Pricing and market structure

The firm's power over prices

In a free and competitive market we know that the quantity bought and sold, and the actual price of the product, are determined by the forces of supply and demand. If demand is in excess of supply, the consequent market shortage will cause the price level to rise. Equally, if supply is in excess of demand, the resulting market surplus will cause the market price to fall. At some point we have an equilibrium or market-clearing price, to which the market will naturally move. In such an environment, the firm cannot have a 'pricing strategy': the price is set for it by the market. It is a price taker.

But, even if a firm were able to identify the market demand and supply schedules, which is not at all certain given the problem of acquiring accurate market information, the market equilibrium price is likely to be short lived as market conditions change and demand and supply shift. This would be particularly the case for those goods or services that are fashionable and subject to changing consumer preferences, or where production technology is undergoing a period of innovation, influencing both the cost structure of the product and the potential output decisions open to the business. The best business could hope for, given the uncertainty of demand and supply, is to be flexible enough to continue making a profit when market conditions shift.

When a firm has a degree of market power, however, it will have some discretion over the price it can charge for its product. The smaller the number of competitors, and the more distinct its product is from those of its rivals, the more inelastic will the firm's demand become and the greater will be the control over price that the business will be able to exert.

We saw in Chapter 12 that, in oligopolistic markets, firms are dependent on each other: what one firm does, in terms of pricing, product design, product promotion, etc., will affect its rivals. The degree of interdependence, and the extent to which firms acknowledge it, will affect the degree to which they either compete or collude. This, in turn, will affect their pricing strategy. The result is that prices may be very difficult to predict in advance and bear little resemblance to those that would have been determined through the operation of free-market forces. At one time there may be an all-out price war, with firms madly trying to undercut each other in order to grab market share, or even drive their rivals out of business. At other times, prices may be very high, with the oligopolists colluding with each other to achieve maximum industry profits. In such cases the price may be even higher than if the industry were an unregulated monopoly, because there might still be considerable *non*-price competition, which would add to costs and hence to the profit-maximising price.

It is clear from this that, under oligopoly, pricing is likely to be highly strategic. One of the key strategic issues is the effect of prices on potential new entrants, and here it is not only the oligopolist, but also the monopolist that

BOX 16.1

Predatory pricing in the airline industry
The case of easyJet and KLM

In April 1996 easyJet began operating services on the Amsterdam–London route. Its lowest price for a return fare was 200 Dutch guilders, less than half the lowest price offered by KLM (406 guilders). On 17 June, KLM reduced its lowest price to 190 guilders.

Was this a 'fair' response to the new competition from easyJet? EasyJet did not think so, and in August 1996 it began legal proceedings against KLM, claiming that KLM was abusing its dominant position on the Amsterdam–London route and was engaging in *predatory pricing*. Predatory pricing is illegal under Article 86 of the Treaty of Rome (see Section 20.1).

Questions

1 How is predatory pricing defined?

2 If the established firm charges a price below the average cost of the new entrant, is this necessarily a case of predatory pricing?

3 If competition is desirable, then is it not always a gain if firms attempt to undercut each other?

4 Why might the new entrant find it more difficult to survive a price war than the established firm?

On 2 August 1996, the *Financial Times* quoted an internal KLM memo, which referred to the need 'to stop the growth and development of easyJet and make sure

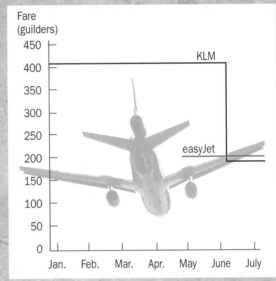

Source: G. Stewart, 'Predatory pricing', *The Economic Review* (February 1997).

that this newcomer will not be able to secure a solid position in the Dutch market'.

5 Does this memo (if correct) suggest that KLM was conducting predatory pricing?

---

must think strategically. If the firm sets its prices too high, will new firms take the risk of entering the market? If so, should the firm keep its price down and thereby deliberately limit the size of its profits so as not to attract new entrants?

Limit pricing

This policy of **limit pricing** is illustrated in Figure 16.1. Two *AC* curves are drawn: one for the existing firm and one for a potential entrant. The existing firm, being experienced and with a capital base and established supply channels, is shown having a lower *AC* curve. The new entrant, if it is to compete successfully with the existing firm, must charge the same price or a lower one. Thus provided the existing firm does not raise price above P_L, the other firm, unable to make supernormal profit, will not be attracted into the industry.

P_L may well be below the existing firm's short-run profit-maximising price, but it may prefer to limit its price to P_L to protect its long-run profits from damage by competition.

> **definition**
>
> **Limit pricing**
> Where a business keeps prices low, restricting its profits, so as to deter new rivals entering the market.

Figure 16.1
Limit pricing

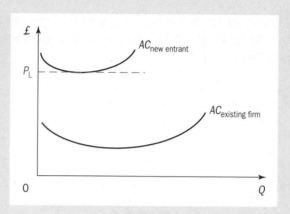

Alternative aims

It is not only market structure that affects pricing policy. The personal objectives of managers might strongly influence pricing policy. A manager who was aiming to maximise profits (as assumed by traditional economic theory) might set a significantly different price from one who was looking to maximise sales or long-run growth. We examined these alternative managerial and behavioural theories of the firm in Chapter 13. They add a further complication to the process by which a business sets the price for its products.

16.2 Alternative pricing strategies

What is the typical procedure by which firms set prices? Do they construct marginal cost and marginal revenue curves (or equations) and find the output where they are equal? Do they then use an average revenue curve (or equation) to work out the price at that output?

To do this requires a detailed knowledge of costs and revenues that few firms possess. To work out *marginal* revenue, the firm requires information not just on current price and sales. It must know what will happen to demand if price *changes*. In other words, it must know the price elasticity of demand for its product. Similarly, to work out *marginal* cost, the firm must know how costs will *change* as output changes. In reality this is highly unlikely. The business environment is in a constant state of change and uncertainty. The costs of production and the potential revenues from sales will be difficult to predict, shaped as they are by many complex and interrelated variables (changes in tastes, advertising, technological innovation, etc.). Under oligopoly in particular, it is virtually impossible to identify a demand curve for the firm's product. Demand for one firm's product will depend on what its rivals do: and that can never be predicted with any certainty. As a consequence, managers' 'knowledge' of future demand and costs will take the form of estimates (or even 'guesstimates'). Trying to equate marginal costs and marginal revenue, therefore, is likely to be a highly unreliable means of achieving maximum profits (if, indeed, that were the aim).

If, then, the marginalist principle of traditional theory is not followed by most businesses, what alternative pricing strategy can be adopted? In practice, firms look for rules of pricing that are relatively simple to apply.

Cost-based pricing

One alternative to marginalist pricing is **average cost** or **mark-up pricing**. In this case, producers derive a price by simply adding a certain percentage (mark-up) for profit on top of average costs (average fixed costs plus average variable costs).

$$P = AFC + AVC + \text{Profit mark-up}$$

The size of the profit mark-up will depend on the firm's aims: whether it is aiming for high or even maximum profits, or merely a target based on previous profit.

Choosing the level of output

Although calculating price in this manner does away with the firm's need to know its marginal cost and revenue curves, it still requires the firm to estimate how much output it intends to produce. The reason is that average cost varies with output. If the firm estimates that it will be working to full capacity, its average cost is likely to be quite different from that if it only works at 80 or 60 per cent of capacity.

Businesses tend to base their mark-up on *short-run* average costs. One reason for this is that estimates of short-run costs are more reliable than those of long-run costs. Long-run costs are based on *all* factors being variable, including capital. But by the time new capital investment has taken place, factors such as technological change and changes in factor prices will have shifted the long-run average cost curve, thereby making initial estimations inaccurate.

Figure 16.2 shows a firm's typical short-run average cost curves. The *AVC* curve is assumed to be saucer shaped. It falls at first as a result of a more

> **definition**
>
> **Mark-up pricing**
> A pricing strategy adopted by business in which a profit mark-up is added to average costs.

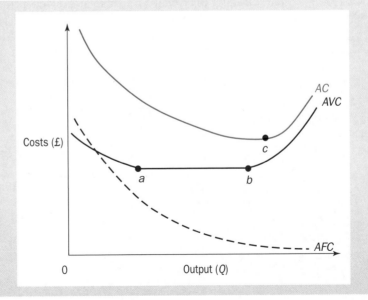

Figure 16.2
A firm's short-run average cost curve

efficient deployment of resources; then is probably flat, or virtually so, over a range of output; then rises as a result of diminishing marginal returns and possibly the need to pay overtime. The flat range of the average variable cost curve reflects the **reserve capacity** held by the business. This is spare capacity that the business can draw upon, if needed, to respond to changes in the market. For example, demand for the product may be subject to seasonal variation. The point is that many businesses can accommodate such changes with very little change in their average variable costs.

Most firms that use average-cost pricing will base their price on this horizontal section of the AVC curve (between points a and b in Figure 16.2). This section represents the firm's *normal* range of output. This normal range of output is that within which the plant has been designed to operate, and the business expects to be producing.

Average fixed costs will carry on falling as more is produced: overheads are spread over a greater output. This is illustrated in Figure 16.2. The result is that average (total) cost (AC) will continue falling over the range of output where AVC is constant, with minimum AC being reached at point c – beyond the flat section of the AVC curve. In practice, many firms do not regard average fixed costs in this way. Instead, they focus on average variable costs and then just add an element for overheads (AFC). This element is probably calculated at the normal level of output (i.e. somewhere in the flat section of the AVC curve), and then assumed to be *constant* as output changes. Although this is clearly wrong, changes in output from the normal level may be sufficiently small as to cause only an insignificantly small change in AFC. Thus AC at point c may be only very slightly below AC at the normal level of output.

Choosing the mark-up

The level of profit mark-up on top of average cost will be influenced by a range of possible considerations, such as fairness and the response of rivals (this will be discussed in more detail below). However, the most significant consideration is likely to be the implications of price for the level of market demand.

The business may well find that, at a given price, it will either be left with unsold stock if the price is too high, or fail to satisfy demand if the price is too low. The reason for this is that a mark-up pricing strategy starts from the principle of covering costs at a normal level of output and then adding a desirable

definition

Reserve capacity
A range of output over which business costs will tend to remain relatively constant.

Figure 16.3
Choosing the output and profit mark-up

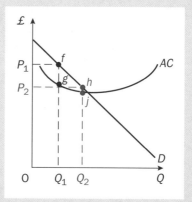

Figure 16.4
A firm's supply
curve for given profit
per unit

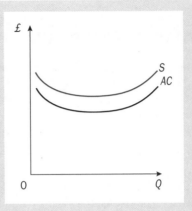

level of profit. As a strategy it may not adequately consider the level of market demand, which may change substantially over time as consumer preferences change. The result is that the price charged may not reflect that which the market can or will bear.

If a firm could estimate its demand curve, it could then set its output and profit mark-up at levels to avoid a shortage or surplus. Thus in Figure 16.3 it could choose a lower output (Q_1) with a higher mark-up (fg), or a higher output (Q_2) with a lower mark-up (hj). If a firm could not estimate its demand curve, then it could adjust its mark-up and output over time by a process of trial and error, according to its success in meeting profit and sales aims.

The equilibrium price and output?

Is it possible to identify an equilibrium price and output for the firm which sets its prices by adding a mark-up to average cost? To answer this, we can identify a supply curve for the firm.

If a firm is aiming for a particular profit *per unit* of output and does not adjust this target, the firm's supply curve will be as in Figure 16.4. It is derived by adding the mark-up to the *AC* curve. If, however, a firm is aiming for a particular level of *total* profit, and does not adjust this target, the firm's supply curve will be as in Figure 16.5. The greater the output, the less the profit per unit

Figure 16.5
A firm's supply
curve for given total
profit

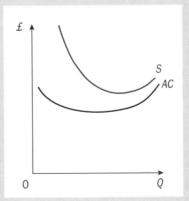

BOX 16.2

How do UK companies set prices?

In 1995 the Bank of England conducted a survey of price-setting behaviour in 654 UK companies.[1] Among other things, the survey sought to establish what factors influenced companies' pricing decisions. The results are given in Table (a).

Companies were asked to rank alternative methods of pricing of their main product ... The most popular response was that prices were set with respect to market conditions. The top preference[2] for almost 40 per cent of respondents was that prices were set at the highest level that the market could bear. An additional 25 per cent of respondents stated that they set prices in relation to their competitors – this was the second choice most popular among companies.

... The survey also confirmed the importance of company-specific factors. The first preference of about 20 per cent of respondents was that price was made up of a direct cost per unit plus a variable percentage mark-up ... A further 17 per cent of

companies, particularly retailing companies, stated that they priced on the basis of costs plus a fixed percentage mark-up.

Cost plus mark-ups tended to be more important for small companies, which cannot afford expensive market research.

The survey also sought to establish those factors which could cause prices to change – either up or down.

The survey asked companies to rank those factors most likely to push prices up or down. It found that there were substantial differences between the factors that influenced price increases and those that influenced price decreases. First, many more companies said that cost rises were likely to push prices up than said that cost reductions were likely to push prices down. Second, a rise in demand seemed less likely to lead to a price increase than a fall in demand was to lead to a price cut.

(a) How are prices determined?

	1st	%	2nd	%	3rd	%
Market level	257	39	140	21	78	12
Competitors' prices	161	25	229	35	100	15
Direct cost plus variable mark-up	131	20	115	18	88	14
Direct cost plus fixed mark-up	108	17	49	8	42	6
Customer set	33	5	52	8	47	7
Regulatory agency	11	2	3	1	5	1

Source: *Bank of England Quarterly Bulletin*, May 1996.

needs to be (and hence the less the mark-up) to give a particular level of total profit.

In either case, price and quantity can be derived from the intersection of demand and supply. Price and output will change if the demand or cost (and hence supply) curve shifts.

However, if the firm adjusts its profit target in the light of its experience or predictions, the mark-up will change. Under such circumstances, it may not be possible to derive a supply curve.

One problem here is that prices have to be set in advance of the firm knowing just how much it will sell and therefore how much it will need to produce. In practice, firms will usually base their assumptions about next year's sales on this year's figures, add a certain percentage to allow for growth

(b) Factors leading to a rise or fall in price

Rise	Number[a]	%	Fall	Number[a]	%
Increase in material costs	421	64	Decrease in material costs	186	28
Rival price rise	105	16	Rival price fall	235	36
Rise in demand	101	15	Fall in demand	146	22
Prices never rise	26	4	Prices never fall	75	12
Increase in interest rates	18	3	Decrease in interest rates	8	1
Higher market share	14	2	Lower market share	69	11
Fall in productivity	5	1	Rise in productivity	22	3

[a] Numbers citing a scenario as most important.
Note: Top preferences only.
Source: *Bank of England Quarterly Bulletin*, May 1996.

... The importance of strategic interaction with competitors suggests that when contemplating a price cut, companies need to consider the chance of sparking off a price war ... The finding that companies were much more likely to match rival price falls than they are to follow rival price rises appears to support the importance of strategic behaviour.

Questions

1 Which of the following is more likely to be consistent with the aim of maximising profits: pricing on the basis of (a) cost per unit plus a *variable* percentage mark-up; (b) cost per unit plus a *fixed* percentage mark-up?

2 Explain the differences between the importance attached to the different factors leading to price increases and those leading to price reductions.

3 Is the strategic behaviour referred to in the second quote consistent with the kinked demand curve theory (see pages 243–4)?

4 Why might we require a more detailed analysis of firm size and the different industrial sectors within the survey in order to evaluate the price-setting data presented above?

[1] Simon Hall, Mark Walsh and Tony Yates, 'How do UK companies set prices?', *Bank of England Quarterly Bulletin*, May 1996.
[2] Companies were able to show more than one response as their top preference. This means the total percentage of companies expressing first preferences for all of the explanations of price determination exceeds 100%.

in demand and then finally adjust this up or down if they decide to change the mark-up.

Variations in the mark-up

In most firms, the mark-up is not rigid. In expanding markets, or markets where firms have monopoly/oligopoly power, the size of the mark-up is likely to be greater. In contracting markets, or under conditions of rising costs and constant demand, a firm may well be forced to accept lower profits and thus reduce the mark-up.

Multiproduct firms often have different mark-ups for their different products depending on their various market conditions. Such firms will often distribute their overhead costs unequally among their products. The potentially most profitable products, often those with the least elastic demands, will probably be required to make the greatest contribution to overheads.

The firm is likely to take account of the actions and possible reactions of its competitors. It may well be unwilling to change prices when costs or demand change, for fear of the reactions of competitors (see the kinked demand curve theory on pages 243–4). If prices are kept constant and yet costs change, either due to a movement along the AC curve in response to a change in demand, or due to a shift in the AC curve, the firm must necessarily change the size of the mark-up.

All this suggests that, whereas the mark-up may well be based on a target profit, firms are often prepared to change their target and hence their mark-up.

16.3 Price discrimination

Up to now we have assumed that a firm will sell its output at a single price. Sometimes, however, firms may practise price discrimination. There are three major varieties of price discrimination:

- **First-degree price discrimination** is where the firm charges each consumer the maximum price he or she is prepared to pay for each unit. For example, stallholders in a bazaar will attempt to do this when bartering with their customers.
- **Second-degree price discrimination** is where the firm charges customers different prices according to how much they purchase. It may charge a high price for the first so many units, a lower price for the next so many units, a lower price again for the next, and so on. For example, electricity companies in some countries charge a high price for the first so many kilowatts. This is the amount of electricity that would typically be used for lighting and running appliances: in other words, the uses for which there is no substitute fuel. Additional kilowatts are charged at a much lower rate. This is electricity that is typically used for heating and cooking, where there are alternative fuels.
- **Third-degree price discrimination** is where consumers are grouped into two or more independent markets and a separate price is charged in each market. Examples include different-priced seats on buses for adults and children, and different prices charged for the same product in different countries. Third-degree price discrimination is much more common than first- or second-degree discrimination.

Conditions necessary for price discrimination to operate

As we shall see, a firm will be able to increase its profits if it can engage in price discrimination. But under what circumstances will it be able to charge discriminatory prices? There are three conditions that must be met:

- The firm must be able to set its price. Thus price discrimination will be impossible under perfect competition, where firms are price takers.
- The markets must be separate. Consumers in the low-priced market must not be able to resell the product in the high-priced market. For example,

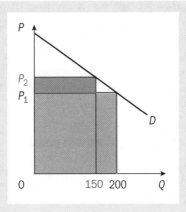

Figure 16.6
Third-degree price discrimination

children must not be able to resell a half-priced child's cinema ticket for use by an adult.
● Demand elasticity must differ in each market. The firm will charge the higher price in the market where demand is less elastic, and thus less sensitive to a price rise.

Advantages to the firm

Price discrimination will allow the firm to earn a higher revenue from any given level of sales. Let us first examine the case of third-degree price discrimination.

Figure 16.6 represents a firm's demand curve. If it is to sell 200 units without price discrimination, it must charge a price of P_1. The total revenue it earns is shown by the grey area. If, however, it can practise third-degree price discrimination by selling 150 of those 200 units at the higher price of P_2, it will gain the green area in addition to the grey area in Figure 16.6.

In the case of first-degree price discrimination, the firm can earn even more revenue. If every unit is sold at the maximum price that each consumer is prepared to pay, the price for each unit can be found from the point on the demand curve above that quantity. Thus in Figure 16.7, the revenue from selling 200 units will be the grey area plus the green area.

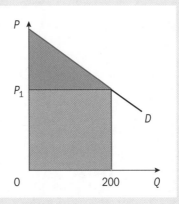

Figure 16.7
First-degree price discrimination

Another advantage to the firm of price discrimination is that it may be able to use it to drive competitors out of business. If a firm has a monopoly in one market (e.g. the home market), it may be able to charge a high price due to relatively inelastic demand, and thus make high profits. If it is under oligopoly in another market (e.g. the export market), it may use the high profits in the first market to subsidise a very low price in the oligopolistic market, thus forcing its competitors out of business.

Profit-maximising prices and output

Assuming that the firm wishes to maximise profits, what discriminatory prices should it charge and how much should it produce? Let us first consider the case of first-degree price discrimination.

First-degree price discrimination

Since an increase in sales does not involve lowering the price for any unit save the *extra* one sold, the extra revenue gained from the last unit (*MR*) will be its price. Thus profit is maximised at Q_1 in Figure 16.8, where $MC = MR$ (= *P* of the *last* unit).

Third-degree price discrimination

Assume that a firm sells an identical product in two separate markets X and Y with demand and *MR* curves as shown in Figure 16.9.

Diagram (*c*) shows the *MC* and *MR* curves for the firm as a whole. This *MR* curve is found by adding the amounts sold in the two markets at each level of *MR* (in other words, the horizontal addition of the two *MR* curves). Thus, for example, with output of 1000 units in market X and 2000 in market Y, making 3000 in total, revenue would increase by £5 if one extra unit were sold, whether in market X or Y.

Total profit is maximised where $MC = MR$: i.e. at an output of 3000 units in total. This output must then be divided between the two markets so that *MC* is equal to *MR* in each market: i.e. $MC = MR = £5$ in each market. *MR* must be the same in both markets, otherwise revenue could be increased by switching output to the market with the higher *MR*.

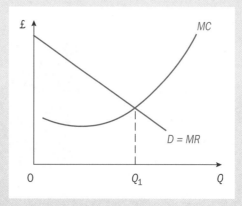

Figure 16.8
Profit-maximising output under first-degree price discrimination

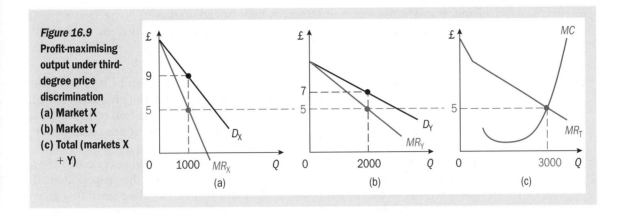

Figure 16.9
Profit-maximising output under third-degree price discrimination
(a) Market X
(b) Market Y
(c) Total (markets X + Y)

The profit-maximising price in each market will be given by the relevant demand curve. Thus, in market X, 1000 units will be sold at £9 each, and in market Y, 2000 units will be sold at £7 each. Note that the higher price is charged in the market with the less elastic demand curve.

Price discrimination by the non-profit-maximising firm

If a firm does not set a profit-maximising price, either because it has some alternative aim, or because it uses cost-based methods of pricing, which, owing to a lack of information, do not lead to the profit-maximising price, then we cannot predict precisely what the discriminatory prices will be. All we can say is that price discrimination will allow the firm to achieve higher profits, which most firms will prefer to lower profits.

The models we have examined show the potential for achieving higher profits. How much, in practice, firms will exploit this potential depends on how important extra profits are to them and how good their information is about the nature of demand in different segments of the market.

Price discrimination and the consumer

No clear-cut decision can be made over the desirability of price discrimination from the point of view of the consumer. Some people will benefit from it; others will lose. This can be illustrated by considering the effects of price discrimination on the following aspects of the market.

Distribution

Those paying the higher price will probably feel that price discrimination is unfair to them. On the other hand, those charged the lower price may thereby be able to obtain a good or service that they could otherwise not afford: e.g. concessionary bus fares for old-aged pensioners. Price discrimination is likely to increase output and make the good or service available to more people.

Competition

As explained above, a firm may use price discrimination to drive competitors out of business. This is known as **predatory pricing** (see Box 16.1). On the other

definition
Predatory pricing
Where a firm sets its average price below average cost in order to drive competitors out of business.

hand, it might use its profits from its high-priced market to break into another market and withstand a possible price war. Competition is thereby increased.

Profits

Price discrimination raises a firm's profits. This could be seen to be against the interests of the consumer, especially if the average price of the product is raised. On the other hand, the higher profits may be reinvested and lead to lower costs in the future. What is more, price discrimination may allow goods or services to be produced that otherwise would not be.

In Figure 16.10 there is no *one* price at which revenue will cover costs. If Q_1 is sold entirely at P_1, the firm will make a loss shown by the striped area. If, however, part of the output is sold at P_2, extra revenue will be gained (the green area) which might be sufficient to eliminate the loss and transform it into a profit.

16.4 Multiple product pricing

Thus far in our analysis of pricing strategy, we have been concerned only with a single product produced by a single firm. However, many businesses produce a range of products. Such products might be totally distinct and sold in different markets, or the firm might offer a range of models in the same market that differ in design and performance. For example, a vacuum cleaner manufacturer might also produce other household appliances such as irons, as well as offering a range of vacuums with different suction abilities and design features.

Each of these products and product ranges will require its own distinct price, and probably a longer-term pricing strategy. However, multiproduct pricing raises a wider set of issues due to the interrelated nature of demand and production.

Interrelated demand

Many of the large supermarkets or DIY stores are in fierce competition for business. It is quite normal to see them offering 'bargain buys', whose prices are cut dramatically in order to attract customers to the store. Often their price is even below average cost. Such cases are known as **loss leaders**. The hope is that

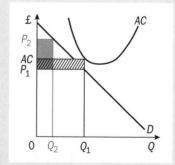

Figure 16.10
How price discrimination could enable a loss-making firm to make a profit

customers will purchase not just the loss leader, but additional amounts of other products with full profit mark-ups, thereby bringing a net gain in profits.

This strategy is known as **full-range pricing** and involves the business assessing the prices of all its products together, and deciding from this how it might improve its profit performance. One of the most important considerations is the price elasticity of demand for the loss leader. The more elastic it is, the more customers will tend to be attracted into the store by the bargain. The business will also consider additional factors such as advertising the loss leaders and their positioning in the store, so as to attract customers to see other items at full price that they had not intended to buy.

Other demand interrelations that might influence the pricing policy of a business are where a business produces either complementary or substitute products. If a business produces complementary products, then increased sales of one product, such as British Telecom telephones, will raise the revenue gained from the other, such as the use of the telephone network. Alternatively, if the products produced by a business are substitutes, such as those of a breakfast cereal manufacturer like Kellogg's, then the increased sales of one product within its range may well detract from the revenue gained from the others. Businesses like BT and Kellogg's should therefore determine the prices of all their substitute and complementary products jointly so as to assess the total revenue implications. Here it is vital for the firm to have estimates of the cross-price elasticities of demand for their products (see section 5.3).

Interrelated production

The production of **by-products** is the most common form of interrelated production. A by-product is a good or service that is produced as a consequence of producing another good or service. For example, whey is a by-product of cheese. By-products have their own distinct market demand. However, the by-product is only produced following demand for the main production good: it may well not be profitable to produce as a separate product.

To consider whether the by-product is profitable to sell, it is important to allocate the correct costs to its production. The raw materials and much of the other inputs to produce it can be considered to have a zero cost, since they have already been paid in producing the main product. But packaging, marketing and distributing the by-product clearly involve costs that have to be allocated directly to it, and the price it sells for must more than cover these costs.

It is not as simple as this, however, since the pricing of the by-product, and the subsequent revenue gained from its sale, might significantly influence the pricing of the main production good. Given that the two products share joint costs, a business must carefully consider how to allocate costs between them and what pricing policy it is going to pursue.

If it is aiming to maximise profits, it should add the marginal costs from both products to get an *MC* curve for the 'combined' product. Similarly, it should add the marginal revenues from both products at each output to get an *MR* curve for the combined product. It should then choose the combined output where the combined *MC* equals the combined *MR*. It should read off the price at this output for each of the two products from their separate demand curves.

In practice, many firms simply decide on the viability of selling by-products *after* a decision has been made on producing the main product. If the specific

> **definition**
>
> **Full-range pricing**
> A pricing strategy in which a business, seeking to improve its profit performance, assesses the pricing of its goods as a whole rather than individually.

> **definition**
>
> **By-product**
> A good or service that is produced as a consequence of producing another good or service.

costs associated with the by-product can be more than covered, then the firm will go ahead and sell it.

16.5 Transfer pricing

The growth of modern business, both national and international, has meant that its organisation has become ever more complex. In an attempt to reduce the diseconomies that stem from co-ordinating such large business enterprises, the setting of price and output levels is frequently decentralised to individual divisions or profit centres. Such divisions or profit centres are assumed to operate in a semi-independent way, aiming to maximise their individual performance and, in so doing, benefit the business as a whole.

However, the decentralisation of pricing and output decision making can become problematic. This is particularly the case when the various divisions within the firm represent distinct stages in the production process. In these instances, certain divisions may well produce intermediate products that they will sell to other divisions within the business. There then arises the difficulty of how such intermediate products should be priced. This is known as the problem of **transfer pricing**.

One implication of this is that a division which is seeking to maximise its own profits when selling to another division will attempt to exploit its 'monopoly' position and increase the transfer price. As it does so, the purchasing division, unless it, in turn, can pass on the higher cost, will see its profits fall. Indeed, if it could, the purchasing division would seek to drive down the purchase price as low as possible.

This conflict between divisions may not necessarily be in the interests of the business as a whole. The solution to this problem is for divisions to base their pricing of intermediate products on marginal costs. The marginal cost of the final product produced by the business will then be a 'true' marginal cost. If the business is seeking to maximise overall profits, it can then compare this final marginal cost with marginal revenue in order to decide on the level of total output. The lesson is that, for maximum company profits, individual divisions should seek to be efficient and produce with the lowest possible marginal costs, but not seek to attempt to maximise their own division's profits.

16.6 Pricing and the product life cycle

New products are launched and then become established. Later they may be replaced by more up-to-date products. Many products go through such a 'life cycle'. Four stages can be identified in a typical life cycle (see Figure 16.11):

1 Being launched.
2 A rapid growth in sales.
3 Maturity: a levelling off in sales.
4 Decline: sales begin to fall as the market becomes saturated, or as the product becomes out of date.

Black and white televisions, twin-tub washing machines and gramophone records have all reached stage 4. Colour televisions, automatic washing

> **definition**
>
> **Transfer pricing**
> The pricing system used within a business organisation to transfer intermediate products between the business's various divisions.

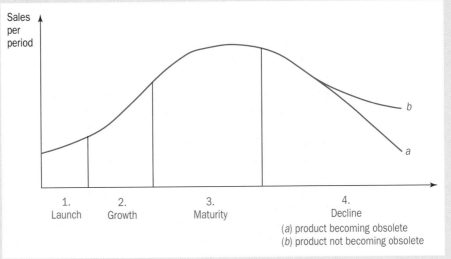

Figure 16.11
The stages in a product's life cycle

Sales per period

1. Launch
2. Growth
3. Maturity
4. Decline

(a) product becoming obsolete
(b) product not becoming obsolete

machines and audio cassettes have reached stage 3. Compact discs, home security systems and stereo video recorders are probably still in stage 2. Mini-disc recorders, computerised personal organisers and CD ROM home entertainment systems are probably still in stage 1.

At each stage, the firm is likely to be faced with quite different market conditions: not only in terms of consumer demand, but also in terms of competition from rivals. What does this mean for pricing strategy?

The launch stage

In this stage the firm will probably have a monopoly (unless there is a simultaneous launch by rivals).

Given the lack of substitutes, the firm may be able to charge very high prices and make large profits. This will be especially true if it is a radically new product – like the ballpoint pen, the pocket calculator and the home computer were. Such products are likely to have a rapidly expanding and price-inelastic demand.

The danger of a high-price policy is that the resulting high profits may tempt competitors to break into the industry, even if barriers are quite high. As an alternative, then, the firm may go for maximum 'market penetration': keeping the price low to get as many sales and as much brand loyalty as possible, before rivals can become established.

Which policy the firm adopts will depend on its assessment of its current price elasticity of demand and the likelihood of an early entry by rivals.

The growth stage

Unless entry barriers are very high, the rapid growth in sales will attract new firms. The industry becomes oligopolistic.

Despite the growth in the number of firms, sales are expanding so rapidly that all firms can increase their sales. Some price competition may emerge, but it is unlikely to be intense at this stage. New entrants may choose to compete in terms of minor product differences, while following the price lead set by the original firm.

The maturity stage

Now that the market has grown large, there are many firms competing. New firms – or, more likely, firms diversifying into this market – will be entering to get 'a piece of the action'. At the same time, the growth in sales is slowing down.

Competition is now likely to be more intense and collusion may well begin to break down. Pricing policy may become more aggressive as businesses attempt to hold on to their market share. Price wars may break out, only to be followed later by a 'truce' and a degree of price collusion.

It is in this stage particularly that firms may invest considerably in product innovation in order to 'breathe new life' into old products, especially if there is competition from new types of product. Thus the upgrading of hi-fi cassette recorders, with additional features such as Dolby S, was one way in which it was hoped to beat off competition from digital cassette recorders.

The decline stage

Eventually, as the market becomes saturated, or as new superior alternative products are launched, sales will start to fall. For example, once most households had a fridge, the demand for fridges fell back as people simply bought them to replace worn-out ones, or to obtain a more up-to-date one. Initially in this stage, competition is likely to be intense. All sorts of price offers, extended guarantees, better after-sales service, added features, etc., will be introduced as firms seek to maintain their sales. Some firms may be driven out of the market, unable to survive the competition.

After a time, however, the level of sales may stop falling. Provided the product has not become obsolete, people still need replacements. This is illustrated by line *b* in the diagram. The market may thus return to a stable oligopoly with a high degree of tacit price collusion.

Alternatively, the product becomes obsolete (line *a*) and sales dry up. Firms will leave the market. It is pointless trying to compete.

SUMMARY

1a Prices are determined by a wide range of factors, principal among which are demand and supply, market structure and the aims of managers.

1b Firms with market power will not always attempt to maximise short-run profits, even if maximum profit is the aim. They may well limit prices so as to forestall the entry of new firms.

2a Traditional economic theory assumes that businesses will set prices corresponding to the output where the marginal costs of production are equal to marginal revenue. They will do so in pursuit of maximum profits.

2b The difficulties that a business faces in deriving its marginal cost and revenue curves suggest that this is unlikely to be a widely practised pricing strategy.

2c Cost-based pricing involves the business adding a profit mark-up to its average costs of production. The profit mark-up set by the business is likely to alter depending upon market conditions, such as the level of consumer demand and the degree of market competition.

3a Many businesses practise price discrimination, in an attempt to maximise profits from the sale of a product. There are different levels of price discrimination that a business might practise.

3b For a business to practise price discrimination it must be able to set prices, separate markets so as

SUMMARY

to prevent resale from the cheap to the expensive market, and identify distinct demand elasticities in each market.

3c Whether price discrimination is in the consumer's interest or not is uncertain. Some individuals will gain and some will lose.

4 Businesses that produce many products need to consider the demand and production interrelations between them when setting prices.

5a The organisation of a business as a series of divisions, each pursuing an independent strategy, has implications for pricing policy, especially

when products are sold within a business enterprise.

5b The optimum transfer price between divisions from the point of view of the whole organisation is likely to be equal to marginal cost.

6a Products will be priced differently depending upon where they are in the product's life cycle.

6b New products can be priced cheaply so as to gain market share, or priced expensively to recoup cost. Later on in the product's life cycle, prices will have to reflect the degree of competition, which may become intense as the market stabilises or even declines.

REVIEW QUESTIONS

1 Explain why a business will find it difficult to set prices following the $MC = MR$ rule of traditional economic theory.

2 'Basing prices on average cost is no less problematical than using marginal cost and marginal revenue.' Assess this statement.

3 Outline the main factors that might influence the size of the profit mark-up set by a business.

4 If a cinema could sell all its seats to adults in the evenings at the end of the week, but only a few on Mondays and Tuesdays, what price discrimination policy would you recommend to the cinema in order for it to maximise its weekly revenue?

5 What is the role of a loss leader and what lessons might a business learn when pricing a range of products? Are there any supermarket products that would *not* be suitable to sell as loss leaders?

6 How will a business's pricing strategy differ at each stage of its product's life cycle? First assume that the business has a monopoly position at the launch stage; then assume that it faces a high degree of competition right from the outset.

F The firm in the factor market

THE FT REPORTS...

THE FINANCIAL TIMES, 30 JUNE 2000

Work in progress

AS EUROPEAN GOVERNMENTS CONGRATULATE THEMSELVES OVER FALLS IN UNEMPLOYMENT, JOHN LLOYD FINDS THAT LABOUR MOBILITY AND FLEXIBLE WORKING HOURS MAY HAVE PLAYED THE BIGGEST PART

As unemployment in Europe begins to fall at last, governments across the Continent have been quick to trumpet their part in its decline. But it remains unclear to what extent their self-congratulation is really justified. Government-run job creation measures have made some impact on joblessness, but of greater significance is the growing flexibility of the labour market combined with a quickening of economic growth across the Continent.

Work is changing as rapidly as it has at any time in the past century, under pressures of foreign competition, rapid technological change, the example of the US in job creation, and the continuing steady decline of manufacturing as a source of employment, even where sectoral output is up.

The status and power of the unions have come under immense pressure. In the Netherlands and Ireland, the numerically strong unions reacted in the 1980s to the pressures for flexibility by agreeing with employers national deals that restrained wages and, in the case of the Netherlands, saw a rise in part-time working to the highest proportion on Europe.

In none of the continental economies has the formal labour market changed as radically as the British one did in the 1980s. All have retained a comparatively well regulated bargaining system between employers and unions, with or without the state's involvement.

But there have been important changes, even in the German system, once a model of regulated corporate capitalism. Federal or regional deals beween employers and unions are still made, but bargaining is increasingly devolved to local factories. High wages costs, and the willingness of large companies to move production to other countries, has shocked German unions into agreeing to part-time and temporary work arrangements.

So far we have considered the role of the firm as a supplier of goods and services. In other words, we have looked at the operation of firms in the goods market. But to produce goods and services involves using factors of production: labour, capital and raw materials. In Part F, therefore, we turn to examine the behaviour of firms in factor markets and, in particular, the market for labour and the market for capital.

In factor markets, the supply and demand roles are reversed. The firm is *demanding* factors of production in order to *produce* goods and services. This demand for factors is thus a *derived* demand: one that is derived from consumers' demand for the firm's products. Households, on the other hand, in order to earn the money to buy goods and services, are *supplying* labour.

Chapter 17 focuses upon labour and the determination of wage rates. It also shows how the existence of power, whether of employers or trade unions, affects the wage rate and the level of employment in a given labour market. In addition to the issue of wage determination, we will consider the problem of low pay and discrimination, and the implications for the labour market of growing levels of flexibility in employment practices.

> **Labour and capital are but different forms of the same thing – human exertion. Capital is produced by labour; it is, in fact, but labour impressed upon matter – labour stored up in matter, to be released again as needed, as the heat of the sun stored up in coal is released in the furnace.**
>
> Henry George (1839–97),
> *Progress and Poverty*,
> Book III, Chapter 1

In Chapter 18 we will consider the employment of capital by firms and look at the relationship between the business and investment. We will consider how businesses appraise the profitability of investment. We will also examine the various sources of finance for investment. The chapter finishes by examining the stock market. We ask whether it is an efficient means of allocating capital.

key terms

Derived demand
Wage taker
Wage setter
Marginal revenue product
Monopsony
Bilateral monopoly
Trade union
Collective bargaining
Efficiency wages
Minimum wage rates
Discrimination
The flexible firm
Core and peripheral workers
Insiders and outsiders
Capital
Capital services
Investment
Discounting
Net present value
Financial intermediaries

Labour markets, wages and industrial relations

In this chapter we will consider how labour markets operate. In particular, we will focus on the determination of wage rates in different types of market: ones where employers are wage takers, ones where they can choose the wage rate, and ones where wage rates are determined by a process of collective bargaining.

We start by examining some of the key trends in the structure of the labour market.

17.1 The UK labour market

The labour market has undergone great change in recent years. Advances in technology, changes in the pattern of output, a need to be competitive in international markets and various social changes have all contributed to changes in work practices and in the structure and composition of the workforce.

Major changes in the UK include the following:

- A shift from agricultural and manufacturing to service-sector employment. Figure 17.1 reveals that employment in agriculture has been falling over a long historical period. The fall in manufacturing employment, however, has been more recent, starting in the 1960s and gathering pace through the 1970s, 1980s and 1990s. By contrast, employment in the service industries has grown steadily since 1946. In fact since 1979, it has expanded by over 3 million jobs.

- A rise in part-time employment, and a fall in full-time employment (see Figure 17.2). In 1971 one in six workers was part time; by 2000 this had risen to one worker in four. In the EU as a whole, the figure is one in six. The fall in full-time employment closely mirrors the decline in manufacturing, where jobs were more likely to be on a full-time basis. At the same time, the growth in part-time work reflects the growth in the service sector, where many jobs are part time. Since 1979 an estimated 1.8 million part-time jobs have been created.

- A rise in female participation rates. Women now constitute approximately half of the paid labour force. The rise in participation rates is strongly associated with the growth in the service sector and the creation of part-time positions. Just under 45 per cent of all female workers, about 5½ million, are in part-time work.

- A rise in the proportion of workers employed on fixed-term contracts, or on a temporary or casual basis. Many firms nowadays prefer to employ only their core workers/managers on a permanent ('continuing') basis. They feel that it gives them more flexibility to respond to changing market

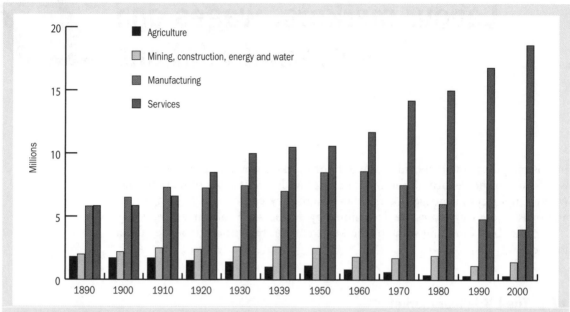

Figure 17.1

Employment in different sectors of the UK economy (1890–2000)

Source: *European Historical Statistics 1750–1970* by B.R. Mitchell (Macmillan Press); *Labour Market Trends* (ONS)

definition

Downsizing
Where a business reorganises and reduces its size, especially in respect to levels of employment, in order to cut costs.

conditions to have the remainder of their workers employed on a short-term basis and, perhaps, to make use of agency staff or to contract out work.

- **Downsizing**. It has become very fashionable in recent years for companies to try to 'trim' the numbers of their employees in order to reduce costs (see Box 3.2 on page 50). There is now, however, a growing consensus that the process may have gone too far. The cost of reducing its workforce may be that a company loses revenue: if it cuts back on people employed to market

Figure 17.2
Full-time and part-time employment in the UK

Source: Based on *Labour Market Trends* (ONS) various editions.

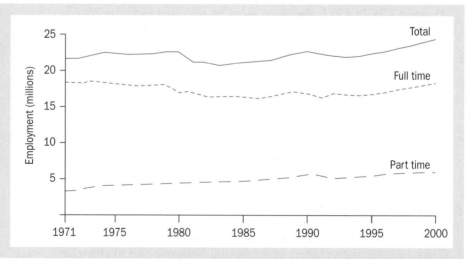

its products, develop new products or ensure that quality is maintained, then it is likely to lose market share. It might reduce unit costs, but total profits could nevertheless fall, not rise.

17.2 Market-determined wage rates and employment

Perfect labour markets

When looking at the market for labour, it is useful to make a similar distinction to that made in the theory of the firm: the distinction between perfect and imperfect markets. Although in practice few labour markets are totally perfect, many do at least approximate to it.

The assumptions of perfect labour markets are similar to those of perfect goods markets. The main one is that everyone is a **wage taker**. In other words, neither employers nor employees have any economic power to affect wage rates. This situation is not uncommon. Small employers are likely to have to pay the 'going wage rate' to their employees, especially where the employee is of a clear category, such as an electrician, a bar worker, a secretary or a porter. As far as employees are concerned, being a wage taker means not being a member of a union and therefore not being able to use collective bargaining to push up the wage rate.

The other assumptions of a perfect labour market are as follows:

- Freedom of entry. There are no restrictions on the movement of labour. For example, workers are free to move to alternative jobs or to areas of the country where wage rates are higher. There are no barriers erected by, say, unions, professional associations or the government. Of course, it takes time for workers to change jobs and maybe to retrain. This assumption therefore applies only in the long run.
- Perfect knowledge. Workers are fully aware of what jobs are available at what wage rates and with what conditions of employment. Likewise employers know what labour is available and how productive that labour is.
- Homogeneous labour. It is usually assumed that, in perfect markets, workers of a given category are identical in terms of productivity. For example, it would be assumed that all bricklayers are equally skilled and motivated.

Wage rates and employment under perfect competition are determined by the interaction of the market demand and supply of labour. This is illustrated in Figure 17.3(b).

Generally it would be expected that the supply and demand curves slope the same way as in goods markets. The higher the wage paid for a certain type of job, the more workers will want to do that job. This gives an upward-sloping supply curve of labour. On the other hand, the higher the wage that employers have to pay, the less labour they will want to employ. Either they will simply produce less output, or they will substitute other factors of production, like machinery, for labour. Thus the demand curve for labour slopes downwards.

Figure 17.3(a) shows how an individual employer has to accept this wage. The supply of labour to that employer is infinitely elastic. In other words, at the

> **definition**
>
> **Wage taker**
> The wage rate is determined by market forces.

BOX 17.1

'Telecommuters'
The electronic cottage

One of the causes of inequality of wages has been the geographical immobility of labour. Within countries this manifests itself in different rates of pay between different regions: often, those regions furthest from the capital city pay the lowest rates.

It also applies between countries. Poorer countries pay lower wages because there is not the mobility of labour between countries to counteract it. Thus in the EU, countries such as Greece, Ireland and Portugal have much lower wages than Germany, France or the Benelux countries. Although there is officially 'free movement of labour' under the terms of the 1993 single market, in practice there are all sorts of social, financial and language barriers that prevent workers in poorer countries moving to higher-paid jobs in the richer EU countries.

Nevertheless within countries people are often prepared to commute long distances in order to earn the higher pay that large cities have to offer. Witness the army of people who travel into London each day from many miles away, getting up early, arriving back late and paying huge sums of money for travelling.

One important development in recent years, however, is helping to reverse this trend. The increasing sophistication of information technology, with direct computer linking, the Internet, fax machines and mobile phones, has meant that many people can work at home. The number of these 'telecommuters' has grown steadily since the information technology revolution of the early 1970s.

It has been found that where 'telecommuting networks' have been established, gains in productivity levels have been significant, when compared with comparable office workers. Most studies indicate rises in productivity of over 35 per cent. With fewer interruptions and less chatting with fellow workers, less working time is lost. Add to this the stress-free environment, free from the strain of commuting, and the individual worker's performance is enhanced.

With further savings in time, in the renting and maintenance of offices (often in high-cost inner city locations) and in heating and lighting costs, the economic arguments in favour of telecommuting seem very persuasive.

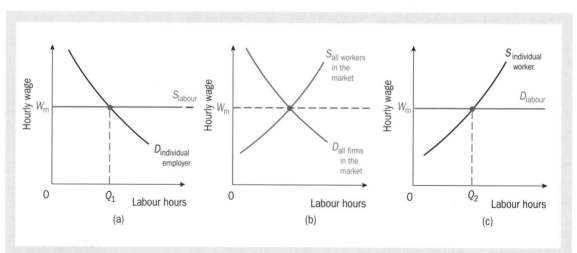

Figure 17.3

A perfectly competitive labour market (a) Individual employer (b) Whole market (c) Individual worker Marginal disutility of work

Then there are the broader gains to society. Telecommuting opens up the labour market to a wider group of workers who might find it difficult to leave the home-groups such as single parents and the disabled. Also, concerns that managers lose control over their employees, and that the quality of work falls, appear unfounded. In fact the reverse seems to have occurred: the quality of work in many cases has improved.

But do such employees feel isolated? For many people, work is an important part of their social environment, providing them with an opportunity to meet others and to work as a team. For those who are unable to leave the home, however, telecommuting may be the *only* means of earning a living: the choice of travelling to work may simply not be open to them.

Ironically, it appears that whereas the industrial revolution destroyed cottage industries and people's ability to work from home, information technology is doing the reverse, and may in the end contribute to the destruction of the office – at least of large central offices.

Small local offices, however, may flourish as the developments in technology (such as video conferencing) mean that people do not have to travel long distances for meetings.

These technological developments have been the equivalent of an increase in labour mobility. Work can be taken to the workers rather than the workers coming to the work. The effect will be to reduce the premium that needs to be paid to workers in commercial centres, such as the City of London.

Questions

1 What effects are such developments likely to have on (a) trade union membership; (b) trade union power?

2 How are the developments referred to in this box likely to affect relative house prices between capital cities and the regions?

market wage W_m, there is no limit to the number of workers available to that employer (but no workers at all will be available below it: they will all be working elsewhere). At the market wage W_m, the employer will employ Q_1 hours of labour.

Figure 17.3(c) shows how an individual worker also has to accept this wage. In this case it is the demand curve for that worker that is infinitely elastic. In other words, there is as much work as the worker cares to do at this wage (but none at all above it).

We now turn to look at the supply and demand for labour in more detail.

The supply of labour

We can look at the supply of labour at three levels. The supply of hours by an individual worker (Figure 17.3(c)), the supply of workers to an individual employer (Figure 17.3(a)) and the total market supply of a given category of labour (Figure 17.3(b)). Let us examine each in turn.

The supply of hours by an individual worker

Work involves two major costs (or 'disutilities') to the worker:

● When people work they sacrifice leisure.
● The work itself may be unpleasant.

Each extra hour worked will involve additional disutility. This **marginal disutility of work** (*MDU*) will tend to *increase* as people work more hours. There are two reasons for this. First, the less the leisure they have left, the greater the disutility they experience in sacrificing a further hour of leisure. Second, the unpleasantness they experience in doing the job will tend to increase due to boredom or tiredness.

This increasing marginal disutility (see Figure 17.4(a)) will tend to give an upward-sloping supply curve of hours by an individual worker (see Figure 17.4(b)). The reason is that, in order to persuade people to work more hours, a higher hourly wage must be paid to compensate for the higher marginal disutility incurred. This helps explain why overtime rates are higher than standard rates.

Under certain circumstances, however, the supply of hours curve might bend backwards (see Figure 17.5). The reason is that, when wage rates go up, there will be two opposing forces operating on the individual's labour supply.

On the one hand, with higher wage rates people will tend to work more hours, since leisure would now involve a greater sacrifice of income and hence consumption. They substitute income for leisure. This is called the **substitution effect** of the increase in wage rates.

On the other hand, people may feel that with higher wage rates they can afford to work less and have more leisure. This is called the **income effect**.

The relative magnitude of these two effects determines the slope of the individual's supply curve. It is normally assumed that the substitution effect outweighs the income effect, especially at lower wage rates. A rise in wage rates acts as an incentive: it encourages a person to work more hours. It is possible, however, that the income effect will outweigh the substitution effect. Particularly at very high wage rates people say, 'There's not so much point now in doing overtime. I can afford to spend more time at home.'

If the wage rate becomes high enough for the income effect to dominate, the supply curve will begin to slope backward. This occurs above a wage rate of W_1 in Figure 17.5.

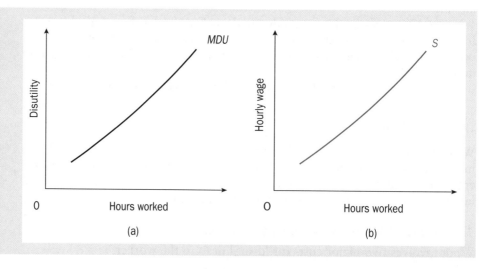

Figure 17.4
(a) The marginal disutility of hours worked
(b) The supply of hours worked

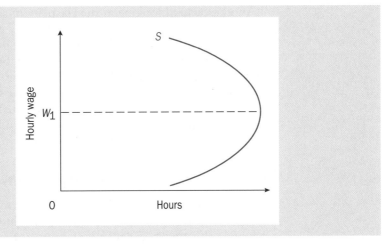

Figure 17.5
Backward-bending supply curve of labour

These considerations are particularly important for a government considering tax cuts. The Conservative governments of the 1980s and 1990s argued that cuts in income taxes are like giving people a pay rise, and thus provide an incentive for people to work harder. This analysis is only correct, however, if the substitution effect dominates. If the income effect dominates, people will work less after the tax cut.

The supply of labour to an individual employer

Under perfect competition, the supply of labour to a particular firm will be perfectly elastic, as in Figure 17.3(a). The firm is a 'wage taker' and thus has no power to influence wages.

The market supply of a given type of labour

This will typically be upward sloping. The higher the wage rate offered in a particular type of job, the more people will want to do that job.

The *position* of the market supply curve of labour will depend on the number of people willing and able to do the job at each given wage rate. This depends on three things:

- The number of qualified people.
- The non-wage benefits or costs of the job, such as the pleasantness or otherwise of the working environment, job satisfaction or dissatisfaction, status, power, the degree of job security, holidays, perks and other fringe benefits.
- The wages and non-wage benefits in alternative jobs.

A change in the wage rate will cause a movement along the supply curve. A change in any of these other three determinants will shift the whole curve.

The elasticity of the market supply of labour

How *responsive* will the supply of labour be to a change in the wage rate? If the market wage rate goes up, will a lot more labour become available or only a little? This responsiveness (elasticity) depends on (a) the difficulties and costs of changing jobs and (b) the time period.

Another way of looking at the elasticity of supply of labour is in terms of the **mobility of labour**: the willingness and ability of labour to move to another job, whether in a different location (geographical mobility) or in a different industry (occupational mobility). The mobility of labour (and hence the elasticity of supply of labour) will be higher when there are alternative jobs in the same location, when alternative jobs require similar skills and when people have good information about these jobs. It is also much higher in the long run, when people have the time to acquire new skills and when the education system has had time to adapt to the changing demands of industry.

The demand for labour: the marginal productivity theory

The traditional 'neoclassical' theory of the firm assumes that firms aim to maximise profits. The same assumption is made in the neoclassical theory of labour demand. This theory is generally known as the **marginal productivity theory**.

The profit-maximising approach

How many workers will a profit-maximising firm want to employ? The firm will answer this question by weighing up the costs of employing extra labour against the benefits. It will use exactly the same principles as in deciding how much output to produce.

In the goods market, the firm will maximise profits where the marginal cost of an extra unit of *goods* produced equals the marginal revenue from selling it: $MC = MR$.

In the labour market, the firm will maximise profits where the marginal cost of employing an extra *worker* equals the marginal revenue that the worker's output earns for the firm: MC of labour $= MR$ of labour. The reasoning is simple. If an extra worker adds more to a firm's revenue than to its costs, the firm's profits will increase. It will be worth employing that worker. But as more workers are employed, diminishing returns to labour will set in (see page 116). Each extra worker will produce less than the previous one, and thus earn less revenue for the firm. Eventually the marginal revenue from extra workers will fall to the level of their marginal cost. At that point the firm will stop employing extra workers. There are no additional profits to be gained. Profits are at a maximum.

Measuring the marginal cost and revenue of labour

Marginal cost of labour (MC$_L$). This is the extra cost of employing one more worker. Under perfect competition the firm is too small to affect the market wage. It faces a horizontal supply curve (see Figure 17.3(a)). In other words, it can employ as many workers as it chooses at the market wage rate. Thus the additional cost of employing one more person will simply be the wage rate: $MC_L = W$.

Marginal revenue of labour (MRP$_L$). The marginal revenue that the firm gains from employing one more worker is called the **marginal revenue product of labour** (*MRP$_L$*). The MRP_L is found by multiplying two elements – the *marginal physical product* of labour (*MPP$_L$*) and the marginal revenue gained by selling one more unit of output (*MR*).

> **definition**
>
> **Mobility of labour**
> The ease with which labour can either shift between jobs (occupational mobility) or move to other parts of the country in search of work (geographical mobility).

> **definition**
>
> **Marginal productivity theory**
> The theory that the demand for a factor depends on its marginal revenue product.

> **definition**
>
> **Marginal revenue product of labour**
> The extra revenue a firm earns from employing one more unit of labour.

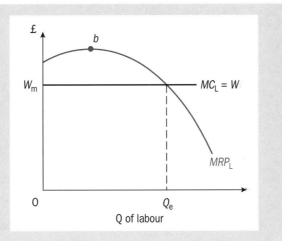

Figure 17.6
The profit-maximising level of employment

$$MRP_L = MPP_L \times MR$$

The MPP_L is the extra output produced by the last worker. Thus if the last worker produces 100 tonnes of output per week (MPP_L), and if the firm earns an extra £2 for each additional tonne sold (MR), then the worker's MRP is £200. This extra worker is adding £200 to the firm's revenue.

The profit-maximising level of employment for a firm

The MPP_L curve was illustrated in Figure 9.2 (see page 170). As more workers are employed, there will come a point when diminishing returns set in (point b). The MPP_L curve thus slopes down after this point. The MRP_L curve will be of a similar shape to the MPP_L curve, since it is merely being multiplied by a constant figure, MR. (Under perfect competition, $MR = P$ and does not vary with output). The MRP_L curve is illustrated in Figure 17.6, along with the MC_L 'curve'.

Profits will be maximised at an employment level of Q_e, where MC_L (i.e. W) = MRP_L. Why? At levels of employment below Q_e, MRP_L exceeds MC_L. The firm will increase profits by employing more labour. At levels of employment above Q_e, MC_L exceeds MRP_L. In this case the firm will increase profits by reducing employment.

Derivation of the firm's demand curve for labour

No matter what the wage rate, the quantity of labour demanded will be found from the intersection of W and MRP_L (see Figure 17.7). At a wage rate of W_1, Q_1 labour is demanded (point a); at W_1, Q_2 is demanded (point b); at W_3, Q_3 is demanded (point c).

Thus the MRP_L curve shows the quantity of labour employed at each wage rate. But this is just what the demand curve for labour shows. Thus the MRP_L curve is the demand curve for labour.

There are three determinants of the demand for labour:

● The wage rate. This determines the position *on* the demand curve. (Strictly speaking, we would refer here to the wage determining the 'quantity demanded' rather than the 'demand'.)

Figure 17.7
Deriving the firm's demand curve for labour

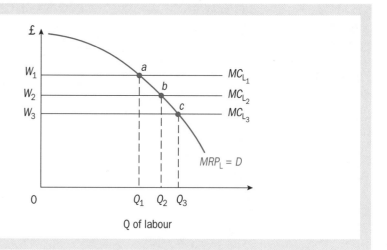

- The productivity of labour (MPP_L). This determines the position *of* the demand curve.
- The demand for the good. The higher the market demand for the good, the higher will be its market price, and hence the higher will be the MR, and thus the MRP_L. This too determines the position of the demand curve. It shows how the demand for labour (and other factors) is a **derived demand**: i.e. one derived from the demand for the good. For example, the higher the demand for houses, and hence the higher their price, the higher will be the demand for bricklayers.

A change in the wage rate is represented by a movement *along* the demand curve for labour. A change in the productivity of labour or in the demand for the good *shifts* the curve.

The elasticity of demand for labour

The elasticity of demand for labour (with respect to changes in the wage rate) will be greater:

- The greater the price elasticity of demand for the good. A fall in W will lead to higher employment and more output. This will drive P down. If the market demand for the good is elastic, this fall in P will lead to a lot more being sold and hence a lot more people being employed.
- The easier it is to substitute labour for other factors of production and vice versa. If labour can be readily substituted for other factors, then a reduction in W will lead to a large increase in labour used to replace these other factors.
- The greater the elasticity of supply of complementary factors. If the wage rate falls, a lot more labour will be demanded if plenty of complementary factors can be obtained at little increase in their price.
- The greater the elasticity of supply of substitute factors. If the wage rate falls and more labour is used, less substitute factors will be demanded and their price will fall. If their supply is elastic, a lot less will be supplied and therefore a lot more labour will be used instead.

definition
Derived demand
The demand for a factor of production depends on the demand for the good which uses it.

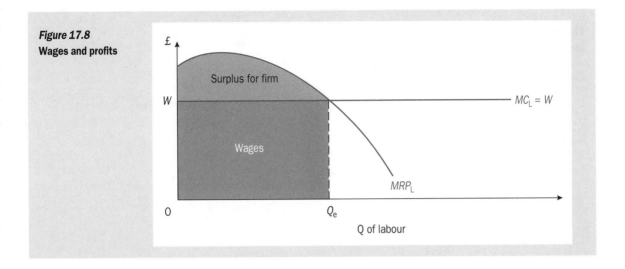

Figure 17.8
Wages and profits

- The greater the wage cost as a proportion of total costs. If wages are a large proportion of total costs and the wage rate falls, total costs will fall significantly; therefore production will increase significantly, and so will the demand for labour.
- The longer the time period. Given sufficient time, firms can respond to a fall in wage rates by reorganising their production processes to make use of the now relatively cheap labour.

Wages and profits under perfect competition

The wage rate (W) will be determined by the interaction of demand and supply in the labour market. This will be equal to the value of the output that the last person produces (MRP_L).

Profits to the individual firm will arise from the fact that the MRP_L curve slopes downward (diminishing returns). Thus the last worker adds less to the revenue of firms than previous workers already employed.

If *all* workers in the firm receive a wage equal to the MRP of the *last* worker, everyone but the last worker will receive a wage less than their MRP. This excess of MRP_L over W of previous workers provides a surplus to the firm (see Figure 17.8). In a simple two-factor model (labour and capital), this surplus will be the same as profits (less fixed capital costs).

Perfect competition between firms will ensure that profits are kept down to *normal* profits. If the surplus over wages is such that *supernormal* profits are made, new firms will enter the industry. The price of the good (and hence MRP_L) will fall, and the wage will be bid up, until only normal profits remain.

17.3 Firms with power in the labour market

In the real world, many firms have the power to influence wage rates: they are not wage takers. This is one of the major types of labour market 'imperfection'.

When a firm is the only employer of a particular type of labour, this situation

Figure 17.9
Monopsony

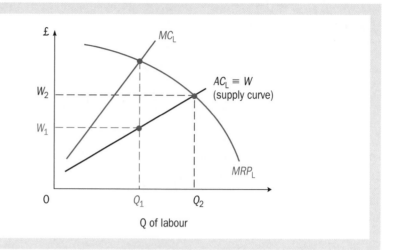

is called a **monopsony**. The Post Office is a monopsony employer of postal workers. Another example is when a factory is the only employer of certain types of labour in that district. It therefore has local monopsony power. When there are just a few employers, this is called **oligopsony**.

Monopsonists (and oligopsonists too) are 'wage setters' not 'wage takers'. Thus a large employer in a small town may have considerable power to resist wage increases or even to force wage rates down.

Such firms face an upward-sloping supply curve of labour. This is illustrated in Figure 17.9. If the firm wants to take on more labour, it will have to pay a higher wage rate to attract workers away from other industries. But conversely, by employing less labour they can get away with paying a lower wage rate.

The supply curve shows the wage that must be paid to attract a given quantity of labour. The wage it pays is the *average cost* to the firm of employing labour (AC_L): i.e. the cost per worker. The supply curve is also therefore the AC_L curve.

The *marginal* cost of employing one more worker (MC_L) will be above the wage (AC_L): see Figure 17.9. The reason is that the wage rate has to be raised to attract extra workers. The MC_L will thus be the new higher wage paid to the new employee *plus* the small rise in the total wages bill for existing employees: after all, they will be paid the higher wage too.

The profit-maximising employment of labour would be at Q_1, where $MC_L = MRP_L$. The wage (found from the AC_L curve) would thus be W_1.

If this had been a perfectly competitive labour market, employment would have been at the higher level Q_2, with the wage rate at the higher level W_2, where $W = MRP_L$. What in effect the monopsonist is doing, therefore, is forcing the wage rate down by restricting the number of workers employed.

definition
Monopsony A market with a single buyer or employer.

definition
Oligopsony A market with just a few buyers or employers.

17.4 The role of trade unions

How can unions influence the determination of wages, and what might be the consequences of their actions?

The extent to which unions will succeed in pushing up wage rates depends on their power and militancy. It also depends on the power of firms to resist and on their ability to pay higher wages. In particular, the scope for unions to gain a better deal for their members depends on the sort of market in which the employers are producing.

Unions facing competitive employers

If the employers are producing under perfect or monopolistic competition, unions can raise wages only at the expense of employment. Firms are only earning normal profit. Thus if unions force up wages, the marginal firms will go bankrupt and leave the industry. Fewer workers will be employed. The fall in output will lead to higher prices. This will enable the remaining firms to pay a higher wage rate.

Figure 17.10 illustrates these effects. If unions force the wage rate up from W_1 to W_2, employment will fall from Q_1 to Q_2. There will be a surplus of people $(Q_3 - Q_2)$ wishing to work in this industry for whom no jobs are available.

The union is in a doubly weak position. Not only will jobs be lost as a result of forcing up the wage rate, but also there is a danger that these unemployed people could undercut the union wage, unless the union can prevent firms employing non-unionised labour.

Wages can be increased without a reduction in the level of employment only if, as part of the bargain, the productivity of labour is increased. This is called a **productivity deal**. The *MRP* curve, and hence the demand curve in Figure 17.10, shifts to the right.

In a competitive market, then, the union is faced with the choice between wages and jobs. Its actions will depend on its objectives.

If it wants to *maximise employment*, it will have to content itself with a wage of W_1 in Figure 17.10, unless productivity deals can be negotiated. At W_1, Q_1 workers will be employed. Above W_1, fewer than Q_1 workers will be *demanded*. Below W_1 fewer than Q_1 workers will be *supplied*.

If the union is more concerned with securing a higher wage rate, it may be prepared to push for a wage rate above W_1 and accept some reduction in

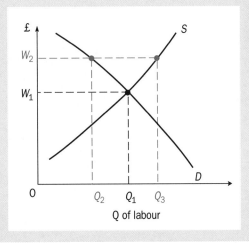

Figure 17.10
Monopoly union facing producers under perfect competition

employment. This is more likely if the reduction can be achieved through 'natural wastage'. This is where people retire, or take voluntary redundancy or simply leave for another job.

Bilateral monopoly

What happens when a union monopoly faces a monopsony employer? What will the wage rate be? What will the level of employment be? Unfortunately, economic theory cannot give a precise answer to these questions. There is no 'equilibrium' level as such. Ultimately, the wage rate and level of employment will depend on the relative bargaining strengths and skills of unions and management.

Unions may in fact be in a stronger position to make substantial gains for their members when they are facing a powerful employer. There is often considerable scope for them to increase wage rates *without* this leading to a reduction in employment, or even for them to increase both the wage rate *and* employment. Figure 17.11 shows how this can be so.

Assume first that there is no union. The monopsonist will maximise profits by employing Q_1 workers at a wage rate of W_1 (Q_1 is where $MRP_L = MC_L$).

What happens when a union is introduced into this situation? Wages will now be set by negotiation between unions and management. Once the wage rate has been agreed, the employer can no longer drive the wage rate down by employing fewer workers. If it tried to pay less than the agreed wage, it could well be faced by a strike, and thus have a zero supply of labour!

Similarly, if the employer decided to take on *more* workers, it would not have to *increase* the wage rate as long as the negotiated wage were above the free-market wage: as long as the wage rate were above that given by the supply curve S_1.

The effect of this is to give a new supply curve that is horizontal up to the point where it meets the original supply curve. For example, let us assume that the union succeeds in negotiating a wage rate of W_2 in Figure 17.11. The supply curve will be horizontal at this level to the left of point x. To the right of this point it will follow the original supply curve S_1, since to acquire more than Q_3 workers the employer would have to raise the wage rate above W_2.

Figure 17.11
Bilateral monopoly

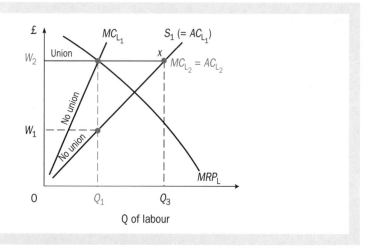

If the supply curve is horizontal to the left of point x at a level of W_2, so too will be the MC_L curve. The reason is simply that the extra cost to the employer of taking on an extra worker (up to Q_3) is merely the negotiated wage rate: no rise has to be given to existing employees. If MC_L is equal to the wage, the profit-maximising employment ($MC_L = MRP_L$) will now be where $W = MRP_L$. At a negotiated wage rate of W_2, the firm will therefore choose to employ Q_1 workers.

What this means is that the union can push the wage right up from W_1 to W_2 and the firm will still *want* to employ Q_1. In other words, a wage rise can be obtained *without* a reduction in employment.

The union could go further still. By threatening industrial action, it may be able to push the wage rate above W_2 and still insist that Q_1 workers are employed (i.e. no redundancies). The firm may be prepared to see profits drop right down to normal level rather than face a strike and risk losses. The absolute upper limit to the wage rate will be that at which the firm is forced to close down.

The actual wage rate under bilateral monopoly is usually determined through a process of negotiation or 'collective bargaining'. The outcome of this bargaining will depend on a wide range of factors, which vary substantially from one industry or firm to another.

Collective bargaining

Sometimes when unions and management negotiate, *both* sides can gain from the resulting agreement. For example, the introduction of new technology may allow higher wages, improved working conditions and higher profits. Usually, however, one side's gain is the other's loss. Higher wages mean lower profits. Either way, both sides will want to gain the maximum for themselves.

The outcome of the negotiations will depend on the relative bargaining strengths of both sides. In bargaining there are various threats or promises that either side can make. For these to be effective, of course, the other side must believe that they will be carried out.

Union *threats* might include strike action, **picketing, working to rule** or refusing to co-operate with management, for example in the introduction of new technology. Alternatively, in return for higher wages or better working conditions, unions might *offer* no strike agreements (or an informal promise not to take industrial action), increased productivity, reductions in the workforce or long-term deals over pay.

In turn, employers might threaten employees with plant closure, **lock-outs**, redundancies or the employment of non-union labour. Or they might offer, in return for lower wage increases, various 'perks' such as productivity bonuses, profit-sharing schemes, better working conditions, more overtime, better holidays or security of employment.

Strikes, lock-outs and other forms of industrial action impose costs on both unions and firms. Unions lose pay. Firms lose revenue. It is usually in both sides' interests, therefore, to settle by negotiation. Nevertheless to gain the maximum advantage, each side must persuade the other that it will carry out its threats if pushed.

The approach described so far has essentially been one of confrontation. The alternative is for both sides to concentrate on increasing the total net income of

> **definition**
>
> **Picketing**
> Where people on strike gather at the entrance to the firm and attempt to dissuade workers or delivery vehicles from entering.

> **definition**
>
> **Working to rule**
> Workers do no more than they are supposed to, as set out in their job descriptions.

> **definition**
>
> **Lock-outs**
> Union members are temporarily laid off until they are prepared to agree to the firm's conditions.

the firm by co-operating on ways to increase efficiency or the quality of the product. This approach is more likely when unions and management have built up an atmosphere of trust over time.

The outcome of negotiations

Given the various 'carrots' and 'sticks' that both sides can wield, what will be the outcome of the bargaining process? This will depend on the following factors.

Power. The greater the power of either side to pursue its objectives, the more likely it is to succeed. A *union's* power depends on factors such as its size, its finances, and support from other unions and from the public in general.

A *firm's* power depends on its financial strength and its ability to substitute machines and non-union labour for the workers in dispute.

Attitudes. It is not just power that is important, but also the determination of either side to win. The more solid the support from members and their families, the more likely the union is to succeed. Similarly, the tougher the management and the more determined it is not to give in, the more likely it is to succeed.

The union's membership. The wage settlement may be higher if the union represents only some of the workers. If it can secure a higher wage rate for its members, who may be **core workers**, non-members may well lose their jobs, or be replaced by part-time or temporary workers. The core workers can be seen as **insiders**. Their union(s) can prevent the unemployed – the **outsiders** – from competing wages down.

Scope for movement by the employer. When firms are operating in a competitive goods market, their scope for giving wage increases is limited. If, however, the firm's rivals are *also* facing similar wage demands, there is more scope for granting them. What is crucial here is the industry-wide demand curve for labour (see Figure 17.10). The less elastic it is (i.e. the fewer the substitutes for labour and for the industry's products), the less will a wage rise be at the expense of employment: the more can the wage rise be simply passed on to the consumer in higher prices.

When the firm has market power in the goods market, its demand curve for the good and hence for labour will be relatively inelastic. It therefore has much more scope to grant wage increases.

Bargaining skills. The more skilful the negotiators are on one side, the more likely they are to gain at the expense of the other.

Information. A lot of bargaining involves bluff and counter-bluff. The bargaining position of each side would be strengthened if it had accurate information about the power, motivation and finances of the other.

The role of government.

The government can influence the outcome of collective bargaining in a number of ways. One is to try to set an example. It may take a tough line in resisting wage demands by public-sector workers, hoping thereby to persuade employers in the private sector to do likewise.

definition

Core workers
Workers, normally with specific skills, who are employed on a permanent or long-term basis.

definition

Insiders
Those in employment who can use their privileged position (either as members of unions or because of specific skills) to secure pay rises despite an excess supply of labour (unemployment).

definition

Outsiders
Those out of work or employed on a casual, part-time or short-term basis, who have little or no power to influence wages or employment.

Alternatively, it could set up arbitration or conciliation machinery. For example, in the UK, the Advisory Conciliation and Arbitration Service (ACAS) conciliates in over 1000 disputes each year. It also provides, on request by both sides, an arbitration service, where its findings will be binding.

Another approach is to use legislation. The government could pass laws that restrict the behaviour of employers or unions. It could pass laws that set a minimum wage rate (see Box 17.2), or prevent discrimination against workers on various grounds. Similarly, it could pass laws that curtail the power of unions. The Conservative governments between 1979 and 1997 put considerable emphasis on reducing the power of trade unions and making labour markets more 'flexible'. Several Acts of Parliament were passed during these years and included the following measures:

- Employees were given the right to join any union, or not to join a union at all. This effectively ended **closed-shop** agreements.
- Secret postal ballots of the union membership were made mandatory for the operation of a political fund, the election of senior union officials, and strikes and other official industrial action.
- Political strikes, sympathy action and action against other non-unionised companies were made illegal.
- Lawful action would be confined to that against workers' own direct employers, even to their own particular place of work. All **secondary action** was made unlawful.
- It was made unlawful for employers to penalise workers for choosing to join or refusing to join a trade union. It was also made unlawful for employers to deny employment on the grounds that an applicant does not belong to a union.

The effect of these measures was considerably to weaken the power of trade unions in the UK.

17.5 The efficiency wage hypothesis

We have seen that a union may be able to force an employer to pay a wage above the market-clearing rate. But wage rates above the equilibrium are not just the result of union power. It may well be in firms' interests to pay higher wage rates, even in non-unionised sectors. The result may be that workers receive a wage rate above that which they would be prepared to accept. Even in times when unemployment is high, and it might be expected wage levels would fall, many firms seem willing to maintain, or even increase, rates of pay (even after taking inflation into account).

One explanation for this phenomenon is the **efficiency wage hypothesis**. This states that the productivity of workers rises as the wage rate rises. As a result, employers are frequently prepared to offer wage rates above the market-clearing level, attempting to balance increased wage costs against gains in productivity. But why may higher wage rates lead to higher productivity? Several explanations have been advanced.

Less 'shirking'. In many jobs it is difficult to monitor the effort that individuals put into their work. Workers may thus get away with shirking or careless

---

definition

Closed shop
Where a firm agrees to employ only members of a recognised union.

definition

Secondary action
Industrial action taken against a firm not directly involved in the dispute.

definition

Efficiency wage hypothesis
A hypothesis that states that a worker's productivity is linked to the wage he or she receives.

behaviour. The business could attempt to reduce shirking by imposing a series of sanctions, the most serious of which would be dismissal, in which case the individual would have to find another job or rely on state benefits. The greater the wage rate currently received, the greater will be the cost to the individual of dismissal, and the less likely it is that workers will shirk. The business will benefit not only from the additional output, but also from a reduction in the costs of having to monitor workers' performance. As a consequence the **efficiency wage rate** for the business will lie above the market-determined wage rate.

Reduced labour turnover. If workers receive on-the-job training or retraining, then to lose a worker once the training has been completed is a significant cost to the business. Labour turnover, and hence its associated costs, can be reduced by paying a wage above the market-clearing rate. By paying such a wage, the business is seeking a degree of loyalty from its employees.

Self-selection. A high wage rate will tend to attract the most productive workers. It therefore acts as a form of selection device, reducing the costs to the business of employing workers of lower quality.

Morale. A simple reason for offering wage rates above the market-clearing level is to motivate the workforce – to create the feeling that the firm is a 'good' employer that cares about its employees. As a consequence, workers might be more industrious and more willing to accept the introduction of new technology (with the reorganisation that it involves).

The paying of efficiency wages above the market-clearing wage will depend upon the type of work involved. Workers who occupy skilled positions, especially where the business has invested time in their training (thus making them costly to replace) are likely to receive efficiency wages considerably above the market wage. By contrast, workers in unskilled positions, where shirking can be easily monitored, little training takes place and workers can be easily replaced, are unlikely to command an 'efficiency wage premium'. In such situations, rather than keeping wage rates high, the business will probably try to pay as little as possible.

17.6 Low pay and discrimination

Low pay

Identifying workers as being low paid clearly involves making certain value judgements about what constitutes 'low'.

We could define low pay in an absolute sense: i.e. pay below a certain figure. This would normally involve relating pay to a worker's standard of living, arguing that living standards below a certain level were unacceptable, or at least are a cause for concern. This is generally the approach adopted by governments when deciding upon the level of social security benefit that a person should receive.

There are two major problems, however, in using this 'absolute' approach. The first is in defining an unacceptable living standard. Different people and

> **definition**
>
> **Efficiency wage rate**
> The profit-maximising wage rate for the firm after taking into account the effects of wage rates on worker motivation, turnover and recruitment.

political parties have different views on what constitutes 'unacceptable'. The second is that pay is only one of the determinants of living standards. Pay of a certain level may give a reasonable living standard for a single person, especially if he or she has property, such as a house and furniture. The same pay may result in dire poverty for a large household with several dependants on that one income, and considerable outgoings.

It is more usual, therefore, to define low pay in relative terms: i.e. the wage rate as a given percentage of average wage rates. The number of workers classified as being low paid will thus depend upon the percentage we select. Predictably, the more generous our percentage, the bigger the low-paid sector will become.

The Council of Europe defines low pay as anything below two-thirds of the mean wage level. It refers to this as the 'decency threshold'. If a minimum hourly wage were to be based on this, then in the UK it would be set at just under £7, and would raise wages for over 9 million workers. Other studies have identified the low-pay threshold at two-thirds of *median* hourly earnings of *male* workers.[1] A minimum hourly wage set at this level would be about £5.95, and would raise wage rates for only 3.4 million workers, 70 per cent of whom would be women.

If the identification of a given wage percentage is seen as a somewhat arbitrary procedure, and open to inevitable debate, an alternative approach to assessing the plight of the low paid is to identify the lowest 10 per cent of income earners and see whether their pay has risen or fallen in comparison to the median wage over a given period of time.

Evidence from various New Earnings Surveys indicates that the top 10 per cent of wage earners have seen their wage rates rise from 167 per cent of the median wage in 1979 to 190 per cent in 1999. By contrast, the bottom 10 per cent have seen their wage rates fall from approximately 70 per cent of the median wage to 56 per cent over the same period.

Low pay is not equally spread throughout all industries within the economy, but concentrated in particular industrial sectors. Catering and textile manufacturing are classic examples. Low pay also occurs disproportionately among certain groups of workers. Studies suggest that about 50 per cent of the low paid are female part-time workers. If we consider the female workforce as a whole, then an estimated 70 per cent of all female workers fall into the low-paid sector.

The growth in low pay

A number of factors can be seen as responsible for the progressive rise in the size of the low-paid sector and the widening disparity between high and low income earners since 1979.

Unemployment due to recession. Very high rates of unemployment in the early 1980s and early 1990s shifted the balance of power from workers to employers. Employers have been able to force many wage rates downwards, especially of unskilled and semi-skilled workers.

---

[1] The mean hourly wage is the arithmetical average: i.e. the total level of gross wage payments divided by the total number of hours worked by the population (over a specified time period). The median hourly wage is found by ranking the working population from lowest to highest paid, and then finding the hourly pay of the middle person in the ranking.

Unemployment due to technological change. Changes in technology have led industry to shift its demand for labour away from unskilled to skilled workers. As might be expected, wage rates for skilled workers have generally risen (except for those with older, now irrelevant skills). By contrast, even though the number of workers with no formal qualifications within the economy fell from 46 per cent to 32 per cent of the labour force from 1979 to the mid-1990s, unemployment among the unskilled worker group still increased from 6.5 per cent at the end of the 1970s to over 16 per cent in the mid-1990s.

Growth in part-time employment. Changes in the structure of the UK economy – in particular, the growth of the service sector and the growing proportion of women seeking work – have led to an increase in part-time work. Many service-sector jobs suit such employment patterns, especially given that demand often varies substantially during the course of the week. In principle, the part-time nature of employment should make little difference to earnings. However, many part-time workers do not receive the same rights, privileges and hourly pay as their full-time equivalents. On the other hand, the work rate of part-time workers is often higher given that, with fewer hours worked, they are often less tired or bored.

Changes in labour laws. The drive to establish a flexible labour market (discussed in section 17.7) encouraged the Conservative governments of the 1980s and 1990s to reform labour market legislation (see page 341). The most significant change with respect to the issue of low pay was the abolition of the Wages Councils in 1993. The Wages Councils were set up in 1945 and at the height of their powers, set minimum wages for about 4.25 million workers, or about 20 per cent of the working population. The year before their abolition, the Councils covered only 2.5 million workers or 10 per cent of the labour force, and many of their powers had been eroded through the passing of the 1986 Wages Act. This Act removed all 18 to 21-year-olds from Wages Council minimum wage protection. The argument used to justify this move was that young people were frequently in positions of training and thus employers might reduce their training commitments if higher wage rates were forced upon them. In addition, the Act reduced the Councils' ability to set minimum wages for different jobs within an industry. Minimum wages had to be set at an industry-wide level. The abolition of the Wages Councils removed one of the few safeguards for workers in the poorest-paid sectors of the economy.

But just what are the costs and benefits of minimum wages? We examine this issue in the next section.

Minimum wages

Before April 1999 there was no statutory minimum wage in the UK. The principle of a minimum or fair wage was based around a voluntary tradition in which, other than in the most poorly paid sectors of the economy, earnings and wages were determined through the process of collective bargaining.

The abolition of the Wages Councils in 1993 had been, according to their critics, a necessary step in creating a flexible labour market, which helped improve the employment prospects of the lowest-paid workers within the economy. To re-establish a national minimum wage rate would simply reverse such benefits and cause unemployment and poverty to rise. The supporters of a national minimum wage, including the Labour government, argued that its introduction would not only help to reduce poverty among the low paid, but would also have little or no adverse effects on unemployment. Some went further. They argued that it would actually *increase* employment.

In order to assess the background to this debate, we need to revisit our earlier analysis of the demand and supply of labour.

Minimum wages in a competitive labour market

In a competitive labour market, workers will be hired up to the point where the marginal revenue product of labour (MRP_L), i.e. the demand for labour, is equal to the marginal cost of labour (MC_L), which gives the supply curve. Referring back to Figure 17.10 on page 337, the free-market equilibrium wage is W_1 and the level of employment is Q_1. A national minimum wage, set at W_2, will reduce the level of employment to Q_2 and increase the supply of labour to Q_3, thereby creating unemployment of the amount $Q_3 - Q_2$.

The level of unemployment created as a result of the national minimum wage will be determined not only by the level of the minimum wage, but also by the elasticity of labour demand and supply. The more elastic the demand and supply of labour, the bigger the unemployment effect will be. Evidence suggests that the demand for low-skilled workers is likely to be relatively wage sensitive. The most likely reason for this is that many of the goods or services produced by low-paid workers are very price sensitive, the firms frequently operating in very competitive markets. It would seem at first sight, therefore, that any increase in wage rates is likely to force up prices and thereby reduce output and employment.

It is important to be careful in using this argument, however. What is relevant is not so much the price elasticity of demand for *individual* firms' products, but rather for the products of the low-paid sector as a whole. If one firm alone raised its prices, it might well lose a considerable number of sales. But with minimum wage legislation applying to *all* firms, if all the firms in an industry or sector put up their prices, demand for any one firm would fall much less. Here the problem of consumers switching away from a firm's products, and hence of that firm being forced to reduce its workforce, would mainly occur (a) if there were cheaper competitor products from abroad, where the new minimum wage legislation would not apply, or (b) if other firms produced the products with more capital-intensive techniques, involving fewer workers to whom the minimum wage legislation applied.

Minimum wages and monopsony employers

In an imperfect labour market where the employer has some influence over rates of pay, the impact of the national minimum wage on levels of employment is even less clear cut.

The situation can be illustrated by referring back to Figure 17.11 on page 338. A monopsonistic employer will employ Q_1 workers: where the MC_L is equal to MRP_L. At this point the firm is maximising its return from the labour it employs. The MC_L curve lies above the supply of labour curve (AC_L), since

BOX 17.2

The UK national minimum wage
The answer to low pay?

Despite the adoption of national minimum wage rates in most of the developed world, the Conservative government in the UK (1979–97), following its philosophy of free-market economics, resisted introducing such a policy. But the number of low-paid workers was increasing. There were many people working as cleaners, kitchen hands, garment workers, security guards and shop assistants, who were receiving pittance rates of pay, sometimes less than £2 per hour.

The incoming Labour government in 1997 was committed to introducing a minimum wage and sought the advice of the Low Pay Commission as to the appropriate rate. The Commission recommended a rate of £3.60 per hour. This, it claimed, would 'offer real benefits to the low paid, while avoiding unnecessary risks to business and jobs'. The government accepted the £3.60 recommendation, subsequently increasing it to £3.70 in October 2000. The government set a lower rate of £3.00 per hour for workers aged between 18 and 21. This was to avoid causing unnecessarily high levels of unemployment among this age group – a group with lower work experience. This rate was raised to £3.20 in June 2000.

The Low Pay Commission estimated that, following the implementation of the national minimum wage,

some 2 million workers would benefit. Of these, 1.5 million would be female, of whom more than half work part time. Some 20 per cent of lone parents would see their wages rise, and 10 per cent of all ethnic minority workers would benefit. The UK's wage bill would rise by approximately 0.5 per cent, although certain sectors, such as retailing, which pays very low wages, would see wage costs rise by far more.

By 2000, just one year after the introduction of the minimum wage, it was clear that there had been virtually no adverse effects on unemployment, and even the Conservative party, previously staunch opponents of a minimum wage, dropped its opposition.

Questions

1 If an increase in wage rates for the low paid led to their being more motivated, how would this affect the marginal revenue product and the demand for such workers? What implications does your answer have for the effect on employment in such cases?

2 If minimum wages encourage employers to substitute machines for workers, will this necessarily lead to higher long-term unemployment in (a) that industry and (b) the economy in general?

Type of worker	Numbers covered (000s)	Proportion of group affected (%)	Increase in group wage bill (%)
All 18+	2050	9	0.6
18–20	235	21	3.9
21+	1815	8	0.6
Male full-time workers	320	3	0.3
Male part-time workers	240	26	3.0
Female full-time workers	340	5	0.7
Female part-time workers	1150	22	2.7

Source: *First Report of the Low Pay Commission*, Department of Trade and Industry (http://www.lowpay.gov.uk/IR/lowpay/summary.htm) (1998), table in Chapter 7.

the additional cost of employing one more unit of labour involves paying all existing employees the new wage. The wage rate paid by the monopsonist will be W_1.

If the minimum wage is set above W_1, but below W_2, the level of employment within the firm is likely to grow! Why should this be so? The reason is that the minimum wage cannot be bid down by the monopsonist cutting back on its workforce. The minimum wage rate is thus both the new AC_L and also the new MC_L: the additional cost of employing one more worker (up to Q_3) is simply the minimum wage rate. The $MC_L = AC_L$ line is thus a horizontal straight line up to the original supply curve ($S_1 = AC_1$). The level of employment that max- imises the monopsonist's profits will be found from the intersection of this new $MC_L = AC_L$ line with the MRP_L curve. With a wage rate between W_1 and W_2 this intersection will be to the right of Q_1: i.e. the imposition of a minimum wage rate will *increase* the level of employment.

Clearly, if the minimum wage rate were very high, then, other things being equal, the level of employment would fall. This would occur in Figure 17.11 if the minimum wage rate were above W_2. But even this argument is not clear cut, given that (a) a higher wage rate may increase labour productivity by improv- ing worker motivation and (b) other firms, with which the firm might compete in the product market, will also be faced with paying the higher minimum wage rate. The resulting rise in prices is likely to shift the MRP_L curve to the right.

On the other hand, to the extent that the imposition of a minimum wage rate reduces a firm's profits, this may lead it to cut down on investment, which may threaten long-term employment prospects.

Evidence on the effect of minimum wages

Which of the views concerning the effects of a national minimum wage are we to believe? The most crucial question appears to be how we might evaluate the monopsonistic status of the firm that employs low-wage labour and how much below their *MRP* low-paid workers are paid.

Unfortunately, there is little evidence to help us assess this point. What evi- dence there is concerning the impact of minimum wage legislation is based upon company employment levels before and after the imposition of a new or increased minimum wage level. Recent findings in the USA have suggested that increases in the minimum wage have had a neutral effect upon employment. It has been found that there exists a 'range of indeterminacy' over which wage rates can fluctuate with little impact upon levels of employment. Even above this 'range', research findings have suggested that, whereas some employers might reduce the quantity of labour they employ, others might respond to their higher wage bill, and hence higher costs, by improving productive efficiency.

Evidence either for or against the employment effects of a national minimum wage appears far from conclusive. The issue may be not so much whether a national minimum wage causes unemployment, as the *level* of minimum wage at which unemployment will begin to rise. Preliminary evidence from the UK suggests that a minimum wage rate set at £3.60 or £3.70 has had no detrimen- tal effect on unemployment. Whether this would be the case if the rate were set at £7.00 (the Council of Europe 'decency threshold' – see page 343) is quite another matter.

Discrimination

Discrimination can take many forms: it can be by race, sex, age, class, dress, etc.; and it can occur in many different aspects of society. What we are con- cerned with here is **economic discrimination**. This is not referring to the fact that different jobs pay different amounts: that skilled workers receive more than

definition
Economic discrimination Where workers of identical *ability* are paid different wages or are otherwise discriminated against because of race, age, sex, etc.

Table 17.1 Average gross hourly earnings, excluding the effects of overtime, for full-time UK employees, aged 18 and over, 1970–99 (pence per hour)

	1970	1974	1978	1980	1984	1986	1988	1990	1992	1994	1996	1998	1999
Men	67	105	200	281	417	482	573	689	810	865	939	1026	1075
Women	42	71	148	206	306	358	429	528	638	688	750	822	870
Differential	25	34	52	74	111	124	144	161	172	177	189	204	205
Women's earnings as a % of men's	63.1	67.4	73.9	73.5	73.5	74.3	75.0	76.6	78.8	79.5	79.9	80.1	80.9

Source: Based on *New Earnings Survey* (ONS) various years.

unskilled workers. It is also not referring to discrimination outside the labour market (e.g. in social or community relationships). Economic discrimination is defined as when otherwise identical workers receive different pay for doing the same job, or are given different chances of employment or promotion. In the following section we will focus upon discrimination on grounds of gender.

Gender and the labour market

One of the key characteristics shown in Table 17.1 is that female gross hourly earnings relative to male gross hourly earnings increased substantially during the early 1970s. Having peaked at around 74 per cent in the late 1970s, they remained at about that level for the next ten years. They then rose again to just above 80 per cent by the late 1990s.

The inequality between male and female earnings can in part be explained by the fact that men and women are occupationally segregated. Seeing that women predominate in poorly paid occupations, the difference in earnings is somewhat to be expected. But if you consider Table 17.2, you can see that quite substantial earning differentials persist *within* particular occupations.

So why has this inequality persisted? There are a number of possible reasons:

- The marginal productivity of labour in typically female occupations may be lower than in typically male occupations. This may in part be due to simple questions of physical strength. More often, however, it is due to the fact that women tend to work in more labour-intensive occupations. If there is less capital equipment per female worker than there is per male worker, then the marginal product of a woman is likely to be less than that of a man.
- Many women take career breaks to have children. For this reason, employers are sometimes more willing to invest money in training men (thereby increasing their marginal productivity), and more willing to promote men.
- Women tend to be less geographically mobile than men. If social norms are such that the man's job is seen as somehow more 'important' than the woman's, then a couple will often move if that is necessary for the man to get promotion. The woman, however, will have to settle for whatever job she can get in the same locality as her partner.
- A smaller proportion of women workers are members of unions than men. Even when they are members of unions, they are often in jobs where unions are weak (e.g. clothing industry workers, shop assistants and secretaries).

Table 17.2	Average gross hourly earnings, excluding the effects of overtime, for selected occupations, full-time UK employees on adult rates, 1999.		
Occupation	Men	Women	Women's earnings as a % of men's
	(£ per hour)		
Social workers	10.97	10.54	96.1
Nurses	10.66	9.99	93.7
Bar staff	4.59	4.28	93.2
Police officers (below sergeant)	13.23	12.13	91.7
Secondary school teachers	16.99	15.23	89.6
Laboratory technicians	9.76	8.64	88.5
Chefs/cooks	6.33	5.41	85.5
Legal professionals	22.05	18.44	83.6
Sales assistants	6.10	5.00	82.0
Medical practitioners	23.99	19.31	80.5
Personnel managers	19.20	15.30	79.7
Computer operators	8.66	6.64	76.7
Assemblers and lineworkers	7.62	5.69	74.7
All occupations	10.75	8.70	80.9
Average *gross weekly* pay	442.40	326.50	73.8
Average weekly hours worked (incl. overtime)	41.4	37.50	
Average weekly overtime (hours)	2.7	0.8	

Source: Adapted from *New Earnings Survey*, April 1999 (ONS).

- Part-time workers (mainly women) have less bargaining power, less influence and less chance of obtaining promotion.
- Custom and practice. Despite equal pay legislation, many jobs done wholly or mainly by women continue to be low paid, irrespective of questions of productivity.
- Prejudice. Some employers may prefer to give senior posts to men on grounds purely of sexual prejudice. This is very difficult to legislate against when the employer can simply claim that the 'better' person was given the job.

Which of the above reasons could be counted as economic discrimination? Certainly the last two would qualify. Discrimination on these grounds would *not* be in the profit interests of the employer. Some of the others, however, are more difficult to classify. They may well reflect some form of discrimination, but the roots can be traced back beyond the workplace: perhaps to the educational system, or to a culture which discourages women from being so aggressive in seeking promotion or in 'self-advertisement', or to the legal right to maternity but not paternity leave. Even if it is a manifestation of profit-maximising behaviour by employers that women in some circumstances are paid less than their male counterparts (and is thus not an example of current economic discrimination), the reason *why* it is more profitable for employers to pay men more than women may indeed reflect discrimination elsewhere or at some other point in time.

17.7 The flexible firm and the market for labour

The past 25 years have seen sweeping changes in the ways that firms organise their workforce. Two world recessions combined with rapid changes in technology have led many firms to question the wisdom of appointing workers on a permanent basis to specific jobs. Instead, they want to have the greatest flexibility possible to respond to new situations. If demand falls, they want to be able to 'shed' labour without facing large redundancy costs. If demand rises, they want rapid access to additional labour supplies. If technology changes, say with the introduction of new computerised processes, they want to have the flexibility to move workers around, or to take on new workers in some areas and lose workers in others.

What many firms seek, therefore, is flexibility in employing and allocating labour. What countries are experiencing is an increasingly flexible labour market, as workers and employment agencies respond to the new 'flexible firm'.

There are three main types of flexibility in the use of labour:

- **Functional flexibility.** This is where an employer is able to transfer labour between different tasks within the production process. It contrasts with traditional forms of organisation where people were employed to do a specific job, and then stuck to it. A functionally flexible labour force will tend to be multiskilled and relatively highly trained.
- **Numerical flexibility.** This is where the firm is able to adjust the size and composition of its workforce according to changing market conditions. To achieve this, the firm is likely to employ a large proportion of its labour on a part-time or casual basis, or even subcontract out specialist requirements, rather than employing such labour skills itself.
- **Financial flexibility.** This is where the firm has flexibility in its wage costs. In large part it is a result of functional and numerical flexibility. Financial flexibility can be achieved by rewarding individual effort and productivity rather than paying a given rate for a particular job. Such rates of pay are increasingly negotiated at the local level rather than being nationally set. The result is not only a widening of pay differentials between skilled and unskilled workers, but also growing differentials in pay between workers within the same industry but in different parts of the country.

Figure 17.12 shows how these three forms of flexibility are reflected in the organisation of a **flexible firm**, an organisation quite different from that of the traditional firm. The most significant difference is that the labour force is segmented. The core group, drawn from the **primary labour market**, will be composed of *functionally* flexible workers, who have relatively secure employment and are generally on full-time permanent contracts. Such workers will be relatively well paid and receive wages reflecting their scarce skills.

The periphery, drawn from the **secondary labour market**, is more fragmented than the core, and can be subdivided into a first and a second peripheral group. The first peripheral group is composed of workers with a lower level of skill than those in the core, skills that tend to be general rather than firm specific. Thus workers in the first peripheral group can usually be drawn from the external labour market. Such workers may be employed on full-time contracts, but they will generally face less secure employment than those workers in the core.

definition

Functional flexibility
Where employers can switch workers from job to job as requirements change.

definition

Numerical flexibility
Where employers can change the size of their workforce as their labour requirements change.

definition

Financial flexibility
Where employers can vary their wage costs by changing the composition of their workforce or the terms on which workers are employed.

definition

Flexible firm
A firm that has the flexibility to respond to changing market conditions by changing the composition of its workforce.

definition

Primary labour market
The market for permanent full-time core workers.

definition

Secondary labour market
The market for peripheral workers, usually employed on a temporary or part-time basis, or a less secure 'permanent' basis.

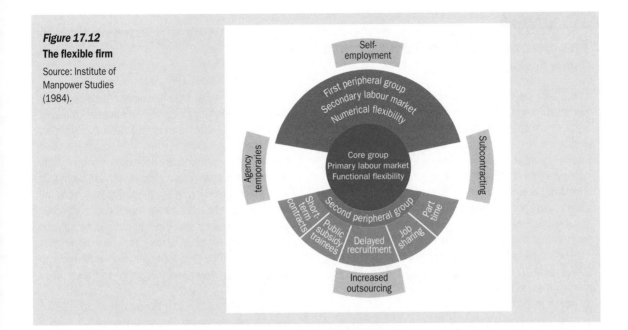

Figure 17.12
The flexible firm
Source: Institute of Manpower Studies (1984).

The business gains a greater level of numerical flexibility by drawing labour from the second peripheral group. Here workers are employed on a variety of short-term, part-time contracts, often through a recruitment agency. Workers in the second peripheral group have little job security.

As well as supplementing the level of labour in the first peripheral group, the second periphery can also provide high-level specialist skills that supplement the core. In this instance the business can subcontract or hire self-employed labour, minimising its commitment to such workers. The business thereby gains both functional and numerical flexibility simultaneously.

The Japanese model

The application of new flexible working patterns is becoming more prevalent in businesses in the UK and elsewhere in Europe and North America. In Japan, flexibility has been part of the business way of life for many years and was crucial in shaping the country's economic success in the 1970s and 1980s. In fact we now talk of a Japanese model of business organisation, which many of its competitors seek to emulate.

The model is based around four principles:

- Total quality management (TQM). This involves all employees working towards continuously improving all aspects of quality, both of the finished product and of methods of production.
- Elimination of waste. According to the 'just-in-time' (JIT) principle, businesses should take delivery of just sufficient quantities of raw materials and parts, at the right time and place. Stocks are kept to a minimum and hence the whole system of production runs with little, if any, slack. For example, supermarkets today have smaller storerooms relative to the total shopping area than they did in the past, and take more frequent deliveries.
- A belief in the superiority of team work. Collective effort is a vital element

BOX 17.3

The Internet and labour mobility
Online flexibility

A firm may be wish to be flexible, but is the *labour market* sufficiently flexible to meet the firm's needs?

It is all well and good a firm looking to expand employment in a prosperous period, but how will it find the individuals it needs, whether they be self-employed, subcontracted or added to the core labour group? This question becomes far more critical, the more highly skilled (and hence scarce) are the workers that the firm requires. Generally, it is the core/skilled workers that flexible firms find most difficulty in recruiting.

The article below, taken from the *Financial Times* of 22 February 2000, considers the impact the Internet is having on the labour market and in particular its impact on labour mobility.

The cinematic cliché of a character searching for a new job is firmly established. The hero pounds the streets, looking in employment agencies' windows; he pores over the classified sections of newspapers, circling likely vacancies in red pen; finally, wearily, he picks up the phone and starts calling.

But modern jobseekers familiar with the Internet can cut out all of this and simply sit in a cafe waiting for a message on their mobile phone. As the labour market increasingly goes on-line, some experts say the speed of information transfer could radically change the traditional process of matching jobseekers – including the unemployed – to work. Paul Rapacioli is head of Reed Online, the Internet branch of the recruitment agency Reed. He says

that although fewer than a quarter of Reed's vacancies are filled through on-line recruitment, the cost savings mean that Internet business is extremely profitable and expanding fast. "People have been talking about labour market flexibility and mobility for years, but until recently the reality has been that a London-based worker prepared to work in Manchester has had to go up there and scout around." Now, he says, the Internet can search the pool of jobs on offer across the country, identify suitable matches and automatically e-mail them to jobseekers, or send text messages to their mobile phones.

Economists say the behaviour of the whole labour market could be revolutionised by such developments. Professor Richard Layard, a leading labour market expert and government adviser at the London School of Economics, says the Internet could help bring a long-awaited improvement in the matching process between the unemployed and available jobs. Although unemployment has fallen over the past 10 years, the number of vacancies – and the average length of time they take to be filled – has risen, indicating the lack of a radical improvement in job-matching efficiency.

Question

Using the article, explain how a flexible firm's flexibility would be enhanced by on-line recruitment.

---

in Japanese working practices. Team work is seen not only to enhance individual performance, but also to involve the individual in the running of the business and thus to create a sense of commitment.

● Functional and numerical flexibility. Both are seen as vital components in maintaining high levels of productivity.

The principles of this model are now widely accepted as being important in creating and maintaining a competitive business in a competitive market place.

SUMMARY

1   Major changes in the UK labour market over recent years include: the movement towards service-sector employment; the rise in part-time working; the growth in female employment levels; a rise in the proportion of temporary, short-term contract and casual employment; and downsizing.

2a Wages in a competitive labour market are determined by the interaction of demand and supply. The individual's supply of labour will be determined by the substitution and income effects from a given increase in the wage rate. At low wage levels, it is likely that individuals will substitute work for leisure. At high wage levels, it is possible that individuals will work less and consume more leisure time, giving a backward-bending supply curve of labour by the individual.

2b The elasticity of labour supply will largely depend upon the geographical and occupational mobility of labour. The more readily labour can transfer between jobs and regions, the more elastic the supply.

2c The demand for labour is traditionally assumed to be based upon labour's productivity. Marginal productivity theory assumes that the employer will demand labour up to the point where the cost of employing one additional worker (MC_L) is equal to the revenue earned from the output of that worker (MRP_L). The firm's demand curve for labour is its MRP_L curve.

2d The elasticity of demand for labour is determined by: the price elasticity of demand for the good that labour produces; the substitutability of labour for other factors; the elasticity of supply of complementary and substitute factors; the proportion of wages to total costs; and time.

3   In an imperfect labour market, where a business has monopoly power in employing labour, it is known as a monopsonist. Such a firm will employ workers to the point where the $MRP_L = MC_L$. Since the wage is below the MC_L, the monopsonist, other things being equal, will employ fewer workers at a lower wage than would be employed in a perfectly competitive labour market.

4a If a union has monopoly power, its power to raise wages will be limited if the employer operates under perfect or monopolistic competition in the goods market. A rise in wage rates will force the employer to cut back on employment, unless there is a corresponding rise in productivity.

4b In a situation of bilateral monopoly (where a monopoly union faces a monopsony employer), the union may have considerable scope to raise wages above the monopsony level, without the employer wishing to reduce the level of employment. There is no unique equilibrium wage. The wage will depend on the outcome of a process of collective bargaining between union and management.

4c Collective bargaining is the process by which employers and unions negotiate wage levels and the terms and conditions of employment. Both sides can use threats and promises to determine the outcome of the negotiating process. The success of such threats and promises depends upon factors such as the power of the union or the business; attitudes and the determination to win; scope for compromise; negotiating skills; information; and the role of government.

5   The efficiency wage hypothesis states that business might hold wages above the market-clearing wage rate so as to: reduce shirking; reduce labour turnover; improve the quality of labour recruited; and stimulate worker morale. The level of efficiency wage will be determined largely by the type of job the worker does, and the level and scarcity of skill they possess.

6a Low pay is difficult to define. There is no accepted definition. The widening disparity in wages between high and low income earners is due to: unemployment resulting from recession; unemployment resulting from a shift in technology; the growth in part-time employment; and changes in labour market legislation.

6b Until April 1999, there was no statutory minimum wage in the UK. The Wages Councils, until their abolition in 1993, set wages for workers in the lowest-paid sectors of the economy. It is argued that in a perfect labour market, where employers are forced to accept the wage as determined by the market place, any attempt to impose a minimum wage above this level will create unemployment. In an imperfect labour market, where an employer has some monopsonistic power, the impact of a minimum wage is uncertain. The impact will depend largely upon how much workers are currently paid

SUMMARY

below their *MRP* and whether a higher wage enourages them to work more productively.

6c Economic discrimination involves paying different rates of pay to otherwise identical workers for doing identical jobs. Differences between male and female earnings between occupations can in part be explained by differences in the types of work that men and women do; they are occupationally segregated. Differences within occupations are less easily accounted for. It would seem that some measure of economic discrimination and other forms of social discrimination are being practised.

7a Changes in technology have had a massive impact upon the process of production and the experience of work. Labour markets and business organisations have become more flexible as a

consequence. There are three major forms of flexibility: functional, numerical and financial. The flexible firm will incorporate these different forms of flexibility into its business operations. It will organise production around a core workforce, to which it will supplement workers and skills drawn from a periphery. Peripheral workers will tend to hold general skills rather than firm-specific skills, and be employed on part-time and temporary contracts.

7b The application of the flexible firm model is closely mirrored in the practices of Japanese business. Commitments to improve quality, reduce waste, build team work and introduce flexible labour markets are seen as key components in the success of Japanese business organisation.

REVIEW QUESTIONS

1 If a firm faces a shortage of workers with very specific skills, it may decide to undertake the necessary training itself. If on the other hand it faces a shortage of unskilled workers it may well offer a small wage increase in order to obtain the extra labour. In the first case it is responding to an increase in demand for labour by attempting to shift the supply curve. In the second case it is merely allowing a movement along the supply curve. Use a demand and supply diagram to illustrate each case. Given that elasticity of supply is different in each case, do you think that these are the best policies for the firm to follow?

2 The wage rate a firm has to pay and the output it can produce varies with the number of workers as follows (all figures are hourly):

Number of workers	1	2	3	4	5	6	7	8
Wage rate (AC_L) (£)	3	4	5	6	7	8	9	10
Total output (TPP_L)	10	22	32	40	46	50	52	52

Assume that output sells at £2 per unit.

(a) Copy the table and add additional rows for TC_L, MC_L, TRP_L and MRP_L. Put the figures for MC_L and MRP_L in the spaces between the columns.

(b) How many workers will the firm employ in order to maximise profits?

(c) What will be its hourly wage bill at this level of employment?

(d) How much hourly revenue will it earn at this level of employment?

(e) Assuming that the firm faces other (fixed) costs of £30 per hour, how much hourly profit will it make?

(f)   Assume that the workers now form a union and that the firm agrees to pay the negotiated wage rate to all employees. What is the maximum to which the hourly wage rate could rise without causing the firm to try to reduce employment below that in (b) above? (See Figure 17.11.)

(g)   What would be the firm's hourly profit now?

3   If, unlike a perfectly competitive employer, a monopsonist has to pay a higher wage to attract more workers, why, other things being equal, will a monopsonist pay a lower wage than a perfectly competitive employer?

4   The following are figures for a monopsonist employer:

Number of workers (1)	Wage rate (£) (2)	Total cost of labour (£) (3)	Marginal cost of labour (£) (4)	Marginal revenue product (£) (5)
1	100	100		230
2	105	210	110	240
3	110	230	120	240
4	115			230
5	120			210
6	125			190
7	130			170
8	135			150
9	140			130
10	145			

Fill in the missing figures for columns (3) and (4). How many workers should the firm employ if it wishes to maximise profits?

5   To what extent could a trade union suceed in gaining a pay increase from an employer with no loss in employment?

6   Do any of the following contradict marginal productivity theory: wage scales related to length of service (incremental scales), nationally negotiated wage rates, discrimination, firms taking the lead from other firms in determining this year's pay increase?

7   What is the efficiency wage hypothesis? Explain what employers might gain from paying wages above the market-clearing level.

8   'Minimum wages will cause unemployment.' Is this so?

9   How might we explain why men earn more than women?

10   Identify the potential costs and benefits of the flexible firm to (a) employers and (b) employees.

18 Investment and the employment of capital

18.1 The pricing of capital and capital services

Capital includes all manufactured products that are used to produce goods and services. Thus capital includes such diverse items as a blast furnace, a bus, a cinema projector, a computer, a factory building and a screwdriver.

Factor prices versus the price of factor services

A feature of most manufactured factors of production is that they last a period of time. A machine may last 10 years; a factory may last 20 years or more. This leads to an important distinction: that between the income that the owner will get from *selling* the factor and that which the owner will get from *using* it or *hiring* it out.

- The income from selling the factor is the factor's *price*. It is a once-and-for-all payment. Thus a factory might sell for £1 million, a machine for £20 000 or a computer disk for £1.
- The income gained from using a factor is its *return*, and the income gained from hiring a factor out is its *rental*. This is income gained not from the sale of the factor, but from its use. This income therefore represents the value or price of the factor's *services*. It is expressed as an income per period of time. Thus a firm might have to pay a rental of £1000 per year for a photocopier.

Obviously the price of capital will be linked to the value of its services: to its return. A highly productive machine will sell for a higher price than one producing a lower output and hence yielding a lower return.

The discussion of the rewards to capital leads to a very important distinction: that between stocks and flows.

A **stock** is a quantity of something held. You may have £1000 in a savings account. A factory may contain 100 machines. These are both stocks: they are quantities held at a given point in time. A **flow** is an increase or decrease in quantity over a specified time period. You may save £10 per month. The factory may invest in another 20 machines next year.

Wages, rental and interest are all rewards to *flows*. Wages are the amount paid not to purchase a person (as a slave!), but for the services of that person's labour for a week. Rental is the amount paid per period of time to use the services of machinery or equipment, not to buy it outright. Likewise interest is the reward paid to people per year for the use of their money.

An important example of stocks and flows arises with capital and investment. If a firm has 100 machines, that is a stock of capital. It may choose to build up its stock by investing. Investment is a flow concept. The firm may choose to invest in 10 new machines each year. This may not add 10 to the stock of machines, however, as some may be wearing out (a negative flow).

The profit-maximising employment of capital

On the demand side, the same rules apply for capital as for labour, if a firm wishes to maximise profits. Namely, it should demand additional capital (K) up to the point where the **marginal cost of capital** equals its **marginal revenue product**: $MC_K = MRP_K$. This same rule applies whether the firm is buying the capital outright, or merely hiring it.

Figure 18.1 illustrates the two cases of perfect competition and monopsony. In both diagrams the MRP curve slopes downwards. This is just another illustration of the law of diminishing returns, but this time applied to capital. If a firm increases the amount of capital while *holding other factors constant*, diminishing returns to capital will occur. Diminishing returns will equally apply whether the firm is buying the extra capital or hiring it.

In diagram (a) the firm is a price taker. The capital price is given at P_{K_1}. Profits are maximised at Q_{K_1} where $MRP_K = P_K$ (since $P_K = MC_K$).

In diagram (b) the firm has monopsony power. The price it pays for capital will vary, therefore, with the amount it uses. The firm will again buy or hire capital to the point where $MRP_K = MC_K$. In this case, it will mean using Q_{K_2} at a price of P_{K_2}.

What is the difference when applying these principles between buying capital and hiring it? Although the $MRP_K = MC_K$ rule remains the same, there are differences. As far as buying capital is concerned, MC_K is the extra outlay for the firm in *purchasing* one more unit of capital – say, a machine – and MRP_K is all the revenue produced by that machine over its *whole life* (but measured in terms

> **definition**
> **Marginal cost of capital**
> The cost of one additional unit of capital.

> **definition**
> **Marginal revenue product**
> The additional revenue earned from employing one additional unit of capital.

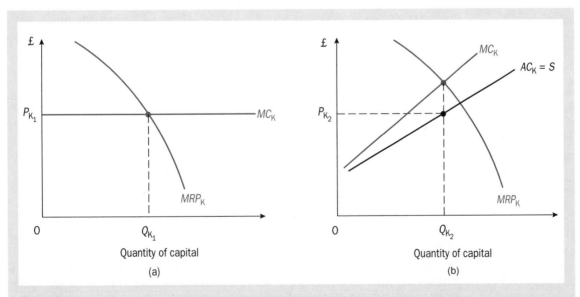

Figure 18.1
(a) Perfectly competitive factor market (b) Firm with monopsony power in factor market

of what this is worth when purchased: see section 18.3). In the case of hiring the machine, MC_K is the extra outlay for the firm in rental *per period of time*, while MRP_K is the extra revenue earned from it *per period of time*.

18.2 The demand for and supply of capital services

In this section we will consider the *hiring* of capital equipment for a given period of time.

Demand for capital services

The analysis is virtually identical to that of the demand for labour. As with labour we can distinguish between an individual firm's demand for capital services (K) and the whole market demand for capital services.

Individual firm's demand

Take the case of a small painting and decorating firm that requires some scaffolding in order to complete a job. It could use ladders, but the job would take longer to complete. It goes along to a company that hires out scaffolding and is quoted a daily rate.

If it hires the scaffolding for one day, it can perhaps shorten the job by two or three days. If it hires it for a second day, it can perhaps save another one or two days. Hiring it for additional days may save extra still. But diminishing returns are occurring: the longer the scaffolding is up, the less intensively it will be used, and the less additional time it will save. Perhaps for some of the time it will be used when ladders could have been used equally easily.

The time saved allows the firm to take on extra work. Thus each extra day the scaffolding is hired gives the firm extra revenue. This is the scaffolding's marginal revenue product of capital (MRP_K). Diminishing returns to the scaffolding means that the MRP_K curve has the normal downward-sloping shape (see Figure 18.1).

Market demand

The market demand for capital services depends on the demand by individual firms. The higher the MRP_K for individual firms, the greater will be the market demand.

Supply of capital services

It is necessary to distinguish (a) the supply *to* a single firm, (b) the supply *by* a single firm and (c) the market supply.

Supply to a single firm

This is illustrated in Figure 18.2(a). The small firm renting capital equipment is probably a price taker. If so, it faces a horizontal supply curve at the going rental rate (R_e). This is the firm's AC_K and MC_K curve. If, however, it has monopsony power, it will face an upward-sloping supply curve as in Figure 18.1(b).

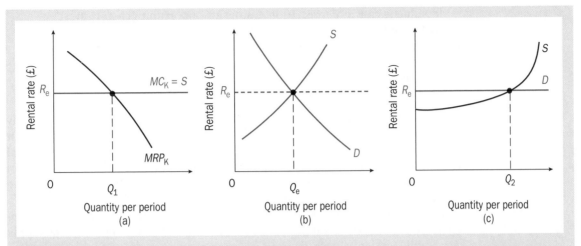

Figure 18.2

Long-run equilibrium rental rate for the services of a particular type of capital (a) Individual user of capital services
(b) Market for capital services (c) Individual supplier of capital services

Supply by a single firm

This is illustrated in Figure 18.2(c). Again, the firm is likely to be a price taker. It has to accept the going rental rate (R_e) established in the market. If it tries to charge more, then customers are likely to turn to rival suppliers. This means that individual suppliers under such conditions will face an infinitely elastic *demand* curve.

But what will the individual supplier's *supply* curve look like? The theory has a lot in common with perfect competition in the goods market: the supply curve is the firm's *MC* curve, only here the *MC* is the extra cost of supplying one more unit of capital equipment for rent over a given time period. But just what will this MC_K be?

The problem with working out the marginal cost of renting out capital equipment is that the piece of equipment probably cost a lot to buy in the first place, but lasts a long time. How are these large costs to be apportioned to each new rental? If scaffolding is hired out for a week, say, what extra costs are incurred? What proportion, if any, of the large costs of buying scaffolding should be included in the calculations? The answer is that it depends on the time period under consideration. Are we talking about the *short run*, where the firm already has its stock of equipment to hire out; or the *long run*, where the firm is considering purchasing additional equipment?

In the short run we do not include the cost of the original purchase or the replacement cost of the equipment when calculating marginal cost. In the case of our scaffolding firm, this is simply the additional expenditures incurred by hiring *existing* scaffolding out. There are no new purchases involved. So what are these additional costs? There are two:

● Depreciation. Scaffolding has second-hand value. The hire company could always sell its equipment second hand. Each time the scaffolding is hired out, however, it deteriorates, and thus its second-hand value falls. This loss in value is called 'depreciation' and is an opportunity cost. It must therefore be included in calculating MC_K.

● Maintenance and handling. When equipment is hired out, it can get damaged and thus incur repair costs. The equipment might need servicing. Also, hiring out equipment involves labour time (e.g. in the office) and possibly transport costs.

The marginal costs of depreciation and maintenance and handling are likely to rise relatively slowly. In other words, for each extra day a piece of equipment is hired out, the company will incur the same or only slightly higher additional costs. This gives a relatively flat supply curve of capital services in Figure 18.2(c) up to the hire company's maximum capacity. Once the scaffolding firm is hiring out all its scaffolding, the supply curve becomes vertical.

In the long run, the hire company will consider purchasing additional equipment. It can therefore supply as much as it likes in the long run. The supply curve will be relatively elastic, or if it is a price taker itself (i.e. if the scaffolding firm simply buys scaffolding at the market price), the supply curve will be horizontal. This long-run supply curve will be vertically higher than the short-run curve, since the long-run MC includes the cost of purchasing each additional piece of equipment.

Market supply

This is illustrated in Figure 18.2(b). The market supply curve of capital services is the sum of the quantities supplied by all the individual firms. It can be either the total supply of a particular type of capital (e.g. scaffolding) or, more narrowly, the supply of a particular type of capital to a certain industry (e.g. the catering industry or the car industry).

In the short run, market supply of a particular type of capital equipment will be relatively inelastic, given that it takes time to manufacture new equipment and that stocks of equipment currently held by manufacturers are likely to be relatively small. Moreover, hire companies may be unwilling to purchase (expensive) new equipment immediately there is a rise in demand: after all, the upsurge in demand may turn out to be short lived.

In the long run, the supply curve will be more elastic because extra capital equipment can be produced. The hire companies will also be more willing to purchase additional equipment if the rental rates continue to be at a higher level.

Determination of the price of capital services

As Figure 18.2(b) shows, in a perfect market the market rental rate for capital services will be determined by the interaction of market demand and supply.

If there is monopsony power on the part of the users of hired capital, this will have the effect of depressing the rental rate below the MRP_K (see Figure 18.1(b)). If, on the other hand, there is monopoly power on the part of hire companies, the analysis is similar to that of monopoly in the goods market (see Figure 11.5 on page 222). The firm, by reducing the supply of capital for hire, can drive up the rental rate. It will maximise profit where the marginal revenue from hiring out the equipment is equal to the marginal cost of so doing: at a rental rate (price) *above* the marginal cost.

18.3 Investment appraisal

The alternative to hiring capital is to buy it outright. This section examines the demand and supply of capital for purchase.

The demand for capital: investment

How many computers will an engineering firm want to buy? Should a steel-works install another blast furnace? Should a removal firm buy another furniture lorry? Should it buy another warehouse? These are all **investment** decisions. Investment is the purchasing of additional capital.

The demand for capital, or 'investment demand', by a profit-maximising firm is based on exactly the same principles as the demand for labour or the demand for capital services. The firm must weigh up the marginal revenue product of that investment (i.e. the money it will earn for the firm) against its marginal cost.

However, the benefits of the investment occur not all at once, but over a number of years. The reason is that capital is durable. It goes on producing goods, and hence yielding revenue for the firm, for a considerable period of time. Calculating these benefits, therefore, involves taking account of their *timing*.

There are two ways of approaching the problem. The first involves calculating the monetary benefits over the life of the investment and comparing them with the monetary costs. This is called the **present value approach**. The second is called the **rate of return approach**. It involves calculating these benefits as a *percentage* of the costs of the investment. This 'rate of return' on the investment is then compared with the rate of interest that the firm would have to pay to borrow the money in order to make the investment.

In both cases the firm is comparing the marginal benefits with the marginal costs of the investment.

Present value approach

To work out the benefit of an investment (its *MRP*), the firm will need to estimate all the future earnings it will bring and then convert them to a *present value*. Let us take a simple example.

Assume that a firm is considering buying a machine. It will produce £1000 per year (net of operating costs) for four years and then wear out and sell for £1000 as scrap. What is the benefit of this machine to the firm? At first sight the answer would seem to be £5000. This, after all, is the total income earned from the machine. Unfortunately, it is not as simple as this. The reason is that money earned in the future is less beneficial to the firm than having the same amount of money today: after all, if the firm has the money today, it can earn interest on it by putting it in the bank or reinvesting it in some other project. (Note that this has nothing to do with inflation. In the case we are considering, we are assuming constant prices.)

To illustrate this, assume that you have £100 today and can earn 10 per cent interest by putting it in a bank. In one year's time that £100 will have grown to £110, in two years' time to £121, in three years' time to £133.10 and so on. This process is known as **compounding**.

From this it follows that, if someone offered to give you £121 in two years' time, that would be no better than giving you £100 today, since, with

definition

Investment
The purchase by the firm of equipment or materials that will add to its stock of capital.

definition

Present value approach to appraising investment
This involves estimating the value *now* of a flow of future benefits (or costs).

definition

Rate of return approach
The benefits from investment are calculated as a percentage of the costs of investment. This rate is then compared to the rate at which money has to be borrowed in order to see whether the investment should be undertaken.

definition

Compounding
The process of adding interest each year to an initial capital sum.

BOX 18.1

Investing in roads
The assessment of costs and benefits

In the UK, the Department of Transport uses the following procedure to evaluate new road schemes, a procedure very similar to that used in many countries.

Estimating demand

The first thing to be done is to estimate likely future traffic flows. These are based on the government's National Road Traffic Forecast. This makes two predictions: a 'low-growth case', based on the assumption of low economic growth and high fuel prices, and a 'high-growth case', based on the assumption of high economic growth and low fuel prices. The actual growth in traffic, therefore, is likely to lie between the two.

Identifying possible schemes

Various road construction and improvement schemes are constantly under examination by the government, especially in parts of the network where traffic growth is predicted to be high and where congestion is likely to occur. In each case forecasts are then made of the likely use of the new roads and the diversion of traffic away from existing parts of the network. Again, two forecasts are made in each case: a 'low-growth' and a 'high-growth' one.

The use of cost–benefit analysis

The costs and benefits of each scheme are assigned monetary values and are compared with those of merely maintaining the existing network. The government uses a computer program known as COBA to assist it in the calculations.

Estimating the benefits of a scheme (relative to the existing network)

Three types of benefit are included in the analysis:

- Time saved. This is broken down into two categories: working time and non-working time (including travelling to and from work).
  The evaluation of working time is based on average national wage rates, while that of non-working time is based on surveys and the examination of traveller behaviour (the aim being to assess the value placed by the traveller on time saved). This results in non-working time per minute being given a value of approximately a quarter of that given to working time.

- Reductions in vehicle operating costs. These include: fuel, oil, tyres, maintenance and depreciation from usage. There will be savings if the scheme reduces the distance of journeys or allows a more economical speed to be maintained.

- Reductions in accidents. There are two types of benefit here: (a) the reduction in casualties (divided

---

interest, £100 would grow to £121 in two years. What we say, then, is that with a 10 per cent interest rate, £121 in two years' time has a *present value* of £100.

The procedure of reducing future values back to a present value is known as **discounting**. When we do discounting, the rate which we use is not called the rate of *interest* but rather the **rate of discount**: in this case 10 per cent. The formula for discounting is given by:

$$PV = \Sigma \frac{X_t}{(1+r)^t}$$

where PV is the present value
X_t is the earnings from the investment in year t.
r is the rate of discount (expressed as a fraction: i.e. 10 per cent = 0.1).
Σ is the sum of each of the years' discounted earnings.

So what is the present value of the investment in the machine that produced

definition

Discounting
The process of reducing the value of future flows to give them a present valuation.

definition

Rate of discount
The rate that is used to reduce future values to present values.

into three categories – fatal, serious non-fatal,_and slight); and (b) the reduction in monetary_costs, such as vehicle repair or replacement, medical costs and police, fire service and ambulance costs.

The reductions in monetary costs are relatively easy to estimate. The benefits from the reduction in casualties are more difficult. The current method of evaluating them is based on the amount people are prepared to pay to reduce the risks of accidents. This clearly has the drawback that people are often unaware of the risks of accidents or of the extent of the resulting pain and suffering.

In 1999, the following figures were used to value each accident prevented: fatal, £1050070: serious non-fatal, £125992; slight, £12372. The human cost element for each type was valued at £685372, £97107 and £7803 respectively.

Estimating the costs of the scheme (relative to the existing network)

There are two main categories of cost: construction costs and additional road maintenance costs. If the new scheme results in a saving in road maintenance compared with merely retaining the existing network, then the maintenance costs will be negative.

The analysis

The costs and benefits of the scheme are assessed for the period of construction and for a standard life (in the UK this is 30 years). The costs and benefits are discounted back to a present value. The rate of discount used in the UK is 8 per cent. If the discounted benefits exceed the discounted costs, there is a positive net present value, and the scheme is regarded as justified on economic grounds. If there is more than one scheme, then their net present values will be compared so as to identify the preferable scheme.

It is only at this final stage that environmental considerations are taken into account. In other words, they are not included in the calculation of costs and benefits, but may have some influence in determining the choice between schemes. Clearly, if a socially efficient allocation of road space is to be determined, such externalities need to be included in the cost and benefit calculations.

Question

Are there any other drawbacks of using a willingness to pay principle to evaluate human costs?

£1000 for four years and then is sold as scrap for £1000 at the end of the four years? According to the formula it is:

$$= \frac{\overset{\text{Year 1}}{£1000}}{1.1} + \frac{\overset{\text{Year 2}}{£1000}}{(1.1)^2} + \frac{\overset{\text{Year 3}}{£1000}}{(1.1)^3} + \frac{\overset{\text{Year 4}}{£2000}}{(1.1)^4}$$

$$= £909 + £826 + £51 + £1366$$

$$= £3852$$

Thus the present value of the investment (i.e. its *MRP*) is £3852, *not* £5000 as it might seem at first sight. In other words, if the firm had £3852 today and deposited it in a bank at a 10 per cent interest rate, the firm would earn exactly the same as it would by investing in the machine.

So is the investment worthwhile? It is now simply a question of comparing the £3852 benefit with the cost of buying the machine. If the machine costs less than £3852, it will be worth buying. If it costs more, the firm would be better off by keeping its money in the bank and earning the 10 per cent rate of interest.

The difference between the present value of the benefits (PV_b) of the investment and its cost (C) is known as the **net present value** (NPV).

$$NPV = PV_b - C$$

If the NPV is positive, the investment is worthwhile.

Rate of return approach

The alternative approach when estimating whether an investment is worthwhile is to calculate the investment's *rate of return*. This rate of return is known as the firm's **marginal efficiency of capital** (MEC) or **internal rate of return** (IRR).

The way this is calculated is to use the formula that we used for calculating present value:

$$PV = \Sigma \frac{X_t}{(1+r)^t}$$

and then to calculate what value of r would make the PV equal to the cost of investment: in other words, to calculate the rate of discount that would make the investment just break even. Say this worked out at 20 per cent. What we would be saying is that the investment will just cover its costs if the current rate of interest (rate of discount) is 20 per cent. In other words, this investment is equivalent to receiving 20 per cent interest: it has a 20 per cent rate of return.

So should the investment go ahead? Yes, if the actual rate of interest (i) is less than 20 per cent. The firm is better off investing its money in this project than keeping its money in the bank. If $IRR > i$, the investment should go ahead.

This is just one more application of the general rule that if $MRP_K > MC_K$ then more capital should be used: only in this case MRP_K is expressed as a rate of return (IRR), and the MC_K is expressed as a rate of interest (i).

The risks of investment

One of the problems with investment is that the future is uncertain. The return on an investment will depend on the value of the goods it produces. But this will depend on the goods market. For example, the return on investment in the car industry will depend on the demand and price of cars. But future markets cannot be predicted with accuracy: they depend on consumer tastes, the actions of rivals and the whole state of the economy. Investment is thus risky.

How is this risk accounted for when calculating the benefits of an investment? The answer is to use a higher rate of discount. The higher the risk, the bigger the premium that must be added to the rate.

> **definition**
> **Net present value of an investment**
> The discounted benefits of an investment minus the cost of the investment.

> **definition**
> **Marginal efficiency of capital** or **internal rate of return**
> The rate of return of an investment: the discount rate that makes the net present value of an investment equal to zero.

The supply of capital

When considering the supply of capital, it is important to distinguish between the supply of *physical* capital and the supply of *finance* to be used by firms for the purchase of capital.

Supply of physical capital. The principles here are just the same as those in the goods market. It does not matter whether a firm is supplying lorries (capital) or cars (a consumer good): it will still produce up to the point where $MC = MR$ if it wishes to maximise profits.

Supply of finance. When firms borrow to invest, this creates a demand for finance (or 'loanable funds'). The supply of loanable funds comes from the deposits that individuals and firms make in financial institutions. These deposits are savings, and represent the resources released when people refrain from consumption. In other words, the less people consume, the more loanable funds there will be available to finance investment.

Among other things, savings depend on the rate of interest that depositors receive. The higher the rate of interest, the more people will be encouraged to save. This is illustrated by an upward-sloping supply curve of loanable funds, as shown in Figure 18.3.

Savings also depend on the level of people's incomes, their expectations of future price changes, and their general level of 'thriftiness' (their willingness to forgo present consumption in order to be able to have more in the future). A change in any of these other determinants will shift the supply curve.

Determination of the rate of interest

What determines the rate of interest: the rate that is used for working out the present value of investment? The answer lies in the demand and supply of loanable funds (see Figure 18.3).

The supply curve is the total supply of savings, which in the long run can be used to build up the capital stock.

The demand curve includes the demand by households for credit and the demand by firms for funds to finance their investment. This demand curve slopes downward for two reasons. First, households will borrow more at lower rates of interest. It effectively makes goods cheaper for them to buy. Second, it reflects the falling rate of return on investment as investment increases. This is simply due to diminishing returns to investment. As rates of interest fall, it will

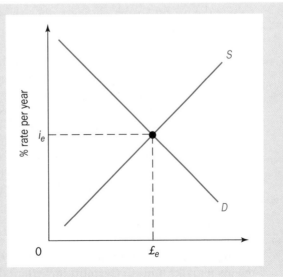

Figure 18.3
The market for
loanable funds

now become profitable for firms to invest in projects that have a lower rate of return: the quantity of loanable funds demanded thus rises.

Equilibrium will be achieved where demand equals supply at an interest rate of i_e and a quantity of loanable funds $£_e$.

How will this market adjust to a change in demand or supply? Assume that there is a rise in demand for capital equipment, due, say, to an improvement in technology which increases the productivity of capital. There is thus an increase in demand for loanable funds. The demand curve shifts to the right in Figure 18.3. The equilibrium rate of interest will rise and this will encourage more savings. The end result is that more money will be spent on capital equipment.

Calculating the costs of capital

When calculating the net present value or internal rate of return of an investment, it is clearly important for the firm to estimate the cost of the investment. The cost does not just include the cost of the equipment that the firm buys: it also includes the costs of raising the finance to pay for the investment.

A firm can finance investment from three major sources:

- Retaining profits.
- Borrowing from the banking sector – either domestic or overseas.
- Issuing new shares (equities) or debentures (fixed-interest loan stock).

It is quite common for a firm to raise finance for a particular project from a mixture of all three sources. The problem is that each source of finance will have a different cost. What is needed, then, for each project is a weighted average of the interest rate (or equivalent) charged or implied by each component of finance.

For investment financed by retained profits, the opportunity cost depends on what would have been done with the profits as the next best alternative. It might be the interest forgone by not putting the money into a bank or other financial institution, or by not purchasing assets. If the next best alternative was to distribute the profits to shareholders, then the opportunity cost would be the cost associated with the increased risks of the firm's share price falling, and the consequent risks of a takeover by another company. (Share prices would fall if shareholders, disillusioned with the reduced dividends, sold their shares.)

For a bank loan, or for debentures, the cost is simply the rate of interest paid on the loan. The only estimation problem here is that of forecasting future rates of interest on loans where the rate of interest is variable.

For equity finance, the cost is the rate of return that must be paid to shareholders to persuade them not to sell their shares. This will depend on the rate of return on shares elsewhere. The greater the return on shares generally, the higher must be the dividends paid by any given firm in order to persuade its shareholders not to switch into other companies' shares.

Leverage and the cost of capital

The cost of capital will increase as the risks for those supplying finance to the company increase: they will need a higher rate of return to warrant incurring the higher risks. One of the most important determinants of the risk to suppliers of finance is the company's leverage. **Leverage** is a measure of the extent to which the company relies on debt finance (i.e. loans) as opposed to equity finance.

There are two common measures of leverage. The first is the **gearing ratio**. This is the ratio of debt finance (debentures and borrowing from banks) to total finance. The other is the **debt/equity ratio**. This is the ratio of debt finance to equity finance.

The higher the company's leverage, the higher will be the risks to creditors and hence the higher will be the interest charged (see Figure 18.4). But why should this be so? The reason is that interest on loans (bank loans and debentures) has to be paid, irrespective of the company's profits. If there is a downturn in the company's profits, then, if it has 'low gearing' (i.e. has low gearing and debt/equity ratios), it can simply cut its dividends and as a result will find it relatively easy to make its interest payments. If, however, it is 'highly geared' (i.e. has high gearing and debt/equity ratios), it may find it impossible to pay all the interest due, even by cutting dividends, in which case it will be forced into receivership.

Given that a highly geared company poses greater risks to creditors, they will demand a higher interest rate to compensate. Similarly with shareholders: given that dividends are likely to fluctuate more with a highly geared company, shareholders will require a higher average dividend over the years. In other words, investors in a highly geared company – whether banks, debenture holders or shareholders – will demand a higher **risk premium**. As gearing increases, so the risk premium, and hence the average cost of capital, will rise at an accelerating rate (see Figure 18.4).

definition
Leverage The extent to which a company relies upon debt finance as opposed to equity finance.

definition
Gearing ratio The ratio of debt finance to total finance.

definition
Debt/equity ratio The ratio of debt finance to equity finance.

definition
Risk premium As a business's gearing rises, investors require a higher average dividend from their investment.

18.4 Financing investment

It is often claimed that the UK has 'fair weather' bankers: that is, bankers who are prepared to lend when things are going well, but less inclined to lend when times are hard. They are accused of taking a short-term perspective in their

**Figure 18.4
The debt/equity
ratio**

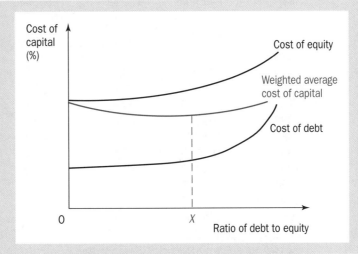

lending practices and of being over-eager to charge high rates of interest on loans, thereby discouraging investment. But the problem for business does not end there. Dealers on the stock market are also accused of focusing their speculative behaviour on short-run returns, thereby generating volatility in share prices and creating business caution, as firms seek ways of maintaining shareholder confidence in their stock (usually through paying high dividends).

In this section we will consider the sources from which business might draw finance, and the roles played by the various UK financial institutions. We will assess the extent to which 'short-termism' is an endemic problem in the capital market.

Sources of business finance

As mentioned in section 18.3 above, the firm can finance growth by borrowing, by retaining profits or by a new issue of shares. The proportions of company investment financed from these sources are shown in Table 18.1 (which reproduces Table 14.1).

Internal sources

As can be seen (and as we noted in Chapter 14), the largest source of finance for investment in the UK is firms' own internal funds (i.e. ploughed-back profit). Given that business profitability depends in large part on the general state of the economy, internal funds as a source of business finance are likely to show considerable cyclical variation. When profits were squeezed in the recessions of the early 1980s and early 1990s, internal finance of investment declined.

It is important to be careful, however, in assessing the figures. Part of the reason, if not the major reason, for a decline in investment in a recession is the lack of *demand* for investment by firms: after all, what is the point in investing if your market is declining? Only part of the reason, therefore, is the lack of supply of internal funds resulting from a decline in profits.

Table 18.1 **Sources of capital funds of UK industrial and commercial companies**

Year	Total from all sources (£ million)	Internal funds[a] (%)	Borrowing from banks, etc. (%)	Shares and debentures (%)	Overseas sources (%)
1970	6336	60.7	22.4	3.2	13.7
1980	28 913	66.1	22.3	4.9	6.7
1986	48 715	58.5	21.6	12.5	7.4
1987	79 475	49.6	21.1	25.3	4.0
1988	99 874	40.8	39.6	11.5	8.1
1989	108 025	32.7	41.7	14.9	10.7
1990	88 058	37.5	33.2	16.2	13.1
1992	53 452	68.3	−5.3	26.8	10.2
1994	82 469	72.9	−2.3	26.9	2.5
1996	114 501	53.0	20.0	19.0	8.0
1997	135 050	41.7	8.7	30.2	19.4

[a] Includes grants and tax relief.

Source: Based on *Financial Statistics* (ONS) various issues.

External sources

Other sources of finance, which include borrowing and the issue of shares and debentures, are known as 'external funds'. These are then categorised as short-term, medium-term or long-term sources of finance.

- Short-term finance is usually in the form of a short-term bank loan or overdraft facility, and is used by firms as a form of working capital to aid them in their day-to-day business operations. Another way of borrowing for a short period of time is for a firm to issue *commercial bills of exchange* (see below, page 373).

- Medium-term finance, again provided largely by banks, is usually in the form of a loan with set repayment targets. It is common for such loans to be made at a fixed rate of interest, with repayments being designed to fit in with the business's expected cash flow. As Table 18.1 shows, bank lending has been the most volatile source of business finance, and has been particularly sensitive to the state of the economy. In the early 1990s, for example, repayments of loans exceeded new loans (hence the negative figures for borrowing in 1992 and 1994 in Table 18.1). While part of the reason is the lower demand for loans during a recession, part of the reason is the caution of banks in granting loans if prospects for the economy are poor.

- Long-term finance, especially in the UK, tends to be acquired through the stock and bond markets. The proportion of business financing from this source clearly depends on the state of the stock market. In the mid-1980s, with a buoyant stock market, the proportion of funds obtained through share issue increased (see Table 18.1). Then with the stock market crash of October 1987, this proportion plummeted, only to rise again as share prices recovered.

  Despite the traditional reliance on the stock market for external long-term sources of finance, there has been a growing involvement of banks in recent years. Banks have become more willing to provide finance for business start-ups and for diversification. Nevertheless, there is still the concern that the relatively cautious attitudes of bankers result in a problem of short-termism, with bankers often demanding a quick return on their money or charging high interest rates.

Another source of external finance is that from outside the country. Part of this is direct investment by externally based companies in the domestic economy. Part is finance from foreign financial institutions. In either case, a major determinant of the amount of finance from this source is the current state of the economy and predictions of its future state. One of the major considerations here is anticipated changes in the exchange rate (see Chapter 26). If the exchange rate is expected to rise, this will increase the value of any given profit in terms of foreign currency. As would be expected, and as can be seen from Table 18.1, this source of finance is particularly volatile.

Comparison of the UK with other European countries

In other European countries, notably Germany and France, the attitude towards business funding is quite different from that in the UK. In these countries, banks provide a significant amount of *long-term*, fixed-rate finance. While this tends to increase companies' gearing ratios and thus increases the risk of bankruptcy,

BOX 18.2

Financing innovation

A flourishing domestic economy is, in no small part, the result of firms successfully innovating and responding to the changing conditions and technologies within the market place. Through such adaptation and innovation the economy prospers, stimulating growth, income and employment. Conversely, an economy that fails to innovate and respond to change is likely to be set upon the rocky road to stagnation and decline.

Given the stark contrast in these alternative realities, not only is the development of new ideas and their diffusion throughout the economy crucial to its vitality, but it is essential that the financial system supports such innovation, and does so in the most efficient way. It must ensure not only that finance is available, but that it goes to those projects with the greatest potential.

Unfortunately, the projects with the greatest potential may involve considerable risk and uncertainty. Because of this, the private sector may be unwilling to fund their development. It may also be unwilling to finance various forms of research, where the outcomes are uncertain: something that is inevitable in much basic research.

As a result of this reluctance by the private sector, innovation funding has traditionally operated at three levels:

- Level one: government financing of 'upstream' or basic research, where outcomes are likely to yield few if any financial returns.
- Level two: self-financed business R&D (i.e. financed out of ploughed-back profit), where the profitability of such R&D activity is difficult to assess, especially by those outside of the business, and thus where banks and other financial institutions would be reluctant to provide finance.
- Level three: external financing using accepted financial assessment criteria for risk and uncertainty.

In this traditional model, the state's role in financing innovation and investment does not end at the level of basic research. It will also compensate for market failures at later stages of the innovation-financing process. For example, it may adopt measures to improve the self-

financing capacity of firms (e.g. tax relief), or measures to facilitate easier access to external finance (e.g. interest rate subsidies), or measures to extend and protect the ownership of intellectual property rights (e.g. tightening up and/or extending patent or copyright legislation).

There is much to suggest, however, that this traditional model is changing, and, along with it, the perceived role of the state in the process of conducting, funding and supporting the innovation process. The most significant of these changes can be found in the liberalisation of global finance.

Three of the major effects of financial liberalisation on innovation financing are as follows:

- Channels of finance have diversified, widening the range of potential investment sources.
- Financial innovations have increased the ability of potential innovators to locate and negotiate favourable financial deals.
- Government regulations over capital market activities have diminished.

The implications of these changes have been to increase the efficiency and flexibility of the financial system. This has resulted in a reduction in international differences in the costs of capital for any businesses having access to global financing. Projects with high earning potential, but high risk, have been able to raise finance from a wider range of sources, national and international.

Although such financial globalisation has not removed the need for state support, it appears that financial changes are certainly diminishing its significance as a supporter of innovation finance.

Questions

1 What market failures could account for a less than optimal amount of innovation in the absence of government support?

2 If financial markets were perfectly competitive and could price risk accurately, would there be any case at all for government support of innovation?

it does provide a much more stable source of finance and creates an environment where banks are much more committed to the long-run health of companies. For this reason the net effect may be to *reduce* the risks associated with financing investment.

The role of the financial sector

Before we look at the financial institutions operating within the UK, and assess their differing financial roles, it should be noted that they all have the common function of providing a link between those who wish to lend and those who wish to borrow. In other words, they act as the mechanism whereby the supply of funds is matched to the demand for funds.

As **financial intermediaries**, these institutions provide four important services.

Expert advice

Financial intermediaries can advise their customers on financial matters: on the best way of investing their funds and on alternative ways of obtaining finance. This should help to encourage the flow of savings and the efficient use of them.

As far as businesses are concerned, banks often play a central role in advising on investment and on possible mergers and acquisitions. With the opening up of the financial sector after the deregulation of 1986 (the 'Big Bang'), and especially with the influx of American and Japanese banks, there is now much more active competition between banks in terms of the advisory services that they offer to businesses.

Expertise in channelling funds

Financial intermediaries have the specialist knowledge to be able to channel funds to those areas that yield the highest return. This too encourages the flow of saving as it gives savers the confidence that their savings will earn a good rate of interest. Financial intermediaries help to ensure that investment projects that are potentially profitable, at least in the short run, are able to obtain finance. They thereby help to increase allocative efficiency.

Maturity transformation

Many people and firms want to borrow money for long periods of time, and yet many depositors want to be able to withdraw their deposits on demand or at short notice. If people had to rely on borrowing directly from other people, there would be a problem: the lenders would not be prepared to lend for a long enough period. If you had £100 000 of savings, would you be prepared to lend it to a friend to buy a house if the friend was going to take 25 years to pay it back? Even if there was no risk whatsoever of your friend defaulting, most people would be totally unwilling to tie up their savings for so long. This is where a bank or building society comes in. It borrows money from a vast number of small savers, who are able to withdraw their money on demand or at short notice. It then lends the money to house purchasers for a long period of time by granting mortgages (typically these are paid back over 20 to 30 years).

This process whereby financial intermediaries lend for longer periods of time than they borrow is known as **maturity transformation**. They are able to do this because with a large number of depositors it is highly unlikely that they would all want to withdraw their deposits at the same time. On any one day, although some people will be withdrawing money, others will be making new deposits.

There is still the problem, however, that long-term loans by banks, especially to industry, often carry greater risks. With banking tradition, especially in the UK, being to err on the side of caution, this can limit the extent to which matu-

> **definition**
>
> **Financial intermediaries**
> The general name for financial institutions (banks, building societies, etc.) which act as a means of channelling funds from depositors to borrowers.

> **definition**
>
> **Maturity transformation**
> The transformation of deposits into loans of a longer maturity.

rity transformation takes place, and can result in a less than optimum amount of investment finance, when viewed from a long-term perspective.

Risk transformation

You may be unwilling to lend money directly to another person in case they do not pay up. You are unwilling to take the risk. Financial intermediaries, however, by lending to large numbers of people, are willing to risk the odd case of default. They can absorb the loss because of the interest they earn on all the other loans. This spreading of risk is known as **risk transformation**. What is more, financial intermediaries may have the expertise to be able to assess just how risky a loan is. Again, however, banks in the UK have been accused of being too cautious, and too unwilling to lend to industry for long-term investment, given the risks associated with such loans.

In addition to channelling funds from depositors to borrowers, certain financial institutions have another important function. This is to provide a means of transmitting payments. Thus by the use of debit cards, credit cards, cheques, standing orders, etc., money can be transferred from one person or institution to another without having to rely on cash.

Financial institutions in the UK

The different types of financial intermediary can be grouped according to the types of deposit taking and lending in which they specialise.

Retail banks

These include the familiar high street banks such as Barclays and the National Westminster. They specialise in providing branch banking facilities to members of the general public, but, as we have seen, they also lend to business, albeit often on a short-term basis. They operate current (cheque-book) accounts, on most of which overdraft facilities can be arranged, and deposit accounts, which, by offering a higher interest rate but no cheque book, are designed to encourage savers. They also provide personal loan facilities and financial advice to their customers. Unlike most other financial institutions, they are involved in operating the *payments* system – the transmission of money through cheques, standing orders, direct debits, etc.

Since the deregulation of the mid-1980s, retail banks have diversified their business, and each one now provides a range of financial services, often through one or more of its subsidiaries. These services include insurance, share dealing, pensions, mortgages and estate agency.

Retail banks are now increasingly moving into the wholesale banking market (see below).

The retail banking sector has been joined in recent years by many former building societies, the first of which was the Abbey National in 1989. Building societies are institutions which specialise in granting loans (mortgages) for house purchase, and which compete for the savings of the general public through a network of high street branches. Building societies have 'mutual' status. This means that people who save with them (their 'members') are, in effect, their owners. Given that there are no shareholders claiming a dividend,

definition

Risk transformation
The process whereby banks can spread the risks of lending by having a large number of borrowers.

the interest paid to savers can, in principle, be higher. By changing their status to a bank, however, and thereby becoming public limited companies with shareholders, the institutions gain increased freedom to diversify their activities. Most of the major building societies have now become banks (including the Halifax, the Woolwich and the Alliance and Leicester).

Investment banks

Investment banks, often known as wholesale banks, specialise in receiving large deposits from and making large loans to industry and other financial institutions: these are known as **wholesale deposits and loans**. These may be for short periods of time to account for the non-matching of the firm's payments and receipts from its business. They may be for longer periods of time, for various investment purposes. These wholesale deposits and loans are very large sums of money. Banks thus compete against each other for them and negotiate individual terms with the firm to suit the firm's particular requirements. The rates of interest negotiated will reflect the current market rates of interest and the terms of the particular loan/deposit. Very large loans to firms are often divided ('syndicated') between several banks.

Merchant banks. One category of investment bank is the merchant banks. Examples include Kleinwort Benson, Morgan Grenfell, Rothschild and Hambro. They often act as 'brokers', arranging loans for companies from a number of different sources. They also offer financial advice to industry and provide assistance to firms in raising new capital through the issue of new shares.

Their traditional business was in 'accepting' **commercial bills of exchange**. Commercial bills of exchange are issued by companies and are a means whereby they can raise money for a short period of time (typically three months). Bills are, in effect, an IOU, with the company that issues them promising to pay the holder a specified sum on a particular date. Since bills do not pay interest, they are sold below their face value in order to enable the purchaser to earn a return. There are financial markets (the 'money market') where these bills can be sold by their holders if they need to get their money back before the due date. This is where the merchant banks come in. They can help to make these bills more marketable by 'accepting' them. This means that the merchant bank will make payment to the holder if the firm issuing the bill fails to do so.

The merchant banks have been particularly affected by the financial deregulation of recent years, with much of their business being threatened by competition from retail banks, overseas banks and other financial institutions. In response to this competition, merchant banks have attempted to diversify their business, and there have been many mergers between merchant banks and other financial institutions.

Overseas banks. Investment banks also include many overseas banks, especially Japanese and American. They have expanded their business in the UK enormously in recent years, especially since the abolition of foreign exchange controls in 1979. Their major specialism is the finance of international trade and capital movements, and they deal extensively in the foreign exchange market. Most of their deposits are in foreign currencies.

> **definition**
>
> **Wholesale deposits and loans**
> Large-scale deposits and loans made by and to firms at negotiated interest rates.

> **definition**
>
> **Commercial bill**
> A certificate issued by a firm promising to repay a stated amount on a certain date, typically three months from the issue of the bill. Bills pay no interest as such, but are sold at a discount and redeemed at their face value, thereby earning a rate of discount for the purchaser.

Finance houses. These specialise in providing hire-purchase finance for the purchase of consumer durables such as cars and electrical goods. This is normally arranged through the retailer, which will offer credit to its customers. Finance houses also lease out capital equipment to firms – something that the retail banks are increasingly doing too. Their main source of funds is the banks, but they also receive deposits from the general public. Several finance houses are subsidiaries of commercial banks.

Conclusions

The trend in banking and finance since the early 1980s has been away from the narrow specialisation of the past and towards the offering of a wider and wider range of services. Inevitably, as this trend continues, so the services offered by the various institutions will increasingly overlap.

18.5 The stock market

During the early 1990s the use of share issues to raise finance for investment increased quite significantly. Almost a quarter of all new finance in the UK was raised in this way.

In this section, we will look at the role of the stock market and consider the advantages and limitations of raising finance through it. We will also consider whether the stock market is efficient.

The role of the Stock Exchange

The London Stock Exchange operates as both a primary and secondary market in capital.

As a **primary market** it is where firms can raise finance by issuing new shares, whether to new shareholders or to existing ones. To raise finance on the Stock Exchange a business must be 'listed'. The Listing Agreement involves directors agreeing to abide by a strict set of rules governing behaviour and levels of reporting to shareholders. Companies must have at least three years' trading experience and make at least 25 per cent of its shares available to the public. In 1998 there were 2609 companies on the Official List. During 1998 £12.6 billion's worth of new capital was raised by selling equity (ordinary shares) and fixed-interest securities on the London Stock Exchange.

As well as those on the Official List, there are a further 312 companies on what is known as the Alternative Investment Market (AIM). Companies listed here tend to be young but with growth potential, and do not have to meet the strict criteria or pay such high costs as companies on the Official List.

As a **secondary market**, the Stock Exchange operates as a market where investors can sell existing shares to one another. In 1998, on an average day's trading, £4.1 billion's worth of trading in UK equities took place.

The advantages and disadvantages of using the stock market to raise capital

As a market for raising capital the stock market has a number of advantages:

- It brings together those that wish to invest and those that seek investment.

---

definition

Primary market in capital
Where shares are sold by the issuer of the shares (i.e. the firm) and where, therefore, finance is channelled directly from the purchasers (i.e. the shareholders) to the firm.

---

definition

Secondary market in capital
Where shareholders sell shares to others. This is thus a market in 'second-hand' shares.

It thus represents a way that savings can be mobilised to create output. Take the growth of 'dot-com' companies in recent years. Technologically innovative ideas that require financing have achieved this through stock market listing – lastminute.com being a good example.

- Firms that are listed on the stock exchange are subject to strict regulations. This is likely to stimulate investor confidence, making it easier for business to raise finance.
- The process of merger and acquisition is facilitated by having a share system. It enables business more effectively to pursue this as a growth strategy.
- The transaction costs of marrying potential investors with potential entrepreneurs are kept low, stimulating economic activity.

The main weaknesses of the stock market for raising capital are:

- The cost to a business of getting listed can be immense, not only in a financial sense, but also in being open to public scrutiny. Directors' and senior managers' decisions will often be driven by how the market is likely to react, rather by what they perceive to be in the business's best interests. They always have to think about the reactions of those large shareholders in the City that control a large proportion of their shares.
- The major weakness of raising finance through the issuing of shares is the potential instability it might cause. If a business is seen by the market to be under-performing, investors may sell their shares. As share values fall, the business may then find itself vulnerable to a take-over bid. In the UK, it is often claimed that the market suffers from **short-termism**. Investors on the Stock Exchange are more concerned with a company's short-term performance and it share value. In responding to this, the business might neglect its long-term performance and potential.

Is the stock market efficient?

One of the arguments made in favour of the stock market is that it acts as an arena within which share values can be accurately or efficiently priced. If new information comes on to the market concerning a business and its performance, this will be quickly and rationally transferred into the business's share value. This is known as the **efficient market hypothesis**. So for example, if an investment analyst found that, in terms of its actual and expected dividends, a particular share was under-priced and thus represented a 'bargain', the analyst would advise investors to buy. As people then bought the shares, their price would rise, pushing their value up to their full worth. So by attempting to gain from inefficiently priced securities, investors will encourage the market to become more efficient.

So how efficient is the stock market in pricing securities? Is information rationally and quickly conveyed into the share's price? Or are investors able to prosper from the stock market's inefficiencies?

We can identify three levels of efficiency.

Weak form of efficiency. Share prices often move in cycles which do not reflect the underlying performance of the firm. If information is imperfect, those with a better understanding of such cycles gain from buying shares at the trough and selling them at the peak of the cycles. They are taking advantage of the market's inefficiency.

definition
Short-termism Where firms and investors take decisions based on the likely short-term performance of a company, rather than on its long-term prospects. Firms may thus sacrifice long-term profits and growth for the sake of quick return.

definition
Efficient (capital) market hypothesis The hypothesis that new information about a company's current or future performance will be quickly and accurately reflected in its share price.

The technical analysis used by investment analysts to track share cycles is a complex science, but more and more analysts are using the techniques. As they do so and knowledge becomes more perfect, so the market will become more efficient and the cycles will tend to disappear. But why?

As more people buy when a share price is low, so this will push the price up more rapidly – but not so far. More people will try to sell quickly, while the price is high. But there will be few buyers, since investors know the stock is nearing its high point. Thus the peak is lower. The same will happen as prices fall. As investors begin to see a 'bargain', they will purchase, thereby pushing the price back up again. As more people react in this way, so the cycle all but disappears: the low price has risen and the high price has fallen. When this happens, **weak efficiency** has been achieved.

If the market was efficient in this sense, then no gain would be made from charting cycles in share prices, as any information would be included in the current share price from buying and selling. As such, it would only be new information that would cause share prices to change. Such information must be by its nature random, and as such cause share prices to move randomly, or follow what we call a **random walk**. Evidence suggests that share prices do tend to follow random patterns and that the stock market is relatively efficient in this weak form.

The semi-strong form of efficiency. **Semi-strong efficiency** is when share prices adjust fully to publicly available information. In practice, not all investors will interpret such information correctly: their knowledge is imperfect. But as investors become more and more sophisticated, and as more and more advice is available to shareholders (though stock brokers, newspapers, published accounts, etc.), and as many shares are purchased by professional fund managers, so the interpretation of public information becomes more and more perfect and the market becomes more and more efficient.

Tests of this level of efficiency have been conducted to see whether new information that would be expected to influence a security's price actually does so, both in the direction expected and quickly. The evidence suggests that the semi-strong form of efficiency holds.

The strong form of efficiency. If the stock market showed the **strong form of efficiency**, then share prices would fully reflect *all* available information – whether public or not. For this to be so, all 'inside' information would have to be reflected in the share price the moment the information is available.

If the market is *not* efficient at this level, then insiders (i.e. those who have access to privileged information) will be able to make large returns from their investments by hiding such information from the public. Gains made from insider dealing are illegal. However, proving whether individuals are engaging in it is very difficult. Nevertheless, there are people in prison for insider dealing: so it does happen! Studies that have been conducted in this area suggest that those that have access to information are able to exploit this to their own advantage. As such the strong-form of stock market efficiency is unlikely to hold.

We can conclude that the stock market is a relatively efficient means of pricing securities. It is only via the use of illegal activities such as insider dealing that the remaining imperfections can be exploited.

---

definition

Weak efficiency (of share markets)
Where share dealing prevents cyclical movements in shares.

definition

Random walk
Where fluctuations in the value of a share away from its 'correct' value are random: i.e. have no systematic pattern. When charted over time, these share price movements would appear like a 'random walk': like the path of someone staggering along drunk!

definition

Semi-strong efficiency (of share markets)
Where share prices adjust quickly, fully and accurately to publicly available information.

definition

Strong efficiency (of share markets)
Where share prices adjust quickly, fully and accurately to all available information, both public and that only available to insiders.

SUMMARY

1a We need to distinguish between factor prices and factor services. A factor's price is income from its sale, whereas a factor's service is the income from its use.

1b The profit-maximising employment of capital will be at the point where the marginal cost of capital equals the marginal revenue product.

2a The demand for capital services will be equal to MRP_K. As a result of diminishing returns, this will decline as more capital is used.

2b The supply of capital services to a firm will be horizontal or upward sloping, depending on whether the firm is perfectly competitive or has monopsony power.

2c The supply curve of capital services *by* a firm in the short run will be relatively elastic up to capacity supply. In the long run, the supply curve will be very elastic, but at a higher rental rate than in the short run, given that the cost of purchasing the equipment must be taken into account in the rental rate.

2d The market supply of capital services is likely to be highly inelastic in the short run, given that capital equipment tends to have very specific uses and cannot normally be transferred from one use to another. In the long run it will be more elastic.

2e The price of capital services will be determined by the interaction of demand and supply.

3a The demand for capital for purchase will depend on the return it earns for the firm. To calculate the return, all future earnings from the investment have to be reduced to present value by discounting at a market rate of interest. If the present value exceeds the cost of the investment, the investment is worthwhile. Alternatively, a rate of return from the investment (IRR) can be calculated and then this can be compared with the return that the firm could have earned by investing elsewhere.

3b The supply of finance for investment depends on the supply of loanable funds, which in turn depends, in large part, on the rate of interest.

3c The rate of interest will be determined by the demand and supply of loanable funds.

3d The costs of capital supplied to the firm will rise the more it is in debt, and hence the more risky the investment becomes.

4a Business finance can come from internal and external sources. External sources of finance include borrowing and the issue of shares.

4b The role of the financial sector is to act as a financial intermediary between those who wish to borrow and those who wish to lend.

4c UK financial institutions specialise in different types of deposit taking and lending.

5a The stock market operates as both a primary and secondary market in capital. As a primary market it channels finance to companies as people purchase new shares. It is also a market for existing shares.

5b It helps to stimulate growth and investment by bringing together companies and people who want to invest in them. By regulating firms and by keeping transaction costs of investment low, it helps to ensure that investment is efficient.

5c It does impose costs on firms, however. It is expensive for firms to be listed and the public exposure may make them too keen to 'please' the market. It can also foster short-termism.

5d The stock market is relatively efficient. It achieves weak efficiency by reducing cyclical movements in share prices. It achieves semi-strong efficiency by allowing share prices to respond quickly and fully to publicly available information. Whether it achieves strong efficiency by adjusting quickly and fully to *all* information (both public or insider), however, is more doubtful.

REVIEW QUESTIONS

1 Draw the MRP_K, AC_K and MC_K curves for a firm which has monopsony power when hiring capital equipment. Mark the amount of capital equipment it will choose to hire and show what hire charge it will pay.

2 Using a diagram like Figure 18.2, demonstrate what will happen under perfect competition (in the short run) when there is an increase in the

productivity of a particular type of capital. Consider the effects on the demand, price (rental rate) and quantity supplied of the services of this type of capital. In what way will the long-run effect differ from the short-run one that you have illustrated?

3   Suppose an investment costs £12 000 and yields £5000 per year for three years. At the end of the three years, the equipment has no value. Work out whether the investment will be profitable if the rate of discount is:
    (a) 5%
    (b) 10%
    (c) 20%.

4   If a project's costs occur throughout the life of the project, how will this affect the appraisal of whether the project is profitable?

5   What factors would cause a rise in the market rate of interest?

6   What is meant by the two terms 'gearing ratio' and 'debt/equity ratio'? What is their significance?

7   Explain the various roles that financial intermediaries play within the finance sector.

8   In what circumstances is the stock market likely to be 'efficient' in the various senses of the term?

G The relationship between government and business

THE FINANCIAL TIMES, 5 OCTOBER 2000

Building bridges across the skills gap

Kevin Brown and Jim Pickard

Britain undoubtedly has a serious basic skills problem. Only half the workforce gained five GCSEs or their vocational equivalents, compared with nearly three-quarters in France and 83 per cent in Germany. One in five adults has severe reading difficulties.

But that is only one factor contributing to the emerging skills shortage. Others include the poor image of industries such as engineering and construction, the uneven pattern of UK economic growth, and the phenomenal expansion in information technology, which is outstripping the local supply of workers.

The scale of the shortages varies greatly across the country and between business sectors. It is most severe in London and the south east, where economic growth is fastest, and virtually non-existent in Scotland and the north east.

There are severe problems in construction, engineering, information technology and hotels and restaurants. But there are local hotspots, too. In the south west aerospace companies report severe recruitment difficulties.

The nature of the missing skills varies widely. Some employers say they cannot find the workers they need in the UK economy at any price. Others say their problems have more to do with getting existing workers to adopt the fresh skills needed to cope with changing business methods such as team working and focusing on customers' needs.

David Blunkett, the education and employment secretary, thinks much of the answer lies in wider provision of state-funded vocational education, on which the government is spending £6bn a year.

This will provide a new internet-based University for Industry, a new range of vocational GCSEs from 2002, and funds to provide every adult in the country with the possibility of taking vocational courses.

Business has given general support to this programme, which many businessmen see as a long-overdue attempt to bring the education system into line with the demand of modern industry.

Despite the fact that most countries today can be classified as 'market economies', governments nevertheless intervene substantially in the activities of business in order to protect the interests of consumers, workers or the environment.

Firms might collude to fix prices, use misleading advertising, create pollution, produce unsafe products, or use unacceptable employment practices. In such cases, government is expected to intervene to correct for the failings of the market system: for example, by outlawing collusion, by establishing advertising standards, by taxing or otherwise penalising polluting firms, by imposing safety standards on firms' behaviour and products, or by protecting employment rights.

In Part G, we explore the relationship between business and government. In Chapter 19 we will consider how markets might fail to achieve ideal outcomes, and what government can do to correct such problems. We will also consider how far firms should go in adopting a more socially responsible position.

In Chapter 20 we will focus upon the relationship between the government and the individual firm, and consider three policy areas: monopolies and oligopolies, research and technology, and training.

In Chapter 21, we will broaden our analysis and look at government policy aimed at the level of the market, and its impact upon all firms. Here we will consider environmental policy, transport policy and the issue of privatisation and regulation.

The government is, in a sense, a super firm (but of a very special kind), since it is able to influence the use of factors of production by administrative decision.

R.H. Coase, 'The problem of social cost', *Journal of Law and Economics*, October 1960, p. 17

key terms

Social efficiency
Equity
Market failure
Externalities
Private and social costs and benefits
Deadweight welfare loss
Public goods
Free-rider problem
Merit goods
Government intervention
Laissez-faire
Social responsibility
Competition policy
Restrictive practices
Technology policy
Training policy
Environmental policy
Transport policy
Privatisation
Regulation
Deregulation
Franchising

Reasons for government intervention in the market

19.1 Markets and the role of government

Government intervention and social objectives

In order to decide the optimum amount of government intervention, it is first necessary to identify the various social goals that intervention is designed to meet. Two of the major objectives of government intervention identified by economists are **social efficiency** and **equity**.

Social efficiency. If the marginal benefits to society (MSB) of producing (or consuming) any given good or service exceed the marginal costs to society (MSC), then it is said to be socially efficient to produce (or consume) more. For example, if people's gains from having additional motorways exceed *all* the additional costs to society (both financial and non-financial) then it is socially efficient to construct more motorways. If, however, the marginal social costs of producing (or consuming) any good or service exceed the marginal social benefits, then it is socially efficient to produce (or consume) less. It follows that if the marginal social benefits of any activity are equal to the marginal social costs, then the current level is the optimum. To summarise: for social efficiency in the production of any good or service:

$MSB > MSC \rightarrow$ produce more

$MSC > MSB \rightarrow$ produce less

$MSB = MSC \rightarrow$ keep production at its current level

Similar rules apply to consumption.

In the real world, the market rarely leads to social efficiency: the marginal social benefits of most goods and services do not equal the marginal social costs. In this chapter we examine why the free market fails to lead to social efficiency and what the government can do to rectify the situation. We also examine why the government itself may fail to achieve social efficiency.

Equity. Most people would argue that the free market fails to lead to a *fair* distribution of resources, if it results in some people living in great affluence while others live in dire poverty. Clearly what constitutes 'fairness' is a highly contentious issue: those on the political right generally have a quite different view from those on the political left. Nevertheless, most people would argue that the government does have some duty in redistributing incomes from the rich to the poor through the tax and benefit system, and perhaps in providing various forms of legal protection for the poor (such as a minimum wage rate).

Although out prime concern in this chapter is the question of social efficiency, we will be touching on questions of distribution too.

19.2 Types of market failure

In the real world, markets frequently fail to achieve social efficiency. Part of the problem is the existence of 'externalities', part is a lack of competition, part is a lack of knowledge on the part of both producers and consumers, and part is the fact that markets may take a long time to adjust to any disequilibrium, given the often considerable short-run immobility of factors of production.

Externalities

The market will not lead to social efficiency if the actions of producers or consumers affect people *other than themselves*. These effects on other people are known as **externalities**: they are the side-effects, or 'third-party' effects, of production or consumption. Externalities can be either desirable or undesirable. Whenever other people are affected beneficially, there are said to be **external benefits**. Whenever other people are affected adversely, there are said to be **external costs**.

Thus the full cost to society (the **social cost**) of the production of any good or service is the private cost faced by firms plus any externalities of production. Likewise the full benefit to society (the **social benefit**) from the consumption of any good is the private benefit enjoyed by consumers plus any externalities of consumption.

There are four major types of externality.

External costs of production (MSC > MC)

When a chemical firm dumps waste in a river or pollutes the air, the community bears costs additional to those borne by the firm. The marginal *social* cost (*MSC*) of chemical production exceeds the marginal private cost (*MC*). Diagrammatically, the *MSC* curve is above the *MC* curve. This is shown in Figure 19.1(a), which assumes that the firm in other respects is operating in a

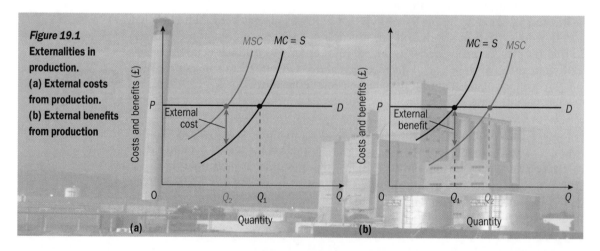

Figure 19.1
Externalities in production.
(a) External costs from production.
(b) External benefits from production

perfect market, and is therefore a price taker (i.e. faces a horizontal demand curve).

The firm maximises profits at Q_1: the output where marginal cost equals price (see section 11.2). The price is what people buying the good are prepared to pay for one more unit (if it wasn't they wouldn't buy it) and therefore reflects their marginal benefit. We assume no externalities from consumption, and therefore the marginal benefit to consumers is the same as the marginal *social* benefit (*MSB*).

The socially optimum output for the firm would be Q_2, where P (i.e. MSB) = MSC. The firm, however, produces Q_1, which is more than the optimum. Thus external costs lead to overproduction from society's point of view.

The problem of external costs arises in a free-market economy because no one has legal ownership of the air or rivers and no one, therefore, can prevent or charge for their use as a dump for waste. Control must, therefore, be left to the government or local authorities.

Other examples include extensive farming that destroys hedgerows and wildlife, acid rain caused by smoke from coal-fired power stations, and nuclear waste from nuclear power stations.

External benefits of production (MSC < MC)

Imagine a bus company that spends money training its bus drivers. Each year some drivers leave to work for coach and haulage companies. These companies' costs are reduced as they do not have to train such drivers. Society has benefited from their training (including the bus drivers themselves, who have acquired marketable skills), even though the bus company has not. The marginal *social* cost of the bus service, therefore, is less than the marginal *private* cost to the company.

In Figure 19.1(b), the *MSC* curve is *below* the *MC* curve. The level of output (i.e. number of passenger miles) provided by the bus company is Q_1, where $P = MC$, a *lower* level than the social optimum, Q_2, where $P = MSC$.

Another example of external benefits in production is that of research and development. If other firms have access to the results of the research, then clearly the benefits extend beyond the firm which finances it. Since the firm only receives the private benefits, it will conduct a less than optimal amount of research. Similarly, a forestry company planting new woodlands will not take into account the beneficial effect on the atmosphere.

External costs of consumption (MSB < MB)

When people use their cars, other people suffer from their exhaust, the added congestion, the noise, etc. These 'negative externalities' make the marginal social benefit of using cars less than the marginal private benefit (i.e. marginal utility to the car user).

Figure 19.2(a) shows the marginal utility and price to a motorist (i.e. the consumer) of using a car. The optimal distance travelled for this motorist will be Q_1 miles: i.e. where $MU = P$ (where price is the cost of petrol, oil, wear and tear, etc. per mile). The *social* optimum, however, would be less than this, namely Q_2, where $MSB = P$.

Other examples include noisy radios in public places, the smoke from cigarettes, and litter.

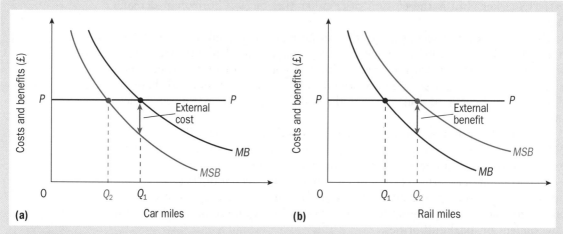

Figure 19.2
Externalities in consumption. (a) External costs from consumption. (b) External benefits from consumption

External benefits of consumption (MSB > MB)

When people travel by train rather than by car, other people benefit by there being less congestion and exhaust and fewer accidents on the roads. Thus the marginal social benefit of rail travel is *greater* than the marginal private benefit (i.e. the marginal utility to the rail passenger). There are external benefits from rail travel. In Figure 19.2(b), the *MSB* curve is *above* the private *MB* curve. The socially optimal level of consumption (Q_2) is thus above the actual level of consumption (Q_1). In other words, when there are 'positive externalities' in consumption, the actual level of consumption will be too low from society's point of view.

Other examples include deodorants, vaccinations and attractive clothing.

In general, whenever there are external benefits, there will be too little produced or consumed. Whenever there are external costs, there will be too much produced or consumed. The market will not equate *MSB* and *MSC*.

The above arguments have been developed in the context of perfect competition with prices given to the producer or consumer by the market. Externalities also occur in all other types of market.

Market power

Whenever markets are imperfect, whether as pure monopoly or monopsony or whether as some form of imperfect competition, the market will fail to equate *MSB* and *MSC*, even if there are no externalities.

Take the case of monopoly. A monopoly will produce less than the socially efficient output. This is illustrated in Figure 19.3. A monopoly faces a downward-sloping demand curve, and therefore marginal revenue is below average revenue (= *P*). Profits are maximised where marginal revenue equals marginal cost (at an output of Q_1 and at a price of P_1). But since price is above marginal revenue, price must also be above marginal cost (P_1 is above MC_1). If there are no externalities and thus $P = MSB$ and $MC = MSC$, the socially efficient output

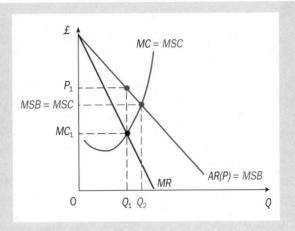

Figure 19.3
The monopolist producing less than the socially efficient level of output

will be Q_2, where $MSB = MSC$. Since Q_2 is greater than Q_1, the firm is clearly producing less than the socially efficient output.

Deadweight loss under monopoly

One way of analysing the welfare loss that occurs under monopoly is to use the concepts of *consumer* and *producer surplus*. Consumer surplus is the excess of consumers' total utility from consuming a good over their total expenditure on it. Producer surplus is just another name for profit. The two concepts are illustrated in Figure 19.4. The diagram shows an industry which is initially under perfect competition and then becomes a monopoly (but faces the same revenue and cost curves).

Under *perfect competition* the industry will produce an output of Q_{pc} at a price of P_{pc}, where $MC(= S) = P(= AR)$: i.e. at point *a*. Consumers' total utility is given by the area under the demand (*MU*) curve (the sum of all the areas 1–7). Consumers' total expenditure is $P_{pc} \times Q_{pc}$ (areas $4 + 5 + 6 + 7$). Consumers surplus is the difference between total utility and total expenditure: in other words, the area between the price and the demand curve (areas $1 + 2 + 3$).

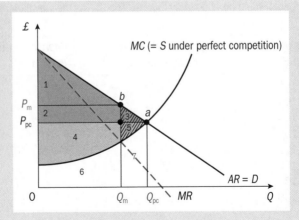

Figure 19.4
Deadweight loss from a monopoly

BOX 19.1

Can the market provide adequate protection for the environment?

In recent years people have become acutely aware of the damage being done to the environment by pollution. But if the tipping of chemicals and sewage into the rivers and seas and the spewing of toxic gases into the atmosphere cause so much damage, why does it continue? If we all suffer from these activities, both consumers and producers alike, then why will a pure market system not deal with the problem? After all, a market should respond to people's interests.

The reason is that the costs of pollution are largely *external* costs. They are borne by society at large and only very slightly (if at all) by the polluter. If, for example, 10 000 people suffer from the smoke from a factory (including the factory owner) then that owner will only bear approximately 1/10 000 of the suffering. That personal cost may be quite insignificant when the owner is deciding whether the factory is profitable. And if the owner lives far away, the personal cost of the pollution will be zero.

Thus the *social* costs of polluting activities exceed the *private* costs. If people behave selfishly and only take into account the effect their actions have on themselves, there will be an *overproduction* of polluting activities.

Thus it is argued that governments must intervene to prevent or regulate pollution, or alternatively to tax the polluting activities or subsidise measures to reduce the pollution.

But if people are purely selfish, why do they buy 'green' products? Why do they buy, for example, 'ozone-friendly' aerosols? After all, the amount of damage done to the ozone layer from their own personal use of 'non-friendly' aerosols would be absolutely minute. The answer is that many people have a social conscience. They *do* sometimes take into account the effect their actions have on other people. They are not totally selfish. They like to do their own little bit, however small, towards protecting the environment.

Nevertheless to rely on people's consciences may be a very unsatisfactory method of controlling pollution. In a market environment where people are all the time being encouraged to consume more and more goods and where materialism is the religion of the age, there would have to be a massive shift towards 'green thinking' if the market were to be a sufficient answer to the problem of pollution.

Certain types of environmental problem may get high priority in the media, like acid rain, the greenhouse effect, damage to the ozone layer and brain damage to children from leaded petrol. However, the sheer range of polluting activities makes reliance on people's awareness of the problems and their social consciences far too arbitrary.

Question
The following table gives the costs and benefits of an imaginary firm operating under perfect competition whose activities create a certain amount of pollution. (It is assumed that the costs of this pollution to society can be accurately measured.)
(a) What is the profit-maximising level of output for this firm?
(b) What is the socially efficient level of output?
(c) Why might the marginal pollution costs increase in the way illustrated in this example?

Output (units)	Price per unit (MSB) (£)	Marginal (private) costs to the firm (MC)(£)	Marginal external (pollution) costs (MEC) (£)	Marginal social costs (MSC = MC + MEC) (£)
1	100	30	20	50
2	100	30	22	52
3	100	35	25	60
4	100	45	30	75
5	100	60	40	100
6	100	78	55	133
7	100	100	77	177
8	100	130	110	240

Producer surplus (profit) is the difference between total revenue and total cost.[1] Total revenue is $P_{pc} \times Q_{pc}$ (areas $4 + 5 + 6 + 7$). Total cost is the area under the MC curve (areas $6 + 7$). Producer surplus is thus the area between the price and the MC curve (areas $4 + 5$). Total consumer plus producer surplus is therefore the area between the demand and MC curves. This is shown by the total shaded area (areas $1 + 2 + 3 + 4 + 5$).

What happens when the industry is under *monopoly*? The firm will produce where $MC = MR$, at an output of Q_m and a price of P_m (at point b on the demand curve). Total revenue is $P_m \times Q_m$ (areas $2 + 4 + 6$). Total cost is the area under the MC curve (area 6). Thus the producer surplus is areas $2 + 4$. This is clearly a *larger* surplus than under perfect competition (since area 2 is larger than area 5). The consumer surplus, however, will fall dramatically. With consumption at Q_m, total utility is given by areas $1 + 2 + 4 + 6$, whereas consumer expenditure is given by areas $2 + 4 + 6$. Consumer surplus, then, is simply area 1. (Note that area 2 has been transformed from consumer surplus to producer surplus.)

Total surplus under monopoly is therefore areas $1 + 2 + 4$: a smaller surplus than under perfect competition. 'Monopolisation' of the industry has resulted in a loss of total surplus of areas $3 + 5$. The producer's gain has been more than offset by the consumers' loss. This loss of surplus is known as **deadweight welfare loss** of monopoly.

Ignorance and uncertainty

Perfect competition assumes that consumers, firms and factor suppliers have perfect knowledge of costs and benefits. In the real world there is often a great deal of ignorance and uncertainty. Thus people are unable to equate marginal benefit with marginal cost.

Consumers purchase many goods only once or a few times in a lifetime. Cars, washing machines, televisions and other consumer durables fall into this category. Consumers may not be aware of the quality of such goods until they have purchased them, by which time it is too late. Advertising may contribute to people's ignorance by misleading them as to the benefits of a good.

Firms are often ignorant of market opportunities, prices, costs, the productivity of factors (especially white-collar workers), the activity of rivals, etc.

Many economic decisions are based on expected future conditions. Since the future can never be known for certain, many decisions will be taken that in retrospect will be seen to have been wrong.

Public goods

There is a category of goods that the free market, whether perfect or imperfect, will underproduce or may not produce at all. They are called **public goods**. Examples include lighthouses, pavements, flood control dams, public drainage, public services such as the police and even government itself.

Public goods have two important characteristics: *non-rivalry* and *non-excludability*:

> **definition**
> **Deadweight welfare loss**
> The loss of consumer plus producer surplus in imperfect markets (when compared with perfect competition).

> **definition**
> **Public good**
> A good or service which has the features of non-rivalry and non-excludability and as a result would not be provided by the free market.

---

[1] Strictly speaking, producer surplus is the excess of total revenue over total *variable* costs (since the sum of all marginal costs gives total *variable* costs). If there are any fixed costs, total profit will be less than total producer surplus.

- If I consume a bar of chocolate, it cannot then be consumed by someone else. If, however, I walk along the pavement or enjoy the benefits of street lighting, it does not prevent you or anyone else doing the same. There is thus what we call **non-rivalry** in the consumption of such goods. These goods tend to have large external benefits relative to private benefits. This makes them socially desirable, but privately unprofitable. No one person on their own would pay to have a pavement built along his or her street. The private benefit would be too small relative to the cost. And yet the social benefit to all the other people using the pavement may far outweigh the cost.
- If I spend money erecting a flood control dam to protect my house, my neighbours will also be protected by the dam. I cannot prevent them enjoying the benefits of my expenditure. This feature of **non-excludability** means that they would get the benefits free, and would therefore have no incentive to pay themselves. This is known as the **free-rider problem**.

When goods have these two features, the free market will simply not provide them. Thus these public goods can only be provided by the government or by the government subsidising private firms. (Note that not all goods and services produced by the public sector come into the category of public goods and services: thus education and health are publicly provided, but they *can* be, and indeed are, privately provided.)

Immobility of factors and time-lags in response

Even under conditions of perfect competition, factors may be very slow to respond to changes in demand or supply. Labour, for example, may be highly immobile both occupationally and geographically. This can lead to large price changes and hence to large supernormal profits and high wages for those in the sectors of rising demand or falling costs. The long run may be a very long time coming!

In the meantime, there will be further changes in the conditions of demand and supply. Thus the economy is in a constant state of disequilibrium and the long run never comes. As firms and consumers respond to market signals and move towards equilibrium, so the equilibrium position moves and the social optimum is never achieved.

Whenever monopoly/monopsony power exists, the problem is made worse as firms or unions put up barriers to the entry of new firms or factors of production.

Protecting people's interests

The government may feel that people need protecting from poor economic decisions that they make on their *own* behalf. It may feel that in a free market people will consume too many harmful things. Thus if the government wants to discourage smoking and drinking, it can put taxes on tobacco and alcohol. In more extreme cases it could make various activities illegal: activities such as prostitution, certain types of gambling, and the sale and consumption of drugs.

On the other hand, the government may feel that people consume too little of things that are good for them: things such as education, health care and sports facilities. When the government feels that it knows better than individuals about

---

definition

Non-rivalry
Where the consumption of a good or service by one person will not prevent others from enjoying it.

definition

Non-excludability
Where it is not possible to provide a good or service to one person without it thereby being available for others to enjoy.

definition

Free-rider problem
When it is not possible to exclude other people from consuming a good that someone has bought.

what items are good for them, such goods are known as **merit goods**. The government could either provide them free or subsidise their production.

19.3 Government intervention in the market

Faced with all the problems of the free market, what is a government to do?

There are several policy instruments that the government can use. At one extreme, it can totally replace the market by providing goods and services itself. At the other extreme, it can merely seek to persuade producers, consumers or workers to act differently. Between the two extremes the government has a number of instruments it can use to change the way markets operate. These include taxes, subsidies, laws and regulatory bodies. In this section we examine these different forms of government intervention.

Taxes and subsidies

When there are imperfections in the market, social efficiency will not be achieved. Marginal social benefit (MSB) will not equal marginal social cost (MSC). A different level of output would be more desirable.

Taxes and subsidies can be used to correct these imperfections. Essentially the approach is to tax those goods or activities where the market produces too much, and subsidise those where the market produces too little.

Taxes and subsidies to correct externalities. The rule here is simple: the government should impose a tax equal to the marginal external cost (or grant a subsidy equal to the marginal external benefit).

Assume, for example, that a chemical works emits smoke from a chimney and thus pollutes the atmosphere. This creates external costs for the people who breathe in the smoke. The marginal social cost of producing the chemicals thus exceeds the marginal private cost to the firm: $MSC > MC$.

This is illustrated in Figure 19.5. For simplicity, it is assumed that the firm is a price taker. It produces Q_1 where $P = MC$ (its profit-maximising output), but in doing so takes no account of the external pollution costs it imposes on society. If the government imposes a tax on production equal to the marginal pollution cost, it will effectively internalise the externality. The firm will now

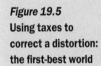

> **definition**
>
> **Merit goods**
> Goods which the government feels that people will underconsume and which therefore ought to be subsidised or provided free.

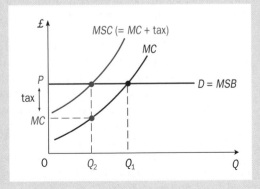

Figure 19.5
Using taxes to correct a distortion: the first-best world

maximise profits at Q_2, which is the socially optimum output where $MSB = MSC$.

Taxes and subsidies to correct for monopoly. If the problem of monopoly that the government wishes to tackle is that of *excessive profits*, it can impose a lump-sum tax on the monopolist: that is, a tax of a fixed absolute amount irrespective of how much the monopolist produces, or the price it charges. Since a lump-sum tax is an additional *fixed* cost to the firm, and hence will not affect the firm's marginal cost, it will not reduce the amount that the monopolist produces (which *would* be the case with a per-unit tax).

If the government is concerned that the monopolist produces *less* than the socially efficient output, it could give the monopolist a per-unit *subsidy* (which would encourage the monopolist to produce more). But would this not *increase* the monopolist's profit? The answer to this is to impose a harsh lump-sum tax in addition to the subsidy. The tax would not undo the subsidy's benefit of encouraging the monopolist producing more, but it could be used to reduce the monopolist's profits below the original (i.e. pre-subsidy) level. The 'windfall tax' imposed in 1997 by the UK Labour government on the profits of various privatised utilities is an example of such a tax.

Advantages of taxes and subsidies

Many economists favour the tax/subsidy solution to market imperfections (especially the problem of externalities) because it still allows the market to operate. It forces firms to take on board the full social costs and benefits of their actions. It also has the flexibility of being adjustable according to the magnitude of the problem. For example, the bigger the external costs of a firm's actions, the bigger the tax can be.

What is more, by taxing firms for polluting, say, they are encouraged to find cleaner ways of producing. The tax thus acts as an incentive over the longer run to reduce pollution: the more a firm can reduce its pollution, the more taxes it can save.

Likewise, by subsidising good practices, firms are given the incentive to adopt more good practices.

Disadvantages of taxes and subsidies

Infeasible to use different tax and subsidy rates. Each firm produces different levels and types of externality and operates under different degrees of imperfect competition. It would be expensive and administratively very difficult, if not impossible, to charge every offending firm its own particular tax rate (or grant every relevant firm its own particular rate of subsidy).

Lack of knowledge. Even if a government did decide to charge a tax equal to each offending firm's marginal external costs, it would still have the problem of measuring that cost. The damage from pollution is often extremely difficult to assess. It is also difficult to apportion blame. For example, the damage to lakes and forests from acid rain has been a major concern since the beginning of the 1980s. But just how serious is that damage? What is its current monetary cost? How long lasting is the damage? What will be the position in twenty years? Just what and who are to blame? These are questions that cannot be answered precisely. It is thus impossible to fix the 'correct' pollution tax on, say, a particular coal-fired power station.

BOX 19.2

Deadweight loss from taxes on goods and services
The excess burden of taxes

Taxation can be used to correct market failures, but taxes can have adverse effects themselves. One such effect is the deadweight loss that results when taxes are imposed on goods and services.

The diagram shows the demand and supply of a particular good. Equilibrium is initially at a price of P_1 and a level of sales of Q_1, (i.e. where $D = S$). Now an excise tax is imposed on the good. The supply curve shifts upwards by the amount of the tax, to $S + tax$. Equilibrium

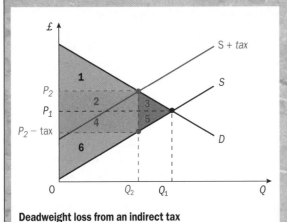

Deadweight loss from an indirect tax

price rises to P_2 and equilibrium quantity falls to Q_2. Producers receive an after-tax price of $P_2 - tax$.

Consumer surplus falls from areas $1 + 2 + 3$, to area 1 (the upper grey area). Producer surplus falls from areas $4 + 5 + 6$ to area 6 (the lower grey area). Does this mean, therefore, that total surplus falls by areas 2

$+ 3 + 4 + 5$? The answer is no, because there is a gain to the government from the tax revenue (and hence a gain to the population from the resulting government expenditure). The revenue from the tax is known as the **government surplus**. It is given by areas $2 + 4$ (the green area).

But, even after including government surplus, there is still a fall in total surplus of areas $3 + 5$. This is the deadweight loss of the tax. It is sometimes known as the **excess burden** of the tax.

Does this loss of total surplus from taxation imply that taxes on goods are always a 'bad thing'? The answer is no. This conclusion would only follow in a 'first-best' world where there were no market failures: where competition was perfect, where there were no externalities and where income distribution was optimum. In such a world, the loss of surplus from imposing a tax on a good would represent a reduction in welfare.

In the real world of imperfect markets and inequality, taxes can do more good than harm. As we have shown in this section, they can help to correct for externalities. They can also be used as a means of redistributing incomes. Nevertheless, the excess burden of taxes is something that ideally ought to be considered when weighing up the desirability of imposing taxes on goods and services, or of increasing their rate.

Question
How far can an economist contribute to this highly political debate over the desirability of an excise tax?

Despite these problems, it is nevertheless possible to charge firms by the amount of a particular emission. For example, firms could be charged for chimney smoke by so many parts per million of a given pollutant. Although it is difficult to 'fine-tune' such a system so that the charge reflects the precise number of people affected by the pollutant and by how much, it does go some way to internalising the externality.

Changes in property rights

One cause of market failure is the limited nature of property rights. If someone dumps a load of rubble in your garden, the law should protect you. It is *your* garden, *your* property, and you can thus insist that it is removed. If, however, someone dumps a load of rubble in his or her *own* garden, which is next door to yours, what can you do? You can still see it from your window. It is still an eyesore. But you have no property rights over the next-door garden.

Property rights define who owns property, to what uses it can be put, the rights other people have over it and how it may be transferred. By *extending* these rights, individuals may be able to prevent other people imposing costs on them, or charge them for doing so.

The trouble is that in many instances this type of solution is totally impractical. It is impractical when *many* people are *slightly* inconvenienced, especially if there are many culprits imposing the costs. For example, if I were disturbed by noisy lorries outside my home, it would not be practical to negotiate with every haulage company involved. What if I wanted to ban the lorries from the street, but my next-door neighbour wanted to charge them 10p per journey? Who gets their way?

The extension of private property rights becomes a more practical solution where the culprits are few in number, are easily identifiable and impose clearly defined costs. Thus a noise abatement act could be passed which allowed me to prevent my neighbours playing noisy radios, having noisy parties or otherwise disturbing the peace in my home. The onus would be on me to report them. Or if I chose, I could agree not to report them if they paid me adequate compensation.

But even in cases where only a few people are involved, there may still be the problem of litigation. I may have to incur the time and expense of taking people to court. Justice may not be free, and there is thus a conflict with equity. The rich can afford 'better' justice. They can employ top lawyers. Thus even if I have a right to sue a large company for dumping toxic waste near me, I may not have the legal muscle to win.

Finally, there is the broader question of *equity*. The extension of private property rights may favour the rich (who tend to have more property) at the expense of the poor. Ramblers may get great pleasure from strolling across a great country estate, along public rights of way. This may annoy the owner. If the owner's property rights were now extended to exclude the ramblers, is this a social gain?

Of course, equity consideration can also be dealt with by altering property rights, but in a different way. *Public* property like parks, open spaces, libraries and historic buildings could be extended. Also the property of the rich could be redistributed to the poor. Here it is less a question of the rights that ownership confers, and more a question of altering the ownership itself.

Laws prohibiting or regulating undesirable structures or behaviour

Laws are frequently used to correct market imperfections. Laws can be of three main types: those that prohibit or regulate behaviour that imposes external costs, those that prevent firms providing false or misleading information, and those that prevent or regulate monopolies and oligopolies (see Chapter 20).

Advantages of legal restrictions

- They are usually simple and clear to understand and are often relatively easy to administer. For example, various polluting activities could be banned or restricted.

- When the danger is very great, it might be much safer to ban various practices altogether (e.g. the use of various toxic chemicals) rather than to rely on taxes or on individuals attempting to assert their property rights through the civil courts.
- When a decision needs to be taken quickly, it might be possible to invoke emergency action. For example, in a city like Athens it has been found to be simpler to ban or restrict the use of private cars during a chemical smog emergency than to tax their use.
- Because consumers suffer from imperfect information, consumer protection laws can make it illegal for firms to sell shoddy or unsafe goods, or to make false or misleading claims about their products.

Disadvantages of legal restrictions

The main problem is that legal restrictions tend to be a rather blunt weapon. If, for example, a firm were required to reduce the effluent of a toxic chemical to 20 tonnes per week, there would be no incentive for the firm to reduce it further. With a tax on the effluent, however, the more the firm reduced the effluent, the less tax it would pay. Thus with a system of taxes there is a *continuing* incentive to cut pollution, to improve safety, or whatever.

Regulatory bodies

Rather than using the blunt weapon of general legislation to ban or restrict various activities, a more 'subtle' approach can be adopted. This involves the use of various regulatory bodies. Having identified possible cases where action might be required (e.g. potential cases of pollution, misleading information or the abuse of monopoly power), the regulatory body would probably conduct an investigation and then prepare a report containing its findings and recommendations. It might also have the power to enforce its decisions. In the UK there are regulatory bodies for each of the major privatised utilities (see section 21.3). Another example is the Office of Fair Trading (OFT), which investigates and reports on suspected cases of anti-competitive practices. The OFT can order such firms to cease or modify these practices. Alternatively it can refer them to the Competition Commission (CC), which then conducts an investigation, and makes a ruling (see section 20.1).

The advantage of this approach is that suspected cases of abuse can be dealt with on a case-by-case basis. All the various circumstances surrounding a particular case can be taken into account, with the result that the most appropriate solution can be adopted.

The problems with this approach are (a) that investigations may be expensive and time consuming, (b) that only a few cases may be examined and (c) that the offending firms may make various promises of good behaviour which may not in fact be carried out owing to a lack of follow-up by the regulatory body.

Price controls

Price controls can be used either to raise prices above, or to reduce them below, the free-market level.

Prices could be raised above the market equilibrium to support the incomes of certain suppliers. For example, under the Common Agricultural Policy of the

European Union, high prices for food are set so as to raise farmers' incomes above the free-market level.

Prices could be lowered in order to protect consumers' interests. For example, the government, or another body, may prevent a monopoly or oligopoly from charging excessive prices. This is one of the major roles of the regulatory bodies for the privatised utilities. Here the industry is not allowed to raise its prices by more than a certain amount below the rate of inflation.

Provision of information

When ignorance is a reason for market failure, the direct provision of information by the government or one of its agencies may help to correct that failure. An example is the information on jobs provided by job centres to those looking for work. They thus help the labour market to work better and increase the elasticity of supply of labour. Another example is the provision of consumer information: for example, on the effects of smoking, or of eating certain foodstuffs. Another is the provision of government statistics on prices, costs, employment, sales trends, etc. This enables firms to plan with greater certainty.

The direct provision of goods and services

In the case of public goods and services, such as streets, pavements, seaside illumination and national defence, the market may completely fail to provide. In this case the government must take over the role of provision. Central government, local government or some other public agency could provide these goods and services directly. Alternatively, they could pay private firms to do so. The public would pay through central and local taxation.

The government could also provide goods and services directly which are *not* public goods. Examples include health and education. There are four reasons why such things are provided free or at well below cost.

Social justice. Society may feel that these things should not be provided according to ability to pay. Rather they should be provided as of right: an equal right based on need.

Large positive externalities. People other than the consumer may benefit substantially. If a person decides to get treatment for an infectious disease, other people benefit by not being infected. A free health service thus helps to combat the spread of disease.

Dependants. If education were not free, and if the quality of education depended on the amount spent, and if parents could choose how much or little to buy, then the quality of children's education would depend not just on their parents' income, but also on how much they cared. A government may choose to provide such things free in order to protect children from 'bad' parents. A similar argument is used for providing free prescriptions and dental treatment for all children.

Ignorance. Consumers may not realise how much they will benefit. If they have to pay, they may choose (unwisely) to go without. Providing health care free may persuade people to consult their doctors for what they perceive to be a minor complaint, which is then diagnosed to be the first symptom of something serious.

19.4 The case for *laissez-faire*

Government intervention in the market can itself lead to problems. The case for non-intervention (*laissez-faire*) or very limited intervention is not that the market is the *perfect* means of achieving given social goals, but rather that the problems created by intervention are greater than the problems overcome by that intervention.

Drawbacks of government intervention

Shortages and surpluses. If the government intervenes by fixing prices at levels other than the equilibrium, this will create either shortages or surpluses.

If the price is fixed *below* the equilibrium, there will be a shortage. For example, if the rent of council houses is fixed below the equilibrium in order to provide cheap housing for poor people, demand will exceed supply. In the case of shortages resulting from fixing prices below the equilibrium, either the government will have to adopt a system of waiting lists, or rationing, or giving certain people preferential treatment, or alternatively it will have to allow allocation to be on a first-come, first-served basis or allow queues to develop. Black markets are likely to develop.

If the price is fixed *above* the equilibrium price, there will be a surplus. For example, if the price of food is fixed above the equilibrium in order to support farmers' incomes, supply will exceed demand. Either government will have to purchase such surpluses and then perhaps store them, throw them away or sell them cheaply in another market, or it will have to ration suppliers by allowing them to produce only a certain quota, or allow them to sell to whom they can.

Poor information. The government may not know the full costs and benefits of its policies. It may genuinely wish to pursue the interests of consumers or any other group and yet may be unaware of people's wishes or misinterpret their behaviour.

Bureaucracy and inefficiency. Government intervention involves administrative costs. The more wide reaching and detailed the intervention, the greater the number of people and material resources that will be involved. These resources may be used wastefully.

Lack of market incentives. If government intervention removes market forces or cushions their effect (by the use of subsidies, welfare provisions, guaranteed prices or wages, etc.), it may remove certain useful incentives. Subsidies may allow inefficient firms to survive. Welfare payments may discourage effort. The market may be imperfect, but it does tend to encourage efficiency by allowing the efficient to receive greater rewards.

Shifts in government policy. The economic efficiency of industry may suffer if government intervention changes too frequently. It makes it difficult for firms to plan if they cannot predict tax rates, subsidies, price and wage controls, etc.

Lack of freedom for the individual. One of the major arguments put forward by those advocating *laissez-faire* is that government intervention involves a loss of freedom for individuals to make economic choices. The argument is not just that the pursuit of individual gain is seen to lead to the social good, but that it is desirable in itself that individuals should be as free as possible to pursue their own interests with the minimum of government interference: that minimum being largely confined to the maintenance of laws consistent with the protection of life, liberty and property.

Advantages of the free market

Although markets in the real world are not perfect, even imperfect markets can be argued to have positive advantages over government provision or even government regulation. These might include the following.

Automatic adjustments. Government intervention requires administration. A free-market economy, on the other hand, leads to the automatic, albeit imperfect, adjustment to demand and supply changes.

Dynamic advantages of capitalism. The chances of making high monopoly/oligopoly profits will encourage capitalists to invest in new products and new techniques. Prices may be high initially, but consumers will gain from the extra choice of products. Furthermore, if profits are high, new firms will sooner or later break into the market and competition will ensue.

A high degree of competition even under monopoly/oligopoly. Even though an industry at first sight may seem to be highly monopolistic, competitive forces may still work as a result of the following:

- A fear that excessively high profits might encourage firms to attempt to break into the industry (assuming that the market is contestable).
- Competition from closely related industries (e.g. coach services for rail services, or electricity for gas).
- The threat of foreign competition.
- Countervailing powers. Large powerful producers often sell to large powerful buyers. For example, the power of detergent manufacturers to drive up the price of washing powder is countered by the power of supermarket chains to drive down the price at which they purchase it. Thus power is to some extent neutralised.
- The competition for corporate control (see page 224).

definition

Social responsibility
Where a firm takes into account the interests and concerns of a community rather than just its shareholders.

19.5 Firms and social responsibility

It is often assumed that firms are simply concerned to maximise profits: that they are not concerned with broader issues of **social responsibility**. What this assumption means is that firms are only concerned with the interests of shareholders (or managers) and are not concerned for the well-being of the community at large.

It is then argued, however, that competitive forces could result in society *benefiting* from the self-interested behaviour of firms: i.e. that profit maximisation will lead to social efficiency under conditions of perfect competition and the absence of externalities. But, as we have seen, in the real world markets are not perfect and there are often considerable externalities. In such cases, a lack of social responsibility on the part of firms can have profoundly adverse effects on society. Indeed, many forms of market failure can be attributed directly to business practices that could not be classified as 'socially responsible': advertising campaigns that seek to misinform, or in some way deceive the consumer; monopoly producers exploiting their monopoly position through charging excessively high prices; the conscious decision to ignore water and air pollution limits, knowing that the chances of being caught are slim.

So should businesses be simply concerned with profit, or should they take broader social issues into account? If they do behave in an anti-social way, is the only answer to rely on government intervention, or are there any social pressures that can be brought to bear to persuade businesses to modify their behaviour?

Two views of social responsibility

The classical view. According to this view, business managers are responsible only to their shareholders, and as such should be concerned solely with profit maximisation. If managers in their business decisions take into account a wider set of social responsibilities, not only will they tend to undermine the market mechanism, but they will be making social policy decisions in fields where they may have little skill or expertise. If being socially responsible ultimately reduces profits then the shareholder loses and managers have failed to discharge their duty. By diluting their purpose in pursuit of *social* goals, businesses extend their influence over society as a whole, which cannot be good given the lack of public accountability to which business leaders are subject.

The socioeconomic view. This view argues that the role of modern business has changed, and that society expects business to adhere to certain moral and social responsibilities. Modern businesses are seen as more than economic institutions, as they are actively involved in society's social, political and legal environments. As such, all businesses are responsible not only to their shareholders but to all **stakeholders**. Stakeholders are all those affected by the business's operations: not only shareholders, but workers, customers, suppliers, creditors and people living in the neighbourhood. Given the far-reaching environmental effects of many businesses, stakeholding might extend to the whole of society.

In this view of corporate social responsibility, it is not just a moral argument that managers should take into account broader social and environmental issues, but also a financial one. It is argued that a business will maximise profits over the *long term* only if its various social responsibilities are taken into account. If a business is seen as ignoring the interests of the wider community and failing to protect society's welfare, then this will be 'bad for business': the firm's reputation and image will suffer.

In many top corporations, **environmental scanning** is now an integral part of the planning process. This involves the business surveying changing social and political trends in order to remain in tune with consumer concerns. For

> **definition**
>
> **Stakeholder**
> An individual affected by the operations of a business.

> **definition**
>
> **Environmental scanning**
> Where a business surveys social and political trends in order to take account of changes in its decision-making process.

example, the general public's growing concern over 'green' issues has significantly influenced many businesses' product development programmes and R & D strategies (see Box 19.3). The more successful a business is in being able to associate the image of 'environmentally friendly' to a particular product or brand, the more likely it is to enhance its sales or establish a measure of brand loyalty, and thereby to strengthen its competitive position.

Many businesses today thus feel that it is not enough to be seen merely *complying* with laws on the environment, product standards or workplace conditions: i.e. just to be doing the legal minimum. There is now a growing philosophy of 'compliance plus', with many businesses competing against each other in terms of their social image.

But does social responsibility not impose costs on firms, which might more than offset any increase in revenue from increased sales? In fact, the opposite can occur. Socially responsible business can reduce the need for government regulation, and the subsequent costs and restrictions that such intervention places upon managerial decision making. Many industries prefer to be self-regulating, not just to avoid government interference and restrictions, but because they can achieve any given social goal at lower costs: after all, a firm is likely to be better placed than government to know how given standards can be met in its own specific case. It is nevertheless the case that there are still many firms that care little about the environment. For them, self-regulation might be preferred because it makes it easier for them to avoid their social responsibilities!

Economic performance and social responsibility

Those who support the classical view argue that 'socially responsible' business will generate costs, which in turn will detract from the business's economic performance. In contrast, supporters of the socioeconomic view argue that any costs incurred in the short run will be offset in the long run as the business retains and enhances its market position.

Unfortunately these arguments are hard to assess. While the short-term effects on costs of a given policy might be relatively easy to measure, the longer-term impact of socially responsible business behaviour is much harder to assess. First there is a problem in identifying precisely what will be entailed over the longer term by social responsibility. Then it is difficult to estimate its effect on profits, given the uncertainties over long-term changes in technology and reactions from competitors.

One way in which we might estimate the impact of social responsibility on business performance is to assess the performance of socially responsible or ethical *investment funds*.

Ethical investment funds (or **ethical unit trusts**) are funds made up of shares in businesses which meet certain ethical standards. Table 19.1 lists the positive and negative criteria used by Friends Provident to identify suitable (or unsuitable) firms for investment.

The performance of ethical investment funds, like that of more traditional non-ethical investment funds, varies widely. Table 19.2 gives some of the more established ethical funds in the UK. It can be seen that ethical funds appear to give as good a return on investment as non-ethical funds. This implies that being a socially responsible business has not significantly hindered business performance or reduced the attractiveness of such stock for investors.

definition

Ethical investment funds
Shares grouped together from companies that meet specified ethical standards.

| Table 19.1 | Friends Provident: ethical investment criteria |

Positive criteria for investing in a company's stock:
- Excellence of products and services which are of long-term benefit to the community.
- Conservation of energy or natural resources.
- Environmental improvement and pollution control.
- Good relations with customers and suppliers.
- High employee welfare standards.
- Strong community involvement.
- A good equal opportunities record.
- Companies which are open about their activities.

Negative criteria for not investing in a company's stock:
- Environmental destruction.
- Unnecessary exploitation of animals.
- Trade with oppressive regimes.
- Pornography.
- Weapons manufacture.
- Tobacco or alcohol production.
- Unsafe products or services.
- Offensive advertising.

In fact, in both the USA and the UK, ethical unit trusts are growing in popularity with shareholders. In the UK, the number of ethical funds is doubling every two years with UK investors putting in an estimated £2.1 billion. In the USA, an estimated $2.1 trillion (approximately £1.35 trillion) of mutual fund

| Table 19.2 | Ethical units trusts and their performance (all funds assumed to start from an initial investment of £1000) |

Fund name	Return over			
	1 year	2 years	5 years	10 years
Abbey Ethical	1226	1207	1762	2577
Allchurches Amity	1018	1028	1619	2159
AXA Sun Life Ethical CI A	1289	–	–	–
Credit Suisse Fellowship	1228	1236	2267	2614
Family Charities Ethical	1674	1758	1613	3955
EPAM Exempt Ethical	1243	1377	–	–
Friends Prov. Stewardship	1243	1297	2088	2768
Friends Prov. Stewardship Inc.	1076	1165	1499	2023
NPI Global Care Income Rtl	1222	1432	–	–
Scot Equitable Ethical A	1263	1266	2107	3004
Sovereign Ethical	1625	1592	2818	3355
Std Life UK Ethical Rtl	1141	–	–	–
Average of ethical funds	1284	1336	2097	2807
Average of all units trusts	1059	1079	1972	3054

Note: Where no figures are given, this is because the respective fund had not been running long enough.
Source: Adapted from *Money Management*, November 2000.

BOX 19.3

The Body Shop
Embodying social responsibility

The Body Shop shot to fame in the 1980s. It stood for environmental awareness and an ethical approach to business. But its success had as much to do with what it sold as what it stood for. It sold natural cosmetics, Raspberry Ripple Bathing Bubbles and Camomile Shampoo, products that were immensely popular with consumers.

Its profits increased from a little over £1 million in 1985 to £33.5 million in 1995. Sales, meanwhile, grew even more dramatically, from £4.9 million to £219.7 million over the same period.

What makes this success so remarkable is that The Body Shop does virtually no advertising. Its promotion has largely stemmed from the activities and environmental campaigning of its founder Anita Roddick, and the company's uncompromising claims that it sells only 'green' products and conducts its business operations with high ethical standards. It actively supports green causes such as saving whales and protecting rainforests, and it refuses to allow its products to be tested on animals. Perhaps most surprising in the world of big business has been its high-profile initiative 'trade not aid', whereby it claimed to pay 'fair' prices for its ingredients, especially those supplied from people in developing countries, who were open to exploitation by large companies.

The growth strategy of The Body Shop, since its founding in 1976, has focused upon developing a distinctive and highly innovative product range, and at the same time identifying such products with major social issues of the day such as the environment and animal rights.

In the 1990s, sales growth was less rapid and in 2000 Roddick announced that she was planning to leave the company. The day after the announcement, the following article appeared in *The Financial Times*.

... At the beginning it was a green fairy tale, the company's commitment to fair trade and the environment and its stance on animal testing was a combination that caught the imagination in the newly affluent 1980s. For over a decade sales and profits continued to grow, on average by 50 per cent a year. Franchises sprung up like mushrooms and following its flotation in 1984 the share price rose from just 5p to a high of 370p in 1992.

With a new shop opening every two and a half days it seemed as if nothing could go wrong for the Roddicks, that is, until they hit America. In 1988 they launched into the US market. Initially the venture was successful. The once successful franchising of the company soon began to disintegrate. "We just got everything wrong", said Ms Roddick, who was criticised for conducting no market research, paying scant attention to marketing and giving little thought to where the shops appeared.

By 1998 the company's earnings had collapsed by 90 per cent and the share price fell to under 117p.

In the City there was a certain amount of *schadenfreude*. Many investors were not impressed with Roddick's cuddly hippie attitude to business and analysts criticised the company for developing new products too quickly.

They were also unimpressed with Ms Roddick's off-hand attitude to finances, especially her comments that finance "bored the pants off her" and her frequent denouncements of the "pin-striped dinosaurs in Throgmorton Street".

When she was forced to step down as chief executive in 1998, following shareholder pressure for "positive and demonstrable change", she compared the experience to handing over a child to complete strangers.

The day-to-day running of Body Shop was handed over to Patrick Gournay, a former vice president at Groupe Danone and Ms Roddick became joint co-chairman with husband Gordon.

When Ms Roddick steps down she said the company will carry on its tradition of ethical trading, even when she leaves. But she will no longer have to "keep on emoting about the shape of a bottle or whether or not we should go for elderberry body butter."

Questions
1 What assumptions has The Body Shop made about the 'rational consumer'?
2 How would you describe the aims of The Body Shop?

and pension money has been put into what are deemed socially responsible stock. In 1999 alone, more than $1 trillion was pulled out of what are called 'sin' stock, i.e. industries such as tobacco, gambling, weapons and alcohol.

In addition to the performance of ethical investment funds, the success of many environmentally friendly and socially aware businesses shows what can be achieved. One such example – The Body Shop – is examined in Box 19.3.

SUMMARY

1 Government intervention in the market sets out to attain two goals: social efficiency and equity. Social efficiency is achieved at the point where the marginal benefits to society for either production or consumption are equal to the marginal costs of either production or consumption. Issues of equity are difficult to judge due to the subjective assessment of what is, and what is not, a fair distribution of resources.

2a Externalities are spillover costs or benefits. Whenever there are external costs, the market will (other things being equal) lead to a level of production and consumption above the socially efficient level. Whenever there are external benefits, the market will (other things being equal) lead to a level of production and consumption below the socially efficient level.

2b Monopoly power will (other things being equal) lead to a level of output below the socially efficient level. It will lead to a deadweight welfare loss: a loss of consumer plus producer surplus.

2c Ignorance and uncertainty may prevent people from consuming or producing at the levels they would otherwise choose. Information may sometimes be provided (at a price) by the market, but it may be imperfect; in some cases it may not be available at all.

2d Public goods will be underprovided by the market. The problem is that they have large external benefits relative to private benefits, and without government intervention it would not be possible to prevent people having a 'free ride' and thereby escaping contributing to their cost of production.

2e Markets may respond sluggishly to changes in demand and supply. The time lags in adjustment can lead to a permanent state of disequilibrium and to problems of instability.

2f In a free market there may be inadequate provision for dependants and an inadequate output of merit goods.

3a Taxes and subsidies are one means of correcting market distortions. Externalities can be corrected by imposing tax rates equal to the size of the marginal external cost, and granting rates of subsidy equal to marginal external benefits.

3b Taxes and subsidies can also be used to affect monopoly price, output and profit. Subsidies can be used to persuade a monopolist to increase output to the competitive level. Lump-sum taxes can be used to reduce monopoly profits without affecting price or output.

3c Taxes and subsidies have the advantages of 'internalising' externalities and of providing incentives to reduce external costs. On the other hand, they may be impractical to use when different rates are required for each case, or when it is impossible to know the full effects of the activities that the taxes or subsidies are being used to correct.

3d An extension of property rights may allow individuals to prevent others from imposing costs on them. This is not practical, however, when many people are affected to a small degree, or where several people are affected but differ in their attitudes towards what they want doing about the 'problem'.

3e Laws can be used to regulate activities that impose external costs, to regulate monopolies and oligopolies, and to provide consumer protection. Legal controls are often simpler and easier to operate than taxes, and are safer when the danger is potentially great. However, they tend to be rather a blunt weapon.

3f Regulatory bodies can be set up to monitor and control activities that are against the public interest (e.g. anti-competitive behaviour of oligopolists). They can conduct investigations of specific cases, but these may be expensive and time consuming, and may not be acted on by the authorities.

3g The government may provide information in cases where the private sector fails to provide an adequate level. It may also provide goods and services directly. These could be either public goods or other goods where the government feels that provision by the market is inadequate. The

SUMMARY

government could also influence production in publicly owned industries.

4a Government intervention in the market may lead to shortages or surpluses; it may be based on poor information; it may be costly in terms of administration; it may stifle incentives; it may be disruptive if government policies change too frequently; it may not represent the majority of voters' interests if the government is elected by a minority, or if voters did not fully understand the issues at election time, or if the policies were not in the government's manifesto; it may remove certain liberties.

4b By contrast, a free market leads to automatic adjustments to changes in economic conditions; the prospect of monopoly/oligopoly profits may stimulate risk taking and hence research and development and innovation, and this advantage may outweigh any problems of resource misallocation;

there may still be a high degree of actual or potential competition under monopoly and oligopoly.

5a There are two views of social responsibility. The first states that it should be of no concern to business, which would do best for society by serving the interests of its shareholders. Social policy should be left to politicians. The alternative view is that business needs to consider the impact of its actions upon society, and to take changing social and political considerations into account when making decisions. This is good business.

5b It is difficult to assess the costs and benefits to economic performance of adopting a socially responsible position.

5c Ethical investment funds have become more numerous, and companies' shares within these funds have, on the whole, done as well as those within non-ethical funds.

REVIEW QUESTIONS

1 Assume that a firm discharges waste into a river. As a result, the marginal social costs (*MSC*) are greater than the firm's marginal (private) costs (*MC*). The following table shows how *MC*, *MSC*, *AR* and *MR* vary with output.

Output	1	2	3	4	5	6	7	8
MC(£)	23	21	23	25	27	30	35	42
MSC(£)	35	34	38	42	46	52	60	72
TR(£)	60	102	138	168	195	219	238	252
AR(£)	60	51	46	42	39	36.5	34	31.5
MR(£)	60	42	36	30	27	24	19	14

(a) How much will the firm produce if it seeks to maximise profits?

(b) What is the socially efficient level of output (assuming no externalities on the demand side)?

(c) How much is the marginal external cost at this level of output?

(d) What size tax would be necessary for the firm to reduce its output to the socially efficient level?

(e) Why is the tax less than the marginal externality?

(f) Why might it be equitable to impose a lump-sum tax on this firm?

(g) Why will a lump-sum tax not affect the firm's output (assuming that in the long-run the firm can still make at least normal profit)?

2 Distinguish between publicly provided goods, public goods and merit goods.

3 Name some goods or services provided by the government or local authorities that are not public goods.

4 Some roads could be regarded as a public good, but some could be provided by the market. Which types of road could be provided by the market? Why? Would it be a good idea?

5 Assume that you wanted the information given in (a)–(h) below. In which cases could you (i) buy perfect information; (ii) buy imperfect information; (iii) be able to obtain information without paying for it; (iv) not be able to obtain information?
(a) Which washing machine is the most reliable?
(b) Which of two jobs that are vacant is the most satisfying?
(c) Which builder will repair my roof most cheaply?
(d) Which builder will make the best job of repairing my roof?
(e) Which builder is best value for money?
(f) How big a mortgage would it be wise for me to take out?
(g) What course of higher education should I follow?
(h) What brand of washing powder washes whiter?

In which cases are there non-monetary costs to you of finding out the information? How can you know whether the information you acquire is accurate or not?

6 Make a list of pieces of information a firm might want to know and consider whether it could buy the information and how reliable that information might be.

7 Why might it be better to ban certain activities that cause environmental damage rather than to tax them?

8 Consider the advantages and disadvantages of extending property rights so that everyone would have the right to prevent people imposing any costs on them whatsoever (or charging them to do so).

9 How suitable are legal restrictions in the following cases?
(a) Ensuring adequate vehicle safety (e.g. that tyres have sufficient tread or that the vehicle is roadworthy).
(b) Reducing traffic congestion.
(c) Preventing the use of monopoly power.
(d) Ensuring that mergers are in the public interest.
(e) Ensuring that firms charge a price equal to marginal cost.

10 Evaluate the following statement: 'Despite the weaknesses of a free market, the replacing of the market by the government generally makes the problem worse.'

11 In what ways might business be socially responsible?

12 What economic costs and benefits might a business experience if it decided to adopt a more socially responsible position? How might such costs and benefits change over the longer term?

20 Government and the firm

In this chapter we shall consider the relationship between government and the individual firm. This relationship is not simply one of regulation and control, but can involve the active intervention of government in attempting to improve the economic performance of business. We shall consider government attitudes and policy towards enhancing research and technology development, and training, as well as the more punitive area of business regulation through the use of monopolies and mergers legislation.

20.1 Policies towards monopolies and oligopolies

Competition policy in the European Union

EU legislation is contained in Articles 85 and 86 of the Treaty of Rome and, since 1990, in additional regulations covering mergers.

Article 85 is concerned with restrictive practices and Article 86 with monopolies and mergers. The Articles are largely confined to firms trading between EU members and thus do not cover monopolies or oligopolies operating solely within a member country. The policy is implemented by the European Commission. If any firm appears to be breaking the provisions of either of the Articles, the Commission can refer it to the European Court of Justice.

EU restrictive practices policy

Article 85 covers *agreements* between firms, *joint decisions*, and concerted *practices* which prevent, restrict or distort competition. In other words it covers all types of oligopolistic collusion that are against the interests of consumers.

Article 85 is not designed to prevent oligopolistic *structures* (i.e. the simple existence of co-operation between firms), but rather collusive *behaviour*. No matter what form collusion takes, if the European Commission finds that firms are committing anti-competitive *practices*, they will be banned from doing so and possibly fined (up to 10 per cent of annual turnover), although firms do have the right of appeal to the European Court of Justice.

Practices considered anti-competitive include firms colluding to do any of the following:

- Fix prices (i.e. above competitive levels).
- Limit production, markets, technical development or investment.
- Share out markets or sources of supply.
- Charge discriminatory prices or operate discriminatory trading conditions, such as to benefit the colluding parties and disadvantage others.

- Make other firms who sign contracts with any of the colluding firms accept unfavourable obligations which, by their nature, have no connection with the subject of such contracts.

In recent years the Commission has adopted a tough stance and has fined many firms.

EU monopoly policy

Article 86 relates to the abuse of market power and has also been extended to cover mergers. As with Article 85, it is the *behaviour* of firms that is the target of the legislation. The following are cited as examples of abuse of market power. As you can see, they are very similar to those in Article 85.

- Charging unfairly high prices to consumers, or paying unfairly low prices to suppliers.
- Limiting production, markets or technical developments to the detriment of consumers.
- Using price discrimination or other discriminatory practices to the detriment of certain parties.
- Making other firms who sign contracts with it accept unfavourable obligations which, by their nature, have no connection with the subject of such contracts.

Under Article 86, such practices can be banned and firms can be fined where they are found to have abused a dominant position. A firm does not have to have some specified minimum market share before Article 86 can be invoked. Instead, if firms are able to conduct anti-competitive practices, it is simply assumed that they must be in a position of market power. This approach is sensible, given the difficulties of identifying the boundaries of a market, either in terms of geography or in terms of type of product.

EU merger policy

The 1990 merger control measures tightened up the legislation in Article 86. They cover mergers where combined worldwide sales exceed €5 billion (approximately £4 billion); where EU sales of at least two of the companies exceed 250 million; and where at least one of the companies conducts no more than two-thirds of its EU-wide business in a single member state. (Less than €4 per cent of mergers involving European companies meet these conditions.)

Such mergers must be notified to the European Commission within one week of their announcement. The merger will then normally be suspended for three weeks. Within one month of the notification, the Commission, on the basis of preliminary investigations (Phase 1), must decide whether to conduct a formal investigation (Phase 2) or to let the merger proceed.

The 1990 measures have made the process of EU merger control very rapid and administratively inexpensive. The measures are also quite tough, if limited in scope (being confined to companies operating in more than one member country). Nevertheless several criticisms have been made of the system.

- The decisions of the Commission are often based on limited and poorly presented analysis and are inconsistent between different cases.
- The Commission, in being willing to show flexibility, can easily be

persuaded by firms, and the conditions imposed on them are often very lax and rely on the firms' co-operation.

● Not enough emphasis is placed on possible cost reductions from mergers. The stress is almost exclusively on questions of competition.

● In the first six years of the merger control measures, 398 mergers were notified, but only 27 proceeded to Phase 2. In many cases (too many, claim critics) the Commission accepted the undertakings of firms. By 1996, only five mergers had been prohibited.

There is considerable disagreement in the EU between those who want to encourage competition *within* the EU and those who want to see European companies being world leaders. For them, the ability to compete in *world* markets normally requires that companies are large, which may well imply having monopoly power within the EU.

UK competition policy

There have been substantial changes to UK competition policy since the first legislation was introduced in 1948 (see Table 20.1). The current approach is based largely on the 1998 Competition Act, which has brought UK policy in line with EU policy, detailed above. The Act has two key sets (or 'Chapters') of prohibitions. Chapter I prohibits various restrictive practices, and mirrors Article 85. Chapter II prohibits various abuses of monopoly power, and mirrors Article 86.

Under the Act, the body charged with ensuring that the prohibitions are carried out is the Office of Fair Trading (OFT). The OFT can investigate any firms suspected of engaging in one or more of the prohibited practices. Its officers have the power to enter and search premises and can require the produc-

Table 20.1 UK competition legislation

Year	Act	Provisions
1948	Monopolies and Restructive Practices Act	Set up Monopolies and Restrictive Practices Commission (MRC) to investigate suspected cases of abuse by a firm or group of firms of a dominant market position.
1956, 1968, 1976	Restrictive Trade Practices Act	Set up Restrictive Practices Court (RPC). All restrictive practices had to be registered. These would then have to be justified to the RPC. MRC renamed Monopolies Commission.
1964, 1976	Resale Prices Acts	Resale price maintenance banned unless firm could demonstrate to the RPC that it was in the public interest.
1965	Monopolies and Mergers Act	Role of Monopolies Commission now extended to examine mergers that would lead to a dominant market position.
1973	Fair Trading Act	Office of Fair Trading established. Its Director-General (DGFT) is responsible for referrals to the RPC or the renamed Monopolies and Mergers Commission (MMC).
1980	Competition Act	Various types of anti-competitive practice were specified. OFT would investigate alleged cases of such practices and possibly refer to MMC.
1989	Companies Act	Simplified and speeded-up mergers investigation procedures.
1998	Competition Act	Brought UK legislation in line with EU legislation. Chapter I prohibition applies to restrictive practices. Chapter II prohibition applies to the abuse of a dominant position. MMC replaced by Competition Commission.

tion and explanation of documents. Where the Director General of Fair Trading (DGFT), who is the head of the OFT, decides that an infringement of one of the prohibitions has occurred, he/she can direct the offending firms to modify their behaviour or cease their practices altogether. Companies in breach of a prohibition are liable to fines of up to 10 per cent of their annual UK turnover. Third parties adversely affected by such breaches can seek compensation through the courts.

The Act also set up a Competition Commission (CC) to which firms can appeal against the findings of the OFT. When an appeal is made, the CC conducts an investigation and makes a ruling.

UK restrictive practices policy

The pre-1998 position. On the surface, the approach adopted towards restrictive practices before 1998 *seemed* very tough. All firms with a formal agreement had to register it with the OFT. If the OFT considered that the agreement was anti-competitive, the firms could choose either to end the agreement or to be taken to the *Restrictive Practices Court* (wound up in 1998) to justify continuing with it. The Court would automatically terminate the agreement unless the firms could prove that it served the public interest.

Between 1956 (when restrictive practices legislation was introduced) and 1998, several thousand agreements were registered, but fewer than 1 per cent came before the Restrictive Practices Court. The remainder were ended voluntarily or judged by the OFT not to be anti-competitive.

Despite the apparent toughness of the policy, there were serious weaknesses. For example, providing no formal agreement was involved, collusion would fall outside the scope of the Restrictive Practices Court. The result was that firms were simply encouraged to engage in tacit collusion! In such cases, any anti-competitive practices would come under monopoly legislation, which, as we shall see below, was relatively weak. What is more, tacit collusion was hard to identify, especially given that the OFT did not have the power to enter and search business premises. Another problem was that, by focusing on *agreements* rather than anti-competitive *practices*, the legislation involved the OFT in having to consider many totally harmless agreements. Indeed, according to the OFT, over 90 per cent of such agreements had insignificant effects on competition.

To summarise: too many agreements were considered that should not have been; too few practices were considered that should have been; and the OFT's powers were too weak.

The current position. Under the Chapter I prohibition of the 1998 Act, any agreement or concerted practice that has the object or effect of preventing, restricting or distorting competition is illegal. The *form* of any agreement (if, indeed, a clearly delineated agreement actually exists) is irrelevant. It is the *effects* of oligopolistic collusion that are the object of the legislation. To contravene the Chapter I prohibition, the effects on competition should be appreciable. It is assumed under the Act that the effects of any agreement will not normally be appreciable if the firms' combined share is less than 25 per cent of the relevant market.

But what are the practices that the Act prohibits? These are identical to the five specified under Article 85 (see above). Within these five categories, the OFT identifies the following practices as being overtly collusive:

- Horizontal price-fixing agreements. These are agreements between competitors to set one or more of the following: fixed prices, minimum prices, the amount or percentage by which prices may be increased, or a range outside which prices may not move. The object is to restrict price competition and thus to keep prices higher than they would otherwise be.

- Vertical price-fixing agreements. These are price agreements between purchasing firms and their suppliers. An example of this is **resale price maintenance**. This is where a manufacturer or distributor sets the price for retailers to charge. It may well distribute a price list to retailers (e.g. a car manufacturer may distribute a price list to car showrooms). Resale price maintenance is a way of preventing competition between retailers driving down retail prices and ultimately the price they pay to the manufacturer. Both manufacturers and retailers, therefore, are likely to gain from resale price maintenance.

- Agreements to share out markets. These may be by geographical area, type or size of customer, or nature of outlet. By limiting or even eliminating competition within each part of the market, such agreements can be an effective means of keeping prices high (or quality low).

- Agreements to limit production. This may involve output quotas or a looser agreement not to increase output wherever this would drive down prices.

- Agreements to limit or co-ordinate investment. By restraining capacity, this will help firms to keep output down and prices up.

- **Collusive tendering**. This is where two or more firms put in a tender for a contract at secretly agreed (high) prices. A well-known case throughout most of the 1980s and 1990s was that of firms supplying ready-mixed concrete agreeing on prices they would tender to local authorities (see Box 20.1).

- Agreements between purchasers. These could be to reduce prices paid to suppliers. For example, large supermarkets could collude to keep prices low to farmers. An alternative form of agreement would be to deal with certain suppliers only.

- Agreements to exchange information which could have the effect of reducing competition. For example, if producers exchange information on their price intentions, it is a way of allowing price leadership, a form of tacit collusion, to continue.

- Agreements to boycott suppliers or distributors who deal with competitors to the colluding firms.

With all these types of agreements (formal or tacit) the Director General has the discretion to decide, on a case-by-case basis, whether or not competition is appreciably restricted, and whether, therefore, they should be terminated or the firms should be exempted. An exemption can be granted if the agreement is likely to lead to technical progress or more efficient production or distribution *and* if consumers benefit from the results.

UK monopoly policy

The pre-1998 position. Until 1998, the approach towards the abuse of monopoly power was relatively permissive. Suspected cases were initially investigated by the OFT (but only where the firm controlled over 25 per cent of the

---

definition

Resale price maintenance
Where the manufacturer of a product (legally) insists that the product should be sold at a specified retail price

---

definition

Collusive tendering
Where two or more firms secretly agree on the prices they will tender for a contract. These prices will be above those which would be put in under a genuinely competitive tendering process.

national or local market). If the OFT considered that firms were engaging in anti-competitive practices, it would first try to get them to comply voluntarily with its recommendations. Failing this, it would refer them to a body known as the *Monopolies and Mergers Commission* (MMC), which was the predecessor of the Competition Commission. The MMC, after an often lengthy investigation, would submit a report to the government trade minister (the Secretary of State for Trade and Industry), who would then decide if action needed taking.

The system was generally regarded as slow and ineffective. The MMC was often prepared to accept firms' assurances, and there was too little follow-up to ensure that firms stuck to their word. During an investigation, firms were free to continue with their behaviour, and even if that behaviour was eventually found to be anti-competitive, the penalties for continuing were relatively mild, and there were no fines for the initial offence. For most companies, then, referral to the MMC was not a serious worry, except for the time and expense that an MMC investigation would incur.

The current position. Under the Chapter II prohibition of the 1998 Competition Act, the policy towards firms with dominant market positions has become much tougher. It is illegal for a dominant firm to exercise its market power in such a way as to reduce competition. Any suspected case is investigated by the OFT, whose Director General of Fair Trading then decides whether a breach of the prohibition has taken place and if so can levy a fine of up to 10 per cent of annual UK turnover.

The OFT uses a two-stage process in deciding whether an abuse has taken place. The first stage is to establish whether a firm has a position of dominance. If it has, the second is to establish whether it is abusing that dominant position.

What constitutes market dominance? According to the OFT, a firm has market dominance if it is able to behave independently of competitive pressures, and can, as a result, charge higher prices than if it faced effective competition. In deciding which firms have dominance, the OFT uses two criteria.

The first is the firm's market share. Although there is no minimum share specified in the Act, the OFT considers that firms will normally need to have at least a 40 per cent share of the market (national or local, whichever is appropriate), if they are to have a position of dominance, although this figure will vary from industry to industry.

The second criterion is the contestability of the market in which the firm is operating (see section 11.4). The higher the barriers to the entry of new firms, the less contestable will be the market, and the more dominant a firm is likely to be for any given current market share. In looking at barriers, the OFT classifies them into three types:

- Absolute advantages. The dominant firm may have patents, copyright or ownership of key factors or outlets.
- Strategic advantages. The dominant firm has advantages from already being in the market. For example, new firms are likely to incur sunk costs (costs that occur on entry, but cannot be recovered on exit: e.g. specialised plant and equipment with little or no second-hand value).
- Expansionary behaviour. The dominant firm may deter entrants through its reputation for aggressive behaviour, such as charging predatory prices (see below), or doing deals with retailers to sell only its products.

If the firm *is* deemed to be dominant, the OFT then decides whether the firm's practices constitute an abuse of its position. As with restrictive practices, Chapter II follows EU legislation. It specifies the same four types of market abuse as does Article 86 (see above). Within these four categories, the OFT identifies the following practices as being overtly anti-competitive:

● Charging excessively high prices. These are prices above those the firm would charge if it faced effective competition. One sign of excessively high prices is abnormally high rates of profit.
● Price discrimination. This is only regarded as an abuse to the extent that the higher prices are excessive or the lower prices are used to exclude competitors.
● Predatory pricing. This is where prices are set at loss-making levels, so as to drive competitors out of business (see page 315). The test is to look at the dominant firm's price in relation to its average costs. If its price is below average variable cost, predation would be assumed. If its price is above average variable cost, but below average total cost, then the Director General would need to establish whether the reason was to eliminate a competitor.
● **Vertical restraints**. This is where a supplying firm imposes conditions on a purchasing firm (or vice versa). Examples include:
 – resale price maintenance. This comes under Chapter II rather than Chapter I, if there is no *agreement* between supplier and purchaser, but rather the *imposition* of conditions on the one by the other.
 – manufacturers imposing rules on retailers about displaying the product or the provision of after-sales service.
 – selective distribution: where manufacturers refuse to supply certain outlets (e.g. perfume manufacturers refusing to supply discount chains, such as Superdrug).
 – exclusive purchasing: where a retailer is only prepared to buy from a particular supplier.
 – **tie-in-sales**: where a firm controlling the supply of a first product insists that its customers buy a second product from it rather than from its rivals.
● Refusal to supply. A firm may refuse to supply competitors with key inputs, or it may be used as a vertical restraint to limit the number of outlets selling its products.

> **definition**
> **Vertical restraints**
> Conditions imposed by one firm on another which is either its supplier or its customer.

The simple *existence* of any of these practices may not constitute an abuse. The Director General has to decide whether their *effect* is to restrict competition. Unlike with the Chapter I prohibition, however, there are no exemptions. *If* the firm is abusing its power so as to restrict competition, then it is illegal.

UK merger policy

The 1998 Act did not cover merger policy. This is covered by the 1973 Fair Trading Act. Companies must give details of any proposed merger to the OFT. These details can be used by the DGFT in making recommendations to the minister, who might then require the firms to sell off some of their assets, so as to reduce the power that would result from the merger. Alternatively the minister could refer the merger to the Competition Commission (to the MMC prior to

> **definition**
> **Tie-in sales**
> Where a firm is only prepared to sell a first product on the condition that its customers buy a second product from it

1999). Whilst investigations are proceeding, companies involved may not acquire each other's shares. If no reference is made within twenty days of the receipt of the details, the merger may proceed.

If reference is made to the CC, there is no presumption that mergers are against the public interest. There are potential costs of greater market power in terms of higher prices and less choice, but also potential benefits from economies of scale, greater research and development, greater investment and greater power to compete internationally. After weighing up the evidence, the CC will recommend to the minister whether or not the merger, or parts of it, should be allowed to proceed.

The vast majority (over 97 per cent) of proposed mergers have not been referred to the CC (or MMC). However, of the 200 or so that have been referred since 1965 (the year when mergers were first investigated by the MMC), most have been abandoned or, after the MMC investigation, blocked by the minister.

This suggests that the policy has not been tough enough, with many mergers not been referred which should have been. Indeed, studies have shown that mergers have generally *not* been in the public interest. Significant benefits from cost reduction and research have not occurred, and yet mergers have contributed to a growing degree of market concentration in the UK. Several commentators have argued that the burden of proof ought to be changed so that the companies would have to demonstrate the *benefits* to the public of the merger if it were to be allowed to proceed.

Nevertheless, by toughening up policy towards the abuse of monopoly power, the 1998 Act has made it much more difficult for firms, once they have merged, to use their newly acquired power to engage in anti-competitive practices.

Assessment of EU and UK competition policy

With UK competition legislation having been brought in line with EU legislation it is possible to consider the two together.

It is generally agreed by commentators that the policy is correct to concentrate on anti-competitive *practices* and their *effects* rather than simply on the existence of agreements or on the size of a firm's market share. After all, economic power is only a problem when it is abused. When, by contrast, it enables firms to achieve economies of scale, or more finance for investment, the result can be to the benefit of consumers. In other words, the assumption that structure determines conduct and performance (see pages 14 and 211) is not necessarily true, and certainly it is not necessarily true that market power is always bad and competitive industries are always good.

Secondly, most commentators favour the system of certain practices being *prohibited*, with fines applicable to the first offence. This acts as an important deterrent to anti-competitive behaviour.

Similar conclusions have been reached in the USA, where the application of competition law has undergone changes in recent years. In the past, the focus was on the structure of an industry. Under the Sherman Act of 1890, oligopolistic collusion in the 'restraint of trade' was made illegal, as was any attempt to establish a monopoly. Although, under the Clayton Act of 1914, various potentially anti-competitive practices (such as price discrimination) were only illegal

BOX 20.1

Cartels set in concrete, steel and cardboard
Experiences in the UK and other European countries

A concrete supplier who attended cartel meetings ... was the key witness in last year's contempt case in which three Oxfordshire firms were fined a total of £56 000 plus costs and two employees were told they had narrowly escaped gaol sentences.

The witness told the Restrictive Practices Court in September that he had occasionally attended meetings between RMC (Thames Valley), Smiths Concrete, Hartigan Readymix, and Pioneer Concrete in 1983 and 1984. During these meetings, held at monthly intervals in pubs in Aylesbury, representatives of the four companies agreed market shares which were recorded in an allocation book. He kept a copy and sent it to the OFT in 1988...

At each meeting representatives would state new jobs they were aware of, discuss prices and decide which firm should get the contract. The other cartel members would then agree to tender higher prices.[1]

When it comes to restrictive practices, few industries can match the poor record of the building materials industry. Firms in many parts of the industry, from glass suppliers to concrete makers, have admitted to operating market share agreements, price rings and other forms of price fixing. The OFT alleges that, in the con-

crete industry alone, at least 29 producers ran over 65 cartels throughout the UK from the late 1970s to the early 1990s. The cost to the consumer is estimated to have been in the region of £65 million.

Such extensive collusion is not confined to the UK. There are many cases throughout Europe and the rest of the world.

The Directorate General IV (DGIV) of the European Competition Department has extensive powers to deal with anti-competitive practices. These powers include raiding companies, seizing documents and levying huge fines (up to 10 per cent of turnover).

In December 1994 record fines of €248 million were imposed on 33 European cement producers and eight national cement associations. It was found that the European Cement Association, by exchanging price information, had managed to reduce price differences between producers in different countries, removing any incentive to export cement overseas, and thereby ensuring that prices remained high. Those producers which did export were encouraged to set their prices at the same level as those of local producers.

Collusion has also been rife in the steel industry, but it is only in recent years that the EU has taken a tough stance against steel cartels. Indeed, in the 1970s the EC even encouraged collusion to help ease the effects of a depression in the steel market. Eurofer,

when they substantially lessened competition, the application of these two 'anti-trust' laws was largely directed to breaking up large firms. Today, the approach is to focus on efficiency, rather than on market share; and on the effects on consumers of any collusion or co-operation between firms, rather than on the simple collusion itself.

A problem with any policy to deal with collusion is the difficulty in rooting it out. When firms do all their deals 'behind closed doors' and are careful not to keep records or give clues, then collusion can be very hard to spot. The cases that have come to light, such as that of collusive tendering between firms supplying ready-mixed concrete, may be just the tip of an iceberg. Nevertheless, as we have seen, under both EU and UK legislation, the OFT has considerable powers of entry to and search of businesses, and can impose heavy fines on firms behaving anti-competitively. It is hoped that this is sufficient of a deterrent to prevent most firms from colluding, or exploiting their monopoly power, who would otherwise be tempted.

the European steel producers association, was established in 1976 and policed this collusion. What followed was a series of formal agreements between the main steel producers. Quotas were set; fines were imposed on members for quota violations; and committees were established to consider market forecasting and pricing.

However, the EC became increasingly unhappy with this collusion. Following a series of large Europe-wide price rises in steel, the Z Club, as it became known, was investigated in 1986, and members were fined.

Then in 1993 the DGIV investigated an alleged cartel between Europe's main steel producers in the supply of steel sections and heavy beams used in the construction industry. With a downturn in construction in the early 1990s, there should have been a fall in the price of steel. In fact, prices did not change. This led to claims that a price ring was in operation. For example, when European steel producers bid for UK contracts, they all tendered prices much the same as British Steel's, even though they could have offered prices some 20–30 per cent lower. In February 1994 the sixteen-strong European and Scandinavian cartel was found guilty by the Commission and fined €104 million. The largest single fine (€32 million) was imposed on British Steel.

In 1991, the same year as the investigation into the European steel industry, carton-board producers were subject to a 'dawn raid' by the Competition Department. Like the steel producers, the carton-board producers were found guilty of extensive price fixing and market manipulation. Operating in an association known as Product Group Paperboard, the cartel of nineteen producers met twelve times a year, most frequently in Zurich, but also in Nice and Barcelona. Behind the façade of a carton-board manufacturers' 'social gathering', the cartel members co-ordinated Europe-wide price rises. This was in part achieved by regulating the supply of carton-board (the largest producers in the cartel frequently engineered plant stoppages in order to keep production levels under control), and by the operation of a strict market-sharing arrangement.

The Commission found that, by controlling supply in this way and creating a shortage of board, the cartel managed to increase prices by 6–10 per cent twice each year from 1987 to 1990. This was in spite of a fall in raw material costs. In 1994 fines totalling €132 million were imposed on the nineteen-member cartel.

Question

If formal collusive arrangements can be discovered by 'dawn raids' and the seizing of incriminating paperwork, why do cartel members not rely on a much looser informal arrangement, with nothing in writing?

[1] *Building*, 27 September 1991.

20.2 Policies towards research and technology development (R&TD)

The impact of technology not only on the practice of business, but on the economy in general is vividly illustrated by the development and use of the Internet. In 1997, worldwide some 40 million people and 25 000 firms used the Internet. By early 2001, there were 400 million users. By 2005 the figure is forecast to be 1 billion. The commercial possibilities of the Internet range from the selling of information and services, to global forms of catalogue shopping where you can browse through a business's product range (or surf the net) and use your credit card number to pay. The Internet is just one example of how technology and technological change are shaping the whole structure and organisation of business (see Chapter 3 on the flat organisation), the experience of work for the worker, and the productivity of business and hence the competitive performance of national economies.

If a business fails to embrace new technology, its productivity and profitability will almost certainly lag behind those businesses that do. It is the same for countries. Unless they embrace new technology, the productivity gap between them and those that do is likely to widen. Once such a gap has been opened, it will prove very difficult to close. Those countries ahead in the technological race will tend to get further ahead as the dynamic forces of technology enhance their competitiveness, improve their profits, and provide yet greater potential for technological advance. How then might countries set about preventing such technological gaps opening, or, once they have become established, set about closing them?

Technology policy refers to a series of government initiatives to affect the process of technological change and its rate of adoption. The nature of the policy will depend on which stage of the introduction of new technology it is designed to affect. Three stages can be identified:

- *Invention*. In this initial stage, research leads to new ideas and new products. Sometimes the ideas arise from general research; sometimes the research is directed towards a particular goal, such as the development of a new type of car engine or computer chip.
- *Innovation*. In this stage, the new ideas are put into practice. A firm will introduce the new technology, and will hopefully gain a commercial advantage from so doing.
- *Diffusion*. In the final stage, the new products and processes are copied, and possibly adapted, by competitor firms. The effects of the new technology thus spread throughout the economy, affecting general productivity levels and competitiveness.

Technology policy can be focused on any or all of these stages of technological change.

Technological change and market failure

Why is a technology policy needed in the first place? The following reasons can be advanced to explain why the market system might fail to provide those factors vital to initiate technological change.

R&TD free riders. If an individual business can benefit from the results of *other* businesses conducting R&TD, with all its associated costs and risks, then it is less likely to conduct R&TD itself. It will simply 'free ride' on such activity. As a consequence, it would be in the interest of the firm conducting R&TD to keep its findings secret or under some kind of property right, such as a patent, so as to gain as much competitive advantage as possible from its investment.

Although it is desirable to encourage firms to conduct R&TD, and for this purpose it may be necessary to have a strict patent system in force, it is also desirable that there is the maximum *social* benefit from such R&TD. This would occur only if such findings were widely disseminated. It is thus important that technology policy finds the optimum balance between the two objectives of (a) encouraging individual firms to conduct research and (b) disseminating the results.

Monopolistic and oligopolistic market structures. The more a market is dominated by a few large producers, the less incentive they will have to conduct

R&TD and innovate as a means of reducing costs. The problem is most acute under monopoly. Nevertheless, despite a lower incentive to innovate, the higher profits of firms with monopoly power will at least put them in a position of being more able to afford to conduct research.

Duplication. Not only is it likely that there is too little R&TD being conducted, there is also the danger that resources may be wasted in duplicating research. The more firms there are conducting R&TD, the greater the likelihood of some form of duplication. Given the scarcity of R&TD resources, any duplication would be a highly inefficient way to organise production.

Risk and uncertainty. Because the payoffs from R&TD activity are so uncertain, there will tend to be a natural caution on the part of both the business conducting R&TD and (if different) the financier. Only R&TD activity which has a clear market potential, or is of low risk, is likely to be considered. It has been found that financial markets in particular will tend to adopt risk-averting strategy and fail to provide an adequate pool of long-term funds. This is another manifestation of the 'short-termism' we considered in section 18.4.

Forms of intervention

Attempts to correct the above market failures and develop a technology policy might include the use of the following.

The patent system. The strengthening of legal rights over the development of new products will encourage businesses to conduct R&TD, as they will be able to reap greater rewards from successful R&TD investment.

Public provision. In an attempt to overcome the free-rider problem and the inefficiency of R&TD duplication, government might provide R&TD itself, either through its own research institutions or via funding to university and other research councils. This is of particular importance in the case of basic research, where the potential outcomes are far less certain that those of applied research.

R&TD subsidies. If the government provided subsidies to businesses conducting R&TD activity, it not only would reduce the cost and hence the risk for business, but could ensure that the outcome from the R&TD activity is more rapidly diffused throughout the economy than might otherwise be expected. This would help improve general levels of technological innovation.

Co-operative R&TD. Given that the benefits of technological developments are of widespread use, the government could encourage co-operative R&TD. The government could take various roles here, from being actively involved in the R&TD process, to acting as a facilitator, bringing private-sector businesses together. The key advantages of this policy are that it will not only reduce the potential for duplication, but also encourage the pooling of scarce R&TD resources.

Diffusion policies. Such policies tend to be of two types: the provision of information concerning new technology, and the use of subsidies to encourage businesses to adopt new technology.

Other policies. A wide range of other policies, primarily adopted for other purposes, might also influence R&TD. These might include: education and training policy; competition policy; national defence policies and initiatives; and policies on standards and compatibility.

Technology policy in the UK and EU

The UK's poor technological performance since 1945 can be attributed to many factors, from a lack of entrepreneurial vision on the part of business, to the excessive short-termism of the UK's financial institutions. Equally there appears to have been a failure on the part of government to initiate suitable strategies to overcome such problems.

In the UK, the current attitude towards technology policy is one in which the role of government is kept to a minimum, and support is given only when 'a worthwhile and viable project is at risk through the failure of the market mechanism'. Actively interventionist strategies, such as the use of R&TD subsidies, are kept to a minimum, and the emphasis of policy is to encourage greater collaboration between companies within the private sector.

This strategy does not appear to have been very successful. Since 1990, UK gross expenditure on research and development (GERD) as a percentage of GDP has been lower than that of its main economic rivals (see Figure 20.1).

In contrast to the UK's approach to R&TD, the EU is more interventionist, and attempts to provide a unified strategy of R&TD subsidies and collaborative R&TD research programmes. EU initiatives range from general programmes such as the European Strategic Programme for Research in Information Technology (ESPRIT), to specific research fields such as that of medicine and health (BIOMED) and communications technology and services (ACTS), to name but two from a wide range of such initiatives. The EU research and tech-

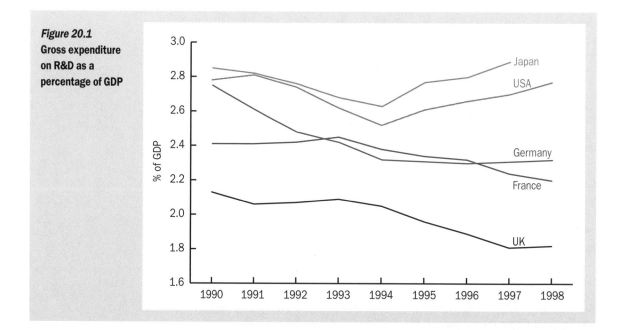

Figure 20.1
Gross expenditure on R&D as a percentage of GDP

nology programme operates within a five-year framework. The fifth research programme, which runs from 1998–2002, has a budget of €14.9 billion.

The EU has in recent years attempted to encourage greater levels of inter-European collaboration on research and technology projects. The European Research Co-ordination Agency (EUREKA) was set up in 1985 (although not formally an EU programme it receives EU backing and funds) and includes all members of the EU and those of EFTA. The European Scientific and Technical Co-operation programme (COST) has a wider membership than EUREKA and extends to businesses in central and eastern Europe. The role of both schemes is to co-ordinate the activities of private business, providing, in most cases, only limited funds. The approach here, therefore, is similar to that adopted in the UK.

Even given the active participation of the EU in funding and encouraging R&TD, there is still some doubt as to whether the various programmes receive adequate finance: whether, if European countries are to remain competitive with their main economic rivals (the USA, Japan and other south-east Asian countries), yet more might be required.

20.3 Policies towards training

It is generally recognised by economists and politicians alike that improvements in training and education can yield significant supply-side gains. Indeed, the UK's failure to invest as much in training as many of its major competitors is seen as a key explanation for the country's poor economic performance since the early 1970s. In the UK some 62 per cent of the manufacturing labour force have no vocational qualifications. In Germany the figure is less than 30 per cent.

Training and economic performance

Training and economic performance are linked in three main ways.

Labour productivity. In various studies comparing the productivity of UK and German industry, education and training was seen as the principal reason for the productivity gap between the two countries. In 1992 this gap was estimated at 22 per cent, of which nearly half was due to the superior skills of German workers.

Innovation and change. A key factor in shaping a firm's willingness to introduce new products or processes will be the adaptability and skills of its workforce. If the firm has to spend a lot of money on retraining, or on attracting skilled workers away from other firms, the costs may prove prohibitive.

Costs of production. A shortage of skilled workers will quickly create labour bottlenecks and cause production costs to increase. This will stifle economic growth.

Training policy

If training is left to the employer, the benefits will become an externality if the workers leave to work elsewhere. Society has benefited from the training, but

BOX 20.2

The R&D scoreboard

For many years it has been suggested that the UK's poor international competitive record has been in no small part due to its failure to invest in research and development. The UK's R&D intensity – that is, the ratio of R&D spending to sales – has been considerably lower than that of its main economic rivals.

Each year the Department of Trade and Industry publishes an R&D Scoreboard. This gives details of the R&D expenditures of the top R&D spending companies in the UK and worldwide. The two tables give extracts from the 2000 Scoreboard (which gives figures for 1999).

The following is an extract from the 'Highlights' of the Scoreboard[1]

R&D sector mix

Sector mix in the UK is very different from that internationally:

- The R&D intensive part of the UK economy is skewed towards chemistry-based (including biology) industries; 60% compared with 40% for physics-based (including engineering). Internationally, physics-based companies dominate with 70%.

- 39% of UK R&D is contributed by one sector – pharmaceuticals – compared with 45% for the top two international sectors (26% IT hardware and 19% automotive).

- The UK Scoreboard has a much higher proportion of its total company sales in low R&D intensive sectors such as oils and construction – nearly 50%, compared with only 12% for the international Scoreboard and 22% for the US.

R&D sector intensity

R&D intensity (R&D as % of sales) is an important comparator at both national and sector levels:

- The overall average UK R&D intensity of 2.1% is less than half the US figure.

- UK R&D intensity is above international levels for the leading sectors – pharmaceuticals and aerospace – and below for most other high and low technology sectors.

- Foreign-owned UK companies contribute significantly to R&D – up to 75% in some sectors – but tend to invest at a lower intensity than either UK or international averages.

(a) World top 21 R&D spenders (1999)

	Industry	Current R&D spending (£m)	% change over previous year	Sales (£m)	R&D (% of sales)
Ford Motor, USA	Automobiles	4 405	13	100 861	4.4
General Motors, USA	Automobiles	4 219	−14	103 846	4.1
DaimlerChrysler, Germany	Automobiles	3 568	15	93 274	3.8
Siemens, Germany	Electronic & electrical	3 133	8	42 653	7.3
IBM, USA	IT hardware	3 127	7	54 320	5.8
Matsushita Electric, Japan	Electronic & electrical	3 031	4	46 313	6.5
Hitachi, Japan	IT hardware	3 011	−3	48 355	6.2
Toyota Motor, Japan	Automobiles	2 954	10	77 337	3.8
Lucent Technologies, USA	IT hardware	2 798	23	23 776	11.8
Ericsson Telefon, Sweden	IT hardware	2 406	18	15 644	15.4
Fujitsu, Japan	IT hardware	2 395	2	31 782	7.5
Volkswagen, Germany	Automobiles	2 356	26	46 748	5.0
NTT, Japan	Telecommunications	2 314	32	58 982	3.9
Sony, Japan	Household goods	2 275	18	38 887	5.9
Motorola, USA	IT hardware	2 133	19	19 192	11.1
NEC, Japan	IT hardware	2 099	−9	28 848	7.3
Intel, USA	IT hardware	1 930	24	18 235	10.6
Toshiba, Japan	IT hardware	1 920	−2	32 134	6.0
Honda Motor, Japan	Automobiles	1 889	9	37 771	5.0
Microsoft, USA	Software & IT services	1 843	6	12 252	15.0
AstraZeneca, UK	Pharmaceuticals	1 813	18	11 444	15.8

Source: Adapted from *R&D Scoreboard*, 2000 (http://www.innovation.gov.uk/finance/rndscore_2000/database/2000csv) (DTI).

R&D and performance

R&D is positively linked to company performance measures:

- *Sales growth.* 40% growth over four years is 75% more likely for high compared to low R&D intensity companies.
- *Productivity.* Generally in high R&D intensity sectors, sales per employee is at least doubled between the high and low spenders measured by R&D per employee.
- *Market value.* Over five years to July 1999, a portfolio of high R&D intensity companies showed twice the market value growth of the FTSE. Since then the relative value has doubled again.

R&D challenge

Given the links between R&D intensity and company performance, and given that:

- overall R&D in the UK represents only one seventh of companies' overall surplus compared with a quarter in the US;
- UK investment in several high intensity sectors

is below international levels in both proportion and intensity; and

- companies investing at high R&D intensity (over 10%) represent 25% of the US Scoreboard but only 4% of a comparable UK sample,

the challenge is for management and investors to identify those sectors where there are opportunities for further quality R&D projects and then invest to generate improved future performance.

Questions

1 What are the economic costs and benefits of R&D spending to the national economy? Distinguish between the short and long run.
2 R&D is only one indicator, albeit an important one, of innovation potential. What other factors are likely to affect innovation?
3 What is the economic case for and against government intervention in the field of R&D?

[1] http://www.innovation.gov.uk/finance/rndscore_2000/introfr.html

(b) UK top 20 R&D spenders (1999)

	Industry	Current R&D spending (£m)	% change over previous year	Sales (£m)	R&D (% of sales)
All companies composite		13 016	8	624 207	2.1
AstraZeneca	Pharmaceuticals	1 813	18	11 444	15.8
Glaxo Wellcome	Pharmaceuticals	1 269	9	8 490	14.9
SmithKline Beecham	Pharmaceuticals	1 018	12	8 381	12.1
BAE Systems	Aerospace & defence	693	61	7 043	9.8
Unilever	Food processors	616	11	26 994	2.3
Marconi	IT hardware	471	64	5 437	8.7
Invensys	Electronic & electrical	378	17	9 034	4.2
Ford	Automobiles	372	−14	8 048	4.6
BT	Telecommunications	345	29	18 715	1.8
Pfizer	Pharmaceuticals	329	26	897	36.6
Shell	Oil & gas	313	−37	65 376	0.5
Rolls-Royce	Aerospace & defence	215	24	4 744	4.5
Reuters	Media & photography	197	−2	3 125	6.3
BP Amoco	Oil & gas	192	−25	51 850	0.4
ICI	Chemicals	181	−19	8 449	2.1
Nycomed Amersham	Health	129	−1	1 292	10.0
IBM	Software & IT services	118	0	5 201	2.3
ICL	Software & IT services	107	50	3 356	3.2
GKN	Automobiles	87	0	3 708	2.3
Roche Products	Pharmaceuticals	77	17	425	18.1

Source: Adapted from *R&D Scoreboard*, 2000 (http://www.innovation.gov.uk/finance/rndscore_2000/database/2000csv) (DTI).

the firm has not. The free market, therefore, will provide a less than optimal amount of training. The more mobile the labour force, and the more 'transferable' the skills acquired from training, the more likely it is that workers will leave, and the less willing will firms be to invest in training.

In the UK, there is a high level of labour turnover. What is more, wage differentials between skilled and unskilled workers are narrower than in many other countries, and so there is less incentive for workers to train.

How can increased training be achieved? There are three broad approaches:

● Workers could be encouraged to stay with their employer so that employers would be more willing to invest in training. Externalities would be reduced.
● The government could provide subsidies for training. Alternatively, the government or some other agency could provide education and training directly.
● Firms could co-operate to prevent 'poaching' and set up industry-wide training programmes, perhaps in partnership with the government and unions.

Training policy in various countries

As far as the first approach is concerned, most countries have seen a movement towards *greater* labour mobility. The rise in the 'flexible firm' has involved the employment of fewer permanent workers and more part-time and temporary workers. Some countries, such as Japan and Germany, however, have a generally lower rate of labour turnover than most. In Japan, in particular, it is common for workers to stay with one employer throughout their career. There the relationship between employer and employee extends well beyond a simple short-term economic arrangement. Workers give loyalty and commitment to their employer, which in return virtually guarantees long-term employment and provides various fringe benefits (such as housing, child care, holiday schemes and health care). It is not surprising that Japanese firms invest highly in training.

In the USA, labour turnover is very high and yet there is little in the way of industry-wide training. Instead, by having a high percentage of young people in further and higher education, the US government hopes that sufficient numbers and quality of workers are available for industry. Almost 30 per cent of the US population graduates, and only just over 0.2 per cent of GDP is spent on training. The problem with the US approach is that many non-graduates are unskilled and receive no training at all.

In Germany the proportion of graduates is considerably lower (less than 14 per cent), but expenditure on training accounts for nearly 1.6 per cent of GDP. Most young people who do not enter higher education embark on some form of apprenticeship. They attend school for part of the week, and receive work-based training for the rest. The state, unions and employers' associations work closely in determining training provision, and they have developed a set of vocational qualifications based around the apprenticeship system. Given that virtually all firms are involved in training, the 'free-rider' problem of firms poaching labour without themselves paying for training is virtually eliminated. The result is that the German workforce is highly skilled. Many of the skills, however, are highly specific. This is a problem when the demand for particular skills declines.

BOX 20.3

The cost of having a skills shortage
Can we leave it to the market?

The UK has a skills shortage. This is hardly surprising: it is a classic sign of an economy that has experienced strong growth over a number of years. If the skills shortage is not addressed, however, the next stage would be a rise in wages and a slowdown in economic growth. Indeed, some are claiming that by 'leaving it to the market', and failing to plug the skills gap, especially in training IT professionals, the economy loses out – not just in the short-run cycle of boom and bust, but over the longer term as well.

In the following extract, taken from *The Guardian* of 23 March 2000, the costs to the EU of having a shortage of IT workers is assessed.

> Between now and 2003, Western Europe stands to lose €380 billion (£232.3 billion) due to the shortage of skilled IT staff.
>
> The figure comes from studies undertaken by researchers Datamonitor, IDC, and Goldman Sachs which, put together, read like a rather grim good news/bad news joke both for the IT industry and the economy in general. The good news, according to a Goldman Sachs report entitled *The Shocking Economic Effect of B2B*, is that business to business (B2B) e-commerce has the potential to increase GDP by 5% over two decades. Better yet says Datamonitor, productivity gains alone from IT could boost EU GDP by 1.5% through 2002.
>
> The bad news is that those figures are dependent on the European countries coming up with an estimated 1.7 million IT professionals who are currently nowhere to be found. As well as losing out on productivity, the EU is set to miss out on €60 billion (£36.7 billion) in tax revenue (personal and corporation) over the next three years unless it plugs the skills gap.
>
> The punchline to the joke is that figures from IDC see demand for IT professionals in the EU topping 13.07 million by 2003, while the supply of same is expected to reach 11.33 million at best. The argument of Microsoft and much of the IT industry is that if the EU is going to put full employment at the top of its wish list, then for the sake of commerce and of its own coffers it should focus on plugging the skills gap.
>
> True, only 5% of the EU workforce is employed in IT, but with an average annual wage of €48 000 (£29 341), compared with the overall average annual wage of €28 700 (£17 543), they contribute heavily in tax. Ironically, as the skills shortage continues, and those wages rise, their individual worth to the EU increases correspondingly. In short, expensive though it may be to train IT staff, their return, both direct and indirect, makes it eminently desirable to cultivate them as the cash cows of GDP.

Question
What solutions might be offered to resolve the EU's IT skills shortage?

In the UK, the former Conservative government's attitude toward training was initially influenced by its free-market approach to supply-side policy. Training was to be left largely to employers. Government schemes such as the Youth Training Scheme (YTS), first introduced in 1983, were seen mainly as a means of reducing youth unemployment, rather than as a means of improving labour productivity. The 'training' element was often very limited or non-existent.

However, with growing worries over the UK's 'productivity gap', the government set up Training and Enterprise Councils (TECs) in 1988. The TECs were to be government funded, and to be responsible for identifying regional skill needs and the manner in which training was to be conducted. By 1998, the TECs' combined budget was approximately £1.3 billion. It bought 403 000 training places: 143 000 for those aged 16 to 24, 133 000 modern apprenticeships and 127 000 adult work-based training places.

Even though most TECs' training records have been good, the future of the TEC system is in doubt. The Department for Education and Employment revealed that the cost of delivering an NVQ3 level qualification through a TEC was £8900, compared with £3900 at a college.

In 1991 the National Vocational Qualification (NVQ) was launched. Students work for an employer and receive on-the-job training. They also attend college on an occasional basis. The NVQ is awarded when they have achieved sufficient experience. In addition, the government launched General National Vocational Qualifications (GNVQs). These further-education qualifications were aimed to bridge the gap between education and work, by ensuring that education was more work relevant.

The GNVQ system was modelled on that in France, where a clear vocational educational route is seen as the key to reducing skills shortages. At the age of fourteen, French students can choose to pursue academic or vocational education routes. The vocational route provides high-level, broad-based skills (unlike in Germany, where skills tend to be more job specific).

Critics of the UK strategy argue that it fails to address fundamental problems of funding, co-ordination and labour market flexibility. Employers still face the threat of having newly trained labour poached; the regional activities of the TECs fail to account for national, long-term training issues; and NVQs often provide too narrow forms of training. Most importantly, the funding devoted to training (0.5 per cent of GDP) is still low compared with most other industrialised countries. Critics claim that the UK system has the worst features of both the US and the German systems: too little training and too specific training.

The failure of the UK to close the productivity gap with the likes of Germany and France, and the continued shortfall in the proportion of adults achieving qualifications at technician and intermediate level, have led the UK government once again to reassess the country's training provision. In a move to co-ordinate training nationally, a new National Learning and Skills Council (NSC) was created, and began operating in April 2001. The NSC co-ordinates a local network of Learning and Skills Councils. These councils have replaced the network of TECs with their links into local skill requirements. In an attempt to improve the quality of training provision, a new independent inspectorate has been created to ensure that funding is closely linked to training outcomes. With an initial budget of £5 billion, it is hoped that the new NSC will deliver what previous training arrangements have failed to do – a closing of the training gap between the UK and its economic rivals.

SUMMARY

1a Competition policy in most countries recognises that monopolies, mergers and restrictive practices can bring both costs and benefits to the consumer. Generally, though, restrictive practices tend to be more damaging to consumers' interests than simple monopoly power or mergers.

1b European Union legislation applies to firms trading between EU countries. Article 85 applies to restrictive practices. Article 86 applies to dominant firms. There are also separate merger control provisions.

1c UK legislation is largely covered by the 1998 Competition Act. The Chapter I prohibition applies to restrictive practices and is similar to Article 85. The Chapter II prohibition applies to dominant firms and is similar to Article 86. Mergers are governed by the 1973 Fair Trading Act.

1d The focus of both EU and UK legislation is on anti-

SUMMARY

competitive practices rather than on the simple existence of agreements between firms or market dominance. Practices that are found after investigation to be detrimental to competition are prohibited and heavy fines can be imposed, even for a first offence.

2a The importance of technology in determining national economic success is growing. There is now a need for government to formulate a technology policy to ensure that the national economy has every chance to remain competitive.

2b Technological change, when left to the market, is unlikely to proceed rapidly enough or to a socially desirable level. Reasons for this include R&TD free riders, monopolistic market structures, duplication of R&TD activities, and risk and uncertainty.

2c Government technology policy might involve intervention at different levels of the technology process (invention, innovation and diffusion). Such intervention might involve extending ownership rights over new products, providing R&TD directly or using subsidies to encourage third parties.

Government might also act in an advisory/co-ordinating capacity.

2d Technology policy in the UK has tended to emphasise the market as the principal provider of technological change. Where possible, government's role has been kept to a minimum. Within the EU, policy has been more interventionist and a wide range of initiatives have been launched to encourage greater levels of R&TD.

3a A well-trained workforce contributes to economic performance by enhancing productivity, encouraging and enabling change, and, in respect to supplying scarce skills to the workplace, helps to reduce wage costs.

3b Training policy in the UK has largely been the responsibility of industry. The result has been a less than optimum amount of training. In other countries, such as Germany, the state plays a far greater role in training provision. Since 1979 training and education policy in the UK has become increasingly vocational.

REVIEW QUESTIONS

1 Try to formulate a definition of the public interest.

2 What are the advantages of the current system of controlling restrictive practices over the pre-1998 one?

3 What problems are likely to arise in identifying which firms' practices are anti-competitive? Should the OFT take firms' assurances into account when deciding whether to grant an exemption?

4 If anti-monopoly legislation is effective enough, is there ever any need to prevent mergers from going ahead?

5 If two or more firms were charging similar prices, what types of evidence would you look for to prove that this was collusion rather than mere coincidence?

6 Should governments or regulators always attempt to eliminate the supernormal profits of monopolists/oligopolists?

7 We can distinguish three clear stages in the development and application of technology: invention, innovation and diffusion. How might forms of technology policy intervention change at each stage of this process?

8 Governments and educationalists generally regard it as desirable that trainees acquire transferable skills. Why may many employers disagree?

9 There are externalities (benefits) when employers provide training. What externalities are there from the undergoing of training by the individual? Do they imply that individuals will choose to receive more or less than the socially optimal amount of training?

Government and the market

In the previous chapter we considered examples of the relationship between the government and the individual firm. In this chapter we turn to examine government policy at the level of the whole market. Although such policies are generally directed at a whole industry or sector, they nevertheless still affect individual businesses, and indeed the effects may well vary from one firm to another.

21.1 Environmental policy

Growing concerns over acid rain, the depletion of the ozone layer, industrial and domestic waste, traffic fumes and other forms of pollution have made the protection of the environment a major political and economic issue. The subject of environmental deterioration lies clearly within the realm of economics, since it is a direct consequence of production and consumption decisions. So how can economic analysis help us to understand the nature of the problem and contribute to the designing of an effective environmental policy?

The environment and production

In Chapter 19 we considered how pollution could be classified as a 'negative externality' of production or consumption. In the case of production, this means that the marginal social costs (MSC) are greater than the marginal private costs (MC) to the polluter. The failure of the market system to equate MSC and marginal social benefit (MSB) is due to the lack of property rights of those suffering the pollution. The fact that no charge is levied on the producer for use of the air or rivers means that the environment is effectively a free good, and as such is overused.

In order to ensure that the environment is taken sufficiently into account by both firms and consumers, the government must intervene. It must devise an appropriate **environmental policy**. Such a policy will involve measures to ensure that at least a specified minimum level of environmental quality is achieved, and ideally that all externalities are fully 'internalised'. This means that firms and consumers are forced to pay the *full* costs of production or consumption: i.e. their marginal private costs *plus* any external costs.

Problems with policy intervention

Valuing the environment

The principal difficulty facing government in constructing its environmental policy is that of *valuing* the environment and hence of estimating the costs of its pollution. If policy is based upon the principle that the polluter pays, then an accurate assessment of pollution costs is vital if the policy is to establish a socially efficient level of production.

Three common methods used for valuing environmental damage are: the financial costs to *other* users; revealed preferences; and 'contingent valuation' (or stated preference).

The financial costs to other users. In this method, environmental costs are calculated by considering the financial costs imposed on other businesses or individuals by polluting activities. For example, if firm A feeds chemical waste into a local stream, then firm B, which is downstream and requires a clean water supply, may have to introduce a water purification process. The expense of this to firm B can be seen as an external cost of firm A.

The main problem with this method is that not all external costs entail a direct financial cost for the sufferers. Many external costs may therefore be overlooked.

Revealed preferences. If the direct financial costs of pollution are difficult to identify, let alone calculate, then an alternative approach to valuing the environment might be to consider how individuals or businesses change their *behaviour* in response to environmental changes. Such changes in behaviour frequently carry a financial cost, which makes calculation easier. For example, the building of a new superstore on a greenfield site overlooked by your house might cause you to move. Moving house entails a financial cost, including the loss in value of your property resulting from the opening of the store. Clearly, in such a case, by choosing to move you would be regarding the cost of moving to be less than the cost to you of the deterioration in your environment.

Contingency valuation. In this method, people likely to be affected are asked to evaluate the effect on them of any proposed change to their environment. In the case of the superstore, local residents might be asked how much they would be willing to pay in order for the development not to take place, or alternatively, how much they would need to be compensated if it were to take place.

The principal concern with this method is how reliable the answers are to the questionnaires. There are two major problems:

- Ignorance. People will not know just how much they will suffer *until* the project goes ahead.
- Dishonesty. People will tend to exaggerate the compensation they would need. After all, if compensation is actually going to be paid, people will want to get as much as possible. But even if it is not, the more people exaggerate the costs to them, the more likely it is that they can get the project stopped.

These problems can be lessened if people are questioned who have already experienced a similar project elsewhere. They are more knowledgeable and have less to gain from being dishonest.

Research on contingency valuation has focused heavily on the questioning process and how monetary values of costs and benefits might be accurately established. Of all the methods, contingency valuation has grown most in popularity over recent years, despite its limitations.

BOX 21.1

Environmental auditing

As environmental issues have grown in importance over the past 20 years, so businesses have been forced to take a closer look at their environmental management. The main way in which this has been done is through the undertaking of an *environmental audit*.

An environmental audit involves the business looking at the environmental impact of using inputs and producing output. So, for example, what are the environmental consequences of bringing raw materials into the factory (e.g. from transporting large amounts of raw materials across long distances)? What environmental consequences are there from the process of production (e.g. from the creation of waste products and pollution)?

The environmental audit has its origins in the USA and was initially undertaken by many businesses as a way of ensuring compliance with government environmental legislation. Legislation in the USA during the 1970s and 1980s, such as the Clean Air Act, made business increasingly responsible for the pollution it caused. It was based on the polluter-pays principle. The environmental audit was therefore seen as a way of helping the business avoid liability for pollution damage, by giving it information on which to base improvements in its environmental management.

The practice of the environmental audit became more widespread during the 1980s. Its arrival in Europe came primarily from the activities of American business subsidiaries. It was not long, however, before many European firms undertook environmental audits themselves, not initially to ensure compliance to legislation, which in Europe was considerably less stringent than in the USA, but to declare their environmental awareness and project a responsible environmental image.

The conducting of the environmental audit is not as yet compulsory within the EU. However, with growing regulations on pollution, the desire for 'eco-labelling' by retailers and consumers, and the establishment of green investing schemes, such environmental audits will become increasingly necessary and commonplace.

Questions

1. What problems are environmental auditors likely to face when attempting to cost the environment?
2. Is environmental auditing consistent with the objective of profit maximisation? Does government environmental legislation make it more so?

Other problems

As well as the problems of value, other aspects of environmental damage make policy making particularly difficult. These include the following:

- Spatial issues. The place where pollution is produced and the places where it is deposited may be geographically very far apart. Pollution crosses borders (e.g. acid rain) or can be global (e.g. greenhouse gases). In both cases, national policies might be of little value, especially if you are a receiver of others' pollution! In such circumstances, international agreements would be needed, and these can be very difficult to reach.

- Temporal issues. Environmental problems such as acid rain and the depletion of the ozone layer have been occurring over many decades. Thus the full effect of pollution on the environment may be identifiable only in the long term. As a consequence, policy initiatives are required to be forward looking and proactive, if the cumulative effects of pollution are to be avoided. Most policy tends to be *reactive*, however, dealing only with problems as they arise. In such cases, damage to the environment may have already been done.

- Irreversibility issues. Much environmental damage might be irreversible: once a species is extinct, for example, it cannot be reintroduced.

Table 21.1 Taxes and charges with beneficial environmental effects: 1997

	Australia	*Belgium*	*Denmark*	*France*	*Germany*	*Hungary*	*Ireland*	*Japan*	*Netherlands*	*Norway*	*Sweden*	*UK*	*USA*
Motor fuel													
Leaded unleaded	●	●	●	●	●	●	●		●	●	●	●	
Diesel (quality differential)			●			●				●	●		
Carbon/energy taxation			●						●	●	●		
Sulphur tax										●	●		
Other excise duties	●	●	●	●	●	●	●	●	●	●	●	●	●
Other energy products													
Carbon/energy tax		●	●						●	●	●		
Sulphur tax or charge		●	●	●				●		●	●		
NO$_2$ charge				●							●		
Other excise duties	●	●	●	●	●	●	●	●	●	●	●	●	●
Vehicle-related taxation													
Large cars > small cars: sales tax		●	●			●	●		●				●
Large cars > small cars: road tax		●	●	●	●	●			●				●
Agricultural inputs													
Fertilisers										●	●		
Pesticides			●							●	●		
Other goods													
Batteries		●	●			●					●		
Plastic carrier bags			●			●							
Disposable containers		●	●			●				●			
Tyres			●			●						●	●
CFCs/halons	●		●			●							●
Disposable razors/cameras		●											
Lubricant oil charge										●			
Oil pollutant charge	●												
Solvents			●										
Direct tax provisions													
Tax relief on green investment	●	●	●	●		●		●	●	●			●
Taxation on free company cars					●								
Employer-paid commuting expenses taxable	●	●	●		●						●	●	●
Employer-paid parking expenses taxable	●												●
Commuter use of public transport tax deductible													●
Air transport													
Noise charges	●	●		●	●	●			●	●	●	●	
Other taxes										●	●		●
Water													
Water charges	●	●	●	●	●	●			●	●	●	●	●
Sewage charges	●	●	●		●	●			●	●	●	●	●
Water effluent charges	●	●	●	●	●				●				
Manure charges									●				
Waste disposal													
Municipal waste charges	●		●	●	●	●			●	●	●		●
Waste-disposal charges	●	●	●	●	●	●	●		●	●		●	
Hazardous waste	●	●		●	●	●				●		●	
Landfill tax or charges									●			●	

Source: *Evaluating Economic Instruments for Environmental Policy,* OECD (1998).

Environmental policy options

Environmental policy can take many forms. However, it is useful to put the different types of policy into three broad categories: market based, non-market based, and mixed. The most important market-based solution is to use taxes and subsidies. Non-market-based solutions usually involve imposing regulations and controls. The most important mixed system is that of tradable permits. Let us examine each of these three categories in turn.

Market-based environmental policy: taxation

Market-based solutions attempt to internalise the costs of the externality, and ensure that the polluter pays. The most common market-based approach to environmental policy is to impose indirect taxes on specific types of polluting activity, such as the use of carbon-based fuels.

Taxes have the advantage of relating the size of the penalty to the amount of pollution. This means that there is continuous pressure to cut down on production or consumption of polluting products or activities in order to save tax.

One approach is to modify *existing* taxes. In most developed countries there are now higher taxes on leaded than unleaded petrol, and lower taxes on low-emission cars. Tax regimes can also be modified which currently *encourage* environmental degradation. For example, lower taxes on diesel could be abolished (given the higher pollution from diesel engines), as could tax relief for commuting expenses. Tax benefits which encourage the use of fertilisers and pesticides in farming, or the felling of trees or hedgerows, could also be abolished.

Increasingly, however, countries are introducing *new* 'green' taxes in order to discourage pollution as goods are produced, consumed or disposed of. Table 21.1 shows the range of green taxes in use in thirteen countries. As you can see, the Scandinavian countries have gone the furthest, reflecting the strength of environmental concerns in these countries.

There are various problems with using the tax weapon in the fight against pollution.

Conflicts with revenue objectives. The more successful a tax is in reducing consumption, the less revenue it will earn for the government. (This is a problem that governments have experienced for years in the use of taxes on tobacco.) In Denmark, where energy used in households has been taxed at higher rates than in most other countries, energy consumption fell by 25 per cent between 1973 and 1989. In Sweden, a sulphur tax reduced the sulphur content of fuel oils by 40 per cent between 1990 and 1992. Clearly, reduced consumption reduces the tax revenue.

But the revenue will still be more than if no tax had been imposed! Provided green taxes are imposed on a wide range of products and at high enough rates, their revenue-earning potential can be considerable. After all, the aim is not to reduce the consumption of energy and many other potentially polluting activities to zero. If it were, it would be simplest just to ban the activity.

Redistributive effects. The poor spend a higher proportion of their income on domestic fuel than the rich. A 'carbon tax' on such fuel will, therefore, have the effect of redistributing incomes away from the poor. Thus, when the UK

Conservative government in 1995 attempted to increase the rate of VAT on domestic fuel from 8 per cent to 17½ per cent (albeit primarily as a revenue-raising measure rather than as an environmental one), there was an outcry from groups representing the poor.

The poor also spend a larger proportion of their income on food than do the rich. Taxes on agriculture, designed to reduce intensive use of fertilisers and pesticides, will again tend to hit the poor proportionately more than the rich.

However, not all green taxes are regressive. The rich spend a higher proportion of their income on motoring than the poor. Thus petrol and other motoring taxes could have a progressive effect. Also, other taxes, such as those on packaging, batteries and disposable items, are likely to be neutral in their impact, since their prime purpose is to encourage people to switch to non-polluting alternatives.

Where adverse redistribution does occur, a solution would be to make compensating payments to the poor, or to reduce other even more regressive taxes, such as VAT.

Problems with international trade. If a country imposes pollution taxes on its industries, its products will become less competitive in world trade. To compensate for this, the industries may need to be given tax rebates for exports. Also taxes would need to be imposed on imports of competitors' products from countries where there is no equivalent green tax.

Evidence on the adverse effect of environmental taxes on a country's exports is inconclusive, however. Over the long term, in countries with high environmental taxes (or other tough environmental measures), firms will be stimulated to invest in low-pollution processes and products. This will later give such countries a competitive advantage if *other* countries then impose tougher environmental standards.

Effects on employment. One of the worries about pollution taxes is that reduced output in the industries affected will lead to a reduction in employ-ment. If, however, the effect was to encourage investment in new cleaner technology, employment might not fall. Where it did, employment opportunities could be generated elsewhere if the extra revenues from the green taxes allowed reductions in taxes on labour (e.g. employers' national insurance contributions).

Given that much of the incidence of green taxes would fall on the consumer (e.g. the motorist), a reduction in employers' national insurance contributions would help to make industry *more* competitive. There could be a net *increase* in employment and exports.

Non-market-based environmental policy: command-and-control systems (laws and regulations)

definition

Command-and-control (CAC) systems
The use of laws or regulations backed up by inspections and penalties (such as fines) for non-compliance.

The traditional way of tackling pollution has been to set maximum permitted levels of emission or resource use, or minimum acceptable levels of environmental quality, and then to fine firms contravening these limits. Measures of this type are known as **command-and-control (CAC) systems**. Clearly, there have to be inspectors to monitor the amount of pollution, and the fines have to be large enough to deter firms from exceeding the limit.

Virtually all countries have environmental regulations of one sort or another. For example, the EU has over 200 items of legislation covering areas such as air and water pollution, noise, the marketing and use of dangerous chemicals, waste management, the environmental impacts of new projects (such as power stations, roads and quarries), recycling, depletion of the ozone layer and global warming.

Typically there are three approaches to devising CAC systems.[1]

- **Technology-based standards** The focus could be on the amount of pollution generated, irrespective of its environmental impact. As technology for reducing pollutants improves, so tougher standards could be imposed, based on the 'best available technology' (as long as the cost was not excessive). Thus car manufacturers could be required to ensure that new car engines meet lower CO_2 emission levels as the technology enabled them to do so.
- **Ambient-based standards**. Here the focus is on the environmental impact. For example, standards could be set for air or water purity. Depending on the location and the number of polluters in that area, a given standard would be achieved with different levels of discharge. If the object is a cleaner environment, then this approach is more efficient than technology-based standards.
- **Social-impact standards**. Here the focus is on the effect on people. Thus tougher standards would be imposed in densely populated areas. Whether this approach is more efficient than that of ambient-based standards depends on the approach to sustainability. If the objective is to achieve social efficiency, then human-impact standards are preferable. If the objective is to protect the environment for its own sake (a 'deeper green' approach), then ambient standards would be preferable.

Assessing CAC systems. Given the uncertainty over the environmental impacts of pollutants, especially over the longer term, it is often better to play safe and set tough emissions or ambient standards. These could always be relaxed at a later stage if the effects turn out not to be so damaging, but it might be too late to reverse damage if the effects turn out to be more serious. Taxes may be a more sophisticated means of reaching a socially efficient output, but CAC methods are usually more straightforward to devise, easier to understand by firms and easier to implement. Also, setting standards is more in accordance with the pro-environment ethic of many environmental pressure groups, such as Greenpeace and Friends of the Earth. Using taxes, by contrast, focuses on the effects on people rather than the environment itself.

Where command-and-control systems are weak is that they fail to offer business any incentive to do better than the legally specified level. By contrast, with a pollution tax, the lower the pollution level, the less tax there will be to pay. There is thus a continuing incentive for businesses progressively to cut pollution levels and introduce cleaner technology.

Tradable permits

A policy measure that has grown in popularity in recent years is that of **tradable permits**. This is a combination of command-and-control and market-based systems. A maximum permitted level of emission is set for a given pollutant for a given factory, and the firm is given a permit to emit up to this amount. If it emits less than this amount, it is given a credit for the difference, which it can then use

---

[1] See R.K. Turner, D. Pearce and I. Bateman, *Environmental Economics* (Harvester Wheatsheaf, 1994), page 198.

---

definition

Technology-based standards
Pollution control that requires firms' emissions to reflect the levels that could be achieved from using the best available pollution control technology.

definition

Ambient-based standards
Pollution control that requires firms to meet minimum standards for the environment (e.g. air or water quality).

definition

Social-impact standards
Pollution control that focuses on the effects on people (e.g. on health or happiness).

definition

Tradable permits
Each firm is given a permit to produce a given level of pollution. If less than the permitted amount is produced, the firm is given a credit. This can then be sold to another firm, allowing it to exceed its original limit.

in another of its factories, or sell to another firm, to enable it to go that amount *over* its permitted level. Thus the overall level of emissions is set by CAC methods, whereas their distribution is determined by the market.

Take the example of firms A and B, which are currently producing 12 units of a pollutant each. Now assume that a standard is set permitting them to produce only 10 units each. If firm A managed to reduce the pollutant to 8 units, it would be given a credit for 2 units. It could then sell this to firm B, enabling B to continue emitting 12 units. The effect would still be a total reduction of 4 units between the two firms. However, by allowing them to trade in pollution permits, pollution reduction can be concentrated in the firms where it can be achieved at lowest cost. In our example, if it cost firm B more to reduce its pollution than firm A, then the permits could be sold from A to B at a price that was profitable to both (i.e. at a price above the cost of emission reduction to A, but below the cost of emission reduction to B). Given the resulting reduced cost of pollution control, it might be politically easier to impose tougher standards (i.e. impose lower permitted levels of emission).

The principle of tradable permits can be used as the basis of international agreements on pollution reduction. Each country could be required to achieve a certain percentage reduction in a pollutant (e.g. CO_2 or SO_2), but any country exceeding its reduction could sell its right to these emissions to other (presumably richer) countries.

A similar principle can be used for using natural resources. Thus fish quotas could be assigned to fishing boats or fleets or countries. Any parts of these quotas not used could then be sold.

Assessing the system of tradable permits. The main advantage of tradable permits is that they combine the simplicity of CAC methods with the benefits of achieving pollution reduction in the most efficient way. The government can simply set the total amount of permitted discharge according to the ability of the environment to absorb the pollutants; and it can do this without any knowledge of the specific costs and benefits of individual firms. This is the main benefit of CAC methods over taxes and charges. Then it can let the market in tradable permits allocate the reduction in pollution to where it can be achieved at least cost (the same effect as with taxes).

How are the permitted levels to be decided? The way that seems to be the most acceptable is to base them on firms' *current* levels, with any subsequent reduction in total permitted pollution being achieved by requiring firms to reduce their emissions by the *same* percentage. This approach is known as **grandfathering**. The main problem with this approach is that it could be seen as unfair by those firms that are already using cleaner technology. Why should they be required to make the same reductions as firms using dirty technology?

definition

Grandfathering
Where each firm's emission permit is based on its *current* levels of emission (e.g. permitted levels for all firms could be 80 per cent of their current levels).

There are other more general problems with tradable permits. One is the possibility that trade will lead to pollution being concentrated in certain geographical areas. Another is that it may reduce the pressure on dirtier factories (or countries) to cut their emissions. An example of this problem is the approach of the USA at international climate conferences, such as that at Buenos Aires in 1998. The USA has advocated an international tradable permits system to allow it to buy up other countries' rights to pollute, and thereby avoiding having to cut pollution itself.

Environmental policy in the UK and EU

In the UK, current policy is embodied in the 1990 Environmental Protection Act. The Act was an attempt to establish an integrated pollution control strategy. This has been the approach in other European countries. In Holland, for example, the first National Environmental Plan was put in place in 1989. Its aim was to establish a series of targets for improving environmental quality. Such goals and targets were then incorporated into government policies and initiatives throughout the economy.

National strategies in European countries to tackle pollution and improve the environment are being increasingly determined by decisions within the EU. It is hoped that eventually there will be a Europe-wide pollution strategy with its own regulatory and enforcement body.

21.2 Transport policy

Traffic congestion is a problem that faces all countries, especially in the large cities and at certain peak times: a problem that has grown at an alarming rate as our lives have become increasingly dominated by the motor car. Sitting in a traffic jam is both time wasting and frustrating. It adds considerably to the costs and stress of modern living.

And it is not only the motorist that suffers. Congested streets make life less pleasant for the pedestrian, and increased traffic leads to increased accidents. What is more, the inexorable growth of traffic has led to significant problems of pollution. Traffic is noisy and car fumes are unpleasant and lead to substantial environmental damage. It is true that the move to unleaded petrol has reduced the problem of lead pollution, but the growing emissions of carbon dioxide and nitrogen dioxide have aggravated the problem of global warming and acid rain.

Between 1983 and 1999 road traffic in Great Britain rose by 58 per cent, whereas the length of public roads rose by only 6 per cent (albeit some roads were widened). Most passenger and freight transport is by road. In 1999, 93 per cent of passenger kilometres and 81 per cent of freight tonnage in Great Britain were by road, whereas rail accounted for a mere 6 per cent of passenger traffic and 5 per cent of freight tonnage. Of road passenger kilometres, over 92 per cent was by car in 1998, and, as Table 21.2 shows, this proportion has been growing. Motoring costs now amount to over 13 per cent of household expenditure.

But should the government do anything about the problem? Is traffic congestion a price worth paying for the benefits we gain from using cars? Or are there things that can be done to ease the problem without greatly inconveniencing the

Table 21.2 **Passenger transport in Great Britain: percentage of passenger kilometres by road**

	Cars	Motor cycles	Buses and coaches	Bicycles
1981	86.1	2.2	10.6	1.1
1990	91.2	0.9	7.1	0.8
1998	92.4	0.6	6.4	0.6

Source: *Annual Abstract of Statistics 2000*, National Statistics © Crown Copyright 2001.

traveller? And if something is to be done, should the government seek to extend the role of the market (e.g. by encouraging the building of private toll roads) or merely to amend market forces (e.g. by subsidising public transport) or should it seek to replace the market (e.g. by banning cars in certain areas)?

The existing system of allocating road space

The allocation of road space depends on both demand and supply. Demand is by individuals who base their decisions on largely private considerations. Supply, by contrast, is usually by the central government or local authorities. Let us examine each in turn.

Demand for road space (by car users)

The demand for road space can be seen largely as a *derived* demand. What people want is not the car journey for its own sake, but to get to their destination. The greater the benefit they gain at their destination, the greater the benefit they gain from using their car to get there.

The demand for road space, like the demand for other goods and services, has a number of determinants. If congestion is to be reduced, it is important to know how responsive demand is to a change in any of these: it is important to consider the various elasticities of demand.

Price. This is the *marginal cost* to the motorist of a journey. It includes petrol, oil, maintenance, depreciation and any toll charges.

The price elasticity of demand for motoring tends to be relatively low. There can be a substantial rise in the price of petrol, for example, and there will be only a modest fall in traffic. After the 1973/4 oil crisis, the price of petrol doubled, but traffic in London fell by only 4 per cent.

The low price elasticity of demand suggests that any schemes to tackle traffic congestion that merely involve raising the costs of motoring will have only limited success.

Income. The demand for road space also depends on people's income. As incomes rise, so car ownership and hence car usage increase substantially. Demand is elastic with respect to income. Figure 21.1 shows the increase in car ownership in various countries.

Price of substitutes. If bus and train fares came down, people might switch from travelling by car. The cross-price elasticity is likely to be relatively low, however, given that most people regard these alternatives as a poor substitute for travelling in their own car. Cars are seen as more comfortable and convenient.

Price of complements. Demand for road space will depend on the price of cars. The higher the price of cars, the fewer people will own cars and thus the fewer will be the cars on the road.

Demand will also depend on the price of complementary services, such as parking. A rise in car parking charges will reduce the demand for car journeys. But here again the cross elasticity is likely to be relatively low. In most cases, the motorist will either pay the higher charge or park elsewhere, such as in side streets.

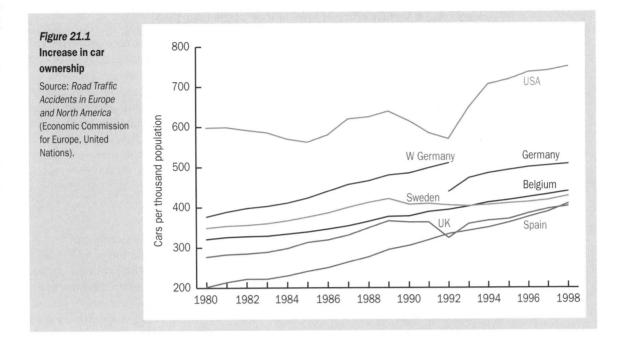

Figure 21.1
Increase in car ownership

Source: *Road Traffic Accidents in Europe and North America* (Economic Commission for Europe, United Nations).

Tastes/utility. Another factor explaining the preference of many people for travelling by car is the pleasure they gain from it compared with alternative modes of transport. Car ownership is regarded by many people as highly desirable, and once accustomed to travelling in their own car, most people are highly reluctant to give it up.

One important feature of the demand for road space is that it fluctuates. There will be periods of peak demand, such as during the rush hour or at holiday weekends. At such times, roads can get totally jammed. At other times, however, the same roads may be virtually empty. The problem is that supply cannot fluctuate to match demand. Empty road space available in the middle of the night cannot be 'stored' and then transferred as additional space during periods of peak demand!

Supply of road space

The supply of road space can be examined in two contexts: the short run and the long run.

The short run. In the short run, the supply of road space is constant. When there is no congestion, supply is more than enough to satisfy demand. There is spare road capacity. At times of congestion, however, there is pressure on this fixed supply. Maximum supply for any given road is reached at the point where there is the maximum flow of vehicles per minute along the road.

The long run. In the long run, the authorities can build new roads or improve existing ones. This will require an assessment of the costs and benefits of such schemes.

Identifying a socially efficient level of road usage (short run)

The existing system of *government* provision of roads and *private* ownership of cars is unlikely to lead to an optimum allocation of road space. So how do we set about identifying just what the social optimum is?

In the short run, the supply of road space is fixed. The question of the short-run optimum allocation of road space, therefore, is one of the optimum usage of existing road space. It is a question of *consumption* rather than supply. For this reason we must focus on the road user, rather than on road provision.

A socially efficient level of consumption occurs where the marginal social benefit of consumption equals its marginal social cost (*MSB = MSC*). So what are the marginal social benefits and costs of using a car?

Marginal social benefit of road usage

Marginal social benefit equals marginal private benefit plus externalities.

Marginal private benefit is the direct benefit to the car user and is reflected in the demand for car journeys, the determinants of which we examined above. For example, the benefit from using your car depends on its relative comfort and convenience compared with alternative modes of transport.

External benefits are few. The one major exception occurs when drivers give lifts to other people.

Marginal social cost of road usage

Marginal social cost equals marginal private cost plus externalities.

Marginal private costs to the motorist were identified when we looked at demand. They include the costs of petrol, wear and tear, and tolls. They also include the time costs of travel.

There may also be substantial external costs. These include the following.

Congestion costs: time. When a person uses a car on a congested road, it will add to the congestion. This will therefore slow down the traffic even more and increase the journey time of *other* car users.

Congestion costs: monetary. Congestion increases fuel consumption, and the stopping and starting increases the costs of wear and tear. So when a motorist adds to congestion, there will be additional monetary costs imposed on other motorists.

Environmental costs. When motorists use a road, they reduce the quality of the environment for others. Cars emit fumes and create noise. This is bad enough for pedestrians and other car users, but can be particularly distressing for people living along the road. Driving can cause accidents, a problem that increases as drivers become more impatient as a result of delays.

The socially efficient level of road usage

The optimum level of road use is where the marginal social benefit is equal to the marginal social cost. In Figure 21.2 costs and benefits are shown on the vertical axis and are measured in money terms. Thus any non-monetary costs or benefits (such as time costs) must be given a monetary value. The horizontal axis measures road usage in terms of cars per minute passing a specified point on the road.

Figure 21.2
Actual and optimum road usage

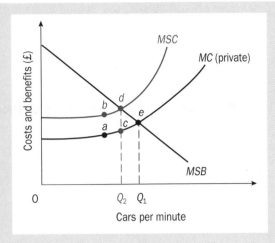

For simplicity it is assumed that there are no external benefits from car use and that therefore marginal private and marginal social benefits are the same. The *MSB* curve is shown as downward sloping. The reason for this is that different road users put a different value on this particular journey. If the marginal (private) cost of making the journey were high, only those for whom the journey had a high marginal benefit would travel along the road. If the marginal cost of making the journey fell, more people would make the journey: people would choose to make the journey at the point at which the marginal cost of using their car had fallen to the level of their marginal benefit. Thus the greater the number of cars, the lower the marginal benefit.

The marginal (private) cost curve (*MC*) is likely to be constant up to the level of traffic flow at which congestion begins to occur. This is shown as point *a* in Figure 21.2. Beyond this point, marginal cost is likely to rise as time costs increase and as fuel consumption rises.

The marginal *social* cost curve (*MSC*) is drawn above the marginal private cost curve. The vertical difference between the two represents the external costs. Up to point *b*, external costs are simply the environmental costs. Beyond point *b*, there are also external congestion costs, since additional road users slow down the journey of *other* road users. These external costs get progressively greater as the level of traffic increases.

The actual level of traffic flow will be at Q_1, where marginal private costs and benefits are equal (point *e*). The socially efficient level of traffic flow, however, will be at the lower level of Q_2, where marginal social costs and benefits are equal (point *d*). In other words, the existing system of allocating road space is likely to lead to an excessive level of road usage.

Identifying a socially optimum level of road space (long run)

In the long run, the supply of road space is not fixed. The authorities must therefore assess what new road schemes (if any) to adopt. This will involve the use of some form of **cost–benefit analysis**.

The socially efficient level of construction will be where the marginal social benefit from construction is equal to the marginal social cost. This means that

definition

Cost–benefit analysis
The identification, measurement and weighing-up of the costs and benefits of a project in order to decide whether or not it should go ahead.

schemes should be adopted as long as their marginal social benefit exceeds their marginal social cost.

We now turn to look at different solutions to traffic congestion. These can be grouped into three broad types.

Solution 1: direct provision (supply-side solutions)

The road solution

One obvious solution to traffic congestion is to build more roads. At first sight this may seem an optimum strategy, provided the costs and benefits of road-building schemes are carefully assessed and only those schemes are adopted where the benefits exceed the costs.

However, there are serious problems with this approach.

The objective of equity. The first problem concerns that of *equity*. After all, social efficiency is not the only possible economic objective. For example, when an urban motorway is built, those living beside it will suffer from noise and fumes. Motorway users gain, but the local residents lose. The question is whether this is fair.

The more the government tries to appeal to the car user by building more and better roads, the fewer will be the people who use public transport, and thus the more will public transport decline. Those without cars lose, and these tend to be from the most vulnerable groups – the poor, the elderly, children and the disabled.

Congestion may not be solved. Increasing the amount of road space may encourage more people to use cars. Apart from the adverse effects of this on the profitability of public transport, it may mean that the problem of congestion persists. The government's forecasts have often underestimated the growth in traffic on new or improved roads.

Thus new roads may simply generate extra traffic, with little overall effect on congestion.

The environmental impact of new roads. New roads lead to loss of agricultural land, the destruction of many natural habitats, noise, the splitting of communities and disruption to local residents. To the extent that they encourage a growth in traffic, they add to atmospheric pollution and a depletion of oil reserves.

Government or local authority provision of public transport

An alternative supply-side solution is to increase the provision of public transport. If, for example, a local authority ran a local bus service and decided to invest in additional buses, open up new routes and operate a low-fare policy, these services might encourage people to switch from using their cars.

Solution 2: regulation and legislation

An alternative strategy is to restrict car use by various forms of regulation and legislation.

Restricting car access

One approach involves reducing car access to areas that are subject to high levels of congestion. The following three measures are widely used:

● Bus and cycle lanes.
● No entry to side streets.
● Pedestrian-only areas.

However, there is a serious problem with these measures. They tend not to solve the problem of congestion, but merely to divert it. Bus lanes tend to make the car lanes more congested; no entry to side streets tends to make the main roads more congested; and pedestrian-only areas often make the roads round these areas more congested.

Parking restrictions

An alternative to restricting road access is to restrict parking. If cars are not allowed to park along congested streets, this will improve the traffic flow. Also, if parking is difficult, this will discourage people from using their cars to come into city centres.

The problems with this solution include the following:

● Possibly *increased* congestion as people drive round and round looking for parking spaces.
● Illegal parking.
● Parking down side streets, causing a nuisance for local residents.

Solution 3: changing market signals

The solution favoured by many economists is to use the price mechanism. As we have seen, one of the causes of traffic congestion is that road users do not pay the full marginal social costs of using the roads. If they could be forced to do so, a social optimum usage of road space could be achieved.

So how can these external costs be charged to the motorist? There are several possible ways.

Extending existing taxes

Three major types of tax are levied on the motorist: fuel tax, taxes on new cars and car licences. Could increasing these taxes lead to the optimum level of road use being achieved?

Increasing the rates of new car tax and car licences may have some effect on reducing the total level of car ownership, but will probably have little effect on car use. The problem is that these taxes do not increase the marginal cost of car use. They are fixed costs. Once you have paid these taxes, there is no extra to pay for each extra journey you make. They do not discourage you from using your car.

Unlike the other two, fuel taxes are a marginal cost of car use. The more you use your car, the more fuel you use and the more fuel tax you pay. They are also mildly related to the level of congestion, since fuel consumption tends to increase as congestion increases. Nevertheless, they are not ideal. The problem is that all motorists would pay an increase in fuel tax, even those travelling on uncongested roads. There is also a political problem. Most motorists regard fuel

---

BOX 21.2

Road pricing in Singapore
Part of an integrated transport policy

It takes only one hour to drive from one end of Singapore to the other. Yet the average Singaporean driver travels an estimated 18 600 km per year, more than the average US driver, and over 50 per cent more than the average Japanese driver. In Singapore in 1996 there were a little over 300 000 cars, giving a vehicle density of 200 motor vehicles per kilometre of road. This compares with a vehicle density in the USA of only 27 motor vehicles per kilometre. It is hardly surprising that traffic congestion has become a major focus of public debate, particularly as the demand for cars is set to increase as consumer affluence grows.

In contrast to its neighbours, many of which are suffering more acute urban traffic congestion problems, Singapore has an integrated transport policy. This includes the following:

- Restricting the number of new car licences, and allowing their price to rise to the corresponding equilibrium. This makes cars in Singapore among the most expensive in the world.
- Investment in a mass rail transit (MRT) system with subsidised fares. Trains are comfortable, clean and frequent. Stations are air-conditioned.
- A programme of building new estates near MRT stations.
- Cheap, frequent buses, serving all parts of the island.

In addition, a 1996 White Paper proposed the following measures:

- Building an extra 56 km of MRT lines running parallel to busy commuter routes.
- A light rail system to serve as feeders to the MRT.
- Private bus companies to operate all routes, including unprofitable ones, with prescribed fares and frequencies.
- 'Premium' buses offering greater comfort and service at higher fares.
- The construction of an extra 225 lane-km of motorways by 2001.
- The possible construction of underground roads in the city centre.

But it is in respect to road usage that the Singaporean authorities have been most innovative.

The first innovation came in 1975. The city centre was made a restricted zone. Motorists who wished to enter this zone had to buy a ticket (an 'area licence') at any one of 33 entry points. Police were stationed at these entry points to check that cars had paid and displayed.

Then in 1990 a quota system for new cars was established. The government decides the total number of cars the country should have, and issues just enough

---

taxes as too high and would resent paying higher rates. The blockade of fuel terminals in the UK and many other countries in late 2000 in protest against high fuel prices demonstrated the strength of feeling on this issue.

Road pricing

Charging people for using roads is a direct means of achieving an efficient use of road space. The higher the congestion, the higher should be the charge.

The scheme most favoured by many economists and traffic planners is that of electronic road pricing. It is the scheme that can most directly relate the price charged to the motorist to the specific level of marginal social cost. It involves having sensors attached to cars, perhaps in the numberplate. When the car passes a recording device in the road, a charge is registered to that car on a central computer. The car owner then receives a bill at periodic intervals, in much the same way as a telephone bill. The charge rate can easily be varied electronically according to the level of congestion (and pollution too). The rates could

licences each month to maintain that total. These licences (or 'Certificates of Entitlement') are for 10 years and are offered at auction. Their market price varies from around £10 000 to £30 000.

A problem with the licences is that they are a once-and-for-all payment, which does not vary with the amount people use their car. In other words, their marginal cost (for additional miles driven) is zero. Many people feel that, having paid such a high price for their licence, they ought to use their car as much as possible in order to get value for money!

With traffic congestion steadily worsening, it was recognised that something more had to be done. Either the Area Licensing Scheme had to be widened, or some other form of charging had to be adopted. The decision was taken to introduce road pricing. This alternative would not only save on police labour costs, but enable charge rates to be varied according to levels of congestion, times of the day, and locality. What, then would be the optimum charge? If the objective is to reduce traffic from Q_1 to Q_2 in Figure 21.2, then a charge of $d - c$ should be levied.

Since 1998 all vehicles in Singapore have been fitted with an in-vehicle unit (IU). Every journey made requires the driver to insert a smart card into the IU. On specified roads, overhead gantries read the IU and deduct the appropriate charge from the card. The charge varies with the time of day. If a car does not have sufficient funds on its smart card, the car's details are relayed to a control centre and a fine is imposed. The system has the benefit of operating on three-lane highways and does not require traffic to slow down. What is more, it is very flexible, with the possibility of adjusting the road price (i.e. the charge) to keep traffic at the desired level.

The system was expensive to set up, however. Cheaper schemes have been adopted elsewhere, such as Norway and parts of the USA. These operate by funnelling traffic into a single lane in order to register the car, but these have the disadvantage of slowing the traffic down.

One message is clear from the Singapore solution. Road pricing alone is not enough. Unless there are fast, comfortable and affordable public transport alternatives, the demand for cars will be highly price inelastic. People have to get to work!

Question

Explain how, by varying the charge debited from the smart card according to the time of day or level of congestion, a socially optimal level of road use can be achieved.

be in bands and the current bands displayed by the roadside so that motorists knew what they were being charged.

An alternative scheme involves having a device fitted to your car that deactivates the car unless a 'smart card' (like a telephone or photocopying card) is inserted. The cards have to be purchased and contain a certain number of units. The device deducts units from the card when the average speed of your car over a specified distance falls below a certain level, or when more than a certain number of stops are made within a specified distance. (Either would be the result of congestion.) Alternatively, beacons or overhead gantries could deduct units from the smart cards at times of congestion.

The most sophisticated scheme, still under development, involves equipping all cars with a receiver. Their position is located by satellites, which then send this information to a dashboard unit, which deducts charges according to location, distance travelled, time of day and type of vehicle. The charges can operate either through smart cards or central computerised billing.

Various road-pricing schemes have been advocated for many cities around the world and pilot schemes are now in operation in several of them.

Subsidising alternative means of transport

An alternative to charging for the use of cars is to subsidise the price of alternatives, such as buses and trains. But cheaper fares alone may not be enough. The government may also have to invest directly in or subsidise an *improved* public transport service: more frequent services, more routes, more comfortable buses and trains.

Subsidising public transport need not be seen as an alternative to road pricing: it can be seen as complementary. If road pricing is to persuade people not to travel by car, the alternatives must be attractive. Unless public transport can be made to be seen by the traveller as a close substitute for cars, the elasticity of demand for car use is likely to remain low.

Subsidising public transport can also be justified on grounds of equity. It benefits poorer members of society who cannot afford to travel by car.

It is unlikely that any one policy can provide the complete solution. Certain or mixes of policies are better suited to some situations than others. It is important for governments to learn from experiences both within their own country and in others, in order to find the optimum solution to each specific problem.

21.3 Privatisation and regulation

One solution to market failure, advocated by some on the political left, is nationalisation. If industries are not being run in the public interest by the private sector, then bring them into public ownership. This way, so the argument goes, the market failures can be corrected. Problems of monopoly power, externalities, inequality, etc. can be dealt with directly if these industries are run with the public interest, rather than private gain, at heart.

The political right is against nationalisation. The failures of the market (which, they claim, are often relatively small) are best dealt with by encouraging more competition, and by generally improving the market. Public ownership, they argue, far from serving the public interest, actually creates more problems than it solves. **Nationalised industries**, they claim, are bureaucratic, inefficient, unresponsive to consumer wishes and often a burden on the taxpayer.

The Thatcher and Major governments thus engaged in extensive programmes of 'privatisation', returning most of the nationalised industries in the UK to the private sector (see Table 21.3). Other countries have followed similar programmes of privatisation in what has become a worldwide phenomenon. Privatisation has been seen as a means of revitalising ailing industries and as a golden opportunity to raise revenues to ease budgetary problems.

> **definition**
>
> **Nationalised industries**
> State-owned industries that produce goods or services that are sold in the market.

The arguments for privatisation

The arguments in favour of privatisation include the following.

Market forces

The first argument is that privatisation will expose these industries to market

Table 21.3	The major nationalised industries in the UK	
Industry	Date and form of nationalisation	Date and form of privatisation
Utilities/fuel		
Electricity	1926 Central Electricity Board (generation and transmission)	1990 Area Electricity Boards
	1948 Area Electricity Boards (supply to customers)	1991 Non-nuclear generation
	1958 Reorganised into Central Electricity Generating Board (CEGB) and 12 Area Electricity Boards	1996 Nuclear generatrion
Coal	1947 National Coal Board	1994– Mines sold off individually
Gas	1949 Gas Council and Area Boards	1986 British Gas
	1973 Re-established as British Gas Corporation (later called British Gas)	1996 Split into TransCo and BG Energy
Water	1973 Regional Water Authorities (10) took over from local government	1989 10 separate companies
Oil	1976 British National Oil Corporation (BNOC) (part of industry)	1982 Privatised as Britoil
Transport and communications		
Posts and telecoms	1961 (Previously a government department)	1984 Privatised as BT
	1981 Split into the Post Office and British Telecom (BT)	
Railways	1948 British Transport Commission	1996– Train operating companies sold individually
	1963 Split into British Railways and London Transport	
	1995 BR split into Railtrack and separate train operating divisions	1996 Railtrack privatised
Buses	1969 National Bus Company	1986 Privatised
Road haulage	1947 Later named National Freight Corporation	1982 Management/worker buyout
Airlines	1940 British Overseas Airways Corporation (non-European)	1987 Privatised as BA
	1946 British European Airways (European)	
	1974 BOAC and BEA combined to form British Airways	
Manufacturing, etc.		
Steel	1951 Iron and Steel Corporation	1953 Privatised
	1967 Renationalised as British Steel Corporation	1988 Privatised as BSC
Shipbuilding	1977 British Shipbuilders	1985–6 Sold as separate companies
Aero-engines	1971 Rolls-Royce nationalised	1987 Privatised
Aerospace	1977 British Aerospace (part of industry only)	1981 Privatised as BAe
Vehicles	1976 British Leyland (part of industry only)	1984 Jaguar division of BL privatised
		1988 Rover group (part of old BL) privatised

forces, from which will flow the benefits of greater efficiency, greater growth and greater responsiveness to the wishes of the consumer.

If privatisation involved splitting an industry into competing companies, this greater competition in the goods market would force the companies to keep their costs as low as possible in order to stay in business.

Privatised companies do not have direct access to government finance. To finance investment they must now go to the market: they must issue shares or borrow from banks or other financial institutions. In doing so, they will be competing for funds with other companies, and thus must be seen as capable of using these funds profitably.

Market discipline will also be enforced by shareholders. Shareholders want a good return on their shares and will thus put pressure on the privatised company to perform well. If the company does not make sufficient profits, shareholders will sell their shares. The share price will fall, and the company will be in danger of being taken over.

Reduced government interference

In nationalised industries, managers may frequently be required to adjust their targets for political reasons. At one time they may have to keep prices low as part of a government drive against inflation. At another they may have to raise their prices substantially in order to raise extra revenue for the government and help finance tax cuts. At another they may find their investment programmes cut as part of a government economy drive.

Privatisation frees the company from these constraints and allows it to make more rational economic decisions and plan future investments with greater certainty.

Reducing the public-sector net cash requirement (PSNCR)

The PSNCR is the amount of money the public sector has to borrow each year to make up the shortfall between public-sector expenditure and public-sector receipts. Reducing the PSNCR was a major aim of the Conservative governments after 1979, which saw it as the way of bringing down the rate of inflation and allowing reductions in the rate of taxation.

The privatisation issue of shares directly earns money for the government and thus reduces the amount it needs to borrow. Effectively, then, the government can use the proceeds of privatisation to finance tax cuts.

Increased share ownership and popular capitalism

This is largely a political/ideological argument. The Conservative Party believes that 'true' public ownership is not state ownership. Although in theory the nationalised industries were owned by everyone in the UK, people did not feel a sense of ownership or participation. Instead the industries were run by 'bureaucrats'. This was not so after privatisation. Shares are now owned by members of the public who thus, it is argued, feel a much greater sense of involvement. In this sense, then, the Conservatives maintain that privatisation is really a return of industries to the public. It is a form of 'popular capitalism'.

The arguments against privatisation

Natural monopolies

The market forces argument for privatisation largely breaks down if a public monopoly is simply replaced by a private monopoly, as in the case of the water companies, which each have a monopoly in their own area. Critics of privatisation argue that at least a public-sector monopoly is not out to maximise profits and thereby exploit the consumer.

The public interest

Will the questions of externalities and social justice not be ignored after privatisation? Critics of privatisation argue that only the most glaring examples of externalities and injustice can be taken into account, given that the whole ethos of a private company is different from that of a nationalised one: private profit is the goal rather than public service. Externalities, they argue, are extremely widespread and need to be taken into account by the industry itself and not just by an occasionally intervening government. A railway or an underground line, for example, may considerably ease congestion on the roads, thus benefiting road as well as rail users. Other industries may cause substantial external costs. Nuclear power stations may produce nuclear waste that is costly to dispose of safely, and/or provides hazards for future generations. Coal-fired power stations may pollute the atmosphere and cause acid rain.

In assessing these arguments, a lot depends on the toughness of government legislation and the attitudes and powers of regulatory agencies after privatisation.

The PSNCR

The privatisation issue of shares will directly reduce the PSNCR, it is true, but there are problems here:

- The nation's *capital* assets are being sold to finance *current* expenditure.
- The profits of nationalised industries also help to reduce the PSNCR. Once sold, there will be no further profits accruing to the state from these industries.
- There is a conflict between reducing the PSNCR and avoiding monopoly exploitation. In order to earn the maximum revenue for the government from the privatisation issue, the industry must have the greatest possible potential for earning profit. This will be so if the industry is sold as a monopoly. But this directly conflicts with the aims of efficiency and the interests of the consumer, which are best served by splitting the industry up and selling it as competing parts.

Regulation

Identifying the short-run optimum price and output

Privatised industries, if left free to operate in the market, will have monopoly power; they will create externalities; and they will be unlikely to take into account questions of fairness. An answer to these problems is for the government or some independent agency to regulate their behaviour so that they produce at the socially optimum price and output. This has been the approach adopted for the major privatisations in the UK.

Regulation in practice

To some extent the behaviour of privatised industries may be governed by general monopoly and restrictive practice legislation. For example, in the UK, privatised firms can be investigated by the Office of Fair Trading and if necessary referred to the Competition Commission.

In addition to this, there is a separate regulatory office to oversee the structure and behaviour of each of the privatised utilities. These regulators are as

BOX 21.3

The right track to reform?
Reorganising the railways in the UK

Over the past 30 years, freight transported by road in Europe has risen by 280 per cent, whereas freight transported by rail has fallen by 8 per cent. While there has been a modest growth in passenger traffic on the railways, it is tiny compared with the growth in journeys by private car. Today more than 70 per cent of all passengers and freight use road transport. The result is that European railways generally operate at a loss, except for a few high-speed routes.

But why has rail transport performed so poorly? Losses on freight are partly the result of the decline in heavy manufacturing industries. A large proportion of freight trains carried coal, iron ore, steel and chemicals. In addition there is the competition from long-distance road haulage, made more competitive with the growth of the motorway network and the long hours worked by lorry drivers.

In the case of passenger services, railways have not managed to match the flexibility of car transport, made increasingly available with the growth in car ownership. Then there is the problem that many road costs are not marginal costs to the motorist. This gives road transport a cost advantage to the traveller. Finally, railways have often been forced to keep unprofitable routes open to meet public-service obligations.

Such has been the strain placed upon public finances that European governments in recent years have been looking for ways of reforming their railways. The most radical approach has been adopted in the UK, which involved dividing up the rail system and privatising its various parts.

The UK Conservative government in 1993 stated that the aim of rail privatisation was to 'improve the qual-

ity of rail services for the travelling public and for freight customers'. The 1993 Railways Act detailed the privatisation programme. The management of rail infrastructure, such as track, signalling and stations, was to be separated from the responsibility for running trains. There would be 25 passenger train operating companies, each having a franchise lasting between seven and fifteen years. These companies would have few assets, being forced to rent track and lease stations from the infrastructure owner (Railtrack), and to lease trains and rolling stock from three new rolling-stock companies. There would be three freight companies, which would also pay Railtrack for the use of track and signalling.

Railtrack would be responsible for maintaining and improving the rail infrastructure, but rather than providing this itself, it would be required to purchase the necessary services from private contractors.

To oversee the new rail network, two new posts were created. The first was a rail franchising director, who would be responsible for specifying the length and cost of franchises, as well as for outlining passenger service requirements, including minimum train frequency, stations served and weekend provision. The second post created was that of the rail regulator, who would be responsible both for promoting competition and for protecting consumer interests, which might include specifying maximum permitted fares.

Although the individual train operators generally have a monopoly over a given route, many see themselves directly competing with coaches and private cars. Several have expressed the intention to replace or refurbish rolling stock and to run additional services.

Despite these apparent benefits, considerable

follows: the Office for Electricity Regulation (OFFER) and the Office of Gas Supply (OFGAS) now combined into the Office for Gas and Electricity Markets (OFGEM), the Office for Telecommunications (OFTEL), the Office of the Rail Regulator (ORR) and the Office of Water Services (OFWAT). The regulators set terms under which the industries have to operate. For example, OFGAS requires the pipeline division of British Gas (TransCo) to allow other gas producers to use its pipelines, and for the same charge as that made to British Gas' supply division (now part of a separate company, Centrica). The terms set by the regulator can be reviewed by negotiation between the regulator and the industry. If

costs have been associated with this privatisation programme. Huge subsidies had to be paid in order to make various parts of the system saleable. The size of the subsidies was determined by the competitive bidding process for the franchises.

It is estimated that total government subsidies will amount to £10 billion in the first ten years. These include fixed subsidies paid to train operating companies over the entire length of their franchise; the writing-off of all but £600 million of Railtrack's £1.5 billion debt prior to its sale in 1996; the payment of a dividend to Railtrack shareholders out of the revenues from the last year of British Rail's operation as a nationalised industry; and, most expensive of all, subsidies for fares. This last concession involved the government compensating companies for pegging two-thirds of their fares at or below the rate of inflation for the first three years after privatisation, and at 1 per cent below the rate of inflation for the following four years. Critics argued that, with such financial backing, the rail companies could not fail to do well and improve upon British Rail's performance in the days of nationalisation.

Critics also argued that the new system would create bureaucracy and a fragmentation of responsibility, with highly complex transactions between the individual companies adding to costs.

Other countries, such as Japan and Germany, have rejected the UK model in favour of maintaining a vertically integrated rail network, where rail infrastructure and train services are managed by the same company. It is suggested that a single management would be far more capable of successfully co-ordinating infrastructure and train service activities than two. As separate bodies, with each management team pursuing its own goals, the best interest of passengers and business might not be served.

Nevertheless, some aspects of the UK model have been adopted under EC Directive 91/440, which allows European train operators access to the rail networks of other companies. This means that several companies (say, from different EU countries) can offer competing services on the same international route.

Government set out new proposals in 2000 for the future of the rail network, as the first set of seven-year franchises drew to an end. The intention was to reintroduce a degree of regional monopoly control back over the rail system. By reducing the number of rail franchises from 25 to 14 (and possibly the number of operators from 11 to 8), it was suggested that the role of the regulator in monitoring and enforcing performance and fare criteria would become less complex and easier to manage. The rail franchising regulator was replaced by a new Strategic Rail Authority, with wider powers and a remit that covered overseeing the integration of the rail network.

In addition, to encourage business to invest long term, new franchise licences would be for 20 years. The original seven-year franchises were argued by many to offer little or no incentive for a rail company to invest or plan long term, when after seven years it might potentially lose its franchise.

Question

Why are subsidies more likely to be needed for commuter services than for medium-to-long-distance passenger services?

agreement cannot be reached, the Competition Commission acts as an appeal court and its decision is binding.

The regulator for each industry also set limits to the prices that certain parts of the industry can charge. These parts are those where there is little or no competition: for example, the charge made to electricity companies by the National Grid Company for transmitting electricity.

The price-setting formulae are essentially of the '*RPI* minus *X*' variety. What this means is that the industries can raise their prices by the rate of increase in the retail price index (i.e. by the rate of inflation) *minus* a certain percentage (*X*) to take account of expected increases in efficiency. Thus if the rate of inflation were 6 per cent, and if the regulator considered that the industry (or firm) could be expected to reduce its costs by 2 per cent ($X = 2\%$), then price rises would be capped at 4 per cent. The $RPI - X$ system is thus an example of **price-cap regulation**. The idea of this system of regulation is that it forces the industry to pass cost savings on to the consumer.

Assessing the system of regulation in the UK

The system that has evolved in the UK has various advantages over that employed in the USA and elsewhere (where regulation often focuses on the level of *profits*).

● It is a *discretionary* system, with the regulator able to judge individual examples of the behaviour of the industry on their own merits. The regulator has a detailed knowledge of the industry which would not be available to government ministers or other bodies such as the Office of Fair Trading. The regulator could thus be argued to be the best person to decide on whether the industry is acting in the public interest.
● The system is *flexible*, since it allows for the licence and price formula to be changed as circumstances change.
● The '*RPI* minus *X*' formula provides an *incentive* for the privatised firms to be as efficient as possible. If they can lower their costs by more than X, they will, in theory, be able to make larger profits and keep them. If on the other hand, they do not succeed in reducing costs sufficiently, they will make a loss. There is thus a continuing pressure on them to cut costs. (In the US system, where *profits* rather than *prices* are regulated, there is little incentive to increase efficiency, since any cost reductions must be passed on to the consumer in lower prices, and do not, therefore, result in higher profits.)

There are, however, some inherent problems with the way in which regulation operates in the UK:

● The '*RPI* minus *X*' formula was designed to provide an incentive for the firms to cut costs. But if *X* is too low, the firm might make excessive profits. Frequently, regulators have underestimated the scope for cost reductions resulting from new technology and reorganisation, and have thus initially set *X* too low. As a result, instead of *X* remaining constant for five years, as intended, new higher values for *X* have been set after only one or two years. But this then leads to the same problem as with the US system. The incentive for the industry to cut costs will be removed. What is the point of being more efficient if the regulator is merely going to insist on a higher value for *X* and thus take away the extra profits?
● A large amount of power is vested in a regulator who is unelected and largely unaccountable. What guarantee is there that the regulator's perception of the public interest is the same as that of the government?
● Regulation is becoming increasingly complex. This makes it difficult for the industries to plan and may lead to a growth of 'short-termism'. One of the claimed advantages of privatisation was to give greater independence to the industries from short-term government interference, and allow them to plan for the longer term. In practice, one type of interference may have been replaced by another.

● As regulation becomes more detailed and complex and as the regulator becomes more and more involved in the detailed running of the industry, so managers and regulators will become increasingly involved in game of strategy: each trying to outwit the other. Information will become distorted and time and energy will be wasted in playing this game of cat and mouse.

● There may also be the danger of **regulatory capture**. As regulators become more and more involved in their industry and get to know the senior managers at a personal level, so they are increasingly likely to see the managers' point of view. They will begin to adopt the values and modes of thinking of the industry and will become less and less tough. Commentators do not believe that this has happened yet: the regulators are generally independently minded. But it is a danger for the future.

Increasing competition in the privatised industries

Where natural monopoly exists, competition is impossible in a free market. Of course, the industry *could* be broken up by the government, with firms prohibited from owning more than a certain percentage of the industry. But this would lead to higher costs of production. Firms would be operating further back up a downward-sloping long-run average cost curve.

But many parts of the privatised industries are not natural monopolies. Generally it is only the *grid* that is a natural monopoly. In the case of gas and water, it is the pipelines. It would be wasteful to duplicate these. In the case of electricity, it is the power lines: the national grid and the local power lines. In the case of the railways, it is the track. *Other* parts of these industries are potentially competitive. There could be many generators of electricity, provided they had access to the national and local grids. There could be many producers of gas, provided they had access to the pipelines. There could be many operators of trains, provided they could all use the same track with central timetabling and signalling.

Since privatisation, most parts of these industries that are not natural monopolies have indeed been opened up to competition. Since 1998, there has been free competition in supplying gas to any home or business; similarly with electricity since 1999. In other words, customers can choose their supplier, even though the suppliers are all using the same pipelines or cables. And it is not just in supply to customers that competition has grown. There has been an increase in the number of gas producers and electricity generators. The telecommunications market too has become more competitive with the growth of mobile phones and lines supplied by cable operators.

To help the opening up of competition, regulators have sometimes restricted the behaviour of the established firms (like BT or British Gas), to prevent them using their dominance in the market as a barrier to entry of new firms. For example, British Gas since 1995 has had to limit its share of the industrial gas market to 40 per cent.

Another approach has been to separate the ownership of the grid from that of supplying companies. Examples include splitting British Gas into separate pipeline and supply companies; re-privatising the national electricity grid in 1996 as a separate company from the twelve regional electricity companies, which had previously owned it; privatising Railtrack (which owns the track, signalling and stations) as a separate company from the train operating companies.

As competition has been introduced into these industries, so price-cap regulation

> **definition**
>
> **Regulatory capture**
> Where the regulator is persuaded to operate in the industry's interests rather than those of the consumer.

has been progressively abandoned. The intention is ultimately to confine price regulation to the operation of the grids: the parts that are natural monopolies.

Even for the parts where there is a natural monopoly, they could be made *contestable* monopolies. One way of doing this is by granting operators a licence for a specific period of time. This is known as **franchising**. This has been the approach used for the railways. Once a company has been granted a franchise, it has the monopoly of passenger rail services over specific routes. But the awarding of the franchise can be highly competitive, with rival companies putting in competitive bids, in terms of both price (or, in the case of railways, the level of government subsidy required) and the quality of service. Another approach is to give all companies equal access to the relevant grid (such as the electricity grid, gas pipelines and the rail network).

But despite attempts to introduce competition into the privatised industries, they are still dominated by giant companies. Even if they are no longer strictly monopolies, they still have considerable market power and the scope for price leadership or other forms of oligopolistic collusion is great. Regulation through the price formula has been progressively abandoned as elements of competition have been introduced. But this assumes that competition really *will* be effective in protecting the public interest!

SUMMARY

1a Pollution is a negative externality, and due to the lack of property rights over the environment, it will be treated as a free good and hence over-used. Environmental policy attempts to ensure that the full costs of production or consumption are paid for by those who produce and consume.

1b The environment is difficult to value, so it is difficult to estimate the costs of environmental pollution. This is a major problem in being able to devise an efficient environmental policy.

1c Environmental policy can be either market based or non-market based, or a mixture of the two. Market-based solutions focus upon the use of taxes and subsidies to correct market signals. Non-market-based solutions involve the use of regulations and controls over polluting activities.

1d The problem with using taxes and subsidies is in identifying the appropriate rates, since these will vary according to the environmental impact.

1e Command-and-control systems, such as making certain practices illegal or putting limits on discharges, are a less sophisticated alternative to taxes or subsidies. However, they may be preferable when the environmental costs of certain actions are unknown and it is wise to play safe.

1f Tradable permits are a mix of command-and-control and market-based systems. Firms are given permits to emit a certain level of pollution and then these can be traded. A firm that can relatively cheaply reduce its pollution below its permitted level can sell this credit to another firm which finds it more costly to do so. The system is an efficient and administratively cheap way of limiting pollution to a designated level. It can, however, lead to pollution being concentrated in certain areas and can reduce the pressure on firms to find cleaner methods of production.

2a The allocation of road space depends on demand and supply. Demand is derived from the demand by travellers to get to their destination. Demand depends on the price to motorists of using their cars, incomes, the cost of alternative means of transport, the price of cars and complementary services (such as parking), and the comfort and convenience of car transport. The price and cross-price elasticities of demand for car usage tend to be low: many people are unwilling to switch to alternative modes of transport. The income elasticity, on the other hand, is high. The demand for cars and car usage grows rapidly as incomes grow.

2b In the short run, with road space fixed, allocation depends on the private decisions of motorists. The problem is that motorists create two types of external cost: pollution costs and congestion costs. Thus $MSC > MC$. Because of these externalities, the actual use of road space (where $MB = MC$) is likely to be greater than the optimum (where $MSB = MSC$).

2c In the long run, the social optimum amount of road space will be where $LRMSB = LRMSC$. New road schemes should be adopted as long as their $LRMSB > LRMSC$. Governments must therefore conduct some form of cost–benefit analysis in order to estimate these costs and benefits. This will include measuring such externalities as reductions in the time taken to make a journey.

2d There are various types of solution to traffic congestion. These include direct provision by the government or local authorities (of additional road space or better public transport); regulation and legislation (such as restricting car access – by the use of bus and cycle lanes, no entry to side streets and pedestrian-only areas – and various forms of parking restrictions); changing market signals (by the use of taxes, by road pricing, and by subsidising alternative means of transport).

2e Problems associated with building additional roads include the decline of public transport, attracting additional traffic on to the roads and environmental costs.

2f The main problem with restricting car access is that it tends merely to divert congestion elsewhere. The main problem with parking restrictions is that they may actually increase congestion.

2g Increasing taxes is effective in reducing congestion only if it increases the *marginal* cost of motoring. Even when it does, as in the case of additional fuel tax, the additional cost is only indirectly related to congestion costs, since it applies to all motorists and not just those causing congestion.

2h Road pricing is the preferred solution of many economists. By the use of electronic devices, motorists can be charged whenever they add to congestion. This should encourage less essential road users to travel at off-peak times or to use alternative modes of transport, while those who gain a high utility from car transport can still use their cars, but at a price. Variable tolls and supplementary licences are alternative forms of congestion pricing, but are generally less effective than the use of electronic road pricing.

2i If road pricing is to be effective, there must be attractive substitutes available. A comprehensive policy, therefore, should include subsidising efficient public transport. The revenues required for this could be obtained from road pricing.

3a From around 1983 the Conservative government in the UK embarked on a large programme of privatisation. The justification was partly ideological and partly to do with the perceived economic failures of the nationalised industries and their better prospects under private ownership.

3b The economic arguments for privatisation include: greater competition, not only in the goods market but in the market for finance and for corporate control; reduced government interference; reducing the PSNCR; and making these industries more accountable to the public via share ownership.

3c The economic arguments against privatisation are largely the market failure arguments that were used to justify nationalisation. In reply the advocates of privatisation argue that these problems can be overcome through appropriate regulation and increasing the amount of competition.

3d Regulation in the UK has involved setting up regulatory offices for the major privatised utilities. These generally operate informally, using negotiation and bargaining to persuade the industries to behave in the public interest. As far as prices are concerned, the industries are required to abide by an '*RPI* minus *X*' formula. This forces them to pass potential cost reductions on to the consumer. At the same time they are allowed to retain any additional profits gained from cost reductions greater than *X*. This provides them with an incentive to achieve even greater increases in efficiency. The regulator can seek a revision of the industry's licence or price formula. If the firm does not agree, an appeal can be made to the Competition Commission whose decision is binding.

3e Many parts of the privatised industries are not natural monopolies. In these parts, competition may be a more effective means of pursuing the public interest. Various attempts have been made to make the privatised industries more competitive, often at the instigation of the regulator. Nevertheless, considerable market power remains in the hands of many privatised firms, and thus the need for regulation will continue.

REVIEW QUESTIONS

1   Why is it so difficult to value the environment? What are the implications of this for government policy on the environment?

2   Is it a good idea to use the revenues from green taxes to subsidise green alternatives (e.g. using petrol taxes for subsidising rail transport)?

3   Compare the relative merits of increased road fuel taxes, electronic road pricing and tolls as means of reducing urban traffic congestion. Why is the price inelasticity of demand for private car transport a problem here, whichever of the three policies is adopted? What could be done to increase the price elasticity of demand?

4   How would you set about measuring the external costs of road transport?

5   Consider the argument that whether an industry is in the public sector or private sector has far less bearing on its performance than the degree of competition it faces.

6   To what extent do the various goals of privatisation conflict?

H Business in the international environment

THE FINANCIAL TIMES, 4 OCTOBER 1999

The single currency has had a significant effect on investment, although the UK – outside the euro-zone – stays ahead of the pack.

Peter Norman

The European single currency has brought new transparency to business decisions in an 11 nation area with a population slightly larger than the US. Yet although costs are now fully comparable and exchange rate uncertainty has been eliminated in the euro-zone, a host of issues relating to the competitiveness of a given location still must be weighted when deciding where best to locate factories and offices in Europe.

Although companies began preparing for the single currency well before its January 1 launch, figures from Eurostat, the European Union's statistical agency, show the UK, which is outside the euro-zone, continued to attract far more direct investment from abroad than its partners last year.

Cultural and linguistics factors play a role. As well as having business friendly governments, Britain and Ireland have the incalculable advantage of English, the world language.

But mainly 'business looks at operating costs and at the bottom line', explains Dirk Hudig, secretary-general of Unice, the Brussels-based union of European business and employers bodies. That means evaluating wage and non-wage labour costs, local skills and education, productivity, capacity for innovation, overall tax burdens and systems of taxation, transport facilities, the financial infrastructure, regulatory environment and legal systems as well as any potential gains and losses from the single currency.

There are huge variations in the cost of labour among EU member-states. Figures cited by Unice in its recent 'benchmarking report' showed labour costs in manufacturing industry ranged between €5.6 an hour in Portugal in 1997 through €14.5 in Britain to €24.4 in Germany. On the other hand, there were wide variations in productivity, with UK manufacturing managing 70 per cent of US levels against 118 per cent in the Netherlands.

With falling barriers to international trade, with improved communications and with an increasingly global financial system, so nations have found that their economies have become ever more intimately linked. Economic events in one part of the world, such as changes in interest rates or a downturn in economic growth, will have a myriad of knock-on effects for the international community at large – from the international investor, to the foreign exchange dealer, to the domestic policy maker, to the business which exports or imports, or which has subsidiaries abroad.

In Part H we explore the international environment and its impact on business. In Chapter 22 we will focus on international trade. We will consider why trading is advantageous and why, nevertheless, certain countries feel the need to restrict trade.

Chapter 23 considers the rise and spread of multinational enterprises within the world economy. It not only looks at why certain businesses become multinational, but evaluates their impact upon host nations, within both the developed and the developing worlds.

Chapter 24 focuses upon the other major change in the global economy over the last 40 years – namely, the rise of the trade bloc. We will outline the advantages and disadvantages of regional trading. We will look briefly at trading blocs in North America and South-East Asia and the Pacific. Then, as an extended case study, we will consider the position of the European Union and the effects of the creation of a single European market on both businesses and consumers.

For European air travellers, 1 April [1997] marked an auspicious date. For the first time, any European airline was able – in theory, at least – to fly any time, any place, any fare. The creation of an open-skies policy in Europe has been 10 years in the making.

The Observer, 11 May 1997

key terms

Comparative advantage
The gains from trade
Terms of trade
Protectionism
Tariffs
Quotas
Infant and senile industries
World Trade Organisation (WTO)
Multinational corporation
Trade bloc
Preferential trading
Free trade areas, customs unions and common markets
Trade creation and diversion
North America Free Trade Association (NAFTA)
Asian-Pacific Economic Co-operation forum (APEC)
European Union (EU)
Single European market

International trade

Without international trade we would all be much poorer. There would be some items like pineapples, coffee, cotton clothes, foreign holidays and uranium that we would simply have to go without. Then there would be other items like wine and spacecraft that we could produce only very inefficiently.

International trade has the potential to benefit *all* participating countries. This chapter explains why.

Totally free trade, however, may bring problems to countries or to groups of people within those countries. Many people argue strongly for restrictions on trade. Textile workers see their jobs threatened by cheap imported cloth. Car manufacturers worry about falling sales as customers switch to Japanese models or other east Asian ones. This chapter, therefore, also examines the arguments for restricting trade. Are people justified in fearing international competition, or are they merely trying to protect some vested interest at the expense of everyone else?

22.1 Trading patterns

In 1985 the value of world merchandise traded stood at a little under $2 trillion. By 2000 the value of world merchandise traded had risen to over $5.6 trillion. Even after allowing for inflation, this still represents a substantial increase in real terms. As can be seen in Figure 22.1, the growth in world trade has, on average, consistently outstripped the growth in world production.

The geography of international trade

The major industrial economies dominate world trade (see Figure 22.2). Some 70 per cent of all merchandise trade is conducted by the developed economies. The EU countries with approximately 41 per cent of exports (by value) and 40 per cent of imports (by value) are the most important trading region. The most important individual country in respect to trade is the USA, followed by Germany and Japan. The USA sells some 12½ per cent of world exports and consumes approximately 18 per cent of world imports. Germany sells about 10 per cent of world exports and consumes about 8 per cent of world imports. The concentration of world trade is further highlighted by the fact that the top eight nations account for over 50 per cent of all world trade.

On a regional basis, Europe exhibits the highest level of intra-regional trading, selling nearly 70 per cent of its exports to other European countries. Other areas such as Latin America and Africa trade very little with themselves and rely heavily on North America and Europe to sell their products. Some 48

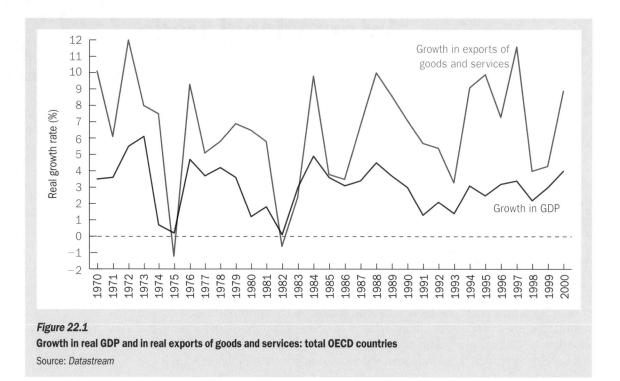

Figure 22.1

Growth in real GDP and in real exports of goods and services: total OECD countries

Source: *Datastream*

per cent of Latin American exports go to North America, whereas over 50 per cent of Africa's exports go to Europe.

Figure 22.3 shows the *growth* of exports and imports by region. China has achieved the most spectacular growth rate in exports (15 per cent annual aver-

Figure 22.2
Share of world merchandise exports, by value (1998)

Note: includes intra EU trade

Source: *Trade Statistics* (WTO, 2000) (http://www.wto.org/english/res_e/statis_e/statis_e.htm)

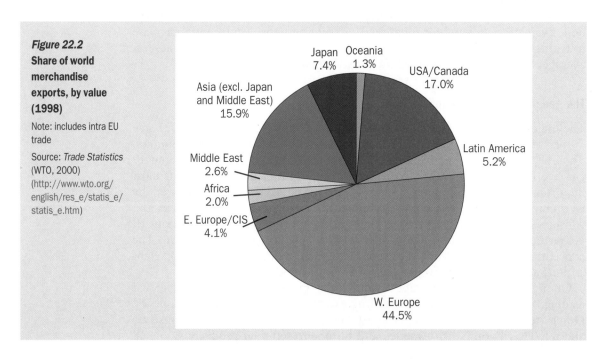

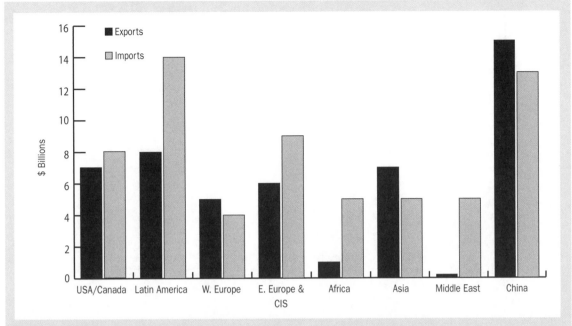

Figure 22.3
Growth in value of merchandise exports and imports by region: average annual percentage, 1990–8
Source: *Trade Statistics* (WTO, 2000) (http://www.wto.org/english/res_e/statis_e/statis_e.htm)

age from 1990–8). Although Latin America growth in exports (8 per cent over the same period) has also been high by international standards, the region's growth in imports (14 per cent) has been much higher. Asian growth in exports has also been high, with the six Asian 'Tigers' (Singapore, Hong Kong, Malaysia, South Korea, Taiwan and Thailand) achieving an average of 8 per cent. In contrast, African countries only managed a 1 per cent growth in exports, but a 5 per cent growth in imports. Middle Eastern countries experienced virtually no growth in export earnings over the period, thanks to the generally falling price of oil. This changed in 1999/2000 as world oil prices surged. In 1999 alone, Middle Eastern export earnings rose by 22 per cent.

The composition of international trade

Trade in goods

By far the largest category of traded goods is that of manufactured products (see Figure 22.4). In 1998 manufactured products accounted for 76.1 per cent of all merchandise exports and 60.8 per cent of *total* exports (which include services). Agricultural products accounted for 10.5 per cent of merchandise exports and mining products 9.5 per cent.

Trade in services

Services in 1998 accounted for about 20 per cent of total trade. As with trade in manufactured products, trade in services is concentrated in the hands of the

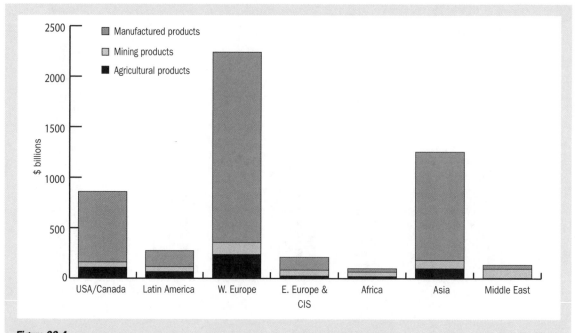

Figure 22.4
Value of merchandise exports by region: $ billions, 1998

Source: *Trade Statistics* (WTO, 2000) (http://www.wto.org/english/res_e/statis_e/statis_e.htm)

largest industrial nations. The USA is by far the largest exporter with some 19 per cent of all service exports, followed by the UK (7.6 per cent) and France (5.9 per cent). The largest importer of services is the USA with 13.7 per cent of the total, followed by Germany (9.5 per cent) and Japan (8.5 per cent).

Trade and the UK

In 1999 the UK sold 5.0 per cent of world exports of goods and services and consumed 5.6 per cent of world imports. Over 54 per cent of the UK's exports of goods went to countries in the eurozone, and 63 per cent to Western Europe as a whole (representing a 4 percentage point rise since 1984). UK imports, like UK exports, are strongly tied to Europe. Some 50 per cent of the imports of goods came from eurozone countries, and 59 per cent from Western Europe as a whole.

In 1999 the UK's earnings from the export of goods relied heavily upon semi-manufactured and finished manufactured goods: some 89 per cent of total earnings came from these two sources. In 1984 earnings from these sources had accounted for only 61 per cent of the total, with earnings from oil exports accounting for 21 per cent. By 1998 oil exports had fallen to only 4.2 per cent of the total earnings from exports but then, with rising oil prices, increased to 7.9 per cent by mid 2000.

As with exports, the UK's imports of goods are dominated by semi-manufactured and manufactured goods. In 1999 such goods represented 87 per cent of the total earnings from imports.

22.2 The advantages of trade

Specialisation as the basis for trade

Why do countries trade with each other and what do they gain out of it? The reasons for international trade are really only an extension of the reasons for trade *within* a nation. Rather than people trying to be self-sufficient and do everything for themselves, it makes sense to specialise.

Firms specialise in producing certain types of goods. This allows them to gain economies of scale and to exploit their entrepreneurial and management skills and the skills of their labour force. It also allows them to benefit from their particular location and from the ownership of any particular capital equipment or other assets they might possess. With the revenues that firms earn, they buy in the inputs they need from other firms and the labour they require. Firms thus trade with each other.

Countries also specialise. They produce more than they need of certain goods. What is not consumed domestically is exported. The revenues earned from the exports are used to import goods which are not produced in sufficient amounts at home.

But which goods should a country specialise in? What should it export and what should it import? The answer is that it should specialise in those goods in which it has a *comparative advantage*. Let us examine what this means.

The law of comparative advantage

Countries have different endowments of factors of production. They differ in population density, labour skills, climate, raw materials, capital equipment, etc. These differences tend to persist because factors are relatively immobile between countries. Obviously land and climate are totally immobile, but even with labour and capital there tend to be more restrictions (physical, social, cultural or legal) on their international movement than on their movement within countries. Thus the ability to supply goods differs between countries.

What this means is that the relative costs of producing goods will vary from country to country. For example, one country may be able to produce 1 fridge for the same cost as 6 tonnes of wheat or 3 compact disc players, whereas another country may be able to produce 1 fridge for the same cost as only 3 tonnes of wheat but 4 CD players. It is these differences in relative costs that form the basis of trade.

At this stage we need to distinguish between *absolute advantage* and *comparative advantage*.

Absolute advantage

When one country can produce a good with less resources than another country, it is said to have an **absolute advantage** in that good. If France can produce wine with less resources than the UK, and the UK can produce gin with less resources than France, then France has an absolute advantage in wine and the UK an absolute advantage in gin. Production of both wine and gin will be maximised by each country specialising and then trading with the other country. Both will gain.

> **definition**
>
> **Absolute advantage**
> A country has an absolute advantage over another in the production of a good if it can produce it with less resources than the other country.

Comparative advantage

The above seems obvious, but trade between two countries can still be beneficial even if one country could produce *all* goods with less resources than the other, providing the *relative* efficiency with which goods can be produced differs between the two countries.

Take the case of a developed country that is absolutely more efficient than a less developed country at producing both wheat and cloth. Assume that with a given amount of resources (labour, land and capital) the alternatives shown in Table 22.1 can be produced in each country.

Despite the developed country having an absolute advantage in both wheat and cloth, the less developed country (LDC) has a *comparative* **advantage** in wheat, and the developed country has a *comparative* advantage in cloth. This is because wheat is relatively cheaper in the LDC: only 1 metre of cloth has to be sacrificed to produce 2 kilos of wheat, whereas 8 metres of cloth would have to be sacrificed in the developed country to produce 4 kilos of wheat. In other words, the opportunity cost of wheat is 4 times higher in the developed country (8/4 compared with 1/2).

On the other hand, cloth is relatively cheaper in the developed country. Here the opportunity cost of producing 8 metres of cloth is only 4 kilos of wheat, whereas in the LDC 1 metre of cloth costs 2 kilos of wheat. Thus the opportunity cost of cloth is 4 times higher in the LDC (2/1 compared with 4/8).

To summarise: countries have a comparative advantage in those goods that can be produced at a lower opportunity cost than in other countries.

If countries are to gain from trade, they should export those goods in which they have a comparative advantage and import those goods in which they have a comparative disadvantage. Given this, we can state a **law of comparative advantage**: provided opportunity costs of various goods differ in two countries, both of them can gain from mutual trade if they specialise in producing (and exporting) those goods that have relatively low opportunity costs compared with the other country.

But why do they gain if they speciualise according to this law? And just what will that gain be? We will consider these questions next.

The gains from trade based on comparative advantage

Before trade, unless markets are very imperfect, the prices of the two goods are likely to reflect their opportunity costs. For example, in Table 22.1, since the less developed country can produce 2 kilos of wheat for 1 metre of cloth, the *price* of 2 kilos of wheat will roughly equal 1 metre of cloth.

Assume, then, that the pre-trade exchange ratios of wheat for cloth are as follows:

definition

Comparative advantage
A country has a comparative advantage over another in the production of a good if it can produce it at a lower opportunity cost: i.e. if it has to forgo less of other goods in order to produce it.

definition

The law of comparative advantage
Trade can benefit all countries if they specialise in the goods in which they have a comparative advantage.

Table 22.1 Production possibilities for two countries

		Kilos of wheat		Metres of cloth
Less developed country	Either	2	or	1
Developed country	Either	4	or	8

LDC   : 2 wheat for 1 cloth
Developed country : 1 wheat for 2 cloth (i.e. 4 for 8)

Both countries will now gain from trade, provided the exchange ratio is somewhere between 2:1 and 1:2. Assume, for the sake of argument, that it is 1:1. In other words, 1 wheat trades internationally for 1 cloth. How will each country gain?

The LDC gains by exporting wheat and importing cloth. At an exchange ratio of 1:1, it now only has to give up 1 kilo of wheat to obtain a metre of cloth, whereas before trade it had to give up 2 kilos of wheat.

The developed country gains by exporting cloth and importing wheat. Again at an exchange ratio of 1:1, it now only has to give up 1 metre of cloth to obtain a kilo of wheat, whereas before it had to give up 2 metres of cloth.

Thus both countries have gained from trade.

The actual exchange ratios will depend on the relative prices of wheat and cloth after trade takes place. These prices will depend on total demand for and supply of the two goods. It may be that the trade exchange ratio is nearer to the pre-trade exchange ratio of one country than the other. Thus the gains to the two countries need not be equal. (We will examine these issues below.)

The limits to specialisation and trade

Does the law of comparative advantage suggest that countries will completely specialise in just a few products? In practice, countries are likely to experience *increasing* opportunity costs. The reason for this is that, as a country increasingly specialises in one good, it will have to use resources that are less and less suited to its production and which were more suited to other goods. Thus ever-increasing amounts of the other goods will have to be sacrificed. For example, as a country specialises more and more in grain production, it will have to use land that is less and less suited to growing grain.

These increasing costs as a country becomes more and more specialised will lead to the disappearance of its comparative cost advantage. When this happens, there will be no point in further specialisation. Thus whereas a country like Germany has a comparative advantage in capital-intensive manufactures, it does not produce only manufactures. It would make no sense not to use its fertile lands to produce food or its forests to produce timber. The opportunity costs of diverting all agricultural labour to industry would be very high.

Other reasons for gains from trade

Decreasing costs. Even if there are no initial comparative cost differences between two countries, it will still benefit both to specialise in industries where economies of scale can be gained, and then to trade. Once the economies of scale begin to appear, comparative cost differences will also appear, and thus the countries will have gained a comparative advantage in these industries.

This reason for trade is particularly relevant for small countries where the domestic market is not large enough to support large-scale industries. Thus exports form a much higher percentage of GDP in small countries such as Singapore than in large countries such as the USA.

Differences in demand. Even with no comparative cost differences and no potential economies of scale, trade can benefit both countries if demand conditions differ.

If people in country A like beef more than lamb, and people in country B like lamb more than beef, then rather than A using resources better suited for lamb to produce beef, and B using resources better suited for producing beef to produce lamb, it will benefit both to produce beef *and* lamb and to export the one they like less in return for the one they like more.

Increased competition. If a country trades, the competition from imports may stimulate greater efficiency at home. This extra competition may prevent domestic monopolies/oligopolies from charging high prices. It may stimulate greater research and development and the more rapid adoption of new technology. It may lead to a greater variety of products being made available to consumers.

Trade as an 'engine of growth'. In a growing world economy, the demand for a country's exports is likely to grow over time, especially when these exports have a high income elasticity of demand. This will provide a stimulus to growth in the exporting country.

Non-economic advantages. There may be political, social and cultural advantages to be gained by fostering trading links between countries.

The terms of trade

What price will our exports fetch abroad? What will we have to pay for imports? The answer to these questions is given by the **terms of trade**. The terms of trade are defined as:

$$\frac{\text{The average price of exports}}{\text{The average price of imports}}$$

expressed as an index, where price changes up or down are measured against a base year in which the terms of trade are assumed to be 100. Thus if the average price of exports relative to the average price of imports have risen by 20 per cent since the base year, the terms of trade will now be 120.

If the terms of trade rise (export prices rising relative to import prices), they are said to have 'improved', since fewer exports now have to be sold to purchase any given quantity of imports. Changes in the terms of trade are caused by changes in the demand and supply of imports and exports and by changes in the exchange rate.

definition

Terms of trade
The price index of exports divided by the price index of imports and then expressed as a percentage. This means that the terms of trade will be 100 in the base year.

22.3 Arguments for restricting trade

We have seen how trade can bring benefits to all countries. But when we look around the world, we often see countries erecting barriers to trade. Their politicians know that trade involves costs as well as benefits.

In looking at the costs and benefits of trade, the choice is not the stark one of whether to have free trade or no trade at all. Although countries may sometimes contemplate having completely free trade, typically countries limit their trade. However, they certainly do not ban it altogether.

Before we look at the arguments for restricting trade, we must first see what types of restriction governments can employ.

Methods of restricting trade

Tariffs (customs duties). These are taxes on imports and are usually **ad valorem**: i.e. a percentage of the price of the import. Tariffs used to restrict imports are most effective if demand is elastic (e.g. when there are close domestically produced substitutes). Tariffs can also be used as a means of raising revenue. Here they will be more effective if demand is inelastic. They can also be used to raise the price of imported goods to prevent 'unfair' competition for domestic producers.

Quotas. These are limits on the quantity of a good that can be imported. Quotas can be imposed by the government, or negotiated with other countries which agree 'voluntarily' to restrict the amount of exports to the first country.

Exchange controls. These include limits on the amount of foreign exchange made available to importers (financial quotas), or to citizens travelling abroad, or for investment. Alternatively, they can be in the form of charges for the purchase of foreign currencies.

Import licensing. The imposition of exchange controls or quotas will often involve importers obtaining licences so that the government can better enforce its restrictions.

Embargoes. This is where the government completely bans certain imports (e.g. drugs) or exports to certain countries (e.g. to enemies during war).

Export taxes. These can be used to increase the price of exports when the country has monopoly power in their supply.

Subsidies. These can be given to domestic producers to prevent competition from otherwise lower-priced imports. They can also be applied to exports in a process known as **dumping**. The goods are 'dumped' at artificially low prices in the foreign market.

Administrative barriers. Regulations may be designed to exclude imports. For example, all lagers that do not meet certain rigid purity standards could be banned. The Germans effectively excluded foreign brands by such measures. Other administrative barriers include taxes which favour locally produced products or ingredients.

Procurement policies. This is where governments favour domestic producers when purchasing equipment (e.g. defence equipment).

Arguments in favour of restricting trade

The infant industry argument. Some industries in a country may be in their infancy but have a potential comparative advantage. This is particularly likely in

> **definition**
> **Ad valorem tariffs**
> Tariffs levied as a percentage of the price of the import.

> **definition**
> **Dumping**
> Where exports are sold at prices below marginal cost – often as a result of government subsidy.

developing countries. Such industries are too small yet to have gained economies of scale; their workers are inexperienced; there is a lack of back-up facilities – communications networks, specialist research and development, specialist suppliers, etc. – and they may have only limited access to finance for expansion. Without protection, these **infant industries** will not survive competition from abroad.

Protection from foreign competition, however, will allow them to expand and become more efficient. Once they have achieved a comparative advantage, the protection can then be removed to enable them to compete internationally.

Similar to the infant industry argument is the *senile industry* argument. This is where industries with a potential comparative advantage have been allowed to run down and can no longer compete effectively. They may have considerable potential, but be simply unable to make enough profit to afford the necessary investment without some temporary protection from foreign competition. This argument has been used to justify the use of special protection for the automobile and steel industries in the USA.

To prevent 'dumping' and other unfair trade practices. A country may engage in dumping by subsidising its exports. Alternatively, firms may practise price discrimination by selling at a higher price in home markets and a lower price in foreign markets in order to increase their profits. Either way, prices may no longer reflect comparative costs. Thus the world would benefit from tariffs being imposed by importers to counteract the subsidy.

It can also be argued that there is a case for retaliating against countries which impose restrictions on your exports. In the *short* run, both countries are likely to be made worse off by a contraction in trade. But if the retaliation persuades the other country to remove its restrictions, it may have a longer-term benefit. In some cases, the mere threat of retaliation may be enough to get another country to remove its protection.

To prevent the establishment of a foreign-based monopoly. Competition from abroad could drive domestic producers out of business. The foreign company, now having a monopoly of the market, could charge high prices with a resulting misallocation of resources.

To reduce reliance on goods with little dynamic potential. Many developing countries have traditionally exported primaries: foodstuffs and raw materials. The world demand for these, however, is fairly income inelastic, and thus grows relatively slowly. In such cases, free trade is not an engine of growth. Instead, if it encourages countries' economies to become locked into a pattern of primary production, it may prevent them from expanding in sectors like manufacturing which have a higher income elasticity of demand. There may thus be a valid argument for protecting or promoting manufacturing industry.

To spread the risks of fluctuating markets. A highly specialised economy – Zambia with copper, Cuba with sugar – will be highly susceptible to world market fluctuations. Greater diversity and greater self-sufficiency, although maybe leading to less efficiency, can reduce these risks.

To reduce the influence of trade on consumer tastes. The assumption of fixed consumer tastes dictating the pattern of production through trade is false.

Multinational companies through their advertising and other forms of sales promotion may influence consumer tastes. Thus some restriction on trade may be justified in order to reduce this 'producer sovereignty'.

To prevent the importation of harmful goods. A country may want to ban or severely curtail the importation of things such as drugs, pornographic literature and live animals.

To take account of externalities. Free trade will tend to reflect private costs. Both imports and exports, however, can involve externalities. The mining of many minerals for export may adversely affect the health of miners; the production of chemicals for export may involve pollution; the importation of juggernaut lorries may lead to structural damage to houses.

The above arguments are of general validity: restricting trade for such reasons could be of net benefit to the world. There are other arguments, however, that are used by individual governments for restricting trade, where their country will gain, but at the expense of other countries, such that there will be a net loss to the world. Such arguments include the following.

The exploitation of monopoly power. If a country, or a group of countries, has monopsony power in the purchase of imports (i.e. they are individually or collectively a very large economy, such as the USA or the EU), then they could gain by restricting imports so as to drive down their price. Similarly, if countries have monopoly power in the sale of some export (e.g. OPEC countries with oil), then they could gain by forcing up the price.

To protect declining industries. The human costs of sudden industrial closures can be very high. In such circumstances, temporary protection may be warranted to allow the industry to decline more slowly, thus avoiding excessive structural unemployment. Such policies will be at the expense of the consumer, who will be denied access to cheaper foreign imports.

To improve the balance of payments. Under certain special circumstances, when other methods of balance of payments correction are unsuitable, there may be a case for resorting to tariffs.

'Non-economic' arguments for restricting trade. A country may be prepared to forgo the direct economic advantages of free trade in order to achieve objectives that are often described as 'non-economic':

- It may wish to maintain a degree of self-sufficiency in case trade is cut off in times of war. This may apply particularly to the production of food and armaments.
- It may decide not to trade with certain countries with which it disagrees politically.
- It may wish to preserve traditional ways of life. Rural communities or communities built round old traditional industries may be destroyed by foreign competition.
- It may prefer to retain as diverse a society as possible, rather than one too narrowly based on certain industries.

Pursuing such objectives, however, will involve costs. Preserving a traditional way of life, for example, may mean that consumers are denied access to cheaper goods from abroad. Society must therefore weigh up the benefits against the costs of such policies.

Problems with protection

Protection will tend to push up prices and restrict the choice of goods available. But apart from these direct costs to the consumer, there are several other problems. Some are a direct effect of the protection, others follow from the reactions of other nations.

Protection as 'second-best'. Many of the arguments for protection amount merely to arguments for some type of government intervention in the economy. Protection, however, may not be the best way of dealing with the problem, since protection may have undesirable side-effects. There may be a more direct form of intervention that has no side-effects. In such a case, protection will be no more than a *second-best* solution.

For example, using tariffs to protect old inefficient industries from foreign competition may help prevent unemployment in those parts of the economy, but the consumer will suffer from higher prices. A better solution would be to subsidise retraining and investment in those areas of the country in *new efficient* industries – industries with a comparative advantage. In this way, unemployment is avoided, but the consumer does not suffer.

World multiplier effects. If the UK imposes tariffs or other restrictions, imports will be reduced. But these imports are other countries' exports. A reduction in their exports will reduce the level of injections into the 'rest-of-the-world' economy, and thus lead to a multiplied fall in rest-of-the-world income. This in turn will lead to a reduction in demand for UK exports. This, therefore, tends to undo the benefits of the tariffs.

Retaliation. If the UK imposes restrictions on, say, Japan, then Japan may impose restrictions on the UK. Any gain to UK firms competing with Japanese imports is offset by a loss to UK exporters. What is more, UK consumers suffer, since the benefits from comparative advantage have been lost.

The increased use of tariffs and other restrictions can lead to a trade war, with each country cutting back on imports from other countries. In the end, everyone loses.

Protection may allow firms to remain inefficient. By removing or reducing foreign competition, tariffs etc. may reduce firms' incentive to reduce costs. Thus if protection is being given to an infant industry, the government must ensure that the lack of competition does not prevent it 'growing up'. Protection should not be excessive and should be removed as soon as possible.

Bureaucracy. If a government is to avoid giving excessive protection to firms, it should examine each case carefully. This can lead to large administrative costs.

22.4 World attitudes towards trade and protection

Pre-war growth in protectionism

After the Wall Street crash of 1929, the world plunged into the Great Depression. Countries found their exports falling dramatically and many suffered severe balance of payments difficulties. The response of many countries was to restrict imports by the use of tariffs and quotas. Of course, this reduced other countries' exports, which encouraged them to resort to even greater protectionism. The net effect of the Depression and the rise in protectionism was a dramatic fall in world trade. The volume of world trade in manufactures fell by more than a third in the three years following the Wall Street crash. Clearly there was a net economic loss to the world from this decline in trade.

Post-war reduction in protectionism and the role of GATT

After the Second World War there was a general desire to reduce trade restrictions, so that all countries could gain the maximum benefits from trade. There was no desire to return to the beggar-my-neighbour policies of the 1930s.

In 1947, 23 countries got together and signed the General Agreement on Tariffs and Trade (GATT). Today there are some 140 members of its successor organisation, the World Trade Organisation (WTO), which was formed in 1995. Between them, the members of the WTO account for over 90 per cent of world trade. The aims of GATT, and now the WTO, have been to liberalise trade. Periodically, member countries have met to negotiate reductions in tariffs and other trade restrictions. There have been eight 'rounds' of such negotiations since 1947. The three major ones were the Kennedy Round (1964–7), the Tokyo Round (1973–9) and the Uruguay Round (1986–93). The Kennedy Round led to tariff reductions averaging 35 per cent. The Tokyo Round involved agreements for tariff reductions of about 33 per cent, but many of the reductions in the event were less than those agreed.

In addition to the negotiated reductions in trade restrictions, GATT, now the WTO, provides various rules governing trade:

- Non-discrimination. Under the 'most favoured nations clause', any trade concession that a country makes to one member must be granted to *all* signatories.
- Reciprocity. Any nation benefiting from a tariff reduction made by another country had to reciprocate by making similar tariff reductions itself.
- The general prohibition of quotas (but with notable exceptions: e.g. agricultural imports).
- Fair competition. If unfair barriers were erected against a particular country, the GATT could sanction retaliatory action by that country. The country was not allowed, however, to take such action without permission.
- Special arrangements for developing countries, to permit them a greater use of protection than developed countries.

The re-emergence of protectionist sentiments in the 1980s

The balance of payments problems that many countries experienced after the oil crisis of 1973 and the recession of the early 1980s led many politicians round

BOX 22.1

Strategic trade theory
The case of Airbus

Supporters of *strategic trade theory* hold that comparative advantage need not be the result of luck or circumstance, but may in fact be created by government. By diverting resources into selective industries, usually high tech and high skilled, a comparative advantage can be created through intervention.

An example of such intervention was the European aircraft industry, and in particular the creation of the European Airbus Consortium.

The European Airbus Consortium was established in the late 1960s, its four members being Aérospatiale (France), British Aerospace (now BAE Systems) (UK), CASA (Spain) and DASA (Germany). The setting up of this consortium was seen as essential for the future of the European aircraft industry for three reasons:

● To share high R&D costs.
● To generate economies of scale.
● To compete successfully with the market's major players in the USA – Boeing and McDonnell Douglas (which have since merged).

The consortium, although privately owned, was sponsored by government and received state aid, especially in its early years when the company failed to make a profit. In more recent times Airbus has become very successful, capturing a larger and larger share of the world commercial aircraft market. By 2001, its share of the large civil aircraft market had risen to 55 per cent. As a consequence, it should come as no surprise to find that the Americans, and Boeing in particular, have brought accusations that Airbus is founded upon unfair trading practices and ought not to receive the level of governmental support that it does (see Box 24.2).

In 1999/2000, there were three major developments. The first was the merger of Aerospatiale-Matra, Dasa (DaimlerChrysler Aerospace) and Casa to form the giant European Aeronautic Defence and Space Company (EADS). The second was the creation of an Airbus Integrated Company (from EADS and BAE Systems) as a single entity to replace the looser Airbus Consortium. Then towards the end of 2000, it was announced that enough orders had been secured for the planned new 550+ seater A3XX for production to go ahead. This new jumbo will be a serious competitor to the long-established Boeing 747.

So does the experience of Airbus support the arguments of the strategic trade theorists? Essentially three kinds of benefit were expected to flow from Airbus and its presence in the aircraft market: lower prices, economic spillovers and profits.

● Without Airbus the civil aircraft market would have been monopolised by two American firms, Boeing and McDonnell Douglas (and possibly one, if the 1997 merger had still gone ahead). Therefore the presence of Airbus would be expected to promote competition and thereby keep prices down. Studies in the 1980s and 1990s tended to support this view, suggesting that consumers have made significant gains from lower prices. One survey estimated that without Airbus commercial aircraft prices would have been 3.5 per cent higher than they currently are, and without both Airbus *and* McDonnell Douglas they would have been 15 per cent higher.
● Economic spillovers from the Airbus Consortium, such as skills and technology developments, might be expected to benefit other industries. Findings are inconclusive on this point. It is clear, however, that although aggregate R&D in the whole aircraft industry has risen, so has the level of R&D duplication.
● Airbus's presence in the market is estimated to have reduced Boeing's profits by as much as $100 billion, and McDonnell Douglas's by two-thirds. Airbus's profits in 1999 were approximately $1 billion.

On balance it appears that Airbus has had many positive effects and that the strategic trade theory that has underpinned state aid, in this instance, has led to a successful outcome. A competitive advantage has been created, and it looks as though it will be maintained into the future, and probably without state aid!

Questions
1 In what other industries could the setting up of a consortium, backed by government aid, be justified as a means of exploiting a potential comparative advantage?
2 Is it only in industries that could be characterised as *world* oligopolies that strategic trade theory is relevant?

the world to call for trade restrictions. Although a tariff war was averted, there was a gradual increase in non-tariff barriers, such as subsidies on domestic products, the prohibition of imports that did not meet precise safety or other specifications, administrative delays in customs clearance, limits on investment by foreign companies, and governments favouring domestic firms when purchasing supplies.

Quotas were increasingly used, especially against Japanese imports. In most cases these were 'voluntary' agreements. Japan, on a number of occasions, agreed to restrict the number of cars it exported to various European countries. Similar restrictions applied to Japanese televisions and videos. Over 200 **voluntary restraint arrangements** (**VRAs**) (also known as **voluntary export restraints** (**VERs**)) were in force around the world in the early 1990s.

The problem of increasing non-tariff barriers were recognised in the Uruguay Round of GATT negotiations, and agreements were sought to dismantle many of them.

The Uruguay Round and the World Trade Organisation

The Uruguay Round

The Uruguay Round was much more comprehensive than previous rounds. Unlike the others, it included negotiations on tariff reductions in agricultural products and in services (as well as in industrial products), and reductions in non-tariff barriers. Despite fears that an agreement would never be reached, negotiations were completed in December 1993 and a deal was signed in April 1994. This involved a programme of phasing in substantial reductions in tariffs and other restrictions up to the year 2002. These included:

- Tariffs on industrial products cut by an average of 38 per cent (more than the original target) and eliminated entirely on certain products.
- Prohibition of export subsidies and voluntary export restraints (VERs).
- Non-tariff measures to be converted to tariffs.
- The Multifibre Agreement, which protected industrialised countries against imports of textiles from developing countries, to be phased out over ten years.
- Tariffs on agricultural products reduced by 36 per cent over six years in industrialised countries and ten years in developing countries.
- An agreement by the EU to cut subsidised farm exports by 21 per cent in volume and by 36 per cent in value within six years. Over the same period, support for domestic farmers would be cut by 20 per cent.
- Protection of intellectual property rights strengthened (including patents, copyrights and trademarks).
- Adoption of rules limiting the power of countries to restrict the provision of services (e.g. banking and insurance) by foreign companies, and to restrict multinational investment (e.g. by forcing them to use a proportion of local inputs). Existing measures to be phased out within seven years.
- Adoption of voluntary codes limiting anti-dumping measures and the practice of government procurement favouring domestic suppliers.

But despite these successes, the cuts in agricultural protection were less than was originally hoped for. Although it was agreed to replace food import quotas into the EU and other industrialised countries by tariff equivalents, the degree

> **definition**
>
> **Voluntary restraint arrangements (VRAs) or voluntary export restraints (VERs)**
> A form of agreed or voluntary quota between the exporting country and the country receiving the exports.

BOX 22.2

The World Trade Organisation and its future
Successes and new challenges[1]

In the years since the signing of the Uruguay Round agreement in 1993, the World Trade Organisation (WTO), which was itself set up as a product of the discussions, has presided over a world economy in which moves towards freer trade have continued.

● More countries have joined the WTO. It now has a membership of 140 countries, compared to the 92 members of GATT when the Uruguay Round started in 1986.

● A new mechanism for settling trade disputes has been set up as part of the Uruguay Round agreement. By 2001 this had been successful in resolving 36 cases requiring some measure of arbitration.

● World trade in goods since 1993 has grown substantially more than world GDP (see Figure 22.1).

● Economic integration through foreign direct investment has also grown much more rapidly than GDP.

The signs are good that trade will continue to become freer and to grow faster than world income. However, there are some possible threats to this process. Not only is there the danger of nations or groups of nations seeking their own advantage (as they have always done) by protecting their industries from international competition, but new challenges have arisen which require resolution if the WTO is to continue to be effective. Three such challenges are as follows:

China. Despite applying to join GATT in 1986, and despite an apparent breakthrough in early 2000, there seems no chance of China being admitted to the WTO before late 2001 at the earliest. Yet China is the world's ninth largest exporter (see panel). This calls into question just how extensively the WTO represents the whole world trading community.

There have been two main stumbling blocks to Chinese membership. First, China has operated a wide variety of trade and foreign investment controls, most of which infringe WTO principles. Although many of these are being dismantled, it is very difficult for the WTO to monitor them. One reason for this is that the distinction between the private and state sectors in China is blurred, and as such it is difficult to identify state subsidies and other aid to industry, let alone regulate it.

Second, there is considerable international concern over China's human-rights record. This, as much as anything, has slowed down discussions, as countries have sought to gain firm guarantees from China.

New issues. Many countries in the WTO have been arguing that a policy to govern world trade and create free

Top exporters
World merchandise trade (1999)

Ranking	Value ($bn)	Share (%)
USA	695.0	12.4
Germany	540.5	9.6
Japan	419.4	7.5
France	299.0	5.3
UK	268.4	4.8
Canada	238.4	4.2
Italy	230.8	4.1
Netherlands	204.1	3.6
China	194.9	3.5
Belgium/Lux.	184.1	3.3
Hong Kong	174.8	3.1
South Korea	144.2	2.6

Source: *Trade Statistics* (WTO, 2000).

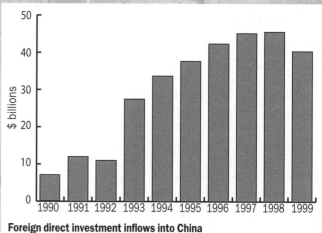

Foreign direct investment inflows into China

Source: *China Statistical Yearbook 1999* (http://www.pnl.gov/china/fdi.htm)

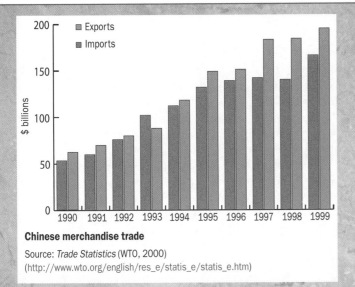

Chinese merchandise trade

Source: *Trade Statistics* (WTO, 2000)
(http://www.wto.org/english/res_e/statis_e/statis_e.htm)

Top importers
World merchandise trade (1999)

Ranking	Value ($bn)	Share (%)
USA	1059.9	18.0
Germany	472.6	8.0
UK	320.7	5.5
Japan	310.7	5.3
France	286.1	4.9
Canada	220.2	3.7
Italy	216.0	3.7
Netherlands	188.9	3.2
Hong Kong	181.7	3.1
Belgium/Lux.	169.4	2.9
China	165.7	2.8
Mexico	148.2	2.5

Source: *Trade Statistics* (WTO, 2000).

and open markets must be extended beyond trading issues. The trading positions of countries can be shaped, and enhanced, by an array of largely domestic policies, over which the WTO has no influence. Three such policy areas are: foreign investment, competition policy and labour standards. It has been suggested that global standards and regulations should be established in each of these areas.

There should, it is argued, be regulations on the offering of 'sweeteners' to attract foreign direct investment. Sweeteners in the form of tax relief or subsidised facilities might be seen as little more than an export subsidy, since many, if not most, of the inward investment results in the company subsequently exporting its products from the country.

Rules governing competition policy are also argued to be necessary, as many businesses can operate international monopolies and cartels beyond the control of national governments and their competition departments.

Equally, universal labour standards are necessary in order to prevent the exploitation of vulnerable groups, especially child labour.

Each of these policy areas attracts far from unanimous support. Many developing economies want nothing to do with setting labour standards. Many countries argue that *they* wish to set the terms on which they receive foreign investment and not follow common principles. As for competition policy, not only are there the difficulties of harmonising existing national and regional competition policy arrangements, but there are funda-

mental disagreements about what aspects of competition policy to discuss.

Regional trading arrangements. Of the 76 free trade areas or customs unions set up since 1948, over half have materialised in the 1990s. Such regional deals range from simple preferential trading arrangements, to agreements covering investment and competition policy, and, in the case of the EU, a lot more besides.

The effect of regional trading agreements on international trade has generally been to encourage trade between member countries and divert it away from other parties outside of the agreement. (For a full discussion of the operation and impact of trade blocs, see Chapter 24). With growing regionalism, trade will become increasingly regional and less multilateral, thus working against the prime aim of the WTO.

The WTO, and its predecessor GATT, may have been hugely successful to date in enhancing global free trade, but it appears that if such success is to be continued into the future then many difficult hurdles still remain to be overcome.

Question

If the gains from global free trade are so obvious, why are nations sometimes so reluctant to embrace measures which might enhance it?

---

[1] This box is adapted from *The Economist*, 7 December 1996.

BOX 22.3

The battle of Seattle
Is the WTO a goody or a baddy?

In November 1999, the 135 members of the World Trade Organisation met in Seattle in the USA. The aim of the meeting was to plan further reductions in trade barriers and to discuss launching a new round of trade negotiations to carry on the work done in the Uruguay round. The free trade movement seemed unstoppable. But stopped it was – at least temporarily.

Amidst riots and street battles, the talks broke up in disarray. Various groups joined in the protests. These ranged from environmentalists, charities, trade unionists and champions of the rights of developing countries, to campaigners against capitalism. They claimed that the WTO is undemocratic: that it is a rich countries' club, protecting the interests of large companies and ignoring the environment and the plight of poor people and poor countries. The process of globalisation, of which the WTO is an agent, is making us all pawns in a game over which we have no control and no democratic rights.

The WTO, not surprisingly, has a different view. Mike Moore, its Director General (from 1999–2002), argued that 'Every member Government supports open trade because it leads to higher living standards for working families which in turn leads to a cleaner environment.' What is the basis of the WTO view?

First is the simple truth that, because of the law of comparative advantage, trade can lead to a net gain to the world. Imagine how much lower our living standards would be if we all had to be self-sufficient and there was no trade at all. Countries that have tried to survive without trade (such as North Korea) have generally suffered lower living standards as a consequence.

Second is the argument that environmental problems result from polluting production processes and waste products, not from trade. The solution then to environmental problems is not to restrict trade but to regulate or tax pollution at source.

Third is the claim that trade leads to greater not less equality. Trade can help to push up wages in poor countries. The reason is that countries are likely to have a comparative advantage in products which require inputs that are relatively cheap. For poor countries, this means labour. By exporting such products, the extra production will push up the price of the inputs used to produce them. Hence the price of labour (i.e. wages) will rise. Thus, says the WTO, it is the champion of the poor, not their enemy. World Bank evidence[1] suggests that growth stimulated by freer trade benefits the poor as much as the rich (in other words it leaves income distribution about the same).

Finally, free trade leads to greater competition as companies are no longer shielded behind protective barriers. Far from protecting the interests of large companies, then, the WTO claims that it is on the side of the consumer.

So is there any basis for the criticisms of the WTO? Were all the protestors at Seattle, and at various anti-globalisation rallies since, missing the point? As is often the case with economic issues, there are valid points on both sides.

Free trade tends not to be fair trade. As trade has become freer, so world inequalities have become deeper. As a report by Christian Aid states:[2]

The poorest countries in the world have seen their share of world trade halved over the last 20 years, until the poorest 10% of the world's population participate in less than half of one percent of the world's trade. And more trade liberalisation won't necessarily help. At the end of the last round of trade talks, it was predicted that Africa would lose out even further, suffering losses of between $300 million and $600 per year after the agreements were implemented.

Though trade rules are made by countries, it is companies that do the trading. And the companies of the richest countries have been able to make most of the gains from freer trade, often at the expense of smaller traders from developing countries. Instead of rushing into new talks on freeing trade, WTO members should address ways to make trade fairer for poor countries and poor people.

The report goes on to look at agriculture, the most important sector for many poor countries.

Trade in agriculture is highly concentrated, with three companies accounting for 83 percent of world trade in cocoa, six companies controlling 85 percent of world grain trade, and three companies accounting for around 80 percent of world banana sales. Though most primary products come from developing countries, all these companies are based in industrialised countries, or the richer developing countries such as Brazil.

Referring to the outcome of the Uruguay round, the report states that:

Trade liberalisation in agriculture was very selective. While developing countries had to open up their markets for primary products, allowing the few companies that dominate these markets to increase their share of the market, often at the expense of smaller firms, industrialised countries have not opened their markets to producers from developing countries. In addition, the protection that large companies enjoy from industrialised country governments has been maintained, while the protections granted to smaller producers have been whittled away. As a result, large companies have made most of the gains from increased market access in both developing and developed countries.

Making world trade freer often gives powerful companies the right to exploit their position of power. For example, under the trade-related intellectual property rights (TRIPS) agreement, large companies are able to establish exclusive rights for their products and brands. The Christian Aid report gives an example of how this can damage the interests of developing countries:

Rice and curry is the staple diet of millions of Indians. Both have been the subject of patents by foreign companies since India implemented the WTO agreement on TRIPs in March 1999. Basmati rice has been patented by the US-based company, RiceTec Inc., in what an Indian academic refers to as 'a direct appropriation of traditional knowledge of Indian farmers'. A Japanese firm have also applied for a patent on curry, described as a process of 'adding extracted spices to ingredients like cut and processed onions, heating the mixture, and adding curry powder, and heating until the mixture

becomes viscous'. Because of TRIPs, Indian farmers and consumers are losing control of their most basic foods to the multinational companies of industrialised countries.

The protection of patents on drugs can deny cheap access to medicines that are vital for saving lives in the poorest countries.

And the problems with free trade do not just concern questions of inequality and poverty. They also concern the environment. Pollution is an external cost to firms. If firms are given total freedom to trade, the environment may suffer.

If countries try to curb the production or importation of goods produced in an environmentally friendly way, they may well fall foul of WTO rules. Take the case of the import of petrol to the USA. Under US law, refiners are subject to strict environmental standards. When the US tried to apply such standards to imported petrol, the WTO ruled against it, forcing it to import petrol made by less environmentally friendly methods. Another case concerned the import of shrimps to the USA from countries that catch shrimps in a way that kills sea turtles. When the USA tried to ban such imports, the WTO ruled against the USA. In doing so, the WTO effectively banned unilateral trade controls designed to protect the environment.

The protests at Seattle and elsewhere are having some positive results. Many multinational companies are redrafting their company mission statements. They know that if they ignore the growing groundswell against them, they may find their profits suffering. For example, companies such as Monsanto cannot ignore the reaction against genetically modified food.

Questions

1 Are there any ways in which free trade *benefits* the environment?

2 In what ways does freer trade lead to (a) more competition; (b) less competition?

---

[1] David Dollar and Aart Kraay, 'Growth is Good for the Poor' (http://www.worldbank.org/research/)

[2] http://www.christian-aid.org.uk/indepth/9911fair/fairshares.htm

of protection remains high, and the industrialised world continues to export food to many developing countries which have a comparative advantage in food production!

The World Trade Organisation

The Uruguay Round deal also led to the setting up of the World Trade Organisation (WTO) in 1995 as the successor to the GATT. Most of the old GATT rules still apply, but the WTO is much more powerful than the GATT, which was merely an inter-governmental treaty, not an international organisation. If there are disputes between member nations, these are settled by the WTO, although there is provision for appeals, and the parties can agree to go to arbitration. However, countries then found to be in the wrong must abide by the ruling or face sanctions.

The greater power of the WTO has persuaded many countries to bring their disputes to it. In the first 5½ years of its existence it had dealt with over 200 disputes (compared with 300 by GATT over the whole of its 48 years). The WTO has also carried on from the Uruguay Round and has completed several new international agreements, for example to lower trade barriers in telecommunications and information technology.

SUMMARY

1a World trade has grown, for many years, significantly faster than the growth in world output.

1b World trade is highly concentrated in the developed world and in particular between the top six trading nations.

1c The composition of world trade is largely dominated by manufacturing products, although trade in services has expanded over recent years.

2a Countries can gain from trade if they specialise in producing those goods in which they have a comparative advantage: i.e. those goods that can be produced at relatively low opportunity costs. This is merely an extension of the argument that gains can be made from the specialisation and division of labour.

2b If two countries trade, then, provided that the trade price ratio of exports and imports is between the pre-trade price ratios of these goods in the two countries, both countries can gain.

2c With increasing opportunity costs there will be a limit to specialisation and trade. As a country increasingly specialises, its (marginal) comparative advantage will eventually disappear.

2d The terms of trade give the price of exports relative to the price of imports expressed as an index, where the base year is 100.

2e Gains from trade also arise from decreasing costs (economies of scale), differences in demand between countries, increased competition from trade and the transmission of growth from one country to another. There may also be non-economic advantages from trade.

3a Countries use various methods to restrict trade, including tariffs, quotas, exchange controls, import licensing, export taxes, and legal and administrative barriers. Countries may also promote their own industries by subsidies.

3b Reasons for restricting trade that have some validity in a world context include the infant industry argument, dumping and other unfair trade practices, the danger of the establishment of a foreign-based monopoly, the problems of relying on exporting goods whose market is growing slowly or even declining, the need to spread the risks of fluctuating export prices, and the problems that free trade may adversely affect consumer tastes, may allow the importation of harmful goods and may not take account of externalities.

3c Often, however, the arguments for restricting trade are in the context of one country benefiting even though other countries may lose more. Countries may intervene in trade in order to exploit their monopoly/monopsony power. In the case of imports, the optimum tariff would be that which

SUMMARY

would reduce consumption to the level where price was equal to the country's marginal cost. In the case of exports, the optimum export tax would be that which reduced production to the level where the country's marginal revenue was equal to marginal cost. Other 'beggar-my-neighbour' arguments include the protection of declining industries and improving the balance of payments.

3d Finally, a country may have other objectives in restricting trade, such as remaining self-sufficient in certain strategic products, not trading with certain countries of which it disapproves, protecting traditional ways of life or simply retaining a non-specialised economy.

3e Arguments for restricting trade, however, are often fallacious. In general, trade brings benefits to countries, and protection to achieve one objective may be at a very high opportunity cost. Other things being equal, there will be a net loss in welfare from

restricting trade, with any gain in government revenue or profits to firms being outweighed by a loss in consumer surplus. Even if government intervention to protect certain parts of the economy is desirable, restricting trade is unlikely to be a first-best solution to the problem, since it involves side-effect costs. What is more, restricting trade may have adverse world multiplier effects; it may encourage retaliation; it may allow inefficient firms to remain inefficient; it may involve considerable bureaucracy and possibly even corruption.

4 Most countries of the world are members of the WTO and in theory are in favour of moves towards freer trade. The Uruguay Round brought significant reductions in trade restrictions, both tariff and non-tariff. Nevertheless, countries have been very unwilling to abandon restrictions if they believe that they can gain from them, even though they might be at the expense of other countries.

REVIEW QUESTIONS

1 What is likely to be the impact of rising levels of intra-regional trade for the world economy?

2 Imagine that two countries, Richland and Poorland, can produce just two goods, computers and coal. Assume that for a given amount of land and capital, the output of these two products requires the following constant amounts of labour:

	Richland	Poorland
1 computer	2	4
100 tonnes of coal	4	5

Assume that each country has 20 million workers.

(a) Draw the production possibility curves for the two countries (on two separate diagrams).

(b) If there is no trade, and in each country 12 million workers produce computers and 8 million workers produce coal, how many computers and tonnes of coal will each country produce? What will be the total production of each product?

(c) What is the opportunity cost of a computer in (i) Richland; (ii) Poorland?

(d) What is the opportunity cost of 100 tonnes of coal in (i) Richland: (ii) Poorland?

(e) Which country has a comparative advantage in which product?

(f) Assuming that price equals marginal cost, which of the following would represent possible exchange ratios?
(i) 1 computer for 40 tonnes of coal; (ii) 2 computers for 140 tonnes of coal; (iii) 1 computer for 100 tonnes of coal; (iv) 1 computer for 60 tonnes of coal; (v) 4 computers for 360 tonnes of coal.

(g) Assume that trade now takes place and that 1 computer exchanges for 65 tonnes of coal. Both countries specialise completely in the product in which they have a comparative advantage. How much does each country produce of its respective product?

(h) The country producing computers sells 6 million domestically. How many does it export to the other country?

(i) How much coal does the other country consume?

3 Why doesn't the USA specialise as much as General Motors or Texaco? Why doesn't the UK specialise as much as ICI? Is the answer to these questions similar to the answer to the questions, 'Why doesn't the USA specialise as much as Luxembourg?', and 'Why doesn't ICI or Unilever specialise as much as the local florist?'

4 To what extent are the arguments for countries specialising and then trading with each other the same as those for individuals specialising in doing the jobs to which they are relatively well suited?

5 The following are four items that are traded internationally: wheat; computers; textiles; insurance. In which one of the four is each of the following most likely to have a comparative advantage? India; the UK; Canada; Japan. Give reasons for your answer.

6 Go through each of the arguments for restricting trade (both those of general validity and those having some validity for specific countries) and provide a counter-argument for not restricting trade.

7 If countries are so keen to reduce the barriers to trade, why do many countries frequently attempt to erect barriers?

8 Debate the following:
'All arguments for restricting trade boil down to special pleading for particular interest groups. Ultimately there will be a net social cost from any trade restrictions.'

9 If rich countries stand to gain substantially from freer trade, why have they been so reluctant to reduce the levels of protection of agriculture?

10 Make out a case for restricting trade between the UK and Japan. Are there any arguments here that could not equally apply to a case for restricting trade between Scotland and England or between Liverpool or Manchester?

Multinational corporations

Since the mid-1980s multinational businesses have been downsizing. They have been shrinking the size of their headquarters, removing layers of bureaucracy, and reorganising their global operations into smaller autonomous profit centres. Gone is the philosophy that big companies will inevitably do better than small ones. In fact, it now appears that multinationals are seeking to create a hybrid form of business organisation, which combines the advantages of size (i.e. economies of scale) with the responsiveness and market knowledge of smaller firms.

The key for the modern multinational is flexibility, and to be at one and the same time both global and local.

In this chapter we shall consider why it is that businesses decide to go multinational, and evaluate what impact they have on their host countries. Before we do this we shall first offer a definition of multinational business and assess the importance of multinational investment for the UK economy.

23.1 What is a multinational corporation?

There are some 35 000 **multinational corporations** (MNCs) worldwide. Between them they control a total of 15 000 foreign subsidiaries. Furthermore, the top 200 MNCs control about one-third of global production.

Even given their obvious gigantic size and overwhelming importance within the global economy, MNCs defy simple definition. At the most basic level, an MNC is a business that either owns or controls foreign subsidiaries in more than one country.

It is this ownership or control of productive assets in other countries which makes the MNC distinct from an enterprise that does business overseas by simply exporting goods or services. However, merely to define an MNC as a company with overseas subsidiaries fails to reflect the immense diversity of multinationals.

Diversity among MNCs

Size. Many, if not most, of the world's largest firms – IBM, Shell, General Motors, etc. – are multinationals. Indeed, the turnover of some of them exceeds the national income of many smaller countries (see Table 23.1). And yet there are also thousands of very small, often specialist multinationals, which are a mere fraction of the size of the giants.

The nature of business. MNCs cover the entire spectrum of business activity, from manufacturing to extraction, agricultural production, chemicals, process-

> **definition**
>
> **Multinational corporations**
> Businesses that either own or control foreign subsidiaries in more than one country.

Table 23.1	Comparison of the eleven largest multinational corporations (by gross revenue) and selected countries (by GDP): 1999	
MNC rank	Country or Company (headquarters)	GDP ($bn) or gross revenue ($bn)
1	General Motors (USA)	189.1
	Turkey	185.2
	Denmark	174.3
2	Wal-Mart Stores (USA)	166.8
3	Exxon Mobil (USA)	163.9
4	Ford Motor (USA)	162.6
5	DaimlerChrysler (Germany)	160.0
	Hong Kong	158.6
	Norway	152.9
	Finland	129.8
	Greece	125.1
	Thailand	123.9
6	Mitsui (Japan)	118.6
7	Mitsubishi (Japan)	117.7
8	Toyota Motor (Japan)	115.7
	Portugal	114.0
9	General Electric (USA)	111.6
10	Itochu (Japan)	109.1
11	Royal Dutch/Shell (UK, Netherlands)	105.4
	Ireland	94.2
	Singapore	84.9
	Malaysia	78.7
	Pakistan	58.1
	New Zealand	54.0
	Hungary	48.4
	Nigeria	34.8
	Kenya	10.4

Sources: companies: *Fortune Global 500* (http://www.fortune.com/fortune/global500/);
countries: *World Economic Outlook* database, IMF, 2000
(http://www.imf.org/external/pubs/ft/weo/2000/02/data/ngdpd_a.csv)

ing, service provision and finance. There is no 'typical' line of activity of a multinational.

Overseas business relative to total business. MNCs differ in respect to how extensive their overseas operations are relative to their total business. Nearly 50 per cent of IBM's sales and profits come from its activities outside the USA. The foreign operations of other MNCs represent only a small fraction of their total business.

Production locations. Some MNCs are truly 'global', with production located in a wide variety of countries and regions. Other MNCs, by contrast, only locate in one other region, or in a very narrow range of countries.

There are, however, a number of potentially constraining factors on the location of multinational businesses. For example, businesses concerned with the extraction of raw materials will locate as nature dictates! Businesses that provide services will tend to locate in the rich markets of developed regions of the world economy, where the demand for services is high. Others locate according to the factor intensity of the stage of production. Thus a labour-intensive stage might be located in a developing country where wage rates are relatively low, while another stage which requires a high level of automation might be located in an industrially advanced country.

Ownership patterns. As businesses expand overseas, they are faced with a number of options. They can decide to go it alone and create wholly owned subsidiaries. Alternatively, they might share ownership and hence some of the risk, by establishing joint ventures. In such cases the MNC might have a majority or minority stake in the overseas enterprise.

In certain countries, where MNC investment is regulated, many governments insist on owning or controlling a share in the new enterprise. Whether governments insist on domestic companies (or themselves) having a majority or minority stake varies from country to country. It also depends on the nature of the business and its perceived national importance. For example, until recently the Indian government insisted on having a majority stake in all multinational business ventures in the high-technology sector of the Indian economy.

Organisational structure. In Chapter 3 we discussed the variety of organisational forms that MNCs might adopt – from the model where the headquarters, or parent company, is dominant and the overseas subsidiary subservient, to that where international subsidiaries operate as self-standing organisations, bound together only in so far as they strive towards a set of global objectives.

The above characteristics of MNCs reveal that they represent a wide and very diverse group of enterprises. Beyond sharing the common link of having production activities in more than one country, MNCs differ widely in the nature and forms of their overseas business, and in the relationship between the parent and its subsidiaries.

23.2 Multinational corporations and the UK economy

When looking at the role played by MNCs in the UK economy, we need to distinguish between UK companies operating overseas, and foreign companies operating in the UK.

We can estimate the size of multinational investment, by both UK business and overseas companies, by looking at figures for foreign direct investment (FDI). FDI represents the finance used either to purchase the assets for setting up a new subsidiary (or expanding an existing one), or to acquire an existing business operation.

Figure 23.1 shows that between 1985 and 1989 outward direct investment rose by £12.1 billion (a rise of nearly 140 per cent). In 1990, however, it fell to half its 1989 level. Since 1991 outward direct investment has risen steeply again, standing at £125.3 billion in 1999, the largest ever recorded figure for direct investment overseas.

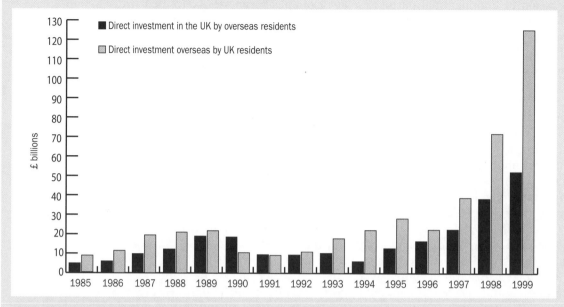

Figure 23.1

Direct investment into and out of the UK: 1985–99

Source: *Financial Statistics* (ONS).

Inward direct investment into the UK increased steadily from 1985 to 1989, reaching £18.6 billion. In 1991 inward investment fell to £9.1 billion and for the following three years showed no signs of recovery, falling to £6.1 billion in 1994. Between 1994 and 1999, however, annual overseas direct investment into the UK increased by £46.2 billion to £52.3 billion. As with outward investment, the 1999 figure for inward direct investment is the highest ever recorded (see Figure 23.1).

The income earned from direct foreign investment is shown in Figure 23.2: both that received from UK investment overseas (credits) and that paid to overseas investors in the UK (debits). The figure shows that since 1985 the UK has experienced an increasing surplus of direct investment income. In 1985 the surplus stood at a modest £0.2 billion. By 1998 the surplus had risen to £20.3 billion (falling to £11.5 billion in 1999). In other words, direct investment income credits have risen significantly faster than debits. This is particularly so since 1993.

FDI and the UK economy: international comparisons

By international comparisons, the UK is both a major investor overseas and a significant receiver of FDI. UK investment abroad accounts for some 15 to 20 per cent of total world outward investment, and FDI into the UK accounts for some 10 per cent of the world total.

During the late 1980s, the USA was the largest receiver of UK direct investment, receiving approximately 60 per cent of all UK direct investment funds. However, by 2000, the USA's share had fallen to around 30 per cent. By con-

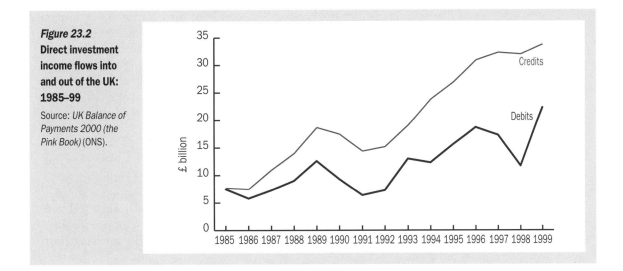

Figure 23.2
Direct investment income flows into and out of the UK: 1985–99

Source: *UK Balance of Payments 2000 (the Pink Book)* (ONS).

trast, the EU's share of UK foreign direct investment, whilst fluctuating with the prospects of the EU economy, has generally risen, to stand at around 40 per cent by 2000.

Some 45 per cent of UK inward investment comes from the USA, 32 per cent from EU countries, 6 per cent from Switzerland and 4 per cent each from Australia and Japan. In 2000 the UK's stock of inward direct investment stood at £300 billion, over six times the level recorded ten years earlier.

In respect to the European market, which attracts two-fifths of all US, Japanese and South Korean investment, approximately 40 per cent of all manufacturing inward investment into the European Union comes to the UK.

Before we consider the potential costs and benefits resulting from having a large multinational sector within the economy, we will first investigate what businesses can hope to gain from going multinational.

23.3 Why do businesses go multinational?

There are many reasons why companies choose to go multinational. These depend on the nature of their business and their corporate strategy. Before identifying the various motives for producing overseas rather than merely exporting to such countries, it is necessary to distinguish different categories of multinational.

- A **horizontally integrated multinational**. This type of multinational seeks to produce essentially the same product in different countries (but perhaps with some variations in product specification to suit the needs of the local market). The primary objective of this strategy is to achieve growth by expanding into new markets.
- A **vertically integrated multinational**. In this case, the multinational undertakes the various stages of production in different countries for a core business. Thus in some countries it will go backwards into the business's supply chain to the components or raw materials stages, and in others it

definition

Horizontally integrated multinational
A multinational that produces the same product in many different countries.

definition

Vertically integrated multinational
A multinational that undertakes the various stages of production for a given product in different countries.

will go forwards into the product's assembly or distribution. Oil companies such as Shell and Exxon (Esso) are good examples of vertically integrated multinationals, undertaking in a global operation the extraction of crude oil, controlling its transportation, refining it and producing by-products, and controlling the retail sale of petrol and other oil products. The principal motive behind such a growth strategy is to be able to exert greater control over costs and reduce the uncertainty of the business environment.

● A **conglomerate multinational**. Such multinationals produce a range of different products in different countries. By this process of diversification, conglomerate multinationals look to spread risks, and maximise returns through the careful buying of overseas assets. Diageo is a good example of a conglomerate multinational. It operates worldwide in various food and drink markets. Its subsidiaries include UDV (spirits and wines), Pillsbury (international food company), Guinness (brewing), and Burger King (fast-food chain).

We can see from the above classification that a clear distinction can be made between MNCs that are using their multinational base primarily as a means of reducing costs (vertically integrated multinationals) and those that are using it to achieve growth (horizontal and conglomerate multinationals). Let us now consider how, by going multinational, such goals might be achieved.

Reductions in costs

Nations, like individuals, are not equally endowed with factors of production. Some nations are rich in labour, some in capital, some in raw materials. In other words, individual nations might have specific advantages over others. Because such factors of production are largely immobile, especially between nations, businesses respond by becoming multinational: that is, they locate where the necessary factors of production they require can be found. In the case of a business that wishes to extract raw materials, it has little choice but to do this. But why might a business wish to move for labour? Here it is not simply a question of the *availability* of labour: rather it is a question of the relative *cost* of labour. For example, it might locate an assembly plant in a developing country (i.e. a country with relatively low labour costs), if that plant uses large amounts of labour relative to the value added to the product at that stage. Thus foreign countries, with different cost conditions, are able to provide business with a more competitive environment within which to produce its products.

Cost differences between countries are ruthlessly exploited by Nike, the American sportswear manufacturer. Nike has organised itself globally such that it can respond rapidly to changing cost conditions in its international subsidiaries. Its product development operations are carried out in the USA, but all of its production operations are subcontracted out to over 40 overseas locations, mostly in south and south-east Asia. If wage rates, and hence costs, rise in one host country, then production is simply transferred to a more profitable subsidiary. So long as Nike headquarters has adequate information regarding the cost conditions of its subsidiaries, management decision-making concerning the location of production simply follows the operation of market forces.

The location of multinational operations does not simply depend on factor *prices*: it also depends on factor *quality*. For example, a country might have a highly skilled or highly industrious workforce, and it is this, rather than simple wage rates, that attracts multinational investment. The issue here is still largely one of costs. Highly skilled workers might cost more to employ *per hour*, but if their productivity is higher, they might well cost less to employ *per unit of output*. It is also the case, however, that highly skilled workers might produce a better quality product, and thus increase the firm's sales.

If a country has both lower-priced factors and high-quality factors, it will be very attractive to multinational investors. In recent years, the UK government has sought to attract multinational investment through its lower labour costs and more flexible employment conditions than those of its European rivals, while still having a relatively highly trained labour force compared with those in developing countries.

Locating production in a foreign country can also reduce costs in other ways. For example, a business locating production overseas would be able to reduce transport costs if those overseas plants served local or regional markets, or used local raw materials. One of the biggest cost advantages concerns the avoidance of tariffs (customs duties). If a country imposes tariffs on imports, then, by locating *within* that country (i.e. behind the 'tariff wall'), the MNC gains a competitive advantage over its rivals which are attempting to import their products from outside the country, and which are thus having to pay the tariff.

Costs might also be reduced as a consequence of the host government's attitude towards MNC investment. In an attempt to attract inward investment, a government might offer the MNC a whole range of financial and cost-reducing incentives, many of which help reduce the fixed (or 'sunk') costs of the investment, thereby reducing the investment's risk. The granting of favourable tax differentials and depreciation allowances, and the provision of premises are all widely used government strategies to attract foreign business. A recent case in the UK saw a potential investor offered financial incentives valued at £37 000 per employee to locate production in an area of Wales!

In highly competitive global markets, even small cost savings might mean the difference between success and failure. Thus MNCs will be constantly searching for ways of minimising costs and locating production where the greatest advantage might be gained.

Growth strategy

Once markets within the domestic economy have become saturated, and opportunities for growth diminish, dynamic firms may seek new markets and hence new opportunities by expanding production overseas. As we saw in Chapter 14, businesses can look to expand in one of two ways: through either internal or external expansion. MNCs are no exception to this rule. They can expand overseas, either by creating a new production facility from scratch (such as Nissan in the north-east of England), or by merging with or taking over existing foreign producers (such as the acquisition of Jaguar by Ford).

Expanding by becoming multinational enables the business to spread its risks (it is no longer tied to the trade cycle of any one country or region, or to the specific market conditions of one particular country), and in addition it enables the business to exploit any specific advantages it might have over its foreign rivals in their home markets. Such advantages might include the following:

- The ownership of superior technology. Given the dominant market positions that many MNCs hold, their possession of the most up-to-date technology is to be expected, and likely to be one of the principal keys to their success. Such ownership will not only enhance the productivity levels of the MNC, but probably also contribute to the production of superior-quality products.
- Entrepreneurial and managerial skills. With the arrival of Japanese multinationals in the UK, it became instantly apparent that Japanese managers conducted business in a very different way from their British counterparts. The most fundamental difference concerned working practices. Japanese MNCs quickly established themselves as among the most efficient and productive businesses in the UK (see section 17.7 on the flexible firm).
- Research and development capacity. Like big business generally, MNCs are likely to invest heavily in R&D in an attempt to maintain their global competitiveness. The global scale of their operations allows them to spread the costs of this R&D over a large output (i.e. the R&D has a low average fixed cost). MNCs, therefore, are often world leaders in process innovation and product development.

The product life cycle and the multinational company

One way in which the MNC might exploit its dominant position – in particular, its R&D advantage – is by extending the life cycle of a given product. By shifting production overseas at a particular point in the product's life cycle, the business is able to reduce costs and maintain competitiveness. In the domestic market, it might be faced with growing competition and static (or even declining) demand. Rivals might also be busy copying its technology. By extending (or switching) its production to different geographical locations, where demand is still growing, where there is less competition and where it has a technological advantage over any local companies, its profitability can be more effectively maintained in the long run.

The product life cycle hypothesis was discussed at length in Chapter 16. However, it is worth reviewing its elements here in order to identify how an MNC, by altering the geographical production of a good, might extend its profitability.

A product's life cycle can be split into four phases: launch, growth, maturity and decline.

The launch phase. This will tend to see the new product produced in the economy where the product is developed. It will be exported to the rest of the world. At this stage of the product's life cycle, the novelty of the product and the monopoly position of the producer enable the business to charge high prices and make high profits.

The growth phase. As the market begins to grow, other producers will seek to copy or imitate the new product. Prices begin to fall. In order to maintain competitiveness, the business will look to reduce costs, and at this stage might consider shifting production overseas to lower-cost production centres.

Maturity. At the early stage of maturity, the business is still looking to sell its product in the markets of the developed economies. Thus it may still be happy to locate some of its plants in such economies. As the original market becomes increasingly saturated, however, the MNC will seek to expand into markets overseas which are at an earlier stage of development. Part of this expansion will be by the MNC simply exporting to these economies, but increasingly it will involve relocating its production there too.

Maturity and decline. By the time the original markets are fully mature and moving into decline, the only way to extend the product's life is to cut costs and sell the product in the markets of developing countries. The location of production may shift once again, this time to even lower-cost countries. By this stage, the country in which the product was developed will almost certainly be a net importer (if there is a market left for the product), but it may well be importing the product from a subsidiary of the same company that produced it within that country in the first place!

Thus we can see that the ability to transfer production to different locations reduces costs and enables profits to be made from a product that could have become unprofitable if its production had continued from its original production base.

Problems facing multinationals

In the vast majority of cases, businesses go multinational for sound business and economic reasons, which we have outlined above. However, multinational corporations may face a number of problems resulting from their geographical expansion:

- Language barriers. The problem of language is less of a difficulty in the developed economies of the world than it is in the developing markets of, for example, Africa or Latin America. The more that the MNC employs expatriate rather than local staff, the greater the problem will be.
- Selling and marketing in foreign markets. Strategies that work at home might fail overseas, given wide social and cultural differences. Many US multinationals, such as McDonald's and Coca-Cola, are frequently accused of imposing American values in the design and promotion of their products, irrespective of the country and its culture. This can lead to resentment and hostility in the host country, which may ultimately backfire on the MNC.
- Attitudes of host governments. Governments will often try to get the best possible deal for their country from multinationals. This could result in governments insisting on part ownership in the subsidiary (either by themselves or by domestic firms), or tight rules and regulations governing the MNC's behaviour, or harsh tax regimes. In response, the MNC can always threaten to locate elsewhere.
- Communication and co-ordination between subsidiaries. Diseconomies of scale may result from an expanding global business. Lines of communication become longer and more complex. These problems are

BOX 23.1

Investing in Wales
Lucky for some[1]

In 1995, Lucky Goldstar (LG) of South Korea, seeking to expand its electronic and semi-conductor empire, decided to embark upon a £1.7 billion project to open two factories in Newport in south-east Wales, one to produce electronic products, the other semi-conductors.

The new investment was to employ 6100 people, the largest job creation programme from inward investment in Europe. However, the potential benefits did not end here. The Welsh Economy Research Unit estimated that a further 8400 jobs would result from LG's investment. This is known as the regional 'multiplier' effect. The table shows where these additional jobs were likely to be created.

Estimated employment in Wales of the LG project (no. of jobs)

Sector	LG Electronics	LG Semiconductors
LG direct employment	4410	1696
Knock-on-effects		
Agriculture	167	73
Energy	154	109
Manufacturing	1821	781
Construction	164	115
Distribution	1638	839
Transport	211	123
Other services	1463	750
Total	10 028	4486

Source: *Financial Times*, November 1996.

New employment would be principally generated by component suppliers either moving into the area or expanding. The EU stipulated that 80 per cent of component sourcing must come from European suppliers by the year 2000. It was estimated that 70 per cent of such sourcing would be from within the UK, and would be worth approximately £300 million. The other area of significant job creation is through the expansion of distribution networks.

Even though it is difficult to estimate the size of this direct employment multiplier, this becomes a relatively minor problem when we try to estimate the long-term impact on jobs. A key influence here is LG's insistence on high standards of product quality from its suppliers. Having to meet such stringent requirements to supply LG, many businesses had to improve their competitive position, subsequently improving their profitability and offering further opportunities for growth and expansion. The job-creating potential was immense.

The Korean hokey-cokey

One important weakness in depending upon foreign direct investment for jobs and growth is the potential uncertainty that it might bring. Companies like Lucky Goldstar are 'footloose' and benefit from being able to locate and relocate where they like within the global economy. So if plant becomes old or obsolete in one country, or if the firm's fortunes suffer a downturn and it seeks to cut costs and streamline its operations, then

likely to be greater, the greater is the attempted level of control exerted by the parent company: in other words, the more the parent company attempts to conduct business as though the subsidiaries were regional branches. Multinational organisational structures where international subsidiaries operate largely independently of the parent state will tend to minimise such problems.

23.4 The advantages of MNC investment for the host state

As mentioned previously, host governments are always on the look-out to attract foreign direct investment, and are prepared to put up considerable

its foreign subsidiaries may disappear from a country as rapidly as they first appeared.

Even more disastrous would be the scenario where foreign investors depart from a country *en masse*, causing widespread unemployment both directly, and indirectly via suppliers. This can have serious effects on a country's growth, investment and even its foreign trading position.

Until recent years, such a scenario would have seemed highly unlikely and would have been dismissed by many as simply scaremongering. However, the collapse and subsequent recession experienced by many of the Asian economies towards the end of 1997 made such an event a real possibility.

The UK may be particularly vulnerable to such a crisis. Its stock of foreign-owned investment is approaching £200 billion; in recent years it has attracted some 40 per cent of all inward investment into the EU. In the year to March 1997, South Korean business invested some £2.7 billion in the UK (the country's second largest inward investor after the United States (£4.0 billion)), and Japanese business contributed a further £883 million.

Inward investment into the UK was severely hit by the Asian recession, and in particular by the crisis in South Korea. Hyundai, the Korean conglomerate, delayed the completion of a £1.1 billion semi-conductor plant in Fife, Scotland. Samsung postponed a £300 million expansion of its electronics complex in north-east England and cut staff at its European Headquarters based in London.

Even in the cases where Asian investors, and in particular those from South Korea, did not pull out of the UK, the reductions and delays in their foreign investment had economic implications for the UK economy over the next few years. What these events illustrate is that, when foreign direct investment is received, usually with open arms, it should not be received without some reservations and caution. As Stefan Wagstyl of the *Financial Times* remarked at the time of the south-east Asian crisis:

If the business world needed a reminder that globalisation brings risks as well as rewards, it has come in the shape of the economic crisis in east Asia. The region which has acted as an engine of global growth for decades has slowed suddenly, shaking almost everybody on board.[2]

Questions

1 Why might the size of the regional employment multiplier effect of inward investment be difficult to estimate?

2 Apart from extra employment, what other benefits might a major inward investment project, like LG's, bring to a regional economy? Might there be any disadvantages?

[1] The first part of this box is adapted from the *Financial Times*, 19 November 1996.
[2] *Financial Times*, 13 January 1998.

finance and make significant concessions to attract overseas business. So what benefits do MNCs bring to the economy?

Employment

MNCs clearly bring investment (even if much of the fixed cost is met by the host nation) and this constitutes a stimulus to economic activity and employment creation. As is the case with the UK, most countries attempt to entice MNCs to depressed regions where investment is low and unemployment is high. Often these will be regions where a major industry has closed (e.g. the coal mining regions of South Wales). The employment that MNCs create is both direct, in the form of people employed in the new production facility, and indirect, through the impact that the MNC has on the local economy. This might be the consequence of establishing a new supply network, or simply the result of the increase in local incomes and expenditure, and hence the stimulus to local business.

It is possible, however, that jobs created in one region of a country by a new MNC venture, with its superior technology and working practices, might cause a business to fold elsewhere, thus leading to increased unemployment in that region. Nationally the level of unemployment may remain the same: all that has changed is its geographical location. The employment-generating effects of MNC investment will also be limited if the investment simply involves the purchase of existing producers, and does not involve the establishment of a new production facility. Thus we need to identify the nature of MNC involvement in the economy in order to estimate its potential employment effects.

The balance of payments

A country's balance of payments is likely to improve on a number of counts as a result of inward MNC investment. First, the investment will represent a direct flow of capital into the country. Second, and perhaps more important (especially in the long term), MNC investment is likely to result in both **import substitution** and export promotion. Import substitution will occur as products, previously purchased as imports, are now produced domestically. Export promotion will be enhanced as many multinationals use their new production facilities as export platforms. For example, many Japanese MNCs invest in the UK in order to gain access to the European Union.

The beneficial effect on the balance of payments, however, will be offset to the extent that profits earned from the investment are repatriated to the parent country, and to the extent that the exports of the MNC displace the exports of domestic producers.

In the UK it is estimated that around half of all output produced by overseas-owned manufacturers is exported, and that the net effect of inward investment represents a positive contribution to the UK balance of payments of about £1 billion a year.

Technology transfer

Technology transfer refers to the benefits gained by domestic producers from the technology imported by the MNC. Such benefits can occur in a number of ways. The most common is where domestic producers copy the production technology and working practices of the MNC. This is referred to as the 'demonstration effect' and has occurred widely in the UK as British businesses have attempted to emulate many of the practices brought into the country by Japanese multinationals.

In addition to copying best practice, technology might also be transferred through the training of workers. When workers move jobs from the MNC to other firms in the industry, or to other industrial sectors, they take their newly acquired technical knowledge and skills with them.

Taxation

MNCs, like domestic producers, are required to pay tax and therefore contribute to public finances. Given the highly profitable nature of many MNCs, the level of tax revenue raised from this source could be highly significant.

> **definition**
>
> **Import substitution**
> The replacement of imports by domestically produced goods or services.

> **definition**
>
> **Technology transfer**
> Where a host state benefits from the new technology that an MNC brings with its investment.

23.5 The disadvantages of MNC investment for the host state

Thus far we have focused on the positive effects resulting from multinational investment. However, multinational investment may not always be beneficial in either the short or the long term.

In our analysis of the benefits resulting from FDI, we noted that the regional employment impacts and repatriation of profits might effectively undermine many or all of the potential gains from multinational investment. In addition to these concerns we might identify the following.

Uncertainty. MNCs are often 'footloose', meaning that they can simply close down their operations in foreign countries and move. This is especially likely with older plants which would need updating if the MNC were to remain, or with plants that can be easily sold without too much loss. The ability to close down its business operations and shift production, while being a distinct economic advantage to the MNC, is a prime concern facing the host nation. If a country has a large foreign multinational sector within the economy, it will become very vulnerable to such footloose activity, and face great uncertainty in the long term. It may thus be forced to offer the multinational 'perks' (e.g. grants, special tax relief or specific facilities) in order to persuade it to remain. These perks are clearly costly to the taxpayer.

Control. The fact that an MNC can shift production locations not only gives it economic flexibility, but enables it to exert various controls over its host. This is particularly so in many developing countries, where MNCs are not only major employers but in many cases the principal wealth creators. Thus attempts by the host state, for example, to improve worker safety or impose pollution controls may be against what the MNC sees as its own best interests. It might thus oppose such measures or even threaten to withdraw from the country if such measures are not modified or dropped. The host nation is in a very weak position.

Transfer pricing. MNCs, like domestic producers, are always attempting to reduce their tax liabilities. One unique way that an MNC can do this is through a process known as *transfer pricing* (see page 318). This enables the MNC to reduce its profits in countries with high rates of profit tax, and increase them in countries with low rates of profit tax. This can be achieved by simply manipulating its internal pricing structure. For example, take a vertically integrated MNC where subsidiary A in one country supplies components to subsidiary B in another. The price at which the components are transferred between the two subsidiaries will ultimately determine the costs and hence the levels of profit made in each country. Assume that in the country where subsidiary A is located, the level of corporation tax is half that of the country where subsidiary B is located. If components are transferred from A to B at very high prices, then B's costs will rise and its profitability will fall. Conversely, A's profitability will rise. The MNC clearly benefits as more profit is taxed at the lower rather than the higher rate. Had it been the other way around, with subsidiary B facing the lower rate of tax, then the components would be transferred at a low price. This would increase subsidiary B's profits and reduce A's.

The practice of transfer pricing has reached such a level in the USA that, according to recent estimates, the federal government is losing over $100 million per day in tax revenue. The extent of this tax evasion was revealed when it was found that a US-based multinational subsidiary purchased toothbrushes from an affiliate for a price of $18 each!

The environment. Many MNCs are accused of simply investing in countries to gain access to natural resources, which are subsequently extracted or used in a way that is not sensitive to the environment. Host nations, especially developing countries, that are keen for investment are frequently prepared to allow MNCs to do this. They often put more store on the short-run gains from the MNC's presence than on the long-run depletion of precious natural resources or damage to the environment. Governments, like many businesses, often have a very short-run focus: they are concerned more with their political survival (whether through the ballot box or through military force) than with the long-term interests of their people.

23.6 Multinational corporations and developing economies

Many of the benefits and costs of MNC investment that we have considered so far are most acutely felt in developing countries. The poorest countries of the world are most in need of investment and yet are most vulnerable to exploitation by multinationals and have the least power to resist it. There tends, therefore, to be a love–hate relationship between the peoples of the developing world and the giant corporations that are seen to be increasingly dominating their lives: from the spread of agribusiness into the countryside through the ownership and control of plantations, to international mining corporations despoiling vast tracts of land; from industrial giants dominating manufacturing, to international banks controlling the flow of finance; from international tour operators and hotels bringing the socially disruptive effects of affluent tourists from North America, Japan, Europe and Australasia, to the products of the rich industrialised countries fashioning consumer tastes and eroding traditional culture.

Although MNCs employ only a small proportion of the total labour force in developing countries, they have a powerful effect on these countries' economies, often dominating the import and export sectors. They also often exert considerable power and influence over political leaders and their policies and over civil servants, and are frequently accused of 'meddling' in politics.

It is easy to see the harmful social, environmental and economic effects of multinationals on developing countries, and yet governments in these countries are so eager to attract overseas investment that they are frequently prepared to offer considerable perks to MNCs and to turn a blind eye to many of their excesses.

The scale of multinational investment in developing countries

The developing countries that receive the most multinational investment are those perceived to have the highest growth potential. They are generally what are known as 'newly industrialised countries' (NICs), and include Asian countries such as China, Singapore, Hong Kong, Malaysia and Thailand, and Latin American countries such as Mexico, Brazil and Argentina. The ten biggest recipients of FDI receive nearly 95 per cent of the total, while all the African countries put together receive less than 4 per cent. The poorest 50 countries of the world between them receive less than 2 per cent.

Originally, most MNC investment in developing countries was in mines and plantations. Today, mining accounts for only about 6 per cent, with manufacturing and services accounting for over half and oil for about one-third of the total.

The value of total MNC investment worldwide is about $1.5 trillion ($1 500 000 000 000), of which approximately one-third is in the developing world. Given the low levels of income of developing countries and their powerless position in world trade, this proportion is very large and shows the dominance of MNCs over their economies.

Does MNC investment aid development?

Whether investment by multinationals in developing countries is seen to be a net benefit or a net cost to these countries depends on what are perceived to be their development goals. If maximising the growth in national income is the goal, then MNC investment has probably made a positive contribution. If, however, the objectives of development are seen as more wide reaching, and include goals such as greater equality, the relief of poverty, a growth in the provision of basic needs (such as food, health care, housing and sanitation) and a general growth in the freedom and sense of well-being of the mass of the population, then the net effect of multinational investment could be argued to be anti-developmental.

Advantages to the host country

In order for countries to achieve economic growth, there must be investment. In general, the higher the rate of investment, the higher will be the rate of economic growth. The need for economic growth tends to be more pressing in developing countries than in advanced countries. One obvious reason is their lower level of income. If they are ever to aspire to the living standards of the rich North, then income per head will have to grow at a considerably faster rate than in rich countries and for many years. Another reason is the higher rates of population growth in developing countries – often some 2 per cent higher than in the rich countries. This means that for income per head to grow at merely the *same* rate as in rich countries, developing countries will have to achieve growth rates 2 per cent higher.

Investment requires finance. But developing countries are generally acutely short of funds: FDI can help to make up the shortfall. Specifically, there are key 'gaps' that FDI can help to fill.

The savings gap. A country's rate of economic growth (g) depends crucially on two factors:

- The amount of extra capital that is required to produce an extra unit of output per year: i.e. the marginal capital/output ratio (k). The greater the marginal capital/output ratio, the lower will be the output per year that results from a given amount of investment.

● The proportion of national income that a country saves (s). The higher this proportion, the greater the amount of investment that can be financed.

There is a simple formula that relates the rate of economic growth to these two factors. It is known as the **Harrod–Domar model** (after the two economists, Sir Roy Harrod and Evsey Domar, who independently developed the model). The formula is:

$$g = s/k$$

Thus if a developing country saved 10 per cent of its national income ($s = 10\%$), and if £4 of additional capital were required to produce £1 of extra output per annum ($k = 4$), then the rate of economic growth would be 10%/4 = 2.5 per cent.

If that developing country wanted to achieve a rate of economic growth of 5 per cent, then it would require a rate of saving of 20 per cent (5% = 20%/4). There would thus be a shortfall of savings: a **savings gap**. Most, if not all, developing countries perceive themselves as having a savings gap. Not only do they require relatively high rates of economic growth in order to keep ahead of population growth and to break out of poverty, but they tend to have relatively low rates of saving. Poor people cannot afford to save much out of their income.

This is where FDI comes in. It can help to fill the savings gap by directly financing the investment required to achieve the target rate of growth.

The foreign exchange gap. There are many items, especially various raw materials and machinery, that many developing countries do not produce themselves and yet which are vital if they are to develop. Such items have to be imported. But this requires foreign exchange, and most developing countries suffer from a chronic shortage of foreign exchange. Their demand for imports grows rapidly: they have a high income elasticity of demand for imports – for both capital goods and consumer goods. Yet their exports tend to grow relatively slowly. Reasons include: the development of synthetic substitutes for the raw material exports of developing countries (e.g. plastics for rubber and metal) and the relatively low income elasticity of demand for primary products (the demand for things such as tea, coffee, sugar cane and rice tends to grow relatively slowly).

FDI can help to alleviate the shortage of foreign exchange: it can help to close the **foreign exchange gap**. Not only will the MNC bring in capital which might otherwise have had to be purchased with scarce foreign exchange, but any resulting exports by the MNC will increase the country's future foreign exchange earnings.

Public finance gap. Governments in developing countries find it difficult to raise enough tax revenues to finance all the projects they would like to. MNC profits provide an additional source of tax revenue.

Skills and technology gaps. MNCs bring management expertise and often provide training programmes for local labour. The capital that flows into the developing countries with MNC investment often embodies the latest technology, access to which the developing country would otherwise be denied.

BOX 23.2

The Maharajah Mac
McDonald's in India

On 13 October 1996, McDonald's opened a restaurant in New Delhi, its first in India. This was a project that had been three years in the planning. Its menu reads like none you would find in the West. To avoid insulting Hindus, there is no beef. To avoid insulting Muslims, there is no pork. The new Maharajah Mac is made from lamb. In order to satisfy vegetarians, veggie dishes are prepared in a separate area of the kitchen so as to avoid all contact with meat.

To make such radical menu changes, which reflect the uniqueness of the Indian consumer, marks a new departure for McDonald's. Previously it had prided itself in providing an identical product virtually anywhere in the world. What also marks a new departure is that McDonald's India has attempted to present itself as a local enterprise. Its ingredients are sourced locally, and it operates in a 50–50 relationship with its Indian partners. With this business strategy, McDonald's believes that it has done everything it can do to be accepted into the Indian market: a market which frequently accuses foreign business, such as McDonald's, of representing a 'cultural invasion', diluting the Indian way of life.

The entry of McDonald's into the Indian market represents a fundamental shift in the Indian government's attitude towards foreign business and overseas investment. Until recently, its economy had been tightly regulated by the state, and in many sectors of the economy multinational investment was restricted to, at most, 50–50 joint ventures with Indian producers. The current Indian government is seeking to encourage greater foreign investment by allowing foreign investors a majority shareholding in a greater number of business sectors. Also, by establishing a series of progressive free-market reforms, it hopes to create the conditions necessary to attract foreign business in the first place.

The 'cultural invasion' feared by many Indians may now be under way, and the Maharajah Mac may be leading the assault.

Questions
1 What justifications might the Indian government claim for limiting the holdings of foreign business in the Indian economy?
2 What drawbacks might the Indian economy experience as a consequence of this policy?

Disadvantages to the host country

Whereas there is the potential for MNCs to make a significant contribution to closing the above gaps, in practice they close them only slightly, or even make them bigger! The following are the main problems:

- They may use their power in the markets of host countries to drive domestic producers out of business, thereby lowering domestic profits and domestic investment.
- They may buy few, if any, of their components from domestic firms, but import them instead: perhaps from one of their subsidiaries.
- The bulk of their profits may simply be repatriated to shareholders in the rich countries, with little, if any, reinvested in the developing country. This, plus the previous point, will tend to make the foreign exchange gap worse.
- Their practice of transfer pricing may give little scope for the host government to raise tax revenue from them. Governments of developing countries are effectively put in competition with each other, each trying to undercut the others' tax rates in order to persuade the MNC to price its intermediate products in such a way as to make its profits in their country.
- Similarly, governments of developing countries compete with each other to offer the most favourable terms to MNCs (e.g. government grants,

government contracts, tax concessions and rent-free sites). The more favourable the terms, the less the gain for developing countries as a whole.

- The technology and skills brought in by the multinationals may be fiercely guarded by the MNC. What is more, the dominance of the domestic market by MNCs may lead to the demise of domestic firms and indigenous technology, thereby worsening the skill and technology base of the country.

In addition to these problems, MNCs can alter the whole course of development in ways that many would argue are undesirable. By locating in cities, they tend to attract floods of migrants from the countryside looking for work, but of whom only a small fraction will find employment in these industries. The rest swell the ranks of the urban unemployed, often dwelling in squatter settlements on the outskirts of cities and living in appalling conditions.

More fundamentally, they are accused of distorting the whole pattern of development and of worsening the gap between the rich and poor. Their technology is capital intensive (compared with indigenous technology). The result is too few job opportunities. Those who are employed, however, receive relatively high wages, and are able to buy their products. These are the products consumed in affluent countries – from cars, to luxury foodstuffs, to household appliances – products that the MNCs often advertise heavily, and where they have considerable monopoly/oligopoly power. The resulting 'coca-colanisation', as it has been called, creates wants for the mass of people, but wants that they have no means of satisfying.

What can developing countries do?

Can developing countries gain the benefits of FDI while avoiding the effects of growing inequality and inappropriate products and technologies? If a developing country is large and is seen as an important market for the multinational, if it would be costly for the multinational to relocate and if the government is well informed about the multinational's costs, then the country's bargaining position will be relatively strong. It may be able to get away with relatively high taxes on the MNC's profits and tight regulation of its behaviour (e.g. its employment practices and its care for the environment). If, however, the country is economically weak and the MNC is footloose, then the deal it can negotiate is unlikely to be very favourable.

The bargaining position of developing countries would be enhanced if they could act jointly in imposing conditions on multinational investment and behaviour. Such agreement is unlikely, however, given the diverse nature of developing countries' governments and economies, and the pro free market, deregulated world of the early 2000s.

SUMMARY

1 There is great diversity among multinationals in respect to size, nature of business, size of overseas operations, location, ownership and organisational structure.

2 The UK has a large multinational sector, in respect both to overseas operations and to receiving foreign business activities in the UK.

3a Why businesses go multinational depends largely upon the nature of their business and their corporate strategy. However, we can draw a clear

SUMMARY

line between businesses which seek to reduce costs by becoming multinational, and those which become multinational in order to achieve growth.

3b An influential theory on MNC development is the product life cycle hypothesis. In this theory, a business will shift production around the world seeking to reduce costs and extend a given product's life. The phases of a product's life will be conducted in different countries. As the product nears maturity and competition grows, reducing costs to maintain competitiveness will force business to locate production in low-cost markets, such as developing economies.

3c Although becoming an MNC is largely advantageous to the business, it can experience problems with language barriers, selling and marketing in foreign markets, attitudes of the host state and the communication and co-ordination of global business activities.

4 Host states find multinational investment advantageous in respect to employment creation, contributions to the balance of payments, the transfer of technology and the contribution to taxation.

5 Host states find multinational investment disadvantageous in so far as it creates uncertainty; foreign business can control or manipulate the country or regions within it; tax payments can be avoided by transfer pricing; and MNCs might misuse the environment.

6a The benefits of MNCs to developing countries depend upon the developing countries' development goals.

6b MNCs bring with them investment, which is crucial to economic growth. They also provide the host state with foreign exchange, which might be crucial in helping purchase vital imports.

6c MNCs might prove to be disadvantageous to developing economies if they drive domestic producers out of business, source production completely from other countries, repatriate profits, practise transfer pricing to avoid tax, force host states to offer favourable tax deals or subsidies for further expansion, and guard technology to prevent its transfer to domestic producers.

REVIEW QUESTIONS

1   What are the advantages and disadvantages to an economy, like that of the UK, of having a large multinational sector?

2   How might the structure of a multinational differ depending upon whether its objective of being multinational is to reduce costs or to grow?

3   If reducing costs is so important for many multinationals, why is it that they tend to locate production not in low-cost developing economies, but in economies within the developed world?

4   Explain the link between the life cycle of a product and multinational business.

5   Assess the advantages and disadvantages facing a host state when receiving MNC investment.

6   Debate the following:
    'Multinational investment can be nothing but good for developing economies seeking to grow and prosper.'

24 Trading blocs

The world economy seems to have been increasingly forming into a series of trade blocs, based upon regional groupings of countries: a European region centred on the European Union, an Asian region on Japan, and a North American region on the United States. Although such trade blocs clearly encourage trade between their members (intra-regional trade has been growing significantly faster than trade between regions), there was growing fear, especially when it seemed that the GATT Uruguay Round of negotiations would fail, that they would become 'trade fortresses'. Even though this did not happen and the GATT agreement was signed, many countries outside these blocs complain that they benefit the members at the expense of the rest of the world. For many developing economies, in need of access to the most prosperous nations in the world, this represents a significant check on their ability to grow and develop.

In this chapter we shall first consider why groups of countries might wish to establish trade blocs, and what they seek to gain beyond the benefits that result from free and open trade. We will then look at the world's trade blocs as they currently stand, paying particular attention to the European Union, which is by far the most advanced in respect to establishing a high level of regional integration.

24.1 Preferential trading

Types of preferential trading arrangement

If a group of countries wish to become more open and trade more freely with each other, but do not want the vulnerability of facing unbridled global competition, they might attempt to remove trade restrictions between themselves, but maintain them with the rest of the world.

There are three possible forms that such trading arrangements might take.

Free trade areas

A **free trade area** is where member countries remove tariffs and quotas between themselves, but retain whatever restrictions *each member chooses* with non-member countries. Some provision will have to be made to prevent imports from outside coming into the area via the country with the lowest external tariff.

Customs unions

A **customs union** is like a free trade area, but in addition members must adopt *common* external tariffs and quotas with non-member countries.

> **definition**
> **Free trade area**
> A group of countries with no trade barriers between themselves.

> **definition**
> **Customs union**
> A free trade area with common external tariffs and quotas.

Common markets

A **common market** is where member countries operate as a *single* market. Like a customs union there are no tariffs and quotas between member countries and there are common external tariffs and quotas. But a common market goes further than this. A full common market includes the following features.

A common system of taxation. In the case of a *perfect* common market, this will involve identical rates of tax in all member countries.

A common system of laws and regulations governing production, employment and trade. For example, in a perfect common market there would be a *single* set of laws governing issues such as product specification (e.g. permissible artificial additives to foods, or levels of exhaust emissions from cars), health and safety at work, the employment and dismissal of labour, the rights of trade unions and their members, mergers and takeovers, and monopolies and restrictive practices.

Free movement of labour, capital and materials, and goods and services. In a perfect common market, this will involve a total absence of border controls between member states, the freedom of workers to work in any member country, the freedom of firms to expand into any member state.

The absence of special treatment by member governments of their own domestic industries. For example, governments are large purchasers of goods and services. In a perfect common market, they should buy from whichever companies within the market offer the most competitive deal and not show favouritism towards domestic suppliers: they should operate a *common procurement policy*.

The definition of a common market is sometimes extended to include the following two features of *economic and monetary union*.

A fixed exchange rate between the member countries' currencies. In the extreme case, this would involve a single currency for the whole market.

Common macroeconomic policies. To some extent this must follow from a fixed exchange rate, but in the extreme case it will involve a single macroeconomic management of the whole market, and hence the abolition of separate fiscal or monetary intervention by individual member states.

The direct effects of a customs union: trade creation and trade diversion

By joining a customs union (or free trade area), a country will find that its trade patterns change. Two such changes can be distinguished: trade creation and trade diversion.

Trade creation

Trade creation is where consumption shifts from a high-cost producer to a low-cost producer. The removal of trade barriers allows greater specialisation according to comparative advantage. Instead of consumers having to pay high prices for domestically produced goods in which the country has a comparative disadvantage, the goods can now be obtained more cheaply from other mem-

> **definition**
> **Common market**
> A customs union where the member countries act as a single market with free movement of labour and capital, common taxes and common trade laws.

> **definition**
> **Trade creation**
> Where a customs union leads to greater specialisation according to comparative advantage and thus a shift in production from higher-cost to lower-cost sources.

bers of the customs union. In return, the country can export to them goods in which it has a comparative advantage.

Trade diversion

Trade diversion is where consumption shifts from a lower-cost producer outside the customs union to a higher-cost producer within the union.

Assume that the most efficient producer of good y in the world is New Zealand – outside the EU. Assume that before membership of the EU (or the European Economic Community (EEC) as it was then called), the UK paid a similar tariff on good y from any country, and thus imported the product from New Zealand rather than from the EEC.

After joining the EEC, however, the removal of the tariff made the EEC product cheaper, since the tariff remained on the New Zealand product. Consumption thus switched to a higher-cost producer. There was thus a net loss in world efficiency. As far as the UK was concerned, consumers still gained, since they were paying a lower price than before. However, there was a loss to producers (from the reduction in protection, and hence reduced prices and profits) and to the government (from reduced tariff revenue). These losses may have been smaller or larger than the gain to consumers: in other words, there may have still been a net gain to the UK, but there could have been a net loss, depending on the circumstances.

Longer-term effects of a customs union

Over the longer term, there may be other gains and losses from being a member of a customs union.

Longer-term advantages

- Increased market size may allow a country's firms to exploit *(internal) economies of scale*. This argument is more important for small countries, which therefore have more to gain from an enlargement of their markets.
- *External economies of scale*. Increased trade may lead to improvements in the infrastructure of the members of the customs union (better roads, railways, financial services, etc.). This in turn could then bring bigger long-term benefits from trade between members, and from external trade too, by making the transport and handling of imports and exports cheaper.
- The bargaining power of the whole customs union with the rest of the world may allow member countries to gain *better terms of trade*. This, of course, will necessarily involve a degree of political co-operation between the members.
- *Increased competition* between member countries may stimulate efficiency, encourage investment and reduce monopoly power. Of course, a similar advantage could be gained by the simple removal of tariffs with any competing country.
- Integration may encourage a *more rapid spread of technology*.

Longer-term disadvantages

- Resources may flow from the country to more efficient members of the customs union, or to the geographical centre of the union (so as to

> **definition**
>
> **Trade diversion**
> Where a customs union diverts consumption from goods produced at a lower cost outside the union to goods produced at a higher cost (but tariff free) within the union.

minimise transport costs). This can be a major problem for a *common market* (where there is free movement of labour and capital). The country could become a depressed 'region' of the community.

- If integration encourages greater co-operation between firms in member countries, it may also encourage *greater oligopolistic collusion*, thus keeping prices higher to the consumer. It may also encourage mergers and takeovers, which would increase monopoly power.
- *Diseconomies of scale.* If the union leads to the development of very large companies, they may become bureaucratic and inefficient.
- *The costs of administering* the customs union may be high. These costs may increase over time if the member countries have inadequate controls over the union's expenditure. This problem is likely to worsen the more there is intervention in the affairs of individual members. This will encourage members to press for higher expenditure when it benefits them specifically, knowing that the costs will be met by the members collectively.

24.2 Preferential trading in practice

Preferential trading has the greatest potential to benefit countries whose domestic market is too small, taken on its own, to enable them to benefit from economies of scale, and where they face substantial barriers to their exports. Most developing countries fall into this category and as a result many have attempted to form preferential trading arrangements.

Examples in Latin America and the Caribbean include the Latin American Integration Association (LAIA),[1] the Andean Community,[2] the Central American Common Market (CACM)[3] and the Caribbean Community (CARICOM).[4] A Southern Common Market (MerCoSur)[5] was formed in 1991, consisting of Argentina, Brazil, Paraguay and Uruguay. It has a common external tariff and most of its internal trade is free of tariffs.

In 1993, the six ASEAN nations (Brunei, Indonesia, Malaysia, the Philippines, Singapore and Thailand) agreed to work towards an ASEAN Free Trade Area (AFTA).[6] ASEAN (the Association of South-East Asian Nations) now has nine members (the new ones being Laos, Myanmar and Vietnam) and is dedicated to increased economic co-operation within the region. What progress has been made towards achieving AFTA? By 2002 the original six members will have reduced internal tariffs to a maximum of 5 per cent on most products and are committed to reducing tariffs to zero on all products as soon as possible. The other three countries will meet similar goals, but a few years later.

In Africa, the Economic Community of West African States (ECOWAS)[7] has been attempting to create a common market between its members.

The most significant and advanced trade blocs, however, are to be found not

---

[1] http://www.aladi.org
[2] http://www.comunidadandina.org/english/who.htm
[3] http://www.imf.org/external/np/sec/decdo/sieca.htm
[4] http://www.caricom.org/
[5] http://www.americasnet.com/mauritz/mercosur/english
[6] http://www.asean.or.id/
[7] http://www.ecowas.net/

BOX 24.1

Crisis in south-east Asia
Birth of a contagion

Stanley Fischer, the First Deputy Managing Director of the International Monetary Fund, refers to Asia's economic success up to 1997 as 'a remarkable historical achievement', where growth and trade performance reached unprecedented levels. The statistics of the region speak for themselves.

- The annual growth rate of GDP in the ASEAN-5 countries (Indonesia, Malaysia, the Philippines, Singapore and Thailand) averaged 8 per cent in the decade up to 1997.
- In the 30 years up to 1997, per capita income levels increased tenfold in Korea, fivefold in Thailand, and fourfold in Malaysia. For nations like Hong Kong and Singapore, per capita income is now well in line with that of many industrial countries.
- It is estimated that only 2 out of 10 people in east Asia are now being paid less than $1 per day, compared with 6 out of 10 in 1975 (at today's prices).
- Prior to the recent crisis, Asia attracted over half of all capital inflows going to developing countries, approximately $100 billion in 1996.
- Asian economies have managed, over the decade up to 1997, to double their share of world exports to almost one-fifth of the world's total.
- Further, such economic success has been achieved within the context of stable inflation, high levels of domestic saving (on average a third of GDP) and sound fiscal management, with some countries, such as Thailand and Indonesia, managing to run significant budget surpluses (1.6 and 1.4 per cent of GDP respectively in 1997).

As well as the directly benefiting the citizens of these countries, the development of the south-east Asian economies has contributed to the economic well-being of the global economy. They have become major consumers of foreign goods; for example, the region purchased 19 per cent of all US exports in 1996. In addition, rising levels of consumption have helped to reduce the scale of downturns in economic activity experienced in the world's developed economies. The south-east Asian economies have also provided attractive investment opportunities to foreign investors, helping to support the remarkable growth of the world's financial markets.

Causes of the crisis

Given this remarkable success how did it go so horribly wrong so quickly?

The crisis broke in Thailand in the summer of 1997. Up to this point, Thailand had been experiencing strong economic growth, averaging about 10 per cent per annum since the mid-1980s. With sound public accounts, the economy presented itself as an attractive investment opportunity for foreign investors. And just as foreign investors were keen to lend, so domestic borrowers were keen to borrow, especially from overseas.

The Thai government operated a pegged exchange rate against the US dollar, and, given the stability of the Thai baht, foreign funds were readily used to meet investment demand. Little attention was paid by domestic borrowers to the extensive foreign exchange risk that they were placing themselves in. What was this risk? Should the baht ever be devalued, interest payments (in dollars) would cost more in local currency.

Things began to go wrong as growth in the Thai economy began to slow and its balance of payments deficit widened. A series of speculative attacks against the Thai baht led the Thai government to unpeg the currency from the dollar. The baht collapsed. The effect then quickly spread to other currencies within the region. This spread or 'contagion' was the result partly of other nations attempting to maintain their competitiveness against the baht, and partly of speculators realising that other economies within the region – Indonesia and Korea, in particular – shared problems very similar to those of Thailand: weak financial markets and a heavily indebted corporate sector.

The region's currencies, interest rates and economic growth have become more synchronised. When Thailand devalued, its neighbours in the Association of south-east Asian Nations (ASEAN) were confronted with intense speculative pressures. Investors identified a regional pattern of slowing export growth, rising current-account deficits and weak banking systems. Market participants realised that concerns about relative competitiveness would cause these currencies to move in tandem since the so-called ASEAN four – Thailand, Malaysia, Indonesia and the Philippines – compete in broadly the same export markets.[1]

As currencies came under pressure from international speculators, those that had borrowed heavily from overseas began to see their debt service costs rise (with weaker currencies, more local currency was needed to pay interest denominated in dollars). With such large foreign debts, they sought desperately to find ways of reducing payments on their external liabilities. However, their actions merely put further pressure on their currencies, intensifying the speculative wave and plunging the region's economies into deeper financial chaos.

The following have been identified as the major contributing factors in the south-east Asian crisis:

- Governments in the region had failed to deal with overheating pressures, growing balance of payments deficits and property and stock-market bubbles.
- Pegged exchange rates were pegged for too long. This gave a false sense of stability and encouraged excessive external borrowing by the corporate sector, with a correspondingly excessive risk from exchange rate devaluation.
- The liberalisation of financial markets in south-east Asia was not accompanied by an increase in regulation and supervision. The result was that banks made excessively risky loans and were inadequately monitored. As Joseph Stiglitz, Senior Vice-President of the World Bank remarked:

In the last decade Thailand has reduced reserve requirements, eased the rules governing non-bank financial institutions, expanded the scope of permissible capital market activities, and increased access to off-shore borrowing. Beginning somewhat earlier, Korea eliminated many interest rate controls, removed restrictions on corporate debt financing and cross-border flows, and permitted intensified competition in financial services. While the advantages of these changes were lauded, the necessary increase in safeguards was not adequately emphasised.[2]

As well as domestic problems, international factors also may have contributed to south-east Asia's problems. For example, weak growth in Japan and Europe, with resulting low domestic interest rates, encouraged investors to search for higher yields overseas, especially in south-east Asia. Lenders, like borrowers, failed to appreciate the risk of their loans and became overexposed in the region.

Consequences for the south-east Asian economies

Joseph Stiglitz expressed the magnitude of the economic collapse for the south-east Asia region when he stated:

> ... capital outflows, and the accompanying depreciating currencies and falling asset prices, exacerbated the strains on private-sector balance sheets. The vicious circle has become even more vicious as financial problems have led to restricted credit, undermining the real economy, and slowing growth. Given the region's financial fragility, the economic downturn may well feed on itself – worsening bankruptcies and weakening confidence. Finally, the economic crisis has fostered political and social instability in some countries, further deepening the crisis.[3]

By early 1998, all leading forecasters expected output in south-east Asia to fall, and had revised their predictions for 1998 to reflect this. The table shows revisions to IMF forecasts. However, there still remained uncertainty as to how great the impact on output would be.

The fall in output reflected both the lower level of consumer and investor confidence and the tighter fiscal and monetary conditions many of the countries were having to embrace in order to: (a) instil greater confidence in their financial systems; (b) meet the conditions imposed by the IMF for financial assistance.

Continued

Revisions to IMF forecasts for 1998 (% points)

	Difference between IMF December 1997 and May 1998 forecasts
G7	−0.3
USA	+0.2
Germany	−0.4
France	−0.3
Italy	−0.1
Japan	−1.8
UK	−0.4
Asian newly industrialised economies	−2.5

Source: *Bank of England Inflation Report* (February 1998).

Global effects

But it would be wrong to see the problem as just south-east Asia's: the consequences of the region's collapse were truly global. With weak demand in these countries, the consumption of imports also declined, thereby reducing the sales of foreign suppliers. In addition, such companies faced enhanced competition in their own domestic economies as south-east Asian producers focused on increasing the sales of their exports, which, given the depressed exchange rate values, had become super-competitive. Of course, the more successful the south-east Asian countries were in expanding their exports, the more this helped to alleviate the effects of their recession.

Speculative pressures on currencies in Brazil, Argentina, Mexico, Greece, Russia and the Ukraine were all argued to have been the consequence of the south-east Asian currency collapse. All were forced to increase interest rates to protect their exchange rates.

The most significant form of long-term contagion is likely to stem from the reduction in foreign capital flows, especially in bank lending. Not only will Asian businesses be affected but businesses around the world are likely to find it harder to acquire foreign capital, as lenders become more cautious and risk averse.

Policy response

In the wake of the collapse, Thailand, Indonesia and South Korea all sought financial assistance from the IMF. A loan of $3.9 billion was agreed for Thailand, $9.9 billion for Indonesia, and a staggering $20.9 billion for South Korea. The purpose of these loans was to help establish a measure of economic stability. As with all IMF financial help, such loans came with various conditions concerning the fiscal and monetary approaches that the countries had to adopt and the financial restructuring that had to be undertaken.

Questions

1 Why did the 'contagion' spread to countries outside south-east Asia?

2 What policy measures could the south-east Asian countries have adopted before the crisis to prevent it occurring?

[1] *Financial Times* (13/10/97)
[2] J. Stiglitz, *The role of International Financial Institutions in the Current Global Economy* (1998), www.worldbank.org
[3] *Ibid.*

in the developing world but in the developed, notably in Europe and North America.

North America Free Trade Association (NAFTA)

Along with the EU, NAFTA is one of the two most powerful trading blocs in the world. It was formed in 1993 and consists of the USA, Canada and Mexico. These three countries have agreed to abolish tariffs between themselves in the hope that increased trade and co-operation will follow. Tariffs between the USA and Canada were phased out by 1999 and those between Mexico and the other two countries will be phased out by 2009. New non-tariff restrictions will not be permitted either, but many existing ones can remain in force, thus preventing the development of true free trade between the members. Indeed, some industries, such as textiles and agriculture, will continue to have major non-tariff restrictions.

NAFTA members hope that, with a market similar in size to the EU (a combined GDP of $11 trillion and over 360 million consumers), they will be able to rival the EU's economic power in world trade. Other countries may join in the future, so NAFTA may eventually develop into a Western Hemisphere free trade association.

NAFTA is, however, at most only a free trade area and not a common market. Unlike the EU, it does not seek to harmonise laws and regulations, except in very specific areas such as environmental management and labour standards. Member countries are permitted total legal independence, subject to the one proviso that they must treat firms of other member countries equally with their own firms. Nevertheless, NAFTA has encouraged a growth in trade between its members, most of which is trade creation rather than trade diversion.

Of the three countries in NAFTA, Mexico potentially has the most to gain from the agreement. With easier access to US and Canadian markets, and the added attractiveness it now has to foreign investors, especially US multinationals looking to reduce labour costs, the Mexican economy could reap huge benefits. Studies have estimated that the Mexican economy might benefit by anything from a 0.1 per cent to an 11.4 per cent rise in real GDP. Estimates of gains for the USA and Canada are more modest: typically a 0.5 per cent rise in real GDP. The estimated employment gains from NAFTA are also subject to some variation. Optimistic estimates anticipate that an additional 600 000 new jobs might be created in Mexico, and 130 000 new jobs in the USA. Pessimistic estimates, in contrast, suggest that the USA might suffer a net loss in employment of up to 500 000 jobs.

Although it is still early days, Mexico seems to have done phenomenally well from the NAFTA agreement. It has become a thriving export economy and attracts sufficient foreign direct investment to finance its total current account deficit. Many EU and south-east Asian businesses are using the Mexican economy to gain access to the USA, although strong demand within Mexico itself is fast making it a valuable market in its own right.

Despite the largely positive effects of NAFTA, the Mexican economy nevertheless faces a number of real and potential threats from the agreement. For example, as trade barriers fall, Mexican companies will be suddenly faced with competition from potentially bigger and more efficient US and Canadian rivals. This is particularly likely in the case of 'high-tech' sectors, such as telecommunications, which will probably become dominated, if not exclusively run, by foreign business.

The Asia-Pacific Economic Co-operation forum (APEC)

The most significant move towards establishing a more widespread regional economic organisation in east Asia appeared with the creation of the Asia-Pacific Economic Co-operation forum. APEC links the economies of the ASEAN nations, NAFTA, Japan, China, Australia and New Zealand: in total 18 countries, which account for half the world's total output. At the 1994 meeting of APEC leaders, it was resolved to create a free trade area across the Pacific by 2010 for the developed industrial countries, and by 2020 for the rest.

Unlike the EU and NAFTA, APEC is likely to remain solely a free trade area and not to develop into a customs union, let alone a common market. Within the region there exists a wide disparity in GDP per capita, ranging from Japan at over $35 000 to Vietnam at a mere $400. Such disparities create a wide range of national interests and goals. Countries are unlikely to share common economic problems or concerns. In addition, political differences and conflicts within the region are widespread, reducing the likelihood that any organisational agreement beyond a simple economic one would succeed.

However, the economic benefits from free trade and the resulting closer regional ties could be immense. If the United States is included in APEC, then it accounts for some 65 per cent of world trade, a truly massive trading zone.

By far the most developed trading bloc is that of the EU. In the remainder of this chapter we will consider the development of the EU and its implications for business.

24.3 The European Union

The European Economic Community (EEC) was formed by the signing of the Treaty of Rome in 1957 and came into operation on 1 January 1958.

The original six member countries of the EEC (Belgium, France, Italy, Luxembourg, Netherlands and West Germany) had already made a move towards integration with the formation of the European Coal and Steel Community in 1952. This had removed all restrictions on trade in coal, steel and iron ore between the six countries. The aim had been to gain economies of scale and allow more effective competition with the USA and other foreign producers.

The EEC extended this principle and aimed eventually to be a full common market with completely free trade between members in all products, and with completely free movement of labour, enterprise and capital. By uniting many of the countries of western Europe, it was hoped too that the conflicts of the two world wars would never be repeated, and that acting together the countries of the EEC could be an effective political and economic force in a world dominated by political giants such as the USA and the USSR, and economic giants such as the USA (and later Japan).

All internal tariffs between the six members had been abolished and common external tariffs established by 1968. But this still only made the EEC a *customs union*, since a number of restrictions on internal trade remained (legal, administrative, fiscal, etc.). Nevertheless the aim was eventually to create a full common market.

In 1973 the UK, Denmark and Ireland joined the EEC. Greece joined in 1981, Spain and Portugal in 1986, and Sweden, Austria and Finland in 1995.

From customs union to common market

The European Union (as it is now known) is clearly a customs union. It has common external tariffs and no internal tariffs. But is it also a common market? For years there have been certain common economic policies.

The Common Agricultural Policy (CAP). The Union sets common high prices for farm products. This involves charging variable import duties to bring foreign food imports up to EU prices and intervention to buy up surpluses of food produced within the EU at these above-equilibrium prices.

Regional policy. EU regional policy provides grants to firms and local authorities in depressed regions of the Union.

Monopoly and restrictive practice policy. EU policy here has applied primarily to companies operating in more than one member state (see section 20.1). For example, Article 85 of the Treaty of Rome prohibits agreements between firms (e.g. over pricing or sharing out markets) which will adversely affect competition in trade between member states.

Harmonisation of taxation. VAT is the standard form of indirect tax throughout the EU. However, there are substantial differences in VAT rates between member states, and rates of other types of indirect tax (such as excise duties) vary considerably between the members, as do rates of direct taxation.

Social policy. Articles 117–28 refer to social policy, and include calls for collaboration between member states on laws relating to employment, health and safety at work and collective bargaining rights, and equal pay for women and men for doing the same work.

In practice, during the 1980s there was little harmonisation of Community social policy. But in 1989 the European Commission presented a *social charter* to the EC heads of state. This spelt out a series of worker and social rights that should apply in all member states. These rights were grouped under twelve headings covering areas such as the guarantee of decent levels of income for both the employed and the non-employed, freedom of movement of labour between EU countries, freedom to belong to a trade union and equal treatment of women and men in the labour market. The social charter was only a recommendation and each element had to be approved separately by the European Council of Ministers.

The social chapter of the Maastricht Treaty (1991) attempted to move the Community forward in implementing the details of the social charter in areas such as maximum working hours, minimum working conditions, health and safety protection, the provision of information to and consultation with workers, and equal opportunities.

The UK government refused to sign this part of the Maastricht Treaty. It maintained that such measures would increase costs of production and would, therefore, make EU goods less competitive in world trade and would increase unemployment. Critics of the UK position argued that the refusal to adopt minimum working conditions (and also a minimum wage rate) would make the UK the 'cheap labour sweat-shop' of Europe. One of the first acts of the incoming Labour government in 1997 was to sign up to the social chapter.

Trade policy. Like tariffs, quotas were eliminated long ago on trade between member states. Nevertheless from time to time they have been imposed by

BOX 24.2

Beyond bananas
EU/US trade disputes

Trade relations between the EU and US seem to be at an all-time low. The World Trade Organisation (WTO), set up to manage trade and prevent such disputes arising, appears helpless in resolving the issues and restoring order.

The current round of bad blood between the EU and US started over bananas.

Bananas

The EU/US 'banana war' has been running since 1993, and although repeated battles have been fought (which the Americans have won on virtually every occasion!), the war rumbles on.

In 1993, the EU adopted a tariff and quota system that favoured banana producers in African, Caribbean and Pacific (ACP) countries, mostly ex-European colonies. However, Latin American banana producers, owned by large American multinationals like Chiquita and Dole, took exception to this move. Latin American producers, with huge economies of scale, were able to produce bananas at considerably lower cost than producers in the ACP countries. But, faced with significant tariffs on entry into the EU market, their bananas became more expensive. Championed by the USA, the Latin American producers won the case at the WTO for removing the agreement.

The EU, however, failed to comply, arguing that the preferential access to EU markets for ACP producers was part of a general development strategy, known as the 'Lomé Convention', to support developing economies. Without preferential access, it was argued, ACP banana producers could simply not compete on world markets. As a European Commission document highlighted, 'The destruction of the Caribbean banana industry would provoke severe economic hardship and political instability in a region already struggling against deprivation.'

As the EU refused to comply with the WTO ruling, the USA imposed $191 million worth of tariffs on EU exports in March 1999. The dispute is still to be resolved.

Hormone-treated beef

If the banana dispute could be resolved, many equally contentious issues could be found to take its place. The dispute between the EU and USA over hormone-treated beef has been going on for a staggering 15 years. The EU, despite being subject to sanctions of $117 million, refuses to import any animal products, live or processed, that have received growth hormones. The ban was made on grounds of public health, and this remains the crux of the dispute. The EU argues that it has not been proven that hormone-treated beef is safe. In reply, the Americans argue that the EU has not provided evidence that it is otherwise.

Genetically modified (GM) foods

A more recent trade dispute, again in the field of public health, concerns the development of GM food. GM strains of maize and soya have been available in the USA for many years, but the export of such products, whether as seed or food, is banned from the EU. The US position is that EU consumers should be free to choose whether they have GM food or not. This, not surprisingly, is rejected by the EU on the basis that GM foods might contaminate the entire food supply once introduced. In July 2000, the EU decided to continue with its GM food ban indefinitely.

Airbus

The most recent branch of the current EU/US trade dispute concerns the Airbus Consortium and EU industrial policy (an area which has been a bone of contention for the USA for many years). The current issue concerns the new superjumbo, the A3XX. The Americans are very unhappy with the loans and subsidies being provided by EU members to companies within the Airbus Consortium to develop the aircraft. The American complaint is that such subsidies are breaking the WTO subsidy code and, as such, are unfair. Estimated at $4 billion, the subsidies will cover a third of the aircraft's development costs. The issue is yet to be brought before the WTO, but it is highly likely to be so, given the current trading climate between the EU and the USA.

Question

Why does the WTO appear to be so ineffective in resolving the disputes between the EU and USA?

individual members on imports from outside the EU (e.g. on the imports of cars and textiles). Where barriers to trade do exist *within* the EU, this is usually the consequence of national economic differences, such as in taxation rates or regulations and norms, or the indirect consequence of other policy actions, such as state procurement policy.

Despite these various common policies, in other respects the Community of the 1970s and 1980s was far from a true common market: there were all sorts of non-tariff barriers, such as high taxes on wine by non-wine-producing countries, special regulations designed to favour domestic producers, governments giving contracts to domestic producers (e.g. for defence equipment), and so on.

The Single European Act of 1986, however, sought to remove these barriers and to form a genuine common market by the end of 1992. One of the most crucial aspects of the Act was its acceptance of the principle of **mutual recognition**. This is the principle whereby if a firm or individual is permitted to do something under the rules and regulations of *one* EU country, it must thereby also be permitted to do it in all other EU countries. This means that firms and individuals can choose the country's rules that are least constraining. It also means that individual governments can no longer devise special rules and regulations that keep out competitors from other EU countries.

The benefits and costs of the single market

It is difficult to quantify the benefits and costs of the single market, given that many occur over a long period. Also it is difficult to know to what extent the changes taking place are the direct result of the single market. Nevertheless it is possible to identify the *types* of benefit and cost that have resulted. The benefits have included the following:

Trade creation. Costs and prices have fallen as a result of a greater exploitation of comparative advantage. Member countries can now specialise further in those goods and services that they can produce at a comparatively low opportunity cost.

Reduction in the direct costs of barriers. This category includes administrative costs, border delays and technical regulations. Their abolition or harmonisation has led to substantial cost savings.

Economies of scale. With industries based on a Europe-wide scale, many firms and their plants can be large enough to gain the full potential economies of scale. Yet the whole European market is large enough for there still to be adequate competition. Such gains vary from industry to industry depending on the minimum efficient scale of a plant or firm.

Greater competition. More effective competition from other EU countries has (a) squeezed profit margins and thus brought prices more in line with costs, and (b) encouraged more efficient use of resources and thus reduced costs. In the long run, greater competition can stimulate greater innovation, the greater flow of technical information and the rationalisation of production.

definition

Mutual recognition
The EU principle that one country's rules and regulations must apply throughout the Union. If they conflict with those of another country, individuals and firms should be able to choose which to obey.

Despite, these gains, the single market has not received universal welcome within the EU. Its critics argue that, in a Europe of oligopolies, unequal ownership of resources, rapidly changing technologies and industrial practices, and factor immobility, the removal of internal barriers to trade has merely exaggerated the problems of inequality and economic power. More specifically, the following criticisms are made.

Radical economic change is costly. Substantial economic change is necessary to achieve the full economies of scale and efficiency gains from a single European market. These changes necessarily involve redundancies – from bankruptcies, takeovers, rationalisation and the introduction of new technology. The severity of this 'structural' and 'technological' unemployment (see section 25.3) depends on (a) the pace of economic change and (b) the mobility of labour – both occupational and geographical.

Adverse regional effects. Firms are likely to locate as near as possible to the 'centre of gravity' of their markets and sources of supply. If, before barriers are removed, a firm's prime market is the UK, it might well locate in the Midlands or the north of England. If, however, with barriers now removed, its market has become Europe as a whole, it may choose to locate in the south of England or in France, Germany or the Benelux countries instead. The creation of a single European market thus tends to attract capital and jobs away from the edges of the Union to its geographical centre.

In an ideal market situation, areas like Cornwall, the south of Italy and Portugal should attract resources from other parts of the Union. Being relatively depressed areas, wage rates and land prices are lower. The resulting lower industrial costs should encourage firms to move there. In practice, however, as capital and labour (and especially young and skilled workers) leave the extremities of the Union, so these regions are likely to become more depressed. If, as a result, their infrastructure is neglected, they then become even less attractive to new investment.

The development of monopoly/oligopoly power. The free movement of capital is likely to lead to the development of giant 'Euro-firms' with substantial economic power. Indeed, recent years have seen some very large European mergers (see Box 14.2). This can lead to higher, not lower prices and less choice for the consumer. It all depends on just how effective competition is, and how effective EU competition policy is in preventing monopolistic and collusive practices.

Trade diversion. Just as trade creation has been a potential advantage of completing the internal market, so trade diversion has been a possibility too. This is more likely if *external* barriers remain high (or are even increased) and internal barriers are *completely* abolished.

Loss of sovereignty. One of the biggest objections raised against the single European market is a political one: the loss of national sovereignty. Governments find it much more difficult to intervene at a microeconomic level in their own economies.

By the mid-1990s it was becoming clear from the evidence that the single market was bringing substantial benefits.

- The elimination of border controls for goods had reduced costs and shortened delivery times and resulted in a larger choice of suppliers.
- The simplification of VAT arrangements had reduced costs.
- Substantial trade creation had taken place.
- Increased competition between firms had led to lower costs, lower prices and a wider range of products available to consumers. This was particularly so in newly liberalised service sectors such as transport, financial services, telecommunications and broadcasting.
- Mergers and other forms of industrial restructuring had resulted in economies of scale and lower prices.

The economic evidence was backed up by the perceptions of business. Firms from across the range of industries felt that the single market project had removed a series of obstacles to trade within the EU and had increased market opportunities.

Nevertheless, the internal market was still not 'complete'. In other words, various barriers to trade between member states still remained. Thus, in June 1997, an Action Plan was adopted by the European Council. Its aim was to ensure that all barriers should have been dismantled by the launch of the euro in January 1999.

The Action Plan was largely, but not totally successful. In 1997, 35 per cent of identified measures to complete the internal market had yet to be implemented. By January 1999, less than 10 per cent remained.

Despite this success, national governments have continued to introduce *new* technical standards, several of which have had the effect of erecting new barriers to trade. Also, infringements of single market rules by governments have not always been dealt with. The net result is that, although trade is much freer today than in the early 1990s, especially given the transparency of pricing with the euro, there still do exist various barriers, especially to the free movement of goods.

In future years, with the euro being used by at least 12 of the member states, trade within the EU is likely to continue to grow as a proportion of GDP. We examine the benefits and costs of the single currency and the whole process of economic and monetary union in the EU in section 31.3.

SUMMARY

1a Countries may make a partial movement towards free trade by the adoption of a preferential trading system. This involves free trade between the members, but restrictions on trade with the rest of the world. Such a system can be either a simple free trade area, or a customs union (where there are common restrictions with the rest of the world), or a common market (where in addition there is free movement of capital and labour, and common taxes and trade laws).

1b A preferential trading area can lead to trade creation where production shifts to low-cost producers within the area, or to trade diversion where trade shifts away from lower-cost producers outside the area to higher-cost producers within the area.

1c Preferential trading may bring dynamic advantages of increased external economies of scale, improved terms of trade from increased bargaining power with the rest of the world, increased efficiency from greater competition between member countries, and a more rapid spread of technology. On the other hand, it can lead to increased regional problems for members, greater oligopolistic collusion and various diseconomies of scale. There may also be large

SUMMARY

costs of administering the system.

2 There have been several attempts around the world to form preferential trading systems. The two most powerful are the European Union and the North America Free Trade Association (NAFTA).

3a The European Union is a customs union in that it has common external tariffs and no internal ones. But virtually from the outset it has also had elements of a common market, particularly in the areas of agricultural policy, regional policy, monopoly and restrictive practice policy, and to some extent in the areas of tax harmonisation, transport policy and social policy.

3b The Single European Act of 1986 sought to sweep away any remaining restrictions and to establish a genuine free market within the EU: to establish a full common market. Benefits from completing the

internal market have included trade creation, cost savings from no longer having to administer barriers, economies of scale for firms now able to operate on a Europe-wide scale, and greater competition leading to reduced costs and prices, greater flows of technical information and more innovation.

3c The actual costs and benefits of EU membership to the various countries vary with their particular economic circumstances – for example, the extent to which they gain from trade creation, or lose from adverse regional multiplier effects – and with their contributions to and receipts from the EU budget.

3d These cost and benefits in the future will depend on just how completely the barriers to trade are abolished, on the extent of monetary union and on any enlargements to the Union.

REVIEW QUESTIONS

1 What factors will determine whether a country's joining a customs union will lead to trade creation or trade diversion?

2 Assume that a group of countries forms a customs union. Is trade diversion in the union more likely or less likely in the following cases?
   (a) Producers in the union gain monopoly power in world trade.
   (b) Modern developments in technology and communications reduce the differences in production costs associated with different locations.
   (c) The development of an internal market within the union produces substantial economies of scale in many industries.

3 Are NAFTA and APEC likely to develop along the same lines as the EU? Explain your answer.

4 Why is it difficult to estimate the magnitude of the benefits of completing the internal market of the EU?

5 Look through the costs and benefits that we identified from the single European market. Do the same costs and benefits arise from a substantially enlarged EU?

6 To what extent do non-EU countries gain or lose from the existence of the EU?

7 If there have been clear benefits from the single market programme, why do individual member governments still try to erect barriers, such as new technical standards?

The macroeconomic environment

THE FINANCIAL TIMES, 7/8 OCTOBER 2000

Input prices put pressure on margins

Chris Flood

Profit margins are being squeezed hard, and next week's data releases will bring no relief. On Monday, the forecast is for a jump of 2.1 per cent in input producer prices during September.

This will take the year-on-year growth rate up to 11.7 per cent from 10.7 per cent previously.

Competitive pressures are preventing manufacturers from passing on costs, so output producer prices will rise more modestly by 2.6 per cent year-on-year.

The trends on core producer prices (excluding energy costs) remain on an upward path because of shortages of many commodities, so September's figures are expected to be above the current four-year high of 1.3 per cent.

In view of high oil prices, the UK's inflation performance remains excellent, especially when measured against its European competitors. The UK's harmonised index of consumer prices (HICP) rate of inflation, at 0.6 per cent, is the lowest in Europe. This compares very favourably with the euro-zone average of 2.4 per cent. A clear indication of the difficulties of a one-fits-all monetary policy.

September's inflation data is due on Tuesday. The current RPIX rate of 1.9 per cent is equal to its 25-year low. The consensus is for a slight increase to 2 per cent, making it the 18th month below the government's target level.

The British Chambers of Commerce will release their third-quarter survey on Thursday. The effect of the fuel crisis may well over-dramatise a further flagging of business confidence, but the underlying message points to slower growth in future. The service sector should hold up better than manufacturing.

Confidence about future profitability will be dented, investment intentions should have weakened and recruitment difficulties will show no signs of easing. A key question will be the extent of any build up in inflationary pressures because of rising pay settlements and higher oil costs.

The success of an individual business depends not only on its own particular market and its own particular decisions. It also depends on the whole *macroeconomic* environment in which it operates, as can be seen in the article opposite.

If the economy is booming, then individual businesses are likely to be more profitable than if the economy is in recession. If the exchange rate rises (or falls), this will have an impact on the competitiveness of businesses trading overseas, and on the costs and profitability of business in general. Similarly, business profitability will be affected by interest rates, the general level of prices and wages and the level of unemployment.

It is thus important for managers to understand the forces that affect the performance of the economy. In the remaining chapters of the book, we will examine these macroeconomic forces and their effects on the business sector.

In Chapter 25 we will identify the main macroeconomic objectives that governments pursue and examine how these objectives are related.

Chapter 26 looks at macroeconomic issues arising from a country's economic relationships with the rest of the world. In particular, it looks at the balance of payments and the role of exchange rates in influencing economic performance.

> It has finally been accepted that the strength of sterling is hurting exporters. But we have seen nothing yet, according to a recent analysis by the National Institute of Economic and Social Research, which states that every 5 per cent appreciation in the average value of the pound eventually depresses UK output by 1 per cent after 2 years, and raises unemployment by 100 000.
>
> *The Observer*, 11 May 1997

Chapter 27 looks at the role of money in the economy and considers the operation of the UK's financial system.

Finally, in Chapter 28 we will examine differing theories about how the economy operates and the implications for business.

key terms

- Actual and potential economic growth
- Aggregate demand
- Aggregate supply
- Business cycle
- Unemployment
- Inflation
- Circular flow of income
- Injections and withdrawals
- The balance of payments
- The exchange rate
- Fixed and floating exchange rates
- Functions of money
- Assets and liabilities (of banks)
- Central bank
- Money market
- Money supply
- Demand for money
- Keynesian
- Monetarist
- The multiplier
- The accelerator
- The quantity theory of money
- Expectations
- The Phillips curve

The macroeconomic environment of business

Government macroeconomic policy aims primarily to achieve two goals:

- To ensure that the key macroeconomic variables (such as economic growth and inflation) are at acceptable levels.
- To create a *stable* economic environment in which the economy can flourish: i.e. to minimise fluctuations in economic activity.

In this chapter we shall identify what the main macroeconomic variables are and how they are related. We shall also have a preliminary look at how the government can influence these variables in order to create a more favourable environment for business. Government macroeconomic policy will be discussed in more detail in Part J.

25.1 Macroeconomic objectives

There are several macroeconomic variables that governments seek to control, but these can be grouped under four main headings.

Economic growth. Governments try to achieve high rates of **economic growth** over the long term: in other words, growth that is sustained over the years and is not just a temporary phenomenon. To this end, governments also try to achieve *stable* growth, avoiding both recessions and excessive short-term growth that cannot be sustained (albeit, governments are sometimes happy to give the economy an excessive boost as an election draws near!).

Unemployment. Governments also aim to ensure that unemployment is as low as possible, not only for the sake of the unemployed themselves, but also because it represents a waste of human resources and because unemployment benefits are a drain on government revenues.

Inflation. By **inflation** we mean a general rise in prices throughout the economy. Government policy here is to keep inflation both low and stable. One of the most important reasons for this is that it will aid the process of economic decision making. For example, businesses will be able to set prices and wage rates, and make investment decisions, with far more confidence. Today we are used to inflation rates of around 2 or 3 per cent, but it was not long ago that inflation in most developed countries was in double figures. In 1991, UK inflation reached 11 per cent; in 1975 it had reached 24 per cent!

The balance of payments. Governments aim to provide an environment in which exports can grow without an excessive growth in imports. They also aim

> **definition**
>
> **Rate of economic growth**
> The percentage increase in output over a twelve-month period.

> **definition**
>
> **Rate of inflation**
> The percentage increase in prices over a twelve-month period.

to make the economy attractive to inward investment. In other words, they seek to create a climate in which the country's earnings of foreign currency at least match, or preferably exceed, the country's demand for foreign currency: they seek to achieve a favourable **balance of payments**.

In order to achieve these goals, the government may seek to control several 'intermediate' variables. These include interest rates, the supply of money, taxes, government expenditure and exchange rates. For example, the achievement of a favourable balance of payments depends, in part, on whether changes in **exchange rates** allow the country's goods and services to remain price competitive on international markets. A lower exchange rate (i.e. fewer dollars, yen, euros, etc. to the pound) will make UK goods cheaper to overseas buyers, and thus help to boost UK exports. The government may thus seek to manipulate exchange rates to make them 'more favourable'.

In later chapters we will be looking at the various types of macroeconomic policy that governments can adopt. First we will look at the four macroeconomic objectives and identify their main determinants. In this chapter we will examine economic growth, unemployment and inflation. In Chapter 26 we will focus on the balance of payments and its relation to the exchange rate.

25.2 Economic growth

The distinction between actual and potential growth

Before examining the causes of economic growth, it is essential to distinguish between *actual* and *potential* economic growth.

Actual growth is the percentage annual increase in national output: the rate of growth in actual output. When statistics on growth rates are published, it is actual growth they are referring to.

Potential growth is the speed at which the economy *could* grow. It is the percentage annual increase in the economy's *capacity* to produce: the rate of growth in **potential output**. Two of the major factors contributing to potential economic growth are:

- An increase in resources – natural resources, labour or capital.
- An increase in the efficiency with which these resources are used, through advances in technology, improved labour skills or improved organisation.

If the potential growth rate exceeds the actual growth rate, there will be an increase in spare capacity and an increase in unemployment: there will be a growing gap between potential and actual output. To close this gap, the actual growth rate would temporarily have to exceed the potential growth rate. In the long run, however, the actual growth rate will be limited to the potential growth rate.

There are thus two major issues concerned with economic growth: the short-run issue of ensuring that actual growth is such as to keep actual output as close as possible to potential output; and the long-run issue of what determines the rate of potential economic growth.

Economic growth and the business cycle

Although growth in potential output will vary to some extent over the years –

---

definition

Balance of payments account
A record of the country's transactions with the rest of the world. It shows the country's payments to or deposits in other countries (debits) and its receipts or deposits from other countries (credits). It also shows the balance between these debits and credits under various headings.

definition

Exchange rate
The rate at which one national currency exchanges for another. The rate is expressed as the amount of one currency that is necessary to purchase one unit of another currency (e.g. DM2.50 = £1).

definition

Actual growth
The percentage annual increase in national output actually produced.

definition

Potential growth
The percentage annual increase in the capacity of the economy to produce.

definition

Potential output
The output that could be produced in the economy if there were a full employment of resources (including labour).

depending on the rate of advance of technology, the level of investment and the discovery of new raw materials – it will nevertheless tend to be much more steady than the growth in actual output.

Actual growth will tend to fluctuate. In some years there will be a high rate of economic growth: the country experiences a boom. In other years, economic growth will be low or even negative: the country experiences a recession. This cycle of booms and recessions is known as the **business cycle** or **trade cycle**.

There are four 'phases' of the business cycle. They are illustrated in Figure 25.1.

1   *The upturn*. In this phase, a stagnant economy begins to recover and growth in actual output resumes.
2   *The expansion*. During this phase, there is rapid economic growth: the economy is booming. A fuller use is made of resources and the gap between actual and potential output narrows.
3   *The peaking out*. During this phase, growth slows down or even ceases.
4   *The slowdown, recession or slump*. During this phase, there is little or no growth or even a decline in output. Increasing slack develops in the economy.

Long-term output trend. A line can be drawn showing the trend of national output over time (i.e. ignoring the cyclical fluctuations around the trend). This is shown as the dashed line in Figure 25.1. If the average level of potential output that is unutilised stays constant from one cycle to another, then the trend line will have the same slope as the potential output line. In other words, the trend rate of growth will be the same as the potential rate of growth. If, however, the level of unutilised potential changes form one cycle to another, then the trend line will have a different slope from the potential output line. For example, if unemployment and unused industrial capacity *rise* from one peak to another, or from one trough to another, then the trend line will move further away from the potential output line (i.e. it will be less steep).

The business cycle in practice

The business cycle illustrated in Figure 25.1 is a 'stylised' cycle. It is nice and

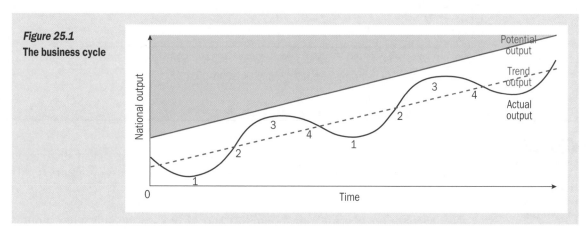

Figure 25.1
The business cycle

National output

Potential output

Trend output

Actual output

Time

BOX 25.1

Output gaps
An alternative measure of excess or deficient demand

If the economy grows, how fast and for how long can it grow before it runs into inflationary problems? What level of growth might be sustainable over the longer term?

To answer this question, economists have developed the concept of 'output gaps'[1] The output gap is the difference between actual output and *sustainable* output. **Sustainable output**[2] is the level of output corresponding to stable inflation. If output is below this level (the gap is negative) there will be a deficiency of demand and hence demand-deficient unemployment, but a fall in inflation. If output is above this level (the gap is positive) there will be excess demand and a rise

in inflation. Generally output will be below this level in a recession and above it in a boom. In other words, output gaps follow the course of the business cycle.

The chart shows output gaps for four countries from 1980 to 2001. As you can see, there was a large positive output gap in the UK in the late 1980s. This corresponded to a rapid rise in output and inflation and a fall in unemployment. You will also see that there was a large negative output gap in Japan in the late 1990s. This corresponded to a deep recession, rising unemployment and inflation just below zero (i.e. a slight decline in prices).

Over the *long* term, the rate of economic growth will

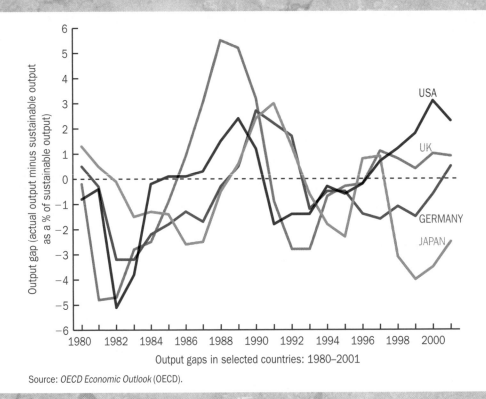

Output gaps in selected countries: 1980–2001

Source: *OECD Economic Outlook* (OECD).

smooth and regular. Drawing it this way allows us to make a clear distinction between each of the four phases. In practice, however, business cycles are highly irregular. They are irregular in two ways.

The length of the phases. Some booms are short lived, lasting only a few months

be approximately the same as the rate of growth of sustainable output. In other words, over the years, the average output gap will tend towards zero.

But how do we measure the output gap? There are two possible methods.

Measuring trend growth. The simplest way of calculating the output gap is by measuring the trend growth rate of the economy (i.e. the average growth rate over the course of the business cycle: see Figure 25.1 on page 521) and then seeing how much actual output differs from trend output. The assumption here is that the sustainable level of output grows steadily. This is, in fact, a major weakness of this method. Technological innovations tend to come in waves, generating surges in an economy's sustainable output. Rates of innovation, in turn, depend upon how flexible the economy is in adapting to such new technologies and how much investment takes place in equipment using this technology and in training labour in the necessary skills.

Business surveys. An alternative way to measure the output gap is to ask businesses directly. The CBI Industrial Trends Survey asks manufacturers, 'Is your present level of output below capacity?' The British Chambers of Commerce Survey asks similar questions of service-sector providers. However, such survey-based evidence can only provide a broad guide to rates of capacity utilisation and whether there is deficient or excess demand. Survey evidence tends to focus on specific sectors, which might, or might not, be indicative of the capacity position of the economy as a whole. So firms might be running above normal capacity (e.g. by overtime working) in one sector of the economy, while firms in another sector might have plenty of spare capacity to continue expansion. Thus survey evidence may give an incomplete picture of overall capacity utilisation in the economy.

Evidence for the UK. The trend growth rate in the UK was just under 2 per cent per year over the full economic cycle to mid-1997 (i.e. from mid-1986: the equivalent point in the previous cycle). But in 1997, the UK economy grew at over 3 per cent – clearly in excess of its sustainable rate. This suggested that economic activity had to slow if domestically generated inflation was to be avoided. Such a conclusion was confirmed by survey evidence, which showed that more companies were experiencing capacity constraints.

The slowdown in the UK economy in 1998 and 1999 meant that the output gap was becoming negative again. Nevertheless, forecasts made in 1999 suggested that the output gap (whether negative or positive) would remain considerably smaller than in the 1980s and early 1990s. The Treasury estimated that the output gap would widen in the year 2000, to about 1 to 1½ per cent and then tend towards zero by the end of 2001.[3]

Question

Under what circumstances would sustainable output (i.e. a zero output gap) move further away from the potential output ceiling shown in Figure 25.1?

[1] See Giorno *et al.*, 'Potential output, output gaps and structural budget balances', *OECD Economic Studies*, No. 24, 1995:1

[2] The level of sustainable output is sometimes referred to as the level of 'potential output'. This, however, is confusing, as the term *potential output* is used elsewhere (including this book) to refer to full-capacity output. Such a level of output, however, would not normally be sustainable over the longer term because of the upward pressure on inflation caused by various bottlenecks in the economy. Thus sustainable output is *below* the level of potential output in the sense that we are using the term 'potential output' (e.g. as in Figure 25.1.).

[3] HM Treasury, *Financial Statement and Budget Report*, March 1999, (ONS)

or so. Others are much longer, lasting perhaps three or four years. Likewise some recessions are short, while others are long.

The magnitude of the phases. Sometimes in phase 2 there is a very high rate of economic growth, perhaps 5 per cent per annum or more. On other occasions in phase 2 growth is much gentler. Sometimes in phase 4 there is a recession, with an actual decline in output (e.g. in the early 1980s and early 1990s). On other occasions, phase 4 is merely a 'pause', with growth simply slowing down.

Nevertheless, despite the irregularity of the fluctuations, cycles are still clearly discernible, especially if we plot *growth* on the vertical axis rather than the *level* of output. This is done in Figure 25.2, which shows the business cycles in selected industrial countries from 1971 to 2001.

Causes of fluctuations in actual growth

definition

Aggregate demand
Total spending on goods and services made in the economy. It consists of four elements, consumer spending (*C*), investment (*I*), government spending (*G*) and the expenditure on exports (*X*), less any expenditure on foreign goods and services (*M*): $AD = C + I + G + X - M$.

The major determinants of variations in the rate of actual growth in the *short run* are variations in the growth of aggregate demand.

Aggregate demand (*AD*) is the total spending on goods and services made within the country. This spending consists of four elements: consumer spending (*C*), investment expenditure by firms (*I*), government spending (*G*) and the expenditure by foreign residents on the country's goods and services (i.e. their purchases of its exports and their new investments in the country) (*X*). From these four must be subtracted any expenditure that goes on imports (*M*), since this is expenditure that 'leaks' abroad and is not spent on domestic goods and services. Thus:

$$AD = C + I + G + X - M$$

A rapid rise in aggregate demand will create shortages. This will tend to stimulate firms to increase output, thereby reducing slack in the economy.

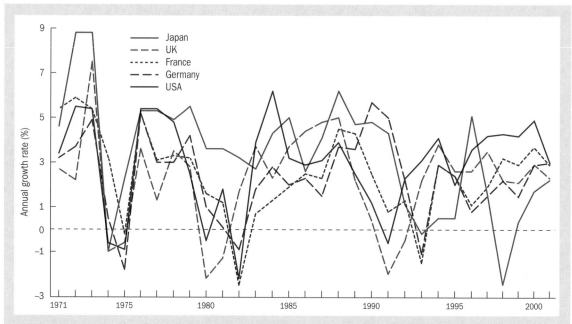

Figure 25.2

Growth rates in selected industrial countries: 1971–2001

Source: *Datastream.*

Likewise, a reduction in aggregate demand will leave firms with increased stocks of unsold goods. They will therefore tend to reduce output.

Aggregate demand and actual output therefore fluctuate together in the short run. A boom is associated with a rapid rise in aggregate demand: the faster the rise in aggregate demand, the higher the short-run rate of actual growth. A recession, by contrast, is associated with a reduction in aggregate demand.

A rapid rise in aggregate demand, however, is not enough to ensure a continuing high level of growth over a *number* of years. Without an expansion of potential output too, rises in actual output must eventually come to an end. Once spare capacity has been used up, once there is full employment of labour and other resources, the rate of growth of actual output will be restricted to the rate of growth of potential output. This is illustrated in Figure 25.1. As long as actual output is below potential output, the actual output curve can slope upward more steeply than the potential output curve. But once the gap between the two curves has been closed, the actual output curve can only slope as steeply as the potential output curve: the two curves cannot cross – actual output cannot be above potential output.

In the long run, therefore, there are two determinants of actual growth:

- The growth in aggregate demand. This determines whether potential output will be realised.
- The growth in potential output.

Causes of potential growth

There are two main determinants of potential output: (a) the amount of resources available and (b) their productivity.

Increases in the quantity of resources

Capital. The nation's output depends on its stock of capital (K). An increase in this stock will increase output. If we ignore the problem of machines wearing out or becoming obsolete and needing replacing, then the stock of capital will increase by the amount of investment. The rise in output that results will depend on the productivity of capital.

As we saw in section 23.6 (page 496), the rate of growth depends on the capital/output ratio (k) (i.e. the amount of capital (K) required to produce one more unit of output (Y) per year: $k = K/Y$). It also depends on the proportion of national income that is invested (i), which, assuming that all saving is invested, will equal the proportion of national income that is saved (s). The formula for growth becomes:

$g = i/k$ (or $g = s/k$)

Thus if 20 per cent of national income went in new investment ($i = 20\%$), and if each £1 of new investment yielded 25p of extra income per year ($k = 4$), then the growth rate would be 5 per cent. A simple example will demonstrate this. If national income is £100 billion, then £20 billion will be invested ($i = 20\%$). This will lead to extra annual output of £5 billion ($k = 4$). Thus national income grows to £105 billion: a growth of 5 per cent.

But what determines the rate of investment? There are a number of determinants. These include the confidence of business people about the future demand for their products, the profitability of business, the tax regime, the rate of growth in the economy and the rate of interest.

Over the long term, if investment is to increase, then *saving* must increase in order to finance that investment. Put another way, people must be prepared to forgo a certain amount of consumption in order to allow resources to be diverted into producing more capital goods: factories, machines, etc.

Note that if investment is to increase, there may need to be an increase in *aggregate demand*. In other words, if firms are to be encouraged to increase their capacity by installing new machines or building new factories, they may need first to see the *demand* for their products growing. Here a growth in *potential* output is the result of a growth in aggregate demand and hence *actual output*.

Labour. If there is an increase in the working population, there will be an increase in potential output. This increase in working population may result from a larger 'participation rate': a larger proportion of the total population in work or seeking work. For example, if a greater proportion of women with children decide to join the labour market, the working population will rise.

Alternatively, a rise in the working population may be the result of an increase in total population. There is a problem here. If a rise in total population does not result in a greater *proportion* of the population working, output *per head* may not rise at all. In practice, many developed countries are faced with a growing proportion of their population above retirement age, and thus a potential *fall* in output per head of the population.

Land and raw materials. Land is virtually fixed in quantity. Land reclamation schemes and the opening up of marginal land can only add tiny amounts to national output.

Whether new raw materials can be discovered is largely a matter of the luck of nature. If a country does discover new raw materials (e.g. oil), it will only result in *short-term* growth: i.e. while the rate of extraction is building up. Once the rate of extraction is at a maximum, economic growth will cease. Output will simply remain at the new higher level, until eventually the raw materials will begin to run out. Output will then fall back again.

The problem of diminishing returns. If a single factor of production increases in supply while others remain fixed, diminishing returns will set in. For example, if the quantity of capital increases with no increase in other factors of production, then diminishing returns to capital will set in. The rate of return on capital will fall. Unless *all* factors of production increase, therefore, the rate of growth is likely to slow down.

The solution to the problem of diminishing returns is for there to be an increase in the *productivity* of resources.

Increases in the productivity of resources

Technological improvements can increase the marginal productivity of capital. Much of the investment in new machines is not just in extra machines, but in superior machines producing a higher rate of return. Consider the microchip revolution of recent years. Modern computers can do the work of many people and have replaced many machines which were cumbersome and expensive to build. Improved methods of transport have reduced the costs of moving goods and materials. Improved communications (such as fax machines and the Internet) have reduced the costs of transmitting information.

As a result of technical progress, the productivity of capital has tended to increase over time. Similarly, as a result of new skills, improved education and training, and better health, the productivity of labour has also tended to increase over time.

Policies to achieve growth

How can governments increase a country's growth rate? Policies differ in two ways.

First, they may focus on the demand side or the supply side of the economy. In other words, they may attempt to create sufficient *aggregate demand* to ensure that firms wish to invest and that potential output is realised. Or alternatively, they may seek to increase *aggregate supply* by concentrating on measures to increase potential output: measures to encourage research and development, innovation and training.

Second, they may be market-orientated or interventionist policies. Many economists and politicians, especially those on the political right, believe that the best environment for encouraging economic growth is one where private enterprise is allowed to flourish: where entrepreneurs are able to reap substantial rewards from investment in new techniques and new products. Such economists therefore advocate policies designed to free up the market. Others, however, argue that a free market will be subject to considerable cyclical fluctuations. The resulting uncertainty will discourage investment. Such economists, therefore, tend to advocate intervention by the government to reduce these fluctuations.

25.3 Unemployment

The meaning of unemployment

Unemployment can be expressed either as a number (e.g. 1.5 million) or as a percentage (e.g. 5 per cent). But just who should be included in the statistics? Should it be everyone without a job? The answer is clearly no, since we would not want to include children and pensioners. We would probably also want to exclude those who were not looking for work, such as parents choosing to stay at home to look after children.

The most usual definition that economists use for the **number unemployed** is: *those of working age who are without work, but who are available for work at current wage rates.* If the figure is to be expressed as a percentage, then it is a percentage of the total **labour force**. The labour force is defined as: *those in employment plus those unemployed.* Thus if 22.5 million people were employed and 2.5 million people were unemployed, the **unemployment rate** would be:

$$\frac{2.5}{22.5 + 2.5} \times 100 = 10 \text{ per cent}$$

---

definition

Number unemployed (economist's definition)
Those of working age who are without work, but who are available for work at current wage rates.

definition

Labour force
The number employed plus the number unemployed.

definition

Unemployment rate
The number unemployed expressed as a percentage of the labour force.

Official measures of unemployment

Claimant unemployment

Two common measures of unemployment are used in official statistics. The first is **claimant unemployment**. This is simply a measure of all those in receipt of unemployment-related benefits. In the UK, claimants receive the 'job-seeker's allowance'.

Claimant statistics have the advantage of being very easy to collect. However, they exclude all those of working age who are available for work at current wage rates, but who are *not* eligible for benefits. If the government changes the eligibility conditions so that fewer people are now eligible, this will reduce the number of claimants and hence the official number unemployed, even if there has been no change in the numbers with or without work. There have been over 30 changes to eligibility conditions since 1979, all but one of which have had the effect of reducing the claimant figures!

Standardised unemployment rates

Two international organisations that publish unemployment statistics for many countries are the International Labour Office (ILO) and the Organisation for Economic Co-operation and Development (OECD). They define the unemployed as persons of working age who are without work, available to start work within two weeks and *actively seeking employment* or waiting to take up an appointment. The figures are compiled from the results of labour force *surveys*. Since 1998, this has been the main measure used by the UK government.

Because these international bodies use the same 'standardised' definition for all countries, international comparisons are easier. But is the **standardised unemployment rate** likely to be higher or lower than the claimant unemployment rate? The standardised rate is likely to be higher to the extent that it includes people seeking work who are nevertheless not entitled to claim benefits, but lower to the extent that it excludes those who are claiming benefits and yet who are not actively seeking work. Clearly, the tougher the benefit regulations, the lower the claimant rate will be relative to the standardised rate.

The costs of unemployment

The most obvious cost of unemployment is to the *unemployed themselves*. There is the direct financial cost of the loss in their earnings, measured as the difference between their previous wage and their unemployment benefit. Then there are the personal costs of being unemployed. The longer people are unemployed, the more dispirited they may become. Their self-esteem is likely to fall, and they are more likely to succumb to stress-related illness.

Then there are the costs to the *family and friends* of the unemployed. Personal relations can become strained, and there may be an increase in domestic violence and the number of families splitting up.

Then there are the *broader costs to the economy*. Unemployment represents a loss of output. In other words, actual output is below potential output. Apart from the lack of income to the unemployed themselves, this under-utilisation of resources leads to less incomes for other people too:

- Firms lose the profits that could have been made, had there been full employment.

---

definition

Claimant unemployment
Those in receipt of unemployment-related benefits.

definition

Standardised unemployment rate
The measure of the unemployment rate used by the ILO and OECD. The unemployed are defined as people of working age who are without work, available for work and actively seeking employment.

- The government loses tax revenues, since the unemployed pay no income tax and national insurance, and, given that the unemployed spend less, they pay less VAT and excise duties. The government also incurs administrative costs associated with the running of benefit offices. It may also have to spend extra on health care, the social services and the police.
- Other workers lose any additional wages they could have earned from higher national output.

The costs of unemployment are to some extent offset by benefits. If workers voluntarily quit their job to look for a better one, then they must reckon that the benefits of a better job more than compensate for their temporary loss of income. From the nation's point of view, a workforce that is prepared to quit jobs and spend a short time unemployed will be a more adaptable, more mobile workforce – one that is responsive to changing economic circumstances. Such a workforce will lead to greater allocative efficiency in the short run and more rapid economic growth over the longer run.

Long-term involuntary unemployment is quite another matter. The costs clearly outweigh any benefits, both for the individuals concerned and for the economy as a whole. A demotivated, deskilled pool of long-term unemployed is a serious economic and social problem.

Unemployment and the labour market

We now turn to the causes of unemployment. These causes fall into two broad categories: *equilibrium* unemployment and *disequilibrium* unemployment. To make clear the distinction between the two, it is necessary to look at the working of the labour market.

Figure 25.3 shows the **aggregate demand for labour** and the **aggregate supply of labour**: that is, the total demand and supply of labour in the whole economy. The *real* average wage rate is plotted on the vertical axis. This is the average wage rate expressed in terms of its purchasing power: in other words, after taking inflation into account.

The aggregate supply of labour curve (AS_L) shows the number of workers *willing to accept jobs* at each wage rate. This curve is relatively inelastic, since the size of the workforce at any one time cannot change significantly. Nevertheless it is not totally inelastic because (a) a higher wage rate will encour-

Figure 25.3
Disequilibrium unemployment

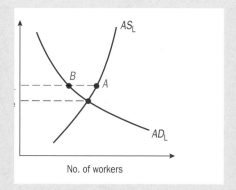

age some people to enter the labour market (e.g. parents raising children) and (b) the unemployed will be more willing to accept job offers rather than continuing to search for a better-paid job.

The aggregate demand for labour curve (AD_L) slopes downward. The higher the wage rate, the more will firms attempt to economise on labour and to substitute other factors of production for labour.

The labour market is in equilibrium at a wage of W_e in Figure 25.3, where the demand for labour equals the supply.

If the wage were above W_e, the labour market would be in a state of disequilibrium. At a wage rate of W_1, there is an excess supply of labour of $A − B$. This is called **disequilibrium unemployment**.

For disequilibrium unemployment to occur, two conditions must hold:

● The aggregate supply of labour must exceed the aggregate demand.
● There must be a 'stickiness' in wages. In other words, the wage rate must not immediately fall to W_e.

Even when the labour market *is* in equilibrium, however, not everyone looking for work will be employed. Some people will hold out, hoping to find a better job. The curve N in Figure 25.4 shows the total number in the labour force. The horizontal difference between it and the aggregate supply of labour curve (AS_L) represents the excess of people looking for work over those actually willing to accept jobs. Q_e represents the equilibrium level of employment and the distance $D − E$ represents the **equilibrium level of unemployment**. This is sometimes known as the *natural level of unemployment*.

Types of disequilibrium unemployment

There are three possible causes of disequilibrium unemployment.

Real-wage unemployment

This is where trade unions use their monopoly power to drive wages above the market-clearing level. In Figure 25.3, the wage rate is driven up above W_e. Excessive real wage rates were blamed by the Thatcher and Major governments for the high unemployment of the 1980s and early 1990s. The possibility of

definition

Disequilibrium unemployment
Unemployment resulting from real wages in the economy being above the equilibrium level.

definition

Equilibrium ('natural') unemployment
The difference between those who would like employment at the current wage rate and those willing and able to take a job.

Figure 25.4
Equilibrium unemployment

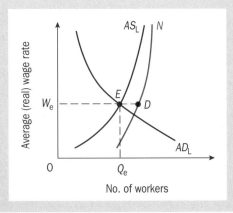

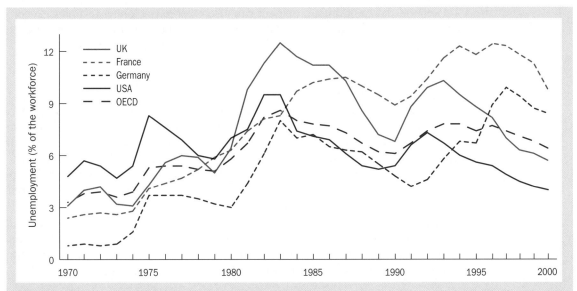

Figure 25.5

Standardised unemployment in selected industrial countries: 1970–2000

Source: *Datastream.*

higher real-wage unemployment was also one of the reasons for their rejection of a national minimum wage.

The solution to real-wage unemployment would seem to be a reduction in real wage rates. However, it may be very difficult to prevent unions pushing up wages. Even if the government did succeed in reducing the average real wage rate, there would then be a problem of reduced consumer expenditure and hence a reduced demand for labour, with the result that unemployment might not fall at all.

Demand-deficient unemployment

Demand-deficient unemployment is associated with economic recessions. As the economy moves into recession, consumer demand falls. Firms find that they are unable to sell their current level of output. For a time they may be prepared to build up stocks of unsold goods, but sooner or later they will start to cut back on production and cut back on the amount of labour they employ. In Figure 25.3 the AD_L curve shifts to the left. The deeper the recession becomes and the longer it lasts, the higher will demand-deficient unemployment become.

As the economy recovers and begins to grow again, so demand-deficient unemployment will start to fall. Because demand-deficient unemployment fluctuates with the business cycle, it is sometimes referred to as 'cyclical unemployment'. Figure 25.5 shows the fluctuations in unemployment in various industrial countries and for the OECD[1] as a whole. If you compare this figure with Figure 25.2, you can see how unemployment tends to rise in recessions and fall in booms.

[1] The Organisation for Economic Co-operation and Development: the 29 major industrialised countries including the Czech Republic, Hungary, Poland, Korea, Mexico and Turkey.

---

definition

Demand-deficient or cyclical unemployment Disequilibrium unemployment caused by a fall in aggregate demand with no corresponding fall in the real wage rate.

Demand-deficient unemployment can also exist in the longer term if the economy is constantly run at below full capacity and labour markets continue not to be in equilibrium. Even at the peak of the trade cycle, actual output may be considerably below potential output.

Growth in the labour supply

If labour supply rises with no corresponding increase in the demand for labour, the equilibrium real wage rate will fall. If the real wage rate is 'sticky' downward, unemployment will occur. This tends not to be such a serious cause of unemployment as demand deficiency, since the supply of labour changes relatively slowly. Nevertheless there is a problem of providing jobs for school leavers each year with the sudden influx of new workers on to the labour market.

There is also a potential problem over the longer term if social trends lead more women with children to seek employment. In practice, however, with the rapid growth of part-time employment and the lower average wage rate paid to women, this has not been a major cause of excess labour supply.

Equilibrium unemployment

If you look at Figure 25.5, you can see how unemployment was higher in the 1980s and 1990s than in the 1970s. Part of the reason for this has been the growth in equilibrium unemployment.

Although there may be overall *macro*economic equilibrium, with the *aggregate* demand for labour equal to the *aggregate* supply, and thus no disequilibrium unemployment, at a *micro*economic level supply and demand may not match. This is when equilibrium unemployment will occur. There are various types of equilibrium unemployment.

Frictional (search) unemployment

Frictional unemployment occurs when people leave their jobs, either voluntarily or because they are sacked or made redundant, and are then unemployed for a period of time while they are looking for a new job. They may not get the first job they apply for, despite a vacancy existing. The employer may continue searching, hoping to find a better-qualified person. Likewise, unemployed people may choose not to take the first job they are offered. Instead they may continue searching, hoping that a better one will turn up.

The problem is that information is imperfect. Employers are not fully informed about what labour is available; workers are not fully informed about what jobs are available and what they entail. Both employers and workers, therefore, have to search: employers search for the right labour and workers search for the right jobs.

Structural unemployment

Structural unemployment is where the structure of the economy changes. Employment in some industries may expand while in others it contracts. There are two main reasons for this.

A change in the pattern of demand. Some industries experience declining demand. This may be due to a change in consumer tastes. Certain goods may

definition

Frictional (search) unemployment
Unemployment that occurs as a result of imperfect information in the labour market. It often takes time for workers to find jobs (even though there are vacancies) and in the meantime they are unemployed.

definition

Structural unemployment
Unemployment that arises from changes in the pattern of demand or supply in the economy. People made redundant in one part of the economy cannot immediately take up jobs in other parts (even though there are vacancies).

go out of fashion. Or it may be due to competition from other industries. For example, consumer demand may shift away from coal and to other fuels. This will lead to structural unemployment in mining areas.

A change in the methods of production (technological unemployment). New techniques of production often allow the same level of output to be produced with fewer workers. This is known as 'labour-saving technical progress'. Unless output expands sufficiently to absorb the surplus labour, people will be made redundant. This creates **technological unemployment**.

Structural unemployment often occurs in particular regions of the country. When it does, it is referred to as **regional unemployment**. This is most likely to occur when particular industries are concentrated in particular areas. For example, the decline in the South Wales coal mining industry led to high unemployment in the Welsh valleys.

Seasonal unemployment

Seasonal unemployment occurs when the demand for certain types of labour fluctuates with the seasons of the year. This problem is particularly severe in holiday areas such as Cornwall, where unemployment can reach very high levels in the winter months.

25.4 Inflation

The rate of inflation measures the annual percentage increase in prices. The most usual measure is that of *retail* prices. The government publishes an index of retail prices each month, and the rate of inflation is the percentage increase in that index over the previous twelve months. Figure 25.6 shows the rates of inflation for the USA, Japan, the UK, the EU and the OECD. As you can see, inflation was particularly severe between 1973 and 1983, and relatively low in the late 1980s and since the mid-1990s.

It is also possible to give the rates of inflation for other prices. For example, indices are published for commodity prices, food prices, house prices, import prices, prices after taking taxes into account and so on. Their respective rates of inflation are simply their annual percentage increase. Likewise it is possible to give the rate of inflation of wage rates ('wage inflation').

Before we proceed, a word of caution: be careful not to confuse a rise or fall in *inflation* with a rise or fall in *prices*. A rise in inflation means a *faster* increase in prices. A fall in inflation means a *slower* increase in prices (but still an increase as long as inflation is positive).

The costs of inflation

A lack of growth is obviously a problem if people want higher living standards. Unemployment is obviously a problem, both for the unemployed themselves and also for society, which suffers a loss in output and has to support the unemployed. But why is inflation a problem? If firms are faced with rising costs, does it really matter if they can simply pass them on in higher prices? Similarly for workers, if their wages keep up with prices, there will not be a cut in their living standards.

definition

Technological unemployment
Structural unemployment that occurs as a result of the introduction of labour-saving technology.

definition

Regional unemployment
Structural unemployment occurring in specific regions of the country.

definition

Seasonal unemployment
Unemployment associated with industries or regions where the demand for labour is lower at certain times of the year.

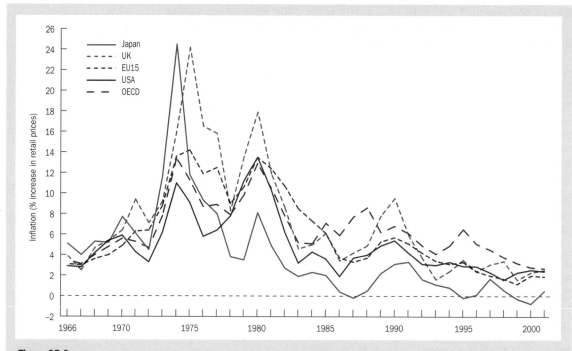

Figure 25.6

Inflation rates in selected industrial countries and groups of countries: 1966–2001

Source: *Datastream*.

If people could correctly anticipate the rate of inflation and fully adjust prices and incomes to take account of it, then the costs of inflation would indeed be relatively small. For us as consumers, they would simply be the relatively minor inconvenience of having to adjust our notions of what a 'fair' price is for each item when we go shopping. For firms, they would again be the relatively minor costs of having to change price labels, or prices in catalogues or on menus, or to adjust slot machines. These are known as **menu costs**.

In reality, people frequently make mistakes when predicting the rate of inflation and are not able to adapt fully to it. This leads to the following problems, which are likely to be more serious the higher the rate of inflation becomes and the more the rate fluctuates.

Redistribution. Inflation redistributes income away from those on fixed incomes and those in a weak bargaining position, to those who can use their economic power to gain large pay, rent or profit increases. It redistributes wealth to those with assets (e.g. property) that rise in value particularly rapidly during periods of inflation, and away from those with savings that pay rates of interest below the rate of inflation and hence whose value is eroded by inflation. Pensioners may be particularly badly hit by rapid inflation.

Uncertainty and lack of investment. Inflation tends to cause uncertainty in the business community, especially when the rate of inflation fluctuates. (Generally, the higher the rate of inflation, the more it fluctuates.) If it is difficult for firms

definition

Menu costs of inflation

The costs associated with having to adjust price lists or labels.

BOX 25.2

Is inflation dead?
No, just kept under control

'What's the big fuss about inflation?' That might seem to be a justified question at the start of the new millennium. After all, inflation rates in developed countries are typically around 2–3 per cent (see Figure 25.6), and that is hardly a cause for concern.

Indeed, having some inflation, provided that it is relatively modest, could even be seen to be an advantage. This is because wages and prices are often 'sticky' downwards: unions are not prepared to accept wage cuts; firms are often unwilling to cut prices. Having a modest amount of inflation allows relative prices and wages in different parts of the economy to be adjusted up *and* down, in line with changes in demand and supply. Where demand has risen (or supply fallen) prices and wages can rise. Where demand has fallen (or supply risen) prices and wages can be held steady. There will be an overall rise in prices and wages in the economy (a modest inflation) and yet *relative* prices and wages will have adjusted.

So why be concerned about inflation, given that it is so low and, at such levels, can be useful? The reason *why* it is so low is that it has been made the main target of macroeconomic policy in many countries. For example, in the UK, the Bank of England tries to keep inflation at 2½ per cent. In the eleven EU countries using the euro, the European Central Bank tries to keep inflation below 2 per cent. In both cases interest rates are adjusted up or down to keep inflation on target. If inflation is predicted to go above its target level, interest rates are raised. The resulting higher cost of borrowing dampens consumer expenditure and investment by firms. The resulting lower aggregate demand leads to a fall in demand-pull inflation.

If controlling inflation was *not* the main target of macroeconomic policy, then it could well rise, causing the problems we have been considering in this section. It is true that inflation is not a problem at present, but only because keeping it low has been given such a high priority.

But has targeting inflation meant giving a lower priority to raising growth and reducing unemployment? Could we have higher growth and lower unemployment if we were prepared to accept a higher rate of inflation? Or is low inflation a means to achieving these other goals? We shall consider these questions in the following chapters.

Question

How is the policy of targeting inflation likely to affect the expected rate of inflation?

to predict their costs and revenues, they may be discouraged from investing. This will reduce the rate of economic growth. On the other hand, as will be explained below, policies to reduce the rate of inflation may themselves reduce the rate of economic growth, especially in the short run. This may then provide the government with a policy dilemma.

Balance of payments. Inflation is likely to worsen the balance of payments. If a country suffers from relatively high inflation, its exports will become less competitive in world markets. At the same time, imports will become relatively cheaper than home-produced goods. Thus exports will fall and imports will rise. As a result the balance of payments will deteriorate and/or the exchange rate will fall. Both of these effects can cause problems. This is examined in more detail in the next chapter.

Resources. Extra resources are likely to be used to cope with the effects of inflation. Accountants and other financial experts may have to be employed by companies to help them cope with the uncertainties caused by inflation.

The costs of inflation may be relatively mild if inflation is kept to single figures. They can be very serious, however, if inflation gets out of hand. If inflation develops into 'hyperinflation', with prices rising perhaps by several hundred or even thousand per cent per year, the whole basis of the market economy will be undermined. Firms constantly raise prices in an attempt to cover their rocketing costs. Workers demand huge pay increases in an attempt to stay ahead of the rocketing cost of living. Thus prices and wages chase each other in an ever-rising inflationary spiral. People will no longer want to save money. Instead they will spend it as quickly as possible before its value falls any further. People may even resort to barter in an attempt to avoid using money altogether.

Aggregate demand and supply and the level of prices

The level of prices in the economy is determined by the interaction of aggregate demand and aggregate supply. The analysis is similar to that of demand and supply in individual markets, but there are some crucial differences. Figure 25.7 shows aggregate demand and supply curves. Let us examine each in turn.

Aggregate demand curve

Remember what we said about aggregate demand earlier in the chapter. It is the total level of spending on the country's products: that is, by consumers, by the government, by firms on investment, and by people residing abroad. But why will the *AD* curve slope downwards: why will people demand fewer products as prices rise? There are three main reasons:

● If prices rise, people will be encouraged to buy fewer of the country's products and more imports instead (which are now relatively cheaper); also the country will sell fewer exports. Thus aggregate demand will be lower.
● As prices rise, people will need more money to pay for their purchases. With a given supply of money in the economy, this will have the effect of driving up interest rates (we will explore this in Chapter 27). The effect of higher interest rates will be to discourage borrowing and encourage saving. Both will have the effect of reducing spending and hence reducing aggregate demand.

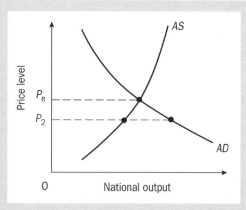

Figure 25.7
Aggregate demand and aggregate supply

● If prices rise, the value of people's savings will be eroded. They may thus save more (and spend less) to compensate.

Aggregate supply curve

The aggregate supply curve slopes upwards – at least in the short run. In other words, the higher the level of prices, the more will be produced. The reason is simple: provided that factor prices (and, in particular, wage rates) do not rise as rapidly as product prices, firms' profitability at each level of output will be higher than before. This will encourage them to produce more.

Equilibrium

The equilibrium price level will be where aggregate demand equals aggregate supply. To demonstrate this, consider what would happen if aggregate demand exceeded aggregate supply: for example, at P_2 in Figure 25.7. The resulting shortages throughout the economy would drive up prices. This would cause a movement up along both the AD and AS curves until $AD = AS$ (at P_e).

Shifts in the AD or AS curves

If there is a change in the price level there will be a movement *along* the AD and AS curves. If any other determinant of AD or AS changes, the respective curve will shift. The analysis here is very similar to shifts and movements along demand and supply curves in individual markets (see pages 60 and 64).

The aggregate demand curve will shift if there is a change in any of its components – consumption, investment, government expenditure or exports. Thus if the government decides to spend more, or if consumers spend more as a result of lower taxes, or if business confidence increases so that firms decide to invest more, the AD curve will shift to the right.

Similarly, the aggregate supply curve will shift to the right if there is a rise in labour productivity or in the stock of capital: in other words, if there is a rise in potential output.

Causes of inflation

Demand-pull inflation

Demand-pull inflation is caused by continuing rises in aggregate demand. In Figure 25.7, the AD curve shifts to the right, and continues doing so. Firms will respond to the rise in aggregate demand partly by raising prices and partly by increasing output (there is a move up along the AS curve). Just how much they raise prices depends on how much their costs rise as a result of increasing output. This in turn depends upon how close actual output is to potential output. The less slack there is in the economy, the more will firms respond to a rise in demand by raising their prices (the steeper will be the AS curve).

Demand-pull inflation is typically associated with a booming economy. Many economists therefore argue that it is the counterpart of demand-deficient unemployment. When the economy is in recession, demand-deficient unemployment will be high, but demand-pull inflation will be low. When, on the other hand, the economy is near the peak of the business cycle, demand-pull inflation will be high, but demand-deficient unemployment will be low.

definition

Demand-pull inflation
Inflation caused by persistent rises in aggregate demand.

Cost-push inflation

Cost-push inflation is associated with continuing rises in costs and hence continuing leftward (upward) shifts in the *AS* curve. If firms face a rise in costs, they will respond partly by raising prices and passing the costs on to the consumer, and partly by cutting back on production (there is a movement back along the *AD* curve).

Just how much firms raise prices and cut back on production depends on the shape of the aggregate demand curve. The less elastic the *AD* curve, the less sales will fall as a result of any price rise, and hence the more will firms be able to pass on the rise in their costs to consumers as higher prices.

The rise in costs may originate from a number of different sources. As a result we can distinguish various types of cost-push inflation.

- *Wage-push inflation.* This is where trades union push up wages independently of the demand for labour.
- *Profit-push inflation.* This is where firms use their monopoly power to make bigger profits by pushing up prices independently of consumer demand.
- *Import-price-push inflation.* This is where import prices rise independently of the level of aggregate demand. An example is when OPEC quadrupled the price of oil in 1973/4.

In all these cases, inflation occurs because one or more groups are exercising economic power. The problem is likely to get worse, therefore, if there is an increasing concentration of economic power over time (for example, if firms or unions get bigger and bigger, and more monopolistic) or if groups become more militant.

Demand-pull and cost-push inflation can occur together, since wage and price rises can be caused both by increases in aggregate demand and by independent causes pushing up costs. Even when an inflationary process *starts* as either demand-pull or cost-push, it is often difficult to separate the two. An initial cost-push inflation may encourage the government to expand aggregate demand to offset rises in unemployment. Alternatively, an initial demand-pull inflation may strengthen the power of certain groups, who then use this power to drive up costs.

Structural (demand-shift) inflation

When the *pattern* of demand (or supply) changes in the economy, certain industries will experience increased demand and others decreased demand. If prices and wages are inflexible downwards in the contracting industries, and prices and wages rise in the expanding industries, the overall price and wage level will rise. The problem will be made worse, the less elastic is supply to these shifts.

Thus a more rapid structural change in the economy can lead to both increased structural unemployment and increased structural inflation. An example of this problem was the so called north–south divide in the UK during the second half of the 1980s. The north experienced high structural unemployment as old industries declined, while the south experienced excess demand. This led to, among other things, rapid house price inflation and rapid increases

---

definition

Cost-push inflation
Inflation caused by persistent rises in costs of production (independently of demand).

BOX 25.3

Disinflation in Europe and Japan

Compared to their US and Japanese rivals, European businesses used to have a reputation for raising prices to make more profits. In an economic environment where inflation is endemic, business can easily hide from its inefficiencies and adopt this short-run strategy.

However, following the recession of the early 1990s – Europe's worst recession since the war – attitudes and practices seem to have changed, and potentially for the better. European business seems to be adopting a more competitive way of doing business and, rather than rising, prices have been falling in many sectors. This process has been dubbed 'disinflation'. It has resulted largely from changes in the external business environment. Here slow growth, financial restraint by central banks attempting to keep inflation within limits, and fierce global competition have led many firms to question whether price rises are necessary or justifiable.

Japanese business has found itself in a very similar position. It too has experienced a lengthy recession, in which prices have fallen as businesses try to shift unwanted stocks. In addition, the high value of the yen and the subsequent reduction in the cost of imports have stimulated a huge rise in foreign competition, which has only succeeded in forcing prices down yet further.

Are general reductions in prices a good thing or a bad thing? The answer to this largely depends upon whether you are a consumer or producer, whether you are looking at the short or long term, and whether any price reduction is met by higher productivity gains and not redundancies.

In the short term, consumers will clearly benefit from lower prices: in effect, their real income will rise. Over the longer term, both producers and consumers are likely to gain as lower underlying rates of inflation enable governments to reduce interest rates. For business this means cheaper capital and greater opportunities for investment and growth.

The down side to disinflation is whether it can be achieved without a massive impact upon levels of income and employment. If businesses simply respond to lower prices, and hence profit margins, by making workers redundant, income levels may begin to fall, stimulating a downward spiral of demand. Thus the key to successful disinflation is to offset falling prices with greater efficiency.

It increasingly appears that only the fit will survive. Those unable to meet these new stringent efficiency goals will not be able to generate profits from higher prices, and will invariably become ripe for takeover by those that can.

Questions

1 If prices and wage rates are forced downward, who are likely to gain and who are likely to lose?
2 What attitudes should trade unions take in such an environment if they are seeking to maximise the interests of their members?
3 What new strategies have businesses been forced to adopt in order to maintain profits in a low-inflation economy?

in incomes for various groups of workers and firms. With many prices and wages being set *nationally*, the inflation in the south then 'spilt over' into the north.

Expectations and inflation

Workers and firms take account of the *expected* rate of inflation when making decisions.

Imagine that a union and an employer are negotiating a wage increase. Let us assume that both sides expect a rate of inflation of 5 per cent. The union will be happy to receive a wage rise somewhat above 5 per cent. That way the members would be getting a *real* rise in incomes. The employers will be happy to pay a wage rise somewhat below 5 per cent. After all, they can put their price up by

5 per cent, knowing that their rivals will do approximately the same. The actual wage rise that the two sides agree on will thus be somewhere around 5 per cent.

Now let us assume that the expected rate of inflation is 10 per cent. Both sides will now negotiate around this benchmark, with the outcome being somewhere round about 10 per cent.

Thus the higher the expected rate of inflation, the higher will be the level of pay settlements and price rises, and hence the higher will be the resulting actual rate of inflation.

In recent years the importance of expectations in explaining the actual rate of inflation has been increasingly recognised by economists, and it has prompted them to discover just what determines people's expectations. As you might expect, there is considerable disagreement, and in fact it is one of the most controversial areas of economics. We explore some of the issues in Chapter 28.

25.5 The business cycle and macroeconomic objectives

In the short term (up to about two years), the four objectives of faster growth in output, lower unemployment, lower inflation and the avoidance of balance of payments deficits are all related. They all depend on aggregate demand and vary with the course of the business cycle. This is illustrated in Figure 25.8.

In the expansionary phase of the business cycle (phase 2), aggregate demand grows rapidly. The gap between actual and potential output will narrow. There will be relatively rapid growth in output, and (demand-deficient) unemployment will fall. Thus two of the problems are getting better. On the other hand, the other two problems will be getting worse. The growing shortages lead to higher (demand-pull) inflation and a deteriorating balance of payments as the extra demand 'sucks in' more imports and as higher prices make domestic goods less competitive internationally.

At the peak of the cycle (phase 3), unemployment is probably at its lowest and output at its highest (for the time being). But growth has already ceased or at least

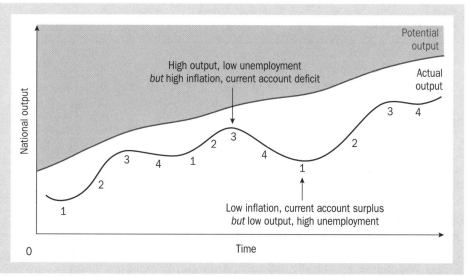

Figure 25.8
The business cycle and the four macroeconomic objectives

slowed down. Inflation and balance of payments problems are probably acute.

As the economy moves into phase 4 (let us assume that this is an actual recession with falling output), the reverse will happen to that of phase 2. Falling aggregate demand will make growth negative and demand-deficient unemployment higher, but inflation is likely to slow down and the balance of payments will improve. These two improvements may take some time to occur, however.

Governments are thus faced with a dilemma. If they reflate the economy, they will make two of the objectives better (growth and unemployment), but the other two worse (inflation and balance of payments). If they deflate the economy, it is the other way round: inflation and the balance of payments will improve, but unemployment will rise and growth, or even output, will fall.

25.6 The circular flow of income

Another way of understanding the relationship between the four objectives is to use a simple model of the economy. This is the circular flow of income, which is shown in Figure 25.9. In the diagram, the economy is divided into two major groups: *firms* and *households*. Each group has two roles. Firms are producers of goods and services; they are also the employers of labour and other factors of production. Households (which is the word we use for individuals) are the consumers of goods and services; they are also the suppliers of labour and various other factors of production. In the diagram there is an inner flow and various outer flows of income between these two groups.

The inner flow, withdrawals and injections

The inner flow

Firms pay money to households in the form of wages and salaries, dividends on shares, interest and rent. These payments are in return for the services of the

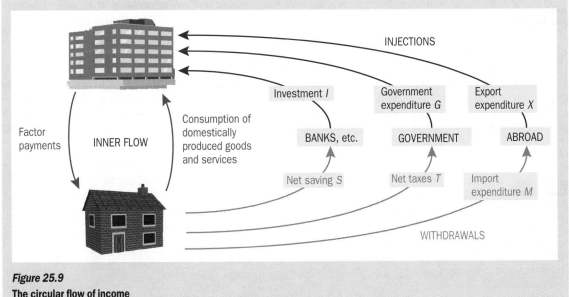

Figure 25.9
The circular flow of income

factors of production – labour, capital and land – that are supplied by households. Thus on the left-hand side of the diagram money flows directly from firms to households as 'factor payments'.

Households, in turn, pay money to domestic firms when they **consume domestically produced goods and services** (C_d). This is shown on the right-hand side of the inner flow. There is thus a circular flow of payments from firms to households to firms and so on.

If households spend *all* their incomes on buying domestic goods and services, and if firms pay out *all* this income they receive as factor payments to domestic households, and if the velocity of circulation does not change, the flow will continue at the same level indefinitely. The money just goes round and round at the same speed and incomes remain unchanged.

In the real world, of course, it is not as simple as this. Not all income gets passed on round the inner flow; some is *withdrawn*. At the same time, incomes are injected into the flow from outside. Let us examine these withdrawals and injections.

Withdrawals

Only part of the incomes received by households will be spent on the goods and services of domestic firms. The remainder will be withdrawn from the inner flow. Likewise, only part of the incomes generated by firms will be paid to domestic households. The remainder of this will also be withdrawn. There are three forms of **withdrawals** (W) (or 'leakages' as they are sometimes called).

Net saving (S). Saving is income that households choose not to spend but to put aside for the future. Savings will normally be deposited in financial institutions such as banks and building societies. This is shown in the bottom right of the diagram. Money flows from households to 'banks, etc'. What we are seeking to measure here, however, is the net flow from households to the banking sector. We therefore have to subtract from saving any borrowing or drawing on past savings by households in order to get the *net* saving flow. Of course, if household borrowing exceeded saving, the net flow would be in the other direction: it would be negative.

Net taxes (T). When people pay taxes (to either central or local government), this represents a withdrawal of money from the inner flow in much the same way as saving: only in this case people have no choice. Some taxes, such as income tax and employees' national insurance contributions, are paid out of household incomes. Others, such as VAT and excise duties, are paid out of consumer expenditure. Others, such as corporation tax, are paid out of firms' incomes before being received by households as dividends on shares.

When, however, people receive *benefits* from the government, such as working families tax credit, child benefit and pensions, the money flows the other way. Benefits are thus equivalent to a 'negative tax'. These benefits are known as **transfer payments**. They transfer money from one group of people (taxpayers) to others (the recipients).

In the model, 'net taxes' (T) represent the *net* flow to the government from households and firms. It consists of total taxes minus benefits.

Import expenditure (M). Not all consumption is of totally home-produced

---

goods. Households spend some of their incomes on imported goods and services, or on goods and services using imported components. Although the money that consumers spend on such goods initially flows to domestic retailers, it will eventually find its way abroad, either when the retailers or wholesalers themselves buy the imports from abroad, or when domestic manufacturers purchase imported inputs to make their products. This expenditure on imports constitutes the third withdrawal from the inner flow. This money flows abroad.

Total withdrawals are simply the sum of net saving, net taxes and the expenditure on imports:

$$W = S + T + M$$

Injections

Only part of the demand for firms' output arises from consumers' expenditure. The remainder comes from other sources outside the inner flow. These additional components of aggregate demand are known as **injections** (J). There are three types of injection.

Investment (I). This is the money that firms spend which they obtain from various financial institutions – either past savings or loans, or through a new issue of shares. They may invest in plant and equipment or may simply spend the money on building up stocks of inputs, semi-finished or finished goods.

Government expenditure (G). When the government spends money on goods and services produced by firms, this counts as an injection. Examples of such government expenditure are spending on roads, hospitals and schools. (Note that government expenditure in this model does not include state benefits. These transfer payments, as we saw above, are the equivalent of negative taxes and have the effect of reducing the T component of withdrawals.)

Export expenditure (X). Money flows into the circular flow from abroad when foreign residents buy our exports of goods and services.

Total injections are thus the sum of investment, government expenditure and exports:

$$J = I + G + X$$

The relationship between withdrawals and injections

There are indirect links between saving and investment, taxation and government expenditure, and imports and exports, via financial institutions, the government (central and local) and foreign countries respectively. If a greater proportion of income is saved, there will be more available for banks and other financial institutions to lend out. If tax receipts are higher, the government may be more keen to increase its expenditure. Finally, if imports increase, foreigners' incomes will increase, which will enable them to purchase more of our exports.

These links, however, do not guarantee that $S = I$ or $G = T$ or $M = X$. For a period of time, financial institutions can lend out (I) more than they receive from depositors (S) or vice versa; governments can spend (G) more than they receive in taxes (T) or vice versa; and exports (X) can exceed imports (M) or vice versa.

A major point here is that the decisions to save and invest are made by different people, and thus they plan to save and invest different amounts. Likewise the demand for imports may not equal the demand for exports. As far as the government is concerned, it may choose not to make $T = G$. It may choose not to spend all its tax revenues: to run a 'budget surplus' ($T > G$); or it may choose to spend more than it receives in taxes: to run a 'budget deficit' ($G > T$), by borrowing or printing money to make up the difference.

Thus planned injections (J) may not equal planned withdrawals (W).

The circular flow of income and the four macroeconomic objectives

If planned injections are not equal to planned withdrawals, what will be the consequences? If, for example, injections exceed withdrawals, the level of expenditure will rise. The extra aggregate demand will generate extra incomes. In other words, *actual* national income will rise. If this rise in actual income exceeds any rise there may have been in potential income, there will be the following effects upon the four macroeconomic objectives:

- There will be economic growth. The greater the initial excess of injections over withdrawals, the bigger will be the rise in national income.
- Unemployment will fall as firms take on more workers in order to meet the extra demand for output.
- Inflation will tend to rise. The more the gap is closed between actual and potential income, the more difficult will firms find it to meet extra demand, and the more likely they will be to raise prices.
- The balance of payments will tend to deteriorate. The higher demand sucks more imports into the country, and higher domestic inflation makes exports less competitive and imports relatively cheaper compared with home-produced goods. Thus imports will tend to rise and exports will tend to fall.

If planned injections were *less* than planned withdrawals then the converse of each of the above would occur.

Changes in injections and withdrawals thus have a crucial effect on the whole macroeconomic environment in which businesses operate. We will examine some of these effects in more detail in the following chapters.

SUMMARY

1. The four main macroeconomic goals that are generally of most concern to governments are economic growth, reducing unemployment, reducing inflation, and avoiding balance of payments and exchange rate problems.

2a. Actual growth must be distinguished from potential growth. The actual growth rate is the percentage annual increase in the output that is actually produced, whereas potential growth is the percentage annual increase in the capacity of the economy to produce (whether or not it is actually produced).

2b. Actual growth will fluctuate with the course of the trade cycle. The cycle can be broken down into four phases: the upturn, the expansion, the peaking-out, and the slowdown or recession. In practice the length and magnitude of these phases will vary: the cycle is thus irregular.

SUMMARY

2c Actual growth is determined by potential growth and by the level of aggregate demand. If actual output is below potential output, actual growth can temporarily exceed potential growth, if aggregate demand is rising sufficiently. In the long term, however, actual output can only grow as fast as potential output will permit.

2d Potential growth is determined by the rate of increase in the *quantity* of resources: capital, labour, land and raw materials; and by the *productivity* of resources. The productivity of capital can be increased by technological improvements and the more efficient use of the capital stock; the productivity of labour can be increased by better education, training, motivation and organisation.

2e Whether governments can best achieve rapid growth through market-orientated or interventionist policies is highly controversial.

3a The two most common measures of unemployment are claimant unemployment (those claiming unemployment-related benefits) and ILO/OECD standardised unemployment (those available for work and actively seeking work or waiting to take up an appointment).

3b The costs of unemployment include the financial and other personal costs to the unemployed person, the costs to relatives and friends, and the costs to society at large in terms of lost tax revenues, lost profits and lost wages to other workers, and in terms of social disruption.

3c Unemployment can be divided into disequilibrium and equilibrium unemployment.

3d Disequilibrium unemployment occurs when the average real wage rate is above the level that will equate the aggregate demand and supply of labour. It can be caused by unions or government pushing up wages (real-wage unemployment), by a fall in aggregate demand but a downward 'stickiness' in real wages (demand-deficient unemployment), or by an increase in the supply of labour.

3e Equilibrium unemployment occurs when there are people unable or unwilling to fill job vacancies. This may be due to poor information in the labour market and hence a time lag before people find suitable jobs (frictional unemployment), to a changing pattern of demand or supply in the economy and hence a mismatching of labour with jobs (structural unemployment – specific types being technological

and regional unemployment), or to seasonal fluctuations in the demand for labour.

4a Inflation redistributes incomes from the economically weak to the economically powerful; it causes uncertainty in the business community and as a result reduces investment; it tends to lead to balance of payments problems and/or a fall in the exchange rate; it leads to resources being used to offset its effects. The costs of inflation can be very great indeed in the case of hyperinflation.

4b Equilibrium in the economy occurs when aggregate demand equals aggregate supply. Inflation can occur if there is a rightward shift in the aggregate demand curve or an upward (leftward) shift in the aggregate supply curve.

4c Demand-pull inflation occurs as a result of increases in aggregate demand. This can be due to monetary or non-monetary causes.

4d Cost-push inflation occurs when there are increases in the costs of production independent of rises in aggregate demand. Cost-push inflation can be of a number of different varieties: wage-push, profit-push or import-price-push.

4e Cost-push and demand-pull inflation can interact to form spiralling inflation.

4f Inflation can also be caused by shifts in the pattern of demand in the economy, with prices rising in sectors of increasing demand but being reluctant to fall in sectors of declining demand.

4g Expectations play a crucial role in determining the level of inflation. The higher people expect inflation to be, the higher it will be.

5 In the short run, the four macroeconomic objectives are related to aggregate demand and the business cycle. In the expansion phase, growth is high and unemployment is falling, but inflation is rising and the current account of the balance of payments is moving into deficit. In the recession, the reverse is the case.

6a The circular flow of income model depicts the flows of money round the economy. The inner flow shows the direct flows between firms and households. Money flows from firms to households in the form of factor payments, and back again as consumer expenditure on domestically produced goods and services.

6b Not all income gets passed on directly round the inner flow. Some is withdrawn in the form of saving, some is paid in taxes, and some goes abroad as expenditure on imports.

6c Likewise not all expenditure on domestic firms is by domestic consumers. Some is injected from outside the inner flow in the form of investment expenditure, government expenditure and expenditure on the country's exports.

6d Planned injections and withdrawals are unlikely to

be the same. What happens when they are not is a major area of debate among macroeconomists.

6e If injections exceed withdrawals, national income will rise, unemployment will tend to fall, inflation will tend to rise and the current account of the balance of payments will tend to deteriorate. The reverse will happen if withdrawals exceed injections.

REVIEW QUESTIONS

1 The following table shows index numbers for real GDP (national output) for various countries (1990 = 100).

	1988	1989	1990	1991	1992	1993	1994	1995	1996	1997	1998	1999	2000
USA	96.4	98.8	100.0	99.4	101.7	104.8	109.1	112.7	116.8	121.7	126.9	132.2	138.7
Japan	90.8	95.2	100.0	104.0	105.1	105.2	105.7	106.5	111.9	113.7	110.9	111.2	113.1
Germany	91.1	94.4	100.0	104.6	105.8	103.8	107.4	108.5	109.4	111.0	113.5	115.2	118.5
France	93.8	97.6	100.0	100.8	102.1	100.6	103.5	106.0	107.2	109.2	112.7	116.0	120.3
UK	97.5	99.6	100.0	98.0	97.5	99.7	103.5	106.0	108.8	112.6	115.0	117.5	120.9

Source: *Datastream*.

(a) Work out the growth rate for each country for each year from 1989 to 2000.

(b) Plot the figures on a graph. Describe the pattern that emerges.

2 Will the rate of actual growth have any effect on the rate of potential growth?

3 Figure 25.1 shows a decline in actual output in recessions. Redraw the diagram, only this time show a mere slowing down of growth in phase 4.

4 At what point of the business cycle is the country now? What do you predict will happen to growth over the next two years? On what basis do you make your prediction?

5 For what possible reasons may one country experience a persistently faster rate of economic growth than another?

6 Would it be desirable to have zero unemployment?

7 What major structural changes have taken place in the UK economy in the past 10 years that have contributed to structural unemployment?

8 What would be the benefits and costs of increasing the rate of unemployment benefit?

9 Do any groups of people gain from inflation?

10 If everyone's incomes rose in line with inflation, would it matter if inflation were 100 per cent or even 1000 per cent per annum?

11 Imagine that you had to determine whether a particular period of inflation was demand pull, or cost push, or a combination of the two. What information would you require in order to conduct your analysis?

12 In terms of the UK circular flow of income, are the following net injections, net withdrawals or neither? If there is uncertainty, explain your assumptions.
  (a) Firms are forced to take a cut in profits in order to give a pay rise.
  (b) Firms spend money on research.
  (c) The government increases personal tax allowances.
  (d) The general public invests more money in building societies.
  (e) UK investors earn higher dividends on overseas investments.
  (f) The government purchases US military aircraft.
  (g) People draw on their savings to finance holidays abroad.
  (h) People draw on their savings to finance holidays in the UK.
  (i) The government runs a budget deficit (spends more than it receives in tax revenues) and finances it by borrowing from the general public.

APPENDIX

Measuring national income and output

Three routes: one destination

To assess how fast the economy has grown, we must have a means of *measuring* the value of the nation's output. The measure we use is called *gross domestic product* (GDP).

GDP can be calculated in three different ways, which should all result in the same figure. These three methods are illustrated in the simplified circular flow of income shown in Figure 25.10.

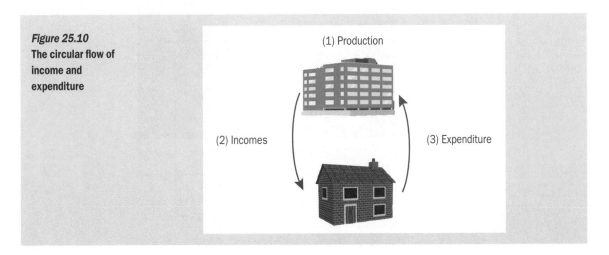

Figure 25.10
The circular flow of income and expenditure

(1) Production

(2) Incomes

(3) Expenditure

The product method

This first method of measuring GDP is to add up the value of all the goods and services produced in the country, industry by industry. In other words, we focus on firms and add up all their production. This method is known as the *product method*.

In the national accounts these figures are grouped together into broad categories such as manufacturing, construction and distribution. The figures for the UK economy for 1998 are shown in Figure 25.11.

When we add up the output of various firms, we must be careful to avoid *double counting*. For example, if a manufacturer sells a television to a retailer for £200 and the retailer sells it to the consumer for £300, how much has this

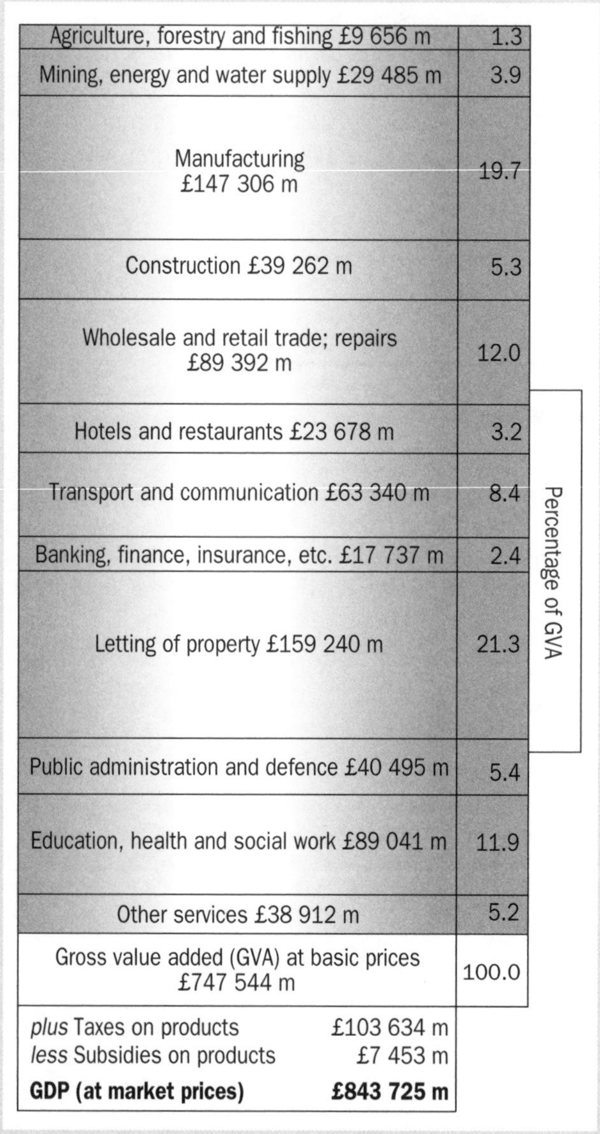

Figure 25.11

UK GDP product-based measure: 1998

Source: *UK National Income and Expenditure* (ONS, 1999).

	Percentage of GVA
Agriculture, forestry and fishing £9 656 m	1.3
Mining, energy and water supply £29 485 m	3.9
Manufacturing £147 306 m	19.7
Construction £39 262 m	5.3
Wholesale and retail trade; repairs £89 392 m	12.0
Hotels and restaurants £23 678 m	3.2
Transport and communication £63 340 m	8.4
Banking, finance, insurance, etc. £17 737 m	2.4
Letting of property £159 240 m	21.3
Public administration and defence £40 495 m	5.4
Education, health and social work £89 041 m	11.9
Other services £38 912 m	5.2
Gross value added (GVA) at basic prices £747 544 m	100.0

plus Taxes on products	£103 634 m
less Subsidies on products	£7 453 m
GDP (at market prices)	**£843 725 m**

television contributed to GDP? The answer is *not* £500. We do not add the £200 received by the manufacturer to the £300 received by the retailer: that would be double counting. Instead we either just count the final value (£300) or the value added at each stage (£200 by the manufacturer + £100 by the retailer).

The sum of all the values added by all the various industries in the economy is known as **gross value added (GVA) at basic prices**.

How do we get from GVA to GDP? The answer has to do with taxes and subsidies on products. Taxes paid on goods and services (such as VAT and duties on petrol and alcohol) and any subsidies on products are *excluded* from gross value added (GVA), since they are not part of the value added in production. Nevertheless the way GDP is measured throughout the EU is at *market prices*: i.e. at the prices actually paid at each stage of production. Thus **GDP at market prices** (sometimes referred to simply as GDP) is GVA *plus* taxes on products *minus* subsidies on products.

The income method

The second approach is to focus on the incomes generated from the production of goods and services. A moment's reflection will show that this must be the same as the sum of all values added at each stage of production. Value added is simply the difference between a firm's revenue from sales and the costs of its purchases from other firms. This difference is made up of wages and salaries, rent, interest and profit. In other words, it consists of the incomes earned by those involved in the production process.

Since GVA is the sum of all values added, it must also be the sum of all incomes generated: the sum of all wages and salaries, rent, interest and profit.

Figure 25.12 shows how these incomes are grouped together in the official statistics. As you can see, the total is the same as that in Figure 25.11, even though the components are quite different.

Note that we do not include *transfer payments* such as social security benefits and pensions. Since these are not payments for the production of goods and services, they are excluded from GVA. Conversely, part of people's gross income is paid in income taxes. Since it is this *gross* (pre-tax) income that arises from the production of goods and services, we count wages, profits, interest and rent *before* the deduction of income taxes.

As with the product approach, if we are working out GVA, we measure incomes before the payment of taxes on products or the receipt of subsidies on products, since it is these pre-tax-and-subsidy incomes that arise from the value added by production. When working out GDP, however, we add in these taxes and subtract these subsidies to arrive at a *market price* valuation.

The expenditure method

The final approach to calculating GDP is to add up all expenditure on final output (which will be at market prices). This will include the following:

● Consumer expenditure (C). This includes all expenditure on goods and services by households and by non-profit institutions serving households (NPISH) (e.g. clubs and societies).

---

definition

Gross value added (GVA) at basic prices
The sum of all the values added by all industries in the economy over a year. The figures exclude taxes on products (such as VAT) and include subsidies on products.

definition

Gross domestic product (GDP (at market prices)
The value of output produced within a country over a 12-month period in terms of the prices actually paid. GDP = GVA + taxes on products − subsidies on products.

Figure 25.12
UK GDP by category of income: 1998

Source: *UK National Income and Expenditure* (ONS, 1999).

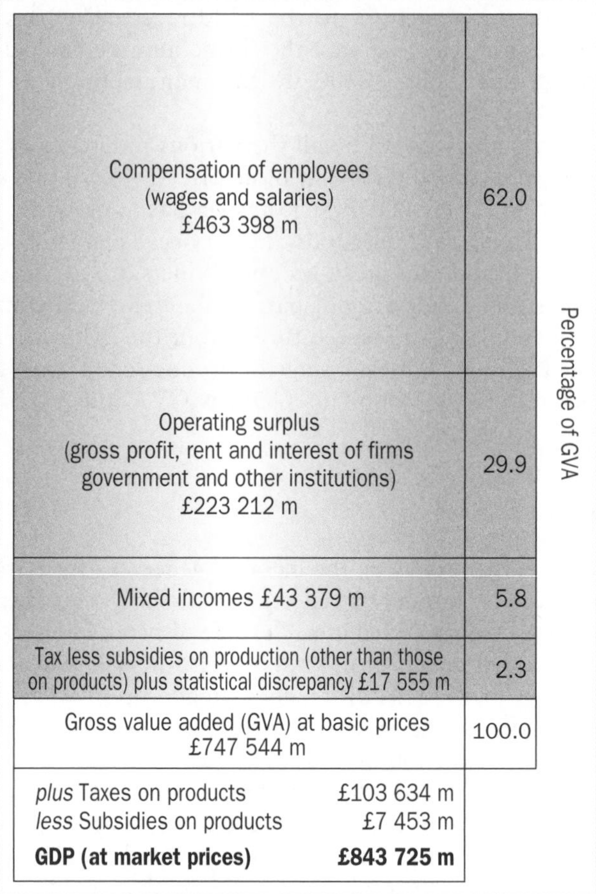

	Percentage of GVA
Compensation of employees (wages and salaries) £463 398 m	62.0
Operating surplus (gross profit, rent and interest of firms government and other institutions) £223 212 m	29.9
Mixed incomes £43 379 m	5.8
Tax less subsidies on production (other than those on products) plus statistical discrepancy £17 555 m	2.3
Gross value added (GVA) at basic prices £747 544 m	100.0

plus Taxes on products	£103 634 m
less Subsidies on products	£7 453 m
GDP (at market prices)	**£843 725 m**

- Government expenditure (*G*). This includes central and local government expenditure on final goods and services. Note that it includes non-marketed services (such as health and education), but excludes transfer payments, such as pensions and social security payments.
- Investment expenditure (*I*). This includes investment in capital, such as buildings and machinery. It also includes the value of any increase (+) or decrease (–) in inventories, whether of raw materials, semi-finished goods or finished goods.
- Exports of goods and services (*X*).
- Imports of goods and services (*M*). These have to be *subtracted* from the total in order to leave just the expenditure on *domestic* product. In other words, we subtract the part of consumer expenditure, government expenditure and investment that goes on imports. We also subtract the imported component (e.g. raw materials) from exports.

GDP (at market prices) $= C + G + I + X - M$

Table 25.1 shows the calculation of UK GDP by the expenditure approach.

Table 25.1	UK GDP at market prices by category of expenditure: 1998		
		£ million	% of GDP
Consumption expenditure of households and NPISH (*C*)		545 124	64.6
Government final consumption (*G*)		153 564	18.2
Gross capital formation (*I*)		151 823	18.0
Exports of goods and services (*X*)		224 202	26.6
Imports of goods and services (*M*)		−232 714	−27.6
Statistical discrepancy		1 726	0.2
GDP at market prices		843 725	100.0

Source: *UK National Income and Expenditure*, National Statistics © Crown Copyright 1999.

From GDP to National income

Gross national income. Some of the incomes earned in the country will go abroad. These include wages, interest, profit and rent earned in this country by foreign residents and remitted abroad, and taxes on production paid to foreign governments and institutions (e.g. the EU). On the other hand, some of the incomes earned by domestic residents will come from abroad. Again, these can be in the form of wages, interest, profit or rent, or in the form of subsidies received from governments or institutions abroad. Gross *domestic* product, however, is concerned with those incomes generated *within* the country, irrespective of ownership. If, then, we are to take 'net income from abroad' into account (i.e. these inflows minus outflows), we need a new measure. This is **gross national income (GNY)**.[2] It is defined as follows:

GNY at market prices = GDP at market prices + net income from abroad

Thus GDP focuses on the value of domestic production, whereas GNY focuses on the value of incomes earned by domestic residents.

Net national income. The measures we have used so far ignore the fact that each year some of the country's capital equipment will wear out or become obsolete: in other words, they ignore capital **depreciation**. If we subtract an allowance for depreciation (or 'capital consumption') we get **net national income (NNY)**:

NNY at market prices = GNY at market prices − Depreciation

Table 25.2 shows GDP, GNY and NNY figures for the UK.

Households' disposable income

Finally, we come to a term called **households' disposable** income. It measures the income people have available for spending (or saving): i.e. after any deductions for income tax, national insurance, etc. have been made. It is the best measure to use if want to see how changes in household income affect consumption.

[2] In the official statistics, this is referred to as *GNI*. We use *Y* to stand for income, however, to avoid confusion with investment.

> **definition**
> **Gross national income (GNY)**
> GDP plus net income from abroad.

> **definition**
> **Depreciation**
> The decline in value of capital equipment due to age or wear and tear.

> **definition**
> **Net national income (NNY)**
> GNY minus depreciation.

> **definition**
> **Households' disposable income**
> The income available for households to spend: i.e. personal incomes after deducting taxes on incomes and adding benefits.

Table 25.2	UK GDP, GNY and NNY at market prices: 1998

	£ million
Gross domestic product (GDP)	**843 725**
Plus net income from abroad	11 737
Gross national income (GNY)	**855 462**
Less capital consumption (depreciation)	−88 771
Net national income (NNY)	**766 691**

Source: *UK National Income and Expenditure*, National Statistics © Crown Copyright 1999.

How do we get from GNY at market prices to households' disposable income? We start with the incomes that firms receive[3] from production (plus income from abroad) and then deduct that part of their income that is *not* distributed to households. This means that we must deduct taxes that firms pay – taxes on goods and services (such as VAT), taxes on profits (such as corporation tax) and any other taxes – and add in any subsidies they receive. We must then subtract allowances for depreciation and any undistributed profits. This gives us the gross income that households receive from firms in the form of wages, salaries, rent, interest and distributed profits.

To get from this what is available for households to spend we must subtract the money households pay in income taxes and national insurance contributions, but add all benefits to households such as pensions and child benefit.

Households' disposable income =

GNY at market prices − Taxes paid by firms + Subsidies received by firms − Depreciation − Undistributed profits − Personal taxes + Benefits

SUMMARY to APPENDIX

1 National income is usually expressed in terms of gross domestic product. This is simply the value of domestic production over the course of the year. It can be measured by the product, expenditure or income methods.

2 The product method measures the values added in all parts of the economy.

3 The income method measures all the incomes generated from domestic production: wages and salaries, rent and profit.

4 The expenditure method adds up all the categories of expenditure: consumer expenditure, government expenditure, investment and exports. We then have to deduct the element of each that goes on imports in order to arrive at expenditure on *domestic*

products. Thus $GDP = C + G + I + X − M$.

5 GDP at *market prices* measures what consumers pay for output (including taxes and subsidies on what they buy). Gross value added (GVA) measures what factors of production actually receive. GVA, therefore, is GDP at market prices minus taxes on products plus subsidies on products.

6 Gross *national* income (GNY) takes account of incomes earned from abroad (+) and incomes earned by people from this country (−). Thus GNY = GDP plus net income from abroad.

7 Net national income (NNY) takes account of the depreciation of capital. Thus NNY = GNY − depreciation.

8 Personal disposable income is a measure of

[3] We also include income from any public-sector production of goods or services (e.g. health and education) and production by non-profit institutions serving households.

REVIEW QUESTIONS TO APPENDIX

1 Should we include the sale of used items in the GDP statistics? For example, if you sell your car to a garage for £2000 and it then sells it to someone else for £2500, has this added £2500 to GDP, or nothing at all, or merely the value that the garage adds to the car, i.e. £500?

2 What items are excluded from national income statistics which would be important to take account of if we were to get a true indication of a country's standard of living?

The balance of payments and exchange rates

In Chapters 22 and 23 we examined the role of international trade for a country and for business, and saw how trade has grown rapidly since 1945. The world economy has become progressively more interlinked, with multinational corporations dominating a large proportion of international business. In this chapter we return to look at international trade and the financial flows associated with it. In particular, we shall examine the relationship between the domestic economy and the international trading environment. This will involve considering both the balance of payments and the exchange rate.

We will first explain what is meant by the balance of payments. In doing so, we will see just how the various monetary transactions between the domestic economy and the rest of the world are recorded.

Then we will examine how rates of exchange are determined, and how they are related to the balance of payments. Then we will see what causes exchange rate fluctuations, and what will happen if the government intervenes in the foreign exchange market to prevent these fluctuations. Finally, we will consider how exchange rates have been managed in practice.

26.1 The balance of payments account

A country's balance of payments account records all the flows of money between residents of that country and the rest of the world. *Receipts* of money from abroad are regarded as *credits* and are entered in the accounts with a positive sign. *Outflows* of money from the country are regarded as *debits* and are entered with a negative sign.

There are three main parts of the balance of payments account: the *current account*, the *capital account* and the *financial account*. Each part is then subdivided. We shall look at each part in turn, and take the UK as an example. Table 26.1 gives a summary of the UK balance of payments for the years 1989 and 1999.

The current account

The **current account** records payments for imports and exports of goods and services, plus incomes flowing into and out of the country, plus net transfers of money into and out of the country. It is normally divided into four subdivisions.

The trade in goods account. This records imports and exports of physical goods (previously known as 'visibles'). Exports result in an inflow of money and are

Table 26.1 UK balance of payments (£m)

	1989		1999	
Current account				
1. Trade in goods	+92 611		+165 204	
a) Exports of goods				
b) Imports of goods	−117 335		−191 815	
Balance on trade in goods	−24 724		−26 611	
2. Trade in services				
a) Exports of services	+29 272		+63 826	
b) Imports of services	−25 355		−52 712	
Balance on trade in services	+3 917		+11 114	
Balance on trade in goods and services		−20 807		−15 497
3. Net income flows (wages and investment income)		−64		+6 848
4. Net current transfers (government and private)		−2 620		−4 112
Current account balance		**−23 491**		**−12 761**
Capital account				
5. Net capital transfers, etc:		+270		+788
Capital account balance		**+270**		**+788**
Financial account				
6. Investment (direct and portfolio)				
a) Net investment in UK from abroad	+36 789		+173 242	
b) Net UK investment abroad	−60 336		−142 568	
Balance of direct and portfolio investment		−23 547		+30 674
7. Other financial flows (mainly short-term)				
a) Net deposits in UK from abroad and borrowing from abroad by UK residents	+72 629		+24 728	
b) Net deposits abroad by UK residents and UK lending to overseas residents	−35 498		−48 213	
Balance of other financial flows		+37 131		−23 485
8. Reserves (drawing on + adding to −)		+5 440		+638
Financial account balance		**+19 024**		**+7 827**
Total of all three accounts		−4 197		−4 146
9. Net errors and omissions		+4 197		+4 146
		0		0

Sources: *Economic Trends Annual Supplement* (ONS); *Financial Statistics* (ONS)

therefore a credit item. Imports result in an outflow of money and are therefore a debit item. The balance of these is called the **balance on trade in goods** or **balance of visible trade** or **merchandise balance**. A *surplus* is when exports exceed imports. A *deficit* is when imports exceed exports.

The trade in services account. This records imports and exports of services (such as transport, tourism and insurance). Thus the purchase of a foreign holiday would be a debit, whereas the purchase by an overseas resident of a UK insurance policy would be a credit to the UK services account. The balance of these is called the **services balance**.

The balance of both the goods and services accounts together is known as the **balance on trade in goods and services** or simply the **balance of trade**.

Income flows. These consist of wages, interest and profits flowing into and out of the country. For example, dividends earned by a foreign resident from shares in a UK company would be an outflow of money (a debit item).

Current transfers of money. These include government contributions to and receipts from the EU and international organisations, and international transfers of money by private individuals and firms. Transfers out of the country are debits. Transfers into the country (e.g. money sent from Greece to a Greek student studying in the UK) would be a credit item.

The **current account balance** is the overall balance of all the above four subdivisions. A *current account surplus* is where credits exceed debits. A *current account deficit* is where debits exceed credits. Figure 26.1 shows the current account balances of the UK, the USA and Japan as a proportion of their GDP (national output).

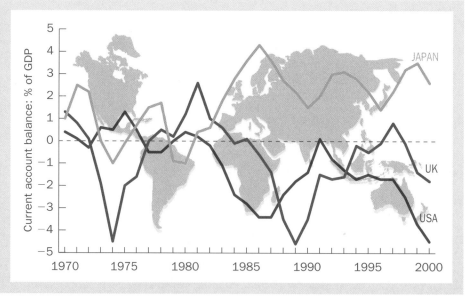

Figure 26.1
Current account balance as % of GDP in selected countries: 1970–2000

Source: *Datastream*.

The capital account

The **capital account** records the flows of funds, into the country (credits) and out of the country (debits), associated with the acquisition or disposal of fixed assets (e.g. land), the transfer of funds by migrants, and the payment of grants by the government for overseas projects and the receipt of EU money for capital projects (e.g. from the Agricultural Guidance Fund).

The financial account[1]

This records the flows of money into and out of the country for the purposes of investment or as deposits in banks and other financial institutions. There are three main sections in the **financial account**.

Investment (direct and portfolio). This account covers primarily long-term investment.

- Direct investment. If a foreign company invests money from abroad in one of its branches or associated companies in the UK, this represents an inflow of money when the investment is made and is thus a credit item. (Any subsequent profit from this investment that flows abroad will be recorded as an *investment income outflow* on the current account.) Investment abroad by UK companies represents an outflow of money when the investment is made. It is thus a debit item.
- Portfolio investment. This is changes in the holding of paper assets, such as company shares. Thus if a UK resident buys shares in an overseas company, this is an outflow of funds and is hence a debit item.

Other financial flows. These consist primarily of various types of short-term monetary movement between the UK and the rest of the world. Deposits by overseas residents in banks in the UK and loans to the UK from abroad are credit items, since they represent an inflow of money. Deposits by UK residents in overseas banks and loans by UK banks to overseas residents are debit items. They represent an outflow of money.

Short-term monetary flows are common between international financial centres to take advantage of differences in countries' interest rates and changes in exchange rates.

Flows to and from the reserves. The UK, like all other countries, holds reserves of gold and foreign currencies. From time to time the Bank of England (acting as the government's agent) will sell some of these reserves to purchase sterling on the foreign exchange market. It does this normally as a means of supporting the rate of exchange (as we shall see below). Drawing on reserves represents a *credit* item in the balance of payments accounts: money drawn from the reserves represents an *inflow* to the balance of payments (albeit an outflow from the reserves account). The reserves can thus be used to support a deficit elsewhere in the balance of payments.

> **definition**
>
> **Capital account of the balance of payments**
> The record of transfers of capital to and from abroad.

> **definition**
>
> **Financial account of the balance of payments**
> The record of the flows of money into and out of the country for the purpose of investment or as deposits in banks and other financial institutions.

---

[1] Prior to October 1998, this account was called the 'capital account'. The account that is *now* called the capital account used to be included in the transfers section of the current account. This potentially confusing change of names was adopted in order to bring the UK accounts in line with the system used by the International Monetary Fund (IMF), the EU and most individual countries.

Conversely, if there is a surplus elsewhere in the balance of payments, the Bank of England can use it to build up the reserves. Building up the reserves counts as a debit item in the balance of payments, since it represents an outflow from it (to the reserves).

When all the components of the balance of payments account are taken together, the balance of payments should exactly balance: credits should equal debits. As we shall see below, if they were not equal, the rate of exchange would have to adjust until they were, or the government would have to intervene to make them equal.

When the statistics are compiled, however, a number of errors are likely to occur. As a result there will not be a balance. To 'correct' for this, a **net errors and omissions item** is included in the accounts. This ensures that there will be an exact balance. The main reason for the errors is that the statistics are obtained from a number of sources, and there are often delays before items are recorded and sometimes omissions too.

26.2 The exchange rate

An exchange rate is the rate at which one currency trades for another on the foreign exchange market.

If you want to go abroad, you will need to exchange your pounds into euros, dollars, Swiss francs or whatever. To do this you will go to a bank. The bank will quote you that day's exchange rates: for example, 2.40 Swiss francs to the pound, or $1.60 to the pound. It is similar for firms. If an importer wants to buy, say, some machinery from Japan, it will require yen to pay the Japanese supplier. It will thus ask the foreign exchange section of a bank to quote it a rate of exchange of the pound into yen. Similarly, if you want to buy some foreign stocks and shares, or if companies based in the UK want to invest abroad, sterling will have to be exchanged into the appropriate foreign currency.

Likewise, if Americans want to come on holiday to the UK or to buy UK assets, or American firms want to import UK goods or to invest in the UK, they will require sterling. They will be quoted an exchange rate for the pound in the USA: say, £1 = $1.64. This means that they will have to pay $1.64 to obtain £1 worth of UK goods or assets.

Exchange rates are quoted between each of the major currencies of the world. These exchange rates are constantly changing. Minute by minute, dealers in the foreign exchange dealing rooms of the banks are adjusting the rates of exchange. They charge commission when they exchange currencies. It is therefore important for them to ensure that they are not left with a large amount of any currency unsold. What they need to do is to balance the supply and demand of each currency: to balance the amount they purchase to the amount they sell. To do this they will need to adjust the price of each currency, namely the exchange rate, in line with changes in supply and demand.

One of the problems in assessing what is happening to a particular currency is that its rate of exchange may rise against some currencies (weak currencies) and fall against others (strong currencies). In order to gain an overall picture of its fluctuations, it is best to look at a weighted average exchange rate against all other currencies. This is known as the **exchange rate index**. The weight given to

---

definition

Net errors and omissions
A statistical adjustment to ensure that the two sides of the balance of payments account balance. It is necessary because of errors in compiling the statistics.

definition

Exchange rate index
A weighted average exchange rate expressed as an index, where the value of the index is 100 in a given base year. The weights of the different currencies in the index add up to 1.

Table 26.2	Sterling exchange rates: 1980–2000						
	US dollar	French franc	Japanese yen	German mark	Italian lira	Euro	Sterling exchange rate index (1990 = 100)
1980	2.33	9.83	526	4.23	1992		124.4
1981	2.03	10.94	445	4.56	2287		127.9
1982	1.75	11.48	435	4.24	2364		123.2
1983	1.52	11.55	360	3.87	2302		115.6
1984	1.34	11.63	317	3.79	2339		111.4
1985	1.30	11.55	307	3.78	2453		111.3
1986	1.47	10.16	247	3.18	2186		101.4
1987	1.64	9.84	236	2.94	2123		99.4
1988	1.78	10.60	228	3.12	2315		105.4
1989	1.64	10.45	226	3.08	2247	(1.45)	102.3
1990	1.79	9.69	258	2.88	2133	(1.40)	100.0
1991	1.77	9.95	238	2.92	2187	(1.43)	100.7
1992	1.77	9.32	224	2.75	2163	(1.36)	96.9
1993	1.50	8.51	167	2.48	2360	(1.28)	89.0
1994	1.53	8.49	156	2.48	2467	(1.29)	89.2
1995	1.58	7.87	148	2.26	2571	(1.22)	84.8
1996	1.56	7.99	170	2.35	2408	(1.25)	86.3
1997	1.64	9.56	198	2.84	2789	(1.45)	100.5
1998	1.66	9.77	217	2.91	2876	(1.48)	103.9
1999	1.62	(9.96)	184	(2.97)	(2941)	1.52	103.8
2000	1.52	(10.77)	163	(3.21)	(3180)	1.64	107.5

Source: *Datastream*

Note: Prior to 1999, a 'synthetic' euro has been used, based on the exchange rates with the countries which have adopted the euro. From 1999, exchange rates into the French franc, German mark and Italian lira are based on the fixed exchange rates of these 'residual' currencies with the euro.

each currency in the index depends on the proportion of transactions done with that country. Table 26.2 shows exchange rates between the pound and various currencies and the sterling exchange rate index from 1980 to 2000.

The determination of the rate of exchange in a free market

In a free foreign exchange market, the rate of exchange is determined by demand and supply. Thus the sterling exchange rate is determined by the demand and supply of pounds. This is illustrated in Figure 26.2.

For simplicity, assume that there are just two countries: the UK and the USA. When UK importers wish to buy goods from the USA, or when UK residents wish to invest in the USA, they will *supply* pounds on the foreign exchange market in order to obtain dollars. In other words, they will go to banks or other foreign exchange dealers to buy dollars in exchange for pounds. The higher the exchange rate, the more dollars they will obtain for their pounds. This will effectively make American goods cheaper to buy, and investment more profitable. Thus the *higher* the exchange rate, the *more* pounds will be supplied. The supply curve of pounds will therefore typically slope upwards.

When US residents wish to purchase UK goods or to invest in the UK, they

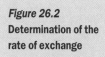

Figure 26.2
Determination of the
rate of exchange

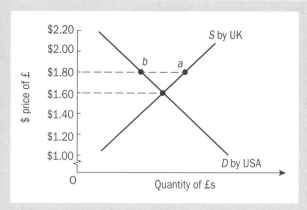

will require pounds. They *demand* pounds by selling dollars on the foreign exchange market. In other words, they will go to banks or other foreign exchange dealers to buy pounds in exchange for dollars. The lower the dollar price of the pound (the exchange rate), the cheaper it will be for them to obtain UK goods and assets, and hence the more pounds they are likely to demand. The demand curve for pounds, therefore, will typically slope downwards.

The equilibrium exchange rate will be where the demand for pounds equals the supply. In Figure 26.2 this will be at an exchange rate of £1 = $1.60. But what is the mechanism that equates demand and supply?

If the current exchange rate were above the equilibrium, the supply of pounds being offered to the banks would exceed the demand. For example, in Figure 26.2 if the exchange rate were $1.80, there would be an excess supply of pounds of *a* − *b*. Banks would not have enough dollars to exchange for all these pounds. But the banks make money by *exchanging* currency, not by holding on to it. They would thus lower the exchange rate in order to encourage a greater demand for pounds and reduce the excessive supply. They would continue lowering the rate until demand equalled supply.

Similarly, if the rate were below the equilibrium, say at $1.40, there would be a shortage of pounds. The banks would find themselves with too few pounds to meet all the demand. At the same time, they would have an excess supply of dollars. The banks would thus raise the exchange rate until demand equalled supply.

In practice, the process of reaching equilibrium is extremely rapid. The foreign exchange dealers in the banks are continually adjusting the rate as new customers make new demands for currencies. What is more, the banks have to watch closely what each other is doing. Banks are constantly in competition with each other and thus have to keep their rates in line. The dealers receive minute-by-minute updates on their computer screens of the rates being offered round the world.

Shifts in the currency demand and supply curves

Any shift in the demand or supply curves will cause the exchange rate to change. This is illustrated in Figure 26.3, which this time shows the euro/sterling exchange rate. If the demand and supply curves shift from D_1 and S_1 to D_2 and S_2 respect-

BOX 26.1

Dealing in foreign exchange
A daily juggling act

Imagine that a large car importer in the UK wants to import 5000 cars from Japan costing ¥15 billion. What does it do?

It will probably contact a number of banks' foreign exchange dealing rooms in London and ask them for exchange rate quotes. It thus puts all the banks in competition with each other. Each bank will want to get the business and thereby obtain the commission on the deal. To do this it must offer a higher rate than the other banks, since the higher the ¥/£ exchange rate, the more yen the firm will get for its money. (For an importer a rate of, say, ¥200 to £1 is better than a rate of, say, ¥180.)

Now it is highly unlikely that any of the banks will have a spare ¥15 billion. But a bank cannot say to the importer 'Sorry, you will have to wait before we can agree to sell them to you.' Instead the bank will offer a deal and then, if the firm agrees, the bank will have to set about obtaining the ¥15 billion. To do this it must offer Japanese who are *supplying* yen to obtain pounds at a sufficiently *low* ¥/£ exchange rate. (The lower the ¥/£ exchange rate, the fewer yen the Japanese will have to pay to obtain pounds.)

The banks' dealers thus find themselves in the delicate position of wanting to offer a *high* enough exchange rate to the car importer in order to gain its business, but a *low* enough exchange rate in order to obtain the required amount of yen. The dealers are thus constantly having to adjust the rates of exchange in order to balance the demand and supply of each currency.

In general, the more of any foreign currency that dealers are asked to supply (by being offered sterling), the lower will be the exchange rate they will offer. In other words, a higher supply of sterling pushes down the foreign currency price of sterling.

Question

Assume that an American firm wants to import Scotch whisky from the UK. Describe how foreign exchange dealers will respond.

---

ively, the exchange rate will fall from €1.60 to €1.40. A fall in the exchange rate is called a **depreciation**. A rise in the exchange rate is called an **appreciation**.

But why should the demand and supply curves shift? The following are the major possible causes of a depreciation:

- *A fall in domestic interest rates.* UK rates would now be less competitive for savers and other depositors. More UK residents would be likely to deposit their money abroad (the supply of sterling would rise), and fewer people abroad would deposit their money in the UK (the demand for sterling would fall).
- *Higher inflation in the domestic economy than abroad.* UK exports will become less competitive. The demand for sterling will fall. At the same time, imports will become relatively cheaper for UK consumers. The supply of sterling will rise.
- *A rise in domestic incomes relative to incomes abroad.* If UK incomes rise, the demand for imports, and hence the supply of sterling, will rise. If incomes in other countries fall, the demand for UK exports, and hence the demand for sterling will fall.
- *Relative investment prospects improving abroad.* If investment prospects become brighter abroad than in the UK, perhaps because of better incentives abroad, or because of worries about an impending recession in the UK, again the demand for sterling will fall and the supply of sterling will rise.

definition

Depreciation
A fall in the free-market exchange rate of the domestic currency with foreign currencies.

definition

Appreciation
A rise in the free-market exchange rate of the domestic currency with foreign currencies.

Dunlop gives Britain the boot
Problems of a strong currency

The strong pound in 1999/2000 had a profound effect on UK exporters. The CBI, in early 2000, predicted that manufacturing growth for the year would be 2.6 per cent. As the year progressed, it had to reduce this forecast to a mere 0.5 per cent. The reduction was blamed almost entirely on the strength of sterling on foreign markets.

The pro-euro 'Britain in Europe' group estimated that many of the 98 000 manufacturing jobs lost between May 1999 and May 2000 resulted from the high value of sterling against the euro.

The Ford motor company cited the high value of sterling as one of its reasons for ending car production at Dagenham. Nissan and Honda also voiced concerns about future investment, if sterling continued to remain so strong on international markets.

Corus, the country's biggest steel manufacturer, threatened further job losses because of the strength of sterling. Since 1997, Corus (or as it was then, British Steel) had reduced its labour force by 7500. Over the same period, the pound rose by almost 40 per cent against the euro. Eighty per cent of Corus's sales are in

Britain and continental Europe. The rise in sterling is credited with reducing Corus's profits by more than £1 billion over the period. Then, in early 2001, a further 6000 redundancies were announced. Again the high pound was cited as a major factor.

Many exporters have simply given up and decided to relocate. The Dunlop Wellington boot factory in Liverpool, which has produced boots for 150 years, is to shift production to Portugal. Half its output is exported to Germany, while on the domestic market it is trying to compete with producers from Italy and France, which can sell Wellingtons for a fraction of the price of those produced in the Liverpool factory.

Questions

1 Other than closure and relocation, what else could exporters do to deal with the problems caused by a high exchange rate?

2 What long-term advantages might there be in having a high exchange rate?

- *Speculation that the exchange rate will fall.* If businesses involved in importing and exporting, and also banks and other foreign exchange dealers, think that the exchange rate is about to fall, they will sell pounds *now* before the rate does fall. The supply of sterling will thus rise.

The exchange rate would rise if the opposite of each of the above occurred.

26.3 Exchange rates and the balance of payments

Exchange rates and the balance of payments: no government intervention

Floating exchange rate
When the government does not intervene in the foreign exchange markets, but simply allows the exchange rate to be freely determined by demand and supply.

In a free foreign exchange market, the balance of payments will *automatically* balance. But why?

The credit side of the balance of payments constitutes the demand for sterling. For example, when people abroad buy UK exports or assets they will demand sterling in order to pay for them. The debit side constitutes the supply of sterling. For example, when UK residents buy foreign goods or assets, the importers of them will require foreign currency to pay for them. They will thus supply pounds. A **floating exchange rate** will ensure that the demand for pounds is equal to the supply. It will thus also ensure that the credits on the balance of payments are equal to the debits: that the balance of payments balances.

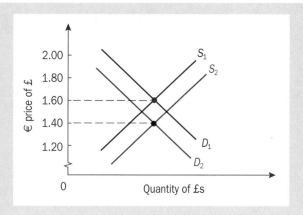

Figure 26.3
Floating exchange rates: movement to a new equilibrium

This does not mean that each part of the balance of payments account will separately balance, but simply that any current account deficit must be matched by a capital plus financial account surplus and vice versa.

For example, suppose initially that each part of the balance of payments did separately balance. Then let us assume that interest rates rise. This will encourage larger short-term financial inflows as people abroad are attracted to deposit money in the UK: the demand for sterling would shift to the right (e.g. from D_2 to D_1 in Figure 26.3). It will also cause smaller short-term financial outflows as UK residents keep more of their money in the country: the supply of sterling shifts to the left (e.g. from S_2 to S_1 in Figure 26.3). The financial account will go into surplus. The exchange rate will appreciate.

As the exchange rate rises, this will cause imports to be cheaper and exports to be more expensive. The current account will move into deficit. There is a movement up along the new demand and supply curves until a new equilibrium is reached. At this point, any financial account surplus is matched by an equal current (plus capital) account deficit.

Exchange rates and the balance of payments: with government intervention

The government may be unwilling to let the country's currency float freely. Frequent shifts in the demand and supply curves would cause frequent changes in the exchange rate. This, in turn, might cause uncertainty for businesses, which might curtail their trade and investment.

The government may thus intervene in the foreign exchange market. But what can it do? The answer to this will depend on its objectives. It may simply want to reduce the day-to-day fluctuations in the exchange rate, or it may want to prevent longer-term, more fundamental shifts in the rate.

Reducing short-term fluctuations

Assume that the government believes that an exchange rate of €1.60 to the pound is approximately the long-term equilibrium rate. Short-term leftward shifts in the demand for sterling and rightward shifts in the supply, however, are causing the exchange rate to fall below this level (see Figure 26.3). What can the government do to keep the rate at €1.60?

Using reserves. The Bank of England can sell gold and foreign currencies from the reserves to buy pounds. This will shift the demand for sterling back to the right.

Borrowing from abroad. The government can negotiate a foreign currency loan from other countries or from an international agency such as the International Monetary Fund. It can then use these moneys to buy pounds on the foreign exchange market, thus again shifting the demand for sterling back to the right.

Raising interest rates. If the government raises interest rates, it will encourage people to deposit money in the UK and encourage UK residents to keep their money in the country. The demand for sterling will increase and the supply of sterling will decrease.

Maintaining a fixed rate of exchange over the longer term

Governments may choose to maintain a fixed rate over a number of months or even years. The following are possible methods it can use to achieve this (we are assuming that there are downward pressures on the exchange rate: e.g. as a result of higher aggregate demand and higher inflation.)

Deflation. This is where the government deliberately curtails aggregate demand by either *fiscal policy* or *monetary policy* or both.

Deflationary fiscal policy will involve raising taxes and/or reducing government expenditure. Deflationary monetary policy will involve reducing the supply of money and raising interest rates. Note that in this case we are not just talking about the temporary raising of interest rates to prevent a short-term outflow of money from the country, but the use of higher interest rates to reduce borrowing and hence dampen aggregate demand.

A reduction in aggregate demand will work in two ways:

- It will reduce the level of consumer spending. This will directly cut imports since there will be reduced spending on Japanese videos, German cars, Spanish holidays and so on. The supply of sterling coming on to the foreign exchange market thus decreases.
- It will reduce the rate of inflation. This will make UK goods more competitive abroad, thus increasing the demand for sterling. It will also cut back on imports as UK consumers switch to the now more competitive home-produced goods. The supply of sterling falls.

Supply-side policies. This is where the government attempts to increase the long-term competitiveness of UK goods by encouraging reductions in the costs of production and/or improvements in the quality of UK goods. For example, the government may attempt to improve the quantity and quality of training and research and development.

Controls on imports and or foreign exchange dealing. This is where the government restricts the outflow of money, either by restricting people's access to foreign exchange, or by the use of tariffs (customs duties) and quotas.

26.4 Fixed versus floating exchange rates

Are exchange rates best left free to fluctuate and be determined purely by market forces, or should the government intervene to fix exchange rates, either rigidly or within bands?

Advantages of fixed exchange rates

Surveys reveal that most business people prefer relatively rigid exchange rates: if not totally fixed, then at least pegged for periods of time. The following arguments are used to justify this preference.

Certainty. With fixed exchange rates, international trade and investment become much less risky, since profits are not affected by movements in the exchange rate.

Assume a firm correctly forecasts that its product will sell in the USA for \$1.50. It costs 80p to produce. If the rate of exchange is fixed at £1 = \$1.50, each unit will earn £1 and hence make a 20p profit. If, however, the rate of exchange were not fixed, exchange fluctuations could wipe out this profit. If, say, the rate appreciated to £1 = \$2, and if units continued to sell for \$1.50, they would now earn only 75p each, and hence make a 5p loss.

Little or no speculation. Provided the rate is *absolutely* fixed – and people believe that it will remain so – there is no point in speculating. For example, with the euro-zone currencies absolutely fixed in terms of the euro from 1999, there has been no speculation that the German mark, say, will change in value against the French franc or the Dutch guilder. (From July 2002, they will cease to exist as separate currencies altogether. Banknotes of the old currencies will no longer be legal tender.)

Prevents governments pursuing 'irresponsible' macroeconomic policies. If a government deliberately and excessively expands aggregate demand – perhaps in an attempt to gain short-term popularity with the electorate – the resulting balance of payments deficit will force it to constrain demand again (unless it resorts to import controls).

Governments cannot allow their economies to have a persistently higher inflation rate than competitor countries without running into balance of payments crises, and hence a depletion of reserves. Fixed rates thus force governments (in the absence of trade restrictions) to keep the rate of inflation roughly to world levels.

Disadvantages of fixed exchange rates

Exchange rate policy may conflict with the interests of domestic business and the economy as a whole. A balance of payments deficit can occur even if there is no excess demand. For example, there can be a fall in the demand for the country's exports as a result of an external shock or because of increased foreign competition. If protectionism is to be avoided, and if supply-side policies work only over the long run, the government (or central bank) will be forced to raise interest rates. This is likely to have two adverse effects on the domestic economy:

- Higher interest rates may discourage business investment. This in turn will lower firms' profits in the long term and reduce the country's long-term rate of economic growth. The country's capacity to produce will be restricted and businesses are likely to fall behind in the competitive race with their international rivals to develop new products and improve existing ones.
- Higher interest rates will have a deflationary effect on the economy by making borrowing more expensive and thereby cutting back on both consumer demand and investment. This can result in a recession with rising unemployment. It will, however, improve the balance of payments. There will be an improvement not only on the financial account, as money flows into the country to take advantage of the higher rates of interest, but also on the current account. The recession will lead to reduced demand for imports, and lower inflation is likely to make exports more competitive and imports relatively more expensive.

The problem is that, with fixed exchange rates, domestic policy is entirely constrained by the balance of payments. Any attempt to cure unemployment by cutting interest rates will simply lead to a balance of payments deficit and thus force governments to raise interest rates again.

Competitive deflations leading to world depression. If deficit countries deflated, but surplus countries *reflated*, there would be no overall world deflation or reflation. Countries may be quite happy, however, to run a balance of payments surplus and build up reserves. Countries may thus competitively deflate – all trying to achieve a balance of payments surplus. But this is beggar-my-neighbour policy. Not all countries can have a surplus. Overall the world must be in balance. The result of these policies is to lead to general world deflation and a restriction in growth.

Problems of international liquidity. If trade is to expand, there must be an expansion in the supply of currencies acceptable for world trade (dollars, pounds, euros, gold, etc.): there must be adequate **international liquidity**. Countries' reserves of these currencies must grow if they are to be sufficient to maintain a fixed rate at times of balance of payments disequilibrium. Conversely, there must not be excessive international liquidity. Otherwise the extra demand that would result would lead to world inflation. It is important under fixed exchange rates, therefore, to avoid too much or too little international liquidity. The problem is whether there is adequate control of international liquidity. The supply of dollars, for example, depends largely on US policy, which may be dominated by its internal economic situation rather than by a concern for the well-being of the international community.

Inability to adjust to shocks. With sticky prices and wage rates, there is no swift mechanism for dealing with sudden balance of payments crises – like that caused by a sudden increase in oil prices. In the short run, countries will need huge reserves or loan facilities to support their currencies. There may be insufficient international liquidity to permit this. In the longer run, countries may be forced into a depression, by having to deflate. The alternative may be to resort to protectionism, or to abandon the fixed rate and **devalue**.

definition

International liquidity
The supply of currencies in the world acceptable for financing international trade and investment.

definition

Devaluation
Where the government refixes the exchange rate at a lower level.

Speculation. If speculators believe that a fixed rate simply cannot be maintained, speculation is likely to be massive. If, for example, there is a large balance of payments deficit, speculative selling will worsen the deficit, and may itself force a devaluation.

Advantages of a free-floating exchange rate

The advantages and disadvantages of free-floating rates are to a large extent the opposite of fixed rates.

Automatic correction. The government simply lets the exchange rate move freely to the equilibrium. In this way, balance of payments disequilibria are automatically and instantaneously corrected without the need for specific government policies.

No problem of international liquidity and reserves. Since there is no central bank intervention in the foreign exchange market, there is no need to hold reserves. A currency is automatically convertible at the current market exchange rate.

Insulation from external economic events. A country is not tied to a possibly unacceptably high world inflation rate, as it could be under a fixed exchange rate. It is also to some extent protected against world economic fluctuations and shocks.

Governments are free to choose their domestic policy. Under a floating rate the government can choose whatever level of domestic demand it considers appropriate, and simply leave exchange rate movements to take care of any balance of payments effect. This is a major advantage, especially when the effectiveness of deflation under fixed exchange rates is reduced by downward wage and price rigidity, and when competitive deflation between countries may end up causing a world recession.

Disadvantages of a free-floating exchange rate

Despite these advantages there are still a number of serious problems with free-floating exchange rates.

Unstable exchange rates. The less elastic are the demand and supply curves for the currency in Figure 26.3, the greater the change in exchange rate that will be necessary to restore equilibrium following a shift in either demand or supply. In the long run, in a competitive world with domestic substitutes for imports and foreign substitutes for exports, demand and supply curves are relatively elastic. Nevertheless, in the short run, given that many firms have contracts with specific overseas suppliers or distributors, the demands for imports and exports are less elastic.

Speculation. In an uncertain world, where there are few restrictions on currency speculation, where the fortunes and policies of governments can change rapidly, and where large amounts of short-term deposits are internationally 'footloose', speculation can be highly destabilising in the short run. If people think that the exchange rate will fall, then they will sell the currency, and this will cause the exchange rate to fall even further, perhaps overshooting the eventual equilibrium.

Uncertainty for traders and investors. The uncertainty caused by currency fluctuations can discourage international trade and investment. To some extent this problem can be overcome by using the **forward exchange market**. Here traders agree with a bank *today* the rate of exchange for some point in the *future* (say, six months' time). This allows traders to plan future purchases of imports or sales of exports at a known rate of exchange. Of course, banks charge for this service, since they are taking on the risks themselves of adverse exchange rate fluctuations.

But dealing in the futures market only takes care of short-run uncertainty. Banks will not be prepared to take on the risks of offering forward contracts for several years hence. Thus firms simply have to live with the uncertainty over exchange rates in future years. This will discourage long-term investment. For example, the possibility of exchange rate appreciation may well discourage firms from investing abroad, since a higher exchange rate will mean that foreign exchange earnings will be worth less in the domestic currency.

Figure 26.4 shows the fluctuations in the dollar/pound exchange rate and the exchange rate index from 1976 to 2000. As you can see, there have been large changes in exchange rates. Such changes not only make it difficult for exporters. Importers too will be hesitant about making long-term deals. For example, a UK manufacturing firm signing a contract to buy US components in 1980, when $2.40 worth of components could be purchased for £1, would find it a struggle to make a profit some four years later when only just over $1.00 worth of US components could be purchased for £1!

Lack of discipline on the domestic economy. Governments may pursue irresponsibly inflationary policies (e.g. for short-term political gain). This will have adverse

> **definition**
>
> **Forward exchange market**
> Where contracts are made today for the price at which a currency will be exchanged at some specified future date.

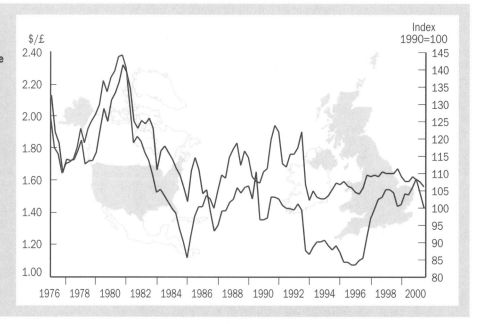

Figure 26.4
$/£ exchange rate and £ exchange rate index: 1976–2000

Source: *Datastream*

effects over the longer term as the government will at some point have to deflate the economy again, with a resulting fall in output and rise in unemployment.

Exchange rates in practice

Most countries today have a relatively free exchange rate. Nevertheless, the problems of instability that this can bring are well recognised, and thus many countries seek to regulate or manage their exchange rate.

There have been many attempts to regulate exchange rates since 1945. By far the most successful was the Bretton Woods system, which was adopted world-wide from the end of World War II until 1971. This was a form of **adjustable peg** exchange rate, where countries pegged (i.e. fixed) their exchange rate to the US dollar, but could re-peg it at a lower or higher level ('devalue' or 'revalue' their exchange rate) if there was a persistent and substantial balance of payments deficit or surplus.

With growing world inflation and instability from the mid-1960s, it became more and more difficult to maintain fixed exchange rates, and the growing likelihood of devaluations and revaluations fuelled speculation. The system was abandoned in the early 1970s. What followed was a period of exchange rate management known as **dirty floating**. Under this system, exchange rates were not pegged but allowed to float. However, central banks intervened from time to time to prevent excessive exchange rate fluctuations. It was thus a form of 'managed flexibility'. This system largely continues to this day.

However, on a regional basis, especially within Europe, there were attempts to create greater exchange rate stability. The European system, which began in 1979, involved establishing exchange rate bands: upper and lower limits within which exchange rates were allowed to fluctuate. The name given to the EU system was the **exchange rate mechanism (ERM)**. The hope was that this would eventually lead to a single European currency. With a single currency there can be no exchange rate fluctuations between the member states, any more than there can be fluctuations between the Californian and New York dollar, or between the English, Scottish and Welsh pound.

The single currency, the euro, finally came into being in January 1999 (although notes and coins would not circulate until January 2002). We examine the euro and its effects on the economies of the member states, and those outside too, in section 31.3.

> **definition**
> **Adjustable peg**
> A system whereby exchange rates are fixed for a period of time, but may be devalued (or revalued) if a deficit (or surplus) becomes substantial.

> **definition**
> **Dirty floating (managed flexibility)**
> A system of flexible exchange rates, but where the government intervenes to prevent excessive fluctuations or even to achieve an unofficial target exchange rate.

> **definition**
> **ERM (the exchange rate mechanism)**
> A semi-fixed system whereby participating EU countries allowed fluctuations against each other's currencies only within agreed bands. Collectively they floated freely against all other currencies.

SUMMARY

1a The balance of payments account records all payments to and receipts from foreign countries. The current account records payments for imports and exports, plus incomes and transfers of money to and from abroad. The capital account records all transfers of capital to and from abroad. The financial account records inflows and outflows of money for investment and as deposits in banks and other financial institutions. It also includes dealings in the country's foreign exchange reserves.

1b The whole account must balance, but surpluses or deficits can be recorded on any specific part of the account. Thus the current account could be in deficit but it would have to be matched by an equal and opposite capital plus financial account surplus.

2a The rate of exchange is the rate at which one currency exchanges for another. Rates of exchange are determined by demand and supply in the foreign exchange market. Demand for the domestic currency consists of all the credit items in the balance of payments account. Supply consists of all the debit items.

BOX 26.3

Currency turmoil
Unleashing the power of speculation

For periods of time, world currency markets can be quite peaceful, with only modest changes in exchange rates. But with the ability to move vast sums of money very rapidly from one part of the world to another and from one currency to another, speculators can suddenly turn this relatively peaceful world into one of extreme turmoil. In this box we examine three periods over just five years when such turmoil occurred.

1995

The problem started towards the end of 1994 with an economic crisis in Mexico. To help its neighbour, the USA quickly arranged a $20 billion aid package. But speculators saw trouble for the dollar. A decline in US sales to Mexico was likely to damage the USA's export recovery. On top of this, market analysts were predicting that US interest rates, which had previously been rising, would now fall as US economic growth slowed. In contrast, interest rates in Germany looked set to rise, as the German authorities faced growing inflationary pressures. Faced by all this, many investors moved out of dollars and into the more stable mark.

On March 6 the dollar reached post-war lows against the German mark and the Japanese yen, standing at DM1.386 and ¥92.40 respectively. The fall in value against the yen represented a 32 per cent depreciation since 1992.

In Europe, the knock-on effect of the strong mark was felt in some measure by all the currencies, especially those within the ERM (see section 12.5). The Spanish peseta, under pressure prior to the mark's rise, was devalued by 7 per cent, and the Portuguese escudo by 3.5 per cent. Both the French and Swedish governments, with their currencies reaching record lows against the mark, were forced to put up interest rates to prevent further depreciation.

The high yen and mark proved to be equally problematic for the Japanese and German governments. The Japanese economy, which is highly dependent on the US economy for its export earnings found its competitive position significantly eroded. On top of this, a surge in cheap imports reduced many Japanese companies' share of their home market and subsequently stifled the recovery of business growth. The high value of the yen

also encouraged many Japanese businesses to shift production facilities overseas, reducing domestic investment still further.

In Germany too, concern was being expressed about the high exchange rate and its impact upon the economy's faltering recovery. It was suggested that if the 13 per cent appreciation of the mark since December 1994 were not to be reversed, economic growth could be reduced by as much as 1 per cent.

The US Federal Reserve seemed unconcerned about the falling dollar and took no steps to support it. This expression of total indifference led speculators to believe that the dollar's fall was not yet over, encouraging yet further selling of dollar balances.

1997

In the summer of 1997, the Thai baht collapsed. It had been pegged to the US dollar and, with strong economic growth, this had encouraged large-scale inward investment. But with a slowing economy in 1997 and a widening trade deficit investors began to question whether the pegged rate could be maintained. There was massive speculative selling of the currency, and hence the collapse.

The massive depreciation of the baht acted as a catalyst, plunging the whole of south-east Asia into financial turmoil. The shock waves, as one currency after another came under speculative attack, spread outwards from the region. Brazil, Argentina, Mexico, Russia and the Ukraine all saw their currencies come under speculative pressure. All were forced to raise interest rates in an attempt to prevent further depreciation of their exchange rates.

As short-term financial flows increase and currency markets become freer, as the growth in information technology and the process of globalisation make the world's financial markets more integrated, and as fear and rumour seem increasingly able to spread like a bush fire around the world's financial capitals, so the greater is the potential for financial volatility and economic crisis.

1999/2000

On 1 January 1999, the euro was launched and

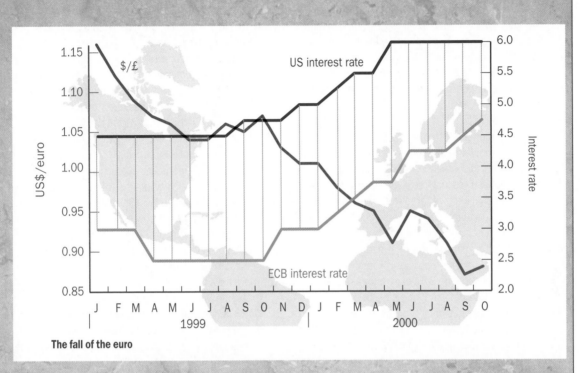

The fall of the euro

exchanged for $1.16. By October 2000 the euro had fallen to $0.85. What was the cause of this 27 per cent depreciation? The main cause was the growing fear that inflationary pressures were increasing in the USA and that, therefore, the Federal Reserve bank would have to raise interest rates. At the same time, the euro-zone economy was growing only slowly and inflation was well below the 2 per cent ceiling set by the ECB. There was thus pressure on the ECB to cut interest rates.

The speculators were not wrong. As the diagram shows, US interest rates rose, and ECB interest rates initially fell, and when eventually they did rise (in October 1999), the gap between US and ECB interest rates soon widened again.

In addition to the differences in interest rates, a lack of confidence in the recovery of the euro-zone economy and a continuing confidence in the US economy encouraged investment to flow to the US. This inflow of finance (and lack of inflow to the euro-zone) further pushed up the dollar relative to the euro.

The low value of the euro meant a high value of the pound relative to the euro. This made it very difficult for

UK companies exporting to euro-zone countries and also for those competing with imports from the euro-zone (which had been made cheaper by the fall in the euro).

In October 2000, with the euro trading at around 85¢, the ECB plus the US Federal Reserve Bank (America's central bank), the Bank of England and the Japanese central bank all intervened on the foreign exchange market to buy euros. This arrested the fall, and helped to restore confidence in the currency. People were more willing to hold euros, knowing that central banks would support it.

The euro had depreciated beyond its long-term equilibrium level, and thus eventually began to rise again – but only after damage had been done.

Question

If in 1995 the Japanese yen was already above its long-term equilibrium exchange rate, and was therefore likely to depreciate some time in the future, why did speculators still continue to buy yen? Similarly, why did people sell euros in 1999?

SUMMARY

2b The exchange rate will depreciate (fall) if the demand for the domestic currency falls or the supply increases. These shifts can be caused by a fall in domestic interest rates, higher inflation in the domestic economy than abroad, a rise in domestic incomes relative to incomes abroad, relative investment prospects improving abroad, or the belief by speculators that the exchange rate will fall. The opposite in each case would cause an appreciation (rise).

3a The government can attempt to prevent the rate of exchange from falling by central bank purchases of the domestic currency in the foreign exchange market, either by selling foreign currency reserves or by using foreign loans. Alternatively, the government can raise interest rates. The reverse actions can be taken if it wants to prevent the rate from rising.

3b In the longer term it can prevent the rate from falling by pursuing deflationary policies, protectionist policies, or supply-side policies to increase the competitiveness of the country's exports.

4a Fixed exchange rates bring the advantage of certainty for the business community, which encourages trade and foreign investment. They also help to prevent governments from pursuing irresponsible macroeconomic policies.

4b Fixed exchange rates bring the disadvantages of conflicting policy goals, the tendency to lead to

competitive deflation seeking to achieve a balance of payments surplus, the problems of ensuring adequate international liquidity to enable intervention, and the restrictions that fixed rates place upon countries when attempting to respond to system shocks.

4c The advantages of free-floating exchange rates are that they automatically correct balance of payments disequilibria; they eliminate the need for reserves; and they give governments a greater independence to pursue their chosen domestic policy.

4d On the other hand, a completely free exchange rate can be highly unstable, especially when the elasticities of demand for imports and exports are low; also speculation may be destabilising. This may discourage firms from trading and investing abroad. What is more, a flexible exchange rate, by removing the balance of payments constraint on domestic policy, may encourage governments to pursue irresponsible domestic policies for short-term political gain.

4e There have been various attempts to manage exchange rates, without them being totally fixed. One example was the Bretton Woods system: a system of pegged exchange rates, but where devaluations or revaluations were allowed from time to time. Another was the ERM, which was the forerunner to the euro. Member countries' currencies were allowed to fluctuate against each other within a band.

REVIEW QUESTIONS

1 The following are the items in the UK's 1998 balance of payments:

	£ billions
Exports of goods	163.7
Imports of goods	184.3
Exports of services	61.8
Imports of services	49.1
Net income flows	+15.8
Net current transfers	−6.4
Net capital transfers	+0.4
Net investment in UK from abroad (direct and portfolio)	61.3
Net UK investment abroad (direct and portfolio)	104.5
Other financial inflows	47.2
Other financial outflows	13.3
Reserves	+0.2

Calculate the following: (a) the balance on trade in goods; (b) the balance on trade (in goods and services); (c) the balance of payments on current account; (d) the financial account balance; (e) the total current plus capital plus financial account balance; (f) net errors and omissions.

2 Assume that there is a free-floating exchange rate. Will the following cause the exchange rate to appreciate or depreciate? In each case you should consider whether there is a shift in the demand or supply curves of sterling (or both) and which way the curve(s) shift(s).

(a) More video recorders are imported from Japan.

Demand curve *shifts left/shifts right/does not shift*
Supply curve *shifts left/shifts right/does not shift*
Exchange rate *appreciates/depreciates*

(b) Non-UK residents increase their purchases of UK government securities.

Demand curve *shifts left/shifts right/does not shift*
Supply curve *shifts left/shifts right/does not shift*
Exchange rate *appreciates/depreciates*

(c) UK interest rates fall relative to those abroad.

Demand curve *shifts left/shifts right/does not shift*
Supply curve *shifts left/shifts right/does not shift*
Exchange rate *appreciates/depreciates*

(d) The UK experiences a higher rate of inflation than other countries.

Demand curve *shifts left/shifts right/does not shift*
Supply curve *shifts left/shifts right/does not shift*
Exchange rate *appreciates/depreciates*

(e) The result of a further enlargement of the EU is for investment in the UK by the rest of the EU to increase by a greater amount than UK investment in other EU countries.

Demand curve *shifts left/shifts right/does not shift*
Supply curve *shifts left/shifts right/does not shift*
Exchange rate *appreciates/depreciates*

(f) Speculators believe that the rate of exchange will fall.

Demand curve *shifts left/shifts right/does not shift*
Supply curve *shifts left/shifts right/does not shift*
Exchange rate *appreciates/depreciates*

3 What is the relationship between the balance of payments and the rate of exchange?

4 Consider the argument that in the modern world of large-scale short-term international financial movements, the ability of individual countries to affect their exchange rate is very limited.

5 To what extent can dealing in forward exchange markets remove the problems of a free-floating exchange rate?

6 What adverse effects on the domestic economy may follow from (a) a depreciation of the exchange rate and (b) an appreciation of the exchange rate?

7 What will be the effects on the domestic economy under free-floating exchange rates if there is a rapid expansion in world economic activity? What will determine the size of these effects?

Money and interest rates

In this chapter we are going to look at the special role that money plays in the economy. The demand and supply of money between them determine the rate of interest, and this has a crucial impact on business. Money and interest rates also have a major effect on the performance of the whole economy, and in particular on the level of national output and prices.

First we define what is meant by money, and examine its functions. Then we look at the operation of the financial sector of the economy and its role in determining the supply of money. We then turn to look at the demand for money, and finally put supply and demand together to show how interest rates are determined.

The control of the financial sector, and the money supply and interest rates in particular, will be considered in more detail in Chapter 29, when we examine monetary policy as one of the means whereby the government or central bank can attempt to manage the economy.

27.1 The meaning and functions of money

Before going any further we must define precisely what we mean by 'money' – not as easy a task as it sounds. Money is more than just notes and coin. In fact the main component of a country's money supply is not cash, but deposits in banks and other financial institutions. Only a very small proportion of these deposits are kept by the banks in their safes or tills in the form of cash. The bulk of the deposits appear merely as bookkeeping entries in the banks' accounts.

This may sound very worrying. Will a bank have enough cash to meet its customers' demands? The answer is yes. Only a small fraction of a bank's total deposits will be withdrawn at any one time, and banks always make sure that they have the ability to meet their customers' demands. The chances of banks running out of cash are practically nil. What is more, the bulk of all but very small transactions are not conducted in cash at all. With the use of cheques, and the growing use of credit cards and debit cards, most money is simply transferred from the purchaser's to the seller's bank account without the need for first withdrawing it in cash.

What items should be included in the definition of money? To answer this we need to identify the *functions* of money.

The functions of money

The main purpose of money is for buying and selling goods, services and assets: i.e. as a **medium of exchange**. It also has three other important functions. Let us examine each in turn.

> **definition**
>
> **Medium of exchange**
> Something that is acceptable in exchange for goods and services.

A medium of exchange

In a subsistence economy where individuals make their own clothes, grow their own food, provide their own entertainments, etc., people do not need money. If people want to exchange any goods, they will do so by barter. In other words, they will do swaps with other people.

The complexities of a modern developed economy, however, make barter totally impractical for most purposes. Someone else may have something you want, but there is no guarantee that they will want what you have to offer them in return. What is more, under a system of capitalism where people are employed by others to do a specialist task, it would be totally impractical for people to be paid in food, clothes, cars, electrical goods, etc. What is necessary is a medium of exchange which is generally acceptable as a means of payment for goods and services, and as a means of payment for labour and other factor services. 'Money' is any such medium.

To be a suitable physical means of exchange, money must be light enough to carry around, come in a number of denominations, large and small, and not be easy to forge. Alternatively, money must be in a form that enables it to be transferred *indirectly* through some acceptable mechanism. For example, money in the form of bookkeeping entries in bank accounts can be transferred from one account to another by the use of such mechanisms as cheques, debit cards, standing orders and direct debits.

A means of storing wealth

Individuals and businesses need a means whereby income earned *today* can be used to purchase goods and services in the *future*. People need to be able to store their wealth: they want a means of saving. Money is one such medium in which to hold wealth. It can be saved.

A means of evaluation

Money is the unit used to value goods, services and assets. It allows the value of one good to be compared with another. In other words, the value of goods is expressed in terms of prices, and prices are expressed in money terms. Money also allows dissimilar things to be added up. Thus a person's wealth or a company's assets can best be expressed in money terms. Similarly, a country's national income is expressed in money terms.

A means of establishing the value of future claims and payments

People often want to agree *today* the price of some *future* payment. For example, workers and managers will want to agree the wage rate for the coming year. Firms will want to sign contracts with their suppliers, specifying the price of raw materials and other supplies. The use of money prices is the most convenient means of measuring future claims.

What should count as money?

What items, then, should be included in the definition of money? Unfortunately, there is no sharp borderline between money and non-money.

Cash (notes and coin) obviously counts as money. It readily meets all the functions of money. Goods (fridges, cars and cabbages) do not count as money.

From building society to bank
Death of the building society movement?

1997 may well become known as the year the building society disappeared. The conversion of the Halifax, Woolwich, Alliance and Leicester, Bristol and West, and Northern Rock building societies into banks represented a huge change in the UK's financial system. For example, the Halifax became the UK's third largest bank following its change in status.

Why were the UK's building societies so keen to become banks? The following reasons have been identified:

● The UK Building Society Act of 1986 restricted the range of financial service activities in which building societies could participate. By converting to bank status, the ex-building societies could more effectively grow as financial service providers.

● The liberalisation of the UK banking sector allowed and encouraged banks to move into building society core business activities: in particular, mortgage lending. In 1980 banks accounted for only 5.5 per cent of mortgages. By 1994 they held 31 per cent.

● Home ownership in the UK, at 67 per cent of households, was believed to be near saturation level. With slow growth in mortgage lending and a more competitive mortgage lending market, future growth prospects in this area looked slim. Thus building societies, in order to maintain growth, needed to diversify – something which their building society status did not allow.

The change in the financial status of the ex-building societies has not only had a significant impact on the financial services sector, but it may have resounding effects upon the economic performance of the UK economy. The source of this impact lies in the change of building societies' legal status, from being mutual societies, where customers were 'members', to becoming public limited companies and hence having shareholders.

The Halifax gave some 9 million people shares; the Woolwich 2.5 million; the Alliance and Leicester 2.4 million; and Northern Rock a further 1 million. In total, over 15 million individuals received shares. In addition to these shares, bonuses were also given to some of the account holders.

The Halifax estimated that its share-out alone would be worth a predicted £11 billion. The total windfall from the conversions could be as high as £20 billion. The great unknown was what people would do with their windfall. Would there be a massive surge in spending, or would the bulk of the windfall be saved?

The experience from the maturing of £18–20 billion worth of Tessas in 1996, where windfall gains were attached to savings, was that there was a surge in savings in other forms, such as unit trusts and National Savings. However, as financial analysts pointed out, people who save in Tessas are naturally savers. Building society pay-outs were going to individuals who were, in many cases, borrowers.

Experience from privatisations suggested that a fairly high proportion of those receiving shares might in time sell them. Ownership of BT shares fell by half between 1984 and 1989. Similarly, ownership of British Gas shares halved over five years. The Abbey National, the first building society to change its status to a bank, had 5.5 million shareholders in 1989 (the year of conversion). By 1994 the figure had fallen to 2.5 million.

One thing was certain: after 1997 the financial services sector would never be the same again.

Questions

1 Would you expect the conversion of building societies into banks to lead to them paying higher or lower interest rates to their savers? Explain.

2 Would the experience of the sale of shares in privatised industries be a good indicator of the likely proportion of people selling their shares in ex-building societies?

But what about various financial assets such as bank and building society accounts, stocks and shares? Do they count as money? The answer is: it depends on how narrowly money is defined.

Countries thus use several different measures of money supply. All include cash, but they vary according to what additional items are included. To understand their significance and the ways in which money supply can be controlled, it is first necessary to look at the various types of account in which money can be held and at the various financial institutions involved.

27.2 The financial system in the UK

In order to understand the role of the financial sector in determining the supply of money, it is important to distinguish different types of financial institution. Each type has a distinct part to play in determining the size of the money supply.

The key role of banks in the monetary system

By far the largest element of money supply is bank deposits. It is not surprising then that banks play an absolutely crucial role in the monetary system.

The most important of the banks in the UK for functioning of the economy and for the implementation of monetary policy are the *retail banks*. These are the familiar high street banks, such as Barclays, Lloyds TSB, HSBC, National Westminster, Co-operative Bank, Royal Bank of Scotland and Bank of Scotland, and ex-building societies such as Woolwich and Halifax. The other major category of banks is the *wholesale* banks (investment banks). These deal primarily with business and are concerned with large-scale deposits and loans at negotiated rates of interest. (See section 18.4 for a more detailed account of their activities.)

Banks are in the business of deposit taking and lending. To understand this, we must distinguish between banks' liabilities and assets. The total liabilities and assets for the UK banks are set out in a balance sheet in Table 27.1.

Liabilities

Customers' deposits in banks (and other depositing-taking institutions such as building societies) are **liabilities** to these institutions. This means simply that the customers have the claim on these deposits and thus the institutions are liable to meet the claims.

There are four major types of deposit: sight deposits, time deposits, certificates of deposit and 'repos'.

Sight deposits. **Sight deposits** are any deposits that can be withdrawn on demand by the depositor without penalty. In the past, sight accounts did not pay interest. Today, however, there are some sight accounts that do.

The most familiar form of sight deposits are current accounts at banks. Depositors are issued with cheque books and/or debit cards (e.g. Switch or Connect) which enable them to spend the money directly without first having to go to the bank and draw the money out in cash. In the case of debit cards, the person's account is electronically debited when the purchase is made and the card is 'swiped' across the machine. This process is known as EFTPOS (electronic funds transfer at point of sale).

An important feature of current accounts is that banks often allow customers to be overdrawn. That is, they can draw on their account and make payments to other people in excess of the amount of money they have deposited.

Time deposits. **Time deposits** require notice of withdrawal. However, they nor-

---

definition

Liabilities
All legal claims for payment that outsiders have on an institution.

definition

Sight deposits
Deposits that can be withdrawn on demand without penalty.

definition

Time deposits
Deposits that require notice of withdrawal or where a penalty is charged for withdrawals on demand.

| Table 27.1 | Balance sheet of UK banks: March 2000 |

Sterling liabilities	£bn	%	Sterling assets	£bn	%
Sight deposits		(31.6)	Notes and coin	5.5	(0.4)
UK banks	39.6		Balances with Bank of England		(0.1)
UK public sector	3.3		Operational deposits	0.1	
UK private sector	344.4		Cash ratio deposits	1.1	
Non-residents	49.5		Market loans		(23.4)
			UK banks	156.9	
Time deposits		(38.4)	UK banks CDs, etc.	71.4	
UK banks	122.4		Building society CDs, etc.	5.4	
UK public sector	6.9		Non-residents	91.2	
UK private sector	277.1		Bills of exchange		(1.0)
Non-residents	124.2		Treasury bills	1.9	
			UK bank bills	10.3	
Certificates of deposit, etc.	150.8	(10.9)	Other	1.2	
			Sale and repurchase agreements		(6.6)
Sale and repurchase agreements (repos)		(6.5)	(reverse repos)		
Government securities	80.0		Government securities	84.1	
Other	9.4		Other	7.3	
			Investments		(7.2)
Items in suspense and transmission	23.4	(1.7)	UK public sector	7.1	
			UK private sector	16.1	
Capital and other funds	147.4	(10.7)	Other	76.1	
			Advances		(56.1)
Notes outstanding and cash loaded cards	2.8	(0.2)	UK public sector	2.5	
			UK private sector	751.0	
			Non-residents	24.5	
			Miscellaneous	71.6	(5.2)
Total sterling liabilities	1381.2	(100.0)	**Total sterling assets**	1385.3	(100.0)
Liabilities in other currencies	1475.7		Assets in other currencies	1471.6	
Total liabilities	2856.9		Total assets	2856.9	

Source: *Monetary and Financial Statistics* (Bank of England).

mally pay a higher rate of interest than sight accounts. With some types of account, a depositor can withdraw a certain amount of money on demand, but will have to pay a penalty of so many days' interest. They are not cheque-book or debit-card accounts. The most familiar forms of time deposits are the deposit and savings accounts in banks and the various savings accounts in building societies. No overdraft facilities exist with time deposits.

Sale and repurchase agreements ('repos'). If banks have a temporary shortage of funds, they can sell some of their financial assets to other banks or to the Bank of England (see below), and later repurchase them on some agreed date, often about a fortnight later. These **sale and repurchase agreements (repos)** are in effect a form of loan, the bank borrowing for a period of time using some of its financial assets as the security for the loan. The most usual assets to use in this way are government bonds, normally called 'gilt-edged securities' or simply

definition
Sale and repurchase agreements (repos) An agreement between two financial institutions whereby one in effect borrows from another by selling it assets, agreeing to buy them back (repurchase them) at a fixed price and on a fixed date.

'gilts' (see below). Sale and repurchase agreements involving gilts are known as *gilt repos*. As we shall see, gilt repos play a vital role in the operation of monetary policy.

Certificates of deposit. CDs are certificates issued by banks to customers (usually firms) for large deposits of a fixed term (e.g. £100 000 for 18 months). They can be sold by one customer to another, and are thus relatively liquid to the depositor but illiquid to the bank. The use of CDs has grown rapidly in recent years. Their use by firms has meant that, at a wholesale level, sight accounts have become *less* popular.

Assets

Banks' financial **assets** are its claims on others. There are three main categories of assets.

Cash and balances in the Bank of England. Banks and certain other financial institutions, such as building societies, need to hold a certain amount of their assets as notes and coin. This is largely used as 'till money' to meet the day-to-day demands by customers for cash. They also keep 'operational balances' in the Bank of England. These are like the banks' own current accounts and are used for clearing purposes. They can be withdrawn in cash on demand and are thus also totally liquid. The banks are also required to deposit a small fraction of their assets as 'cash ratio deposits' with the Bank of England.

Cash and balances in the Bank of England, however, earn no interest for banks. The vast majority of banks' assets are therefore in the form of various types of loan – to individuals and firms, to other financial institutions and to the government. These are 'assets' since they represent claims that the banks have on other people. Loans can be grouped into two types: short and long term.

Short-term loans. These are in the form of *market loans*, *bills of exchange* or *reverse repos*.

- **Market loans** are made primarily to other banks or financial institutions. They consist of (a) money lent 'at call' (i.e. reclaimable on demand or at 24 hours' notice), (b) money lent 'at short notice' (i.e. money lent for a few days) and (c) CDs (i.e. certificates of deposit made in other banks or building societies).
- **Bills of exchange** are loans either to companies (guaranteed by another bank and hence called 'bank bills') or to the government (Treasury bills). As explained in section 18.4, these are, in effect, an IOU, with the company issuing them (in the case of bank bills) or the Bank of England (in the case of Treasury bills) promising to pay the holder a specified sum on a particular date (normally in three months' time). Since bills do not pay interest, they are sold below their face value (at a 'discount') in order to enable the purchaser to earn a return.
- **Reverse repos.** When a sale and repurchase agreement is made, the financial institution *purchasing* the assets (e.g. gilts) is, in effect, giving a short-term loan. The other party agrees to buy back the assets (i.e. pay back the loan) on a set date. The assets temporarily held by the bank making the loan are known as 'reverse repos'.

---

definition

Certificates of deposit
Certificates issued by banks for fixed-term interest-bearing deposits. They can be resold by the owner to another party.

definition

Assets
Possessions, or claims held on others.

definition

Market loans
Loans made to other financial institutions.

definition

Bill of exchange
A certificate promising to repay a stated amount on a certain date, typically three months from the issue of the bill. Bills pay no interest as such, but are sold at a discount and redeemed at face value, thereby earning a rate of discount for the purchaser.

definition

Reverse repos
When gilts or other assets are *purchased* under a sale and repurchase agreement. They become an asset of the purchaser.

BOX 27.2

Are the days of cash numbered?
EFTPOS versus ATMs

Banking is becoming increasingly automated, with computer debiting and crediting of accounts replacing the moving around of pieces of paper. What was once done by a bank clerk is often now done by computer.

One possible outcome of this replacement of labour by computers is the gradual elimination of cash from the economy – or so some commentators have claimed.

The most dramatic example of computerisation in recent years has been EFTPOS (electronic funds transfer at the point of sale). This is where you pay for goods in the shops by means of a card – either a credit card (like Access or Visa) or a debit card (like Switch or Connect). The card is simply 'swiped' across a machine at the till which may then require you to enter your PIN (personal identification number). The details of the transaction (the amount, the retailer and your card number) are then transmitted down the line to the EFTPOS UK processing centre. If necessary, the information is then directed down the line to the card issuer for authorisation. If the card is valid and the transaction acceptable, then within seconds the machine will issue a slip for you to sign and the purchase is complete. Subsequently your account will be automatically debited and the retailer's account automatically credited.

The advantage of this system is that it does away with the processing by hand of pieces of paper. In particular it does away with the need for (a) credit-card slips when used in conjunction with credit cards and (b) cheques. Both cheques and credit-card slips have to be physically moved around and then read and processed by *people*. If this EFTPOS system were to become widely

used for *small* transactions, it could well reduce the need for cash. But reducing the need for cash is not the prime purpose of EFTPOS. Its prime purpose is to do away with cheques and credit-card slips.

So are we moving towards a cashless society? Probably not. Cash is still the simplest and most efficient way of paying for a host of items, from your bus ticket to a newspaper to a packet of mints. What is more, another technical innovation is moving us in the direction of using *more* cash, not less! This is the cash machine – or *ATM* (automated teller machine), to give it its official title. The spread of cash machines to virtually every bank and building society branch and to many larger stores has been rapid in recent years. The sheer simplicity of obtaining cash at all hours from these machines, not only from your current account but also on your credit card, is obviously a huge encouragement to the use of cash.

So are we using more cash or less cash? The evidence suggests a gradual decline in cash in circulation as a proportion of GDP. It fell from just over 5 per cent of GDP in 1980 to around 2½ per cent in 2000.

But although the effects of EFTPOS and ATMs may be quite different in terms of the use of cash, they both have the same advantage to banks: they reduce the need for bank staff and thereby reduce costs.

Question

Under what circumstances are cheques more efficient than cash and vice versa? Would you get the same answer from everyone involved in transactions: individuals, firms and banks?

Longer-term loans. These consist primarily of loans to customers, both personal customers and businesses. These loans, also known as *advances*, are of three main types: fixed-term (repayable in instalments over a set number of years, typically six months to five years), overdrafts (often for an unspecified term) and mortgages (typically for 25 years).

Banks also make *investments*. These are partly in government bonds ('gilts'), which are effectively loans to the government. The government sells bonds, which then pay a fixed sum each year as interest. Once issued, they can then be bought and sold on the Stock Exchange. Banks are normally only prepared to buy bonds that have less than five years to maturity (the date when the government redeems the bonds). Banks also invest in various subsidiary financial institutions and in building societies.

Liquidity and profitability

As we have seen, banks keep a range of liabilities and assets. The balance of items in this range is influenced by two important considerations: profitability and liquidity.

Profitability. Profits are made by lending money out at a higher rate of interest than that paid to depositors.

Liquidity. The **liquidity** of an asset is the ease with which it can be converted into cash without loss. Cash itself, by definition, is perfectly liquid.

Some assets, such as money lent at call to other financial institutions, are highly liquid. Although not actually cash, these assets can be converted into cash on demand with no financial penalty. Other assets, however, are much less liquid. Personal loans to the general public or mortgages for house purchase can only be redeemed by the bank as each instalment is paid. Other advances for fixed periods are only repaid at the end of that period.

Banks must always be able to meet the demands of their customers for withdrawals of money. To do this, they must hold sufficient cash or other assets that can be readily turned into cash. In other words, banks must maintain sufficient liquidity.

Profitability is the major aim of banks and most other financial institutions. However, the aims of profitability and liquidity tend to conflict. In general, the more liquid an asset, the less profitable it is, and vice versa. Personal and business loans to customers are profitable to banks, but highly illiquid. Cash is totally liquid, but earns no profit. Thus financial institutions like to hold a range of assets with varying degrees of liquidity and profitability.

The ratio of an institution's liquid assets to total assets is known as its **liquidity ratio**. For example, if a bank had £100 million of assets, of which £10 million were liquid and £90 million were illiquid, the bank would have a 10 per cent liquidity ratio. If a financial institution's liquidity ratio is too high, it will make too little profit. If the ratio is too low, there will be the risk that customers' demands will not be able to be met: this would cause a crisis of confidence and possible closure. Institutions thus have to make a judgement as to what liquidity ratio is best – one that is neither too high nor too low.

The Bank of England

The Bank of England is the UK's central bank. All countries have a central bank and they fulfil two vital roles in the economy.

The first is to oversee the whole monetary system and ensure that banks and other financial institutions operate as stably and as efficiently as possible.

The second is to act as the government's agent, both as its banker and in carrying out monetary policy. The Bank of England traditionally worked in very close liaison with the Treasury and there used to be regular meetings between the Governor of the Bank of England and the Chancellor of the Exchequer.

---

definition

Liquidity
The ease with which an asset can be converted into cash without loss.

definition

Liquidity ratio
The proportion of a bank's total assets held in liquid form.

Although the Bank may have disagreed with Treasury policy, it always carried it out. With the election of the Labour government in 1997, however, the Bank of England was given independence to decide the course of monetary policy. In particular, this meant that the Bank of England and not the government would now decide interest rates.

Another example of an independent central bank is the European Central Bank (ECB). The ECB operates monetary policy for the countries using the euro and it alone, not the member governments, determines common interest rates for these countries. Similarly, the Federal Reserve Bank of America (the US central bank) is independent of both President and Congress, and its chairman is generally regarded as having great power in determining the country's economic policy. Although the degree of independence of central banks from government varies considerably around the world, there has nevertheless been a general trend to make central banks more independent.

If the UK adopts the euro, there will be a much reduced role for the Bank of England. At present, however, within its two broad roles, it has a number of different functions.

It issues notes

The Bank of England is the sole issuer of banknotes in England and Wales (in Scotland and Northern Ireland retail banks issue banknotes). The amount of banknotes issued by the Bank of England depends largely on the demand for notes from the general public. If people draw more cash from their bank accounts, the banks will have to draw more cash from their balances in the Bank of England.

It acts as a bank

To the government. It keeps the two major government accounts: 'The Exchequer' and the 'National Loans Fund'. Taxation and government spending pass through the Exchequer. Government borrowing and lending pass through the National Loans Fund. The government tends to keep its deposits in the Bank of England to a minimum. If the deposits begin to build up (from taxation), the government will probably spend them on paying back government debt. If, on the other hand, the government runs short of money, it will simply borrow more.

To the banks. As we have seen, banks hold operational balances in the Bank of England. These are used for clearing purposes between the banks and to provide them with a source of liquidity.

To overseas central banks. These are deposits of sterling held by overseas authorities as part of their official reserves and/or for purposes of intervening in the foreign exchange market in order to influence the exchange rate of their currency.

It manages the government's borrowing programme

Whenever the government runs a budget deficit (i.e. spends more than it receives in tax revenue), it will have to finance that deficit by borrowing. It can borrow by issuing either bonds (gilts), National Savings Certificates or Treasury bills.

The Bank of England organises this borrowing. Even when the government runs a budget surplus, the Bank of England will still have to manage the national debt (the accumulated borrowing from the past). The reason is that old bonds will be maturing and new issues of bonds will probably be necessary to replace them.

It provides liquidity, as necessary, to banks

It ensures that there is always an adequate supply of liquidity to meet the legitimate demands of depositors in banks. As we shall see below, it does this through the discount and gilt repo markets.

It used to supervise the activities of banks to ensure that they were behaving prudently, were not operating with excessive levels of risk and were generally behaving in the interests of their customers. Since 1997, however, this supervisory role has passed to the regulatory agency, the Financial Services Authority (FSA).

It operates the country's monetary and exchange rate policy

Monetary policy. By careful management of the issue and repurchasing of government bonds and Treasury bills, the Bank of England can manipulate interest rates and influence the size of the money supply. This is explained in Chapter 29.

Exchange rate policy. The Bank of England manages the country's gold and foreign currency reserves. This is done through the **exchange equalisation account**. As we saw in Chapter 26, by buying and selling foreign currencies on the foreign exchange market, the Bank of England can affect the exchange rate.

The role of the London money market

It is through the London money market that the Bank of England exercises its control of the economy. The market deals in short-term lending and borrowing. It is normally divided into the 'discount and repo' markets and the 'parallel' or 'complementary' markets.

The discount and repo markets

The markets for bills of exchange (the discount market) and for repos play a crucial role in ensuring that banks have sufficient liquidity to meet all their needs.

Assume that bank customers start drawing out more cash. As a result, banks find themselves short of liquid assets. What can they do? The answer is that they borrow from the Bank of England. There are two ways in which this can be done.

The first is to enter a repo agreement, whereby the Bank of England buys gilts from the banks (thereby supplying them with money) on the condition that the banks buy the gilts back at a fixed price and on a fixed date, typically two weeks later. The repurchase price will be above the sale price. The difference is the equivalent of the interest that the banks are being charged for having what amounts to a loan from the Bank of England. The repurchase price (and hence the 'repo rate') will be set by the Bank of England to reflect its chosen rate of

definition

Exchange equalisation account
The gold and foreign exchange reserves account in the Bank of England.

interest: i.e. the rate chosen by the Bank of England's Monetary Policy Committee (see section 29.3). This eight-member committee, consisting of four independent experts and four senior members of the Bank of England (with the Governor in the chair), meets once per month.

The second method is to sell Treasury bills back to the Bank of England before they have reached maturity (i.e. before the three months are up). This process is known as **rediscounting**. The Bank of England will pay a price below the face value, thus effectively charging interest to the banks.

In being prepared to rediscount bills or provide money through gilt repos, the Bank of England is thus the ultimate guarantor of sufficient liquidity in the monetary system and is known as **lender of last resort**.

The need for banks to acquire liquidity in this way is not uncommon: the 'last resort' occurs on most days! It is generally a deliberate policy of the Bank of England to create a shortage of liquidity in the economy to force banks to obtain liquidity from it. But why should the Bank of England do this? It does it as a means of controlling interest rates. If the banks are forced to obtain liquidity from the Bank of England, they will be borrowing at the Bank of England's *chosen rate* (i.e. the repo rate). The banks will then have to gear their other rates to it, and other institutions will gear their rates to those of the banks.

The way in which the Bank of England creates a shortage of liquidity and the way in which it forces through changes in interest rates are examined in section 29.3.

The parallel money markets

The parallel money markets include the following:

- The inter-bank market (wholesale loans from one bank to another from one day to up to several months).
- The market for certificates of deposit.
- The inter-companies deposit market (short-term loans from one company to another arranged through the market).
- The foreign currencies market (dealings in foreign currencies deposited short term in London).
- The finance house market (short-term borrowing to finance hire purchase).
- The building society market (wholesale borrowing by the building societies).
- The commercial paper market (borrowing in sterling by companies, banks and other financial institutions by the issue of short-term (less than one year) 'promissory notes'. These, like bills of exchange, are sold at a discount and redeemed at their face value.)

The parallel markets have grown in size and importance in recent years. The main reasons for this are (a) the opening-up of markets to international dealing, given the abolition of exchange controls in 1979, (b) the deregulation of banking and money-market dealing and (c) the volatility of interest rates and exchange rates, and thus the desire of banks to keep funds in a form that can be readily switched from one form of deposit to another, or from one currency to another. The main areas of growth have been in inter-bank deposits, certificates of deposit and the foreign currency markets.

Although the Bank of England does not deal directly in the parallel markets and does not provide 'last resort' lending facilities, it nevertheless closely mon-

definition
Rediscounting bills of exchange
Buying bills before they reach maturity.

definition
Lender of last resort
The role of the Bank of England as the guarantor of sufficient liquidity in the monetary system.

itors the various money-market rates of interest and, if necessary, seeks to influence them, through its dealings in the repo and discount markets.

27.3 The supply of money

If money supply is to be monitored and possibly controlled, it is obviously necessary to measure it. But what should be included in the measure? Here we need to distinguish between the *monetary base* and *broad money*.

The **monetary base** (or 'high-powered money') consists of cash (notes and coin) in circulation outside the central bank. It is sometimes referred to as the 'narrow monetary base' to distinguish it from the **wide monetary base**, which also includes banks' balances with the central bank. In the UK, the wide monetary base in known as *M0*.

But the monetary base gives us a very poor indication of the effective money supply, since it excludes the most important source of liquidity for spending: namely, bank deposits. The problem is which deposits to include. We need to answer three questions:

- Should we include just sight deposits, or time deposits as well?
- Should we include just retail deposits, or wholesale deposits as well?
- Should we include just bank deposits, or building society deposits as well?

In the past there has been a whole range of measures, each including different combinations of these accounts. However, financial deregulation, the abolition of foreign exchange controls and the development of computer technology have led to huge changes in the financial sector throughout the world. This has led to a blurring of the distinctions between different types of account. It has also made it very easy to switch deposits from one type of account to another. For these reasons, the most usual measure that countries use for money supply is **broad money**, which in most cases includes both time and sight deposits, retail and wholesale deposits, and bank and building society (savings institutions) deposits.

In the UK this measure of broad money is known as *M4*. In most other European countries and the USA it is known as *M3*. There are, however, minor differences between countries in what is included. (Official UK measures of money supply are given in Box 27.3.)

As we have seen, bank deposits of one form or another constitute by far the largest component of (broad) money supply. To understand how money supply expands and contracts, and how it can be controlled, it is thus necessary to understand what determines the size of bank deposits. Banks can themselves expand the amount of bank deposits, and hence the money supply, by a process known as 'credit creation'.

The creation of credit

To illustrate this process in its simplest form, assume that banks have just one type of liability – deposits – and two types of asset – balances with the Bank of England (to achieve liquidity) and advances to customers (to earn profit).

Banks want to achieve profitability while maintaining sufficient liquidity. Assume that they believe that sufficient liquidity will be achieved if 10 per cent

---

definition

Monetary base
Notes and coin outside the central bank.

definition

Wide monetary base (M0)
Notes and coin outside the central bank plus banks' operational deposits with the central bank.

definition

Broad money
Cash in circulation plus retail and wholesale bank and building society deposits.

Table 27.2 Banks' original balance sheet

Liabilities	£bn	Assets	£bn
Deposits	100	Balances with the B. of E.	10
		Advances	90
Total	100	Total	100

of their assets are held as balances with the Bank of England. The remaining 90 per cent will then be in advances to customers. In other words, the banks operate a 10 per cent liquidity ratio.

Assume initially that the combined balance sheet of the banks is as shown in Table 27.2. Total deposits are £100 billion, of which £10 billion (10 per cent) are kept in balances with the Bank of England. The remaining £90 billion (90 per cent) are lent to customers.

Now assume that the government spends more money – £10 billion, say, on roads or the National Health Service. It pays for this with cheques drawn on its account with the Bank of England. The people receiving the cheques deposit them in their banks. Banks return these cheques to the Bank of England and their balances correspondingly increase by £10 billion. The combined banks' balance sheet now is shown in Table 27.3.

But this is not the end of the story. Banks now have surplus liquidity. With their balances in the Bank of England having increased to £20 billion, they now have a liquidity ratio of 20/110. If they are to return to a 10 per cent liquidity ratio, they need only retain £11 billion as balances at the Bank of England (£11 billion/ £110 billion = 10 per cent). The remaining £9 billion they can lend to customers.

Assume now that customers spend this £9 billion in shops and the shopkeepers deposit the cheques in their bank accounts. When the cheques are cleared, the balances in the Bank of England of the customers' banks will duly be debited by £9 billion, but the balances in the Bank of England of the shopkeepers' banks will be credited by £9 billion: leaving *overall balances in the Bank of England unaltered*. There is still a surplus of £9 billion over what is required to maintain the 10 per cent liquidity ratio. The new deposits of £9 in the shopkeepers' banks, backed by balances in the Bank of England, can thus be used as the basis for *further* loans. Ten per cent (i.e. £0.9 billion) must be kept back in the Bank of England, but the remaining 90 per cent (i.e. £8.1 billion) can be lent out again. When the money is spent and the cheques are cleared, this £8.1 billion will still remain as surplus balances in the Bank of England and can therefore be used as the basis for yet more loans. Again, 10 per cent must be retained and the remaining 90 per cent can be lent out. This process goes on and on until eventually the position is as shown in Table 27.4.

Table 27.3 The initial effect of an additional deposit of £10 billion

Liabilities	£bn	Assets	£bn
Deposits (old)	100	Balances with the B. of E. (old)	10
Deposits (new)	10	Balances with the B. of E. (new)	10
		Advances	90
Total	110	Total	110

Table 27.4 The full effect of an additional deposit of £10 billion			
Liabilities	*£bn*	*Assets*	*£bn*
Deposits (old)	100	Balances with the B. of E. (old)	10
Deposits (new: initial)	10	Balances with the B. of E. (new)	10
(new: subsequent)	90	Advances (old)	90
		Advances (new)	90
Total	200	Total	200

The initial increase in balances with the Bank of England of £10 billion has allowed banks to create new advances (and hence deposits) of £90 billion, making a total increase in money supply of £100 billion.

This effect is known as the **bank (or deposits) multiplier**. In this simple example with a liquidity ratio of $\frac{1}{10}$ (i.e. 10 per cent), the deposits multiplier is 10. An initial increase in deposits of £10 billion allowed total deposits to rise by £100 billion. In this simple world, therefore, the deposits multiplier is the inverse of the liquidity ratio (L).

$$\text{Deposits multiplier} = \frac{1}{L}$$

The creation of credit: the real world

In practice, the creation of credit is not as simple as this. There are three major complications.

Banks' liquidity ratio may vary

Banks may choose a different liquidity ratio. At certain times, banks may decide that it is prudent to hold a bigger proportion of liquid assets. If Christmas or the summer holidays are approaching and people are likely to make bigger cash withdrawals, banks may decide to hold more liquid assets. They may also do so if they anticipate that their liquid assets may soon be squeezed by government monetary policy.

On the other hand, there may be an upsurge in consumer demand for credit. Banks may be very keen to grant additional loans and thus make more profits, even though they have acquired no additional assets. They may simply go ahead and expand credit, and accept a lower liquidity ratio.

Customers may not want to take up the credit on offer. Banks may wish to make additional loans, but customers may not want to borrow. There may be insufficient demand. But will the banks not then lower their interest rates, thus encouraging people to borrow? Possibly, but if they lower the rate they charge to borrowers, they must also lower the rate they pay to depositors. But then depositors may switch to other institutions such as building societies. Thus, just because banks have acquired additional liquid assets, it does not automatically follow that they will create credit on the basis of them.

Banks may not operate a simple liquidity ratio

The fact that banks hold a number of fairly liquid assets, such as money at call, bills of exchange and certificates of deposit, makes it difficult to identify a

---

definition

Bank (or deposits) multiplier
The number of times greater the expansion of bank deposits is than the additional liquidity in banks that caused it: $1/L$ (the inverse of the liquidity ratio).

BOX 27.3

UK monetary aggregates
How long is a piece of string?

In the recent past, measures of 'money supply' in the UK have included M0, non-interest-bearing M1, M1, M2, M3, M3H, M3c, M4, M4c, M5. This confusing array of measures reflected the many different types of deposit that might be considered to be part of money.

Today, there are just four official measures: M0, M2, M4 and M3 (EU measure). The government regards M0 and M4 as the most important. M0 is referred to as the 'wide monetary base' and M4 is referred to as 'broad money' or simply as 'the money supply'. The definitions of the three UK aggregates are:

M0. Cash in circulation with the public and cash held by banks and building societies, plus banks' operational balances with the Bank of England.

M2. Cash in circulation with the public (but not cash in banks and building societies), plus private-sector retail sterling deposits in banks and building societies.

M4. M2 plus private-sector wholesale sterling deposits in banks and building societies, plus sterling certificates of deposit.

The table gives the figures for all these aggregates for the end of August 2000.

Question

Why is cash in banks and building societies included in M0 but not in the other measures?

UK monetary aggregates, end August 2000

		£ million
	Cash outside Bank of England	31 445
+	Banks' operational deposits with Bank of England	194
=	**M0**	**31 639**
	Cash outside banks (i.e. in circulation with the public and non-bank firms)	25 383
+	Private-sector retail bank and building society deposits	546 057
=	**M2**	**571 440**
+	Private-sector wholesale bank and building society deposits + CDs	293 256
=	**M4**	**864 696**

simple liquidity ratio. If the banks use extra cash to buy such liquid assets, can they then use these assets as the basis for creating credit? It is largely up to banks' judgements on their overall liquidity position.

Some of the extra cash may be withdrawn from the banks

If extra cash comes into the banking system, and as a result extra deposits are created, part of them may be held by the public as cash *outside* the banks. In other words, some of the extra cash leaks out of the banking system. This will result in an overall multiplier effect that is smaller than the full deposits multiplier.

What causes money supply to rise?

The money supply might rise as a consequence of the following.

Banks choose to hold a lower liquidity ratio

If banks collectively choose to hold a lower liquidity ratio, they will have surplus liquidity. The banks have tended to choose a lower liquidity ratio over time because of the increasing use of cheques and debit-card and credit-card transactions. Surplus liquidity can be used to expand advances, which will lead to a multiplied rise in the money supply.

An important trend in recent years has been the growth in *inter-bank lending*. These wholesale loans are often short term and are thus a liquid asset to the bank making them. Short-term loans to other banks and CDs are now the two largest elements in banks' liquid assets. Being liquid, these assets may be used by a bank as the basis for expanding loans and thereby starting a chain of credit creation. But although these assets are liquid to an *individual* bank, they do not add to the liquidity of the banking system *as a whole*. Thus by using them as the basis for credit creation, the banking system is in effect operating with a lower *overall* liquidity ratio.

An inflow of funds from abroad

Sometimes the Bank of England will choose to build up the foreign currency reserves. To do this it will buy foreign currencies on the foreign exchange market using sterling. When the recipients of this extra sterling deposit it in UK banks, or spend it on UK exports and the exporters deposit in UK banks, credit will be created on the basis of it, leading to a multiplied increase in money supply.

A public-sector deficit: a PSNCR

The public-sector net cash requirement (PSNCR) is the difference between public-sector expenditure and public-sector receipts. To meet this deficit the government has to borrow money by selling interest-bearing securities (Treasury bills and gilts). In general, the bigger the PSNCR, the greater will be the growth in the money supply. Just how the money supply will be affected, however, depends on who buys the securities.

Such securities could be sold to the Bank of England. In this case the Bank of England credits the government's account to the value of the securities it has purchased. When the government spends the money, it pays with cheques drawn on its account with the Bank of England. When the recipients of these cheques pay them into their bank accounts, the banks will present the cheques to the Bank of England and their balances at the Bank will be duly credited. These additional balances will then become the basis for credit creation. There will be a multiplied expansion of the money supply.

Similarly, if the government borrows through additional Treasury bills, and if these are purchased by the banking sector, there will be a multiplied expansion of the money supply. The reason is that, although banks' balances at the Bank of England will go down when the banks purchase the bills, they will go up again when the government spends the money. In addition, the banks will now have additional liquid assets (bills), which can be used as the basis for credit creation.

If, however, the government securities are purchased by the 'non-bank private sector' (i.e. the general public and non-bank firms), then the money supply will remain unchanged. When the public buy the bonds or bills, they will draw

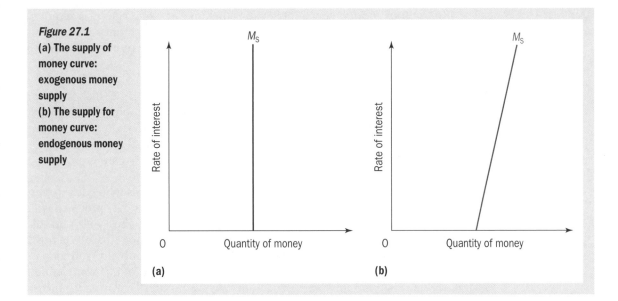

Figure 27.1
(a) The supply of money curve: exogenous money supply
(b) The supply for money curve: endogenous money supply

money from their banks. When the government spends the money, it will be redeposited in banks. There is no increase in money supply. It is just a case of existing money changing hands.

The government could attempt to minimise the boost to money supply by financing the PSNCR through the sale of bonds.

The relationship between money supply and the rate of interest

Simple monetary theory often assumes that the supply of money is totally independent of interest rates. The money supply is 'exogenous'. This is illustrated in Figure 27.1(a). The supply of money is assumed to be determined by government: what the government chooses it to be, or what it allows it to be by its choice of the level and method of financing the PSNCR.

Some economists, however, argue that money supply is 'endogenous', with higher interest rates leading to increases in the supply of money. This is illustrated in Figure 27.1(b). The argument is that the supply of money is responding to the demand for money. If people start borrowing more money, the resulting shortage of money in the banks will drive up interest rates. But if banks have surplus liquidity or are prepared to operate with a lower liquidity ratio, they will create extra credit in response to the increased demand and higher interest rates: money supply has expanded.

27.4 The demand for money

The demand for money refers to the desire to *hold* money: to keep your wealth in the form of money, rather than spending it on goods and services or using it to purchase financial assets such as bonds or shares. It is usual to distinguish three reasons why people want to hold their assets in the form of money.

The transactions motive. Since money is a medium of exchange, it is required for conducting transactions. But since people only receive money at intervals (e.g. weekly or monthly) and not continuously, they require to hold balances of money in cash or in current accounts.

The precautionary motive. Unforeseen circumstances can arise, such as a car breakdown. Thus individuals often hold some additional money as a precaution. Firms too keep precautionary balances because of uncertainties about the timing of their receipts and payments. If a large customer is late in making payment, a firm may be unable to pay its suppliers unless it has spare liquidity.

The speculative or assets motive. Certain firms and individuals who wish to purchase financial assets such as bonds, shares or other securities may prefer to wait if they feel that their price is likely to fall. In the meantime they will hold idle money balances instead. This speculative demand can be quite high when the price of securities is considered certain to fall. Some clever (or lucky) individuals anticipated the 1987 stock market crash. They sold shares and 'went liquid'. Money when used for this purpose is a means of temporarily storing wealth.

The relationship between the demand for money and the rate of interest

The demand for money balances is called 'liquidity preference' (L). What determines liquidity preference and how is it related to the rate of interest?

Active balances

Money balances held for transactions and precautionary purposes are called **active balances**, since they are held to be used as a medium of exchange. The major determinant of active balances is the level of national income (Y). The bigger people's income, the more their purchases and the bigger their demand for active balances. The transactions and precautionary demands are also determined by the frequency with which individuals and businesses are paid. The less frequently they are paid, the greater the level of money balances that will be required to tide them over until the next payment. The rate of interest is another, albeit less important, determinant of active balances. At high rates of interest, people will be encouraged to risk reducing their holdings of money, and to keep their assets in a form that will earn the high interest.

> **definition**
>
> **Active balances**
> Money held for transactions and precautionary purposes.

> **definition**
>
> **Idle balances**
> Money held for speculative purposes: money held in anticipation of a fall in asset prices.

Idle balances

Money balances held for speculative purposes are called **idle balances**. People who possess wealth, whether they are wealthy or simply small savers, have to decide the best form in which to hold that wealth. Do they keep it in cash or in a current account in a bank; or do they put it in some interest-bearing time account; or do they buy stocks and shares or government bonds; or do they buy some physical asset such as a car or property?

The speculative demand for money has two major determinants. The first is the rate of interest (or 'rate of return') on various financial assets, such as stocks and shares. The higher the rate of interest, the higher the opportunity cost of holding money, and the lower is the speculative demand for money.

The second determinant is people's expectations about the future. For

Figure 27.2
A liquidity
preference curve

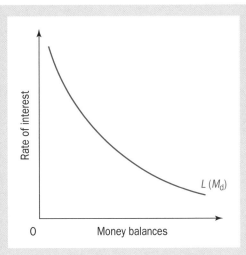

example, if people believe that share prices are about to rise rapidly on the stock market, they will buy shares and hold smaller speculative balances of money. If they think share prices will fall, they will sell them and hold money instead.

The speculative demand for money also depends on expectations about changes in the exchange rate of foreign currencies into the pound. If businesses believe that the exchange rate is about to appreciate (rise), they will hold idle balances of sterling in the meantime, hoping to buy foreign currencies with them when the rate has risen (since they will then get more foreign currency per pound).

The liquidity preference curve

The demand for money with respect to interest rates is given by a 'liquidity preference' curve. This is shown in Figure 27.2. It is downward sloping, showing that lower interest rates will encourage people to hold additional money balances (mainly for speculative purposes).

A change in interest rates is shown by a movement along the liquidity preference curve. A change in any other determinant of the demand for money (such as national income or expectations about exchange rate movements) will cause the whole curve to shift: a rightward shift represents an increase in demand; a leftward shift represents a decrease.

27.5 Equilibrium

Equilibrium in the money market

Equilibrium in the money market occurs when the demand for money (L) is equal to the supply of money (M_s). This equilibrium is achieved through changes in the rate of interest.

In Figure 27.3 the equilibrium rate of interest is r_e and the equilibrium quantity of money is M_e. If the rate of interest were above r_e, people would have

Figure 27.3
Equilibrium in the money market

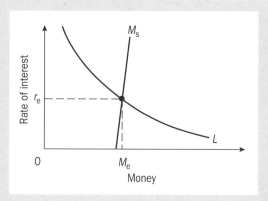

money balances surplus to their needs. They would use these to buy stocks and shares and other assets. This would drive up the price of these assets. But the price of assets is inversely related to interest rates. The higher the price of an asset (such as a government bond), the less will any given interest payment be as a percentage of its price (e.g. £10 as a percentage of £100 is 10 per cent, but as a percentage of £200 is only 5 per cent). Thus a higher price of assets will correspond to lower interest rates.

As the rate of interest fell, so there would be a contraction of the money supply (a movement down along the M_s curve) and an increase in the demand for money balances, especially speculative balances (a movement down along the liquidity perference curve). The interest rate would go on falling until it reached r_e. Equilibrium would then be achieved.

Similarly, if the rate of interest were below r_e, people would have insufficient money balances. They would sell securities, thus lowering their prices and raising the rate of interest until it reached r_e.

A shift in either the M_s or the L curve will lead to a new equilibrium quantity of money and rate of interest at the new intersection of the curves. For example, a rise in the quantity of money will cause the rate of interest to fall, whereas a rise in the demand for money will cause the rate of interest to rise.

Equilibrium in the foreign exchange market

Changes in the money supply will not only affect interest rates, they will also have an effect on exchange rates. Assume, for example, that the money supply increases. This has three direct effects:

● *Part* of the excess balances will be used to purchase foreign assets. This will therefore lead to an increase in the supply of pounds coming on to the foreign exchange markets.
● The excess supply of money in the domestic money market will push down the rate of interest. This will reduce the return on UK assets below that on foreign assets. This, like the first effect, will lead to an increased demand for foreign assets and thus an increased supply of pounds on the foreign exchange market.
● Speculators will anticipate that the higher supply of sterling will cause the

exchange rate to depreciate. They will therefore sell sterling and buy foreign currencies.

The effect of all three is to cause the exchange rate to depreciate.

The full effect of changes in the money supply

The effect of changes in the money supply on interest rates and exchange rates will in turn affect the level of activity in the economy. Assume that there is a rise in money supply. The sequence of events is as follows:

- A rise in money supply will lead to a fall in the rate of interest: this is necessary to restore equilibrium in the money market.
- The fall in the rate of interest will lead to a rise in investment and other forms of borrowing. (Since borrowing money will be cheaper, investment will cost less.)
- The fall in the domestic rate of interest and the resulting outflow of money from the country, plus the increased demand for foreign assets resulting from the increased money supply, will cause the exchange rate to depreciate.
- The fall in the exchange rate will mean that people abroad have to pay less for a pound. This will make UK exports cheaper and hence more will be sold. People in the UK will get less foreign currency for a pound. This will make imports more expensive and hence less will be purchased.
- The rise in investment and exports will mean increased injections into the circular flow of income (see section 25.6), and the fall in imports will mean reduced withdrawals from it. The effect will be a rise in aggregate demand and a resulting rise in national income and output, and possibly a rise in inflation too.

Just how much will aggregate demand, national income and inflation change as a result of changes in the money supply? This is a controversial issue, and one that we will examine in the next chapter. Then in Chapter 29 we will examine how the government can attempt to *control* the level of aggregate demand: both by changing the money supply and interest rates ('monetary policy') and by changing taxation and/or government expenditure ('fiscal policy').

SUMMARY

1 Money's main function is as a medium of exchange. In addition it is a means of storing wealth, a means of evaluation and a means of establishing the value of future claims and payments.

2a Banks aim to make profits, but they must also maintain sufficient liquidity. Liquid assets, however, tend to be unprofitable and profitable assets tend to be illiquid. Banks therefore hold a range of assets of varying degrees of profitability and liquidity.

2b Banks' liabilities include both sight and time deposits. They also include certificates of deposit and repos. Their assets include in descending order

of liquidity: notes and coin, balances with the Bank of England, market loans, bills of exchange, investments (government bonds and inter-bank investments) and advances to customers (the biggest item, including overdrafts, personal loans and mortgages).

2c The Bank of England is the UK's central bank. It issues notes; it acts as banker to the government, to the banks, to various overseas central banks and to certain private customers; it manages the government's borrowing programme; it provides liquidity to the banking sector; it operates the

SUMMARY

country's monetary and exchange rate policy.

2d The money market is the market in short-term deposits and loans. It consists of the discount and repo markets and the parallel money markets. The Bank of England operates in the discount and repo markets. By buying (rediscounting) bills and through gilt repos, it provides liquidity to the banks at its chosen rate of interest.

2e The parallel money markets consist of various markets in short-term finance between various financial institutions.

3a Money supply can be defined in a number of different ways, depending on what items are included. M0, the narrowest definition, only includes cash and banks' operational balances in the Bank of England. M2 is cash in circulation plus all retail deposits (including time deposits and building society deposits). M4 is M2 plus all wholesale bank and building society deposits.

3b Bank deposits are a major proportion of money supply (except M0). The expansion of bank deposits is the major element in the expansion of the money supply.

3c Bank deposits expand through a process of credit creation. If banks' liquid assets increase, they can be used as a base for increasing loans. When the loans are redeposited in banks, they form the base for yet more loans, and thus takes place a process of multiple credit expansion. The ratio of the increase of deposits to an expansion of banks' liquidity base is called the 'bank multiplier'. It is the inverse of the liquidity ratio.

3d In practice it is difficult to predict the precise amount by which money supply will expand if there is an increase in cash. The reasons are that banks may choose to hold a different liquidity ratio; customers may not take up all the credit on offer; there may be no simple liquidity ratio given the range of near money assets; and some of the extra cash may leak away into extra cash holdings by the public.

3e Money supply will rise if (a) banks choose to hold a lower liquidity ratio and thus create more credit for an existing amount of liquidity; (b) there is a total currency flow surplus; (c) the government runs a PSNCR and finances it by borrowing from the banking sector or from abroad.

3f Simple monetary theory assumes that the supply of money is independent of interest rates. In practice, a rise in interest rates will often lead to an increase in money supply. But conversely if the government raises interest rates, the supply of money may fall in response to a lower demand for money.

4a The three motives for holding money are the transactions, precautionary and speculative (or assets) motives.

4b The transactions-plus-precautionary demand for money (L_1) depends primarily on the level of national income, the frequency with which people are paid and institutional arrangements (such as the use of credit or debit cards). It also depends to some degree on the rate of interest. The transactions-plus-precautionary demand for very narrow money is more interest elastic than for broader money.

4c The speculative demand for money (L_2) depends on the rate of interest on financial assets. The higher the rate of interest, the lower will be the speculative demand for money. It also depends on people's expectations about future movements in asset prices and the rate of exchange. If asset prices are expected to rise or the exchange rate to fall, then people's speculative demand for money will be low.

5 Equilibrium in the money market is where the supply of money is equal to the demand. Equilibrium is achieved through changes in the interest rate and the exchange rate.

REVIEW QUESTIONS

1 Imagine that the banking system receives additional deposits of £100 million and that all the individual banks wish to retain their current liquidity ratio of 20 per cent.

(a) How much will banks choose to lend out initially?

(b) What will happen to banks' liabilities when the money that is lent out is spent and the recipients of it deposit it in their bank accounts?

(c) How much of these latest deposits will be lent out by the banks?

(d) By how much will total deposits (liabilities) eventually have risen, assuming that none of the additional liquidity is held outside the banking sector?

(e) How much of these are matched by (i) liquid assets; (ii) illiquid assets?

(f) What is the size of the bank multiplier?

(g) If one half of any additional liquidity is held outside the banking sector, by how much less will deposits have risen compared with (d) above?

2   What is meant by the terms *narrow money* and *broad money*? Does broad money fulfil all the functions of money?

3   Why do banks hold a range of assets of varying degrees of liquidity and profitability?

4   Define the term 'liquidity ratio'. How will changes in the liquidity ratio affect the process of credit creation? Why might a bank's liquidity ratio vary over time?

5   Why might the relationship between the demand for money and the rate of interest be an unstable one?

6   What effects will the following have on the equilibrium rate of interest? (You should consider which way the demand and/or supply curves of money shift.)

(a) Banks find that they have a higher liquidity ratio than they need.

(b) A rise in incomes.

(c) A growing belief that interest rates will rise from their current level.

28 Economic ideas – Keynesian and monetarist explanations of business activity

28.1 Background to the debate

There is no universal agreement among economists as to how the economy functions at a macroeconomic level. Instead there are various schools of thought.

These schools of thought see very different roles for the government in managing the economy. Some economists argue that the economy is more likely to achieve the various macroeconomic objectives if businesses are allowed to function pretty well freely, without hindrance from the government. Other economists argue that the government must intervene if macroeconomic objectives are to be met.

Although there are many of these schools, they are often grouped into two broad categories: *Keynesian* and *monetarist*.

In general, Keynesians argue that free markets will fail to meet the macroeconomic objectives of rapid economic growth and low unemployment with simultaneously low inflation and the avoidance of balance of payments problems. They thus argue that the government should intervene to manage the economy. This was the position taken by the economist John Maynard Keynes in the 1930s. The UK, like most of the rest of the world, was suffering from a deep and prolonged recession (the Great Depression). Keynes argued that the government should have intervened to expand aggregate demand, since the problem was essentially one of a lack of spending.

Monetarists generally argue that government intervention should be kept to a minimum. The role of government, they argue, is not to *manage* the economy, but simply to create a sound financial environment in which the free-enterprise economy can flourish. This means essentially two things:

- Ensuring that the money supply does not expand too rapidly. This is the way of keeping inflation in check.
- Deregulation. Government intervention, according to monetarists, normally does more harm than good. Thus governments should adopt a 'hands-off' approach to industry and commerce.

A more extreme version of this school of thought is the 'new classical' school. New classicists argue that free markets work very well indeed in achieving the macroeconomic goals.

Most of the debate, then, between Keynesians and monetarists centres on the working of the market mechanism: just how well or how badly it will achieve the various macroeconomic objectives. There are three major areas of disagreement: (a) how flexible are wages and prices, (b) how flexible is aggregate supply and (c) what is the role of expectations. Let us examine each in turn.

Issue 1: The flexibility of prices and wages

Monetarists argue that prices and wage rates are relatively flexible. Markets tend to clear, they say, and clear fairly quickly.

Disequilibrium unemployment (real-wage and demand-deficient unemployment) is therefore likely to be fairly small, according to their view, and normally only a temporary, short-run phenomenon. Any long-term unemployment will be equilibrium (or 'natural') unemployment. To cure this, they argue, encouragement must be given to the free play of market forces: to a rapid response of both firms and labour to changes in market demand and supply, to a more rapid dissemination of information on job vacancies, and generally to greater labour mobility, both geographical and occupational.

Keynesians reject the assumption of highly flexible prices and wages. If there is a deficiency of demand for labour in the economy, during a recession say, there will be a resistance from unions to cuts in real wages and certainly to cuts in money wages. Any cuts that do occur will be insufficient to eliminate the disequilibrium and will anyway only serve further to reduce aggregate demand so that workers have less money to spend. The aggregate demand for labour curve in Figure 25.3 (on page 529) would shift to the left.

The prices of goods may also be inflexible to changes in demand. As industry has become more concentrated and more monopolistic over the years, firms, it is argued, have become less likely to respond to a general fall in demand by cutting prices. Instead, they are likely to build up stocks if they think the recession is temporary, or cut production and hence employment if they think the recession will persist.

Thus markets cannot be relied upon automatically to correct disequilibria and hence cure disequilibrium unemployment.

Issue 2: The flexibility of aggregate supply

The question here is: how responsive is national output (i.e. aggregate supply), and hence also employment, to a change in aggregate demand?

Monetarists argue that aggregate supply does not respond, except perhaps in the short run, to changes in aggregate demand. Aggregate supply is determined *independently* of demand. It depends on the quantity and productivity of factors of production, *not* on the level of aggregate demand. An expansion of aggregate demand will merely lead to (demand-pull) inflation. It cannot lead to a long-term growth in output and employment. Likewise a contraction in aggregate demand will not lead to a long-term fall in output and a rise in unemployment. It will merely lead to a fall in prices.

If the government wants to expand aggregate supply and get more rapid economic growth, it is no good, they argue, concentrating on demand. Instead, governments should concentrate directly on *supply* by encouraging enterprise and competition, and generally by encouraging markets to operate more freely. For this reason, this approach is often labelled **supply-side economics.**

Keynesians argue that rises in aggregate demand *will* cause aggregate supply to rise, and if the rise in aggregate demand is sufficient, unemployment will fall. This rise in output and employment can persist into the long run if governments maintain a high and expanding level of aggregate demand. Buoyant and expanding markets for their products will encourage firms to produce up to

definition
Supply-side economics An approach which focuses directly on aggregate supply and how to shift the aggregate supply curve outwards.

capacity, to employ more people and to invest for the future, thus increasing capacity further.

However, these conditions will not be achieved, they argue, if the government pursues a non-interventionist, *laissez-faire* policy. The government instead must seek to control aggregate demand, to ensure that it continues to grow, and at a steady, non-fluctuating rate.

But will an expansion of aggregate demand also be inflationary? Some argue that the effects on inflation can be minimal. If a rise in aggregate demand causes a real growth in output, and productivity, workers can have real wage rises without it being inflationary. Others argue that inflation could be quite high with such policies and get worse over time as people come to expect ever bigger rises in their standard of living and/or ever bigger rises in prices. (See issue 3 below.)

All these arguments centre on the nature of the aggregate supply curve (*AS*). Three different *AS* curves are shown in Figure 28.1. The *AD* curves are drawn as downward sloping, showing that the higher the level of prices, the less will people purchase for a given level of money supply in the economy. In each of the three cases, it is assumed that the government now raises aggregate demand, by, say, increasing the amount of money in the economy. Aggregate demand shifts from AD_1 to AD_2. The effect on prices and output will depend on the shape of the *AS* curve.

Monetarists argue that there will be little or no effect on output (certainly in the long run, and for new classicists in the short run too). Instead, the rise in aggregate demand will simply lead to a rise in prices. They therefore envisage an *AS* curve like that in diagram (a).

Keynesians argue that a rise in aggregate demand will lead to a rise in output. In the extreme case, prices will not rise at all. In this case the *AS* curve is like that in diagram (b). Output will rise to Y_2 with the price level remaining at *P*.

It is more likely, however, that both prices and output will rise. In this case, the short-term curve will be like that in diagram (c). If there is plenty of slack in the economy – idle machines, unemployed labour, etc. – output will rise a lot and prices only a little. But as slack is taken up, the *AS* curve becomes steeper. Firms, finding it increasingly difficult to raise output in the short run, simply respond to a rise in demand by raising prices. In the longer term, if increased

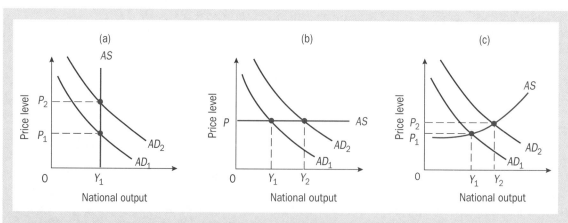

Figure 28.1
Different aggregate supply curves

demand leads to more investment and increased capacity (potential output), the short-run *AS* curve will shift to the right. A long-term *AS* curve, in this view, would be more elastic than the short-term one.

Issue 3: The role of expectations in the working of the market

How quickly and how fully will individuals and firms anticipate changes in prices and changes in output? How are their expectations formed and how accurate are they? What effect do these expectations have? This is the third major controversial topic.

Monetarists argue that people's expectations adjust fully and fairly rapidly to changing economic circumstances (new classicists argue that the response is instantaneous). They emphasise the role of expectations of *price* changes.

If aggregate demand expands, they argue, people will expect higher prices. Workers will realise that the apparently higher wages they are offered are an illusion. The higher wages are 'eaten up' by higher prices. Thus workers are not encouraged to work longer hours and unemployed workers are not encouraged to take on employment more readily. Likewise firms realise that any increased demand for their products is an illusion. Very soon all firms will raise their prices in response to the demand increase, and given that firms' costs are rising due to higher wages and the higher prices of raw materials, machinery, etc., their price rises will fully choke off the extra demand. There will be no increase in sales and hence no increase in output and employment.

Thus, they argue, increased aggregate demand merely fuels inflation and can do no more than give a very temporary boost to output and employment. If anything, the higher inflation could damage business confidence and thus worsen long-term output and employment growth by discouraging investment.

Keynesians argue that the formation of expectations is more complex than this, and whether people expect an increase in demand to be fully matched by inflation depends on the current state of the economy and how any increase in demand is introduced.

If there is a lot of slack in the economy – if unemployment is very high and there are many idle resources – and if an increase in demand is in the form, say, of direct government spending on production (on roads, hospitals, sewers and other infrastructure), then output and employment may quickly rise. Here the effect of expectations may be beneficial. Rather than expecting inflation from the increased demand, firms may expect faster growth and an expansion of markets. As a result they may choose to invest, and this in turn will produce further growth in output and employment.

Views on expectations therefore parallel views on aggregate supply. Monetarists argue that a boost to demand will not produce extra output and employment (certainly in the long run): aggregate supply is inelastic (as in Figure 28.1(a)) and therefore the higher demand will merely fuel expectations of inflation. Keynesians argue that a boost to aggregate demand will increase aggregate supply and employment. Firms will expect this and therefore produce more.

Policy implications

Generally, then, monetarists tend to favour a policy of *laissez-faire*. At most, governments should intervene to remove hindrances to the free and efficient operation of markets: for example, by legislation to reduce the power of trade unions. This way, they argue, disequilibrium unemployment will be removed and the greatest opportunity given for long-term growth in output and the reduction in equilibrium unemployment. Any intervention by government to boost demand will merely be inflationary and will thus damage long-term growth and employment.

In contrast, Keynesians argue that a gap between actual and potential output, and the accompanying disequilibrium unemployment, may persist for many years and be very great. The answer is for active government intervention to ensure a sufficient level of aggregate demand. On the other hand, the government must also ensure that actual output does not grow too fast, otherwise inflation will result. If output does begin to grow too rapidly, the government should intervene to dampen aggregate demand.

In the following sections we examine the main arguments of Keynesians and monetarists. We begin with the Keynesian theory of output and employment determination: the theory that output and employment depend on the level of aggregate demand.

28.2 The Keynesian theory of national income determination

The Keynesian analysis of output and employment can be explained most simply in terms of the circular flow of income diagram. Figure 28.2 shows a simplified version of the circular flow with injections entering at just one point, and likewise withdrawals leaving at just one point (this simplification does not affect the argument).

If injections (J) do not equal withdrawals (W), a state of disequilibrium exists. What will bring them back into equilibrium is a change in national income and employment.

Start with a state of equilibrium, where injections equal withdrawals. If there is now a rise in injections – say, firms decide to invest more – aggregate demand ($C_d + J$) will be higher. Firms will respond to this increased demand by using more labour and other resources and thus paying out more incomes (Y) to households. Household consumption will rise and so firms will sell more.

Firms will respond by producing more, and thus using more labour and other

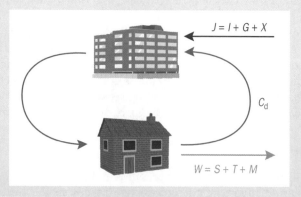

Figure 28.2
The circular flow of income

$J = I + G + X$

C_d

$W = S + T + M$

resources. Household incomes will rise again. Consumption and hence production will rise again, and so on. There will thus be a multiplied rise in incomes and employment. This is known as the **multiplier effect**.

The process, however, does not go on for ever. Each time household incomes rise, households save more, pay more taxes and buy more imports. In other words, withdrawals rise. When withdrawals have risen to match the increase in injections, equilibrium will be restored and national income and employment will stop rising. The process can be summarised as follows:

$$J > W \rightarrow Y\uparrow \rightarrow W\uparrow \text{ until } J = W$$

Similarly, an initial fall in injections (or rise in withdrawals) will lead to a multiplied fall in national income and employment:

$$J < W \rightarrow Y\downarrow \rightarrow W\downarrow \text{ until } J = W$$

Thus equilibrium in the circular flow of income can be at *any* level of output and employment.

If aggregate demand is too low, there will be a recession and high unemployment. In Figure 28.3, it is assumed that there is some potential level of national income and output (Y_p), at which there would be full employment of resources. This represents a limit to output. If aggregate demand were initially at AD_1, equilibrium would be at Y_1, considerably below the full-employment potential. In this case, argue Keynesians, governments should intervene to boost aggregate demand. For example, a rise in aggregate demand to AD_2 would raise national income to Y_2, and so on. As Y_p is approached, however, so the effect of rises in aggregate demand will increasingly be felt in higher prices.

Identifying the equilibrium level of national income

Withdrawals and injections and their relationship with national income can be plotted on a diagram. This is shown in Figure 28.4. National income is plotted on the horizontal axis. Withdrawals and injections are plotted on the vertical axis.

As national income rises, so withdrawals (saving, taxes and imports) will rise. Thus the withdrawals curve slopes upwards. But the amount that businesses

definition

Multiplier effect
An initial increase in aggregate demand of £xm leads to an eventual rise in national income that is greater than £xm.

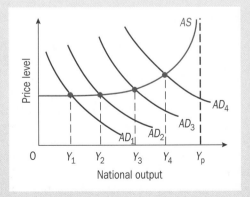

Figure 28.3
The effects of increases in aggregate demand on national output

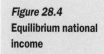

Figure 28.4
Equilibrium national income

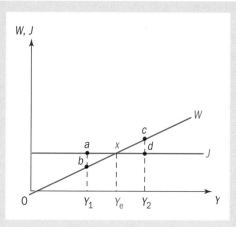

plan to invest, that the government plans to spend and that overseas residents plan to import from the UK (i.e. UK exports) are all only slightly affected by the current level of UK national income. Thus injections, for simplicity, are assumed to be independent of national income. The injections line is therefore drawn as a horizontal straight line. (This does not mean that injections are constant over time: merely that they are constant with respect to national income. If injections rise, the whole line will shift upwards.)

Withdrawals equal injections at point x in the diagram. Equilibrium national income is thus Y_e. If national income were below this level, say at Y_1, injections would exceed withdrawals (by an amount $a - b$). This additional net expenditure injected into the economy would encourage firms to produce more. This in turn would cause national income to rise. But as people's incomes rose, so they would save more, pay more taxes and buy more imports. In other words, withdrawals would rise. There would be a movement up along the W curve. This process would continue until $W = J$ at point x.

If, on the other hand, national income were initially at Y_2, withdrawals would exceed injections (by an amount $c - d$). This deficiency of demand would cause production and hence national income to fall. As it did so, there would be a movement down along the W curve until again point x was reached.

The multiplier

When injections rise this will cause national income to rise. But by how much? The answer is that there will be a *multiplied* rise in national income: i.e. it will rise by more than the rise in injections.

Assume that injections rise from J_1 to J_2 in Figure 28.5. Equilibrium will move from point a to point b. Income will thus rise from Y_{e1} to Y_{e2}. But this rise in income (ΔY) is bigger than the rise in injections (ΔJ) that caused it. This is the multiplier effect. The multiplier is therefore given by: $\Delta Y/\Delta J$. Thus if a £10 million rise in injections caused a £30 million rise in national income, the multiplier would be 3 (i.e. £30m/£10m).

It can be seen that the size of the multiplier depends on the *slope of the W curve*. The shallower the slope, the bigger will be the multiplier: i.e. the bigger will be the rise in national income from any given rise in injections. The slope

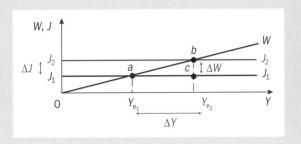

Figure 28.5
The multiplier: a shift in injections

of the W curve is given by $\Delta W/\Delta Y$. This is the proportion of a rise in national income that is withdrawn, and is known as the **marginal propensity to withdraw** (mpw).

The point here is that the less is withdrawn each time money circulates, the more will be recirculated and hence the bigger will be the rise in national income. The size of the multiplier thus varies inversely with the size of the mpw. The bigger the mpw, the smaller the multiplier; the smaller the mpw, the bigger the multiplier. In fact the **multiplier formula** is simply the inverse of the mpw:

Multiplier $= 1/mpw$

Thus if the mpw were ¼, the multiplier would be 4. So if J increased by £10 million, Y would increase by £40 million.

But why is the multiplier given by the formula $1/mpw$? This can be illustrated by referring to Figure 28.5. The mpw is the slope of the W line. In the diagram this is given by the amount $(b - c)/(c - a)$. The multiplier is defined as $\Delta Y/\Delta J$. In the diagram this is the amount $(a - c)/(b - c)$. But this is merely the inverse of the mpw. Thus the multiplier equals $1/mpw$.

The Keynesian analysis of unemployment and inflation

'Full-employment' national income

In simple Keynesian theory it is assumed that there will be a maximum level of national output, and hence real income, that can be obtained at any one time. If the equilibrium level of income is at this level, there will be no deficiency of aggregate demand and hence no disequilibrium unemployment. This level of income is referred to as the **full-employment level of national income** (Y_F). (In practice, there would still be some unemployment at this level because of the existence of equilibrium unemployment – structural, frictional and seasonal.)

The deflationary gap

If the equilibrium level of national income (Y_e) is below the full-employment level (Y_F), there will be excess capacity in the economy and hence demand-deficient unemployment. This situation is illustrated in Figure 28.6(a). If national income is to be raised from Y_e to Y_F, injections will have to be raised and/or withdrawals lowered so as to close the gap $a - b$. This gap is known as the **deflationary gap**.

Note that the size of the deflationary gap is *less* than the amount by which Y_e falls short of Y_F. This is another illustration of the multiplier. If injections are

definition

Marginal propensity to withdraw
The proportion of an increase in national income that is withdrawn from the circular flow: $mpw = \Delta W/\Delta Y$, where $mpw = mps + mpt + mpm$.

definition

(Injections) multiplier formula
The formula for the multiplier is $k = 1/mpw$ or $1/(1 - mpc_d)$.

definition

Full-employment level of national income
The level of national income at which there is no deficiency of demand.

definition

Deflationary gap
The shortfall of injections below withdrawals at the full-employment level of national income.

Figure 28.6
(a) Deflationary gap
(b) Inflationary gap

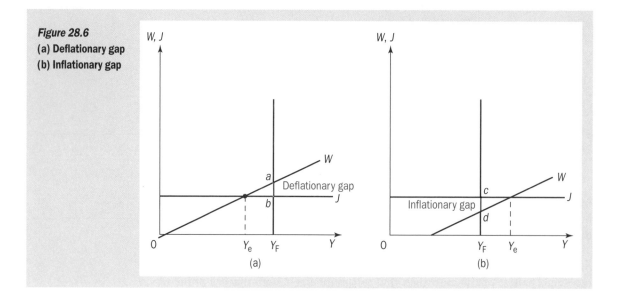

(a)

(b)

raised by $a - b$, national income will rise by $Y_F - Y_e$. The multiplier is thus given by:

$$\frac{Y_F - Y_e}{a - b}$$

The inflationary gap

If, at the full-employment level of income, national expenditure *exceeds* national income, there will be a problem of excess demand. Y_e will be above Y_F. The problem is that Y_F represents a real ceiling to output. In the short run, national income *cannot* expand beyond this point. Y_e cannot be reached. The result will be demand-pull inflation.

This situation is illustrated in Figure 28.6(b). If withdrawals were raised and/or injections lowered so as to close the gap $c - d$ (known as the **inflationary gap**, then the excess demand would be eliminated, and Y_e would equal Y_F. This can be done by a deliberate government policy of deflation. This could be either a deflationary *fiscal* policy of lowering government expenditure or raising taxes, or a deflationary *monetary* policy of reducing the amount of money in the economy and/or deliberately raising interest rates.

Keynesians thus advocate an active policy of demand management: raising aggregate demand (for example, by raising government expenditure or lowering taxes) to close a deflationary gap, and reducing aggregate demand to close an inflationary gap.

definition

Inflationary gap
The excess of injections over withdrawals at the full-employment level of national income.

Unemployment and inflation at the same time

The simple analysis of deflationary and inflationary gaps implies that the aggregate supply curve looks like AS_1 in Figure 28.7. Up to Y_F, output and employment can rise with no rise in prices at all. The deflationary gap is being closed. At Y_F no further rises in output are possible. Any further rise in aggregate

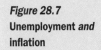

Figure 28.7
Unemployment *and*
inflation

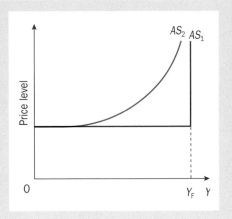

demand is entirely reflected in higher prices. An inflationary gap opens. In other words, this implies that either inflation *or* unemployment can occur, but not both simultaneously.

Keynesians make two important qualifications to this analysis to explain the occurrence of both unemployment *and* inflation at the same time.

First, there are *other* types of inflation and unemployment not caused by an excess or deficiency of aggregate demand: for example, cost-push and expectations-generated inflation; frictional and structural unemployment.

Thus, even if a government could manipulate national income so as to get Y_e and Y_F to coincide, this would not eliminate all inflation and unemployment – only demand-pull inflation and demand-deficient unemployment. Keynesians argue, therefore, that governments should use a whole package of policies, each tailored to the specific type of problem. But certainly one of the most important of these policies will be the management of aggregate demand.

Second, not all firms operate with the same degree of slack. This may be due to different policies of firms over how much spare capacity to maintain and how many stocks to carry. It may be due to shifts in consumer demand away from some firms and towards others.

The implication of this is that a rise in aggregate demand can lead to *both* a reduction in unemployment *and* a rise in prices: some firms respond to the rise in demand by taking up slack and hence increasing output; other firms, having little or no slack, respond by raising prices; others do both. Similarly, labour markets have different degrees of slack and therefore the rise in demand will lead to various mixes of higher wages and lower unemployment.

Thus the *AS* curve will look like AS_2 in Figure 28.7.

The Phillips curve

The relationship between inflation and unemployment was examined by A.W. Phillips in 1958. He showed the statistical relationship between wage inflation and unemployment in the UK from 1861 to 1957. With wage inflation ($\dot{W}$) on the vertical axis and the unemployment rate (U) on the horizontal axis, a scatter of points was obtained. Each point represented the observation for a particular year. The curve that best fitted the scatter has become known as the

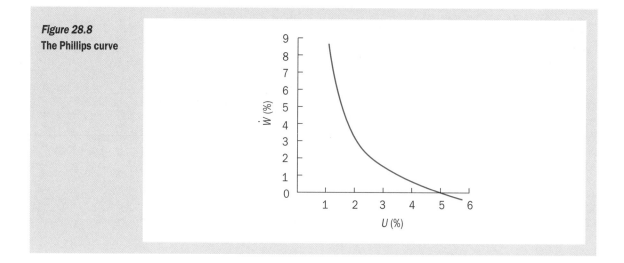

Figure 28.8
The Phillips curve

Phillips curve. It is illustrated in Figure 28.8 and shows an inverse relationship between inflation and unemployment.

Given that wage increases over the period were approximately 2 per cent above price increases (made possible by increases in labour productivity), a similar-shaped, but lower curve could be plotted showing the relationship between *price* inflation and unemployment.

The curve has often been used to illustrate the effects of changes in aggregate demand. When aggregate demand rose (relative to potential output), inflation rose and unemployment fell: there was an upward movement along the curve. When aggregate demand fell, there was a downward movement along the curve.

The Phillips curve was bowed in to the origin. The usual explanation for this is that as aggregate demand expanded, at first there would be plenty of surplus labour, which could be employed to meet the extra demand without the need to raise wage rates very much. But as labour became increasingly scarce, firms would find that they had to offer increasingly higher wage rates to obtain the labour they required, and the position of trade unions would be increasingly strengthened.

The *position* of the Phillips curve depended on *non*-demand factors causing inflation and unemployment: frictional and structural unemployment; and cost-push, structural and expectations-generated inflation. If any of these non-demand factors changed so as to raise inflation or unemployment, the curve would shift outward to the right. The relative stability of the curve, over the 100 years or so observed by Phillips, suggested that these non-demand factors had changed little.

The Phillips curve seemed to present governments with a simple policy choice. They could trade off inflation against unemployment. Lower unemployment could be bought at the cost of higher inflation, and vice versa. Unfortunately, the experience since the late 1960s has suggested that no such simple relationship exists beyond the short run. Both inflation and unemployment were generally worse in the 1970s, 1980s and early to mid-1990s than in the 1950s and 1960s, but have both improved in recent years.

28.3 Keynesian analysis of cyclical fluctuations in unemployment

and inflation

Keynesians blame fluctuations in output and employment on fluctuations in aggregate demand. Theirs is therefore a 'demand-side' explanation of the business cycle. In the upturn (phase 1), aggregate demand starts to rise (see Figure 25.1 on page 521). It rises rapidly in the expansionary phase (phase 2). It then slows down and may start to fall in the peaking-out phase (phase 3). It then falls or remains relatively stagnant in the recession (phase 4).

Keynesians seek to explain why aggregate demand fluctuates, and then to devise appropriate stabilisation policies to iron out these fluctuations. A more stable economy, they argue, will provide a better climate for investment and the growth of both individual businesses and the economy as a whole.

Instability of investment: the accelerator

One of the major factors contributing to the ups and downs of the trade cycle is the instability of investment.

In a recession, investment in new plant and equipment can all but disappear. After all, what is the point of investing in additional capacity if you cannot even sell what you are currently producing? When an economy begins to recover from a recession, however, and confidence returns, investment can rise very rapidly. In percentage terms the rise in investment may be *several times that of the rise in income*. When the growth of the economy slows down, however, investment can fall dramatically.

The point is that investment depends not so much on the *level* of national income and consumer demand, as on their *rate of change*. The reason is that investment (except for replacement investment) is to provide *additional* capacity, and thus depends on how much demand has risen, not on its level. But growth rates change by much more than the level of output. For example, if economic growth is 1 per cent in 2001 and 2 per cent in 2002, then in 2002 output has gone up by 2 per cent, but growth has gone up by 100 per cent! (i.e. it has doubled). Thus changes in investment tend to be much more dramatic than changes in national income. This is known as the **accelerator theory**.

These fluctuations in investment, being injections into the circular flow, will then have a multiplied effect on national income and will thus magnify the upswings and downswings of the business cycle.

Fluctuations in stocks

Firms hold stocks of finished goods. These stocks tend to fluctuate with the course of the business cycle, and these fluctuations in stocks themselves contribute to fluctuations in output.

Imagine an economy that is recovering from a recession. At first, firms may be cautious about increasing production. Doing so may involve taking on more labour or making additional investment. Firms may not want to make these commitments if the recovery could soon peter out. They may therefore run down their stocks rather than increase output. Initially, the recovery from recession will be slow.

> **definition**
>
> **Accelerator theory**
> The *level* of investment depends on the *rate of change* of national income, and the result tends to be subject to substantial fluctuations.

BOX 28.1

Business expectations and their effect on investment
Recent European experience

In the boom years of the late 1980s, business optimism was widespread throughout Europe. Investment was correspondingly high, and with it there was a high rate of economic growth.

Surveys of European business expectations in the early 1990s, however, told a very different story. Pessimism was rife. Europe was in the grip of a recession (see Table (a)). Growth slowed right down and output actually fell in 1993. Along with this decline in growth and deteriorating levels of business and consumer confidence, there was a significant fall in investment.

Not only was the total level of investment falling, but the proportion of that investment used to expand capacity was also falling (see Figure (a)). By contrast, the proportion of investment devoted to 'rationalisation' schemes had risen: firms were increasingly having to look for ways of cutting their costs through restructuring their operations. One of the consequences of this was a growth in structural unemployment (as well as in demand-deficient unemployment).

But whereas these reductions in costs, and corresponding increases in labour productivity, provided a partial solution to the short-run difficulties faced by firms during the recession, in the long run productivity gains became increasingly difficult to achieve without investment in new capacity. This suggested that it was vital for firms to have confidence that their market *would* expand.

So were there any signs that confidence would pick up? As Table (b) and Figure (b) show, pessimism began to decrease after 1993, but it was not until the last quarter of 1994 that the average industrial confidence indicator for the EU as a whole became positive and the consumer confidence indicator. (The figures in the table show the percentage excess of confident over pessimistic replies to business questionnaires: a negative figure meaning that there was a higher percentage of pessimistic responses.) Indeed, after mid-1995, the recovery in Europe began to slow down, and as a result both industrial and consumer confidence waned. The growth in investment slowed from 4.0 per cent in 1995 to 1.4 per cent in 1996.

Since 1996, each year has seen EU growth rates above 2 per cent (although growth temporarily fell below this in the winter of 1998/9). This improved growth performance has been mirrored in improving consumer confidence and, except for 1999, improving industrial confidence. Between 1998 and 2000 investment growth was over 5 per cent per year.

(a) Macroeconomic indicators for the EU countries

	1989	1990	1991	1992	1993	1994	1995	1996	1997	1998	1999	2000
GDP growth (%)	3.5	3.0	1.6	1.1	−0.5	3.0	2.4	1.8	2.5	2.7	2.3	3.4
Investment (% change)	7.1	4.0	−0.2	−0.9	−6.4	2.4	4.0	1.4	3.3	6.0	5.5	5.3
Unemployment (%)	9.0	8.4	8.8	9.4	10.7	11.1	10.7	10.9	10.6	9.9	9.2	8.4
Inflation (%)	5.2	5.7	5.1	4.5	3.6	3.1	3.0	2.7	1.7	1.3	1.2	2.1
Net government borrowing (% of GDP)	−2.6	−3.9	−4.4	−5.2	−6.4	−5.7	−5.4	−4.1	−2.4	−1.5	−0.7	1.2
Current account balance (% of GDP)	−0.1	−0.5	−1.1	−1.1	0.1	0.3	0.6	0.9	1.4	0.8	0.2	−0.3

Source: Based on *European Economy Annual Report*, various issues and *European Economy Supplement A, October 2000* (http://europa.eu.int/comm/economy_finance/document/eesuppal/a2000autumnforecast_en.pdf) (Commission of the European Communities).

(b) Industrial confidence indicator

Country	Trough 1991–5	Peak 1988–91	1989	1991	1993	1995	1996	1997	1998	1999	2000
Belgium	−33	4	0	−15	−29	−9	−18	−3	−8	−9	2
Denmark	−18	5	4	−8	−12	6	−9	6	−1	−13	6
France	−41	12	8	−20	−35	−2	−18	−5	5	−2	12
Germany	−36	11	5	0	−34	−3	−21	−10	−5	−14	−2
Ireland	−22	14	10	−9	−13	8	−1	3	3	5	10
Italy	−22	13	8	−13	−17	6	−12	0	0	−4	11
Netherlands	−12	3	1	−5	−10	4	−2	3	2	0	4
UK	−40	21	−2	−32	−11	3	−5	−1	−16	−14	−7
EU	−28	6	4	−14	−26	0	−14	−4	−3	−8	4

Source: Based on *European Economy Supplement B* (Commission of the European Communities) various years.

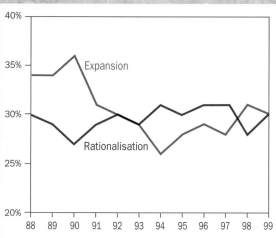

(a) Purposes of industrial investment
(% of total investment)

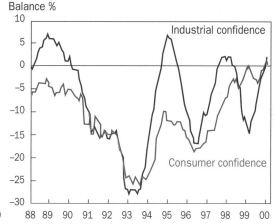

(b) Confidence indicators in the EU

Source: *European Economy* (Commission of the European Communities).

Questions

1 How is the existence of surveys of business confidence likely to affect firms' expectations and actions?

2 Why, if the growth in output slows down (but is still *positive*), is investment likely to *fall* (i.e. the growth in investment be *negative*)? If you look at Table (a) you will see that this happened in 1991 and 1992. (See section on the accelerator on page 609.)

If the recovery continues, however, firms will start to gain more confidence and will increase their production. Also they will find that their stocks have got rather low and will need building up. This gives a further boost to production, and for a time the growth in output will exceed the growth in demand. This extra growth in output will then, via the multiplier, lead to a further increase in demand.

Once stocks have been built up again, the growth in output will slow down to match the growth in demand. This slowing down in output will, via the accelerator and multiplier, contribute to the ending of the expansionary phase of the business cycle.

As the economy slows down, firms may for a time be prepared to carry on producing and build up stocks. The increase in stocks thus cushions the effect of falling demand on output and employment.

If the recession continues, firms will be unwilling to go on building up stocks. But as firms attempt to reduce their stocks back to the desired level, production will fall *below* the level of sales, despite the fact that sales themselves are lower. This could therefore lead to a dramatic fall in output and, via the multiplier, to an even bigger fall in sales.

Eventually, once stocks have been run down to the minimum, production will have to rise again to match the level of sales. This will contribute to a recovery and the whole cycle will start again.

Determinants of the course of the business cycle

Keynesians seek to answer two key questions: why do booms and recessions last for several months or even years, and why do they eventually come to an end? Let us examine each in turn.

Why do booms and recessions persist for a period of time?

Time lags. It takes time for changes in injections and withdrawals to be fully reflected in changes in national income, output and employment. The multiplier process takes time. Moreover, consumers, firms and government may not all respond immediately to new situations. Their responses are spread out over a period of time.

'Bandwagon' effects. Once the economy starts expanding, expectations become buoyant. People think ahead and adjust their expenditure behaviour: they consume and invest more *now*. Likewise in a recession, a mood of pessimism may set in. The effect is cumulative. The multiplier and accelerator interact: they feed on each other.

Why do booms and recessions come to an end? What determines the turning points?

Ceilings and floors. Actual output can go on growing more rapidly than potential output only as long as there is slack in the economy. As full employment is approached and as more and more firms reach full capacity, so a ceiling to output will be reached.

There is a basic minimum level of consumption that people tend to maintain. During a recession, people may not buy much in the way of luxury and durable goods, but they will continue to buy food and other basic goods. There is thus a floor to consumption.

The industries supplying these basic goods will need to maintain their level of replacement investment. Also there will always be some minimum investment demand as firms, in order to survive competition, need to install the latest equipment. There is thus a floor to investment too.

Echo effects. Durable consumer goods and capital equipment may last several years, but eventually they will need replacing. The replacement of goods and capital purchased in a previous boom may help to bring a recession to an end.

The accelerator. For investment to continue rising, consumer demand must rise at a *faster and faster* rate. If this does not happen, investment will fall back and the boom will break.

Random shocks. National or international political, social or natural events can affect the mood and attitudes of firms, governments and consumers, and thus affect aggregate demand.

Changes in government policy. In a boom, a government may become most worried by inflation and balance of payments deficits and thus pursue contractionary policies. In a recession, it may become most worried by unemployment and lack of growth and thus pursue expansionary policies. These government policies, if successful, will bring about a turning point in the cycle.

Keynesians argue that governments should attempt to reduce cyclical fluctuations by the use of active stabilisation policies. A more stable economy will provide a better climate for long-term investment, which will lead to faster growth in both potential and actual output. The policy most favoured by Keynesians for stabilising the economy is fiscal policy. This is considered in section 29.1.

28.4 The role of money in Keynesian and monetarist models

Monetarists argue that inflation can be attributed entirely to increases in the money supply. The faster money supply expands, the higher will be the rate of inflation. Keynesians see a much looser association between money and prices. The debate can best be understood in terms of the **quantity theory of money**. The theory is simply that the level of prices in the economy depends on the quantity of money.

A development of the quantity theory is the *equation of exchange*.

The equation of exchange

The **equation of exchange** shows the relationship between national expenditure and national income. This identity may be expressed as follows:

$$MV = PQ$$

M is the supply of money in the economy. V is the **velocity of circulation**. This is the average number of times per year that money is spent on buying goods

> **definition**
>
> **Quantity theory of money**
> The price level (P) is directly related to the quantity of money in the economy (M).

> **definition**
>
> **The equation of exchange**
> $MV = PQ$. The total level of spending on GDP (MV) equals the total value of goods and services produced (PQ) that go to make up GDP.

> **definition**
>
> **Velocity of circulation**
> The number of times annually that money on average is spent on goods and services that make up GDP.

and services that have been produced in the economy that year (national output). P is the average level of prices. Q is the quantity of national output sold in that year.

PQ will thus be the money value of national output sold (i.e. GDP: see appendix to Chapter 25). MV will be the total spending on national output, and therefore must be equal to PQ. For example, if money supply was £10 billion, and money as it passed from one person to another was spent on average 8 times a year on national output, then total spending (MV) would be £80 billion a year. And thus the value of goods sold (PQ) must also equal £80 billion.

The equation of exchange (or 'quantity equation') is true by definition. MV is *necessarily* equal to PQ because of the way the terms are defined. What a change in M does to P, however, is a matter of debate. The controversy centres on whether and how V and Q are affected by changes in the money supply (M). The way in which a change in M affects V and Q will determine what happens to P.

The velocity of circulation (V)

Monetarists argue that in the long run V is determined *totally independently* of the money supply (M). Thus an increase in M will leave V unaffected and bring a corresponding change in expenditure (MV):

$$M{\uparrow}, \bar{V} \to MV{\uparrow}$$

where the bar over the V term means that it is exogenously determined: i.e. determined *independently* of M.

Monetarists therefore claim that monetary policy is an extremely powerful weapon for controlling aggregate demand.

Keynesians argue that V tends to vary inversely with M, but also rather unpredictably. An increase in money supply will not necessarily have much effect on spending; instead, people may simply increase their holdings of idle speculative balances, with a corresponding decline in the speed with which money circulates (V). How much extra idle balances people hold will depend on their expectations of changes in interest rates, prices and exchange rates. Since expectations are difficult to predict, the amount by which V will fall is also difficult to predict:

$$M{\uparrow} \to V{\downarrow} \; (?) \to MV?$$

Keynesians therefore claim that monetary policy is an extremely unreliable weapon for controlling aggregate demand.

The quantity of national output (Q)

Monetarists argue that aggregate supply is inelastic in the long run (see Figure 28.1(a)), and therefore output (Q) is determined independently of aggregate demand. Any rise in MV will be totally reflected in a rise in prices (P):

$$MV{\uparrow} \to P{\uparrow}, \bar{Q}$$

The stock of money therefore determines the price level, and the rate of increase in money supply determines the rate of inflation. Thus monetary policy is the means of controlling inflation, and in the long run, control of the money supply will not affect output (Q) and employment.

Keynesians argue that aggregate supply is relatively elastic except when full employment is approached (see Figure 28.1(b) and (c)). Thus Q is variable. A tight monetary policy, to the extent that it does affect aggregate demand, is likely to reduce Q as well as P, especially when there is resistance from monopolistic firms and unions to price and wage cuts:

$$MV\downarrow \rightarrow P\downarrow \text{ and } Q\downarrow$$

If monetary policy is successful in reducing aggregate demand, it can lead to a lasting recession.

The amount that changes in money supply affect aggregate demand depends on the variability of V. This is the subject of this section. The effect of changes in aggregate demand on national output depends on the variability of Q. That is the subject of section 28.5.

The Keynesian view

As we saw in the last chapter, changes in money supply affect aggregate demand through the following mechanism:

1   A rise in money supply will lead to a fall in the rate of interest.
2   (a) The fall in the rate of interest will lead to a rise in investment and other forms of borrowing.
2   (b) The fall in the domestic rate of interest and the resulting outflow of money from the country, plus the increased demand for foreign assets resulting from the increased money supply, will cause the exchange rate to depreciate.
3   The fall in the exchange rate will cause an increased demand for exports and a decreased demand for imports.
4   The rise in investment and exports, and the fall in imports will mean a rise in aggregate demand and a resulting rise in national income and output, and possibly a rise in inflation too.

However, according to Keynesians, stages 1–3 are unreliable, and often weak.

Problems with stage 1: the money–interest link

According to Keynesians, the speculative demand for money is highly responsive to changes in interest rates. The speculative demand can be quite large. Keynesians point to the large sums of money that move around the money market as firms and financial institutions anticipate changes in interest rates. Thus only a small fall in interest rates may be necessary to persuade people to hold all the extra money as idle balances.

A more serious Keynesian criticism is that the demand for money is *unstable*. People hold speculative balances of money when they anticipate that interest rates will rise (security prices fall). But it is not just the current interest rate that affects people's expectations of the future direction of interest rates. Many factors could affect such expectations, such as changes in foreign interest rates, changes in exchange rates, statements of government intentions on economic policy, good or bad industrial news, or newly published figures on inflation or money supply. With an unstable demand for money it is difficult to predict the effect on interest rates of a change in money supply.

Problems with stage 2(a): the interest rate–investment link

The problem here is that investment may be insensitive to changes in interest rates. Businesses are more likely to be influenced in their decision to invest by predictions of the future buoyancy of markets. Interest rates do have some effect on businesses, investment decisions, but the effect is unpredictable, depending on the confidence of investors.

Problems with stage 2(b): the interest rate–exchange rate link

Just how much people will switch out of sterling depends on *how much* they think the exchange rate will depreciate. The effect may be quite strong, especially given the large amount of speculative money ('hot money') moving from country to country. But these expectations are highly unpredictable, and thus the effect on exchange rates is likely to be unpredictable too.

Problems with stage 3: the exchange rate–trade link

Given time, the demand by consumers abroad for UK exports and demand in the UK for imports may be quite elastic. In the short run, however, the effect may be rather limited. But here again, the size of the effect is uncertain and *could* be quite large. It depends on people's expectations of exchange rate movements. If people think that the exchange rate will fall further, importers will buy *now* before the rate does fall and they have to pay more for the imports. Exporters, on the other hand, will hold back as long as possible before shipping their exports: if the rate does fall, they will earn more sterling per dollar's worth of exports. These actions will tend to push the exchange rate down. But such speculation is very difficult to predict as it depends on often highly volatile expectations.

To summarise: the effects of a change in the money supply *might* be quite strong, but their precise magnitude is usually highly unpredictable.

The monetarist view

Monetarists argue that money has a strong and direct effect on aggregate demand. If money supply increases, people will have more money than they require to hold. They will spend this surplus. Much of this spending will go on goods and services, thereby directly increasing aggregate demand:

$$M_s\uparrow \rightarrow M_s > M_d \rightarrow AD\uparrow$$

The theoretical underpinning for this is given by the *theory of portfolio balance*. People have a number of ways of holding their wealth. They can hold it as money, or as financial assets such as bills, bonds or shares, or as physical assets such as houses, cars and televisions. In other words, people hold a whole portfolio of assets of varying degrees of liquidity – from cash to central heating.

If money supply expands, people will find themselves holding more money than they require: their portfolios are unnecessarily liquid. Some of this money will be used to purchase financial assets, and some to purchase *goods and services*. As more assets are purchased, this will drive up their price. This will effectively reduce their 'yield'. For bonds and other *financial* assets, this means a reduction in their rate of interest. For goods and services, this means a reduction in their marginal utility/price ratio: a higher level of consumption will reduce their marginal utility and drive up their price. The process will stop when a balance has been restored in people's portfolios. In the meantime, there will have been extra consumption and hence an increase in aggregate demand.

Monetarists also see monetary policy operating through the interest rate and exchange rate mechanisms we described above. What they argue, however, is that these mechanisms are relatively *strong*. Borrowing, they claim, whether for investment or by consumers, *will* be relatively responsive to changes in interest rates. For example, if interest rates go up and mortgage rates follow suit, people will suddenly be faced with higher monthly repayments and will therefore have to cut down their expenditure on goods and services.

Monetarists also argue that, in an open economy with free-floating exchange rates, the effect of an increase in the money supply is very strong. Any fall in interest rates will have such a strong effect on international financial flows and the exchange rate that the rise in money supply will be relatively quickly and fully transmitted through to aggregate demand.

Short-run variability of V. Despite arguing that changes in money supply will have a strong effect on aggregate demand, monetarists do recognise that there will often be a time lag before these effects take place. In other words, they do admit to some variability of the velocity of circulation (V) in the short run. The demand for money can shift unpredictably in the short run with changing expectations of prices, interest rates and exchange rates. Thus V is unpredictable in the *short* run, and hence the effect of monetary policy on aggregate demand is also unpredictable in the short run. For these reasons monetarists argue that monetary policy cannot be used for short-run demand management. Here at least, then, there is a measure of agreement between Keynesians and monetarists.

28.5 Expectations and the Phillips curve

The main contribution of monetarists to the theory of unemployment and inflation is the incorporation of expectations into the Phillips curve. This is then used to derive a *vertical* long-run Phillips curve. In other words, it is used to explain the monetarist contention that there is *no* trade-off between inflation and unemployment in the long run, and that therefore government policy to expand aggregate demand will not create more jobs (except perhaps in the very short term).

The monetarist theory of the vertical long-run Phillips curve is known as the *accelerationist theory.*

The expectations-augmented Phillips curve

In its simplest form, the **expectations-augmented Phillips curve** is given by the following:

$$\dot{P} = f(1/U) + \dot{P}^e \tag{1}$$

What this states is that inflation ($\dot{P}$) depends on two things:

> **definition**
>
> **Expectations-augmented Phillips curve**
> A (short-run) Phillips curve whose position depends on the expected rate of inflation.

- The inverse of unemployment ($1/U$). This is simply the normal Phillips curve relationship. The higher the rate of (demand-deficient) unemployment, the lower the rate of inflation.
- The expected rate of inflation ($\dot{P}^e$). The higher the rate of inflation that people expect, the higher will be the level of wage demands and the more willing will firms be to raise prices. Thus the higher will be the actual rate of inflation and thus the vertically higher will be the whole Phillips curve.

Let us assume for simplicity that the rate of inflation people expect this year ($\dot{P}^e_t$) (where t represents the current time period: i.e. this year) is the same rate that inflation actually was last year ($\dot{P}_{t-1}$).

$$\dot{P}^e_t = \dot{P}_{t-1} \tag{2}$$

Thus if unemployment is such as to push up prices by 4 per cent ($f(1/U) = 4\%$) and if last year's inflation was 6 per cent, then inflation this year will be 4 per cent + 6 per cent = 10 per cent.

The accelerationist theory

Let us trace the course of inflation and expectations over a number of years in an imaginary economy. To keep the analysis simple, assume there is no growth in the economy.

Year 1. Assume that at the outset, in year 1, there is no inflation at all; that none is expected; that $AD = AS$; and that equilibrium unemployment is 8 per cent. The economy will be at point a in Figure 28.9 and Table 28.1.

Year 2. Now assume that the government expands aggregate demand in order to reduce unemployment. Unemployment falls to 6 per cent. The economy moves to point b along curve I. Inflation has risen to 4 per cent, but people, basing their expectations of inflation on year 1, still expect zero inflation. There is therefore no shift as yet in the Phillips curve. Curve I corresponds to an expected rate of inflation of zero.

Year 3. People now revise their expectations of inflation to the level of year 2. The Phillips curve shifts up by 4 percentage points to position II. If aggregate

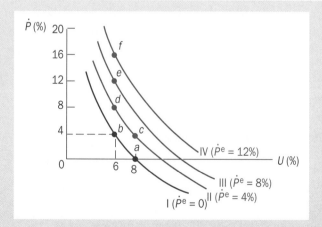

Figure 28.9
The accelerationist theory of inflation and inflationary expectations

Table 28.1 The accelerationist theory of inflation and inflationary expectations

Year	Point on graph	$\dot{P}$	=	$f(1/U)$	+	$\dot{P}^e$
1	a	0	=	0	+	0
2	b	4	=	4	+	0
3	c	4	=	0	+	4
4	d	8	=	4	+	4
5	e	12	=	4	+	8
6	f	16	=	4	+	12

monetary demand continues to rise at the same rate, the whole of the increase will now be absorbed in higher prices. *Real* aggregate demand will fall back to its previous level and the economy will move to point *c*. Unemployment will return to 8 per cent. There is no *demand-pull* inflation now, ($f(1/U) = 0$), but inflation is still 4 per cent due to expectations, ($\dot{P}^e = 4\%$).

Year 4. Assume now that the government expands *real* aggregate demand again so as to reduce unemployment once more to 6 per cent. This time it must expand aggregate *monetary* demand *more* than it did in year 2, because this time, as well as reducing unemployment, it also has to validate the 4 per cent expected inflation. The economy moves to point *d* along curve II. Inflation is now 8 per cent.

Year 5. Expected inflation is now 8 per cent (the level of actual inflation in year 4). The Phillips curve shifts up to position III. If at the same time the government tries to keep unemployment at 6 per cent, it must expand aggregate monetary demand 4 per cent faster in order to validate the 8 per cent expected inflation. The economy moves to point *e* along curve III. Inflation is now 12 per cent.

Year 6. To keep unemployment at 6 per cent, the government must continue to increase aggregate monetary demand by 4 per cent more than the previous year. As the expected inflation rate goes on rising, the Phillips curve will go on shifting up each year.

Thus in order to keep unemployment below the initial equilibrium rate, inflation must go on *accelerating* each year. For this reason, this theory of the Phillips curve is sometimes known as the **accelerationist theory**.

The more the government reduces unemployment, the greater the rise in inflation that year, and the more the rise in expectations the following year and each subsequent year; and hence the more rapidly will price rises accelerate. Thus the true longer-term trade-off is between unemployment and the rate of increase in inflation.

The long-run Phillips curve and the natural rate of unemployment

As long as there are demand-pull pressures ($f(1/U) > 0$), inflation will accelerate as the expected rate of inflation ($\dot{P}^e$) rises. In the long run, therefore, the

> **definition**
>
> **Accelerationist theory**
> The theory that unemployment can only be reduced below the natural rate at the cost of accelerating inflation.

BOX 28.2

The political business cycle
The art of looping the loop

Imagine that a politically naïve government has been fulfilling election promises to cure unemployment, cut taxes and increase welfare spending. In the figure this is shown by a move from points *a* to *b* to *c*.

To its dismay, by the time the next election comes, inflation is accelerating and unemployment is rising again. The economy is moving from point *d* to *e* to *f*. You would hardly be surprised to learn that it loses the election!

But now suppose a much more politically adroit government is elected. What does it do? The answer is that it does politically unpopular things at first, so that before the next election it can do nice things and curry favour with the electorate.

The first thing it does is to have a tough Budget and to raise interest rates. 'We are having to clear up the economic mess left by the last government.' It thus engineers a recession and begins to squeeze down inflationary expectations. The economy moves from point *f* to g to *h*.

But people have very short memories (despite opposition attempts to remind them). After a couple of years of misery, the government announces that the economy has 'begun to turn the corner'. Things are looking up. Inflation has fallen and unemployment has stopped rising. The economy has moved from point *h* to *i* to *j*.

'Thanks to prudent management of the economy', claims the Chancellor, 'I am now in a position to reduce taxes and to allow modest increases in government expenditure.' Unemployment falls rapidly; the economy grows rapidly; the economy moves from point *j* to *a* to *b*.

The government's popularity soars; the pre-election 'give-away' Budget is swallowed by the electorate who trustingly believe that similar ones will follow if the government is returned to office. The government wins the election.

Then comes the nasty medicine again. But who will be blamed this time?

Questions

1 Why might a government sometimes 'get it wrong' and find itself at the wrong part of the Phillips loop at the time of an election?

2 Which electoral system would most favour a government being re-elected: the US fixed-term system with presidents being elected every four years, or the UK system where the government can choose to hold an election any time within five years of the last one?

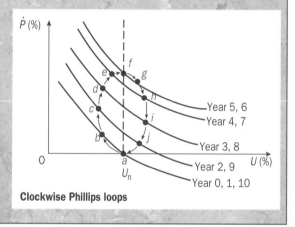

Clockwise Phillips loops

Phillips curve will be vertical at the rate of unemployment where *real* aggregate demand equals *real* aggregate supply. This is the rate of unemployment that monetarists call the **natural rate** (U_n). It sometimes also known as the **non-accelerating-inflation rate of unemployment** (**NAIRU**). In Figure 28.9 the NAIRU is 8 per cent.

The implication for government policy is that expansionary monetary and fiscal policy can only reduce unemployment below U_n in the *short* run. In the long run, the effect will be purely inflationary. On the other hand, a policy of restraining the growth in the money supply will *not* in the long run lead to higher unemployment: it will simply lead to lower inflation at the natural rate of unemployment. The implication is that governments should make it a priority to control money supply.

Rational expectations

New classical economists go further than the monetarist theory described above. They argue that even the short-run Phillips curve is vertical: that there is *no* trade-off between unemployment and inflation, even in the short run. They base their arguments on two key assumptions:

- Prices and wage rates are flexible and thus markets clear very rapidly. This means that there will be no disequilibrium unemployment. All unemployment will be equilibrium unemployment – or 'voluntary unemployment' as new classical economists prefer to call it.
- Expectations are 'rational', but are based on imperfect information.

In the accelerationist theory, expectations are based on *past* information and thus take time to catch up with changes in aggregate demand. Thus for a short time a rise in aggregate demand will raise output and reduce unemployment below the natural level, while prices and wages are still relatively low.

The new classical analysis is based on **rational expectations**. Rational expectations are not based on past rates of inflation. Instead they are based on the current state of the economy and the current policies being pursued by the government. Workers and firms look at the information available to them – at the various forecasts that are published, at various economic indicators and the assessments of them by various commentators, at government pronouncements, etc. Then, on the basis of this information, they predict as well as they can what the rate of inflation will be. It is in this sense that the expectations are 'rational': people use their reason to assess the future on the basis of current information.

But forecasters frequently get it wrong, and so do economic commentators! And the government does not always do what it says it will. Thus workers and firms will be basing expectations on *imperfect information*. The crucial point about the rational expectations theory, however, is that these errors in prediction are *random*. People's predictions of inflation are just as likely to be too high as too low.

If the government raises aggregate demand in an attempt to reduce unemployment, people will anticipate that this will lead to higher prices and wages, and that there will be *no* effect on output and employment. If their expectations of higher inflation are correct, this will thus *fully* absorb the increase in aggregate monetary demand such that there will have been no increase in *real* aggregate demand at all. Firms will not produce any more output or employ any more people: after all, why should they? If they anticipate that people will spend 10 per cent more money but that prices will rise by 10 per cent, their *volume* of sales will remain the same.

Output and employment will only rise, therefore, if people make an error in their predictions (i.e. if they underpredict the rate of inflation and interpret an increase in money spent as an increase in *real* demand). But they are as likely to *over*predict the rate of inflation, in which case output and employment will fall! Thus there is no systematic trade-off between inflation and unemployment, even in the short run.

Real business cycles

If unemployment and output fluctuate only *randomly* from the natural level, and then only in the short run, how can the new classical economists explain

definition
Rational expectations Expectations based on the *current* situation. These expectations are based on the information people have to hand. While this information may be imperfect and therefore people will make errors, these errors will be random.

booms and recessions? How can they explain the business cycle? Their answer, unlike Keynesians, does not lie in fluctuations in aggregate demand. Rather it lies in shifts in aggregate *supply*. In a recession, the vertical short- and long-run aggregate supply curves will shift to the left (output falls) and the vertical short- and long-run Phillips curves will shift to the right (unemployment rises). The reverse happens in a boom. Since the new classical theory of cyclical fluctuations focuses on supply, it is known as **real business cycle theory**.

But what causes aggregate supply to shift in the first place, and why, once there has been an initial shift, will the aggregate supply curve *go on* shifting, causing a recession or boom to continue?

The initial shift in aggregate supply could come from a structural change, such as a shift in demand from older manufacturing industries to new service industries. Because of the immobility of labour, not all those laid off in the older industries will find work in the new industries. Structural unemployment (part of equilibrium unemployment) rises and output falls. *Aggregate* demand may be the same, but because of a change in its pattern, aggregate supply shifts to the left and the Phillips curve shifts to the right.

Alternatively, the initial shift in aggregate supply could come from a change in technology. For example, a technological breakthrough in telecommunications could shift aggregate supply to the right. Or it could come from an oil price increase, shifting aggregate supply to the left.

But why, when a shift occurs, does the effect persist? Why is there not a single rise or fall in aggregate supply? There are two main reasons. The first is that several changes may take months to complete. For example, a decline in demand for certain older industries, perhaps caused by growing competition from abroad, does not take place overnight. Likewise, a technological breakthrough does not affect all industries simultaneously.

The second reason is that these changes will affect the profitability of investment. If investment rises, this will increase firms' capacity and aggregate supply will shift to the right. If investment falls (as a result, say, of the election of a government less sympathetic to industry), aggregate supply will shift to the left. In other words, investment is causing changes in output not through its effect on aggregate *demand* (through the multiplier), but rather through its effect on aggregate *supply*.

So far we have seen how the theory of real business cycles explains persistent rises or falls in aggregate supply. But how does it explain *turning points*? Why do recessions and booms come to an end? The most likely explanation is that, once a shock has worked its way through, aggregate supply will stop shifting. If there is then any shock in the other direction, aggregate supply will start moving back again. For example, after a period of recession, an eventual rise in business confidence will cause investment to rise and hence aggregate supply to shift back to the right. Since these 'reverse shocks' are likely to occur at irregular intervals, they can help to explain why real-world business cycles are themselves irregular.

The Keynesian response

Keynesians today accept that the original analysis of the Phillips curve was an oversimplification and that expectations have to be taken into account. Nevertheless, Keynesians still maintain that output and employment depend on the

definition

Real business cycle theory
The new classical theory which explains cyclical fluctuations in terms of shifts in aggregate supply, rather than aggregate demand.

level of aggregate demand, and that excessive expansion of aggregate demand will lead to inflation: in other words, that there *is* a trade-off between inflation and unemployment, even in the long run.

How is it then that both inflation *and* unemployment were generally worse in the 1970s, 1980s and early 1990s than in the 1950s, 1960s, late 1990s and early 2000s? Keynesians argue that there still is a Phillips curve, but that it has shifted: first to the right, then back to the left. They give a number of explanations for this.

Changes in equilibrium unemployment

Structural unemployment. Most Keynesians include growth in equilibrium unemployment (NAIRU) as part of the explanation of a rightward shift in the Phillips curve in the 1970s and 1980s. In particular, Keynesians highlight the considerable structural rigidities in the economy in a period of rapid industrial change. The changes included the following:

- Dramatic changes in technology. The microchip revolution, for example, has led to many traditional jobs becoming obsolete.
- Competition from abroad. The introduction of new products from abroad, often of superior quality to domestic goods, or produced at lower costs, has led to the decline of many older industries: e.g. the textile industry.
- Shifts in demand away from the products of older labour-intensive industries to new capital-intensive products.

Keynesians argue that the free market simply could not cope with these changes without a large rise in structural/technological unemployment. Labour is not sufficiently mobile – either geographically or occupationally – to move to industries where there are labour shortages or into jobs where there are skill shortages. A particular problem here is the lack of investment in education and training, with the result that the labour force is not sufficiently flexible to respond to changes in demand for labour.

Hysteresis If a recession causes a rise in unemployment which is not then fully reversed when the economy recovers, then there is a problem of **hysteresis**. This term, used in physics, refers to the lagging or persistence of an effect, even when the initial cause has been removed. In our context it refers to the persistence of unemployment even when the initial demand deficiency no longer exists.

The recessions of the early 1980s and early 1990s created a growing number of people who were both deskilled and demotivated. Many in their forties and fifties who had lost their jobs were seen as too old by prospective employers. Many young people, unable to obtain jobs, became resigned to 'life on social security' or to doing no more than casual work. What is more, many firms, in an attempt to cut costs, cut down on training programmes. In these circumstances, a rise in aggregate demand again will not simply enable the long-term unemployed to be employed again. The effect was a rightward shift in the Phillips curve: a rise in the NAIRU. To reverse this, argue Keynesians, the government should embark on a radical programme of retraining.

Recessions also cause a lack of investment. The reduction in their capital stock means that many firms cannot respond to a recovery in demand by making significant increases in output and taking on many more workers. Instead they are more likely to raise prices. Unemployment may thus only fall

> **definition**
>
> **Hysteresis**
> The persistence of an effect even when the initial cause has ceased to operate. In economics it refers to the persistence of unemployment even when the demand deficiency that caused it no longer exists.

modestly and yet inflation may rise substantially. The NAIRU has increased: the Phillips curve has shifted to the right.

If the economy achieves sustained expansion, with no recession, as occurred after 1992, then gradually these effects can be reversed. In other words, the hysteresis is not permanent. As firms increase their investment, the capital stock will expand; firms will engage in more training; the long-term unemployed will fall. The Phillips curve will shift back to the left again and the NAIRU will fall.

The persistence of demand-deficient unemployment

If there is demand-deficient unemployment, why will there not be a long-run fall in real wage rates so as eliminate the surplus labour (see Figure 25.3 on page 529)? Keynesians give two major explanations for the persistence of real wage rates above equilibrium.

Efficiency wages. The argument here is that wage rates fulfil two functions. The first is the traditional one of balancing the demand and supply of labour. To this Keynesians add the function of motivating workers. If real wage rates are reduced when there is a surplus of labour (demand-deficient unemployment), then those workers already in employment may become dispirited and work less hard. If, on the other hand, firms keep wage rates up, then by maintaining a well-motivated workforce, by cutting down on labour turnover and by finding it easier to attract well-qualified labour, firms may find that their costs are reduced: a higher real wage is thus more profitable for them. The maximum-profit real wage rate (the **efficiency wage rate**) is likely to be above the market-clearing real wage rate (see page 342). Demand-deficient unemployment is likely to persist.

Insider power. If those still in employment (the insiders) are members of unions while those out of work are not (the outsiders), or if the insiders have special skills or knowledge that give them bargaining power with employers while the outsiders have no influence, then there is no mechanism whereby the surplus labour – the outsiders – can drive down the real wage and eliminate the demand-deficient unemployment.

These two features help to explain why real wage rates did not fall during the recessions of the early 1980s and early 1990s.

Keynesian analysis of expectations

Keynesians criticise the monetarist/new classical approach of focusing exclusively on price expectations. Expectations, argue Keynesians, influence *output* and *employment* decisions, not just pricing decisions.

Unless the economy is at full employment or very close to it, Keynesians argue that an expansion of demand *will* lead to an increase in output and employment, even in the long run after expectations have fully adjusted. If there is a gradual but sustained expansion of aggregate demand, firms, seeing the economy expanding and seeing their orders growing, will start to invest more and make longer-term plans for expanding their labour force. People will generally *expect* a higher level of output, and this optimism will cause that higher level of output to be produced. In other words, expectations will affect output and employment as well as prices.

---

definition

Efficiency wage rate
The profit-maximising wage rate for the firm after taking into account the effects of wage rates on worker motivation, turnover and recruitment.

Graphically, the increased output and employment from the recovery in investment will shift the Phillips curve to the left, offsetting (partially, wholly or more than wholly) the upward shift from higher inflationary expectations.

The lesson here for governments is that a sustained, but moderate, increase in aggregate demand can lead to a sustained growth in aggregate supply. What should be avoided is an excessive and unsustainable expansion of aggregate demand, as occurred in the late 1980s. This will lead to a boom, only to be followed by a 'bust' and a consequent recession.

The Keynesian criticisms of non-intervention

Keynesians are therefore highly critical of the monetarist/new classical conclusion that governments should not intervene other than to restrain the growth of money supply. High unemployment may persist for many years and become deeply entrenched in the economy without a deliberate government policy of creating a steady expansion of aggregate demand.

28.6 Common ground between economists?

Clearly, there is considerable disagreement between economists over the nature of the aggregate supply and Phillips curves, and hence over the effects of changes in aggregate demand. Nevertheless, it is important not to get the impression that economists disagree over everything. There is, in fact, quite a lot of common ground between the majority of economists over the issues we have examined so far in this chapter. Here are three major areas of agreement.

In the short run, changes in aggregate demand will have a major effect on output and employment.

With the exception of extreme new classical economists, who argue that markets clear instantly and that expectations are formed rationally, all other economists would accept that the short-run aggregate supply curve is upward sloping, albeit getting steeper as potential output is approached. Similarly they would argue that the short-run Phillips curve is downward sloping. There are two major implications of this analysis.

- Reductions in aggregate demand can cause reductions in output and increases in unemployment. In other words, too little spending will cause a recession.
- An expansion of aggregate demand by the government (whether achieved by fiscal or monetary policy, or both) will help to pull an economy out of a recession. There may be considerable time lags, however, before the economy fully responds to such expansionary policies.

In the long run, changes in aggregate demand will have much less effect on output and employment and much more effect on prices

As we have seen, new classical economists and monetarists argue that both the long-run aggregate supply curve and the long-run Phillips curve are vertical. Most Keynesian economists, while arguing that these curves are not vertical, would still see them as less elastic than the short-run curves. Nevertheless, many

Keynesians argue that changes in aggregate demand *will* have substantial effects on long-term output and employment via changes in investment and hence in potential output.

Expectations have important effects on the economy

Virtually all economists argue that expectations are crucial in determining the success of government policy on unemployment and inflation. Whatever people expect to happen, their actions will tend to make it happen.

If people believe that an expansion of money supply will merely lead to inflation (the monetarist position), then it will. Firms and workers will adjust their prices and wage rates upwards. Firms will make no plans to expand output and will not take on any more labour. If, however, people believe that an expansion of demand will lead to higher output and employment (the Keynesian position), then, via the accelerator mechanism, it will.

Similarly, just how successful a deflationary policy is in curing inflation depends in large measure on people's expectations. If people believe that a deflationary policy will cause a recession, then firms will stop investing and will cut their workforce. If they believe that it will cure inflation and restore firms' competitiveness abroad, firms may increase investment.

To manage the economy successfully, therefore, the government must convince people that its policies will work. This is as much a job of public relations as of pulling the right economic levers.

SUMMARY

1a There is considerable debate among economists and politicians over how the market mechanism works at a macroeconomic level. Monetarists argue that markets work relatively well and adjust quickly to changes in demand and supply. Their critics argue that there are various rigidities and that disequilibrium may persist.

1b Monetarists argue (a) that prices and wages are relatively flexible, (b) that aggregate supply is determined independently of aggregate demand and (c) that people's price and wage expectations adjust rapidly to shifts in aggregate demand so as to wipe out any output effect.

1c Keynesians argue (a) that prices and wages are inflexible downwards, (b) that output depends on the level of aggregate demand and that aggregate supply is relatively elastic when there is slack in the economy and (c) that people's expectations of prices and wages depend on their expectations of output and employment, and anyway may be relatively slow to adjust to shifts in aggregate demand.

2a In the simple Keynesian model, equilibrium national income is where withdrawals equal injections: where $W = J$.

2b If there is an increase in injections (or a reduction in withdrawals), there will be a multiplied rise in national income. The multiplier is defined as $\Delta Y/\Delta J$.

2c The size of the multiplier depends on the marginal propensity to withdraw (*mpw*). The smaller the *mpw*, the less will be withdrawn each time incomes are generated round the circular flow, and thus the more will go round again as *additional* demand for domestic product. The multiplier formula is $1/mpw$.

2d If equilibrium national income (Y_e) is below the full-employment level of national income (Y_F), there will be a deflationary gap. This gap is equal to $W - J$ at Y_F. This gap can be closed by expansionary fiscal or monetary policy, which will then cause a multiplied rise in national income (up to a level of YF) and will eliminate demand-deficient unemployment.

2e If equilibrium national income exceeds the full-employment level of income, the inability of output to expand to meet this excess demand will lead to demand-pull inflation. This excess demand gives an inflationary gap, which is equal to $J - W$ at Y_F. This gap can be closed by contractionary policies.

2f This simple analysis tends to imply that the AS

SUMMARY

curve will be horizontal up to Y_F and then vertical. If allowance is made for other types of inflation and unemployment, the *AS* curve will be upward sloping but getting steeper as full employment is approached and as bottlenecks increasingly occur.

2g The Phillips curve showed the trade-off between two of the problems: inflation and unemployment. There seemed to be a simple inverse relationship between the two.

3a Keynesians explain cyclical fluctuations in the economy by examining the causes of fluctuations in the level of *demand*.

3b A major part of the Keynesian explanation of the business cycle is the instability of investment. The accelerator theory explains this instability. It relates the level of investment to *changes* in national income and consumer demand. An initial increase in consumer demand can result in a very large percentage increase in investment; but as soon as the rise in consumer demand begins to level off investment will fall; and even a slight fall in consumer demand can reduce investment to virtually zero.

3c The accelerator effect will be dampened by the carrying of stocks, the cautiousness of firms, forward planning by firms and the inability of producer goods industries to supply the capital equipment.

3d Keynesians identify other causes of cyclical fluctuations, such as cycles in the holding of stocks, time lags, 'bandwagon' effects, ceilings and floors to output, echo effects, swings in government policy and random shocks.

4a The quantity equation $MV = PQ$ can be used to analyse the possible relationship between money and prices. Monetarists argue that the velocity of circulation (V) and the level of output (Q) are independent of money supply (M), and that therefore increases in money supply will simply raise prices (P).

4b Keynesians argue that V varies inversely, but unpredictably, with M and that Q will depend on aggregate demand (MV) according to the degree of slack in the economy.

4c Keynesians argue that the interest rate transmission mechanism between changes in money and changes in national income is unreliable and possibly weak. The reasons are (a) an unstable and possibly elastic demand for money and (b) an unstable and possibly inelastic investment demand.

4d They argue that the exchange rate transmission mechanism is stronger but still very unpredictable.

4e Monetarists argue that the transmission mechanisms are strong and relatively stable in the long run. If people have an increase in money in their portfolios, they will attempt to restore portfolio balance by purchasing assets, including goods. Thus an increase in money supply is transmitted directly into an increase in aggregate demand. The interest rate and exchange rate mechanisms are also argued to be strong. The demand for money is seen to be stable in the long run. This leads to a long-run stability in V (unless it changes as a result of other factors, such as institutional arrangements for the handling of money).

5a The moderate monetarist analysis of the relationship between inflation and unemployment is based on the adaptive expectations hypothesis. In its simplest form the hypothesis states that the expected rate of inflation this year is what it actually was last year: $\dot{P}^e_t = \dot{P}_{t-1}$.

5b If there is excess demand in the economy, producing upward pressure on wages and prices, initially unemployment will fall. The reason is that workers and firms will believe that wage and price increases represent *real* wage and price increases. Thus workers are prepared to take jobs more readily and firms choose to produce more. But as people's expectations adapt upwards to these higher wages and prices, so ever increasing rises in aggregate monetary demand will be necessary to maintain unemployment below the natural rate. Price and wage rises will accelerate: i.e. inflation will rise.

5c The Phillips curve, according to monetarist analysis, is thus vertical at the natural rate of unemployment.

5d The new classical theory assumes flexible prices and wages in the short run as well as in the long run. It also assumes that people base their expectations of inflation on a rational assessment of the *current* situation.

5e People may predict wrongly, but they are equally likely to underpredict or to overpredict. On average over the years they will predict correctly.

5f The rational expectations theory implies that not only the long-run but also the short-run *AS* and Phillips curves will be vertical. If people correctly

SUMMARY

predict the rate of inflation, they will correctly predict that any increase in aggregate *monetary* demand will simply be reflected in higher prices. Total output and employment will remain the same: at the natural level.

5g With a vertical aggregate supply curve, cyclical fluctuations must arise from shifts in aggregate supply, not shifts in aggregate demand. Real business cycle theory thus focuses on aggregate supply shocks, which then persist for a period of time. Eventually their effect will peter out, and supply shocks in the other direction can lead to turning points in the cycle.

5h Modern Keynesians incorporate expectations into their analysis of inflation and unemployment. They also see an important role for cost-push factors in inflation. Like the monetarists, they accept that equilibrium unemployment has increased since the 1950s and 1960s.

5i Demand-deficient unemployment may persist because real wage rates may be sticky downwards, even into the longer term. This stickiness may be the result of efficiency real wage rates being above market-clearing real wage rates and/or outsiders not being able to influence wage bargains struck between employers and insiders.

6a Despite there being different schools of thought, there is a large measure of agreement between macroeconomists.

6b The areas of agreement include the following: (a) in the short run, changes in aggregate demand will have an effect on output and employment; (b) in the long run, changes in aggregate demand will have a smaller or even no effect on output and employment; instead, there will be a significant effect on prices; (c) expectations play a major role in determining the outcome of government policy changes.

REVIEW QUESTIONS

1 Assume that the multiplier has a value of 3. Now assume that the government decides to increase aggregate demand in an attempt to reduce unemployment. It raises government expenditure by £100 million with no increase in taxes. Firms, anticipating a rise in their sales, increase investment by £200 million, of which £50 million consists of purchases of foreign machinery. How much will national income rise? (Assume *ceteris paribus*.)

2 What factors could explain why some countries have a higher multiplier than others?

3 How can the interaction of the multiplier and accelerator explain cyclical fluctuations in national income?

4 Compare Keynesian and monetarist assumptions about the V and Q terms in the quantity equation $MV = PQ$. What are the implications of these respective assumptions for the effectiveness of controlling the amount of money in the economy as a means of controlling inflation?

5 In the accelerationist model, if the government tries to maintain unemployment below the natural rate, what will determine the speed at which inflation accelerates?

6 For what reasons might the natural rate of unemployment increase?

7 How can adaptive expectations of inflation result in clockwise Phillips loops? Why would these loops not be completely regular?

8 What implications would a vertical short-run aggregate supply curve have for the effects of demand management policy?

9 Given the Keynesian explanation for the persistence of high levels of unemployment after the 1980s recession, what policies would you advocate to reduce unemployment?

Macroeconomic policy

J

THE FINANCIAL TIMES, 21 SEPTEMBER 2000

Interest rates held after MPC split

By DAVID TURNER

The Bank of England's nine-member monetary policy committee rejected an interest rate rise this month by the narrowest possible margin, minutes for the MPC's September meeting revealed yesterday.

... The minutes showed that the debate between the four hawks and five doves continued to rage over whether 25-year lows in the unemployment rate were compatible with restrained earnings growth and therefore with moderate consumption growth and inflation. Some of the doves said jobs and earnings figures suggested that 'the rate of unemployment at which inflation tended to increase might have fallen'.

The number of unemployment benefit claimants as a proportion of the total workforce fell 0.1 percentage points in both July and August, reaching 3.6 per cent in the latter month. However, anecdotal evidence that this has caused skills shortages has not translated into earnings figures, with average annual earnings growth at 3.9 per cent in the three months to July,

down from 4.6 per cent just two months before.

The hawks pointed out that although average earnings figures had been lower than expected, this 'perhaps reflected transitory movements in bonuses'.

Richard Jeffrey, chief economist at Charterhouse Securities, said: 'What worries me about the economy is the labour market, which is exceptionally tight.' He pointed to the high ratio of vacancies to claimants.

Even some of the MPC members who voted for unchanged rates admitted 'there remained upside risks from higher import prices and buoyant growth in some parts of the economy'.

Retail sales volumes rose a strong 4.1 per cent in the year to July, with growth falling only 0.1 percentage points in August, according to figures published after the MPC's meeting. However, raising interest rates would be hard to justify when RPIX inflation is nearer the 1.5 per cent rate below which it is officially seen as too low by the government than to the 2.5 rate that is the target.

The role of government in managing macroeconomic affairs has always been a contentious one. Sometimes government action is welcomed when, for example, the economy is languishing in recession. Yet on other occasions, as in the quote below, the removal of government influence and interference can be equally praised.

Even when the type of intervention is agreed upon, the decision makers still have to agree on precisely what action to take. As the article opposite shows, even those who should know best cannot always be sure of the best course of action.

In this final part of the book, we consider the alternative policies open to government in its attempt to manage or influence the macroeconomy. Chapter 29 focuses on fiscal and monetary policy, which are used by government to regulate aggregate demand. We shall consider how such policies are supposed to work and how effective they are in practice. Chapter 30, by contrast, focuses on aggregate supply and considers the role of government in attempting to improve economic performance by supply-side reforms: i.e. reforms designed to increase productivity and efficiency and achieve a growth in *potential* output. Both free-market and interventionist supply-side strategies will be considered.

Finally Chapter 31 takes an international perspective. We shall see how, in a world of interdependent economies, national governments try to harmonise their policies so as to achieve international growth and stability. Unfortunately, there is frequently a conflict between the broader interests of the international community and the narrow interests of individual countries, and in these circumstances, national interests normally dictate policy.

Business yesterday gave a resounding welcome to the government's decision to give the Bank of England operational independence. Business leaders said it would help keep politics out of economic management and aid the development of macro-economic stability. They said it would also help the UK meet the criteria set by the Maastricht Treaty for entry into European monetary union.

Financial Times, 7 May 1997

key terms

Fiscal policy
Fiscal stance
Fine tuning
Automatic fiscal stabilisers and discretionary fiscal policy
Pure fiscal policy
Crowding out
Monetary policy
Open-market operations
Demand management
Market-orientated and interventionist supply-side policies
Regional and urban policy
Industrial policy
International business cycle
Policy co-ordination
International convergence
Economic and monetary union in Europe (EMU)
Single European currency
Currency union

Demand-side policy

There are two major types of demand-side policy: fiscal and monetary. In each case we shall first describe how the policy operates and then examine its effectiveness.

In Chapter 28 we outlined the theoretical distinction between the Keynesian and monetarist approaches to the operation of the national economy. We saw that Keynesians advocate active intervention by the government to manage the level of demand, so as to avoid excess demand and inflation on the one hand, and deficient demand and recessions on the other. Monetarists prefer to use demand-side policy merely to create a stable financial environment with zero or low inflation: an environment in which market forces will operate most effectively. For them, demand-side policy should be seen as a 'steady as you go' policy.

29.1 Fiscal policy

Fiscal policy involves the government manipulating the level of government expenditure and/or rates of tax so as to affect the level of aggregate demand. An *expansionary* fiscal policy will involve raising government expenditure (an injection into the circular flow of income) or reducing taxes (a withdrawal from the circular flow). This will increase aggregate demand and lead to a *multiplied* rise in national income. A *deflationary* (i.e. a contractionary) fiscal policy will involve cutting government expenditure and/or raising taxes.

During the 1950s and 1960s, when fiscal policy was seen by both governments and economists as the major way of controlling the economy, it was used to perform two main functions:

- To prevent the occurrence of *fundamental* disequilibrium in the economy. In other words, expansionary fiscal policy could be used to prevent mass unemployment, and deflationary fiscal policy could be used to prevent excessive inflation.
- To smooth out the fluctuations in the economy associated with the business cycle. This would involve reducing government expenditure or raising taxes during the boom phase of the cycle. This would dampen down the expansion and prevent 'overheating' of the economy, with its attendant rising inflation and deteriorating balance of payments. Conversely, during the recessionary phase, as unemployment grew and output declined, the government should cut taxes or raise government expenditure in order to boost the economy. If these stabilisation policies are successful, they will amount merely to **fine tuning**. Problems of excess

definition

Fine tuning
The use of demand management policy (fiscal or monetary) to smooth out cyclical fluctuations in the economy.

or deficient demand will never be allowed to get severe. Any movement of aggregate demand away from a steady growth path will be immediately 'nipped in the bud'.

Deficits and surpluses

Central government deficits and surpluses

Since an expansionary fiscal policy will involve raising government expenditure and/or lowering taxes, this will have the effect of either increasing the **budget deficit** or reducing the **budget surplus**. A budget deficit in any one year is where central government's expenditure exceeds its revenue from taxation. A budget surplus is where tax revenues exceed central government expenditure. With the exception of short periods in 1969–70, 1987–90 and since 1998, governments in the UK, like most governments around the world, have run budget deficits.

Public-sector deficits and surpluses

To get a complete view of the overall **stance of fiscal policy** – just how expansionary or contractionary it is – we would need to look at the deficit or surplus of the entire public sector: namely, central government, local government and public corporations.

If the public sector spends more than it earns (through taxes and the revenues of public corporations, etc.), the amount of this deficit is known as the **public-sector net cash requirement (PSNCR)** (previously known as the public-sector borrowing requirement (PSBR)). The reason for the name 'public-sector borrowing requirement' is simple. If the public sector runs a deficit in the current year of, say, £1 billion, then it will have to borrow £1 billion this year in order to finance it. It will borrow by issuing government securities: Treasury bills or government bonds (gilts).

If the public sector runs a surplus (a negative figure for the PSNCR), then this will be used to reduce the accumulated debts from the past. The accumulated debts of central government are known as the **national debt**. The accumulated debts of the entire public sector are known as the *public-sector debt*. Table 29.1 shows the PSNCR and the national debt for the UK from 1986 to 1999.

The use of fiscal policy

Automatic fiscal stabilisers

To some extent, government expenditure and taxation will have the effect of *automatically* stabilising the economy. For example, as national income rises, the amount of tax people pay automatically rises. This rise in withdrawals from the circular flow of income will help to damp down the rise in national income.

definition

Budget deficit
The excess of central government's spending over its tax receipts.

definition

Budget surplus
The excess of central government's tax receipts over its spending.

definition

Fiscal stance
How deflationary or reflationary the Budget is.

definition

Public-sector net cash requirement (PSNCR)
The (annual) deficit of the public sector (central government, local government and public corporations), and thus the amount that the public sector must borrow.

definition

National debt
The accumulated budget deficits (less surpluses) over the years: the total amount of government borrowing.

| Table 29.1 | UK public-sector borrowing and debt |

Year	1986	1988	1990	1991	1992	1993	1994	1995	1996	1997	1998	1999
PSNCR (£bn) (+ = deficit)	−2.4	+11.6	+2.1	−7.7	−28.7	−42.5	−39.3	−35.4	−24.8	−11.9	+6.4	+1.8
PSNCR as % of GDP	+0.6	−2.5	−0.4	+1.3	+4.8	+6.8	+5.8	+5.0	+3.3	+1.5	−0.8	−0.2
National debt (£bn)	158.4	178.1	160.0	163.7	180.4	225.8	289.1	330.1	367.6	391.9	393.9	392.3

Source: *Financial Statistics* (ONS)

This effect will be bigger if taxes are *progressive* (i.e. rise by a bigger percentage than national income). Some government expenditure will have a similar effect. For example, total government expenditure on unemployment benefits will fall, if rises in national income cause a fall in unemployment. This again will have the effect of dampening the rise in national income.

Discretionary fiscal policy

If there is a fundamental disequilibrium in the economy or substantial fluctuations in national income, these automatic stabilisers will not be enough. The government may thus choose to *alter* the level of government expenditure or the rates of taxation. This is known as **discretionary fiscal policy**.

If government expenditure on goods and services (roads, health care, education, etc.) is raised, this will create a full multiplied rise in national income. The reason is that all the money gets spent and thus all of it goes to boosting aggregate demand.

Cutting taxes (or increasing benefits), however, will have a smaller effect on national income than raising government expenditure on goods and services by the same amount. The reason is that cutting taxes increases people's *disposable* incomes, of which only part will be spent. Part will be withdrawn into extra saving, imports and other taxes. In other words, not all the tax cuts will be passed on round the circular flow of income as extra expenditure. Thus if one-fifth of a cut in taxes is withdrawn and only four-fifths is spent, the tax multiplier will only be four-fifths as big as the government expenditure multiplier.

29.2 The effectiveness of fiscal policy

How successful will fiscal policy be? Will it be able to 'fine tune' demand? Will it be able to achieve the level of national income that the government would like it to achieve?

The effectiveness of fiscal policy depends on a number of factors, including the following:

- The accuracy of forecasting. Governments would obviously like to act as swiftly as possible to prevent a problem of excess or deficient demand. The more reliable are the forecasts of what is likely to happen to aggregate demand, the more able will the government be to intervene quickly.
- The extent to which changes in government expenditure (G) and taxation (T) will affect total injections and withdrawals. Will changes in G or T be partly offset by changes in *other* injections and withdrawals? If so, are these changes predictable?
- The extent to which changes in injections and withdrawals affect national income. Will it be possible to predict the size of the multiplier and accelerator effects?
- The timing of the effects. It is no good simply being able to predict the *magnitude* of the effects of fiscal policy. It is also necessary to predict how long they will take. If there are long time lags with fiscal policy, it will be far less successful as a means of reducing fluctuations.
- The extent to which changes in aggregate demand will have the desired effects on output, employment, inflation and the balance of payments.

> **definition**
>
> **Discretionary fiscal policy**
> Deliberate changes in tax rates or the level of government expenditure in order to influence the level of aggregate demand.

- The extent to which fiscal policy has undesirable side-effects, such as higher taxes reducing incentives.

Discretionary fiscal policy: problems of magnitude

Before changing government expenditure or taxation, the government will need to calculate the effect of any such change on national income, employment and inflation. Predicting these effects however, is often very unreliable for a number of reasons.

Predicting the effect of changes in government expenditure

A rise in government expenditure of £x may lead to a rise in total injections (relative to withdrawals) that is smaller than £x. This will occur if the rise in government expenditure *replaces* a certain amount of private expenditure. For example, a rise in government expenditure on social services could lead to a fall in private consumer expenditure. For example, a rise in expenditure on state education may dissuade some parents from sending their children to private schools. Similarly, an improvement in the National Health Service may lead to fewer people paying for private treatment.

Crowding out. Another reason for the total rise in injections being smaller than the rise in government expenditure is a phenomenon known as **crowding out** (something that monetarists see as being particularly significant). If the government relies on **pure fiscal policy** – that is, if it does not finance an increase in the budget deficit by increasing the money supply – it will have to borrow the money from individuals and firms. It will thus be competing with the private sector for finance and will have to offer higher interest rates. This will force the private sector also to offer higher interest rates, which may discourage firms from investing and individuals from buying on credit. Thus government borrowing *crowds out* private borrowing. In the extreme case, the fall in consumption and investment may completely offset the rise in government expenditure, with the result that aggregate demand does not rise at all. We examine crowding out in more detail in section 29.5.

Predicting the effect of changes in taxes

A rise in taxes, by reducing people's real disposable income, will reduce not only the amount they spend, but also the amount they save. The problem is that it is not easy to predict just how much people will cut down on their spending and how much on their saving. In part it will depend on whether people feel that the rise in tax is only temporary, in which case they may well cut savings in order to maintain their level of consumption, or permanent, in which case they may well reduce their consumption.

Predicting the resulting multiplied effect on national income

Even if the government *could* predict the net initial effect on injections and withdrawals, the extent to which national income will change is still hard to predict for the following reasons:

- The size of the *multiplier* may be difficult to predict, since it is difficult to predict how much of any rise in income will be withdrawn. For example, the amount of a rise in income that households save or consume will

---

definition

Crowding out
Where increased public expenditure diverts money or resources away from the private sector.

---

definition

Pure fiscal policy
Fiscal policy which does not involve any change in money supply.

depend on their expectations about future price and income changes. The amount of a rise in income spent on imports will depend on the exchange rate, which may fluctuate considerably.

● Induced investment through the *accelerator* is also extremely difficult to predict. It may be that a relatively small fiscal stimulus will be all that is necessary to restore business confidence, and that induced investment will rise substantially. In such a case, fiscal policy can be seen as a 'pump primer'. It is used to *start* the process of recovery, and then the *continuation* of the recovery is left to the market. But for pump priming to work, businesspeople must *believe* that it will work. If they are cautious and fear that the recovery will falter, they may hold back from investing. This lack of investment will probably mean that the recovery *will* falter and that the effects of the fiscal expansion are very modest. The problem is in predicting just how the business community will react. Business confidence can change very rapidly and in ways that could not have been foreseen a few months earlier.

Random shocks

Forecasts cannot take into account the unpredictable. For that you would have to consult astrologers or fortune tellers! Unfortunately unpredictable events, such as a war or a major industrial dispute, do occur and may seriously undermine the government's fiscal policy.

Discretionary fiscal policy and the problem of timing

Fiscal policy can involve considerable time lags. If these are long enough, fiscal policy could even be *de*stabilising. Expansionary policies that are taken to cure a recession may only come into effect once the economy has *already* recovered and is experiencing a boom. Under these circumstances, expansionary policies will be quite inappropriate: they will simply worsen the problems of overheating. Similarly, deflationary policies that are taken to prevent excessive expansion may only start taking effect once the economy has peaked and is already plunging into recession. The deflationary policies will only deepen the recession.

This problem is illustrated in Figure 29.1. Path (a) shows the course of the

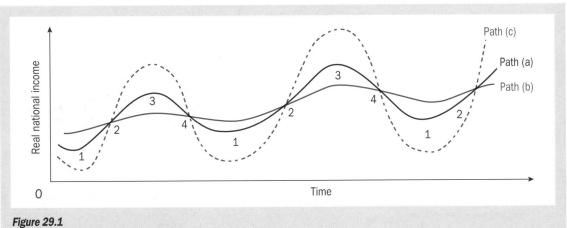

Figure 29.1
Fiscal policy: stabilising or destabilising?

Following the golden rule
Fiscal policy in a strait-jacket?

If the government persistently runs a budget deficit, the national debt will rise. If it rises faster than GDP, then it will account for a growing proportion of GDP. There is then likely to be an increasing problem of 'servicing' this debt: i.e. paying the interest on it. The government could find itself having to borrow more and more to meet the interest payments, and so the national debt could rise faster still. As the government borrows more and more, so it has to pay higher interest rates to attract finances. If it is successful in this, borrowing and hence investment by the private sector could be crowded out (see page 636).

Recognising these problems, many governments in recent years have attempted to reduce their debts.

Preparing for EMU

In signing the Maastricht Treaty in 1992, the EU countries agreed that to be eligible to join the single cur-rency, they should have sustainable deficits and debts. This was interpreted as follows: the general government deficit should be no more than 3 per cent of GDP and general government debt should be no more than 60 per cent of GDP, or should at least be falling towards that level at a satisfactory pace.

But in the mid-1990s, several of the countries which were subsequently to join the euro, had deficits and debts substantially above these levels. Getting them down proved a painful business. Government expendi-ture had to be cut and taxes increased. Fiscal policy, unfortunately, proved to be powerful! Unemployment rose and growth remained low.

The EU Stability and Growth Pact

In June 1997, at the European Council in Amsterdam, the EU countries agreed that governments adopting the euro should seek to balance their budgets (or even aim

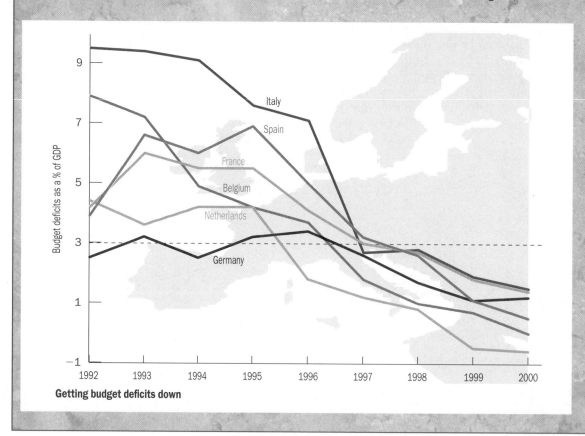

Getting budget deficits down

for a surplus) averaged over the course of the business cycle, and that deficits should not exceed 3 per cent of GDP in any one year. A country's deficit is only permitted to exceed 3 per cent if its GDP has declined by at least 2 per cent (or 0.75 per cent with special permission from the Council of Ministers). Otherwise, countries with deficits exceeding 3 per cent are required to make deposits of money with the European Central Bank. These then become fines if the excessive budget deficit is not eliminated within two years.

There are two main aims of targeting a zero budget deficit over the business cycle. The first is to allow automatic stabilisers to work without 'bumping into' the 3 per cent deficit ceiling in years when economies are slowing. The second is to allow a reduction in government debts as a proportion of GDP (assuming that GDP grows on average at around 2–3 per cent per year).

The main criticism of aiming for a zero deficit over the cycle has been that this would mean a further reduction in deficits, which by the start of the euro in 1999 were typically only just meeting the 3 per cent ceiling. In other words, meeting the zero deficit target would mean further deflationary fiscal policies: something that most political leaders in Europe felt to be inappropriate at a time when there were fears of a world recession.

But if the zero target was not achieved and deficits remained at around the 3 per cent level, then automatic stabilisers would not be allowed to work (so long as the 3 per cent ceiling was adhered to).

Labour's golden rule

The Labour government in the UK has adopted a similar approach to that of the Stability and Growth Pact. Under its 'golden rule', the government pledges that over the economic cycle, it will borrow only to invest (e.g. in roads, hospitals and schools) and not to fund current spending (e.g. on wages, administration and benefits). Investment is exempted from the zero borrowing rule, because it contributes towards the growth of GDP. Indeed, in its 1998 'Comprehensive Spending Review', the government announced that government investment expenditure would double as a percentage of GDP. The

government has also set itself the target of maintaining a stable public-sector debt/GDP ratio below 40 per cent.

To allow the golden rule to operate, government departments are set three-year spending limits and each has separate current and capital (investment) budgets.

As with the Stability and Growth Pact, the argument is that by using an averaging rule over the cycle, automatic stabilisers will be allowed to work. Deficits of receipts over current spending can occur when the economy is in recession or when growth is sluggish, helping to stimulate the economy. Surpluses can occur in boom periods, helping to dampen the economy.

But, as with the Stability and Growth Pact, the golden rule had not previously been met. Between 1985/6 and 1996/7, average annual current public spending had exceeded receipts by over 1½ per cent of GDP. If the golden rule was to be met, therefore, there would have to be a fiscal tightening. Again, this was a concern given the slowdown of the economy in 1998.

Loosening the strait-jacket?

Once average zero current deficits in the case of the UK, and overall deficits in the case of the euro-zone countries, have been achieved over the course of a cycle, then fiscal policy can cease to be so deflationary and can operate more effectively as an automatic stabiliser. The question is, however, whether automatic stabilisers are enough. As the Asian crisis of 1998 spread around the world as a 'contagion', so more and more governments turned to discretionary fiscal policy as a means of boosting their economies.

Question

What effects will government investment expenditure have on public-sector debt (a) in the short run; (b) in the long run?

business cycle without government intervention. Ideally, with no time lags, the economy should be dampened in stage 2 and expanded in stage 4. This would make the resulting course of the business cycle more like path (b), or even, if the policy were perfectly stabilising, a straight line. With the presence of time lags, however, deflationary policies taken in stage 2 may not come into effect until stage 4, and reflationary policies taken in stage 4 may not come into effect until stage 2. In this case the resulting course of the business cycle will be more like path (c). Quite obviously, in these circumstances 'stabilising' fiscal policy actually makes the economy *less* stable.

There are five possible lags associated with fiscal policy.

Time lag to recognition. Since the business cycle can be irregular and forecasting unreliable, governments may be unwilling to take action until they are convinced that the problem is serious.

Time lag between recognition and action. Most significant changes in government expenditure have to be planned well in advance. The government cannot increase spending on motorways overnight or suddenly start building new hospitals.

Changes in taxes and benefits cannot be introduced overnight either. They normally have to wait to be announced in the Budget and will not be instituted until the new financial year or at some other point in the future. As Budgets normally occur annually, there could be a considerable time lag if the problems are recognised a long time before the Budget.

Time lag between action and changes taking effect. A change in tax rates may not immediately affect tax payments. For example, income tax codings take two or three months to be changed by the Inland Revenue.

Time lag between changes in government expenditure and taxation and the resulting change in national income, prices and employment. The multiplier round takes time. Accelerator effects take time. The multiplier and accelerator go on interacting. It all takes time.

Consumption may respond slowly to changes in taxation. If taxes are cut, consumers may respond initially by saving the extra money. They may only later increase consumption.

If the fluctuations in aggregate demand can be forecast, and if the lengths of the time lags are known, then all is not lost. At least the fiscal measures can be taken early and their delayed effects can be taken into account.

Side-effects of discretionary fiscal policy

The purpose of fiscal policy is to control aggregate demand. In doing so, however, it may create certain undesirable side-effects.

Cost inflation. If the economy is overheating and inflation is rising, the government may raise taxes. Although this will lower aggregate demand, a rise in expenditure taxes and corporation taxes will usually be passed on in full or in part to the consumer in higher prices. This in turn could lead to higher wage claims, as could a rise in income tax.

Welfare and distributive justice. The use of fiscal policy may conflict with various social programmes. The government may want to introduce cuts in public expenditure in order to reduce inflation. But where are the cuts to be made? Cuts will often fall on people who are relatively disadvantaged. After all, it is these people who are the most reliant on the welfare state and other public provision (such as state education).

Incentives. Both automatic stabilisers, in the form of steeply progressive income taxes, and discretionary rises in taxes could be a disincentive to effort. What is the point in working more or harder, people might say, if so much is going to be taken in taxes? It could work the other way, however: faced with higher tax bills, people may feel the need to work more in order to maintain their living standards.

Steady as you go

Given the problems of pursuing active fiscal policy, many governments today take a much more passive approach. Instead of changing the policy as the economy changes, a rule is set for the level of public finances. This rule is then applied year after year, with taxes and government expenditure being planned to meet that rule. For example, a target could be set for the PSNCR, with government expenditure and taxes being adjusted to keep the PSNCR at or within its target level. Box 29.1 looks at some examples of fiscal targets.

29.3 Monetary policy

Control of the money supply over the medium and long term

One of the major sources of monetary growth is government borrowing. If the government wishes to prevent excessive growth in the money supply over the longer term, therefore, it will have to be careful not to have an excessively high PSNCR (see page 590).

The precise effect of government borrowing on the money supply will depend on how the PSNCR is financed. If it is financed by borrowing from the Bank of England or by the sale of Treasury bills to the banking sector, the money supply will increase. If, however, it is financed by selling bills or bonds outside the banking sector or by selling bonds to the banks, the money supply will not increase (see page 590).

If there is no increase in money supply, the increased demand for loans by the government will 'crowd out' lending to the private sector. To attract money the government will have to offer higher interest rates on bonds. This will force up private-sector interest rates and reduce private-sector borrowing and investment. This is known as **financial crowding out**.

If governments wish to reduce monetary growth and yet avoid financial crowding out, they must therefore reduce the level of the PSNCR.

Monetarists argue that governments should make reductions in the PSNCR

definition
Financial crowding out Where an increase in government borrowing diverts money away from the private sector.

(as a proportion of national income) the central part of their medium- and longer-term monetary strategy. Not only is this desirable as a means of restricting monetary growth, but if it involves cutting government expenditure (as opposed to increasing taxes), it will also increase the size of the private sector relative to the public sector: and it is the private sector that monetarists see as the main source of long-term growth in output and employment.

Short-term monetary control

Monetary policy may be off target. Alternatively, the government may wish to alter its monetary policy. Assume, for example, that the government wishes to operate a tighter monetary policy in order to reduce aggregate demand. What can it do?

The government could use various techniques for conducting monetary policy. These can be grouped into three categories: (a) controlling the money supply; (b) controlling interest rates; (c) rationing credit.

Figure 29.2 shows the demand for and supply of money. Assume that the government wants to tighten monetary policy, such that the equilibrium quantity of money moves from Q_1 to Q_2. It could (a) seek to shift the supply of money curve to the left, from M_s to M_s' (resulting in the equilibrium rate of interest rising from r_1 to r_2), (b) raise the interest rate directly from r_1 to r_2, and then manipulate the money supply to reduce it to Q_2, or (c) keep interest rates at r_1, but reduce money supply to Q_2 by rationing the amount of credit granted by banks and other institutions.

definition

Open-market operations
The sale (or purchase) by the authorities of government securities in the open market in order to reduce (or increase) money supply.

Techniques to control the money supply

The possible techniques available to the authorities have one major feature in common: they involve manipulating the liquid assets of the banking system. The aim is to influence the total money supply by affecting the amount of credit that banks can create.

Open-market operations. **Open-market operations** are the sale (or purchase) by the Bank of England of government securities (bonds or Treasury bills) in the

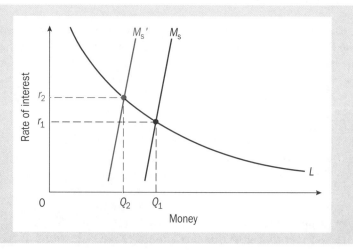

Figure 29.2
The demand for and supply of money

BOX 29.2

The daily operation of monetary policy
What goes on at Threadneedle Street?

The Bank of England does not attempt to control money supply directly. Instead it seeks to control short-term interest rates by conducting open-market operations in the discount and gilt 'repo' markets (see page 584). These operations, as we shall see, will determine short-term interest rates, which will then have a knock-on effect on longer-term rates, as returns on different forms of assets must remain competitive with each other.

Let us assume that the Monetary Policy Committee of the Bank of England is worried that inflation is set to rise, perhaps because there is excessive growth in the money supply. At its monthly meeting, therefore, it decides to raise interest rates. What does it do?

The first thing is that it will *announce* a rise in interest rates. But the Bank must do more than this. It must back up the announcement by using open-market operations to ensure that its announced interest rate is the *equilibrium rate*. In fact, it has to conduct open market operations every day to keep interest rates at the chosen level.

How do these open-market operations work? In general, the Bank of England seeks to keep banks short of liquidity. It achieves this through its weekly sales of Treasury bills to the banks and other financial institutions (collectively known as the Bank's 'counterparties').

The counterparties will thus have to borrow from the Bank of England. They do this by entering into sale and repurchase agreements (repos). This entails them selling gilts to the Bank, with an agreement that they will repurchase them from the Bank at a fixed date in the future (typically about two weeks). The difference between the sale and repurchase prices will be set by the Bank of England to reflect its chosen rate of interest. By the Bank determining the repo rate in this way, there will then be a knock-on effect on other interest rates throughout the banking system.

Each morning at 9.45 the Bank of England forecasts that day's shortage (forecasts that are updated during the day). It then contacts its counterparties to offer them assistance (i.e. to enter repo agreements). The assistance is provided at the published rate in two rounds of open market operations: at 12.00 noon and at 2.30 pm, with an additional 'early round' at 9.45 am if the predicted shortage of liquidity is large.

At about 3.45 pm the Bank publishes a final update for the day's liquidity shortage. If it is greater than was forecast earlier in the day, the Bank may make a further repo facility available, for which banks must apply by 3.55 pm.

Although there is usually a shortage of liquidity in the banking system, on some days there may be a *surplus*. To prevent this driving market interest rates down, the Bank will invite its counterparties to bid for outright purchase of short-dated Treasury bills (i.e. ones part-way through their life) at prices set by the Bank to reflect its current (above equilibrium) interest rate: i.e. at prices lower than the market would otherwise set. At such prices, the Bank has no difficulty in selling them and hence in 'mopping up' the surplus liquidity.

Question

Assume that the Bank of England wants to reduce interest rates. Trace through the process during the day by which it achieves this.

---

open market. These sales (or purchases) are to fund additional (or reduced) government borrowing, and are best understood, therefore, in the context of an unchanged PSNCR.

If the Bank of England wishes to *reduce* the money supply, it sells more securities. When people buy these securities, they pay for them with cheques drawn on banks. Thus banks' balances with the Bank of England are reduced. If this brings bank reserves below their prudent ratio (or statutory ratio, if one is in force), banks will reduce advances. There will be a multiple contraction of credit and hence of money supply.

Funding. **Funding** is where the Bank of England, if it wishes to reduce the money supply, issues more government bonds, but at the same time fewer Treasury bills. Banks' balances with the Bank of England will be little affected, but to the extent that banks hold fewer bills, there will be a reduction in their liquidity. Funding is thus the conversion of one type of government debt (liquid) into another (illiquid).

Reduced central bank lending to the banks. The central bank in most countries is prepared to provide extra money to banks (through rediscounting bills, gilt repos or straight loans). In some countries, it is the policy of the central bank to keep its interest rate to banks *below* market rates, thereby encouraging banks to borrow (or sell back securities) whenever such facilities are available. By controlling the amount of money it is willing to provide at these low rates, the central bank can control the banks' liquid assets. By cutting back the amount it provides, it can reduce the money supply.

In other countries, such as the UK, it is not so much the amount of money made available that is controlled, but rather the rate of interest (or discount). The lower this rate is relative to other market rates, the more will banks be willing to borrow, and the more, therefore, will the monetary base expand. Raising this rate, therefore, will have the effect of reducing the money supply.

Variable minimum reserve ratios. In some countries (such as the USA), banks are required to hold a certain proportion of their assets in liquid form. The assets which count as liquid are known as 'reserve assets'. These include assets such as balances in the central bank, bills of exchange, certificates of deposit and money market loans. The ratio of such assets to total liabilities is known as the **minimum reserve ratio**. If the central bank raises this ratio (in other words requires the banks to hold a higher proportion of liquid assets), then banks will have to reduce the amount of credit. The money supply will fall.

A version of variable minimum reserves was used in the UK up to 1981. Banks could be required to deposit a given percentage of their deposits in a special account at the Bank of England. These *special deposits* were frozen, and could not be drawn on until the authorities chose to release them. They provided a simple means of reducing banks' liquidity and hence their ability to create credit.

Techniques to control interest rates

The approach to monetary control today in most countries is to focus directly on interest rates. In the UK, interest rate changes are made by the Bank of England's Monetary Policy Committee (MPC) at its monthly meetings. The MPC announces a rate change. This is then backed up through the Bank's operations in the discount and gilt repo markets. Let us assume that the MPC decides to raise interest rates. What should the Bank of England do?

In general, the Bank of England seeks to keep banks short of liquidity. This will happen automatically on any day when tax payments by banks' customers exceed the money they receive from government expenditure. This excess is effectively withdrawn from banks and ends up in the government's account at the Bank of England. Even when this does not occur, sales of Treasury bills by the Bank of England to banks, discount houses and other financial institutions will effectively keep the banking system short of liquidity.

definition

Funding
Where the authorities alter the balance of bills and bonds for any given level of government borrowing.

definition

Minimum reserve ratio
A minimum ratio of cash (or other specified liquid assets) to deposits (either total or selected) that the central bank requires banks to hold.

This 'shortage' can then be used as a way of forcing through interest rate changes. Banks will obtain the necessary liquidity from the Bank of England through gilt repos (see pages 584–5) or by selling it back bills. The Bank of England can *choose the rate of interest to charge* (i.e. the gilt repo rate or the bill rediscount rate). This will then have a knock-on effect on other interest rates throughout the banking system. (See Box 29.2 for more details on just how the Bank of England manipulates interest rates on a day-to-day basis.)

Techniques to ration credit

In the past, and particularly in the late 1960s, governments attempted to keep interest rates low so as not to discourage investment. This frequently meant that the demand for money exceeded the supply of money that the authorities were prepared to permit.

Faced with this excess demand, the authorities had to ration credit. Credit was rationed in two main ways. First, the Bank of England could ask banks to restrict their total lending to a certain amount, or to reduce lending to more risky customers or for non-essential purchases. The Bank of England had the power to order banks to obey, but in practice it always relied on persuasion. This was known as *suggestion and request* (or 'moral suasion'). Second, the authorities could restrict *hire-purchase credit*, by specifying minimum deposits or maximum repayment periods.

The use of credit rationing has been abandoned by most countries in recent years.

29.4 The effectiveness of monetary policy

Controlling the money supply over the medium and long term

A government committed to a sustained reduction in the growth of the money supply over a number of years will find this very difficult unless it restricts the size of the public-sector deficit. The Thatcher government in the 1980s recognised this and made reducing the PSNCR (then known as the PSBR – the public-sector borrowing requirement) the central feature of its 'medium-term financial strategy'. There are serious problems, however, in attempting to reduce the PSNCR if it is currently high, principal among which is the difficulty in cutting government expenditure.

Cuts in government expenditure are politically unpopular. The Thatcher government as soon as it came into office met considerable opposition in Parliament, from public opinion, from local authorities and from various pressure groups, to 'cuts'. What is more, much of government expenditure is committed a long time in advance and cannot easily be cut. As a result the government may find itself forced into refusing to sanction *new* expenditure. But this will mean a decline in capital projects such as roads, housing, schools and sewers, with the net result that there is a decline in the country's infrastructure and long-term damage to the economy.

The less successful a government is in controlling the PSNCR, the more it will have to borrow through bond issue, to prevent money supply growing too fast. This will mean high interest rates and the problem of crowding out, and a growing burden of national debt with interest on it that has to be paid from taxation, from

BOX 29.3

Monetary policy in the euro-zone
The role of the ECB

The European Central Bank (ECB) is based in Frankfurt and is charged with operating the monetary policy of those EU countries that have adopted the euro. Although it has the overall responsibility for the euro-zone's monetary policy, the central banks of the individual countries, such as the Bank of France and the Bundesbank, have not been abolished. They are responsible for distributing euros and for carrying out the ECB's policy with respect to institutions in their own countries. The whole system of the ECB and the national central banks is known as the European System of Central Banks (ESCB).

In operating the monetary policy of a 'euro economy' roughly the size of the USA, and in being independent from national governments, the ECB's power is enormous. So what is the structure of this new giant on the European stage, and how does it operate?

The structure of the ECB

The ECB has two major decision-making bodies: the Governing Council and the Executive Board.

● The Governing Council consists of the members of the Executive Board and the governors of the central banks of each of the euro-zone countries. The Council's role is to set the main targets of monetary policy and to take an oversight of the success (or otherwise) of that policy.

● The Executive Board consists of a president, a vice president and four other members. Each serves for an eight-year, non-renewable term. The Executive Board is responsible for implementing the decisions of the Governing Council and for preparing policies for the Council's consideration. Each member of the Executive Board has a responsibility for some particular aspect of monetary policy.

The ECB is one of the most independent central banks in the world. It has very little formal accountability to elected politicians. Although its president can be called before the European Parliament, the Parliament has virtually no powers to influence the ECB's actions. Also its deliberations are secret. Unlike meetings of the Bank of England's Monetary Policy Committee, the minutes of the Council meetings are not published.

The targets of monetary policy

The overall responsibility of the ECB is to achieve price stability in the euro zone. The target set at the launch of the euro in 1999 was a rate of inflation below 2 per cent. This is an *average* rate for all 11 members (12 after Greece joined in January 2001), not a rate that has to be met by every member individually.

The ECB also sets a target for the growth of M3, the broad measure of the money supply (similar, although not identical to the UK's M4 measure). The target set

---

further cuts in government expenditure, or from further borrowing. The problems in controlling public expenditure will be explored more fully in section 29.5.

Short-term monetary control

In order to control the money supply, governments in the past, and particularly in the 1960s, resorted to various forms of credit rationing, such as ceilings on bank lending, requests to banks to discriminate between customers, and hire-purchase controls.

However, the problems of credit rationing can be serious:

● With credit rationing, there will be surplus liquidity that rationed banks are prevented from using for creating credit. To prevent business merely flowing from rationed banks (e.g. UK high street banks) to non-rationed banks (e.g. foreign banks, finance companies, clearing banks' subsidiaries),

at the launch of the euro was 4½ per cent. The target for M3 is only an *intermediate* target, seen as a means of achieving the target rate of inflation. If the M3 target turns out to be too high or too low to achieve the target rate of inflation (perhaps because money circulates faster or slower than originally thought: see section 28.4) then the M3 target is altered.

On the basis of its inflation and money supply targets, the ECB then sets the rates of interest. It sets three rates: a rate for 'refinancing operations' of the ESCB (i.e. the rate of interest charged by the ESCB for liquidity on offer to banks); a (higher) 'last resort' rate; and a (lower) 'deposit rate' (the rate paid to banks for depositing surplus liquidity with the ESCB). In October 2000, these rates were 4.75, 5.75 and 3.75 per cent respectively.

Interest rates are set by the Governing Council by simple majority. In the event of a tie, the president has the casting vote.

The operation of monetary policy

The ECB sets a minimum reserve ratio. It argues that this gives greater stability to the system and reduces the need for day-to-day intervention by the ECB. The ECB argues that if there were no minimum reserves, with banks free to use as much of their reserves with the ESCB as they chose, then they will do so if there is an upsurge in demand from customers. After all, the banks know that they can always *borrow* from the ESCB to meet any liquidity requirements. In such a situation, the ECB would be forced to rely much more on open-market operations to prevent excessive lending by banks to their customers, and hence excessive borrowing from the ESCB, and this would mean much greater fluctuations in interest rates.

The minimum reserve ratio is not designed to be used to make *changes* in monetary policy. In other words it is not used as a *variable* minimum reserves ratio, and for this reason is set at a low level of 2 per cent.

The main instrument for keeping the ECB's desired interest rate as the equilibrium rate is open-market operations in government bonds and other recognised assets, mainly in the form of repos. These repo operations are conducted by the national central banks, which must ensure that the repo rate does not rise above the emergency overnight rate or below the rate at which banks can deposit surplus funds with the ESCB.

Question

What are the arguments for and against publishing the minutes of the meetings of the ECB's Governing Council and Executive Board?

---

credit rationing would have to extend to all institutions. The more complex the banking system, and the more open it is to international competition and international financial flows, the more difficult it is to do this.

- Banks might also resist the attempts at rationing. They would *like* to lend and have the liquidity to do so. They may thus find ways to get round the controls.
- Hire-purchase controls may have serious disruptive effects on certain industries (e.g. cars and other consumer durables), whose products are bought largely on hire-purchase credit.

As long as people *want* to borrow, banks and other financial institutions will normally try to find ways of meeting the demand. In other words, in the short run at least, the supply of money is to a large extent demand-determined. It is for this reason that the authorities prefer to control the *demand* for money by controlling interest rates.

The effectiveness of changes in interest rates

Even though this is the current preferred method of monetary control, it is not without its difficulties. The problems centre on the nature of the demand for loans. If this demand is (a) unresponsive to interest rate changes or (b) unstable because it is significantly affected by other determinants (such as anticipated income or foreign interest rates), then it will be very difficult to control by controlling the rate of interest.

Problem of an inelastic demand for loans. If the demand for loans is inelastic, any attempt to reduce demand will involve large rises in interest rates. The problem will be compounded if the demand curve shifts to the right, due, say, to a consumer spending boom. High interest rates lead to the following problems:

● They may discourage investment and hence long-term growth.
● They add to the costs of production, to the costs of house purchase and generally to the cost of living. They are thus cost inflationary.
● They are politically unpopular, since the general public do not like paying higher interest rates on overdrafts, credit cards and mortgages.
● The necessary bond issue to restrain liquidity will commit the government to paying high rates on these bonds for the next twenty years or so.
● High interest rates encourage inflows of money from abroad. This drives up the exchange rate. A higher exchange rate makes UK goods expensive relative to goods made abroad. This can be very damaging for export industries and industries competing with imports. Many firms suffered badly in 1999/2000 when a policy of raising interest rates (among other things) caused the exchange rate with the euro to soar.

Evidence suggests that the demand for loans may indeed be quite inelastic. The reasons include the following:

● A rise in interest rates, particularly if it deepens a recession, may force many firms into borrowing merely to survive. This increase in 'distress borrowing' may largely offset any decline in borrowing by other firms or individuals.
● Although investment *plans* may be curtailed by high interest rates, *current* borrowing by many firms cannot easily be curtailed. Similarly, high interest rates may discourage householders from taking on *new* mortgages, but existing mortgages are unlikely to be reduced.
● High interest rates may discourage many firms from taking out long-term fixed-interest loans. But instead of reducing total borrowing, some firms may merely switch to shorter-term variable-interest loans. This will reduce the overall fall in demand for bank loans, thus making the demand less elastic.

Problem of an unstable demand. Accurate monetary control requires the authorities to be able to predict the demand curve for money (in Figure 29.2). Only then can they set the appropriate level of interest rates. Unfortunately, the demand curve may shift unpredictably, making control very difficult. The major reason is *speculation*:

● If people think interest rates will rise and bond prices fall, in the meantime they will demand to hold their assets in liquid form. The demand for money will rise.

BOX 29.4

Should central banks be independent of government?

In the mid-1990s there was much discussion in the UK among both economists and politicians as to whether the Bank of England should be independent. The Conservative governments under Margaret Thatcher and John Major felt that it was important for the government to retain control over monetary policy, if it was to achieve its macroeconomic objectives: a view also held by many on the left of the Labour party.

In contrast to these views, the advocates of independence frequently cited the experience of Germany. Before the launch of the euro in 1999, Germany's monetary policy was conducted by its central bank, the Bundesbank. This was fiercely independent of the German government, and was credited with being instrumental in Germany's economic success. The Bundesbank's philosophy was simple: monetary and price stability are of overriding importance in the pursuit of growth. Inflation should be tightly controlled at all times.

This philosophy has been continued by the European Central Bank (ECB) in operating the euro-zone's monetary policy. It is keen to stress its independence from member governments in setting interest rates and it resists attempts by politicians to influence its policy.

The arguments in favour of an independent central bank are strong.

- An independent central bank is free from political manipulation. It can devote itself to attaining long-run economic goals, rather than to helping politicians achieve short-run economic success in time for the next election.
- Independence may strengthen the *credibility* of monetary policy. This may then play an important part in shaping expectations: workers may put in moderate wage demands and businesses may be more willing to invest.
- An independent central bank like the ECB and the Bank of England has a clear legal status and set of responsibilities. It is the 'protector of the currency' and as such it is not subordinate to government. This is important given the political nature of economic policy-making, in both a domestic and an international context.

Evidence suggests that the greater the independence of a country's central bank, the lower and more stable is its rate of inflation. If this is the goal of economic policy, it would seem that more, rather than less, independence is desirable.

Certainly the incoming Labour government in 1997 was convinced of these arguments. Indeed, granting independence to the Bank of England was the very first act of the Chancellor, Gordon Brown. The decision could also have been affected by two other arguments.

The first was a political one: any blame for rises in interest rates would be deflected from the government. Indeed the government was keen to stress that the several rises in interest rates announced by the Bank of England's Monetary Policy Committee in 1997 and 1998 were the MPC's decision alone!

The second was concerned with the possibility of the UK joining the single currency at some future date. Given that the ECB is independent, the transition to a single currency would be simpler if the Bank of England were already independent.

One of the major arguments *against* having an independent central bank is that it makes it more difficult to integrate monetary management into wider economic policy objectives. On some occasions, for example, it might be desirable to accept a *higher* rate of inflation – if this were the consequence of a growth stimulus aimed at reducing unemployment. But with an independent central bank committed to monetary stability, it may be difficult for the government to achieve such economic policy goals. As Kenneth Clarke, the Chancellor in the outgoing Conservative government, argued: 'What you are going to see is tighter monetary policy than you might otherwise have got from a perfectly responsible Chancellor of the Exchequer.'

In fact, these very arguments were used by various EU governments in 1999 when there were fears of an impending recession. Centre-left leaders in countries such as Germany, Italy and France were keen for the ECB to focus more on stimulating demand to help stave off recession, rather than on keeping inflation below the 2 per cent target it had set.

Question

Is there any case for an independent body to determine fiscal policy? If so what would its role be?

- If people think exchange rates will rise, they will demand sterling while it is still relatively cheap. The demand for money will rise.
- If people think inflation will rise, the transactions demand for money may rise. People spend now while prices are still relatively low.
- If people think the economy is going to grow faster, the demand for loans will increase as firms seek to increase their investment.

It is very difficult for the authorities to predict what people's expectations will be. Speculation depends so much on world political events, rumour and 'random shocks'.

If the demand curve shifts very much, and if it is inelastic, then monetary control will be very difficult. Furthermore, the authorities will have to make frequent and sizeable adjustments to interest rates. These fluctuations can be very damaging to business confidence and may discourage long-term investment.

Using monetary policy

It is impossible to use monetary policy as a precise means of controlling aggregate demand. It is especially weak when it is pulling against the expectations of firms and consumers and when it is implemented too late. However, if the authorities operate a tight monetary policy firmly enough and long enough, they should eventually be able to reduce lending and aggregate demand. But there will inevitably be time lags and imprecision in the process.

An expansionary monetary policy is even less reliable. If the economy is in recession, no matter how low interest rates are driven, people cannot be forced to borrow if they do not wish to. Firms will not borrow to invest if they predict a continuing recession.

Despite these problems, changing interest rates can be quite effective. After all, they can be changed very rapidly. There are not the time lags of implementation that there are with fiscal policy. Indeed, since the early 1990s, the government has used interest rate changes as its major means of keeping aggregate demand and inflation under control. A target is set for the rate of inflation. If forecasts suggest that inflation is going to be above target, the Bank of England's Monetary Policy Committee will raise interest rates at its next monthly meeting.

The main objective of the Bank of England in controlling interest rates is to keep inflation at the target level of 2½ per cent. The advantage of this is that it sends a very clear message to people that inflation *will* be kept under control. People will therefore be more likely to adjust their expectations accordingly and keep their borrowing in check.

29.5 Trends in public expenditure and the crowding-out debate

Trends in public expenditure

Figure 29.3 reveals that since 1901 general government expenditure (GGE) as a percentage of GDP has been rising. This rise, however, has not been steady. On occasions, such as during the First and Second World Wars, the level of GGE rose dramatically (but without returning afterwards to previous levels).

In 1989, GGE as a percentage of GDP was 39.8 per cent – its lowest level for

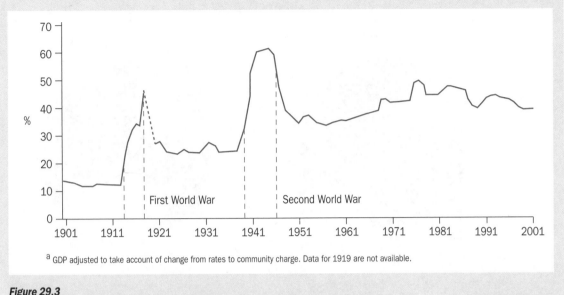

a GDP adjusted to take account of change from rates to community charge. Data for 1919 are not available.

Figure 29.3
UK general government expenditure as a percentage of GDP[a]: 1901–2001

22 years. However, the deep and protracted recession experienced by the UK in the early 1990s pushed the expenditure rate back upwards again to reach 45.4 per cent by 1993. Nevertheless, with continued economic growth since then, the rate has progressively fallen to stand at 39.3 per cent in 1999. However, in absolute terms GGE is still rising. It rose from £250.4 billion in 1981 to £346.8 billion in 1999 (both in 1999 prices).

Figure 29.4 shows that the four largest areas of GGE are social protection, health, education and defence. Only defence has declined as a percentage of GGE (thanks to the ending of the 'cold war').

Attempts to control public expenditure since 1979

The Conservative governments in the 1980s and 1990s adopted a number of tough measures to reduce the level of public expenditure (or to improve its efficiency). Such measures included the following:

- Cash limits on various government departments and local authorities. The aim was to limit their spending and force them to become more efficient. Local authorities are subject to Standard Spending Assessments (SSA). The government calculates an SSA for each local authority based on government estimates of how much the authority needs to spend in order to provide a 'standard' level of service. If a local authority's spending exceeds its SSA, then the council tax (the local tax) will be increased by proportionately *more* than this, thus effectively imposing a penalty on 'high spending' authorities.
- A reduction in grants and subsidies. The grant to local authorities from the government was reduced from 61 per cent of local authority expenditure in 1979 to 54 per cent in 1986 to 47 per cent in 1989 (but was increased

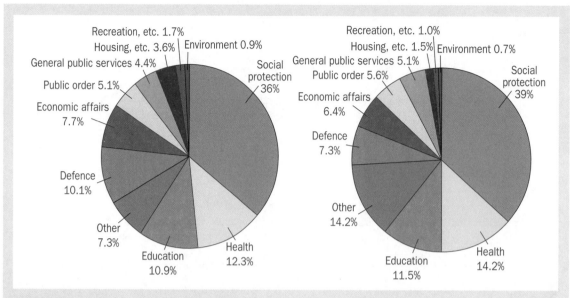

Figure 29.4

UK general government expenditure by function (%)

Sources: *UK National Income and Expenditure* (ONS); *Financial Statement and Budget Report 1999/2000* (HM Treasury).

again thereafter). Subsidies to nationalised industries were reduced and many nationalised industries were forced to raise their prices.

- Continuous attempts to reduce staffing in the civil service.
- Appointment of tough managers (in the early 1980s) in several nationalised industries, in order to bring about radical reorganisation and substantial increases in efficiency. In several cases this meant redundancies. The government was prepared to withstand lengthy industrial disputes in the pursuit of this policy, such as the bitter miners' dispute in 1984–5 over pit closures.
- A tough line on public-sector pay. Here too the government was prepared to withstand union action.

However, these policies were not without problems:

- In some sectors the effect was to cut services rather than increase efficiency.
- It was found much easier to cut long-term capital expenditure than current expenditure (e.g. wages). Thus there was a sharp decline in new roads, schools, public-sector housing, etc. Public investment was cut from 2.6 per cent of GDP in 1979 to 1.8 per cent in 1981 to 1.6 per cent in 1989. Recognising the importance of infrastructure expenditure for the long-run growth of the economy, the Major government made some attempt to reverse this trend in the early 1990s.
- Reducing the overall size of the public sector was very difficult when the government was also trying to reduce inflation by tight monetary policy. The dramatic rise in unemployment after 1979 led to large increases in expenditure on unemployment and other social security benefits. Up to 1982 government expenditure actually rose as a proportion of GDP. The problem re-emerged in the recession of the early 1990s.

Despite the government's desire to achieve savings in public expenditure, most of the cuts have only been at the margin. In real terms GGE has continued to rise. Of all the government's budgets, only housing, cut by 67 per cent between 1979 and 1990 and by a further 58 per cent between 1991 and 1999, has been dramatically reduced. It is only by trimming the big four – social security (social 'protection'), health, education and defence, which together account for over 70 per cent of all spending – that GGE can be significantly reduced. But such trimming is very difficult, especially in such politically sensitive areas. No politician wants to be seen reducing spending on health and education!

Why is controlling public expenditure seen as such an important economic goal? The answer lies in what is known as the 'crowding-out debate'.

The crowding-out debate

If increased government expenditure is used to stimulate output and employment, will the effect be neutralised by *crowding out*? Will, for example, a programme of public works to bring the economy out of recession merely lead to a reduction in private expenditure? To answer this, it is important to distinguish two types of crowding out: *resource crowding out and financial crowding out.*

Resource crowding out. This is when the government uses resources such as labour and raw materials that would otherwise be used by the private sector. This would clearly be possible if the economy were operating near full capacity. Workers cannot be in two places at once. If they work for the government, they cannot at the same time work for a private company.

The argument is far less convincing, however, if there is slack in the economy. If the government merely mobilises otherwise *idle* resources, there need be no reduction in private-sector output. Quite the opposite: if there is a growth in public-sector output and employment, this will stimulate a demand for goods produced by the private sector too. If these private-sector firms have spare capacity, they will respond by producing more themselves. This is the argument put forward by Keynesians: extra aggregate demand will stimulate extra production.

Financial crowding out. This occurs when extra government spending diverts funds from private-sector firms and thus deprives them of the finance necessary for investment.

If the government spends more (without raising taxes or printing more money), it will have to borrow more. In order to attract people to buy government securities or put their money in National Savings, the government will have to offer higher rates of interest. Private companies in turn will then have to offer higher rates of interest themselves in order to attract funds. Alternatively, if they borrow from banks, and banks have less funds, the banks will charge them higher interest rates. Higher interest rates will discourage firms from borrowing and hence discourage investment.

In short, if the government spends more money, there will be less money for the private sector to spend.

The weakness with this argument is that it assumes that the supply of money is fixed. If the government spends more but *increases* the amount of money in the economy, it need not deprive the private sector of finance. Interest rates will not be bid up.

But would that not be inflationary? No, say Keynesians, not if there are idle resources and hence the extra money can be spent on extra output. Only if *resource* crowding out took place would it be inflationary.

What if the government *reduces* its expenditure: will this result in a release of resources and funds, and will this lead to extra private expenditure? This is an even more contentious claim, given that a successful reduction in government expenditure would lead to a direct reduction in aggregate demand, whereas any fall in interest rates, made possible by the reduction in government borrowing and the consequent release of funds to the private sector, would only stimulate private investment expenditure if there was confidence that the economy would expand.

29.6 The management of aggregate demand in practice

Attitudes towards demand management

The debate between Keynesians and monetarists over the control of demand has shifted ground somewhat in recent years. There is less debate today over the relative merits of fiscal and monetary policy. There is general agreement now that a *combination* of fiscal and monetary policies will have a powerful effect on demand.

The debate today is much more concerned with whether the government ought to pursue an active demand management policy at all, or whether it ought merely to adhere to a set of policy rules.

Keynesians believe that governments should manage the level of aggregate demand, both to remove persistent inflationary and deflationary gaps, and to smooth out cyclical fluctuations in national income.

Monetarists believe that governments should not engage in demand management policies. Such policies, they claim, will be at best ineffective and at worst actually destabilising. Monetarists therefore prefer a 'steady as you go' approach. They prefer to set firm rules: e.g. targets for the steady growth in money supply in line with potential output.

In summary: Keynesians prefer discretionary policy – changing policy as circumstances change. Monetarists prefer to set firms rules and then stick to them.

Policy in action

During the 1950s and 1960s both Labour and Conservative governments embraced Keynesian ideas. They pursued active demand management policies in an attempt to smooth out cyclical fluctuations and to keep national income as close as possible to the full-employment level.

The main weapon for this was changes in tax rates. But use was also made of government expenditure changes and monetary policy. As a result, a 'package deal' of policies was frequently adopted.

Economic performance during the 1950s and 1960s compares very favourably with the periods both before and after.

The demise of fine tuning in the 1970s: the problem of stagflation

Attempts at fine tuning the economy became impossible in the 1970s because of the rising problem of **stagflation**. Demand management policies were still used, but they could no longer achieve an acceptable combination of inflation and unemployment. The Phillips curve had broken down.

Sometimes reflationary policies were used to get a modest reduction in unemployment, but then inflation would be very high. At other times, deflationary policies were used to reduce inflation, but then unemployment rose very rapidly.

The Keynesian response to stagflation was to recommend supplementing demand management with interventionist supply-side policies, such as regional policy, import restrictions and retraining policies.

The monetarist response was to recommend abandoning discretionary demand management of the stop–go variety altogether, and moving to a policy of sticking to monetary targets. In addition, they advocated the use of *market-orientated* supply-side policies such as tax reform (so as to increase the incentives for work and investment), legislation to reduce the monopoly power of unions, abandoning minimum wages (set by government bodies such as wages councils) and lower unemployment benefits.

Monetarism under Mrs Thatcher

With the election of the Conservatives in 1979, the UK for the first time had a government committed to monetarist policies.

On the supply side, the government pursued policies to free up the market. The prices and incomes policy of the previous Labour government was abandoned; legislation was introduced to curb trade union power; foreign exchange controls were lifted; in order to increase incentives the standard rate of income tax was cut from 33 per cent to 30 per cent (with VAT being raised to compensate for the loss of revenue); the government made it clear that it would not bale out 'lame duck' industries that were unable to survive the rigours of the market; and later on it pursued a comprehensive policy of privatisation.

On the demand side, the cornerstone of the government's policy on inflation was the medium-term financial strategy (MTFS). Discretionary demand management in an attempt to fine tune the economy was totally abandoned. Instead, progressively descending targets were adopted for the growth of the money supply each year for the following four years. Money supply was to be kept on target in the short term by changes in interest rates. In the medium term, the achievement of the targets would require a progressive reduction in the PSBR as a proportion of GDP (if crowding out was to be avoided).

Initially, the UK experienced the deepest recession since the 1930s. What is more, unlike the 1930s there was also high inflation. The abandonment of incomes policy, the doubling of oil prices from 1979 to 1981 and the rise in VAT from 7 per cent to 15 per cent led to a rise in inflation from 8.3 per cent in 1978 to 18 per cent in 1980. At the same time, fiscal and monetary policy had a highly deflationary effect. Interest rates rose rapidly, with banks' base rates reaching 17 per cent in late 1979. The high interest rates, plus an improving balance of payments due to North Sea oil, led to a rapid rise in the exchange rate, fuelled by speculation of further rises.

The combination of low demand, high interest rates, a high exchange rate and

definition

Stagflation
A term used in the 1970s to refer to the combination of stagnation (low growth and high unemployment) and high inflation.

656 CHAPTER 29 DEMAND-SIDE POLICY

rapidly rising costs led to a severe recession, and unemployment rocketed from 4.7 per cent in 1979 to nearly 10 per cent in 1981.

The continuing tight monetary policy with high real interest rates allowed only a slow recovery from recession. It was not until 1985 that the economy appeared to turn the corner. At this time, demand management policy reverted to a more traditional stop–go pattern. Discretion seemed to be replacing rules. Interest rate policy became increasingly determined by short-run considerations of managing the exchange rate or responding to upward pressures on inflation.

The problem of more than one target and only one instrument

In the mid-1980s there was a growing belief that, with closer links being forged with Europe, and with the desirability of a stable exchange rate between the pound and other European currencies, the *exchange rate* ought to be targeted. But the government now effectively had only one instrument of policy: interest rates. In fact, the opposition, using a golfing analogy, often referred to Nigel Lawson as 'the one-club Chancellor'. The problem is that you cannot use just one instrument (interest rates) at one and the same time to control *both* the level of aggregate demand (and hence inflation) *and* the rate of exchange. In 1988 high interest rates were required to control the rapidly expanding credit, but low interest rates were required to prevent the exchange rate rising above its target level of around £1 = DM3.00[1], a rise that would be damaging to exports. Which to choose was a matter of fierce political debate – not least between the Prime Minister, who saw control of inflation as the immediate objective, and the Chancellor (Nigel Lawson), who saw control of the exchange rate as the immediate objective, albeit as a means, among other things, of controlling inflation. The debate, however, resolved itself. With a *falling* pound in 1989, high interest rates were desirable for both exchange rate and counter-inflationary reasons.

ERM membership: 1990–2

In October 1990 the UK joined the exchange rate mechanism (ERM) of the European Community. The requirement to keep the pound within an exchange rate band of approximately DM2.78–3.13 meant that there was now effectively an exchange rate target. But with essentially only one instrument of macroeconomic policy – the rate of interest – all other macroeconomic goals had to be subordinated to this target.

In a fixed exchange rate system, UK interest rates were largely governed by those of the other countries within the system. The reunification of Germany had involved a large expansion of German money supply. In response the Bundesbank (the German central bank), in order to prevent inflation rising, raised interest rates substantially. To maintain sterling's value within the ERM, the UK government therefore had to pursue a high interest rate policy. But given that the German inflation rate was still only 2.8 per cent and the UK inflation rate was nearly 11 per cent, this meant that UK interest rates had to be considerably above the German level.

Within a few months it was clear that the UK was plunging into recession. On domestic grounds alone, lower interest rates would have been desirable. But by

[1] DM stands for Deutschmark, the German mark.

mid-1991 the pound was again under pressure in the ERM and so monetary policy had to be kept tight. Inflation was now falling rapidly, but interest rates were only reduced slightly. This meant that *real* interest rates had risen. In the twelve months after joining the ERM, UK inflation fell by 7 percentage points whereas interest rates fell by only 3 percentage points. There was thus a growing policy conflict between the *external* requirement of maintaining the exchange rate and the internal requirement of reflating a depressed domestic economy.

Throughout 1991 and the first part of 1992 the government stuck resolutely to the policy of maintaining sterling's value in the ERM. Ministers repeatedly justified this as being the best means of continuing the fight against inflation. But, as we saw in Chapter 26, by September 1992 massive speculation against the pound had forced the UK to abandon ERM membership.

A return to domestic-orientated policies: targeting inflation

With the need to defend the value of the pound removed, the government could focus once more on the domestic situation. Within four months interest rates had been reduced by 4 per cent. This loosening of monetary policy gave a welcome boost to the economy, which was still only just beginning to pull out of recession.

The government was not worried that this would lead to an unwelcome growth in money supply and inflation. Indeed, the control of inflation was now to be the main objective of monetary policy. An initial target rate of inflation of 1–4 per cent was set, to be backed up by 'monitoring ranges' of 0–4 per cent for M0 and 3–9 per cent for M4 until 1997, by which time inflation should be between 1 and 2½ per cent.

Targeting inflation was based on the belief that monetary policy cannot influence *real* variables such as output and employment in the long run. It can only influence inflation. It is better, therefore, to focus on achieving low inflation in order to provide the best environment for businesses to thrive. But to achieve an inflation target meant doing two things.

First, given the time lags between changing interest rates and their effect on inflation, interest rates would have to be changed in response to inflation *forecasts*, rather than the current rate of inflation. Second, people would have to be made to believe that the government could and would achieve the target. To this end, a number of steps were taken:

- The Bank of England published inflation forecasts, which the government publicly used to assess whether policy was on target.
- The Chancellor and the Governor of the Bank of England met monthly to consider the necessary interest rate policy to keep inflation within the target range.
- Minutes of these meetings were published six weeks later, in order to give transparency to the process.
- Although interest rate changes would be determined at these meetings (with the Chancellor having the final say), the *timing* of their introduction would be determined by the Bank of England. The idea here was to stress a new semi-autonomous role for the Bank.
- Each time interest rates were changed, a press notice would be issued

explaining the reasons. The idea here was to show the government's commitment to keeping to the target.

Was the policy a success? Inflation remained within the target bands, and the government claimed that this was the result of the policy. In fact, the reduction in inflation from 1992 to 1994 was the lagged result of the tight monetary conditions during the previous two years when the UK was in the ERM. Indeed, the government *reduced* interest rates several times between September 1992 and February 1994. After 1994, however, the policy *did* help to keep inflation down, with the government raising interest rates whenever inflationary forecasts were adverse.

As far as fiscal policy was concerned, with the PSNCR for the year ending March 1993 being a massive £36.3 billion, there was a serious problem that, if monetary growth was kept in check, government borrowing would crowd out private-sector growth. The government thus saw the need to get a 'better' balance between fiscal and monetary policy. It therefore announced a series of tax increases to be phased in over the coming years. It also stated its intention to examine ways of reducing government expenditure.

The PSNCR peaked at £45.4 billion in 1993/4, but remained high throughout 1995 and 1996. The government thus felt unable to make significant tax cuts in the November 1995 and 1996 Budgets, even though there were worries about a fall in economic growth.

Current demand-side policy in the UK

Fiscal policy

Since 1998, the government has set targets for government expenditure, not for just one year, but for a three-year period. Does this mean, therefore, that fiscal policy as a means of adjusting aggregate demand had been abandoned? In one sense, this is the case. The government is now committed to following its 'golden rule', whereby public-sector receipts should cover all current spending, averaged over the course of the business cycle (see Box 29.1). In fact, in supporting sticking to the golden rule, the Chancellor explicitly rejected Keynesian fine tuning:

> In today's deregulated, liberalised financial markets, the Keynesian fine tuning of the past, which worked in relatively sheltered, closed national economies and which tried to exploit a supposed long-term trade-off between inflation and unemployment, will simply not work.[2]

But despite this apparent rejection of short-term discretionary fiscal adjustments, there is still a role for *automatic* fiscal stabilisers: with deficits rising in a recession and falling in a boom. There is also still the possibility, within the golden rule, of financing additional *investment* by borrowing, thereby providing a stimulus to a sluggish economy.

Monetary policy

In 1997, the incoming Labour government set a target for inflation of 2½ per cent. Unlike its predecessor, however, it decided to make the Bank of England

[2] Extract from the Chancellor's Mansion House speech, 11 June 1998.

independent. Indeed, this was the first action taken by the Chancellor when the government came to power.

But why did the government give up its right to set interest rates? First, there is the political advantage of taking 'blame' away from the government if interest rates need to be raised in order to prevent inflation rising above its target. Second, an independent central bank, free to set interest rates in order to achieve a clear target, is more likely to be consistent in pursuit of this objective than a government concerned about its popularity. Then there is the question of transparency in decision making.

> If inflation is more than 1 percentage point higher or lower than the target, an open letter will be sent by the Governor to the Chancellor so that the public is fully informed as to why the divergence has occurred; the policy action being taken to deal with it; the period within which inflation is expected to return to the target; and how this approach meets the government's monetary policy objectives. Monetary policy decision-making is now among the most transparent and accountable in the world.[3]

Transparency is enhanced by the publication of the minutes of the monthly meetings of the Bank's Monetary Policy Committee (MPC) at which interest rates are set. One of the main purposes of transparency is to convince people of the seriousness with which the Bank of England will adhere to its targets. This, it is hoped, will keep people's *expectations* of inflation low: the lower expected inflation is, the lower will be the actual rate of inflation.

With monetary policy geared to an inflation target and fiscal policy geared to following the golden rule, there seems to be virtually no scope for discretionary demand management policy. Rules appear to have replaced discretion.

> When there are ever more rapid financial flows across the world that are unpredictable and uncertain, the answer is to ensure stability through establishing the right long-term policy objectives and to build credibility in the policy through well-understood procedural rules that are followed for fiscal and monetary policy.[4]

There is, however, a new form of fine tuning: the frequent adjustment of interest rates, not to smooth out the business cycle, but to make sure that the inflation rule is adhered to.

SUMMARY

1a The government's fiscal policy will determine the size of the budget deficit or surplus and the size of the PSNCR.

1b Automatic fiscal stabilisers are tax revenues that rise and benefits that fall as national income rises. They have the effect of reducing the size of the multiplier and thus reducing cyclical upswings and downswings.

1c Discretionary fiscal policy is where the government deliberately changes taxes or government expenditure in order to alter the level of aggregate demand. Changes in government expenditure on goods and services will have a full multiplier effect. Changes in taxes and benefits will have a smaller multiplier effect as some of the tax/benefit changes will merely affect other withdrawals and thus have a

---

[3] *The Government's Overall Economic Strategy* (http://www.hm-treasury.gov.uk/pub/html/e_info/overview/1_goes.html).
[4] Extract from the Chancellor's Mansion House speech, 11 June 1998.

SUMMARY

smaller net effect on consumption of domestic product.

2a The effectiveness of fiscal policy depends on the accuracy of forecasting. It also depends on the predictability of the outcome of the fiscal measures: the effect of changes in G and T on other injections and withdrawals, the size and timing of the multiplier and accelerator effects, the relative effects of changes in aggregate demand on the various macroeconomic objectives, and whether there are any side-effects. It also depends on whether there are any random shocks.

2b Automatic stabilisers take effect as soon as aggregate demand fluctuates, but they can never remove fluctuations completely. They also create disincentives and act as a drag on recovery from recession.

2c There are problems in predicting the magnitude of the effects of discretionary fiscal policy. Expansionary fiscal policy can act as a pump primer and stimulate increased private expenditure, or it can crowd out private expenditure. The extent to which it acts as a pump primer depends crucially on business confidence – something that is very difficult to predict beyond a few weeks or months. The extent of crowding out depends on monetary conditions and the government's monetary policy.

2d There are five possible time lags involved with fiscal policy: the time lag before the problem is diagnosed, the lag between diagnosis and new measures being announced, the lag between announcement and implementation, the lag while the multiplier and accelerator work themselves out, and the lag before consumption fully responds to new economic circumstances.

2e Discretionary fiscal policy can involve side-effects, such as disincentives, higher costs and adverse effects on social programmes.

2f Today many governments prefer a more passive approach towards fiscal policy. Targets are set for one or more measures of the public-sector finances, and then taxes and government expenditure are adjusted so as to keep to the target.

3a In the medium and long term, the major sources of monetary growth are banks choosing to operate with a lower liquidity ratio and government borrowing.

3b Banks choosing to operate with a lower liquidity ratio could be prevented by the authorities imposing statutory reserve requirements on banks. This practice is commonplace throughout the world, but the authorities in the UK regard it as 'anti-market'. Instead they have chosen to rely on using interest rates to curb the *demand* for credit.

3c In the short term, the government can use monetary policy to restrict the growth in aggregate demand in one of three ways: (a) reducing money supply direct, (b) reducing the demand for money by raising interest rates, or (c) rationing credit.

3d The money supply can be reduced directly by using open-market operations. This involves selling more government securities and thereby reducing banks' reserves when their customers pay for them from their bank accounts. Alternatively, funding can be used. This is where the government increases the ratio of bonds to bills. In some countries, banks are required to observe a minimum reserve ratio. By increasing this ratio, the central bank can force banks to reduce credit, thereby reducing the money supply.

3e The current method of control involves the Bank of England's Monetary Policy Committee announcing the interest rate and then the Bank of England bringing this rate about by its operations in the discount and repo markets. It keep banks short of liquidity, and then supplies them with liquidity largely through gilt repos, at the chosen interest rate (gilt repo rate). This then has a knock-on effect on interest rates throughout the economy.

3f Credit rationing in the UK has not been used since the late 1970s.

4a It is difficult to control the growth of the money supply over the longer term without controlling the growth of the PSNCR. This will be difficult in a recession, when automatic fiscal stabilisers will cause a growth in government expenditure and a cut in tax revenues.

4b All forms of short-term monetary policy involve problems. If the government is successful in controlling the money supply, there then arises the problem of severe fluctuations in interest rates if the demand for money fluctuates and is relatively inelastic.

SUMMARY

4c Credit rationing is a means of directly reducing aggregate demand without having to raise interest rates. It stifles competition between banks, however, and encourages banks to discriminate (perhaps unfairly) between customers. Banks may also try to evade the controls, and business may simply flow to those institutions that are not controlled.

4d The form of monetary policy that has been favoured in recent years is the control of interest rates. Higher interest rates, by reducing the demand for money, effectively also reduce the supply. However, with an inelastic demand for loans, interest rates may have to rise to very high levels in order to bring the required reduction in monetary growth. They are politically unpopular and discriminate against those with high borrowing commitments. They also drive up the exchange rate, which can damage exports. Controlling aggregate demand through interest rates is made even more difficult by fluctuations in the demand for money. These fluctuations are made more severe by speculation against changes in interest rates, exchange rates, the rate of inflation, etc.

4e Nevertheless, controlling interest rates is a way of responding rapidly to changing forecasts, and can be an important signal to markets that inflation will be kept under control, especially when, as in the UK, there is a firm target for the rate of inflation.

5a Since 1945 the trend has been for public expenditure to grow steadily, although in recent years, with continued economic growth, it has fallen somewhat as a percentage of GDP. Attempts to control public expenditure growth intensified following 1979.

5b The crowding out of the private sector by the public sector became a point of debate in the 1980s. The crowding-out debate concerns the possible crowding out of both resources and finance.

6a In the 1950s and 1960s, both Labour and Conservative governments pursued active demand management policies. The dominating constraints on these policies were the balance of payments and electoral considerations. Demand management was little more than stop–go policy dictated by the state of the balance of payments and the need to win elections.

6b The 1950s and 1960s was a period of relative economic success. But whether this was due to the pursuit of Keynesian demand management policies or to other factors such as a buoyant world economy and economic optimism is a matter of debate.

6c In the 1970s stagflation became a major problem due to a number of factors, including expansionary fiscal and monetary policies in the early 1970s, the adoption of floating exchange rates, a large rise in oil prices, growing domestically generated cost-push pressures, a decline in the competitiveness of UK exports, technological change and increasingly pessimistic expectations.

6d The Conservative government in the 1980s initially pursued a tight monetary policy and targeted the PSNCR and the growth in the money supply. The exchange rate rose and the economy plunged into a deep recession. The economy started to grow again after 1982, but for a time a tight monetary policy was retained (along with monetary targets) in order to keep a downward pressure on inflation.

6e Then, after 1985, targets for monetary growth were abandoned and for a time targeting the exchange rate became the main focus of monetary policy. But with only one instrument (interest rates) there was a conflict between keeping exchange rates down and controlling inflation.

6f The UK joined the ERM in October 1990 and the conflict between domestic and exchange rate policy became acute. The economy was moving rapidly into recession, but the government was unable to make substantial cuts in interest rates because of the need to defend the value of the pound. Eventually in September 1992, with huge speculation in favour of the Deutschmark and against sterling and the lira, the UK and Italy were forced to leave the ERM.

6g Since 1992, there has been a return to using interest rates to manage domestic demand in line with inflation targets.

6h Today, fiscal policy is geared to achieving a balanced budget over the course of the business cycle. The only exception to this is borrowing for public *investment*. Monetary policy is geared to achieving a target rate of inflation of 2½ per cent. The Bank of England adjusts interest rates in order to keep to this target.

REVIEW QUESTIONS

1 'The existence of a budget deficit or a budget surplus tells us very little about the stance of fiscal policy.' Explain and discuss.

2 Adam Smith remarked in *The Wealth of Nations* concerning the balancing of budgets, 'What is prudence in the conduct of every private family can scarce be folly in that of a great kingdom.' What problems might there be if the government decided to follow a balanced budget approach to its spending?

3 When the Bank of England announces that it is putting up interest rates, how will it achieve this, given that interest rates are determined by demand and supply?

4 What is the crowding-out debate?

5 What was stagflation? What reasons have been advanced to explain the stagflation experienced by the British economy during the 1970s? What problems did stagflation create for the management of economic affairs during this period?

6 Would you describe the policies pursued by the Conservative government in the UK in the 1980s as strictly monetarist?

7 Is there a compromise between purely discretionary policy and adhering to strict targets?

8 Under what circumstances would adherence to an inflation target lead to (a) more stable interest rates, (b) less stable interest rates than pursuing discretionary demand management policy?

Supply-side policy 30

30.1 The supply-side problem

In considering economic policy up to this point we have focused our attention upon the demand side, where unemployment and slow growth are due to a lack of aggregate demand, and inflation and a balance of payments deficit are due to excessive aggregate demand. Many of the causes of these problems lie on the supply side, however, and as such require an alternative policy approach.

Unemployment and supply-side policies

Equilibrium unemployment – frictional, structural, etc. – is caused by various rigidities or imperfections in the market. There is a mismatching of aggregate supply and demand, and vacancies are not filled despite the existence of unemployment. Perhaps workers have the wrong qualifications, or are poorly motivated, or are living a long way away from the job, or are simply unaware of the jobs that are vacant. Generally, the problem is that labour is not sufficiently mobile, either occupationally or geographically, to respond to changes in the job market. Labour supply for particular jobs is too inelastic.

Supply-side policies aim to influence labour supply. They aim to make workers more responsive to changes in job opportunities. Alternatively, they may aim to make employers more adaptable and willing to operate within existing labour constraints.

Inflation and supply-side policies

If inflation is caused by cost-push pressures, supply-side policy can help to reduce these cost pressures in two ways:

- By reducing the power of unions and/or firms (e.g. by anti-monopoly legislation), and thereby encouraging more competition in the supply of labour and/or goods.
- By encouraging increases in productivity through the retraining of labour, or by investment grants to firms, or by tax incentives, etc.

Growth and supply-side policies

Supply-side economics focuses on *potential* income. Supply-side policies aim to increase the total quantity of factors of production (e.g. policies designed to encourage the building of new factories) or they can be used to encourage greater productivity of factors of production (e.g. policies to encourage the training of labour, or incentives for people to work harder).

The term 'supply-side policy' is often associated with monetarism. Monetarists advocate policies to 'free up' the market: policies that encourage private enterprise, risk taking and competition; policies that provide incentives and reward initiative, hard work and productivity. Section 30.2 examines these *market-orientated* supply-side policies.

Although the term 'supply-side policy' is often used to refer specifically to free-market-orientated policies, there are other supply-side policies which are *interventionist* in nature and are designed to counteract the deficiencies of the free market. Such policies are considered in sections 30.3 and 30.4, which focus upon regional and urban, and industrial policy initiatives.

30.2 Market-orientated supply-side policies

Radical market-orientated supply-side policies were first adopted in the early 1980s by the Thatcher government in the UK and the Reagan administration in the USA. The essence of these supply-side policies was to encourage and reward individual enterprise and initiative, and to reduce the role of government; to put more reliance on market forces and competition, and less on government intervention and regulation. The policies were associated with the following:

- Reducing government expenditure so as to release more resources for the private sector.
- Reducing taxes so as to increase incentives.
- Reducing the monopoly power of trade unions so as to encourage greater flexibility in both wages and working practices and to allow labour markets to clear.
- Reducing the automatic entitlement to certain welfare benefits so as to encourage greater self-reliance.
- Reducing red tape and other impediments to investment and risk taking.
- Encouraging competition through policies of deregulation and privatisation.
- Abolishing exchange controls and other impediments to the free movement of capital.

Such policies were increasingly copied by other governments around the world, so that by the mid-1990s most countries had adopted some or all of the above measures.

Reducing government expenditure

The desire of many governments to cut government expenditure is not just to reduce the PSNCR and hence reduce the growth of money supply; it is also an essential ingredient of their supply-side strategy.

In most countries the size of the public sector, relative to national income, has grown substantially since the 1950s (see Table 30.1). A major aim of Conservative governments throughout the world has been to reverse this trend. The public sector is portrayed as more bureaucratic and less efficient than the private sector. What is more, it is claimed that a growing proportion of public money has been spent on administration and other 'non-productive' activities, rather than on the direct provision of goods and services.

Two things are needed, it is argued: (a) a more efficient use of resources

Table 30.1	General government outlays as a percentage of GDP					
	1961–70	*1971–80*	*1981–5*	*1986–90*	*1991–5*	*1996–2000*
Belgium	33.7	50.0	61.5	55.6	54.4	51.2
Germany	37.0	45.3	48.2	46.0	48.1	47.8
France	38.3	42.4	51.5	50.2	52.8	52.3
Japan	–	26.8	33.2	32.0	33.8	38.2
Netherlands	39.9	49.3	59.5	54.7	52.7	46.2
UK	36.5	41.2	44.6	39.9	42.6	40.5
USA	29.1	33.1	36.5	34.9	35.4	32.5

Source: Adapted from *European Economy Supplement A* December 2000 (European Commission).

within the public sector and (b) a reduction in the size of the public sector. This would allow private investment to increase with no overall rise in aggregate demand. Thus the supply-side benefits of higher investment could be achieved without the demand-side costs of higher inflation.

However, as we saw in section 29.5, it is difficult in practice to cut government expenditure without cutting services and the provision of infrastructure.

Tax cuts: the effects on labour supply and employment

Cutting the marginal rate of income tax was a major objective of the Thatcher and Major governments. In 1979 the standard rate of income tax in the UK was 33 per cent and the top rate was 83 per cent. By 1997 the standard rate was only 23 per cent (with a starting rate of just 20 per cent), and the top rate was only 40 per cent. The Blair government continued with this policy, so that by 2000 the standard rate was 22 per cent and the starting rate was only 10 per cent. Cuts in the marginal rate of income tax have been claimed to have many beneficial effects: for example, people work longer hours; more people wish to work; people work more enthusiastically; unemployment falls; employment rises. The evidence regarding the truth of these claims, however, is less than certain.

For example, do more people wish to work? This applies largely to second income earners in a family, mainly women. A rise in after-tax wages may encourage more women to look for jobs. It may now be worth the cost in terms of transport, child minders, family disruption, etc. However, the effect of a 1 or 2 per cent cut in income tax rates is likely to be negligible. A more significant effect may be achieved by raising tax allowances: the amount of income that can be earned before taxes are paid. Part-time workers, especially, could end up paying no taxes. Then there is the question of whether the government will welcome more people seeking employment. This depends on the level of unemployment. If unemployment is already high, the government will not want to increase the labour force.

Whether people will be prepared to work longer hours is also questionable. On the one hand, each hour worked will be more valuable in terms of take-home pay, and thus people may be encouraged to work more and have less leisure time. On the other hand, a cut in income tax will make people better off, and therefore they may feel less need to do overtime than before. The evidence on these two effects suggests that they just about cancel each other out.

One of the main arguments is that tax cuts, especially at the lower end (by having a low starting rate of tax, or high personal allowances), will help to reduce unemployment. If income taxes are cut (especially if unemployment benefits are also cut), there will be a bigger difference between after-tax wage rates and unemployment benefit. More people will be motivated to take jobs rather than remain unemployed.

Despite the cuts in marginal rates of income tax, there have been significant tax *increases* elsewhere. In particular, VAT stood at only 8 per cent in 1979; in 1997 it was 17½ per cent. The marginal rate of national insurance contributions was 6½ per cent in 1979; in 1997 it was 10 per cent. The net effect was that taxes as a proportion of national income rose from 34.2 per cent in 1979 to 37 per cent in 2000.

To the extent that tax cuts do succeed in increasing take-home pay, there is a danger of 'sucking in' imports. There tends to be a high income elasticity of demand for imports. Extra consumer incomes may be spent on Japanese videos and hi-fi, Japanese or European cars, holidays abroad, and so on. Tax cuts can therefore have a serious effect on the balance of payments.

Tax cuts for business and other investment incentives

A number of financial incentives can be given to encourage investment. Market-orientated policies seek to reduce the general level of taxation on profits, or to give greater tax relief to investment.

A cut in corporation tax will increase after-tax profits. This will create more money for ploughing back into investment, and the higher after-tax return on investment will encourage more investment to take place. In 1983 the main rate of corporation tax in the UK stood at 52 per cent. A series of reductions have taken place since then, and by 2000/1 the rate was 30 per cent for large companies and 20 per cent for small ones, with a starting rate of only 10 per cent.

Reducing the power of labour

The argument here is that if labour costs to employers are reduced, their profits will probably rise. This could encourage and enable more investment and hence economic growth. If the monopoly power of labour is reduced, then cost-push inflation will also be reduced.

The Thatcher government took a number of measures to weaken the power of labour. These included restrictions on union closed shops, restrictions on secondary picketing and enforced secret ballots on strike proposals. It set a lead in resisting strikes in the public sector. Unlike previous Labour governments, it did not consult with union leaders over questions of economic policy. It was publicly very critical of trade union militancy and blamed the unions for many of the UK's economic ills. As a result, unions lost a lot of political standing and influence.

Reducing welfare

Monetarists claim that a major cause of unemployment is the small difference between the welfare benefits of the unemployed and the take-home pay of the employed. This causes voluntary unemployment (i.e. frictional unemployment). People are caught in a 'poverty trap': if they take a job, they lose their benefits.

A dramatic solution to this problem would be to cut unemployment benefits.

In the early 1980s the gap between take-home pay and welfare benefits to the unemployed did indeed widen. However, over the same period unemployment rose dramatically. This suggests that too high benefits were not a significant cause of growing unemployment over this period. Nevertheless, the claim that there was too little incentive for people to work was still a major part of the Thatcher government's explanation of growing unemployment.

A major problem is that, with changing requirements for labour skills, many of the redundant workers from the older industries are simply not qualified for new jobs that are created. What is more, the longer people are unemployed, the more demoralised they become. Employers would probably be prepared to pay only very low wages to such workers. To persuade these unemployed people to take low-paid jobs, the welfare benefits would have to be slashed. A 'market' solution to the problem, therefore, may be a very cruel solution. A fairer solution would be an interventionist policy: a policy of retraining labour.

Another alternative is to make the payment of unemployment benefits conditional on the recipient making a concerted effort to find a job. In the job-seeker's allowance introduced in 1996, claimants must be available for and actively seeking work and must complete a Jobseeker's Agreement, which sets out the types of work the person is willing to do and the plan to find work. Payment can be refused if the claimant refuses to accept jobs offered.

Policies to encourage competition

If the government can encourage more competition, this should have the effect of increasing national output and reducing inflation. Five major types of policy were pursued under this heading.

Privatisation. If privatisation simply involves the transfer of a natural monopoly to private hands (e.g. the water companies), the scope for increased competition is limited. However, where there is genuine scope for increased competition (e.g. in the supply of gas and electricity), privatisation can lead to increased efficiency, more consumer choice and lower prices.

Alternatively, privatisation can involve the introduction of private services into the public sector (e.g. private contractors providing cleaning services in hospitals, or refuse collection for local authorities). Private contractors may compete against each other for the franchise. This may well lower the cost of provision of these services, but the quality of provision may suffer unless closely monitored. The effects on unemployment are uncertain. Private contractors may offer lower wages and thus may use more labour. But if they are trying to supply the service at minimum cost, they are likely to employ less labour.

Deregulation. This involves the removal of monopoly rights: again, largely in the public sector. The deregulation of the bus industry is a good example of this initiative (see Box 30.1). An example in the private sector was the 'Big Bang' on the Stock Exchange in 1986. Under this the monopoly power of 'jobbers' to deal in stocks and shares on the Stock Exchange was abolished. In addition, stock-brokers now compete with each other in the commission rates they charge.

Introducing market relationships into the public sector. This is where the government tries to get different departments or elements within a particular

BOX 30.1

Private Finance Initiative (PFI) projects
Are they good value for money?

With more than 200 PFI deals signed by 2000, the UK government had already committed itself to £84 billion in revenue expenditure over the following 25 years. More immediately, some £20 billion worth of private capital will be put into public services through PFI projects between 2000 and 2003. Projects include the Channel Tunnel rail link, capital investment in the London Underground, moves to modernise and privatise air traffic control and a range of health, education and transport initiatives.

A recent report conducted by the London School of Economics, considered 29 PFI projects and compared the costs if the public sector bought the equivalent projects in the normal way. The report estimates that the average PFI cost saving was about 17 per cent.

As well as such cost savings, what other benefits might be gained by opening up public services to private enterprise? The article below, taken from the *Financial Times* of 27 November 1999, considers the advantages of the PFI to fund the redevelopment and modernisation of the London Underground.

A study last year placed London behind the Tokyo metro for frequency, reliability and punctuality, but slightly ahead of New York and Paris. Try telling that to passengers crammed into dirty carriages or stranded on platforms. Billions of pounds of investment are needed.

The government wants three public–private partnerships [PPPs] to take over the infrastructure, through a form of private finance initiative. Mr Livingstone (the Lord Mayor of London) prefers to keep the Tube in the public sector, and finance the investment with revenue bonds.

The Treasury's argument is two-fold. First, with the delays and £1.5 billion cost over-run of the newly opened Jubilee line extension fresh in its mind, it does not trust London Underground's public-sector management to deliver. But second, it maintains the PFI offers the advantage of transferring to the private sector the risk of maintaining the track, signalling and tunnels. Tim Stone, head of corporate finance at KPMG and a leading PFI practitioner whose firm is not involved in the Tube deal, says: 'Those who advocate a bond issue are radically missing the point'. PFI requires the private sector to take a long-term, closer to life-time approach to assets that, in the case of the Tube, can easily last for 30 years and more, he argues. It will invest more upfront to save running costs later and it will have big incentives to perform.

'It is not just that there are penalties. If the trains can't run because of infrastructure problems,

part of the public sector to 'trade' with each other, so as to encourage competition and efficiency. The most well-known examples are within health and education.

The process often involves 'devolved budgeting'. For example, under the local management of schools scheme (LMS), schools have become self-financing. Rather than the local authority meeting the bill for teachers' salaries, the schools have to manage their own budgets. The hope is that it will encourage them to cut costs, thereby reducing the burden on council tax payers. However, one result is that schools have tended to appoint inexperienced (and hence cheaper) teachers rather than those who can bring the benefits of their years of teaching.

Perhaps the most radical example of devolved budgeting was the introduction by the Thatcher government of an 'internal market' into the national health service. General practitioners were offered the opportunity to control their own budget. The size of the budget was determined by the number of patients and

you don't get paid at all,' Mr Stone says. 'And you get paid poorly if the service is poor. Bonds on their own simply cannot deliver that.'

Evidence in the government's favour can be found within Britain and outside it. An extension to the Docklands Light Railway, a PFI-type deal, has been completed on budget and two months early, despite engineering problems. 'Under PPP,' says Tony Poulter of Pricewaterhouse Coopers, who is advising the government on the Underground deal, 'it was down to the private sector to sort it out, and they did.' The Dutch government plans a high-speed rail line structured similarly to the deal planned for the Tube. The public sector will operate the trains, but the infrastructure will come from the private sector.

'We don't need to do this to attract the money,' says Alexander van Altena, project manager in the Ministry of Transport. 'If it (the PFI approach) falls through, there is public money reserved for it. But we will get a better deal from using the private sector.'

Not everyone is convinced. 'The PFI is an elegant solution and it does have the advantages claimed for it,' says Stephen Glaister, professor of transport and infrastructure at Imperial College. 'It would have been ideal if the Tube had been a simpler situation. But it is so complicated and the risks are so very, very difficult to assess that when the bids come in I believe it will turn out to be a very expensive way of raising the money.'

The Treasury rejects that. The public sector will retain certain disaster risks – tunnel collapse, for example, or London's rising water table making the Tube inoperable. But cost-overruns in refurbishment, maintenance, delays and train unavailability will all fall to the private sector. Calculations undertaken for the Treasury suggest a saving of £2.5 – £3 billion over the public-sector alternative in a deal that will see £12 billion spent on the Tube's infrastructure over the next 15 years – about £7.5 billion of it new investment, the remainder, maintenance. That saving 'will heavily outweigh the extra cost of some hundreds of millions in raising the finance through a PPP', Mr Poulter says.

Questions

1 Other than cost savings, what are the advantages of opening the London Underground to private-sector investment?

2 Why might the London Underground PFI 'turn out to be a very expensive way of raising the money'? What government measures could reduce the likelihood of this happening?

by their age and health profiles. GP fundholders purchased services directly from hospitals and had to cover their drugs bill. The suppliers of treatment, the hospitals, depended for much of their income on attracting the business of GP purchasers. They were thus put in competition with other hospitals.

Advocates of the internal market in the NHS argued that it created greater efficiency through competition. Critics, however, claimed that it led to growing inequalities of service between practices and between hospitals, and increased the administrative costs of the NHS.

The Private Finance Initiative. In 1993 the government introduced its Private Finance Initiative (PFI). This became the new way in which public projects were to be financed and run. Instead of the government or local authority planning, building and then running a public project (such as a new toll bridge, a maintenance depot, a prison, a records office or a block of inner-city workshops), it merely decides in broad terms the service it requires, and then seeks tenders from the private sector for designing, building, financing and running such projects. The capital costs are borne by the private sector, but then, if the provision of the service is not self-financing, the public sector pays the private-sector firm for providing it. Thus instead of the public sector being a provider, it is merely an enabler, buying services from the private sector.

The aim of PFI is to introduce competition (through the tendering process) and private-sector expertise into the provision of public services. It is hoped that the extra burden to the taxpayer of the private-sector profits will be more than offset by gains in efficiency.

Free trade and capital movements. The opening up of international trade and investment is central to a market-orientated supply-side policy. One of the first measures of the Thatcher government (in October 1979) was to remove all exchange controls, thereby permitting the free inflow and outflow of capital, both long term and short term. Most other industrialised countries also removed or relaxed exchange controls during the 1980s and early 1990s.

The Single European Act of 1987, which came into force in 1993, was another example of international liberalisation. As we saw in section 24.3, it created a 'single market' in the EU: a market without barriers to the movement of goods, services, capital and labour.

In addition to adopting supply-side measures that focus on the economy as a whole, governments might decide to target specific regions of the economy, or specific industries for policy initiatives. Such initiatives might be market based. However, they are more likely to be interventionist in nature, as our investigation of regional and industrial policy will show.

30.3 Regional and urban policy in the UK and Europe

Unemployment is not evenly distributed around the UK. Northern Ireland and parts of the north and west of England, parts of Wales and parts of Scotland have unemployment rates substantially higher than in the south-east of England.

Similarly, there are regional disparities in average incomes, rates of growth and levels of prices, as well as in health, crime, housing, etc. These disparities grew wider in the mid-1980s as the recession hit the north, with its traditional heavy industries, much harder than the south. In the recession of the early 1990s, however, it was the service sector that was hardest hit, a sector more concentrated in the south. Regional disparities therefore narrowed somewhat. Disparities are not only experienced at regional level. They are often more acutely felt in specific *areas*, especially inner cities and urban localities subject to industrial decline.

Within the Europe Union differences exist not only within individual countries, but between them. For example, in the EU some countries are much less prosperous than others. Thus, especially with the opening up of the EU in 1993 to the free movement of factors of production, capital and labour may flow to the more prosperous regions of the Union, such as Germany, France and the Benelux countries, and away from the less prosperous regions such as Portugal, Greece and southern Italy.

Causes of regional imbalance and the role of regional policy

If the market functioned perfectly, there would be no regional problem. If wages were lower and unemployment were higher in the north, people would simply move to the south. This would reduce unemployment in the north and help to fill vacancies in the south. It would drive up wage rates in the north and reduce wage rates in the south. The process would continue until regional disparities were eliminated.

The capital market would function similarly. New investment would be located in the areas offering the highest rate of return. If land and labour were cheaper in the north, capital would be attracted there. This too would help to eliminate regional disparities.

In practice, the market does not behave as just described. There are three major problems:

Labour and capital immobility. Labour may be geographically immobile. The regional pattern of industrial location may change more rapidly than the labour market can adjust to it. Thus jobs may be lost in the depressed areas more rapidly than people can migrate.

Similarly, the existing capital stock is highly immobile. Buildings and most machinery cannot be moved to where the unemployed are! *New* capital is much more mobile. But there may be insufficient new investment, especially during a recession, to halt regional decline, even if some investors are attracted into the depressed areas by low wages and cheap land.

Regional multiplier effects. The continuing shift in demand may in part be due to **regional multiplier effects**. In the prosperous regions, the new industries and the new workers attracted there create additional demand. This creates additional output and jobs and hence more migration. There is a multiplied rise in income. In the depressed regions, the decline in demand and loss of jobs causes a multiplied downward effect. Loss of jobs in manufacturing leads to less money spent in the local community; transport and other service industries lose custom. The whole region becomes more depressed.

Externalities. Labour migration imposes external costs on non-migrants. In the prosperous regions, the new arrivals compete for services with those already there. Services become overstretched; house prices rise; council house waiting lists lengthen; roads become more congested, etc. In the depressed regions, services decline, or alternatively local taxes must rise for those who remain if local services are to be protected. Dereliction, depression and unemployment cause emotional stress for those who remain.

Causes of urban decay

Throughout the post-war period there has been a general movement of people from the inner areas of the big cities to the suburbs, to smaller towns and cities, and to rural areas within easy commuting distance of towns. This movement of population has been paralleled by a decline in employment in the inner cities. But with an increasing number of urban jobs being taken by people commuting into the cities, the unemployment problem for those living in these areas grew

definition

Regional multiplier effects
When a change in injections into or withdrawals from a particular region causes a multiplied change in income in that region. The regional multiplier is given by $1/mpw_r$, where the import component of mpw_r consists of imports into that region either from abroad or from other regions of the economy.

dramatically. Moreover, many of the older manufacturing industries were located in the inner cities and it was these industries that were hardest hit by the recession of the early 1980s. The picture today is one of large differences in living standards and unemployment rates between the inner-city areas and the rest of the country.

The run-down nature of many inner cities has caused the more mobile members of the workforce to move away. Spending in these areas has thus declined, causing a local multiplier effect. The jobs that poor people living in these areas do manage to find are often low-paid, unskilled jobs in the service sector (such as shops and the hotel and catering trade) or in petty manufacturing (like garment workshops).

Many of the newer industries prefer to locate away from the inner-city areas on sites where land is cheaper, rates are lower and there is easy access to the motorway network. At the same time, for financial reasons local authorities have found it difficult to offer inducements to firms to move into the inner cities. Nor can they afford to spend large amounts on improving the infrastructure of the blighted areas. Their council taxes are also higher, which again provides an inducement for the more mobile to move away, as well as a disincentive for new firms to move into the area.

Approaches to regional and urban policy

Market-orientated solutions

Supporters of market-based solutions argue that firms are the best judges of where they should locate. Government intervention would impede efficient decision taking by firms. It is better, they argue, to remove impediments to the market achieving regional and local balance. For example, they favour either or both of the following.

Locally negotiated wage agreements. Nationally negotiated wage rates mean that wages are not driven down in the less prosperous areas and up in the more prosperous ones. This discourages firms from locating in the less prosperous areas. At the same time, firms find it difficult to recruit labour in the more prosperous ones, where wages are not high enough to compensate for the higher cost of living there. Thus the Conservative governments of the 1980s and 1990s advocated replacing nationally negotiated wage rates with locally negotiated ones.

Reducing unemployment benefits. A general reduction in unemployment benefits and other welfare payments would encourage the unemployed in the areas of high unemployment to migrate to the more prosperous areas, or enable firms to offer lower wages in the areas of high unemployment.

The problem with these policies is that they attempt initially to widen the economic divide between workers in the different areas in order to encourage capital and labour to move. Such policies would hardly be welcomed by workers in the poorer areas!

Interventionist solutions

Interventionist policies involve encouraging firms to move. Such policies include the following.

Subsidies and tax concessions in the depressed regions. Businesses could be given general subsidies, such as grants to move, or reduced rates of corporation tax. Alternatively, grants or subsidies could be specifically targeted on increasing employment (e.g. reduced employer's national insurance contributions) or on encouraging investment (e.g investment grants or other measures to reduce the costs of capital).

The provision of facilities in depressed regions. The government or local authorities could provide facilities such as land and buildings at concessionary, or even zero, rents to incoming firms; or spend money on improving the infrastructure of the area (roads and communications, technical colleges, etc.).

The siting of government offices in the depressed regions. The government could move some of its own departments out of the capital and locate them in areas of high unemployment.

It is important to distinguish policies that merely seek to *modify* the market by altering market signals, from policies that *replace* the market. *Regulation* replaces the market, and unless very carefully devised and monitored may lead to ill-thought-out decisions being made. *Subsidies* and *taxes* merely modify the market, leaving it to individual firms to make their final location decisions.

Regional and urban policy in the UK

Regional policy

Certain areas are identified as requiring government financial assistance. These are known as **assisted areas** (AAs) and cover around 29 per cent of the UK population. They are divided into two categories. Tier 1 areas are those suffering the most acute economic problems. There are four of these areas: Cornwall, South Yorkshire, Merseyside and much of Wales. Tier 2 areas include large parts of Scotland and the north-east of England and many smaller areas affected by economic decline. The assistance comes from both the UK government (the Department of Trade and Industry) and the EU. UK government aid is in two major forms.

Regional selective assistance (RSA) consists of discretionary grants given to firms for investment projects that provide skilled jobs. Grants of up to 40 per cent of investment costs are available in Tier 1 areas and up to 20 per cent in Tier 2 areas. £785 million of RSA is available in the period 2000–3.

Regional enterprise grants (REGs) are a means of providing assistance to small and medium-sized firms in England employing up to 250 people in Enterprise Grant Areas (Tier 3 areas). These areas extend beyond Tiers 1 and 2, and include local authority districts with high unemployment rates and various rural development areas. £45 million of REGs is available in the period 2000–3. Separate support for small and medium-sized businesses is available in Scotland and Wales.

The largest amount of regional assistance comes from the *European Regional Development Fund* (ERDF) (see next section). The money is intended to be *additional* to any supplied by member governments. However, some countries, including the UK, have tended to use ERDF grants to *replace* domestic assistance, and have thus come into dispute with the EU.

definition

Assisted areas
Areas of high unemployment qualifying for government regional selective assistance (RSA) and grants from the European Regional Development Fund (ERDF).

In 1998 the government set up eight **Regional Development Agencies** (RDAs) for the different regions of England (and a ninth for London in 2000). These, along with the Scottish Parliament and Welsh Assembly, are responsible for administering economic policies for their particular parts of the UK and for developing strategies for improving local infrastructure, encouraging inward investment and promoting investment in skills and training.

Urban policy

During the 1980s the thrust of policy shifted away from regional and towards urban policy. Several new schemes were introduced, involving the creation of various new categories of deprived area.

Enterprise zones are very small districts in urban areas suffering acute industrial decline. Firms setting up in enterprise zones received 100 per cent capital allowances on property, exemption from rates and land tax, fewer planning regulations and less bureaucratic intervention generally. By the mid-1990s there were 27 such zones.

Simplified planning zones (SPZs) were set up in 1990 to provide a cheaper means of encouraging firms to set up in deprived inner-city areas. SPZs are similar to enterprise zones in having fewer planning regulations, but there are no financial incentives available to firms.

Urban Development Corporations (UDCs) were first established in the early 1980s. Their role was to stimulate private-sector-led regeneration of inner city areas. They could grant planning permission; acquire, hold and manage land and property (including making compulsory purchases); and provide grants and other assistance to firms. By the mid-1990s there were twelve UDCs in operation. They were all wound up between 1995 and 1998.

Currently there are four major elements of regeneration policy:

- The *Single Regeneration Budget* (SRB). This was established in 1994 and is now administered through the nine Regional Development Agencies (see above). The aim is to encourage a partnership between government and the private sector (the Private Finance Initiative (PFI)) and to ensure that maximum benefit is gained from European Structural Funds. The SRB provides grants for schemes which meet various local objectives, such as increased employment, training, new businesses, better housing, crime prevention and support for ethnic minorities. Monies are allocated to partnerships drawn from local authorities, TECs, and the private, community and voluntary sectors.

  In 1999 the government predicted that, between 1995 and 2001, £3.9 billion of government expenditure under the SRB would have been matched by £7.6 billion of private-sector expenditure. It also predicted that 672 000 jobs would have been created, 5 921 000 pupils would have benefited from projects, 83 800 new businesses would have started up and 259 000 dwellings would have been improved.

- *New Deal for Communities* was established in 1998 to provide help for some of the most deprived neighbourhoods. The aim is that local people, local businesses, community and voluntary organisations, local authorities and public agencies form partnerships in each area. These partnerships draw up plans for the economic and social development of the area and submit them to the government, which then awards funds according to the plans' viability.

---

definition

Regional Development Agencies (RDAs). Nine agencies, based in English regions, which initiate and administer regional policy within their area.

- *English Partnerships*, originally the *Urban Regeneration Agency (URA)*, aims to promote the reclamation and development of derelict or contaminated land. It acts as a partner with private firms, local authorities and the voluntary sector. It provides grants, loans, guarantees and partnership investment to encourage private companies to develop and move into such areas.
- *Housing Action Trusts* (HATs) are public bodies dedicated to the regeneration of run-down housing estates in six areas of England. They repair and improve houses and improve the local environment and amenities. Between 1991 and 1999, the six HATs had provided 2322 new and 2335 renovated homes.

Regional policy in the EU

With the signing of the Maastricht Treaty, which established the European Union in November 1993, member states agreed to work together to ensure that:

- The distribution of benefits from European unification were spread fairly.
- Economic and social development was speeded up in the less prosperous countries, so that they might play a fuller part in the EU's future development.
- Economic imbalances between countries did not distort the operation of the internal market between member states.
- Structural reforms were in place, such that the EU would be well prepared for the next century.

In pursuit of these goals, the EU currently allocates some 40 per cent of its total budget to their achievement. In 1998 the EU spent €34 billion (£22 billion), and over the funding period 1994–1999 expects to have spent some €158 billion in total. In order to allocate these vast resources. the EU operates a series of inter-related funds, which are collectively known as the Structural Funds.

The structural funds

The European Regional Development Fund (ERDF). This fund is managed by the Directorate-General for Regional Affairs, which allocates grants of up to 50 per cent of the value of projects designed to aid development in poorer regions of the EU. In particular it focuses upon:

- Investment to create and maintain employment.
- Investment in infrastructure.
- Investments in education and health.
- Measures to enhance research and development.
- Collective measures used to support economic activity.

The European Social Fund (ESF). The ESF is managed by the Directorate-General for Employment and Social Affairs. It allocates funds to vocational training programmes, to job creation and the adaptation of worker skills to industrial change.

The Guidance section of the European Agricultural Guidance and Guarantee Fund (EAGGF). The EAGGF is managed by the Directorate-General for

Agriculture and allocates funds for the development and restructuring of agriculture and rural areas in general.

The Financial Instrument for Fisheries Guidance (FIFG). The FIFG is managed by the Directorate-General for Fisheries. As with EAGGF, FIFG is concerned solely with one sector of the EU economy, namely fishing, and the problems faced by communities which rely on it.

Cohesion Fund. This fund offers additional assistance to the four poorest nations within the EU: Greece, Portugal, Spain and Ireland. Its aim is to support the development of infrastructure projects, and enhance measures that help protect and improve the quality of the environment: for example, improving the quality of water supply and the treatment of waste.

The European Investment Bank (EIB). In addition to the Structural Funds, the EIB also offers support to the less prosperous regions within the EU (approximately two-thirds of its budget goes to such regions). However, unlike the Structural Funds, the EIB offers loans, not grants, and hence requires repayment. The EIB generally offers loans up to 50 per cent of the cost of the project, and these loans generally run for between 4 and 18 years. With only a small fee for administration, and with the EIB operating on a non-profit-making basis, interest rates changed by the EIB are low.

The allocation of structural funds

Given the diversity of funding alternatives, how are the resources available allocated? Support from the ERDF, ESF, EAGGF and FIFG focuses upon one or more of the following 'objectives':

Objective 1.	To promote the development and structural adjustment of regions which lag behind the rest of the EU. This receives by far the largest share of the Structural Funds budget (see chart). In order to achieve objective 1 status, a region's per capita GDP must be 75 per cent or less of the EU level for the last three years. This objective is funded by the ERDF, ESF and EAGGF.
Objective 2.	To support regions adversely affected by industrial decline. In order to qualify for assistance under this objective, a region must have an unemployment rate above the EU average over the last three years. This objective is funded by the ERDF and ESF.
Objective 3.	To combat long-term unemployment, and help other groups excluded from the labour market.
Objective 4.	To help workers to adapt to industrial change. All EU members are eligible to apply for grants under objectives 3 and 4, which are both funded by the ESF.
Objective 5a.	To aid structural adjustment in agriculture and fisheries. This is also open to all EU members. It is funded by the EAGGF and the FIFG.
Objective 5b.	To aid the development and restructuring of rural areas. This is also open to all EU members. It is funded not only by the EAGGF but also by the ERDF and the ESF.

Objective 6.   To help in the development of areas that are sparsely populated. This is only open to Sweden and Finland. A region in these countries is eligible for money if it has eight or less inhabitants per km square. Objective 6 is funded by all the Structural Funds.

The distribution of the structural funds between the objectives and between countries is shown in Figure 30.1.

Agenda 2000

In the late 1990s a full-scale review of the EU's Structural Funds was undertaken. There were two reasons for this. First, the existing spending round was due to end in 1999. Second, the enlargement of the EU, in particular into Eastern Europe, is likely to place great strains on the EU's budget, and in particular that part of the budget devoted to the Structural Funds. It is suggested that, without any reform of the funding system, the cost to the EU of the Structural Funds would double.

Agenda 2000 is the name given to this review of EU funding in the light of its anticipated enlargement. It makes the following proposals for EU regional policy and Structural Funds:

- The seven objectives of funding should be reduced to three. The proposed objective 1 is much like the old objective 1, focusing upon those regions lagging behind the rest of the EU. The proposed objective 2 would be a merging of the old objectives 2 and 5b, with the focus being on structural change. The proposed objective 3 would be an amalgamation of old

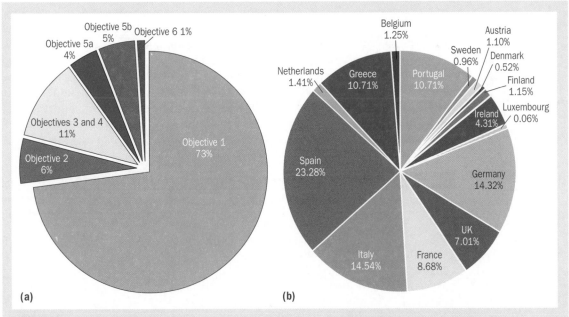

(a)   (b)

Figure 30.1
(a) Distribution of structural funds between objectives. (b) Distribution of structural funds between countries

objectives 3 and 4, with the focus being on labour markets and long-term unemployment. Access to funds under this new objective 3 would remain open to all EU members.

● Eligibility for objectives 1 and 2 should be tightened, so as to concentrate expenditure on the most affected regions.

The impact of Agenda 2000 on the UK would be a reduction in money received from the Structural Funds. On a strict enforcement of the rules of eligibility, only two regions, Merseyside and South Yorkshire (with an income per capita of 71 and 72 per cent of the EU average), would qualify. Northern Ireland and the Highlands and Islands of Scotland would not.

30.4 Industrial policy in the UK and Europe

The poor performance of UK industry

For decades, the UK has had a lower level of investment relative to national income than other industrialised countries. This is illustrated in Table 30.2.

This low level of investment has been a major reason for the UK's poor growth performance. It has also meant that for many industries there has emerged a widening technological gap between the UK and its major competitors such as Japan and Germany. This is reflected in the poor quality and high cost of many UK products. To some extent, however, this has been offset by the fact that wage rates in the UK have been lower than in competing countries. This has at least made the UK relatively attractive to inward investment, especially by Japanese, Korean and US companies seeking to set up production plants within the EU.

The poor performance of UK manufacturing firms has resulted in a growing import penetration of the UK market. Imports of manufactured products have grown more rapidly than UK manufactured exports, and since 1983 the UK has become a net importer of manufactured products.

These problems have led many economists to call for a much more active supply-side policy: one which involves government intervention, especially in the fields of education and training, research and development, and the provision of infrastructure. This has been the approach in many countries, including France, Germany and Japan.

Table 30.2 Gross fixed capital formation as a percentage of GDP: 1960–99

Year (average)	UK	Germany[a]	Japan	EU	OECD (total)
1960–7	17.7	25.2	31.0	22.8	21.0
1968–73	18.9	24.5	34.6	23.6	22.3
1974–80	19.2	21.0	31.8	22.2	22.2
1981–5	16.5	20.4	28.7	19.8	20.7
1986–90	18.9	19.9	29.8	20.1	20.8
1991–4	16.6	22.4	30.0	19.8	20.6
1995–9	16.8	20.2	27.3	18.6	20.9

[a] West Germany prior to 1991.
Source: *European Economy* (Commission of the European Communities).

Approaches to industrial policy

Industrial policy involves the attempt to increase investment and halt or slow-down the shrinking of the industrial sector. There are two approaches to industrial policy: a demand-side approach and a supply-side one.

On the *demand side*, we have already examined (in Chapter 28) the Keynesian approach of trying to maintain a high level of activity in the economy by demand management policy. It is based on the premise that the major determinant of investment is consumer demand.

Supply-side approaches aim to provide more incentives to invest for any given level of aggregate demand. They also attempt to improve industrial efficiency and competitiveness for any given level of investment.

The advocates of such policies highlighted a number of supply-side weaknesses of the UK economy in the 1970s: overstaffing, union restrictive practices, an outdated educational and training system insufficiently geared to industry's needs, too little research and development, misdirected research and development, and poor management that is unwilling to go out into world markets and compete aggressively. Some of these problems have eased somewhat in recent years. Others, however, such as a lack of training and too little research and development, are argued by many to have got worse.

Supply-side industrial policy can be interventionist or market orientated in nature.

Interventionist industrial policy

Research and development. The government may sponsor research and development in certain industries (e.g. aerospace) or in specific fields (e.g. microprocessors). The amount of government support in this field has been very small in the UK compared with Japan, France and the USA. What is more, the amount of support declined between the mid-1980s and the late 1990s. In 1999, however, the Labour government introduced a system of tax credits for small firms which invest in research and development.

Rationalisation. The government may encourage mergers or other forms of industrial reorganisation that would lead to greater efficiency and/or higher levels of investment. This could be done through government agencies or government departments.

Advice and persuasion. The government may engage in discussions with private firms in order to find ways to improve efficiency and innovation. It may bring firms together to exchange information so as to co-ordinate their decisions and create a climate of greater certainty. It may bring firms and unions together to try to create greater industrial harmony.

Information. The government may provide various information services to firms: technical assistance, the results of public research, information on markets, etc.

Direct provision. Improvements in infrastructure – such as a better motorway system – can be of direct benefit to industry. Alternatively, the government could provide factories or equipment to specific firms.

---

definition

Industrial policies
Policies to encourage industrial investment and greater industrial efficiency.

Training. Well-targeted training can lead to substantial improvements in labour productivity. We examined training policy in section 20.3.

Market-orientated supply-side policy

Supporters of the free market claim that interventionist industrial policy is based on a false analysis. They suggest that industry's poor investment performance is due to market rigidities, such as managerial inertia and union restrictive practices. Government intervention to support industry weakens market forces and in the long run reduces, not increases, industrial efficiency.

They argue that if the government is to help industry, it is best to reduce the tax burden on industry generally, so as to increase the return on investment and improve the operation of the market system. It is also best to resist the introduction of minimum wage rates and to reduce the power of labour through trade union reform. Finally, it is better to have open markets and open competition: for example, by having no trade barriers and no restrictions on international capital movements.

Industrial policy in Japan and Europe

Japan and the Ministry of International Trade and Industry (MITI)

Japan is now the world's largest manufacturer of steel, ships, cars and lorries, motor cycles, engines, cameras, calculators, big memory chips, televisions, video tape recorders and photocopiers. Between 1960 and 1995 investment averaged 31 per cent of GDP, industrial output grew by over 5 per cent per annum, real GDP grew by 5.7 per cent per annum and the rate of automation outpaced all Japan's economic rivals.

Part of the explanation for the rapid growth in industrial output in the 1960s and 1970s was the fact that Japan was starting from a low base and was copying and adapting technology developed in the West. But, despite a slowing down in growth after 1973 and particularly in the late 1990s, investment remains higher than in Europe and North America (see Table 30.2) and the development of new products and processes is actively encouraged by the Japanese government.

Industrial policy in Japan is guided by the Ministry of International Trade and Industry (MITI), whose role is to encourage co-operation between private companies and to help stimulate investment in new technology and product development. Using a mixture of state aid and legislative power, MITI wields a considerable amount of influence. However, this power is seldom in evidence as most Japanese industry is only too willing to take advantage of the services MITI can offer.

MITI encourages older industries to close down or to adapt, and provides grants for this purpose. But it is for its help to the 'sunrise' industries that MITI is best known. It provides subsidies and helps these industries to raise finance. It has also used tariffs and quotas to protect them from international competition while they are becoming established. It provided help in the 1950s to the steel, shipbuilding and electricity industries, and in the 1960s and 1970s to the chemical, car and electrical goods industries.

BOX 30.2

A new approach to industrial policy

As with many other areas of economic policy, industrial policy throughout most of the world has undergone a radical reorientation in recent years. The government's role has shifted from one of direct intervention in the form of subsidies and protecting industry from competition, to one of focusing upon the external business environment and the conditions that influence its competitiveness.

The reasons for such a change are both philosophical and structural:

● The 1980s saw the efficacy of government intervention questioned, and the re-emergence of the belief that, where possible, the productive potential of an economy ought to be developed by free-market forces.

● Growing government debt, and a desire to curb public expenditure, acted as a key incentive to reduce the state's role in industrial affairs. This was argued to be one of the driving forces behind the European privatisation process from the 1980s onwards.

● The declining role of the manufacturing sector – the sector which received most state support – meant that less intervention was required.

● During the 1980s, industry became progressively more global in its outlook. As such, its investment decisions were increasingly being determined by external environmental factors, such as comparative labour costs in different countries and countries' transport and communication links. Old-style industrial policy, which focuses on the national economy in isolation and on distinct sectors within it, has become increasingly less effective and relevant in meeting the needs of national economies operating in an open trading environment, where business investment and strategy are assessed in global terms.

The new approach to industrial policy, being widely adopted by many advanced countries, is to focus on improving those factors which shape a nation's competitiveness. This involves shifting away from particular sectors to targeting what are referred to as 'framework conditions for industry'.

Such 'conditions' have been the subject of a series of recent reviews by the OECD, which found that the following initiatives are forming the basis of a new industrial competitiveness policy:

● The promotion of investment in physical and human capital. Human capital in particular, and the existence of a sound skills base, are seen as crucial for attracting global business and ensuring long-run economic growth.

● A reduction in non-wage employment costs, such as employers' social security and pension contributions. Many governments see these costs as too high and as a severe limitation on competitiveness and employment creation.

● The promotion of innovation and the encouragement of greater levels of R&D.

● Support for small and medium-sized enterprises. SMEs have received particular attention due to their crucial role in enhancing innovation, creating employment and contributing to skills development, especially in high-tech areas (see Chapter 15).

● The improvement of infrastructure. This includes both physical transport, such as roads and railways, and information highways.

● The protection of intellectual property by more effective use of patents and copyright. By reinforcing the law in these areas, it is hoped to encourage firms to develop new products and commit themselves to research.

These new initiatives, if they are to be truly effective, are likely to require co-ordination and integration, since they represent a radical departure from established industrial policy. As a consequence, a new Department of Competitiveness may not be out of the question as industrial policy enters the new millennium.

Questions

1 In what senses could these new policies be described as (a) non-interventionist; (b) interventionist?

2 Does globalisation, and in particular the global perspective of multinational corporations, make industrial policy in the form of selective subsidies and tax relief more or less likely?

In the 1980s and 1990s, it gave substantial support to the computer industry. In 1981 it announced a ten-year project of research into 'next generation computer technology'. This encompassed twelve distinct projects covering investigations into new materials, bio-technology and semi-conductors.

Long-term industrial policy on this scale helps to give Japanese companies a competitive advantage and encourages them to adopt a long-term investment strategy.

Industrial policy in the EU

The Japanese use of industrial policy to help create a vibrant and world-beating industrial sector is an approach that has been readily embraced by the European Union. During the 1960s and 1970s the EU's industrial policy amounted to little more than the use of 'protectionism' (see section 24.3), using restrictions on imports to shelter domestic producers from the rigours of global competition. Today the EU's approach is more mature and recognises that a successful industrial sector is built upon far broader foundations.

> The EU industrial policy aims at creating a knowledge-based society with enterprises operating on markets open to international competition. The policy fosters innovation, sustainable development and the removal of obstacles to change. It encourages flexibility, investment in knowledge and risk-taking as well as the spread of information and know-how.[1]

The EU's main means of creating greater industrial competitiveness is the deepening of the internal market by the removal of all barriers to trade between the member states (see section 24.3). But EU industrial policy does not end here. The White Paper on Growth, Competitiveness and Employment (1993) stressed the weaknesses of the market in providing adequate levels of research and development (R&D) and training, and the difficulties businesses might have in identifying others with whom they might work in developing new products and processes. As a result, the White Paper advocated that, in order to create a favourable environment for industry, the EU should actively promote investment, especially in the fields of training and R&D, and that it should encourage various forms of industrial co-operation. This would be achieved by setting up various bodies to support industry and by the provision of finance.

Currently, the EU's research and technology programme has a budget of €16.3 billion over the five-year period, 1998–2002. This represents an increase of 3 per cent over the previous five-year period. Research initiatives, such as the European Strategic Programme for Research in Information Technology (ESPRIT) and the setting up of the European Research Co-ordination Agency (EUREKA), have, as their primary objective, the co-ordination of R&D activities of private business in order to create an internationally competitive industrial sector. In other words, they have a role very similar to that of MITI in Japan.

---

[1] *A Common Approach to Enhanced Competitiveness*, (DGXIII, 1998).

SUMMARY

1a Demand-side policies (fiscal and monetary) may be suitable for controlling demand-pull inflation or demand-deficient unemployment, but supply-side policies will be needed to control the other types of inflation and unemployment.

1b Demand-side policies can be used to increase the actual rate of economic growth if there is slack in the economy. In the long term, however, economic growth can be increased only if there is an increase in the *potential* rate of economic growth. To achieve this the government will require supply-side policies.

2a Market-orientated supply-side policies aim to increase the rate of growth of aggregate supply by encouraging private enterprise and the freer play of market forces.

2b Reducing government expenditure as a proportion of GDP is a major element of such policies. This can involve the use of cash limits on government departments and local authorities, reducing grants and subsidies, reducing the number of civil servants and other public employees, resisting pay increases in the public sector, and reorganising public-sector industries and departments in order to achieve greater efficiency.

2c Tax cuts can be used to encourage more people to take up jobs, and people to work longer hours and more enthusiastically. They can be used to reduce equilibrium unemployment and encourage employers to take on more workers. Likewise tax cuts for businesses or increased investment allowances may encourage higher investment. The effects of tax cuts will depend on how people respond to incentives.

2d Reducing the power of trade unions by legislation could reduce disequilibrium unemployment and cost-push inflation. It could also lead to a redistribution of income to profits, which could increase investment and growth (but possibly lead to greater inequality).

2e A reduction in welfare benefits, especially those related to unemployment, will encourage workers to accept jobs at lower wages and thus decrease equilibrium unemployment.

2f Privatisation and deregulation are two examples of policies that could be used to encourage greater competition. In practice, there will be little or no gain in competition from privatisation if industries are sold as monopolies.

2g A policy of free trade and free capital movements can be used to encourage greater competition from abroad.

3a Regional and local disparities arise from a changing pattern of industrial production. With many of the older industries concentrated in certain parts of the country and especially in the inner cities, and with an acceleration in the rate of industrial change, so the gap between rich and poor areas has widened.

3b Regional disparities can in theory be corrected by the market, with capital being attracted to areas of low wages and workers being attracted to areas of high wages.

3c In practice, regional disparities persist because of capital and labour immobility and regional multiplier effects.

3d The market-orientated solution is to remove impediments to the market achieving regional balance. Policies include local, rather than national, pay bargaining, reducing unemployment benefits, adopting uniform business rates and limiting local authority expenditure.

3e Interventionist solutions focus on measures to encourage firms to move to areas of high unemployment. These measures might include subsidies or tax concessions for firms which move, the provision of facilities and improved infrastructure in the depressed area, the siting of government offices in the depressed areas and the prevention of firms expanding in the prosperous ones. Employment subsidies will create more jobs than general subsidies, which in turn will create more jobs than capital subsidies.

3f In the UK there has been a movement away from general grants towards discretionary grants based on job creation. There are also regional grants from the EU and grants and initiatives for the regeneration of the inner cities.

3g The success of regional and urban policies has been limited by the relatively low level of government grants and by the fact that some of the money has gone to projects which would have gone ahead anyway.

3h Regional policy in the EU became formalised in 1975 with the creation of the European Regional Development Fund. The Maastricht Treaty saw the creation of a Cohesive Fund to focus on the regional needs of the EU's poorest members.

SUMMARY

4a The UK has had a lower rate of investment than most other industrialised countries. This has contributed to a historically low rate of economic growth and a growing trade deficit in manufactures.

4b Those in favour of interventionist industrial policy point to failings of the market, such as the externalities involved in investment and training, the imperfections in the capital market and the short-term perspective of decision makers.

4c Intervention can take the form of grants, the encouragement of mergers and other forms of rationalisation, advice and persuasion, the provision of information and the direct provision of infrastructure.

4d Industrial policy in Japan is guided by the Ministry of International Trade and Industry (MITI). Its principal role is to encourage co-operation between private companies in new technology and product development.

4e Industrial policy in the EU is a mixture of market-orientated measures (ensuring that the internal market in goods, capital and labour is free) and interventionist measures, especially in the encouragement of research.

REVIEW QUESTIONS

1 Define *demand-side* and *supply-side* policies. Sometimes it is said that Keynesians advocate demand-side policies and monetarists advocate supply-side policies. Is there any accuracy in this statement?

2 Outline the main supply-side policies that have been introduced in the UK since 1979. Does the evidence suggest that they have achieved what they set out to do?

3 Compare the relative merits of pro-market and interventionist solutions to regional decline.

4 In what ways does the EU approach to regional and industrial policy differ from that of the UK?

5 Is the decline of older industries necessarily undesirable?

6 In what ways can interventionist industrial policy work *with* the market, rather than against it? What are the arguments for and against such policy?

International economic policy

31.1 International business cycles

So long as nations trade with one another, the domestic economic actions of one nation will have implications for those which trade with it. For example, if the US administration feels that the US economy is growing too fast, it might adopt various deflationary fiscal and monetary measures, such as higher tax rates or interest rates. US consumers will not only consume fewer domestically produced goods, but also reduce their consumption of imported products. Thus *foreign* producers will experience a fall in demand and, if this persists, may respond by cutting back on production and reducing the size of their labour force. This reduction in the demand for factors of production will then have effects on other firms. The process is likely to be repeated many times as the **international trade multiplier** sends ripples throughout the global economy.

The more open an economy, the more vulnerable it will be to changes in the level of economic activity in the rest of the world. This problem will be particularly acute if a nation is heavily dependent on trade with one other nation (e.g. Canada on the USA) or region (e.g. Switzerland on the EU).

As a consequence of both trade and financial interdependences, the world economy, like the economy of any individual nation, tends to experience periodic fluctuations in economic activity – an *international* business cycle. The implication of this is that nations will tend to share common problems and concerns at the same time. At one time the most pressing problem may be world inflationary pressures; at another time it may be a world recession.

In order to avoid 'beggar-my-neighbour' policies, it is better to seek *common* solutions to these common problems: i.e. solutions that are international in scope and design rather than narrowly based on national self-interest. For example, during a world recession, countries are likely to suffer from rising unemployment. An individual nation might like to stimulate aggregate demand, but be reluctant to do so if it fears that this will merely create a balance of payments problem. Indeed, faced with falling export sales as a result of the recession, it might even be persuaded to *curb* aggregate demand in order to reduce inflation and make its exports more competitive. But this will then only worsen the position for other countries. However, if other nations (which will also be experiencing higher unemployment) can be convinced to co-ordinate their policy actions, then an expansionary *international* economic policy will remove the worries of going it alone. In addition to the resulting rise in their imports, all nations will also experience rising export sales.

Even if national policies are not in the strictest sense co-ordinated, discussions between nations regarding the nature and magnitude of the problems they face help to improve the policy-making process. The sharing of information

definition

International trade multiplier
The impact of changing levels of international demand on levels of production and output.

concerning their economies' performance and their intended actions enables them to assess the likely success or otherwise of their own initiatives. Would they be pursuing an incompatible policy goal? Would the cumulative actions of individual nations cause the global economy to grow too fast? With such knowledge, fluctuations in international economic activity might be more effectively regulated, if not totally removed.

Although co-operation is the ideal, in practice discord often tends to dominate international economic relations. Co-operation merely occurs in episodes, some of very short duration. Where co-operation does occur, it varies in intensity, ranging from the integration of economic strategy to the mere issuing of statements.

In the following sections we shall consider how international economic policy tends to be conducted in practice.

31.2 International harmonisation of economic policies

One of the major causes of currency fluctuations is the very different conditions existing in different countries and the different policies they pursue. For example, an expansionary fiscal policy plus a tight monetary policy can lead to huge currency appreciation if other countries do not follow suit. This is what happened to the dollar in 1983/4 and 1999/2000. Conversely, a persistent current account deficit, plus a policy of interest rate reductions in order to stimulate the economy, can lead to large-scale currency depreciation. This happened to sterling after it left the ERM in 1992.

Changes in exchange rates that result from such imbalances are often amplified by speculation. And this problem is becoming worse. Approximately one trillion dollars per day passes across the foreign exchange markets. The scale of such movements makes any significant speculation simply too great for individual countries to resist. And on some occasions even the concerted action of groups of countries cannot maintain exchange rate stability.

The four main underlying causes of exchange rate movements are divergences in *interest rates*, *growth rates*, *inflation rates* and *current account balance of payments*. Table 31.1 shows the levels of these and other indicators for the seven major industrialised countries. As can be seen, the variations between countries have been considerable.

For many years now the leaders of these countries have met once a year (and more frequently if felt necessary) at an economic summit conference. Top of the agenda in most of these 'Group of Seven' (G7) meetings has been how to generate world economic growth without major currency fluctuations. But to achieve this it is important that there is a **harmonisation** of economic policies between nations. In other words, it is important that all the major countries are pursuing consistent policies aiming at common international goals.

But how can policy harmonisation be achieved? As long as there are significant domestic differences between the major economies, there is likely to be conflict not harmony. For example, if one country, say the USA, is worried about the size of its budget deficit, it may be unwilling to respond to world demands for a stimulus to aggregate demand to pull the world economy out of recession. What is more, speculators, seeing differences between countries, are likely to exaggerate them by their actions, causing large changes in exchange

Table 31.1 Macroeconomic indicators for the G7 countries

	1991							1999						
	USA	Japan	Germany	France	Italy	UK	Canada	USA	Japan	Germany	France	Italy	UK	Canada
Economic growth (% change in real GDP)	−0.5	3.8	5.0	1.1	1.4	−1.5	−1.9	4.2	0.3	1.5	2.9	1.4	2.1	4.2
Output gap (%)	−1.8	3.0	2.2	0.2	0.1	−0.8	−3.5	1.8	−4.0	−1.5	−0.6	−2.5	0.4	−0.4
Standardised unemployment (%)	6.8	2.1	4.2	9.5	8.6	8.9	10.3	4.2	4.7	8.7	11.3	11.4	6.1	7.6
Inflation: GDP deflator (%)	3.6	2.7	3.9	3.0	7.6	6.7	2.7	1.5	−0.9	1.0	0.3	1.5	2.9	1.7
Short-term interest rate (% average)	5.9	7.4	9.2	9.6	12.2	11.5	8.8	5.4	0.2	3.0	3.0	3.0	5.4	4.9
Current account (% of GDP)	0.1	2.0	−1.0	−0.5	−2.1	−1.5	−3.8	−3.7	2.5	−0.9	2.6	1.0	−1.4	−0.5
General government borrowing Requirement (% of GDP)	−5.0	2.9	−2.9	−2.4	−10.0	−2.8	−7.2	1.0	−7.0	−1.1	−1.8	−1.9	1.1	2.8
General government gross debt (% of GDP)	71.4	57.9	40.1	40.3	107.4	40.1	82.2	65.1	105.3	63.5	65.0	116.6	53.0	93.0
Effective exchange rate (1995 = 100)	85.4	59.3	79.4	85.1	124.1	110.9	115.7	124.7	99.3	98.4	99.1	114.3	127.4	97.9

rates. The G7 countries have therefore sought to achieve greater **convergence** of their economies. However, convergence may be a goal of policy, but in practice it has proved elusive.

Because of a lack of convergence, there are serious difficulties in achieving international policy harmonisation:

- Countries' budget deficits and national debt differ substantially as a proportion of their national income. This puts very different pressures on the interest rates necessary to service these debts.
- Harmonising rates of monetary growth would involve letting interest rates fluctuate with the demand for money. Without convergence in the demand for money, interest rate fluctuations could be severe.
- Harmonising interest rates would involve abandoning both monetary targets and exchange rate targets (unless interest rate 'harmonisation' meant adjusting interest rates so as to maintain monetary targets or a fixed exchange rate).
- Countries have different internal structural relationships. A lack of convergence here means that countries with higher endemic *cost* inflation would require higher interest rates and higher unemployment if international inflation rates were to be harmonised, or higher inflation if interest rates were to be harmonised.
- Countries have different rates of productivity increase, product development, investment and market penetration. A lack of convergence here means that the growth in exports (relative to imports) will differ for any given level of inflation or growth.
- Countries may be very unwilling to change their domestic policies to fall into line with other countries. They may prefer the other countries to fall

<table>
<tr><td>definition</td></tr>
<tr><td>Convergence of economies
When countries achieve similar levels of growth, inflation, budget deficits as a percentage of GDP, balance of payments, etc.</td></tr>
</table>

into line with them! Japan, for example, on several occasions in the early 1990s was reluctant to reflate. Likewise Germany, following the inflationary effects of reunification in 1990, was unwilling to reflate and kept interest rates high. This forced other countries, despite being in recession, to keep their interest rates high if they were to maintain fixed exchange rates with the Deutschmark.

If any one of the four – interest rates, growth rates, inflation rates or current account balance of payments – could be harmonised across countries, it is likely that the other three would then not be harmonised.

One solution would be to concentrate monetary and fiscal policies entirely on targeting the exchange rate. If governments were prepared to accept large interest rate fluctuations, it might be possible to keep the exchange rate reasonably stable. But this is little more than a return to fixed exchange rates with a resulting total constraint over domestic policies!

Total convergence and thus total harmonisation may not be possible. Nevertheless most governments favour some movement in that direction: some is better than none.

Response to the south-east Asian crisis

The need to establish greater co-operation was demonstrated by the south-east Asian crisis in 1997/8 and the shock waves it sent round the global economy (see Box 24.1 on pages 504–6). The fact that the crisis came as a total surprise to governments, international institutions, international financiers and speculators, clearly revealed the need to monitor more closely, and when necessary, regulate the world economy.

Following weeks of negotiations with the IMF and World Bank, the finance ministers and central bank governors of the G7 countries met in October 1998 to agree a package of measures designed to prevent a repeat of the 'Asian contagion' and to restore greater stability to the international financial system. The agreement included the following:

- The provision of credit facilities, through the IMF and the World Bank, for 'well-run' economies whose currencies were victims of speculative attack. The IMF would have $90 billion for this purpose.
- The establishment of closer links between national and international regulatory bodies in order to provide more effective regulation of financial markets.
- Greater fiscal openness by governments, in order to make policy co-ordination between countries easier.

On the central issue of exchange rate regimes, however, the G7 had little to say, merely calling for 'consideration of the elements necessary for the maintenance of sustainable exchange rate regimes in emerging markets, including consistent macroeconomic policies'. But does this mean that countries would be better off with floating exchange rates, pegged exchange rates or exchange rates irrevocably fixed to some major currency, such as the dollar? On this the G7 was silent. (We considered the problems associated with various alternative exchange rate regimes in Chapter 26. We explore some possible ways forward later in this chapter.)

BOX 31.1

Monitoring the world economy

In 1995 the world's capital markets supplied some $228 billion of funds to the developing world. One might instantly look to assert that this can only be a good thing. As developing countries grow, investment opportunities flourish, and finance, whether national or international, will look to exploit such opportunities.

However, growing concern is being expressed about the rate at which these flows of capital are expanding, and whether certain countries would, in the face of economic trouble, be able to deal with the volatility that a mass exodus of investment might cause.

The case of Mexico at the tail end of 1994 revealed the financial fragility that many countries currently face. Mexico had to be bailed out to the tune of $37.8 billion by the US treasury and the IMF as the peso collapsed on a wave of adverse speculation.

So what is to be done in order to avoid such instability, and yet maintain the capital market's interest in investing in developing economies? The G7 countries and the IMF believe that the market needs more information and better surveillance of the financial positions of vulnerable countries so that further Mexicos might be avoided.

In *Euromoney* of September 1995, details were given of what, according to the G7 and the IMF, needed to be done.

At their annual June summit in Canada, the G7 heads of state published this homily: 'The growth and integration of global capital markets have created both enormous opportunities and new risks . . . [To deal with these risks] an improved early warning system [is required] so that we can act more quickly to prevent or handle financial shocks. We urge the IMF to:

  a) establish benchmarks for timely publication of key economic and financial data;

  b) establish a procedure for the regular public identification of countries which comply with these benchmarks;

  c) insist on full and timely reporting by member countries of standard sets of data.'

In July of that year, IMF staff presented executive directors with a blueprint for enhanced surveillance. This blueprint invited governments to join an 'honour roll' of nations publishing standardised data on monetary stocks, central bank foreign reserves, and other measures of economic soundness in a world of global capital flows. The point of the honour roll was to single out and embarrass emerging market nations not supplying minimum standards of data to the IMF.

Whether such measures will be sufficient over the longer term has been questioned. The crisis in southeast Asia exposed the weakness in financial surveillance and reporting, and also revealed dramatically the greatest problem of all – capital market liberalisation. In the 1990s, some $1300 billion of private capital went into emerging market economies. This compares with a meagre $170 billion in the previous decade.

For many this is the big issue facing the IMF. Reformers argue that the IMF should continue to upgrade its financial reporting and moves to create transparency within the world financial system. It should also focus more on monitoring its short-term credit facilities, rather than its longer-term 'extended structural adjustment facility', which focuses on poverty and growth. Wherever possible, *long*-term investment should be left to the market or the World Bank.

Question

Why is an open and transparent financial system seen as so crucial for successfully managing the global economy?

31.3 European economic and monetary union

European economic and monetary union (EMU) involves the complete economic and financial integration of the EU countries. It is not just a common market, but a market with a single currency, a single central bank and a single monetary policy. This European monetary union is thus like the current 'British monetary union' – the economic union of England, Scotland, Wales and Northern Ireland – or the economic and monetary union of the USA.

The ERM

The forerunner to EMU was the exchange rate mechanism (ERM). This came into existence in March 1979 and the majority of the EU countries were members. The UK, however, chose not to join. When Greece joined the EU in 1984, it too stayed outside the ERM. Spain joined in 1989, the UK joined in 1990 and Portugal in April 1992. Then in September 1992, the UK and Italy indefinitely suspended their membership of the ERM, but Italy rejoined in November 1996 as part of its bid to join the single European currency. Austria joined in 1995, Finland in 1996 and Greece in 1998. By the time the ERM was replaced by the single currency in 1999, only Sweden and the UK were outside the ERM.

Features of the ERM

Under the system, each currency was given a central exchange rate with each of the other ERM currencies in a grid. However, fluctuations were allowed from the central rate within specified limits. The central rates could be adjusted from time to time by agreement, thus making the ERM an **adjustable peg** system. All the currencies floated jointly with currencies outside the ERM.

Each currency's fluctuations were limited to a certain percentage either side of each other currency. For most countries these bands were set at ±2¼ per cent. However, in 1993 the bands were widened to ±15 per cent. Despite this, countries attempted to maintain their currencies within much narrower limits and were generally successful in this.

If a currency approached the upper or lower limit against *any* other ERM currency, the two countries had to intervene to maintain their currencies within the band. This could take the form of their central banks selling the stronger currency and buying the weaker one, or reducing interest rates in the case of the strong currency and raising interest rates in the case of the weak currency.

The ERM in practice

In a system of pegged exchange rates, countries should harmonise their policies to avoid excessive currency misalignments and hence the need for large devaluations or revaluations. There should be a convergence of their economies: they should be at a similar point on the business cycle and have similar inflation rates and interest rates.

The ERM in the 1980s. In the early 1980s, however, French and Italian inflation rates were persistently higher than German rates. This meant that there had to be several realignments (devaluations and revaluations). After 1983 realignments became less frequent, and then from 1987 to 1992 they ceased altogether. This was due to a growing convergence of members' internal policies.

By the time the UK joined the ERM in 1990, it was generally seen by its existing members as being a great success. It had created a zone of currency stability in a world of highly unstable exchange rates, and had provided the necessary environment for the establishment of a truly common market by the end of 1992.

definition

Adjustable peg
A system whereby exchange rates are fixed for a period of time, but may be devalued (or revalued) if a deficit (or surplus) becomes substantial.

Crisis in the ERM. For most of the period 1990–2, there was optimism that convergence could continue in the enlarged ERM and would remove the need for realignments. After all, there had been no realignments since 1987, and there seemed a genuine collective commitment to defend the agreed parities. The anchor was the German economy, with its history of monetary stability and low inflation.

But all was not well. The German economy was becoming subject to increasing strains from the reunification process. The finance of reconstruction in the eastern part of Germany was causing a growing budget deficit. The Bundesbank thus felt obliged to maintain high interest rates in order to keep inflation in check. At the same time, the UK was experiencing a massive current account deficit (partly the result of entering the ERM at what many commentators argued was too high an exchange rate). It was thus obliged to raise interest rates in order to protect the pound, despite the fact that the economy was sliding rapidly into recession. The French franc and Italian lira were also perceived to be overvalued, and there were the first signs of worries as to whether their exchange rates within the ERM could be retained

At the same time, the US economy was moving into recession and, as a result, US interest rates were cut. This led to a large outflow of capital from the USA. With high German interest rates, much of this capital flowed to Germany. This pushed up the value of the German mark and with it the other ERM currencies. Then in September 1992, with a further fall in US interest rates and further buying of the German mark, things reached crisis point. First the lira was devalued. Then two days later, on 'Black Wednesday' (16 September), the UK and Italy were forced to suspend their membership of the ERM: the pound and the lira were floated. At the same time the Spanish peseta was devalued by 5 per cent.

Turmoil returned in the summer of 1993. The French economy was moving into recession and there were calls for cuts in French interest rates. But this was only possible if Germany was prepared to cut its rates too, and it was not. Speculators began to sell francs and it became obvious that the existing franc/mark parity could not be maintained. In an attempt to rescue the ERM, the EU finance ministers agreed to adopt wide ±15 per cent bands. The result was that the franc and the Danish krone depreciated against the mark.

A return of calm. The old ERM appeared to be at an end. The new ±15 per cent bands hardly seemed like a 'pegged' system at all. However, the ERM did not die. Within months, the members were again managing to keep fluctuations within a very narrow range (for most of the time, within ±2¼ per cent!). The scene was being set for the abandonment of separate currencies and the adoption of a single currency: the euro.

The Maastricht Treaty

The ERM was conceived as a stage on the road to complete economic and monetary union (EMU). If achieved, this would involve the complete economic and financial integration of the EU countries. Details of the path towards EMU were finalised in the Maastricht Treaty, which was signed in February 1992. The timetable for EMU was divided into three stages.

Stage 1. This was to be a preliminary stage, during which a 'Monetary Committee' of the European Union would monitor monetary policy in the member states and provide advice to the Council of Ministers on monetary convergence. During this stage preparations would be made for the establishment of a European Monetary Institute (EMI), an institution which would be the forerunner of a European central bank.

Stage 2. This would begin on 1 January 1994, at which point the EMI would be established. It would seek to co-ordinate monetary policy and encourage greater co-operation between EU central banks. It would also monitor the operation of the ERM and would prepare the ground for the establishment of a European central bank in stage 3.

During stage 2, the member states would seek to achieve convergence of their economies. In order to progress to full economic and monetary union in stage three, a country would have to meet five convergence criteria:

● Inflation: should be no more than 1½ per cent above the average inflation rate of the three countries in the EU with the lowest inflation.
● Interest rates: the rate on long-term government bonds should be no more than 2 per cent above the average of the three countries with the lowest inflation.
● Budget deficit: should be no more than 3 per cent of GDP.
● National debt: should be no more than 60 per cent of GDP.
● Exchange rates: the currency should have been within the normal ERM bands for at least two years with no realignments or excessive intervention.

Before the end of stage 2, the Council of Ministers would have to decide which countries had met the convergence criteria and would thus be eligible to progress to stage 3.

Stage 3. This would commence at the latest on 1 January 1999. At the beginning of this stage, the countries which met the five criteria would form a **currency union** by fixing their currencies permanently to the new single currency: the euro. Their national currencies would therefore effectively disappear.

At the same time a European System of Central Banks (ESCB) would be created, consisting of a European Central Bank (ECB) and the central banks of the member states. The ECB would be independent, both from governments and from EU political institutions. It would operate the monetary policy on behalf of the countries which had adopted the single currency.

Any member state not initially meeting the convergence criteria would proceed to full EMU when the criteria had subsequently been met. The UK and Denmark, however, negotiated an 'opt-out' from the Maastricht Treaty. They do not have to proceed to stage 3, if they so choose. In October 2000, the Danes voted in a referendum not to join the euro, despite having met the criteria.

Birth of the euro

definition

Currency union
A group of countries (or regions) using a common currency.

In March 1998, the European Commission ruled that 11 of the 15 member states were eligible to proceed to EMU in January 1999. The UK and Denmark were to exercise their opt out and Sweden and Greece failed to meet one or more of the convergence criteria.

All 11 countries unambiguously met the interest rate and inflation criteria, but doubts were expressed by many 'Eurosceptics' as to whether they all genuinely met the other three criteria.

- Exchange rates. Neither Finland nor Italy had been in the ERM for 2 years (Finland had joined the ERM in October 1996 and Italy had rejoined in November 1996), and the Irish punt was revalued by 3 per cent on 16/3/98. However, the Commission regarded these three countries as being sufficiently close to the reference value.
- Government deficits. All 11 countries met this criterion, but some countries only managed to achieve a deficit of 3 per cent or below by taking one-off measures, such as a special tax in Italy, and counting privatisation receipts in Germany.
- Government debt. Only four countries had debts that did not exceed 60 per cent (France, Finland, Luxembourg and the UK). However, the Maastricht Treaty allowed countries to exceed this value as long as the debt was 'sufficiently diminishing and approaching the reference value at a satisfactory pace'.

At a meeting of EU heads of state in May 1998, it was agreed that the 11 countries would join the single currency. By December 1998 the European Central Bank (ECB) would be formally established and the euro would come into existence on 1 January 1999, but euro banknotes and coins would not be introduced until 2002. In the meantime, national currencies continue to exist alongside the euro, but are irrevocably fixed to it. Notes and coins of existing currencies are in odd denominations of the euro.

On 1 January 2002 the ECB will introduce euro banknotes and coins, and for 6 months these will circulate alongside the old currencies. On 1 July 2002 national banknotes and coins of the euro-zone countries will lose their legal tender status and will be withdrawn from circulation.

How desirable is EMU?

Advantages of a single currency

Elimination of the costs of converting currencies. With separate currencies in each of the EU countries, costs are incurred each time one currency is exchanged into another, the elimination of these costs is probably the least important benefit from a single currency. The European Commission estimated that the effect would be to increase the GDP of the countries concerned by an average of only 0.4 per cent. The gains to countries like the UK, which have well-developed financial markets, would be even smaller.

Increased competition and efficiency. Despite the advent of the single market, large price differences remained between member states. Not only does the single currency eliminate the need to convert one currency into another (a barrier to competition), but it brings more transparency in pricing, and puts greater downward pressure on prices in high-cost firms and countries.

Elimination of exchange-rate uncertainty (between the members). Even with a narrow-banded ERM, realignments might still have occurred from time to time if separate currencies had remained. As the events of 1992 and 1993 showed, this could cause massive speculation if it was believed that currencies were out of line. Removal of this uncertainty has helped to encourage trade between euro-zone countries. Perhaps more importantly, it has encouraged investment by firms that trade between these countries, given the greater certainty in calculating costs and revenues from such trade.

Conversely, the exchange rate uncertainty for the countries which have remained outside has been damaging to investment. The high €/£ exchange rate in 1999/2000 (see Table 26.2 on page 559) squeezed profits of UK firms. At an exchange rate of over €1.60 = £1 (i.e. under 60p to a euro), the sterling value of exports sold to the euro-zone countries was often too low to be profitable. BMW blamed the high value of the pound as its main reason for pulling out of Rover.

Increased inward investment. Investment from the rest of the world is likely to increase, attracted to a euro-zone of over 300 million customers, where there is no fear of internal currency movements. The EU countries, by contrast, which have not joined could find that inward investment was diverted away from them to the euro-zone countries. Even before the launch of the euro, companies such as General Motors and Toyota were warning that investment might be diverted away from the UK to countries inside the euro-zone if the UK stayed outside for very long.

Lower inflation and interest rates. A single monetary policy forces convergence in inflation rates (just as inflation rates are very similar between the different regions *within* a country). Provided the ECB succeeds in remaining independent from short-term political manipulation, this is likely to result in a lower average inflation rate in the euro-zone countries. This, in turn, will help to convince markets that the euro will be strong relative to other currencies. The result will be lower long-term rates of interest. This, in turn, would further encourage investment in the euro-zone countries, both by member states and by the rest of the world.

In practice, the value of the euro fell relative to the dollar in 1999 and early 2000 (see Box 26.3 on pages 570–1). This, however, was the result largely of much lower rates of interest in the euro-zone than in the USA. In the USA, the main worry was an overheating economy with rising inflation. In the euro-zone, by contrast, inflation was very low and the main worry was one of too little growth and high unemployment.

Opposition to EMU

Monetary union has been bitterly opposed, however, by certain groups. Many 'Eurosceptics' see within it a surrender of national political and economic sovereignty. The lack of an independent monetary and exchange rate policy is a serious problem, they argue, if an economy is at all out of harmony with the rest of the Union. For example, if countries like the UK, Italy and Spain have higher endemic rates of inflation (due, say, to greater cost-push pressures – perhaps caused by a lower growth in productivity than in other EU countries), then how are they to make their goods competitive with the rest of the Union? With separate currencies these countries could devalue or run a deflationary monetary policy. With a single currency, however, they could become depressed 'regions' of Europe, with rising unemployment and all the other regional problems of

BOX 31.2

Optimal currency areas
When it pays to pay in the same currency

Imagine that each town and village used a different currency. Think how inconvenient it would be having to keep exchanging one currency into another, and how difficult it would be working out the relative value of items in different parts of the country.

Clearly there are benefits of using a common currency, not only within a country but across different countries. The benefits include greater transparency in pricing, more open competition, greater certainty for investors and the avoidance of having to pay commission when you change one currency into another. There are also the benefits from having a single monetary policy if that is delivered in a more consistent and effective way than by individual countries.

So why not have a single currency for the whole world? The problem is that the bigger a single-currency area gets, the more likely the conditions are to diverge in the different parts of the area. Some parts may have high unemployment and require reflationary policies. Others may have low unemployment and suffer from inflationary pressures. They may require *deflationary* policies. What is more, different members of the currency area may experience quite different shocks to their economies, whether from outside the union (e.g. a fall in the price of one of their major exports) of from inside (e.g. a prolonged strike). These 'asymmetric shocks' (see page 696) would imply that different parts of the currency area should adopt different policies. But with a common monetary policy and hence common interest rates, and with no possibility of devaluation/revaluation of the currency of individual members, the scope for separate economic policies is reduced

The costs of asymmetric shocks (and hence the costs of a single-currency area) will be greater, the less the mobility of labour and capital, the less the flexibility of prices and wage rates, and the fewer the alternative policies there are that can be turned to (such as fiscal and regional policies).

So is the euro zone an optimal currency area? Certainly strong doubts have been raised by many economists.

- Labour is relatively immobile.
- There are structural differences between the member states.
- The transmission effects of interest rate changes are different between the member countries, given that countries have proportions of borrowing at variable interest rates and different proportions of consumer debt to GDP.
- Exports to countries outside the euro-zone account for different proportions of the members' GDP, and thus their economies are affected differently by a change in the rate of exchange of the euro against other currencies.
- Wage rates are relatively inflexible.
- Under the Stability and Growth Pact (see Box 29.1), the scope for using discretionary fiscal policy is curtailed.

This does not necessarily mean, however, that the costs of having a single European currency outweigh the benefits. Also, the problems outlined above should decline over time as the single market develops. Finally, the problem of asymmetric shocks can be exaggerated. European economies are highly diversified; there are often more differences *within* economies than between them. Thus shocks are more likely to affect different industries or localities, rather than whole countries. Changing the exchange rate, if that were still possible, would hardly be an appropriate policy in these circumstances.

Question

Why is a single currency area likely to move towards becoming an optimal currency area over time?

depressed regions *within* a country. This may then require significant regional policies – policies which may not be in place or, if they were, would be seen as too interventionist by the political right.

The answer given by proponents of EMU is that it is better to tackle the problem of high inflation in such countries by the disciplines of competition from other EU countries, than merely to feed that inflation by keeping separate currencies and allowing repeated devaluations, with all the uncertainty that that brings. If such countries become depressed, they argue, it is better to have a fully developed *fiscal* policy for the Union which will divert funds into investment in such regions. What is more, the high inflation countries tend to be the poorer ones with lower wage levels (albeit faster wage *increases*). With the high mobility of labour and capital that will accompany the development of the single market, resources are likely to be attracted to such countries. This could help to narrow the gap between the richer and poorer member states. The critics of EMU argue that labour is relatively immobile, given cultural and language barriers. Thus an unemployed worker in Wales could not easily move to a job in Turin or Helsinki. What the critics are arguing here is that the EU is not an **optimal currency area** (see Box 31.2).

Another problem for members of a single currency occurs in adjusting to a shock when that shock affects members to different degrees. These are known as **asymmetric shocks**. For example, a sudden change in the price of oil would affect an oil-exporting country like the UK differently from oil importing countries. This problem is more serious, the less the factor mobility between member countries and the less the price flexibility within member countries.

This problem, however, should not be overstated. The divergences between economies are often the result of a lack of harmony between countries in their demand-management policies: something that is impossible in the case of monetary policy, and more difficult in the case of fiscal policy, for countries in the euro-zone. Also, many of the shocks that face economies today are global and have similar (albeit not identical) effects on all countries. Adjustment to such shocks would often be better with a single co-ordinated policy, something that would be much easier with a single currency and a single central bank.

Even when shocks are uniformly felt in the member states, however, there is still the problem that policies adopted centrally will have different impacts on each country. For example, in the UK, a large proportion of borrowing is at variable interest rates. In Germany, by contrast, much is at fixed rates. Thus if the ECB were to raise interest rates, the deflationary effects would be felt disproportionately in the UK. Of course, were this balance to change – and there is some evidence that types of borrowing are becoming more uniform across the EU – this problem would diminish.

The problem for economists is that the issue of monetary union is a very emotive one. 'Europhiles' often see monetary union as a vital element in their vision of a united Europe. Many Eurosceptics, however, see EMU as a surrender of sovereignty and a threat to nationhood. In such an environment, a calm assessment of the arguments and evidence is very difficult.

31.4 Alternative policies for achieving currency stability

One important lesson of the expulsion of the UK and Italy from the ERM in 1992, the dramatic fall of the Mexican peso and rise of the yen in 1995, the collapse of various south-east Asian currencies and the Russian rouble in 1997/8, and the decline of the euro in 1999/2000, is that concerted speculation has become virtually unstoppable. In comparison with the vast amounts of short-

---

definition

Optimal currency area
The optimal size of a currency area is one that maximises the benefits from having a single currency relative to the costs. If the area were to be increased or decreased in size, the costs would rise relative to the benefits.

definition

Asymmetric shocks
Shocks (such as an oil price increase or a recession in another part of the world) that have different-sized effects on different industries, regions or countries.

term finance flowing across the foreign exchanges each day, the reserves of central banks seem trivial.

If there is a consensus in the markets that a currency will depreciate, there is little that central banks can do. For example, if there were a 50 per cent chance of a 10 per cent depreciation in the next week, then selling that currency now would yield an 'expected' return of just over 5 per cent for the week (i.e. 50% of 10%): equivalent to more than 5000 per cent at an annual rate!

For this reason, many commentators have argued that there are only two types of exchange rate system that can work over the long term. The first is a completely free-floating exchange rate, with no attempt by the central bank to support the exchange rate. With no intervention, there is no problem of a shortage of reserves!

The alternative is to share a common currency with other countries: to join a common-currency area, such as the euro-zone or to adopt the US dollar, and let the common currency float freely. The country would give up independence in its monetary policy, but at least there would be no problem of exchange rate instability within the currency area.

Either any attempt to peg exchange rates, they argue, will end in failure as the country succumbs to a speculative attack, or its monetary policy will have to be totally dedicated to maintaining the exchange rate.

So is there any way of 'beating the speculators' and pursuing a policy of greater exchange rate rigidity without establishing a single currency? Or must countries be forced to accept freely floating exchange rates, with all the uncertainty for traders that such a regime brings?

We shall examine two possible solutions. The first is to reduce international financial mobility, by putting various types of restriction on foreign exchange transactions. The second is to move to a new type of exchange rate regime which offers the benefits of a degree of rigidity without being susceptible to massive speculative attacks.

Controlling exchange transactions

Until the early 1990s, many countries retained restrictions of various kinds on financial flows. Such restrictions made it more expensive for speculators to gamble on possible exchange rate movements. It is not the case, as some commentators argue, that it is impossible to reimpose controls. Indeed Malaysia did just that in 1998 when the ringgit was under speculative attack. Many countries in the developing world still retain controls, and the last ERM countries to give them up only did so in 1991. It is true that the complexity of modern financial markets provides the speculator with more opportunity to evade controls, but they will still have the effect of dampening speculation.

In September 1998, the IMF said that controls on inward movements of capital could be a useful tool, especially for countries which were more vulnerable to speculative attack. In its 1998 annual report it argued that the Asian crisis of 1997–8 was the result not only of a weak banking system, but also of open capital accounts, allowing massive withdrawals of funds.

The aim of capital controls is not to prevent capital flows. After all, capital flows are an important source of financing investment. Also if capital moves from countries with a lower marginal productivity of capital to countries where it is higher, this will lead to an efficient allocation of world savings. The aim of capital controls must therefore be to prevent speculative flows which are based on rumour or herd instinct rather than on economic fundamentals.

Types of control

In what ways can movements of short-term capital be controlled? There are various alternatives, each one with strengths and drawbacks:

Quantitative controls. Here the authorities would restrict the amount of foreign exchange dealing that could take place. Perhaps financial institutions would be allowed to exchange only a certain percentage of their assets. Alternatively special emergency measures could be introduced to restrict capital movements in times of a currency crisis.

According to Article 73c, the European Commission can consider 'special measures relating to capital transactions with non-EU countries'. Article 73f allows 'precautionary measures' if there is an extraordinary threat to the 'normal operation of economic and monetary union'. Article 73g allows members to take 'unilateral action to regulate the movement of capital and payments to and from non-EU countries'.[1]

Developed countries and most developing countries have rejected this approach, however, since it is seen to be far too anti-market. Certainly, although EU countries *could* impose such controls, they would be highly unlikely to do so.

A 'Tobin' tax. This is named after James Tobin, who in 1978 advocated the imposition of a small tax (say 0.5 per cent) on all foreign exchange transactions, or on just capital account transactions.[2] This would discourage destabilising speculation (by making it more expensive) and would thus impose some 'friction' in the foreign exchange markets, making them less volatile.

A problem with such a tax is that it would penalise transactions that were for normal trading or investment purposes as well as those for speculative purposes. Another problem is that the tax might have to be quite high to prevent speculation in times of uncertainty, and this would be very damaging to trade and investment. A possibility here would be to impose the tax only at times of exchange market turbulence, or to impose a higher tax at such times. At least a tax is far less distortionary than quantitative controls.

Non-interest-bearing deposits. Here a certain percentage of inflows of capital would have to be deposited with the central bank in a non-interest-bearing account for a set period of time. Chile in the late 1990s used such a system. It required that 30 per cent of all inflows be deposited with Chile's central bank for a year. This clearly amounted to a considerable tax (i.e. in terms of interest sacrificed) and had the effect of discouraging short-term speculative flows. The problem was that it meant that interest rates in Chile had to be higher in order to attract capital.

One objection to all these measures is that they are likely only to dampen speculation, not eliminate it. If speculators believe that currencies are badly out of equilibrium and will be forced to realign, then no taxes on capital movements or artificial controls will be sufficient to stem the flood.

---

[1] See D. Shirreff, 'Can anyone tame the currency market?', *Euromoney*, September 1993, p. 66.
[2] J. Tobin, 'A proposal for international monetary reform', *The Eastern Economic Journal*, 4, no. 3–4 (1978), pp. 153–9.

There are two replies to this objection. The first is that if currencies are badly out of line then exchange rates *should* be adjusted. The second is that dampening speculation is probably the ideal. Speculation *can* play the valuable role of bringing exchange rates to their long-term equilibrium more quickly. Controls are unlikely to prevent this aspect of speculation: adjustments to economic fundamentals. If they help to lessen the wilder forms of destabilising speculation, so much the better.

Exchange-rate target zones

One type of exchange rate regime that has been much discussed in recent years is that proposed by John Williamson, of Washington's Institute for International Economics.[3] Williamson advocates a form of 'crawling peg' within broad bands. This system would involve a pegged central rate, where fluctuations around that rate would be allowed within bands (i.e. like the ERM). Unlike, the ERM, however, the central value could be adjusted frequently, but only by small amounts: hence the term 'crawling'. The system would have four major features:

- Wide bands. For example, currencies could be allowed to fluctuate by 10 per cent of their central parity.
- Central parity set in *real* terms, at the 'fundamental equilibrium exchange rate' (FEER): i.e. a rate that is consistent with long-run balance of payments equilibrium.
- Frequent realignments. In order to stay at the FEER, the central parity would be adjusted frequently (e.g. monthly) to take account of the country's rate of inflation. If its rate of inflation were 2 per cent per annum above the trade weighted average of other countries, then the central parity would be devalued by 2 per cent per annum. Realignments would also reflect other changes in fundamentals, such as changes in the levels of protection, or major political events, such as German reunification.
- 'Soft buffers'. Governments would not be forced to intervene at the 10 per cent mark or at some specified fraction of it. In fact, from time to time the rate might be allowed to move outside the bands. The point is that the closer the rate approached the band limits, the greater would be the scale of intervention.

This system has two main advantages. First, the exchange rate would stay at roughly the equilibrium level, and therefore the likelihood of large-scale devaluation or revaluation, and with it the opportunities for large-scale speculative gains, would be small. The reason why the narrow-banded ERM broke down in 1992 and 1993 was that the central parities were *not* equilibrium rates.

Second, the wider bands would leave countries freer to follow an independent monetary policy: one that could therefore respond to domestic needs.

The main problem with the system is that it removes the pressure on high inflation countries to bring their inflation under control: after all, if inflation causes the balance of payments to deteriorate, the exchange rate can simply be allowed to crawl down. Also, if the rate of exchange has to be maintained

---

[3] See, for example, J. Williamson and M. Miller, 'Targets and Indicators: A Blueprint for the Co-ordination of Economic Policy', *Policy Analyses in International Economics* No. 22, IIE, 1987.

within the zone, then monetary policy may sometimes have to be used for that purpose rather than controlling inflation.

Nevertheless, crawling bands have been used relatively successfully by various countries, such as Chile and Israel over quite long periods of time. What is more, in 1999, Germany's finance minister at the time, Oskar Lafontaine, argued that they might be appropriate for the euro relative to the dollar and yen. A world with three major currencies, each changing gently against the other two in an orderly way has a lot to commend it.

SUMMARY

1a The more open the world economy, the more effect changes in economic conditions in one part of the world economy will have on world economic performance.

1b Changes in aggregate demand in one country will affect the amount of imports purchased and thus the amount of exports sold by other countries and hence their national income. There is thus an international trade multiplier effect.

1c Changes in interest rates in one country will affect financial flows to and from other countries, and hence their exchange rates, interest rates and national income.

2a Currency fluctuations can be lessened if countries harmonise their economic policies. Ideally this will involve achieving common growth rates, inflation rates, balance of payments (as a percentage of GDP) and interest rates. The attempt to harmonise one of these goals, however, may bring conflicts with one of the other goals.

2b Leaders of the G7 countries meet regularly to discuss ways of harmonising their policies. Usually, however, domestic issues are more important to the leaders than international ones, and frequently they pursue policies that are not in the interests of the other countries.

2c Attempts to harmonise and manage the international economy by the G7 nations have generally proved unsuccessful.

3a One means of achieving greater currency stability is for a group of countries to peg their internal exchange rates and yet float jointly with the rest of the world. The exchange rate mechanism of the EU (ERM) was an example. Members' currencies were allowed to fluctuate against other member currencies within a band. The band was ±2¼ per cent for the majority of the ERM countries until 1993.

3b The need for realignments seemed to have diminished in the late 1980s as greater convergence was achieved between the members' economies. Growing strains in the system, however, in the early 1990s, led to a crisis in September 1992. The UK and Italy left the ERM. There was a further crisis in July 1993 and the bands were widened to ±15 per cent.

3c Thereafter, as convergence of the economies of ERM members increased, fluctuations decreased and remained largely within ±2¼ per cent.

3d The ERM was seen as an important first stage on the road to complete economic and monetary union (EMU) in the EU.

3f The Maastricht Treaty set out a timetable for achieving EMU. This would culminate in stage 3 with the creation of a currency union: a single European currency with a common monetary policy operated by an independent European Central Bank.

3g The advantages claimed for EMU are that it will eliminate the costs of converting currencies and the uncertainties associated with possible changes in inter-EU exchange rates. What is more, a common central bank, independent from domestic governments, will provide the stable monetary environment necessary for a convergence of the EU economies and the encouragement of investment and inter-Union trade.

3h Critics claim, however, that it might make adjustment to domestic economic problems more difficult. The loss of independence in policy making is seen by such people to be a major issue, not only because of the loss of political sovereignty, but also because domestic economic concerns may be at variance with those of the Union as a whole. A single monetary policy is claimed to be inappropriate for dealing with asymmetric shocks. What is more, countries and regions at the periphery of the Union

SUMMARY

may become depressed unless there is an effective regional policy.

4a Many economists argue that, with the huge flows of short-term finance across the foreign exchanges, governments are forced to adopt one of two extreme forms of exchange rate regime: free floating or being a member of a currency union.

4b If financial flows could be constrained, however, exchange rates could be stabilised somewhat.

4c Forms of control include: quantitative controls, a tax on exchange transactions and non-interest-bearing deposits of a certain percentage of capital inflows with the central bank. Such controls can dampen speculation, but may discourage capital flowing to where it has a higher marginal productivity.

4d An alternative means of stabilising exchange rates is to have exchange rate target zones. Here exchange rates are allowed to fluctuate within broad bands around a central parity which is adjusted to the fundamental equilibrium rate in a gradual fashion.

4e The advantage of this system is that, by keeping the exchange rate at roughly its equilibrium level, destabilising speculation is avoided, and yet there is some freedom for governments to pursue an independent monetary policy. Monetary policy, however, may still from time to time have to be used to keep the exchange rate within the bands. The system also has the drawback of removing the pressure on governments to maintain a low rate of inflation.

REVIEW QUESTIONS

1 What are the implications for a country attempting to manage its domestic economy if it is subject to an international business cycle? How might it attempt to overcome such problems?

2 What are the economic (as opposed to political) difficulties in achieving an international harmonisation of economic policies so as to avoid damaging currency fluctuations?

3 To what extent can international negotiations over economic policy be seen as a game of strategy? Are there any parallels between the behaviour of countries and the behaviour of oligopolies?

4 What are the causes of exchange rate volatility? Have these problems become greater or lesser in the last ten years? Explain why.

5 Why did the ERM with narrow bands collapse in 1993? Could this have been avoided?

6 Did the exchange rate difficulties experienced by countries under the ERM strengthen or weaken the arguments for progressing to a single European currency?

7 By what means would a depressed country in an economic union with a single currency be able to recover? Would the market provide a satisfactory solution or would (union) government intervention be necessary, and if so. what form would the intervention take?

8 Is the euro-zone likely to be an optimal currency area now? Is it more or less likely to be so over time? Explain your answer.

9   Assume that just some of the members of a common market like the EU adopt full economic and monetary union, including a common currency. What are the advantages and disadvantages to those members joining the full EMU and to those not joining?

10   Assess the difficulties in attempting to control exchange transactions: might such a policy restrict the level of trade?

11   Would the Williamson system allow countries to follow a totally independent monetary policy?

12   If the euro were in a crawling peg system against the dollar, what implications would this have for the ECB in sticking to its inflation target of no more than 2 per cent?

Web appendix

All the following Web sites can be accessed from this book's own Web site (http://www.booksites.net/sloman). When you enter the site, click on **Student Resources,** and then click on **Hot Links** in the left-hand panel. You will find all the following sites listed. Click on the one you want and the 'hot link' will take you straight to it.

(A) General news sources

As the title of this section implies, the Web sites here can be used for finding material on current news issues or tapping into news archives. Most archives are offered free of charge. However, some do require you to register. As well as key UK and American news sources, you will also notice some slightly different places from where you can get your news, such as the St Petersburg Times and Kyodo News (from Japan). Check out site no. 33 for links to newspapers across the world.

1. BBC news
2. The Economist
3. The Financial Times
4. The Guardian
5. The Independent
6. ITN
7. The Observer
8. The Telegraph
9. The Times, Sunday Times
10. The New York Times
11. Fortune
12. Time Magazine
13. The Washington Post
14. Moscow Times (English)
15. St Petersburg Times (English)
16. Straits Times
17. New Straits Times
18. Megastories
19. Economic Strategy Institute
20. Euromoney
21. Money World
22. Market News International
23. Nexus
24. Prospect Magazine
25. CNN Financial Net
26. Wall Street Journal
27. Asia related news
28. AfricaNews Online
29. Greek News Agencies
30. Kyodo News (Japanese)
31. Radio Free Europe
32. Sydney Morning Herald
33. My Virtual Newspaper (links to a whole range of news sources)
34. Japan Times
35. Economist Intelligence Unit
36. Stratfor.com (economic and political articles)

(B) Sources of economic and business data

Using Web sites to find up-to-date data is of immense value to the economist. The data sources below offer you a range of specialist and non-specialist data information. Universities have free access to site no. 12, which is a huge data base of statistics. No. 35 is a very useful source of key UK and world statistics, and is updated monthly.

1. Acquisitions monthly
2. Biz/ed Gateway to economic and company data
3. Business information
4. Data Archive (Essex)
5. Econ Links
6. Economic Resources (About)
7. Halifax House Price Index
8. House Web (data on housing market)
9. Incomes Data Services
10. Keynote Publications Ltd
11. Land Registry (house prices, etc.)
12. Manchester Information and Association Services (MIMAS)
13. Mintel Market Intelligence
14. PACIFIC International trade and business reference page
15. NatWest Economic Forecasts
16. Products On-Line
17. Resources for economists on the Internet
18. Joseph Rowntree Foundation
19. Social Science Information Gateway
20. Central European Business Daily
21. Ed Yardeni's Economics Network (mainly US data)
22. CIA world statistics site
23. The Whitehouse (US and international data)
24. World Bank statistics
25. Japanese Economic Foundation
26. Ministry of International Trade and Industry (Japan)
27. Nomura Research Institute (Japan)
28. Nanyang Technological University, Singapore: Statistical Data Locators
29. Richard Tucker's Data Resources site
30. Oanda Currency Converter
31. World Economic Outlook Database (IMF)
32. Barclays annual country reports (separate economic reports for 51 countries)
33. Economist Intelligence Unit
34. OFFSTATS links to data sets
35. Treasury Pocket Data Bank (source of UK and world economic data)

(C) Sites for students and teachers of economics

The following Web sites offer useful ideas and resources to those who are studying or teaching economics. It is worth browsing through some just to see what is on offer. Try out the first four and nos 7, 8 and 14. Site no. 6 provides a very helpful tutorial for economics students on using the Internet.

1. Economics Subject Centre of the UK Learning and Teaching Support Network (LTSN)
2. Biz/ed
3. EcEdWeb
4. Econ Links: student resources
5. Economics and Business Education Association
6. The Internet Economist (tutorial on using the Internet)

7. Tutor2U
8. Economics America
9. Oxford School of Learning
10. Teaching resources for economists
11. Resources for University Teachers of Economics (University of Melbourne)
12. Federal Reserve Bank of San Francisco: Economics Education
13. Federal Reserve Bank of Minneapolis Economic Education
14. WebEc resources
15. BibEc papers
16. Wimmeranet Global Grocery List Project
17. Wimmeranet Currency Comparison
18. The Idea Channel
19. History of Economic Services (Individual Economists)
20. History of Economic Services (Themes)
21. Resources for Economist on the Internet (RFE)
22. Rationalexpectations.com (resources and news of the discipline)
23. VCE Economics (Economics teaching resources – Australian)
24. JokEc: economics jokes!

(D) Economic models and simulations

Economic modelling is an important aspect of economic analysis. There are a number of sites that offer access to a model for you to use, e.g. Virtual economy (where you can play being Chancellor of the Exchequer). Using such models can be a useful way of finding out how economic theory works within an environment that claims to reflect reality.

1. Virtual economy
2. Virtual factory
3. WinEcon
4. About.com Economics
5. Estima (statistical analysis)
6. SPSS (statistical analysis)
7. National Institute of Economic and Social Research
8. Software available on Economics LTSN site

(E) UK government and UK organisations' sites

If you want to see what a government department is up to, then look no further than the list below. Government departments' Web sites are an excellent source of information and data. They are particularly good at offering information on current legislation and policy initiatives.

1. Gateway site
2. Advertising Standards Authority
3. Central Office of Information
4. Competition Commission
5. DfEE
6. Department for International Development
7. DETR
8. Department of Health
9. DSS
10. DTI
11. Environment Agency
12. UK euro information site
13. Low Pay Unit
14. MAFF
15. OFFER (OFGEM)

16. OFGEM
17. Official Documents OnLine
18. Office of Fair trading
19. Office of the Rail Regulator (ORR)
20. OFGAS (OFGEM)
21. OFTEL
22. OFWAT
23. Office for National statistics (ONS)
24. ONS Statstore and Statbase
25. Strategic Rail Authority
26. Patent Office
27. Parliament web site
28. Scottish Abstract
29. Scottish Environment Agency
30. Treasury
31. Equal Opportunities Commission
32. Trades Union Congress (TUC) (see Biz/ed link)
33. Confederation of British Industry
34. Adam Smith Institute
35. Royal Institute of International Affairs
36. Institute of Fiscal Studies

(F) Sources of monetary and financial data

As the title suggests, the following is a list of Web sites for finding information on financial matters. You will see that the list comprises mainly central banks, both within Europe and further afield.

1. Bank of England
2. Bank of England Monetary and Financial Statistics
3. Banque de France (English)
4. Bundesbank (German central bank) (English)
5. Central Bank of Ireland
6. European Central Bank (ECB)
7. Eurostat
8. US Federal Reserve Bank
9. Netherlands Central Bank
10. Bank of Japan (English)
11. Reserve Bank of Australia
12. Bank Negara Malaysia (English)
13. Monetary Authority of Singapore
14. National Bank of Canada
15. National Bank of Denmark (English)
16. Reserve Bank of India
17. About.com link to central banks

(G) European Union and related sources

For information on European issues, the following is a wide range of useful sites. The sites maintained by the European Union are an excellent source of information and are provided free of charge.

1. Economic and Financial Affairs (EC DG)
2. European Central Bank
3. EU official web site
4. Euromonitor
5. Eurostat
6. Site for information on the euro and EMU
7. Enterprise: (EC DG)
8. Competition: (EC DG)
9. Agriculture: (EC DG)
10. Energy and Transport: (EC DG)
11. Environment: (EC DG)
12. Regional Policy: (EC DG)
13. Taxation and Customs Union (EC DG)

14. Education (EC DG)
15. European Patent Office
16. Resource Centre for Access to Data on Europe

17. Association for the Monetary Union of Europe

(H) International organisations

This section casts its net beyond Europe and lists the Web addresses of the main international organisations in the global economy. You will notice that some sites are run by pressure groups, such as Jubilee 2000, while others represent organisations set up to manage international affairs, such as the International Monetary Fund and the United Nations.

1. Food and Agricultural Organisation
2. International Air Transport Association (IATA)
3. International Labour Office (ILO)
4. International Monetary Fund (IMF)
5. Organisation for Economic Co-operation and Development (OECD)
6. OPEC
7. World Bank
8. World Health Organisation
9. United Nations
10. United Nations Industrial Development Organisation
11. Friends of the Earth
12. Jubilee 2000
13. Oxfam
14. Christian Aid (reports on development issues)
15. European Bank for Reconstruction and Development (EBRD)
16. World Trade Organisation (WTO)
17. United Nations Development Program
18. UNICEF
19. EURODAD – European Network on Debt and Development
20. NAFTA
21. MERCOSUR
22. ASEAN

(I) Economics search and link sites

If you are having difficulty finding what you want from the list of sites above, the following sites offer links to other sites and are a very useful resource when you are looking for something a little bit more specialist. Once again, it is worth having a look at what these sites have to offer in order to judge their usefulness.

1. Gateway for UK official sites
2. Search for UK official sites
3. Data Archive Search
4. Inomics (search engine for economics information)
5. International Digital Electronic Access Library
6. Links to economics resources sites
7. Social Science Information Gateway
8. WebEc
9. One World (link to economic development sites)

10. Economic development sites (list)
11. Biz/ed internet catalogue
12. Web links for economists from the Economics LTSN subject centre
13. Yahoo's links to economic data
14. OFFSTATS links to data sets
15. UniGuide academic guide to the Internet (Economics)

(J) Internet search engines

The following search engines have been found to be useful.

1. Altavista
2. Google
3. Go To
4. Excite
5. Infoseek
6. Search.com
7. MSN
8. UK Plus
9. Yahoo

Index